HANDBOOK FOR ACHIEVING SEX EQUITY THROUGH EDUCATION

Advisory Board

WITHDRAWN

Jessie Bernard, author of many books on women.

Mary Frances Berry, Commissioner, U.S. Commission on Civil Rights; Professor of History and Law and Senior Fellow in the Institute for the Study of Educational Policy, Howard University, Washington, D.C.

Raphaela Best, Reading Specialist and In-Service Human Relations Instructor, Montgomery County (Maryland) Public Schools.

Phyllis W. Cheng, Member of the California Commission on the Status of Women.

Hendrik Gideonse, Dean, College of Education, University of Cincinnati; President of the Association of Colleges and Schools of Education in State Universities and Land Grant Colleges and Affiliated Private Universities.

Dolores "D" Grayson, Director, Educational Equity Office, Office of the Los Angeles County Superintendent of Schools.

Maxine Greene, William F. Russell Professor in Foundations of Education, Teachers College, Columbia University.

Carol Nagy Jacklin, Professor and Chair, Program for the Study of Women and Men in Society, University of Southern California, Los Angeles.

Bernice Resnick Sandler, Director, Project on the Status and Education of Women, Association of American Colleges.

Charol Shakeshaft, Professor, Hofstra University; Director, Doctoral Program, Administration and Policy Studies; Chair of the American Educational Research Association Committee on the Role and Status of Women in Educational R&D.

Joy R. Simonson, Coordinator, Citizens' Council on Women's Education.

Robert E. Stake, Director, Center for Instructional Research and Curriculum Evaluation, University of Illinois.

Carol Kehr Tittle, Professor, University of North Carolina, Greensboro; at-large member of the AERA Executive Council.

Leslie R. Wolfe, Director, Project on Equal Education Rights, NOW Legal Defense and Education Fund.

Handbook for Achieving Sex Equity through Education

EDITED BY Susan S. Klein

THE JOHNS HOPKINS UNIVERSITY PRESS
Baltimore and London

*This work is published with the endorsement of
the American Educational Research Association.*

The Johns Hopkins University Press, Baltimore, Maryland 21218
The Johns Hopkins Press Ltd, London

Library of Congress Cataloging in Publication Data
Main entry under title:

Handbook for achieving sex equity through education.

Includes index.
1. Educational equalization—United States—Addresses,
essays, lecture. 2. Sex discrimination in education—
United States—Addresses, essays, lecture. 3. Sexism—
United States—Addresses, essays, lectures. I. Klein,
Susan S.
LC213.2.H36 1984   370.19'345   84–7866
ISBN 0–8018–3172–5

*Although Dr. Klein performed some preliminary work on this handbook as part of her official
Department of Education duties, all final editorial work and writing was completed outside of her
governmental responsibilities. The views expressed by Dr. Klein are her own and are not necessarily
those of the National Institute of Education, U.S. Department of Education. Copyright is claimed for
the entire work except for the Preface.*

Contents

PREFACE   xi
ACKNOWLEDGMENTS   xv

  1. Examining the Achievement of Sex Equity in and through
      Education, *by Susan S. Klein, Lillian N. Russo, Patricia B.*
      Campbell, and Glen Harvey   1

PART I. **Assumptions about the Nature and Value**
         of Sex Equity   13
           Part Editor: Carol Kehr Tittle

  2. Economic Considerations for Achieving Sex Equity through
      Education, *by Glen Harvey and Elizabeth Noble*   17
  3. Sex Equity as a Philosophical Problem, *by Maxine Greene*   29
  4. The New Scholarship on Women, *by Sari Knopp Biklen and*
      Charol Shakeshaft   44
  5. Facts and Assumptions about the Nature of Sex Differences,
      by Marcia C. Linn and Anne C. Petersen   53
  6. Educational Equity and Sex Role Development,
      by Candace Garrett Schau   78

PART II. **Administrative Strategies for Implementing**
          Sex Equity   91
           Part Editor: Patricia A. Schmuck

  7. Administrative Strategies for Institutionalizing Sex Equity in
      Education and the Role of Government, *by Patricia A. Schmuck,*
      Judith A. Adkison, Barbara Peterson, Susan Bailey, Georgia S.
      Glick, Susan S. Klein, Scott McDonald, Jane Schubert,
      and Stephen L. Tarason   95
  8. Strategies for Overcoming the Barriers to Women in Educational
      Administration, *by Charol Shakeshaft*   124

9.   The Treatment of Sex Equity in Teacher Education,
by David Sadker and Myra Sadker   145

**PART III.   General Educational Practices for Promoting
Sex Equity**   163
Part Editor: Patricia B. Campbell

10.   Sex Equity in Testing, *by Esther E. Diamond
and Carol Kehr Tittle*   167
11.   Sex Equity in Classroom Organization and Climate,
by Marlaine E. Lockheed   189
12.   Sex Equity and Sex Bias in Instructional Materials,
by Kathryn P. Scott and Candace Garrett Schau   218

PART IV.   Sex Equity Strategies in the Content Areas   233
*Part Editors: Peggy J. Blackwell
and Lillian N. Russo*

13.   Increasing the Participation and Achievement of Girls and
Women in Mathematics, Science, and Engineering,
*by Elizabeth K. Stage, Nancy Kreinberg, Jacquelynne Eccles
(Parsons), and Joanne Rossi Becker*   237
14.   Sex Equity in Reading and Communication Skills, *by Kathryn P.
Scott, Carol Anne Dwyer, and Barbara Lieb-Brilhart*   269
15.   Sex Equity in Social Studies, *by Carole L. Hahn
and Jane Bernard-Powers*   280
16.   Sex Equity in Visual Arts Education, *by Renee Sandell,
Georgia C. Collins, and Ann Sherman*   298
17.   Sex Equity in Physical Education and Athletics,
by Patricia L. Geadelmann   319
18.   Sex Equity in Career and Vocational Education,
by Helen S. Farmer and Joan Seliger Sidney   338

PART V.   Sex Equity Strategies for Specific Populations   361
Part Editor: Saundra Rice Murray

19.   Achieving Sex Equity for Minority Women, *by Shelby Lewis*   365
20.   Gifted Girls and Women in Education, *by Barbara J. A. Gordon
and Linda Addison*   391
21.   Rural Women and Girls, *by Stuart A. Rosenfeld*   416
22.   Educational Programs for Adult Women, *by Ruth B. Ekstrom
and Marjory G. Marvel*   431

**PART VI.   Sex Equity from Early through
Postsecondary Education**   455
Part Editor: Carol Anne Dwyer

23.   Educational Equity in Early Education Environments,
by Selma Greenberg   457

24. Improving Sex Equity in Postsecondary Education,
by Karen Bogart   470

25. Summary and Recommendations for the Continued Achievement
of Sex Equity in and through Education, *by Susan S. Klein,
Lillian N. Russo, Carol Kehr Tittle, Patricia A. Schmuck,
Patricia B. Campbell, Peggy J. Blackwell, Saundra Rice
Murray, Carol Anne Dwyer, Marlaine E. Lockheed, Barb
Landers, and Joy R. Simonson*   489

LIST OF EDITORS AND MAJOR AUTHORS   521
INDEX   525

Preface

We have written this handbook with two general complementary purposes in mind. The long-range purpose is to aid in the achievement of sex equity *through* education by helping individuals use educational strategies to attain sex equity in society. The second (related and often prerequisite) purpose is to aid in the achievement of sex equity *in* educational activities and settings, whether or not the instructional content is dealing with sex equity issues. To accomplish these purposes, we have described key sex equity issues in our respective areas of expertise and have come to an agreement on some answers about how sex equity may be achieved in and through education.

The achievement of sex equity goals in society by the reduction of sex discrimination and sex stereotyping is valued for a wide variety of personal, political, economic, and philosophic reasons. Some personal and societal reasons for supporting sex equity are to optimize human development potential so that all females and males are able to develop themselves as individuals without limitations of gender-prescribed roles. For example, males as well as females should be encouraged to play nurturing roles toward their families and others. Key political reasons favoring sex equity focus on the need to provide basic human rights essential for a democracy and to eliminate discrimination against groups of people based on stereotypes. Some historians have also noted that less sex-stereotyped societies have had fewer wars than more sex-stereotyped societies. Economic reasons for advocating sex equity are based on concerns for adequate resource use. When certain groups are relegated to limited production responsibilities regardless of their qualifications, output is reduced. Philosophic reasons for sex equity are based on a variety of principles, including those that focus on justice, ethics, human dignity, and an accurate portrayal of the world as it is, or can be, without the continuing neglect of the contributions of the 51% of the world's population that is female.

The possibility that sex equity goals can be at least partially achieved through education is a basic assumption of this handbook. We, the authors, like many others now and in the past, view education as a primary vehicle for equalizing the opportunities and potential success of individuals who come from lower-status groups in our society. Women, as a generally lower-status group, have recently made some progress toward equity through education. More women have been trained to work in male-dominated, higher-paid fields and have become more aware of their legal rights and history. Men have also made progress toward sex equity through education. For example, many have gained key consumer skills as a result of participation in new coeducational courses in this area, and others have found that teaching young children is a satisfying occupation for males as well as females. We realize, however, that education alone will not create equality, even if the education received is completely equitable.

We also realize that many changes are needed to ensure the achievement of sex equity in educational activities and settings. Such equity with respect to sex, race, ethnicity, handicap, age, religion, and so on, is a matter of simple justice, whether or not it has a measurable causal effect on achieving larger educational or societal goals. Our educational institutions do not yet provide full equality for females and males. Many obvious types of inequalities in providing educational opportunities for both sexes—such as restrictions on enrollments for certain courses—have decreased, but subtle types of discrimination leading to differential learning opportunities and inequitable benefits still exist. Recent progress, setbacks, and continued gaps in the achievement of sex equity in American education are summarized in the education chapters of *The Women's Annual, 1983: A Year in Review* (Klein & Pritchard, Eds., 1984) and by one of his book's initial supporters, the National Advisory Council on Women's Educational Programs, in its 1981 report, *Title IX: The Half Full, Half Empty Glass*. Title IX of the 1972 Education Amendments prohibits discrimination on the basis of sex in education activities and programs that receive federal financial assistance. To provide positive incentives for state and local compliance with Title IX, Congress also passed program statutes and appropriated funds primarily through the Women's Educational Equity Act of 1974 (WEEA), Title IV of the 1964 Civil Rights Act (CRA IV), and the Vocational Education Amendments of 1976. These federal laws and a wide variety of state laws which support sex equity in education are written to help males as well as females receive the desired educational outcomes or benefits. For example, in elementary schools in the United States an important concern is for boys to increase their reading scores to reach parity with girls' scores. But since sex discrimination has more frequently harmed females, as authors we have given greater attention to the unique needs of females and to solutions that will help girls and women achieve parity with boys and men rather than the reverse.

Many believe that the democratic principles of our society call for equal educational opportunities. However, despite federal and state civil rights and sex equity legislation, some individuals do not believe that the achievement of equity is sufficient by itself, and believe that its value should be additionally justified on the basis of its enhancement of other aspects of education. Although we and many others believe that educational equity is appropriate for its own sake, we felt the need for a careful scrutiny of various sex equity strategies to determine which are the most and least effective contributors to the achievement of other educational outcomes. Furthermore, we believe that information about the effects of sex equity activities should add to the general knowledge about improving education. For example, information on institutionalizing sex equity in state education agencies, school districts, and schools may provide guidance on institutionalizing other types of educational programs.

While several recent books have focused on the phenomena of sex bias and stereotyping in society, and a few on sex discrimination in education, none of these publications has focused on the key issues and the effective strategies designed to achieve sex equity in or through education. This handbook is designed to fill this gap. As such, this effort is distinctive in the following ways: First, it addresses key concerns in those sex equity and education fields that have not been addressed systematically before but that are essential to achieving goals in either field. Second, it provides a set of assumptions about sex equity phenomena in education which are set forth for examination, clarification, and modification where necessary. Third, it provides individuals concerned with increasing sex equity with a scholarly, yet practical, examination and discussion of the relationships between the current issues facing them and the answers (principles and practices) designed to achieve sex equity in education. Most previous books on women's equity documented the barriers or problems, but not the possible answers. Fourth, it approaches issues and answers about achieving sex equity from a variety of education perspectives ranging from administrative structures and activities to general instructional strategies, specific content areas, and diverse types of populations. Fifth, its authors have used evidence as documentation for arriving at, or supporting, their recommendations on how to achieve sex equity both in and through education. In placing emphasis on describing current knowledge about the answers or solutions to problems, the authors have addressed the same basic questions about how sex equity activities in their domain contribute to attitudinal, motivational, perceptual, or behavioral outcomes of females compared to males; decrease sex stereotyping in general for females and males; and affect other educationally significant outcomes that are important to parents, educators, or society.

And finally, this book was developed by a unique confluential effort involving over two hundred researchers, evaluators, developers, disseminators, and practitioners with expertise in sex equity and education who served voluntarily and without financial remuneration as authors, reviewers, and editors. In these capacities they synthesized evidence from empirical and qualitative research and evaluation studies and from their personal sex equity program development and implementation experiences. Such synthetic activities helped them arrive at agreements on their recommendations for achieving sex equity in and through education.

SUSAN SHURBERG KLEIN

March 5, 1984

Acknowledgments

This *Handbook for Achieving Sex Equity through Education* was developed through a unique collaborative process. The editors, authors, and contributors worked together to synthesize and consolidate an enormous amount of critical research, evaluation, and practical information on sex equity. Most chapters were written by more than one author, and all benefited from 3 to 30 additional experts' contributions and critiques. During the almost three years spent writing and revising this book some chapters changed considerably, but all were written to mesh with the emerging conceptual framework for achieving sex equity in and through education described in chapter 1. Thus, we first acknowledge each other's help.

We also acknowledge the support and assistance of the following groups: (1) from April 1981 to July 1982, the members and staff of the National Advisory Council on Women's Educational Programs under executive director Joy Simonson; (2) the National Coalition for Sex Equity in Education, composed of professional educators at the local, state, and national levels with responsibility for sex equity who meet annually and exchange information via a newsletter; (3) Women Educators, which monitors sex equity in the federal arena and sponsors annual awards for research, curricular development, and activism; (4) the Special Interest Group: Research on Women and Education of the American Educational Research Association (AERA), which encourages scholarly research on equity issues and, through its newsletter, its annual midyear conference, and sessions at the AERA annual meeting, provides a mechanism for sharing information about research relating to women; (5) the Committee on the Role and Status of Women in Educational R&D of the AERA, which brings the concerns of women members to the attention of the AERA Council and to the membership at large through activities including sponsoring program sessions at the annual meeting, assisting in the coordination of AERA-sponsored research efforts in equity areas, and maintaining contact among equity groups; and (6) the American Educational

Research Association and particularly its Publications Committee and Executive Council, which agreed that AERA should sponsor this book, in part to help AERA implement its Equity Resolution, which states: "AERA resolves to use its influence to promote equity in all areas of education by supporting the maintenance of strong civil rights laws and Federal and state programs and activities which support equity in education."

We want to thank the Polaroid Corporation and to express our appreciation for the collaborative efforts of Barbara Nelson and Alison Bernstein of the Ford Foundation, which joined with another foundation to provide a matching grant to enable the Johns Hopkins University Press to sell this large handbook at a lower than normal price.

We appreciate the insight and skill of Johns Hopkins University Press science editor Wendy Harris, who recognized the promise in this book and worked to make it a reality; and Carol Ehrlich, manuscript editor, who had the unenviable task of working with over 50 authors.

We thank the members of our Advisory Board for their ongoing role in advising us and others on the implications of this work and on how it might be shared and improved in the next edition.

Finally, we all thank our supportive colleagues, friends, and families, who understand the importance of our efforts to achieve sex equity in and through education.

1
Examining the Achievement of Sex Equity in and through Education

Susan S. Klein, Lillian N. Russo,
Patricia B. Campbell, and Glen Harvey

In this chapter we present the conceptual framework that guided the volume authors' examination of the issues and answers related to the achievement of sex equity in and through education. This framework contains both descriptive and prescriptive perspectives. The descriptive aspects help us examine the relationship between education and sex equity in society; the nature of sex differences and similarities from both individually-oriented psychological perspectives and group-oriented sociological perspectives; and the relationship among the various input, process, and outcome factors related to differential treatment of females and males and to the nature of sex role stereotyping in education.

The prescriptive aspects help us evaluate the extent to which what we are measuring comes close to achieving our sex equity goals. In developing the prescriptive aspects of our conceptual framework, we have also arrived at some common assumptions about the nature of these equity process and outcome goals. The prescriptive dimension of our conceptual framework is a necessary part of this book because it guided the selection of research perspectives and descriptive information to focus attention on areas of concern for sex equity in education; issues or needs related to sex equity goals or values; and common answers or responses to the equity issues.

THE DESCRIPTIVE DIMENSION OF THE CONCEPTUAL FRAMEWORK

The descriptive components of our conceptual framework are shown in figure 1 and table 1. Figure 1 illustrates how we view the relationship of sex equity in education to sex equity in society. The arrows from the inner "sex equity in education" circle to the outer "sex equity in society" and "society"

The authors gratefully acknowledge the assistance of Rita Bornstein in developing the conceptual framework.

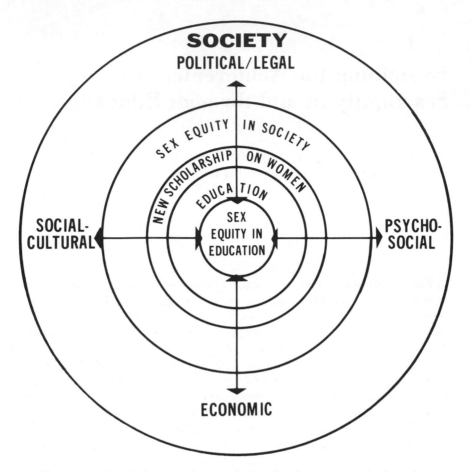

Figure 1.   The relationship of sex equity in education to sex equity in society.

circles show how we view the achievement of sex equity *through* education. The arrows go in both directions to indicate that we recognize the equal roles of the general economic, social-cultural, political-legal, psychosocial, and other factors in influencing the nature of sex equity in education. We also realize that sex equity concerns are just one type of concern in the larger domains of education and society. Many aspects of our shared assumptions about the nature of these relationships are described in part I of the book. The narrow circle, "new scholarship on women," is included to show that we share common sex equity goals and understandings about sex differences and similarities and sex role development as well as about appropriate methodological approaches for sex equity research. Thus, figure 1 provides a general framework for subsequent descriptions of how sex equity may be achieved *through* education. As shown in table 1, we were able to be even more explicit about common ways to describe and measure sex equity *in* education.

Table 1 charts most of the complexities that we have considered in describing issues and answers about sex equity in our areas of expertise. Following the guidance provided by this aspect of the conceptual framework, the authors put major emphasis on sex equity as it involves the learner and used the initial input, process, and outcome dimensions as they described their evidence. This table has also been used to remind the authors to describe assumptions and evidence about the causes of sex-based inequities or progress toward equity. In doing so, they have been asked to examine two types of phenomena: comparisons of female and male learners to study sex discrimination, and sex role stereotyping as it relates to both sexes. While it is possible to merge the dimensions relating to these two interrelated concepts of sex discrimination and sex stereotyping by subsuming sex stereotyping under sex discrimination, such a merger would have made it difficult to clarify important distinctions between these two concepts. Thus, we have found it more useful to differentiate the two concepts and discuss them separately.

Measuring Sex Discrimination in Education: Comparisons by Sex

The "learner attributes" column in the top half of table 1 is used to remind the authors to note relevant ascribed nonmalleable learner characteristics such as sex, race, ethnicity, age, and permanent disability status. There is some debate about the extent to which some learner characteristics such as intelligence and aptitude are malleable or likely to be changed by education. Although we believe that many of the "external preprocess influences" mentioned in column 1.2 may not be directly relevant to sex equity concerns and that the relationship between these factors and subsequent process or outcome variables is hard to determine, we have included this category for authors who find it relevant.

The major education process categories include "access" (2.1) and "treatment" (2.2). In describing these categories it is important to examine content, staff and students, and instructional materials. Thus, authors may describe whether the same cognitive, affective, and psychomotor items are taught to female and male learners, in either sex-segregated or coeducational settings. For example, are boys taught advanced science and girls shorthand? In the staff and student category it is likely that teachers, other personnel, peers, and sometimes even investigators interact differentially with students by sex. In investigating sex differences, it is important to note subtle as well as overt differences and differences that may arise when the learner is a token representative of her/his sex, race, or other ascribed category.

Column 3.1 contains a list of learner variables of particular interest in past studies of sex differences, which will be described in more detail in the chapters

Table 1. Measuring Sex Equity in Education

Factors	1. Initial input		2. The educational process as it involves the learner		3. Outcomes	
	1.1. Learner attributes	1.2. External preprocess influences	2.1. Access	2.2. Treatment	3.1. Learner outcomes	3.2. Related outcomes
Comparisons by sex	Compare females and males according to their ascribed characteristics such as race, ethnicity, age, handicap as well as any pretreatment experiences or scores on outcome or other measures known to correlate consistently for females and males with the outcome measures. Discuss assumptions about the causes of any sex differences such as whether they are genetic (biochemical) or learned (psychosocial).	Describe relevant institutional input, per pupil expenditures, educational facilities, male-female personnel ratio, expectations for learners, attitudes toward learners, which may differentially influence females and males.	Describe access to educational treatments (policies and practices which influence learners' opportunities to participate, e.g. recruitment, admissions, and mentoring). Note whether access is the same or different for the sexes. If the same, describe whether it is separate, but equal. If different, is it provided on the basis of need, merit, or both? Measurement should consider the importance of and difficulty in obtaining access.	Describe educational treatments (activities, programs, products, or practices which involve the learner such as courses, materials, and classroom interactions). Note whether the treatments are the same or different for the sexes. If the same, describe whether they are separate, but equal. If different, are they provided on the basis of need, merit, or both? Include relevant information on the content of instruction, role of educators, and role of educational products and practices as they re-	Compare female and male learners on variables such as the following: Nonbehavioral: attitudes, expectations, motivations, aspirations, self-assessments, moral development, cognitive achievement Short-term behavioral: anxiety, empathy, sociability, nurturance, cooperation, level of activity, aggression, dependency, competitive behavior, enrollment in courses, equal status cross-sex interactions Summative behavioral: educational attainment, incomes, success in parent-	These outcomes do not need to be composed of results from learners and may be by-products of the sex equity process. Examples include: ○ Measures of organizational effectiveness —school attendance rate —school climate ○ Increased teacher effectiveness if teachers were not considered the learners. ○ Costs of the sex equity process —costs in time, money, effort for educators —feasibility to educators in terms of ease of use, con-

flicts with other activities
—satisfaction of teacher, administration or training, nurturing, career choices, civic activities

Sex-based comparisons of the above outcomes may be measured on the basis of whether they are:
○ the same (identical)
○ proportional
○ minimal standards
○ same progress (gains)
○ equivalent, but not identical

er with the equity process

Describe common learner outcomes in terms of:
○ Nonbehavioral measures such as attitudes and expectations about sex stereotyping, masculinity and femininity scales.
○ Short-term behavioral indicators:
—knowledge of equal rights on the basis of sex, contributions of both sexes, awareness of inaccurate sex stereotypes
—affective measures such as information on sexual harassment or segregation patterns, sexism in language
—experiential measures of nontraditional career choice, compliance with Title IX
○ Summative behavioral indicators such as employment in nontraditional jobs, or assuming nonstereotyped family roles.

late to female and male learners.

Measurement should consider adequacy and frequency of the activity as it affects the learners.

Describe the nature and extent of sex role stereotyping in any of the two above categories of the educational process as it involves the learner by answering questions such as:

Are the policies or activities:
○ sex-biased or stereotyped?
○ about sex stereotyping in society and equity laws?

Are teachers, peers, and others teaching sex stereotyping or the elimination of same by their actions relating to direct instruction such as assignment of sex-stereotyped tasks or by modeling sex-stereotyped behavior.

Are the instructional materials sex biased, sex fair, or sex affirmative?

Extent of sex stereotyping

Describe sex role stereotypes commonly shared by both sexes and the degree to which learners and educators believe that these stereotypes can be changed. For each category of outcome measures, describe those which measure sex stereotyping specifically (i.e., attitudes toward desirability of sex role stereotyping). Focus on learners' internalized sex stereotyped views or self-perceptions, particularly as they are perceived in relation to the opposite sex. Where possible, describe the interaction of sex role stereotypes with racial, ethnic, age, disability, or other pertinent stereotypes. Focus on the organizational role in providing a context for sex stereotyping.

on sex differences and sex role development. This column also contains suggestions on diverse ways to measure sex-based comparisons of learners ranging from proportional relationships to differences in rates of change. The "related outcomes" suggested in column 3.2 are intended to remind authors to look for ways that sex equity in education contributes to important organizational and cost-effectiveness outcomes such as a decrease in school violence or the identification of effective, easy-to-use, low-cost instructional strategies that benefit students of both sexes.

Measuring the Extent of Sex Stereotyping in Education

The bottom half of table 1, although organized like the top half, focuses on sex stereotyping—or attributing abilities, motivations, behaviors, values, and roles to a person or group solely because of sex. These dimensions in the top half of table 1 address sex differences that may or may not have been sex stereotyped. The dimensions in the bottom half of table 1, unlike those in the top half, assume that sex stereotyping, much like skills in mathematics or human relations, is learned and performed by both sexes and sometimes results in the same behavior for each sex.

In column 1, "initial input," authors are reminded to note their assumptions about sex stereotypes by, among other things, stating their assumptions about whether some sex-stereotyped learner characteristics may be malleable or learnable for one sex and nonmalleable for the other. For instance, some people believe that boys need to learn nurturing, caring skills while girls inherit these skills and just need the proper environment for them to appear naturally. It is fairly easy to distinguish sex stereotypes in the educational process from the simple sex differential processes described in the top half of this column. To identify sex stereotyping in content, the authors have described whether the same information presented to female and male students in the same way is sex biased or stereotyped. The nature and effects of sex stereotyping in content and instructional materials are described in the chapter on that topic. To identify sex stereotyping in interpersonal interactions, authors may note the extent to which the teachers and students are either teaching each other traditional sex roles and to sex-segregate themselves, or teaching, modeling, and facilitating nonsexist responsibilities and behaviors and cross-sex interactions. This research is synthesized in the chapter on classroom organization and climate.

Although learner outcome indicators of sex stereotyping could be included in examples for column 3.1, which is focused on comparing scores by sex, we have singled many of them out for special attention in the bottom half of column 3, which focuses on sex stereotyping for both sexes. Thus, examples of nonbehavioral measures of stereotypes include attitudes, perceptions, and expectations toward sex stereotyping and scales designed to measure masculinity and femininity. However, we urge caution in using masculinity/femininity scales as outcome measures because of various problems inherent in validating the stereotypes upon which they are based.

Summarizing Our Descriptive Perspectives

In summary, figure 1 contains a framework for describing the relationship of sex equity in education to sex equity in society, and table 1 contains a framework for measuring and describing sex equity in education. Table 1 is primarily focused on the learner. It assumes that the authors will describe systematic and causal relationships among the input, process, and outcome columns. While it has been designed to be a circular continuum reading from the left "initial input" column to the far right "outcomes" column and back to the "initial input" column, there is no absolute distinction among the columns. As Borich and Jemelka (1982, p. 59) point out, "Any event or condition can be viewed as occupying space on a continuum such that it is simultaneously an end to those events and conditions that preceded it and a means to those that follow." Thus, an outcome, such as a satisfactory test score, may also determine access to a course. Table 1 is based on many systems models of educational research and recent equity continuums developed by Bornstein (1981) and Campbell and Klein (1982). It has been designed to highlight information dealing with educational equity and with gender or sex—but not sexuality. Finally, while the focus of table 1 is primarily on describing sex equity in education, some of the summative outcome variables may indicate ways that sex equity in education relates to achieving sex equity in society.

THE PRESCRIPTIVE DIMENSION OF THE CONCEPTUAL FRAMEWORK

As previously discussed in relation to figure 1, which focuses attention on achieving sex equity through education, our prescriptive aspects of the conceptual framework are partially represented by the thin circle in that figure called "new scholarship on women." This and related concepts and assumptions about sex equity in society will be discussed more extensively in the chapters in part I. Some other aspects of our prescriptive dimensions, which primarily systematize our descriptive dimensions to explain sex equity in education, underlie the categories presented in table 1. These other prescriptive aspects are our normative values about what sex equity should be and our assumptions about how we want the causal relationships among the columns in table 1 to operate. Although we have fairly clear agreement among ourselves and with our peers in the field of educational equity about what we generally want sex equity to be, we are just beginning to build our knowledge base and consensus about the precise nature of our sex equity goals.

We have based the following outline of our four basic sex equity goals on the horizontal process and outcome categories and the vertical sex discrimination and sex stereotyping dimensions in table 1.

1. Process goals: eliminate sex discrimination by
   • Providing the same access and treatment to female and male learners
     —within the same context

—possibly in a separate (sex-segregated) but equal context
  • Providing differential access and treatment to female and male learners based on their needs, their merit, or their needs and merit combined
2. Outcome goals: the elimination of sex discrimination when
  • Both females and males acquire the most valued characteristics and skills, whether or not they are generally attributed to the opposite sex or to their own sex
  • Both sexes achieve at least minimum levels of competency in the desired outcomes
  • Members of the less dominant sex achieve parity with members of the dominant sex group
  • The range of desirable outcomes is extended beyond those formerly restricted on the basis of sex
  • There is a trend toward less sex differentiation in achievements
  (These goals may apply to nonbehavioral short-range outcomes, medium-range behavioral education outcomes, or long-range outcomes that indicate societal change.)
3. Process goals: decrease sex stereotyping and sex segregation in education by
  • Decreasing sex-role expectations and behavior that limit the opportunities of members of either sex to maximize their individual talents
  • Increasing knowledge and use of sex equitable (sex fair and sex affirmative) processes by examining and counteracting sex stereotyping in society
4. Outcome goals: the reduction of sex stereotyping and sex segregation in education and society when
  • Fewer jobs, roles, activities, and expectations are differentiated by sex
  • There is decreased use of sex stereotypes in decision making by and about individuals
  • Sex segregation in education and society caused by sex stereotyping is reduced

This outline reveals that our goals are not entirely definitive or mutually exclusive. They reflect the complexity of what we are dealing with and the uncertainty of our knowledge about, and subsequent prescriptions for, cause-effect relationships that will advance sex equity. Our goals are multifaceted and likely to differ according to the particular learner and educational context. For example, if we were certain that sex-integrated settings were best for reaching the same goals for females and males in all circumstances, we might never select separate but equal process goals. However, since such causal evidence is not yet available, some authors may find that special kinds of sex-differential treatment in the short term may be needed to reach longer-term goals.

Most laws to provide sex equity are concerned with a combination of process and outcome goals dealing with sex discrimination. For example, state Equal Rights Amendments (ERAs) and Title IX prohibit differential coverage on the basis of sex. What they cover—such as the ERAs' "equality of rights" or Title

IX's "nondiscrimination," "exclusion from participation in," or "denial of benefits under any education program or activity"—could be considered as either process or outcome goals. Although goals 3 and 4 focusing on decreasing sex stereotypes may be viewed as enabling educators to eliminate nonbiological sex differences (that is, the anti-sex discrimination goals), some laws, such as the sex equity provisions of the 1976 federal Vocational Education Act Amendment and state laws designed to decrease sex stereotyping in instructional materials, also specifically emphasize decreasing sex stereotypes as both process and outcome goals.

These goals have also guided us in our selection and discussion of issues and answers in each of the chapters. Something is an issue only because it describes what exists or what should exist in relation to our goals. For example, we would define the need for high school females to improve their achievement in math as an issue because we found females generally have lower scores than their male peers. This inequitable relationship is incongruent with our outcome goal 2, favoring the elimination of sex discrimination or differential results on desirable educational outcomes. A nonissue for our purposes would be a relationship with no apparent relevance to our sex equity goals, such as the total per pupil expenditure as it relates to student achievement in coeducational schools. Answers indicate causal, evidence-based knowledge that shows how one process goal contributes to the achievement of other process goals or how the process goals relate to the achievement of outcome goals. Answers may also be viewed as the identification of criteria or goals which will then be used to find more answers. Clusters of answers which support each other can be viewed as general principles to guide the practice of sex equity in education or as theories to facilitate the development of sex equity as a field of inquiry.

OTHER CONSIDERATIONS

Although we believe that no social research is completely objective, we have provided a balanced report on the many desirable and the few undesirable effects of sex equity activities. Our assumptions are stated throughout the volume so that readers will be able to put the issues, answers, and recommendations in perspective. Generally researchers are inclined to put greater emphasis on describing what works rather than what doesn't work. However, we have tried to balance this positive inclination in two ways. First, we have included information on costs. These costs may include undesirable or negative effects that seem to be associated with the desirable or positive effects. An example of such a situation may occur if the funds for female and male sports are equalized and in the process the funds available for predominantly male sports are decreased. The second way was to report undesirable effects of sex equity programs. For example, some sex equity activities that have focused on girls are difficult to use in coeducational classes. To the extent possible, we have used both empirical and qualitative types of evidence from a variety of sources to document and justify the key issues and answers in the chapters.

ORGANIZATION OF THE BOOK

The 25 chapters are grouped in the following major sections: Assumptions about the Nature and Value of Sex Equity; Administrative Strategies to Implement Sex Equity; General Educational Practices to Promote Sex Equity; Sex Equity Strategies in the Content Areas; Sex Equity Strategies for Specific Populations, and Sex Equity from Early Education through Postsecondary.

The authors of chapters in Part I have tried to document major understandings and assumptions that are shared by all the editors and authors to avoid repetition in individual chapters. Similarly, the subsequent parts are organized so that general information that is most likely to be a component of other chapters is included in the earlier sections of the book. Therefore, part II on Administrative Strategies to Implement Sex Equity and part III on General Educational Practices to Promote Sex Equity precede part IV on Sex Equity Strategies in the Content Areas. They also cover three major concerns of educators: administration, instruction, and curriculum.

Although the chapters and topics covered in this book represent the major areas of sex equity research and practice in education, we realize that some educational areas have been omitted. Many of these other pertinent sex equity topics will be identified in the overviews for each part.

Since we are attempting to achieve fairly comprehensive coverage of what is known about sex equity activities in American education, there are some redundancies among chapters. For example, practices to promote sex equity in teacher and student classroom interactions have been tried in sex equity content areas such as physical education or math instruction and with learners at different age levels. Where we have emphasized similar types of activities, we have cross-referenced each others' chapters.

To facilitate the use of comparable information from several chapters of interest, authors in parts II through VI used a parallel structure for their chapters. The authors first described the rationale or key sex equity needs and issues in their area. Then they described how best to respond to the issues, based on evidence of the effectiveness of various strategies in achieving the sex equity process or outcome goals. Although all these authors were encouraged to give relatively more attention to the answers than the issues, some were less able to comply because less is known about what works to promote sex equity in some areas of education than in others. The final chapter in the book contains recommendations for policy makers, developers, educational practitioners, sex equity advocates, researchers, and evaluators.

REFERENCES

Borich, G. D., & Jemelka, R. P. (1982). *Programs and systems: An evaluation perspective*. New York: Academic Press.

Bornstein, R. (1981). *Title IX compliance and sex equity: Definitions, distinctions, costs, and benefits (Urban Diversity Series,* No. 73, ERIC Clearinghouse on Urban Education). New York: Columbia University, Teachers College.

Campbell, P. B., & Klein, S. (1982). Equity issues in education. In *Encyclopedia of educational research* (5th Ed.). New York: Macmillan.

PART I

Assumptions about the Nature and Value of Sex Equity

Carol Kehr Tittle

Sex equity is a broad term with different meanings for the students, parents, teachers, administrators, researchers, and others who are concerned participants in the schools. In this first section the authors examine research and scholarly writing that gives meaning to the concept of sex equity, those ideas and findings that provide the foundations for the efforts that are being made to achieve sex equity in the schools. Three main assumptions can be drawn from these chapters: (1) there are both pragmatic and philosophical bases for sex equity in education; (2) there is a strong interdisciplinary basis for sex equity in the new scholarship on women; and (3) there is a supporting base of social and behavioral sciences research from which to derive sex equitable approaches to education. The five chapters in this section both expand and provide the rationale for these assumptions.

Harvey and Noble find that the economic and legal status of women forms the pragmatic reasons for sex equity. The year-to-year stability of sex differences in wages and types of occupations entered means fewer resources for women to deal with the day-to-day impact of changing family structures: higher divorce rates and more female-headed families. These economic inequities become more cruel as increasing numbers of women enter the labor force, and women now constitute 42% of the total labor force. Some recognition of these inequities is found in legal remedies, but these have not had much of an overall impact on the key indicators of inequity in status: lower wages and occupational segregation. Thus, there is a critical need to give high priority to sex equity efforts in education to support legislative and regulatory efforts.

There is another rationale for sex equity efforts in education, one found in the ethical argument advanced by Greene. Historically the private and public realms of social arrangements and politics have been constructed in opposition to each other. The nature of the public realm, the definition of feminine reality in terms of "natural" virtues, and the linking of the "natural" to the subordinate has had harmful consequences: the implication that the matter of human rights, like the matter of justice, is irrelevant when it comes to women's lives. Reconsideration of the ethical argument justifies the claims and courses of action such as those described in the sex equity programs in later chapters and further supports the pragmatic rationale developed by Harvey and Noble.

Biklen and Shakeshaft report on the evolution of the new scholarship on women. Feminist theory and visions, along with the development of women's studies courses focusing on women's roles and perspectives in the academic disciplines, have resulted in a gradual and continuing base of scholarship on women's participation in and contributions to all human endeavors. This new scholarship on women has found increasing acceptance in the academy and is now in the forefront of the transformation of the curriculum in postsecondary institutions of education. The sex equity efforts in the schools draw on the research findings of these scholars and will follow the movement to integrate further the research on women into the curriculum in elementary and secondary schools. This important development is another stage in the attainment of sex equity in education, following efforts to remove stereotypes, increase representation of women in curriculum materials, and broaden career choices for women.

Just as the philosophic rationale rejects the "natural" virtues ascribed to women as the basis of inequity, research in the social and behavioral sciences finds little evidence of "natural" sex differences in the social and cognitive skills of boys and girls in schools. Research *cannot* justify discouraging girls from courses in mathematics and the sciences or discouraging boys from the careers of teaching and nursing. Quite the contrary. Linn and Petersen examine the facts about individual and sex differences in studies of the biological, cognitive, and psychosocial areas. They provide a perspective on sex differences by considering one of the major issues in such studies: the assignment of causal influences to heredity or environment in explaining any observed differences in performance on psychological tasks. They conclude that no clear evidence exists for genetic explanations of the few and small sex differences in cognitive skills which are found, nor is there such evidence for psychosocial characteristics.

Many of the differences thought to exist between the sexes in various stages of their development (for example, play activities), as well as in their roles in adult life, are the result of what one researcher has suggested occurred during the 1800s when "virtually all human relations were reshaped by a vast system of what modern sociologists would call sex-role stereotyping" (Demos, cited in Collins, 1982, p. B10). Schau describes theory and research on the development of sex roles and their implications for sex equity in education. The tendency to sex-stereotype behaviors and other attributes of females and males in our culture has a strong and pervasive influence throughout our lives. Yet changes are occurring in the work and parenting roles of women. Many of the educational equity materials have been directed at reducing stereotyping in these areas in an attempt to reflect what actually happens to men and women in their current lives. There are further role analyses and equity materials to be developed; these developments will focus less on single roles in isolation, such as that of worker, and more on patterns of adult roles, thus examining the conflicts and tensions variously identified as role ambiguity, role strain, and role proliferation.

In part I, then, the authors have emphasized the value of sex equity in educational settings as well as describing the research basis for the assumptions that guide sex equity programs. Sex equity in education is a part of human rights, but Greene tells us that equity must be claimed, and then attained through "demystification"—through knowing the status of women in our culture, through increased knowledge of women's lives and attainments in all areas, through being aware that there is no evidence of educationally relevant sex differences for abilities and characteristics required in schooling and adult life, and through understanding the influence of sex role expectations and the changing life cycle of women. Beyond the demystification steps are the acts of critiquing and adding further to our knowledge about both women and men and, finally, of taking positive steps to attain sex equity in education. The remaining parts of this book continue the critiques and describe our progress in developing interventions to achieve sex equity in and through education.

REFERENCE

Collins, G. (1982, May 17). New perspectives on father and his role. *New York Times,* p. B10.

2
Economic Considerations for Achieving Sex Equity through Education

Glen Harvey and Elizabeth Noble

Education is only one of many aspects of society which affects the achievement of sex equity. Since it is not possible to examine adequately all of these influential factors, this book has been intentionally narrowed to focus primarily on the role of education in attaining equity between the sexes. In reading the following educationally focused chapters, however, it is important to keep in mind that the context in which sex equity is to be achieved is not a simple one involving only educational factors. It is complex, involving the interactions of a variety of factors, some of which enhance the effectiveness of education in achieving sex equity while others restrict its impact. Understanding these other influential factors and the complex, interactive context that they form can yield insight into the successes and failures of educational efforts to achieve sex equity and can suggest ways in which less successful efforts can be modified to interact more positively with these other factors.

The purpose of this chapter is to illustrate the complex, interactive nature of the larger context formed by these other influential factors and to examine the impact of education on the achievement of sex equity within such a context. This will be accomplished through an examination of the relationship of education to the achievement of sex equity in the economic arena. Economic factors are considered by many to be the most informative and reliable indicators of whether and in what areas equity has been achieved. The concept of equity itself is often interpreted as a distributional term denoting "the preferred shape of the distributional curve or just distribution of economic resources in society" (Hewlett, 1977, p. 31) and is examined extensively in economic literature. The economic sphere also illustrates the complexity of the relationships among economic factors, education, and sex equity as well as indicating the difficulty of actually attaining the goal of sex equity.

The authors wish to thank Wolfgang Gurr, Susan Klein, and Carol Tittle for their assistance in critiquing this chapter.

17

In addition to discussing economic and educational factors, major legal and regulatory remedies designed to address gender-related economic inequities; will be indicated whenever appropriate. Occasional references to related psychosocial and social-cultural factors will also be made, although these factors will be examined extensively in later chapters.

ECONOMIC FACTORS

While there are a variety of ways in which equity can be specifically defined, the concept generally involves issues of access, treatment, and/or outcomes (Harvey, 1982); and, as Weale (1978) suggests,

> equity arguments are normally used in a context where one social group is being benefited relative to another. . . . The normal method of arguing is to say that one group should be better treated than it is because another group like it in relevant respects receives better treatment. (p. 28)

This is precisely the line of argument advocated by many proponents of sex equity in the economic sphere, particularly when the focus is narrowed to issues of the labor market. When such a method of argument is applied, there is little evidence to suggest that sex equity has been achieved in the economic arena. There is, in fact, considerable evidence to indicate that women are not equitably treated, even when, in Weale's terms, women are equivalent to their male counterparts in all "relevant respects."

Progress in lessening gender-related economic inequities has, at best, been mixed. The impact of education on achieving sex equity in the economic arena has also been mixed. In some areas, education positively affects the reduction of gender-related economic inequities; in other areas, the impact is negligible; and in still others, education may even have some negative effect.

In order to identify where gender-related economic inequities have been reduced and to examine the impact of education upon these inequities, four major aspects of the labor market will be examined: labor force participation, unemployment, occupational choice, and wages.

Labor Force Participation

In 1980, 52% of all women were participating in the labor force, constituting 42% of the total work force. This represents a dramatic increase in female labor force participation. In 1950, for example, females constituted a mere 29% of the total work force with only 34% of all women participating in the labor force (Sherman, Sheeran, Thornton, & Hill, 1982).

A variety of factors can be associated with this sharp rise in female labor force participation. Wilson (1981) suggests that one such factor is the increase in the level of educational attainment of females. Female-male differences in average educational attainment are now minimal, and female participation in higher education is rapidly increasing. During the period 1976/77 to 1978/79 alone, females registered marked increases in the number of earned bachelor's degrees (up 4.7%), doctor's degrees (up 13.6%), and first-professional degrees (law, theology, medicine—up 35.2%) (Dearman & Plisko, 1981).

A comparison between the rate of labor force participation and the level of educational attainment indicates that females with higher levels of education have correspondingly higher rates of participation in the labor force. In the fall of 1979, for example, the rate of labor force participation of female school dropouts was 48.4% compared to a rate of 78.8% for high school graduates, 83.9% for women with 1 to 3 years of college, and 93.4% for women with 4 or more years of college (Dearman & Plisko, 1981). This suggests a positive relationship between increased equity between the sexes in education (in this case, raising the levels of educational attainment of females to correspond more to those of males) and increased sex equity in labor force participation.

Education is not the only factor associated with the increase in female participation in the labor force, however. Wilson (1981) also points to changes in family planning and the availability of labor demand. For example, the number of women delaying childbirth rose during the previous decade, with first births occurring to women 21 years old or younger declining from 55.9% in 1965–69 to 47.4% in 1975–79. During the same time period, the average number of lifetime births expected by 18–24-year-old married women declined from 2.9 in 1967 to 2.2 in 1979 (U.S. Department of Commerce, 1980). In addition, more than half of all women with children under the age of 18 were participating in the labor force by 1979, including nearly half of the mothers with preschoolers (NACWEP, 1981).

Changes in the economy and the family structure during the 1970s are also suggested as factors associated with this increase. Families headed by single parents increased from 1 in 9 families in 1970 to 1 in 5 by 1978 (Reder, 1981). The majority of these single-parent families are headed by females (WREI, 1982), thus expanding the number of women with responsibility for the support of themselves and others. A disproportionate number of these female-headed families are poor. In fact, single mothers constitute "the fastest growing poverty group" in the United States (WREI, 1982, p. 8). In 1978, 1 in every 3 female-headed households was poor, while only 1 in 18 male-headed households was poor; 60% of 15–24-year-old female heads of households lived in poverty; and 50.6% of black female heads of households were poor (Reder, 1981).

Changing expectations of females, increased educational and employment opportunities for women, the efforts of the civil rights and women's rights movements, and the impact of legal and regulatory remedies such as affirmative action and Title IX suggest still other factors that could be associated with this rise in participation rates.

It remains unclear which, if any, of these factors can be attributed with primary responsibility for the rise in the number of females participating in the labor force. It is likely that it is the complex interactions of a variety of factors which have resulted in the increase. It is safe to say, however, that education is a major factor affecting this increase, both directly, for example, through increased levels of educational attainment, and indirectly, for example, through the impact of education on other potentially significant factors such as family planning.

Unemployment

Historically, women have experienced higher unemployment rates than men, and there is little evidence to indicate that this trend will change significantly in the near future. In 1976, for example, the unemployment rate for adult women was systematically higher than for men within racial and ethnic categories: 5.9% (white men) compared to 8.7% (white women); 16.3% (Puerto Rican men) compared to 22.3% (Puerto Rican women); and 15.9% (black men) compared to 18.9% (black women) (President's Commission for a National Agenda for the Eighties, 1980).

The discrepancies between female and male unemployment rates fluctuate with the economy. Gender-related differences are maximized during periods of strong economic growth and minimized during periods of recession. This is largely the result of the concentration of women in clerical and service occupations, which are affected less by a slow economy than are the construction and industrial occupations dominated by men. Far from being an advantage for women, however, the concentration of females in particular occupations results in the continued occupational sex segregation of females in low-paying jobs, as will be discussed in the following section.

More positively, female unemployment rates—similar to labor force participation rates—appear to be affected by the level of educational attainment. In 1979 the overall unemployment rate for women was 12.4%. When the level of educational attainment is taken into consideration, however, the rate of female unemployment steadily decreases as the level of education increases. For example, dropouts experienced a 24.7% rate; high school graduates, 10.0%; those with 1 to 3 years of college, 7.1%; and those with 4 or more years of college, 4.6% (Dearman & Plisko, 1981).

This suggests that the overall female unemployment rate may begin to decrease in response to the increase in female educational attainment discussed in the previous section. The probability of this occurring remains slight, however. A recent study of earned doctorates since 1940, for example, indicates that involuntary unemployment for female 1975–78 Ph.D.'s was two and one-half times higher than for male Ph.D.'s (Ahern & Scott, 1981). Thus, equal educational attainment has not resulted in equal rates of unemployment *within* educational levels. In addition, since women are normally the last hired and generally have less status, power, and seniority than their male counterparts, it is more likely that female unemployment rates will remain disproportionately high. The seniority rule of "last hired, first fired" continues to work to the disadvantage of women and minorities. In 1981, there was some cause for optimism when the lower federal courts weakened the seniority rule by ordering that layoffs in the Boston police and fire departments not affect the percentages of minorities in those departments. On November 1, 1982, however, the Supreme Court agreed to review the Boston case (*Boston Firefighters Union v. Boston Chapter, NAACP, et al.*), thus throwing the previous ruling into question.

Occupational Choice

As was discussed in the previous section, the segregation of females in low-paying occupations continues to persist, indicating another aspect of the labor market where equity between the sexes has yet to be achieved. Seventy percent of men in the labor force are in occupations dominated by men; 54% of women are in occupations dominated by women. Of 553 classified occupations in the 1970 U.S. Census, 310 had at least 80% male incumbents and 50 had at least 80% female incumbents (Treiman & Hartmann, 1981). Although this dominance of particular occupations by one or the other sex is not by necessity negative, as Trieman and Hartmann (1981) point out, "Not only do women do different work than men, but also the work women do is paid less, and the more an occupation is dominated by women the less it pays" (p. 28).

While a variety of factors have been suggested as possible causes of occupational sex segregation, it is often through education and training that a solution is sought. Considerable attention has been focused on providing the necessary education and training to enable women to move into traditionally male-dominated, higher-paying occupations. A variety of specific educational strategies and programs, many of which will be discussed in later chapters, have been developed to address the problem of occupational sex segregation. Legislative remedies, such as the 1976 Vocational Education Amendments and Title IX of the 1972 Higher Education Act, have been used to lend support to these educational strategies. Executive Orders 11246 and 11375 further support these efforts more directly in the labor market through the concept of affirmative action.

The success of these and other efforts to reduce occupational sex segregation as well as promote sex equity in general has been mixed. On the positive side, between 1972 and 1978 female enrollment in high school and post-high school vocational education programs increased by 60%, and the proportion of females in male-dominated vocational programs also showed a minor increase (NACWEP, 1981). Similarly, in higher education during 1978, 24% of all master's degrees in science and engineering fields were earned by women, as were 19% of doctor's degrees. While these degrees were heavily weighted toward the social and biological sciences, the number of women earning bachelor's degrees in the physical sciences and engineering has also increased (NSF/DOE, 1980). Occupational employment rates have tended to reflect such increases in educational attainment: for example, 10.4% of the science and engineering labor force in 1977 was female, an increase from 8.5% in 1973. While this participation rate remains extremely low, the rate of increase in the number of female scientists and engineers was nearly double that of men between 1974 and 1976 (15% compared to 8%) (NSF/DOE, 1980). The number of women receiving degrees in other traditionally male fields such as agriculture, architecture, and business and management has also increased (NACWEP, 1981).

On the negative side, females still tend to be concentrated in particular areas of academic specialization and/or vocational training. In higher education women continue to be represented disproportionately in the more general cultural fields such as English, languages, and fine arts, as well as education and the social sciences. They are poorly represented in disciplines with a strong scientific or technical emphasis such as mathematics and engineering. Similarly, in vocational programs, traditionally female areas such as nursing and general office and secretarial programs continue to be dominated by females; traditionally male areas such as electrical technology and auto mechanics are still dominated by males (Sherman et al., 1982).

Moreover, Dearman and Plisko (1981) report that

> women with any college experience were more likely than men to be professional and technical workers, but men at similar levels of college education were at least twice as likely as women to be managers or administrators. In addition, a full 44 percent of women with some college and 21 percent who held college degrees were employed as clerical workers in 1979. (p. 219)

This suggests that the positive effects of education on the achievement of sex equity have not always been as strong as had been hoped. Women with high levels of educational attainment still tend to remain in sex-segregated, lower-paying occupations such as clerical work, and those who enter more male-dominated occupations are significantly less likely to have positions of authority.

Wages

A comparison of female and male wages indicates still another area where economic inequities remain. A recent EEOC-commissioned study of measurement of job comparability indicates the persistent nature of female and male earning differentials. For example, in 1955–59, white women (full-time, year-round workers) had a median income 63.2% of that of white men; black and other women had a median income of 36.4% of that of white men. By 1965–69, the income of white women was 57.8%; for black and other women, 42.8%. And in 1975–78, it was 58.6% (white) and 55.8% (black/other). In 1978, the mean earnings of all adult (18 years or older) women (year-round, full-time, civilian workers) were 55.3% of the mean earnings of their white male counterparts. White women earned 55.6%, black women 52.3%, and women of Spanish origin 48.2% (Treiman & Hartmann, 1981).

Furthermore, males systematically receive higher wages within occupational categories, even within those occupations dominated by females. Ninety-six percent of registered nurses are female, yet the 1980 median weekly wage of males in the field was $311.32 compared to $296.98 earned by females. The discrepancy between female and male cashiers (86.9% female) was even greater: $149.27 (female) compared to $216.47 (male). The pattern is the same in male-dominated occupations. In the field of electrical engineering (96% male), for example, women had a 1980 median weekly wage of $344.21 compared to $505.12 earned by men; male carpenters (99.2% male) earned $304.03 compared to $196.40 (female); and male computer specialists (74.8% male) earned $439.47, while females in the same occupation earned only $335.19 (Sherman et al., 1982).

Explanations of female-male wage differentials have differed widely, often focusing on such factors as differences in female and male worker characteristics (experience, education, and work history, for example). Such explanations have not proved accurate, however. An analysis of studies designed to explain such wage differentials indicates that

> only two of the studies can explain more than one-fifth of the difference between men's and women's average earnings in terms of differences in worker characteristics. The two studies whose findings go furthest . . . account for less than half of the difference. (Treiman & Hartmann, 1981, p. 19)

The 1982 Working Conference on Women's Employment and Economic Status reached a similar conclusion in its Final Report: "Research on the wage discrepancy between men and women has shown that about half the difference can be explained by differences in skill and experience. The other half is due to discrimination" (WREI, 1982, p. 15).

Recent studies support these conclusions. A study of white-collar federal employees found that controlling for such influential factors as an employee's education, supervisory status, disabled veteran status, and age, white women still earned an average of $3,416 less than white men, and minority women earned $3,970 less than white men (Stasz, 1982).

A study of female and male scientists by the National Academy of Sciences' National Research Council indicates similar findings. Matching females and males by race, year, doctoral field, reputation of degree-granting department, and prestige of institution where employed and where the degree was earned did not eliminate salary and rank differences between females and males (Project on the Status and Education of Women, 1982).

It is clear from these studies that increased equality in female educational attainment has not eliminated, or even decreased, female-male wage differentials. The 1980 U.S. Census indicates that even when education is controlled for, mean annual earnings of full-time year-round female workers in 1978 remained substantially lower than those of white males. White women with less than 8 years of education earned 59.8% of what their white male counterparts earned, while black women earned even less—56.5%. With 4 years of high school, the percentage remained essentially the same—58% (white) and 57% (black). A college education made little difference, and the difference it did make was negative: 4 years of college—51.6% (white) and 54.6% (black); 5 or more years of college—56.8% (white) and 49.3% (black) (Treiman & Hartmann, 1981).

Theoretically, female-male wage differentials of the type cited above are illegal. The Equal Pay Act of 1963 prohibits discrimination in salaries and fringe benefits. Similarly, Title VII of the 1964 Civil Rights Act (from which much of the legal basis for prohibiting gender-related discrimination in employment derives) prohibits employment discrimination (including hiring, firing, compensation, promotion, and so forth) on the basis of race, color, religion, sex, and/or national origin. Additional laws, such as the Intergovernmental Personnel Act of 1970, which prohibits sex bias in merit systems for state or local government agencies receiving federal aid, and the 1978 Civil Service Reform Act, also (theoretically) prohibit such wage differentials. Pending court cases involving issues of comparable worth hold the potential for expanding interpretations of these legislative efforts to include the notion of equal pay for comparable work.

Seemingly, this body of laws and regulations should have been sufficient to prevent the wage differentials that continue to persist between females and males. And, in fact, there have been individual and class action suits that have been successful in challenging wage discrimination. In the area of equal pay, for example, there were 7,878 compliance actions from June 1964 to the end of fiscal 1977 involving over $147 million owed to more than 253,000 workers (Treiman & Hartmann, 1981). Yet these "successes" appear to have accomplished little in changing the overall inequitable situation; the discrepancy between female and male wages persists. As the above-cited report of the 1982 Working Conference on Women's Employment and Economic Status has stated, "Laws . . . banning discrimination on account of age, sex, or race are not monitored or enforced" (WREI, 1982, p. 15). Recent federal government efforts to weaken affirmative action, vocational education, and Title IX regulations and in general to reduce the federal commitment to the civil rights of women and minorities portend an even more inequitable situation in the future.

Still more negatively, education appears to have had even less of an impact on reducing this wage differential than have legal remedies. To briefly reiterate the previously cited data, during the period of 1955–59, the median income of white women was 63.2% of that of white men. This percentage decreased to 58.6% by 1975–78, even though the levels of educational attainment had risen for females. Similarly, in 1978 white women with less than 8 years of education earned a *higher* percentage of what their white male counterparts earned (59.8%) than did white women with 5 or more years of college (56.8%). The situation was even worse for black women: 49.3% (5 or more years of college) compared to 56.5% (less than 8 years of education). This, of course, is not to say that increases in educational equity have not had some positive effects on the wages of females. It does suggest, however, that increases in educational equity have not been successful in reducing the discrepancy between female and male wages and that efforts to achieve such a reduction must take into consideration not one but many factors that continue to perpetuate this economic inequity.

FURTHER THOUGHTS: THE SOCIAL UTILITY
OF SEX EQUITY

The above discussion illustrates the complexity of the relationships between economic factors and education and among economic factors, education, and sex equity. The relationships are not consistent, and often it is not even possible to determine their strength or direction. In some instances, education appears to positively affect the achievement of sex equity in the labor market as, for example, in the case of increased educational attainment of women apparently resulting in increased participation in the labor force. In other instances, neither the strength nor the direction of the relationship are clear as, for example, when the labor market exhibits a demand for particular occupations. In such cases, it is probable that women move to fill these positions in response to market demand rather than education, but the role of education in facilitating this movement is not known. And in still other instances, there appears to be no relationship between education and economic factors in achieving sex equity as, for example, in the area of wages, where equal or equivalent educational qualifications do not result in equal economic benefits.

On balance, increased sex equity in education has not been as successful as many had hoped in reducing gender-related economic inequities. Why is this the case? Why haven't the variety of efforts to promote sex equity been more successful in the economic arena?

One clue to better understanding such limited success lies in the nature of equity itself. Discussions of equity can often be reduced to questions of distribution—who gets what goods and services. When one person or group benefits, another normally loses. Thus, even if there is agreement concerning the causes of gender-related inequities, as well as agreement concerning effective remedies, there may not be agreement about what steps, if any, should be taken to eliminate such inequities or what our responsibility is to take such steps (Harvey, 1978). This suggests that values are integrally linked with equity policy—values often pragmatically based on self-interest.

This points to a major obstacle facing proponents of sex equity. Many men believe that sex equity is achieved at their expense. Convincing them that a sex equitable society is actually to their advantage is not an easy task. In the following chapter, Maxine Greene provides a persuasive philosophical argument for sex equity. Unfortunately, however, when the issue involves the redistribution of wealth, power, benefits, and status, self-interest often prevails over appeals to justice and equality. In such instances, the ethical justification for sex equity requires a supporting pragmatic justification, indicating how a sex equitable society ultimately benefits everyone.

Fullenwider's (1981) recent analysis of preferential hiring of blacks indicates a potentially viable model for this much-needed pragmatic rationale—what Fullenwider labels the "Social Utility Argument." This argument

> takes the form of showing that the aggregate well-being of society is promoted by some policy. . . . If the social "utility" (i.e., aggregate well-being) is raised, and raised at least as high as it would be by any other alternative, then the policy is said to be "in the public interest," or "for the common good." (Fullenwider, 1981, pp. 18–19)

A similar argument can and should be developed in support of sex equity, specifying the benefits of sex equity for society. These benefits are of many types, incorporating the more ethically-oriented (and social) benefits implicit in Maxine Greene's philosophical rationale with the more pragmatic (economic and social) benefits, some of which can be inferred from the previous discussion of economic factors.

A report on science and engineering education, jointly prepared by the National Science Foundation and the Department of Education (1980), suggests the skeleton of one aspect of such an argument.

> Education has long been the route by which upward mobility has been achieved by disadvantaged groups in our society. . . . Increased emphasis must be given to aiding those who have been excluded, for too long, from careers in science and engineering. We stress this imperative both for reasons of equity and to increase the size of the pool of talent from which the Nation's scientists, engineers, and technicians can be drawn. (p. 3)

"Reasons of equity" implies a philosophical argument; "pool of talent" implies a pragmatic argument (in this case, labor market demand).

It is this latter point—labor market demand—that provides an example of one essential argument for sex equity both in education and in the labor market. The NSF/DOE report suggests that our society's need for more highly qualified scientists and engineers is not being met and concludes that "women still remain the largest pool of talent available for increasing the size and quality of the science and engineering labor force" (p. 64).

The clear implication of this statement is that there would be a definite benefit to society if more women entered these traditionally male-dominated fields. But is it reasonable to expect that women will move into these fields under current conditions? The response to such a query must be negative. Large increases in the numbers of females in these fields would be possible, however, if (1) females were treated more equitably in the educational arena—for example, if they were provided appropriate educational opportunities, encouragement, financial assistance, counseling, and so forth—and if (2) the labor market provided more incentives for a woman to invest her resources and energy in a career such as electrical engineering, where she knows that at present her median weekly earnings will be $160.91 less than her male counterpart's—and that she is significantly more likely to lose her job (should she find one) than is her male co-worker. With significant reductions in gender-related incquities in both the educational and economic arenas, a larger labor pool of scientists and engineers which includes substantially greater numbers of women could and probably would occur. This, in turn, would result in increased benefits (social utility) to be shared by all of society.

This is but one example of the type of point that should be further developed to provide a thorough social utility argument for sex equity in society. Substantial evidence exists to support the value of sex equity in society, but it has yet to be fully developed into a cohesive, sound, and convincing rationale for sex equity based on the notion of social utility.

The purpose here has been merely illustrative, but it is clear that the need to develop such a rationale is critical, both to justify the importance and benefit of sex equity to society and to indicate more precisely the role of education in achieving sex equity. This book addresses the second component of this needed rationale—the role of education in achieving sex equity. Through extensive syntheses and analyses of the available literature on sex equity in and through education, the following chapters go a long way toward providing a major portion of this rationale.

REFERENCES

Ahern, N., & Scott, E. (1981). *Career outcomes in a matched sample of men and women Ph.D.'s*. Washington, DC: National Academy Press.

Dearman, N., & Plisko, V. (1981). *The condition of education: Statistical report* (1981 ed.). Washington, DC: National Center for Education Statistics.

Fullenwider, R. (1981). *The reverse discrimination controversy: A moral and legal analysis*. Totowa, NJ: Rowman & Littlefield.

Harvey, G. (1978). Response to Ennis. *Educational Theory, 28*(2), 147–151.

Harvey, G. (1982). *Competing interpretations of equity*. Washington, DC: National Institute of Education.

Hewlett, S. (1977). *Inequality and its implications for economic growth*. In I. Horowitz (Ed.), *Equity, income, and policy* (pp. 29–48). New York: Praeger.

National Advisory Council on Women's Educational Programs. (1981). *Title IX: The half full, half empty glass*. Washington, DC: author.

National Science Foundation & Department of Education. (1980). *Science and engineering: Education for the 1980s and beyond*. Washington, DC: U.S. Government Printing Office.

President's Commission for a National Agenda for the Eighties. (1980). *Government and the advancement of social justice: Health, welfare, education, and civil rights in the eighties*. Washington, DC: U.S. Government Printing Office.

Project on the Status and Education of Women. (1982). Misconceptions about women Ph.D.'s challenged. *On Campus with Women, 34*, 6–7.

Reder, N. (1981). *Human needs: Unfinished business on the nation's agenda.* Washington, DC: League of Women Voters Education Fund.

Sherman, R., Sheeran, A., Thornton, M., & Hill, C. (1982). *Women and vocational training: A step up or a come down?* Washington, DC: League of Women Voters Education Fund.

Stasz, C. (1982). Room at the bottom. *Working Papers, 9*(1), 28–36.

Treiman, D., & Hartmann, H. (Eds.). (1981). *Women, work, and wages: Equal pay for jobs of equal value.* Washington, DC: National Academy Press.

U.S. Department of Commerce, Bureau of the Census. (1980). Fertility of American women. *Current Population Reports: Population Characteristics* (Series P-20, No. 358). Washington, DC: U.S. Government Printing Office.

Weale, A. (1978). *Equality and social policy.* London: Routledge & Kegan Paul.

Wilson, E. (1981). The limits of the law. *Update, 5*(3), 18–28, 58–59.

The Women's Research and Education Institute & the Committee on Women's Employment and Related Social Issues of the National Academy of Sciences. (1982). *Working conference on women's employment and economic status: Final report.* Washington, DC: WREI.

3
Sex Equity as a Philosophical Problem

Maxine Greene

Muriel Rukeyser, in a poem called "Käthe Kollwitz," wrote:

> *What would happen if one woman told the truth*
> *about her life?*
> *The world would split open.* (Goulianos, 1973, p. 377)

She meant the conventional world, the taken-for-granted world; she meant what is arbitrarily defined as "reality." Much the same might be said about the doing of philosophy, if philosophy is understood to signify "a battle against the be-witchment of intelligence by means of language" (Wittgenstein, 1968, p. 49) or, alternatively, a matter of "thinking what the known demands" (Dewey, 1916, p. 381). It entails as well, for many inquirers, a critical reflection upon historical situations and presently lived situations, an examination of major premises, a challenge to what is "given" and habitually assumed. Inequities, exclusions, and humiliations are in part maintained by the "bewitchment" of the general intel-ligence (including women's intelligence) and by mystifications of diverse kinds. They are maintained, also, by an unwillingness (or a refusal) to look at what the human sciences actually claim with respect to female and male realities and, surely, by an incapacity to think seriously about "what the known demands." Moreover, the dearth of reflection on what has been called "natural" and what must be grasped as social or cultural in part accounts for the continuing acquies-cence to man-made paradigms and to the fiction of what is "objectively" the case where women are concerned. An educational undertaking that is routinized and conventional, that is concerned primarily with basic literacy and socialization into frequently inequitable structures, cannot but perpetuate such acquiescence. A particular kind of wide-awakeness is required of those responsible for the undertaking, a break with what Virginia Woolf called the "cotton wool" (1976, p. 70) of their daily lives, if the lacks and deficiencies that obstruct sex equity are to be overcome. A break with what Hannah Arendt called "thoughtlessness" is

29

required—with the "heedless recklessness or hopeless confusion or complacent repetition of 'truths' that have become trivial and empty" (1958, p. 5). As Arendt proposed, they need, quite simply, to think what they are doing.

THE HISTORICAL CONTEXT

The ethical arguments for sex equity, however, are not self-evident, and the ground must be cleared to some degree before any are proposed. Attention must be paid, for example, to the presuppositions underlying the standard arguments having to do with human rights, equality, and what John Rawls calls "the morality of association" (cited in Wolff, 1977, pp. 467–472): presuppositions having to do with the nature of the person, with differences between men and women, with autonomy and the "sense of justice," with the public and the private spheres. The most common argument assumes a universality with respect to human beings and human rights; and it rests, most often, upon an eighteenth-century view of a society composed of unrelated equals governed by and responsive to general rules and principles. We need only think back to John Locke, Thomas Jefferson, and other pioneers of liberalism. "Men being by nature all free, equal, and independent," wrote Locke, "no one can be put out of this estate and subjected to the political power of another without his own consent" (Somerville & Sanroni, 1963, p. 178). As atomic, self-sufficient individuals, they come together by means of a social contract to protect their natural rights and preserve their property. "We hold these truths to be self-evident," wrote Jefferson, "that all men are created equal" (1940, p. 33). From his perspective, of course, they come together to protect their rights to "life, liberty and the pursuit of happiness" from depredation by tyranny; but, again, it is the individual right that must be protected by a civil authority or a set of laws acceptable to rational minds. In liberal thought, the classical notion of "essence" still prevailed: the idea that human beings were distinguished from all other living beings by the possession of a "soul" associated with active reason— reason conceived as the perfection or the purpose of the body. It was because of the capacity of reason that man, as Shakespeare's Hamlet put it, was "the paragon of animals." And it was reason that defined man's "nature," as it were. This view, John Dewey pointed out, overlooked "the part played by interaction with the surrounding medium, especially the social, in generating impulses and desires" (Dewey, 1960, p. 269). Nonetheless, it was the view that gave rise to the conviction that all men were equal "by nature." The feminist tendency has been to challenge the focus on "all men" and, on similar premises, to assert that the so-called "essence" must be seen to inhere in every living person, obviously including women. And, indeed, the woman question has traditionally been conceived to be a philosophical question by those who take this universalist point of view. It is important to note that the idea of "essence" gradually was linked to a concept of the *individual* as a rational being living with others by contract or convention, governed by law.

Arguing, then, in the light of a conception of universal "human-ness," many feminists have simply affirmed that women are entitled to all those rights that apply to human beings qua human beings. For them, being a woman is "accidental"; and any acknowledgment of a polarity beyond sex differences, they say, can only make women vulnerable to continuing unequal treatment. Others say that there is no universal human nature, that sex differences are "essential or categorial." Consider, for instance, Carol Gilligan's view that women "impose a distinctive construction on moral problems" and that there is a "centrality of the concepts of responsibility and care in women's constructions of the moral domain" (1982, p. 105). Gilligan, a developmental psychologist, does not see this distinctiveness as God-given or innate, but she clearly views developmental differences as more than accidental. So do a number of French feminist critics and writers. Ronnie Scharfman, for one, writes of the "relationship between reproduction and bonding on the one hand, and textual production on the other" (Scharfman, 1981, p. 88). The philosopher Carol Gould claims that the concrete and the particular are, in any case, as appropriate for philosophical discussion as the universal. She says that "the oppression of women as well as all significant differences between men and women are thoroughly *historical, social, and cultural.*" She goes on to comment "that being human is essentially a social, historical and cultural matter," and "differences which are rooted in such contexts are therefore philosophically relevant differences" (Gould, 1976, p. 7).

Such matters as equity—yes, and dignity and self-respect and rationality— can be approached from a nonuniversalist point of view. The argument for sex equity can be and should be developed without reliance on an idea of "essence" or a single definition of "human nature." It is possible, for instance, to take an existential view and assert that each existing being must (by choosing) create her/his own "nature." We need only recall Simone de Beauvoir's conception of women and men as human beings, free and in quest of themselves. She wrote at the end of *The Second Sex* that "in both sexes is played out the same drama of the flesh and the spirit, of finitude and transcendence; both are gnawed away by time and laid in wait for by death; they have the same essential need for one another; and they can gain from their liberty the same glory" (1957, p. 728). She knew (and knows) well the effects of oppression; she acknowledged and indeed celebrated difference; she thought women could and should *choose* their "ascent." She did not rely on some predetermined or "natural" equality; she spoke of "natural behavior" becoming "human"; but she knew that each person had to choose—or to struggle for—his or her "humanity."

It would appear that, for all the lingering universalist views, there is a general acknowledgment that women's long association with the natural, as opposed to the sociopolitical order, is and was a function of political and then social and economic arrangements. So is and was their confinement to the so-called private sphere. The roots of such separation can be traced back through history, perhaps as far back as the Greek polis, perhaps even before. Indeed, there are many who find the origins in the passage from the matriarchate to the patriarchate (De Beauvoir, p. 70), so remarkably dramatized in Aeschylus's

Eumenides. In that tragedy, rendering the trial of Orestes for killing his mother, the Chorus asks how a man can be acquitted for such a crime. Apollo, defending Orestes, says: "The mother is no parent of that which is called/her child, but only nurse of the new-planted seed that grows. The parent is he who mounts" (Aeschylus, p. 158). This forgiving of the killing of Clytemnestra has been viewed as a function of crucial economic changes in once agricultural Attica, changes that led to the triumph of the patriarchate.

What is crucial is the recognition that women's relegation to private life is neither biologically based nor given in the nature of things. What is of particular interest today is the way in which liberal individualism, coupled with the rise of laissez-faire capitalism, rationalized and in some manner depended upon the identification of women with the "natural" or the private sphere. It was in this context and with the personal and social consequences in mind that Mary Wollstonecraft, John Stuart Mill and Harriet Taylor, Elizabeth Cady Stanton, and others defined their protests. There were and are those who speak of the contribution of the bourgeois family to social reproduction generally; there are those who describe the exploitative relations within families as a reflection of the exploitation without; there are those, like Nancy Chodorow today (1978), who explain the social organization of gender and the "reproduction of mothering" as essential for the maintenance of the division of labor and the modes of production that characterize capitalist society. And there is considerable evidence of felt needs to exclude mutuality and reciprocity from the public spaces of a competitive system, to thrust them into sometimes hallowed private places where alienated men could express their urges to power freely and at once be nurtured and restored. To do this, of course, they had to impress on women conceptions of duty and the need for self-sacrifice. We might think of Charlotte Brontë's Jane Eyre telling Mr. Rochester that once men—even like Hercules and Samson—get married, "they would no doubt by their very severity as husbands have made up for their softness as suitors; and so will you, I fear. I wonder how you will answer me a year hence, should I ask a favour it does not suit your convenience or pleasure to grant." Or we might recall Kate Chopin's Edna Pontellier, in *The Awakening,* thinking before her suicide of the "soul's slavery." But, once again, such things do not occur "naturally."

The economic and social realities that led to such peculiar couplings were mediated and articulated in diverse ways by thinkers of the eighteenth, nineteenth, and twentieth centuries. Of particular moment, when it comes to the differentiation of the sexes and the spheres assigned to each, are the works of Rousseau, Hegel, and Freud. Obviously, were it not for the match between social contract theories and the development of eighteenth-century liberalism, such views as Rousseau's would not have been so consequential. The same is true of Hegel's views on the family and civil society, conservative though Hegel is believed to have been. In any event, Rousseau made the point in *The Social Contract* that the family had preceded civil society and existed apart from it.

Rooted in procreation and in "natural" ties of love and affection, the family was the natural form of social relationship (1968, p. 50). Civil society, in contrast, was an affair of conventions and contractual relationships. The natural, for Rousseau, represented the good; it was part of the order of things as compared with the artifices of society. When he wrote that males were the natural holders of authority in the family, he could only affirm that to be good as well. Not surprisingly, he wrote in his *Emile* that women were naturally made to be "at the mercy of man's judgment" (1911, p. 138) and that their education should be of the sort that encouraged the development of their feelings and affections, since those were what maintained the family.

Feelings and affections, however, were—and often are—conceived to be at odds with the sense of justice considered basic to the civil order. As Carole Pateman points out, this has led to a viewing of women as a threat to public order, sometimes to civil order itself (1980, pp. 20–21). Hegel's *Philosophy of the Right* extended the notion that the family, not being contractual in character, was particularistic and opposed to the universalistic and impersonal sphere of public life. This meant, in his context, that wives were bound to play a subordinate role in the world, were not to be educated as citizens, and were fated to live their lives in a privileged private realm. It goes without saying that because they were barred from the public sphere, they had no claim to "human"—or what we now call "option"—rights.

Years later, Sigmund Freud wrote that the family is a naturally social institution whose primary virtue is love (not fairness, certainly not equity). Civilization, he believed, was the work of men capable of sublimations women could never achieve (1953). And, like his forerunners, he thought that women (because their oedipal experiences were different from those of males) were unable to develop a sense of justice. This insistence on the antithesis between the natural order and the civic order, between the virtue of love and the virtue of justice, was sustained by the language of "natural law" and, in time, by the language of instincts (Pierce, 1971, pp. 160–172). Not only did these languages intensify the traditional mystifications, they carried with them conceptions of biological and psychological determinism. Even as women have moved increasingly from the family sphere into the wider spheres of economic life, many have carried with them the notion that the virtues so long associated with them (affection, sympathy, concern) are marks of inferiority and incapacity where the public realm is concerned. But, at once, they continue to suffer shame or guilt when they opt for self-determination or self-development, thereby turning their backs on the self-sacrifice that seemed the inevitable accompaniment of concern. It is all too evident that many males (perhaps, particularly, males in power) have internalized the same spectrum of values and associated the same virtues (and the related self-sacrifices) with unmanliness. This partially explains the competitiveness, the game playing, the lack of reciprocity and mutuality that still characterize the worlds of industry, politics, and institutionalized education.

THE PROBLEMATIC OF THE PUBLIC REALM

The matter of justification is closely related to the ways in which the public realm is conceived. At the same time, it has to do with the ways in which such virtues as mutuality and care are viewed. The fact that these have been historically defined as "natural" and therefore linked to subordination and exclusion from the public realm in no sense lessens their significance or the need to hold them in mind when arguing for sex equity. It is true that because human rights (like justice itself) were so long considered irrelevant to life in the private sphere, inequity in education was long maintained by treating schools as an extension of the private. Female teachers were infantilized; they were praised as "good daughters" to superintendents (Tyack, 1974, pp. 60 ff.); they were required, until well into the present century, to remain unmarried, to remain "girls" in presumed need of protection. And "girls," according to our history, were never considered fully responsible for their actions and therefore not mature enough to govern themselves by rational principles. It was only when teachers began to take responsibility for themselves in unions and other associations that they felt themselves in a position to claim their rights as persons and professionals. Their struggle for equality had necessarily to be a struggle for equal rights; and, since the possession of rights was associated with participation in the public sphere, equal opportunities for participation had to be fought for, including suffrage and (always) all that was represented by "a room of one's own" and (at the very least) "five hundred a year" (Woolf, 1957).

Historical experience, however, does not entail an uncritical acceptance of the public realm as traditionally defined, for all the fact that entry into it was so prized and so hard-won. As has been suggested, what is generally understood to be that realm even today has its origin in early Enlightenment liberalism and, as well, in laissez-faire capitalism. It is a sphere frequently conceived in formal terms, often regarded as in some manner timeless, ahistorical (like Immanuel Kant's "kingdom of ends" [1949, p. 30]) in which persons seen to be rational agents guide themselves according to objective, rational principles of morality. The world of contingencies—the world of habit, impulse, fallibility, change—is set apart; so are the life histories and the personal idiosyncrasies of those involved. The individual is thought to possess dignity as a rational moral agent, not as a mortal being caught up in concrete relationships with others. Both his rights and his freedoms are functions of his rationality, since it is by virtue of his rationality that he can make choices and abide by abstract rules. The pronoun "his" is used deliberately, since the liberal ideal, with a stress on autonomy and self-sufficiency, has been in many senses akin to the traditional masculine view of human perfection (at least in the Western world). Virginia Woolf's description cannot but come to mind. She was talking about the dependence of men's sense of superiority on their views of women as inferior, and about men's restiveness under women's criticism. "For if she begins to tell the truth, the figure in the looking glass shrinks; his fitness for life is diminished. How is he to go on giving judgment, civilising natives, making laws, writing books, dressing up and speechifying at banquets, unless he can see himself at breakfast and at dinner at least twice the size he really is? . . . The looking-glass vision is of supreme importance because it charges the vitality. . . . Take it away and man may die" (1957, p. 36).

It is in the sphere of the rational, articulate, self-regarding, and self-determining person that justice becomes the primary virtue for many philosophers. John Rawls's conception of justice as fairness and his view of the "original position" in which the principles of justice are (hypothetically) defined are in many ways exemplary (1971, pp. 17–22). Rawls posits a situation in which people come to agreement about the principles of justice by pulling a "veil of ignorance" over knowledge of their social positions, their incomes, and "those contingencies which set men at odds and allow them to guided by their prejudices" (1971, p. 19). Moreover, they have no idea of their purposes, plans, and interests. It is supposed that all parties involved are equal, "with the same rights in the procedure for choosing principles." They are equal as moral persons, creatures with "a conception of their good and capable of a sense of justice" (1971, p. 19). What Rawls is concerned with is finding out whether certain principles of justice are justified when they are agreed to in an initial position of equality; and he presumes that under the veil of ignorance there will be a unanimous choice of justice as fairness. The principle is intended to apply to society in the large, in its widest institutional arrangements, not to small groups, families, local communities. A society Rawls believes, "is a more or less self-sufficient association of persons who in their relations to one another recognize certain rules of conduct as binding and who for the most part act in accordance with them." The rules themselves specify a system of cooperation "designed to advance the good of those taking part in it."

Robert Paul Wolff, stressing the abstractness of the theory and the remoteness of what is described from existing actuality, asserts that *A Theory of Justice* "can be placed historically in the tradition of utopian liberal political economy. . . . One could characterize it . . . as a philosophical *apologia* for an egalitarian brand of liberal welfare-state capitalism" (1977, p. 195). The fact that (as Wolff indicates) a "formal model of a bargaining game" lies at the center of the theory is not as important where women are concerned as the neglect of the social and historical realities that have led to the exclusion of women (and still lead to the exclusion of many) from the domain where rational activity is seen as *the* good for the individual. There is certainly something appealing to the individual in search of ethical justifications for equity in the notion that "all primary goods—liberty and opportunity, income and wealth, and the bases of self-respect—are to be distributed equally unless an unequal distribution of any or all of these goods is to the advantage of the least favored" (Rawls, 1971, p. 303). But Alasdair MacIntyre, among others, points out that Rawls is primarily concerned about those "worst off" with regard to income, wealth, and other goods. Comparing Rawls with Robert Nozick and his view of "entitlement" on the part of those who have acquired what they have by a just act of original acquisition and through some just act of transfer from someone else (Nozick, 1974), MacIntyre writes that both views are individualistic and geared to persons who are "*only* rational.*" If this is so, they cannot but evoke recollections of time past, of the "rational animal" who was thought of as exclusively male. MacIntyre continues: "Thus Rawls and Nozick articulate with great power a shared view which envisages entry into social life as—at least ideally—the voluntary act of at least potentially rational individuals with prior interests who have to ask the question 'What kind of social contract with others is it reasonable for me to enter into?' Not surprisingly, it is a consequence of this that their views exclude any account of human community in which the notion of desert in relation to contributions to the common tasks of that community in pursuing shared goods could provide the judgments about virtue and injustice" (1981, p. 233). It should be clear that a concern with shared goods and common tasks does not and need not exclude the growth of rationality, intelligence, insight, all of which are relevant to the life of any community. What is being questioned is the so-called "rationalist prejudice," the association of advanced cognitive development with the right to participate and the attainment of dignity. It would appear that if we are to deal with the matter of equity in a concrete and particular context, if we are to frame an argument geared to social actualities, we cannot consider merely those who are "*only* rational" any more than we can neglect the idea of community.

SEEKING GROUNDED JUSTIFICATIONS

To do philosophy with respect to all this is to keep visible the historical inventions that have given rise to conceptions of contracts and law-governed rational orders in some fashion separated from the world of actualities. By now, we have come to understand the problematic character of atomistic conceptions of the individual and the degree to which human individuality is a function of relationships, communication, and community (Mead, 1948, pp. 135–226). We have also come to recognize the transformation of the liberal individualist society into one largely oriented to technological and bureaucratic controls, a society in which rationality has become increasingly depersonalized and "neutral," a society in which communication has become increasingly distorted (Habermas, 1971, pp. 80–122). It is impossible not to entertain the notion that the old liberalism, with its deficient and ahistorical views of the person, its repression of feeling, and its attempted transcendence of relationship and community, carried within it the potentiality of technicism.

Such critiques as those of Dewey, who objected so strenuously to the idea of an "original endowment of rights, powers, and wants" and to liberalism's focus on the elimination of obstructions to the free play of "the natural equipment of individuals" (Dewey, 1960, p. 271), may have led temporarily to an increased concern for general welfare and equality, but they did not stop the seeds of technicism from sprouting. Without mentioning women, Dewey did write that the removal of obstructions may have led to the liberation of individuals "antecedently possessed of the means, intellectual and economic, to take advantage of the changed social conditions. But it left all others at the mercy of the new social conditions brought about by the freed powers of those advantageously situated" (1960, p. 271). He may not have had women in mind, but it is difficult to read the sentence now without distinguishing between those "antecedently possessed by the means" and "all others" without imagining women among those "others." Dewey called continually, it happens, for a regard for totality, interconnectedness, sociality, and social concern. But he said relatively little about the problematic of the "natural" and the "civic," relatively little about the subordination of women or the denials of sex equity. For Dewey, the public "consists of all those who are affected by the indirect consequences of transactions to such an extent that it is deemed necessary to have those consequences systematically cared for" (1954, pp. 12–13). There is no sure knowing what would have happened to what is thought of as the public sphere if more voices had been audible, if the consequences of oppression were made clear, if more women had "told the truth" about their worlds.

In any case, at the present moment, a management ideal (or a game-player paradigm) frequently absorbs and distorts the value of autonomy. As compassion and social concern seem to diminish in the public domain, women's rights are being eroded on all sides: the right to choose, where abortions are concerned; the "welfare mother's" rights to health care and child care; the right to affirmative action in hiring. Insistent talk of "family protection" threatens a new effort to thrust women back into the private sphere. Economic stringencies are affecting equity efforts in the domains of schooling, as federal resources diminish and school systems do less to compensate for longstanding discrimination in classrooms, as they do less to correct the unfairness to females inherent in sex-biased schoolbooks and sexist language. Meanwhile, access to private colleges and universities is being curtailed because of the absence of loans and other supports; and there are fewer and fewer opportunities, therefore, for young women to attempt recently opened ladders to high status in the professions, the arts, and the sciences.

As never before, there is a need to reconceive curricula, to rethink the traditional subjects (for example, history, philosophy, literature, political science). Female students need to be able to confront their own history, to develop a critical awareness of the obliteration of women from fields like philosophy and literature and the arts. Occasions must be provided, also, for them to engage with such reconceptions of female development as that made available by Carol Gilligan's *In a Different Voice*. Her research led her to recognize that the concept of human rights enabled many young women to acknowledge the legitimacy of their own self-interest and to give up the "morality of self-sacrifice and self-abnegation." But she also discovered that the "concern for care" extended "from an injunction not to hurt others to an ideal of responsibility in social relationships" (1982, p. 164). Mercy, as Gilligan suggests, can be seasoned with justice; and "the tensions between responsibilities and rights sustains the dialectic of human development." It is important to note that this view challenges one of the oldest of either/ors: namely, that mercy and love exist in one sphere, justice in another. The point of exposing young women to such ideas, like the reason for empowering them for conceptual understanding of their shared worlds, is to release them for further and further cognitive action, for sisterly action, and for choice.

ARGUMENTS FOR EQUITY

How do we argue for equity where access and treatment are concerned? (Harvey, 1982). How do we make a philosophical case for an acknowledgment of difference and diversity while asserting that each person has an equal right to grow, to choose, to be? In a discussion of feminism and philosophy, Nancy Sherman has said that "for the most part, it is to be used in analyzing the issues of rights and justice and the goals of an egalitarian society. As such, part of its task is to establish a vision of a society which provides mutual supports for self-respect and which minimizes the hostilities caused by scarcity and envy" (1980, p. 91). Most commonly, as this suggests, formal arguments are used and formal, rule-governed systems are posited. Rawls's approach is one example. Brian Barry provides another, when he writes about the advantage of appealing to equity (or "the principle that equals should be treated equally and unequals equally" [1965, p. 152]). He says that an appeal of that sort in cases suited to it has the advantage that "one can derive results from it without having to bring in any independent criteria at all; they may instead be found within the system to which the principle of equity is being applied. One may simply say: in this system, x is admitted as relevant yet *here* it is not allowed to make a difference between the treatment of A's who have x and B's who haven't x; or, conversely, x is not admitted to be relevant yet *here* it *does* make a difference. All that is needed is a sharp eye for inconsistency. Thus, one may criticize a series of decisions or a set of rules as inconsistent with one another without having to look any further and see whether there is anything wrong with the general principles or laws underlying the decisions" (1965, pp. 152–153).

Where, say, reasonably qualified women are concerned, and where the rules governing recruitment to a teaching position specify reasonable qualifications, we are (following Barry) persuaded to take a stand on the principle that such women should be treated as men are treated because they are alike in what the rules specify to be relevant. There is no need, Barry suggests, to commit ourselves to questions having to do with the criteria that ought to govern hiring on the various levels of schooling or anything else. But this is another example of the deficiency in the purely formal argument, since it not only leaves out the necessity (in actuality) of affirmative action procedures to insure that women are treated as men are treated, but it also does not allow for acknowledgment of the difficulty experienced by female students who cannot perceive themselves as chemists, school administrators, foundation executives, and the like, no matter what formal criteria exist.

For all that, it is generally agreed that if we are to justify a claim or a course of action, we are required to refer to the kinds of general principles that give relevance to our reasons. R. S. Peters is fairly representative when he points out that "to say a principle is general is to say that what ought to be done in any particular situation or by any particular person ought to be done in any other situation or by any other person unless there is some relevant difference in the situation or person in question. The mere fact that situations or persons are not identical must never be taken as a ground for making distinctions. If reasons hold in one situation then they hold in another, unless further reasons can be adduced which indicate a relevant difference" (1978, p. 22). This is known as the formal principle of fairness or justice, depending upon the existence of a universe of rational discourse. But, once more, the deficiencies come clear. Someone has to make a conscious choice to proceed according to such a principle. It may be that someone else has to make a deliberate demand that a choice of that order be made.

There is no denying that the principle gives relevance to the reason that it is wrong to offer more direct instruction to high-achieving males than to high-achieving females, and that therefore the amount of direct instruction should be equalized. If there is a good reason, say, for praising a high-achieving boy, there is an equally good reason for praising a high-achieving girl. The formal principle enables us to condemn the effects of unfairness or to turn our attention toward them, but it does not permit us to conceptualize or even to deal with its causes. In the case of discrimination with regard to direct instruction, we may know that the abstract principle has been violated; but there is nothing to tell us that the discrimination was on the basis of sex. Nor does this way of thinking help us understand the intentions of the teacher who was guilty of discrimination, nor why sex became a relevant factor in the situation. Most importantly, a concentration on principle does not permit attention to be turned to the actual decisions made within the particular situation, nor to the existing alternatives, nor to neglected possibilities. As has been suggested, the realm governed by formal principles (even so confined a realm as a public school) exists apart from the temporal realm of relationship, feelings, intentions, and actions. The awareness of principle may provide a perspective, a means of selecting those features of a situation that need attending to; but living, fallible persons have deliberately to take responsibility, even as they have to develop some sensitivity to the plight of others. There must be some ability to enter into dialogue with others, to look through others' eyes at what is being lived in common, to *name* what is wrong, and then (in the midst of determinants) to choose—freely, authentically—to remove (in this case) existing inequities, in some manner to transform.

There is no question but that those being discriminated against are entitled to claim that their rights are being violated. There are at least *pro forma* agreements that each individual is entitled to protection against encroachments on her/his freedom (to choose, to learn, to grow). If freedom does signify the power to act and to choose, if freedom does refer to the release of capacities, then surely educational inequities must be considered to be infringements on fundamental rights. We recognize, however, that such considerations mean little if those involved or affected do not care, if they are unable to structure their realities in terms of reciprocity, if there exists no social concern. Moreover, formal considerations mean little if conditions are not consciously and deliberately created to defend or to secure those rights.

We need only recall the presumed guarantee of equal educational opportunity to see how little it actually meant until people came together to demand compensations for disadvantages, to demand that differential opportunities be provided for diverse young persons. They were making claims when they marched and petitioned and held their meetings. It is doubtful whether rights were ever conferred without demand and claim. There are those, like Joel Feinberg, who speak of "valid claims," the official recognition of which is called for by existing rules or principles. "To have a *claim*," Feinberg writes, ". . . is to have a case meriting consideration, that is, to have reasons or grounds that put one in a position to engage in performative and propositional claiming. The activity of claiming . . . as much as any other thing, makes for self-respect and respect for others, gives a sense to the notion of personal dignity" (Feinberg, 1978, p. 31). Again, we see a linking—from a somewhat different perspective— of rights and responsibilities, or (in this case) "respect for others." Bertram Bandman writes that rights ought to be understood as warrants for making claims, that a right is a "justification for claiming." Then he says that "a just (or justified) entitlement for making effective claims and demands is what we understand by a right" (Bandman & Bandman, 1978). Like Feinberg, he has in mind a context or rules or principles that give relevance to a person's "reasons or grounds" for making her claims; but the significant point is that a mere abstract acknowledgment (due, let us say, to a sense of justice) is coupled with and realized in the act or acts of claiming, of demanding. Action of this sort, where sex equity is concerned, must take place in the changing, complex, intersubjective world of schools—where persons are empowered to reason but must also care and attend.

William James once wrote about concrete living persons making claims upon one another and about the sense in which claims create obligations. He believed that every claim any person made ought to be satisfied unless some other claim could be shown to conflict with it (1956, pp. 194–195). It is not difficult to imagine conflicting claims in the present difficult time: conflicts between those who say they are entitled to equal treatment and those who claim the right to compensatory discrimination; conflicts between those who affirm their rights to seniority and those who think merit should be rewarded, seniority or no. One philosopher has made the point that it may be unjust for larger rewards to be provided for tasks that require superior intelligence. "This is simply the way things work out in a technologically advanced society," he wrote, "with a market economy. It does not reflect a social judgment that smart people *deserve* the opportunity to make more money than dumb people" (Nagel, 1973, p. 348). If sex equity is to be achieved in education, it may be that the matter of economic justice ought to be separated from the question of equity in the distribution of employment. If it were, it might be possible to diversify the opportunities made available in the light of an expanded vision of merit and competency, an altered approach to rewards. Surely, equal opportunities should not be reserved only for the smart or the superior. The point, after all, of the struggle for sex equity in education is to provide the opportunity—the equal opportunity—for growth and development in self-chosen ways to women as well as men.

It remains crucial, however, for women to continue making their demands and creating obligations. Jill Conway made the important point some years ago that women should not be content until they found places at the center of those academic institutions that create and transmit the culture of the West. "On the one hand," she said, "to be in command of that culture women must master skills in mathematics and the hard sciences which have been traditionally defined as unfeminine and neglected in the education of females. On the other hand, if these skills in abstract reasoning are to be applied in a manner which draws upon the inner springs of creativity, they must be acquired in a way which is no threat to the female identity. This can be achieved by an educational experience which is critical of many of the assumptions of a male-controlled culture and which takes the female as the norm rather than the deviant exception to the life of the mind. One precondition for such a view of intellectual life is a sense of solidarity with female colleagues" (1971, p. 241).

Again, the point is made that some of our taken-for-grantedness regarding self-sufficient rational agents, focally concerned with the protection of their own individual rights, ought to be questioned, and that an enriched ethic of responsibility and solidarity ought to be linked to the traditional orientation. It remains entirely possible to develop a notion of justice grounded in the sense of mutuality and respect. Hannah Arendt thought that "what love is in its own, narrowly circumscribed sphere, respect is in the larger domain of human affairs" (1958, p. 243). Respect, like friendship, is directed toward the person and finds expression when persons come together in speech and action. To come together freely in this manner, acknowledging distinctiveness and equal worth, is quite different from the contractual relation; and the capacity to do so may derive from what is most valuable in female experience—precisely that which was for so long denigrated and denied.

Even this, of course, is not enough at the present moment of our history. If sex equity is to be secured, there must be intellectual action among women of a force and vibrancy never attempted before. As the French writer Catherine Clement says, there must be "knowledge of the real relationship between intellectual activity and the overall totality of forces that seek to change society." She believes that that is the condition of all intellectual action; and it surely seems to be so for women in this country today. Then Clement continues: "Feminine crisis does not truly signify, it does not produce any change. . . . Enclosed as an enclave by all of the group and individual constraints, feminine crisis remains enslaved. That women's language must first be a stuttering, when it's about real suffering, is true in fact; can we make a weapon of this shackle? A means must be elaborated to unhinge entire panels of ideology; a rigorous activity is needed which for the sake of rigor must think out and measure its relation to social activities as a whole" (1981, pp. 135–136).

Demystification, critique, and intellectual action: these are the phases in the doing of philosophy where the problem of women and the matter of equity are concerned. The magician's tricks, the old illusions of the "natural" order must be exposed; the historical and social origins of inequity must be disclosed; and women must make their demands and their claims along with others—make them powerfully and passionately. Only then can discrimination and stereotyping be effectively eliminated; only then can individuals be empowered to make use of education to attain sex equity; only then may equity be expanded in educational activities. To work for sex equity in education and the social order as a whole is to move to alter the oppressiveness that makes individual autonomy antithetical to social concern. It is to rediscover what it signifies to be a person and a woman, while discovering what it signifies to transform.

REFERENCES

Aeschylus. (1959). *The Eumenides* (R. Lattimore, Trans.). D. Grene & R. Lattimore, eds.), *Aeschylus* (Vol. 1, *The complete Greek tragedies*). Chicago: University of Chicago Press.

Arendt, H. (1958). *The human condition.* Chicago: University of Chicago Press.

Bandman, B. (1978). 'Rights and claims.' In E. L. Bandman & B. Bandman (eds.), *Bioethics and human rights* (pp. 35–43) Boston: Little, Brown.

Barry, B. (1965). *Political argument.* New York: Humanities Press.

Chodorow, N. (1978). *The reproduction of mothering.* Berkeley and Los Angeles: University of California Press.

Clement, C. (1981). Warnings. In E. Marks & I. De Courtivron (Eds.), *New French feminism* (pp. 130–136). New York: Shocken.

Conway, J. (1971). Coeducation and women's studies: Two approaches to the question of woman's place in the contemporary university. *Daedalus, 1,* 239–249.

De Beauvoir, S. (1959). *The second sex* New York: Knopf.

Dewey, J. (1916). *Democracy and education.* New York: Macmillan.

Dewey, J. (1954). *The public and its problems.* Chicago: Swallow.

Dewey, J. (1960). Philosophies of freedom. In R. J. Bernstein (Ed.), *On experience, nature, and freedom* (pp. 262–281). New York: Liberal Arts.

Feinberg, J. (1978). The nature and value of rights. In E. L. Bandman & B. Bandman (Eds.), *Bioethics and human rights* (pp. 19–31). Boston: Little, Brown.

Freud, S. (1953). *Civilization and its discontents.* London: Hogarth.

Gilligan, C. (1982). *In a different voice*. Cambridge: Harvard University Press.

Gould, C. (1976). The woman question: Philosophy of liberation and the liberation of philosophy. In C. C. Gould & M. W. Wartofsky (Eds.), *Women and philosophy: Toward a theory of liberation* (pp. 5–44). New York: Capricorn.

Habermas, J. (1971). *Toward a rational society*. Boston: Beacon.

Harvey, G. (1982). *Competing interpretations of equity*. Washington, DC: National Institute of Education.

James, W. (1956). *The will to believe*. New York: Dover.

Jefferson, T. (1940). Political philosophy. In J. Dewey (Ed.), *The living thoughts of Thomas Jefferson* (p. 33). New York: David McKay.

Kant, I. (1949). *Fundamental principles of the metaphysics of morals*. Indianapolis: Bobbs-Merrill.

Locke, J. (1963). An essay concerning the true original extent and end of civil government. In J. Somerville & R. E. Santoni (Eds.), *Social and political philosophy* (pp. 169–175). Garden City, NY: Doubleday Anchor.

MacIntyre, A. (1981). *After virtue*. Notre Dame: University of Notre Dame Press.

Mead, G. F. H. (1948). *Mind, self, and society*. Chicago: University of Chicago Press.

Nagel, T. (1973). Equal treatment and compensatory discrimination. *Philosophy and Public Affairs, 2*(4), 342–350.

Nozick, R. (1974). *Anarchy, state, and utopia*. New York: Basic Books.

Pateman, C. (1980). "The disorder of women": Women, love, and the sense of justice. *Ethics, 91*(1), 30–34.

Peters, R. S. (1978). *Ethics and education*. London: Allen & Unwin.

Pierce, C. (1971). Natural law language and women. In V. Gornick & B. K. Moran (Eds.), *Woman in sexist society* (pp. 160–172). New York: Basic Books.

Rawls, J. (1971). *A theory of justice*. Cambridge: Harvard University Press.

Rousseau, J. J. (1911). *Emile*. London: Dent.

Rukeyser, M. (1973). Käthe Kollwitz. In J. Goulianos (Ed.), *by a woman writt* (p. 377). Indianapolis: Bobbs-Merrill.

Scharfman, R. Mirroring and mothering in Simone Schwartz-Bart's *Pluie et vent sur Telumee Miracle* and Jean Rhys' *Wide sargasso sea*. *Yale French Studies: Feminist readings: French texts/ American contexts,* (62), 88–106.

Sherman, N. (1980). Philosophical issues in feminism. *Harvard Educational Review, 50*(1), 86–91.

Tyack, D. (1974). *The one best system*. Cambridge: Harvard University Press.

Wittgenstein, L. (1968). *Philosophical investigations*. New York: Macmillan.

Wolff, R. P. (1977). *Understanding Rawls*. Princeton: Princeton University Press.

Woolf, V. (1967). *A room of one's own*. New York: Harcourt, Brace & World.

Woolf, V. (1976). A sketch of the past. In J. Schulkind (Ed.), *Moments of being*. New York: Harcourt Brace Jovanovich.

4
The New Scholarship
on Women

Sari Knopp Biklen and Charol Shakeshaft

Any research, including educational research on sex equity, relies on a conceptual framework, on a chosen view of the human condition. Researchers, however, are not always aware of the assumptions that underlie the work they do, particularly if that work is part of the tradition of conventional scholarship. For this reason, feminist scholars have placed greater emphasis in recent years on the need to identify all such frameworks.

In this chapter, we examine the conceptual framework for sex equity research. We call this understanding of gender relations, which is neither narrow nor inflexible, the new scholarship on women. The term itself has only recently come into use; it was developed in order to define more clearly the content it proscribed: scholarship that rested on an androcentric understanding of gender relations. How does the new scholarship on women relate to the larger social movement for sex equity? How does it differ from women's studies? What is this understanding of gender relations? These are the questions with which we grapple.

It is also important to note that we take an evolutionary perspective on the new scholarship on women. That is, over time, new fields of scholarship as well as movements for social change (equal rights for women) develop greater sophistication. As a result of this sophistication, our scholarly horizons expand, our research questions change. We address these changes as well. We start with feminism, the broadest perspective, discuss the evolution of women's studies, and finally focus on the research directions of the new scholarship on women.

The authors would like to acknowledge assistance from Ann Fitzgerald and Joan Shapiro on some of the women's studies information.

FEMINISM

The basis of the conceptual framework of the new scholarship on women is feminism. Feminist perspectives vary and are shaped by the sociopolitical values of those who consider themselves feminists. Hence, feminists can be distinguished as liberal feminists, socialist feminists, radical feminists, and marxist feminists. Basic to feminist thought, however, is the "belief that the unequal and inferior status of women is unjust and needs to be changed" (Jagger, 1978, p. 5). Feminism touches all areas of social, political, and economic life, providing both an activist mode for changing inequalities and a theoretical base from which the new scholarship emerges. We focus here on the theoretical base.

Two interrelated feminist principles have particularly influenced our scholarship. First, to understand and value women's lives, we must put them at the center of our inquiry. We must ask how all issues affect women as well as men. A major effect of feminism on scholarship, then, has been to change the scholarly focus. In education, for example, scholars began to question the effects of elementary schools on girls (where earlier the research focus had been on boys), to examine the ways textbooks portrayed girls, and to research the historical relationship between women and teaching.

Human activity, then, becomes what both men and women do, not just what men do. Feminists agree with Pleck & Pleck (1980) that in conventional scholarship "the activity and behavior of men are seen as human activity, that of women as distinctly female" (p. 1), and they work to eliminate this bias. Feminism attempts to overcome the image of woman as "the stranger" (Smith, 1979) or as "the other" (de Beauvoir, 1951). We must then substitute an alternative framework to replace this rejected view of gender relations.

The second feminist principle to have influenced our scholarship is that the obstacles women face are structural (Scott, 1981). The personal situations that women confront, then, are derived from a larger, group inequality. At the same time, this social devaluation may be individually internalized. The new scholarship reflects this feminist principle, taking into account the structural causes of inequity and considering the position of women as a group.

The particular goal of sex equity in education is part of this larger agenda to shape a future in which gender is not a basis for discrimination, where one sex is not valued more highly than another, and where what we know about human beings is based on the study of women's and girls' as well as men's and boys' lives. These are the common values that permeate and bind together the chapters in this book.

WOMEN'S STUDIES

If we think of the relationship between the terms we are defining as a pyramid, we see that feminism represents the broadest aspects, the intellectual and theoretical base. Women's studies represents the center level of the pyramid because it too encompasses a broad range of activities and interests. An outgrowth of feminism, women's studies was originally used to refer to all educational efforts—whether in colleges and universities, high schools, elementary schools, day care centers, continuing education facilities, or women's centers—to redress the inequities women have faced.

An evolutionary look at descriptions of women's studies shows that the term has become focused over time. In 1972, for instance, Gerda Lerner suggested two characteristics. The first was that the approach must be interdisciplinary because the study of women's lives could not be confined by a single discipline. The second was that it had to involve more than students' intellects: it also had to reach their feelings and philosophy. Consciousness raising had to be an integral part of women's studies (Lerner, 1972).

By 1975, some definitions began to emphasize that women's studies was that part of the women's movement that occurred in educational settings:

> Women's studies represents an on-going effort to put women's contributions to humanity into proper perspective. It is the "academic" end of the women's movement, with "academic" redefined to include the process of becoming as the vital core of our subject matter. Our methods are subversive of disciplines which in the past have ignored or excluded matters of utmost concern to us as women. (Schramm, 1975, p. 1)

The academic interdisciplinary approach and the concern with process were still emphasized. At this stage, women's studies practitioners felt that the disciplines could not retain their existing shape if they were to include women's lives centrally.

More recently Florence Howe, one of the founders of women's studies as we know it in these decades, summarized the goals of women's studies programs. While the consciousness-raising aspect was still present, research was emphasized and educational objectives clarified. The goals were

1. to raise the consciousness of students and faculty alike about the need to study women;
2. to begin to compensate for the absence of women, or for the unsatisfactory manner in which they were present in some disciplines, through designing new courses focusing on women;
3. to build a body of research about women;
4. with that body of research, to reenvision the lost culture and history of women;
5. using all four goals, to improve the education of women and men through changing what we have come to call the "mainstream" curriculum. (Howe, 1982)

A change in language accompanies this focus on research.

Discontent with the term "women's studies" has grown. Women's studies referred to an educational arena so large that it had become confusing. Its content area ranged from high school curriculum development to research in the academic disciplines. Women's studies confused people, as well, because it was often difficult to differentiate it from the women's movement (Stimpson, 1980).

THE NEW SCHOLARSHIP ON WOMEN

Finally, we reach the top third of our pyramid, which consists of feminist scholarship about women's lives. The new scholarship about women "concerns itself with ideas, facts, concepts, data," and has three major goals: "to deconstruct error about women, an extensive task; to add to the existing body of knowledge to compensate for the absence of women in the past; and to transform consciousness through such processes" (Stimpson, 1980, pp. 1–2).

As this last goal suggests, the new scholarship on women will increase our understanding of human behavior and society, since an inadequate conceptualization of the female experience distorts our perspectives on the human experience as a whole. Research on sex equity in education is one example of the new scholarship on women. The emphasis on equity implies that studies of sex equity will compare men to women rather than focus on women. The new comparative questions, however, may offer new insights into the lives of men because they do not assume that male activities are the norm for human activities.

As a result of assumptions that male activities define those of women as well, many existing paradigms and theoretical models in the social sciences reflect imprecise, inaccurate, and imbalanced scholarship in their attempts to understand and explain human behavior. Historians who write the new scholarship of women, for example, suggest that most current designations of historical periods reflect major events in the lives of men, but not those in the lives of women. Hence, Joan Kelly (1976) asked, "Did women have a renaissance?" If they did, she suggested, it was not during the same period that men had theirs.

The new scholars' response to the old scholarship on women has been twofold. First, they have critiqued the narrowness of the perspective of these "conventional modes of establishing social knowledge" (Westkott, 1979). Second, they have undertaken new research that puts women at the center of the inquiry in order to relate and incorporate female experience. This approach seeks to broaden and enlarge the body of knowledge in the social sciences.

The new scholarship on women takes place in stages. The first stage of inquiry has reflected a documentation of how things are for women. It has not yet removed man as the measure—whether it is a measure of career patterns, teachers' work, or schooling practices. Thus, this first stage of inquiry has looked at the female experience, but from a framework that originated in a masculine consciousness. At this stage we find the description and documentation of pervasive sexism as a social fact and attempts to redress these inequities in the mission, structure, and practices of social institutions.

A second stage of the new scholarship on women questions the knowledge base itself. At this stage, researchers suggest that most existing conceptual and methodological frameworks and practices are based upon man as the measure, and thus may be neither relevant to the female experience nor adequate for explaining female behavior (see, for example, Kaufman and Richardson's [1982] critique of models of women's achievement). As Gilligan (1979) describes it, we must stop "seeing life through men's eyes."

This changing emphasis has resulted in alternative questions, questions which for the first time do not look at women as defined exclusively in relationship to men (Westkott, 1979). We have begun to ask: How have ordinary women shaped institutions to fit their needs? What are the ways that women define and conceptualize educational issues? How have women created community in the places they have found themselves? What does the female world look like? (Bernard, 1981).

Writers of the new scholarship on women have suggested different frameworks for analyzing human experience. Stimpson (1980), for example, posits a male and a female world as two subworlds of a patriarchal world. These two worlds exist in relation to each other, and on particular occasions members of each enter the other's domain. In many other ways, Stimpson suggests, "sexually, psychologically, economically, and culturally" these worlds are dependent on each other (Stimpson, 1980).

Sklar (1980) sets up her model a little differently. Her conceptual framework focuses on "the historical study of past female experience." Female experience has

> two basic dimensions—human-specific dimensions that women share to a
> considerable degree with men, and female-specific dimensions that women have
> in common with one another and for the most part do not share with men.
> Both dimensions are shaped by cultural and biological imperatives; both are
> informed by material and ideological considerations. (p. 473)

Sklar suggests that her model is a humanistic concept rather than a scientific model because it represents ideal types that cannot exist in everyday life. Along with Stimpson, Sklar suggests that these two dimensions are interrelated. Since women are humans, and since even the purest kinds of female-specific experiences have consequences for men, they cannot exist as totally separate entities in real life.

THE NEW SCHOLARSHIP ON WOMEN
WITHIN EDUCATIONAL THOUGHT

The chapters in this book are all examples of the new scholarship on women. They examine important issues for women (and consequently for all human beings) in educational fields. In this section, we examine several examples of the theoretical work presently being undertaken in education, and then discuss the state of the art.

The theoretical work in the philosophy of education reveals how philosophical definitions of teaching have excluded work women have done over the years as mothers. Martin (1982) suggests that the historical exclusion of aspects of mothering from definitions of teaching reveals the narrowness of our definitions of education and a bias against women. Her work also suggests that scholars have tended to recognize work in the public realm that is institutionalized but not that which happens more informally in the private realm. This has historical antecedents:

> A typical pattern would be that women perceived a social or community need, began to meet it in practical, unstructured ways, then continued to expand their efforts into building a small institution, often financed by funds they raised through voluntary activities. Thus women built orphanages, homes for wayward children, old-age homes, kindergartens, libraries in community after community. Usually, when the institution had existed long enough and established itself, it became incorporated, registered, licensed, possibly taken over as a community institution. At that point it would usually be taken over by a male board of directors. It would also—incidentally—enter history, its official status making of its records historical sources. The women who had done the work, if they appeared in the record at all, would be visible only as a ladies' auxiliary group or as unpaid, unrecognized volunteers. (Lerner, 1979, p. 179)

Gilligan's work indicates that developmental psychologists and moral behaviorists have taken account of men's lives but not women's. When she did take women's lives into account, she found that not only is there a model of justice built on the orientation toward individual rights, but also one built on an ethic of care (Gilligan, 1977, 1979, 1982). Listening to women's voices, Gilligan first recognized the inadequacy of a model based on a sample of males for explaining the complexity of moral development. As she explored the relational and contextual concerns of women as they faced moral dilemmas, she broadened her understanding of human decision making rather than just female decision making.

The new scholarship on women in education influences the ways we examine our basic understanding of important issues, as these two examples suggest. The chapters in this book document the influence of research and inquiry into these concerns. Theoretical work in education has lagged behind other fields, however, for several reasons.

First, education is a multidisciplinary field. It draws continually on anthropology, history, psychology, sociology, and philosophy to define its orientation, and perhaps, as a subfield within education, women's scholarship can only draw on insights from these other fields.

Second, education has always been the second cousin to the liberal arts in terms of prestige and status. Many disdain the field of education and its work for being too practical, too concerned with "how to" rather than "why." And in women's studies, this view is paralleled as well. Education as a topic is low in the women's studies status hierarchy. The *Guide to Social Science Resources in*

Women's Studies (Oakes & Sheldon, 1978), for example, has no heading for education. And in another bibliographic reference, *Women's Studies Abstracts*, the heading "Education and Socialization" refers only to the process of students getting educated and socialized in educational settings such as schools, universities, and continuing education programs. Research on educational workers goes under the subheading "Employment."

Third, those concerned with women's issues in education face a different set of problems than those in more traditional social science fields—most importantly, the needs of schools. Educational practices have so often lacked sex equity that many educational researchers and activists felt it imperative to focus on applied areas. Curricula, practices, and structures that perpetuate discrimination have absorbed our attention rather than the more theoretical, less practical concerns. Motivated by a desire to change these practices for the next generations, women's studies practitioners in education have focused on schools. As this book amply demonstrates, the need for this work has not slackened. Educators must focus on the practice of education, for it is as Emile Durkheim said close to a century ago, the "means by which society prepares, within the child, the essential conditions of its very existence" (Durkheim, 1956).

THE NEW SCHOLARSHIP ON WOMEN AND METHODS OF INQUIRY

Educators do, however, conduct more theoretical research on these issues that may not be immediately applicable to the classroom. Additionally, researchers have begun to examine the ways in which research is conducted. As Campbell (1981) has shown, research methods are affected in a variety of ways by race and sex bias at all the different points in a research cycle, from choosing the problem to data analysis. These effects have important implications both for the knowledge base of human behavior, which has already been established in the social sciences, and for the understanding that researchers hope to bring to the female experience.

Feminist researchers will always call upon a variety of research methods to accomplish their goals, particularly because we are concerned that the problem shape the method, and not the reverse (see, for example, Richardson and Wirtenberg, 1983). Whatever method we choose, however, we must be highly self-conscious because we are covering new terrain, mapping it as we go. We must place tremendous importance on the process of discovering the questions that will get to the heart of women's experiences. These kinds of questions will no longer use a framework that is constructed solely from men's experiences. We no longer take what we had assumed were basic definitions and perspectives for granted. If we immerse ourselves in looking at the world from women's perspective we will, of course, lose the mythical construction of human reality we have previously framed.

We will need to depend on a variety of research styles and methods to reach this goal. The new emphasis on letting women speak in their own voices has heightened interest in qualitative methods, since these approaches provide participants an opportunity to construct their social realities. Stimpson has suggested two characteristics of the new scholarship on women that are in this sense phenomenological: "The investigator tries to extend affection and esteem toward her subject. . . . Next, the investigator tends to assume that women are sincere, not chatty fibbers of legend, but reliable witnesses of their own experience" (Stimpson, 1980, p. 5). Both of these characteristics emphasize that researchers concern themselves with how the world looks to women by using what have been called qualitative methods—for example, participant observation, in-depth interviewing, life histories, all of which are methods used more typically in anthropology, sociology, and history (see, for example, Biklen, 1983).

There will be more attempts to develop collaborative research efforts. Such collaboration may include research participants as well as researchers trained in qualitative and quantitative methods. Focusing on women's experiences and construction of their reality may encourage an inductive approach to the further understanding of sex equity in education. The new scholarship on women in education will build on the particulars of women's worlds to create new ways of looking at the education of both men and women.

REFERENCES

Bernard, J. (1981). *The female world*. New York: Free Press.
Biklen, S. (1983). *Teaching as occupation for women: A case study* (NIE report) (Grant No. NIE–G–81–0007). Syracuse: Education Designs Group.
Campbell, P. (1981, February). *The impact of societal biases on research methods*. Paper prepared for the National Institute of Education, Washington, DC.
de Beauvoir, S. (1952). *The second sex*. NY: Knopf.
Durkheim, E. (1977). *Education and sociology*. Glencoe, IL: Free Press.
Gilligan, C. (1977). Women's conceptions of the self and of morality. *Harvard Educational Review, 47*, 481–517.
Gilligan, C. (1979). Woman's place in man's life cycle. *Harvard Educational Review, 49*, 431–446.
Gilligan, C. (1982). *In a different voice*. Cambridge: Harvard University Press.
Howe, F. (1982). Feminist scholarship: The extent of the revolution. *Change, 14*(3), 12–30.
Jagger, A. (1978). Political philosophies of women's liberation. In M. Vetterline-Braggin, F. A. Elliston, & J. English, (Eds.), *Feminism and philosophy* (pp. 5–21). NJ: Littlefield, Adam.
Kaufman, D., & Richardson, B. (1982). *Achievement and women*. NY: Free Press.
Kelly, J. (1976). The social relation of the sexes: Methodological implications of women's history. *Signs, 1*, 809–823.
Lerner, G. (1972). On the teaching and organization of feminist studies. In Rae Lee Siporin (Ed.), *Female Studies V* (pp. 34–37). Pittsburgh: KNOW, Inc.
Lerner, G. (1979). *The majority finds it past*. New York: Oxford University Press.

Martin, J. R. (1982). Excluding women from the educational realm. *Harvard Educational Review, 52,* 133–148.

Oakes, E., & Sheldon, K. (1978). *Guide to social science resources in women's studies.* Santa Barbara, CA: Clio Books.

Pleck, E., & Pleck, J. H. (Eds.). (1980). *The American man.* Englewood Cliffs, NJ: Prentice-Hall.

Richardson, B., & Wirtenberg, J. (1983). *Sex role research: Measuring social change.* NY: Praeger.

Schramm, S. S. (1975). Do it yourself: Women's studies. In S. S. Schramm (Ed.), *Female Studies VIII* (pp. 1–4). Pittsburgh: KNOW, Inc.

Scott, J. (1981). Politics and professionalism: Women historians in the 1980s. *Women's Studies Quarterly, 9*(3), 23–31.

Sklar, K. K. (1980). A conceptual framework for the teaching of U.S. women's history. *The History Teacher, 13,* 471–481.

Smith, D. (1974). Women's perspective as a radical critique of sociology. *Sociological Inquiry, 44,* 7–13.

Stimpson, C. (1980). The new scholarship about women: The state of the art. *Annals of Scholarship,* No. 2, 2–14.

Westkott, M. (1979). Feminist criticism of the social sciences. *Harvard Educational Review, 49,* 422–430.

5

Facts and Assumptions about
the Nature of Sex Differences

Marcia C. Linn and Anne C. Petersen

This chapter provides a framework for subsequent chapters by clarifying gender differences in individual (that is, biological, cognitive, and psychosocial) factors which are frequently assumed to cause other gender differences. We also discuss methodological and logical issues that are critical to causal inference. Finally, we describe the implications of these issues for educational programs aimed at increasing equitable access to schooling and careers.

As an ultimate objective, investigations of gender similarities and differences should serve to ensure pluralism and diversity in society, independent of gender. Equity means access to societal and personal accomplishments, including economic reward, for both men and women. Equity means freedom for both sexes to choose school and career activities without social censure. These conditions encourage individuals to achieve their own potential and to serve their own and others' needs.

CAUSES OF GENDER DIFFERENCES:
THE ROLE OF HEREDITY AND ENVIRONMENT

Since there are biological differences between males and females, many individuals assume that other gender-related differences reflect genetic factors. No noncontroversial evidence for genetic explanations of gender differences in cognitive and psychosocial factors exists. Since environmental differences for the sexes emerge at birth and continue throughout the life span (see, for example, Haugh, Hoffman, & Cowan, 1980), genetic explanations have limited power. As

The authors would like to acknowledge the helpful assistance of Maryse Tobin-Richards, Carol Weissbrod, and Lisa Crockett.

This material is based upon research supported by the National Science Foundation under grant numbers 81–12631 and 79–19494. Any opinions, findings and conclusions, or recommendations expressed in this publication are those of the authors and do not necessarily reflect the views of the National Science Foundation.

Cronbach (1969) noted, "Human development is a cumulative, active process of utilizing environmental inputs, not an unfolding of genetically given structures" (p. 5). Thus, our attention will be devoted to understanding and enhancing the environmental inputs rather than to seeking elusive evidence for genetic influences. The evidence from the past decade of dramatic changes in educational and career choices of males and females clearly demonstrates the powerful impact of environmental factors on behavioral differences between males and females.

The tendency to assume that all differences between males and females are genetically determined and resistant to change is well illustrated by the controversial reporting of Benbow and Stanley's (1980) research on mathematics achievement. Benbow and Stanley's study of mathematically gifted volunteer subjects was erroneously interpreted as suggesting that gender differences in mathematics performance were genetically determined. Media reports overstated the research findings (for example, "Males inherently have more mathematical ability than females" ["Gender Factor," 1980]) and suggested unproven causal relationships (for example, "Do males have a math gene?" [Williams & King, 1980]). Although Benbow and Stanley did not examine genetic influences, they interpreted the lack of support in their data for differential course-taking by boys and girls as evidence for genetic factors in gender differences in mathematics performance. Given societal biases about gender differences, researchers must take extreme care in reporting potentially misinterpretable findings.

Misunderstandings such as those demonstrated in the media treatment of Benbow and Stanley's findings can have serious consequences. Vocational counselors who believe that females have less ability in math and science may discourage females from entering these careers. Parents, believing that their daughters' difficulties in mathematics reflect an innate predisposition, may not help or encourage them as much as they do their sons (for example, Parsons, 1982).

A general problem with the logic of the genetic hypothesis is that it is basically a "black box" proposition, since the mechanism for the effect is not specified. Few investigators have examined the mechanism by which genes might produce sex differences. The purely genetic possibilities are quite limited and unlikely to produce sex differences in characteristics such as these (Petersen, 1982). In contrast to the dearth of evidence for hereditary influences on gender differences, dramatic environmental influences on behavior of males and females have been documented. For example, females now hold many jobs previously held only by males. Women graduates of professional schools increase yearly; in 1968, only 9% of medical school graduates were women, compared to 24% in 1979 (Grant, 1982). Although their numbers are still small, women increasingly figure in that sign of corporate status: transfers. Moving ahead by moving around, women now account for close to 10% of corporate transfers, up from 5% three years ago (O'Toole, 1982).

The profound nature of these changes is illustrated in the response of advertisers—a force frequently implicated in the preservation of sex role stereotypes. Advertisements change in response to societal change. As Rena Bartos, a senior vice-president at J. Walter Thompson advertising agency, remarked, "Think of the old [10 years] Geritol commercial in which the man said, 'My wife, I think I'll keep her.' Nobody could do that today" (O'Toole, 1982, p. 78).

These dramatic changes in career and media roles for women serve to illustrate both the potential and the power of environmental influences on gender differences in academic performance. The potential is illustrated by the effect of access to valued schooling or career equity for the sexes; the power is illustrated by the pervasive media reinforcements of sex role stereotypes. Any claim for genetic influence on differential school and career performance of males and females must account for the impact of sex role expectations and other environmental factors, including education.

METHODOLOGICAL CONCERNS IN RESEARCH ON GENDER DIFFERENCES

Before turning to research findings of gender differences, we shall consider three methodological difficulties: magnitude of effects, definition of constructs, and bias of researchers.

Magnitude of Effects

In contrast to large gender differences in some academic majors (for example, 92% of 1979 undergraduate engineering degrees were awarded to men [*Chronicle of Higher Education,* 1980]), gender differences in cognitive and psychosocial factors are generally fairly small.

The limited magnitude of gender differences in cognitive and psychosocial factors has led some researchers to question their relevance to psychological themes (for example, Hyde, 1981; Linn & Pulos, 1983a; Plomin & Foch, 1982). Many have noted that small average score differences indicate that distributions are largely overlapping (for example, Jacklin, 1981). Yet small differences in average scores may be of interest at the extremes of the score distribution and may interact with other factors to have greater impact.

First, at the extremes of the distribution the ratio of males to females becomes meaningful even when gender differences account for only minor percentages of the total variance. Suppose that 5% of spatial orientation ability performance is attributed to gender, but that because of some unknown aspect of the career of interior design, one needs to be at the 95th percentile to succeed. As Hyde (1981) has calculated, 7.35% of the males and 3.22% of the females will be above the cutoff. Thus, twice as many males as females would be eligible for the career. Such conjecture is hardly sufficient to account for the observed ratios of males and females in certain careers, but it does illustrate the possible impact of small differences at the extremes of the distribution.

A similar problem concerns possible discontinuities at the tails of distributions. Jacklin (1981) has reported in one study that the mean differences in activity level for the sexes are solely attributable to a small group of very active males. These subjects form a "bump" at the top of the distribution, which raises the group mean. However, they compose a separate group, which is also discontinuous with the remainder of the boys and with all the girls. The existence of unusual groups at the extremes may explain some observed gender differences that are not characteristic of the sexes as a whole.

Definition of Constructs

Labeling of the constructs which allegedly lead to male-female differences in school performance often determines the content of remedial programs. For example, differences thought to reflect spatial visualization may be remedied by training in visualizing problems, but two difficulties may emerge: first, the constructs may be improperly labeled, making attempts at remediation fruitless. Second, the observed relationship between a construct and school performance may be the result of another factor which moderated the observed relationship (for example, a gender difference in motivation rather than ability could produce sex differences in performance).

Labeling of constructs may reflect the beliefs of the experimenter, the instruments chosen, or a currently popular theory. Since differences are small to start with, inconsistent findings that reflect chance fluctuations may form the basis for refinement of constructs. For example, it is possible that the variety of spatial ability constructs may all stem from one small, unstable ability that influences performance on each test, or they may stem from several distinct abilities. Each of these views could be supported by selected research studies. Constructs revealing gender differences might be based on a variety of abilities, or on just one. For this reason, the constructs are troublesome to define and may be improperly labeled in some research.

Further, unnamed constructs might mediate observed causal relationships. Many constructs that yield gender differences such as attributions for failure or spatial visualization are assumed to be the cause of the observed differences, although another variable may actually explain the relationship between the measured construct and gender differences.

Consider an example. Suppose we administer a questionnaire and find that females attribute failure in mathematics to their lack of ability, while males attribute failure to different factors on each item. Such a finding could be due either to differences in verbal ability (perhaps females understood the questions better and answered reliably, while males answered randomly) or to differences in self-disclosure (perhaps females answer questionnaires with their honest feelings, while males second-guess the experimenter and attempt to sound sophisticated). Each of these explanations for gender differences in responses to the questionnaire (attributional patterns, verbal ability, or propensity to self-disclosure) leads to different actions by those wishing to increase equity for the sexes.

Clearly, causal statements concerning gender differences should be made with caution. Investigations that use several measures of a construct are more likely to reach useful conclusions (and also are more likely to reveal contradictory findings) than studies using a single measure. Replications can also enhance the validity of constructs showing gender differences.

Bias of Researchers

Two kinds of bias deserve mention. First, researchers investigating the role of individual factors in gender differences have focused on biological explanations and on the accomplishments of males (Petersen, 1980). Second, since journals generally prefer studies that show some effect, and since researchers put more energy into interpreting studies that have significant findings, reported studies may include more significant gender effects than actually occur.

BIOLOGICAL SEX DIFFERENCES

Genes

Maleness and femaleness can be defined by biological features, but as Grady (1977) has said, sex is, in fact, primarily a social variable. No test of biological sex is generally given—except in the Olympics. We usually accept a self-report of sex and have developed an elaborate system of social cues for the purpose of identification (for example, short versus long hair, skirts, high heels).

Sex differences in genetic material act in two ways: through sex limitation or through sex linkage. Very few characteristics are sex-limited (that is, seen only in one sex). A trait that is sex-linked is carried on the X chromosome but is differentially distributed to males and females because females have two X chromosomes while males have only one. No known behavioral characteristics are sex-linked, and the few biological characteristics (for example, hemophilia) are maladaptive.

Hormones

Hormones, particularly sex hormones, constitute another biological sex difference. Both males and females have some amounts of all kinds of hormones, including sex hormones. What differs between males and females is the distribution, or ratio, of each of these hormones. In addition, hormone action is a complex process involving vast individual differences, including gender differences.

Furthermore, the human endocrine system is an open system, interacting with the central nervous system and other factors. The endocrine system can be influenced by behavior and social interactions. For example, stress in males can decrease testosterone levels. Reciprocal relationships between hormones and behavior have been demonstrated with a variety of variables. Thus, hormonal influences reflect both individual and contextual factors, and therefore cannot be given direct explanatory power.

Developmental Changes in Hormones

The endocrine system that controls reproduction is established prenatally. There appear to be few sex differences in the development of this system except that the levels, or ratios, of gonadal hormones are different for adult males and females.

Somatic Development

Prior to puberty there are few somatic differences in boys and girls apart from genitalia. The pubertal growth spurt occurs about two years earlier in girls than in boys. Although the amount of growth occurring during the adolescent growth spurt is about the same for boys and girls, the fact that it happens earlier in girls means that their prepubertal linear growth is curtailed sooner by the growth spurt, giving them an ultimate height that is shorter than that of boys. Gender differences in weight are based primarily on the smaller size of girls. The importance of these size differences has been largely neglected in research; size may, however, be the only important biological influence on other gender differences.

Distribution of body hair is somewhat more exclusive in males, but both boys and girls grow substantial amounts of "sexual" hair (pubic hair and axillary, or underarm, hair) during puberty. Although boys typically develop hair in a more extensive pattern, due to greater levels of androgen, the most notable sex difference is the growth of facial hair. At puberty, body proportions show sexual dimorphism. Both shoulder and hip width increase in pubertal boys and girls, but shoulders increase relatively more in males, and hips increase relatively more in females.

The timbre and pitch of voices deepens with puberty, though the effect is greater in boys than in girls. Sociocultural expectations for high-pitched female voices and low-pitched male voices probably exaggerate this biologically-based difference (Sachs, Liebeman, & Erickson, 1973). Some (for example, Henley, 1977), have noted that pitch of voice has come to be linked to attributions of power.

Other biological sex differences (for example, muscle and fat development) may reflect differences in the physical activity of boys and girls. It is now known that strenuous exercise affects such pubertal events as menarche, body shape, and muscle development (Frisch, 1983; Warren, 1983).

Organization of the Brain

Recently, much attention has been focused on sex differences in organization of the brain. Most of the data showing sex differences are obtained with rodents; data on some other mammals show no such differences. Hier (1981) has argued than no evidence for a sex difference in the anatomical structure of the human brain has been found, although a recent study with very small samples presented evidence for a sex difference in the anatomy of the corpus callosum (de Lacoste-Utamsing & Holloway, 1982).

A popular hypothesis is that cognitive functions such as verbal or spatial processing may be more lateralized in one hemisphere for males and the other for females. McGlone (1980), however, in her recent review of sex differences in laterality, concluded that males are more likely than females to show left hemisphere dominance in processing verbal material, and at the same time seem to exhibit greater right hemisphere dominance for nonverbal material. Females are thought to be less lateralized for either function. There is some evidence that extent of laterality is dynamic rather than fixed, raising the possibility that laterality can be influenced by experiences, can change developmentally, and perhaps can change in response to intervention. Thus, differences in laterality may reflect experiential or biological differences or both.

Timing of Maturation

Girls appear to mature faster than boys in utero and throughout early development. At birth girls are more mature than boys by 4 to 6 weeks, and at puberty by about 2 years. Waber (1976, 1977) proposed that sex differences in cognition are due to male-female differences in the timing of puberty. She hypothesized that the relatively longer period of maturation in boys permits more time for brain lateralization, and that the greater brain lateralization in males is responsible for the observed sex differences in cognition. Her data support the proposed link between timing of maturation, brain lateralization, and cognition.

Subsequent studies have corroborated Waber's finding of association between timing of maturation and spatial ability (Newcombe, Bandura, & Taylor, in press; Petersen & Gitelson, in preparation). They have not, however, found associations between brain lateralization and either timing of maturation or spatial ability.

Sherman (1967, 1978) has proposed a different version of the timing hypothesis. She posits that girls' early maturational advantage in speech leads them to develop brain pathways facilitating verbal proficiency to a greater extent than boys. Through continued reinforcement, verbal pathways predominate, making it less likely that girls will develop the neural pathways underlying alternative skills for communication and perception, such as spatial skills. Another version of this hypothesis is that girls' relative precocity in social skills may encourage further development of a person-orientation rather than the object-orientation thought by some to be the usual pattern for boys. This hypothesis appears promising, based on the limited existing data.

In general, studies have not addressed the possible effects of sex-related experiences on brain development and functioning. Studies have shown that experiences, training, and so forth, can influence brain development, but no investigations have applied these approaches to the possible etiology of sex differences.

Summary

Human males and females differ in genetic makeup, hormone levels and functioning, and timing of maturation. Since human biological systems are open, it would be inaccurate to assume that these factors are fixed and unalterable. The central nervous system of the human interacts in a dynamic, reciprocal way with other aspects of human functions and with the external environment.

The methodological and logical factors identified above have significance for conclusions about biological sex differences. Thus, heredity appears to set potentials for biological factors such as brain lateralization, hormonal levels, and timing of puberty, but within these potentials the biological factors appear to be modifiable by environmental events such as learning experiences, emotional states, and levels of exercise.

Establishment of causal relationships involving biological gender differences such as hormonal levels, timing of puberty, and brain lateralization must consider the difficulties in measuring and defining these factors. Construct definition also confounds efforts at causal inference. For example, brain lateralization is usually assessed by using a behavioral measure that may be imprecise. All these impediments to accurate causal inferences involving biological sex differences suggest the importance of using multiple measures of potential constructs and of closely examining the justification of causal inferences that have been made.

COGNITIVE SEX DIFFERENCES

Tests of cognitive, or mental, abilities include many that are variously grouped into constructs. Two broad types generally reveal gender differences: tests of verbal ability (favoring females) and spatial ability (favoring males). In this chapter we intentionally exclude tests of achievement (for example, in math or social studies), which are discussed in subsequent chapters. Tests of problem solving such as letter series, mechanical reasoning, or Piagetian reasoning appear to yield gender differences only when they require specific knowledge of a given subject. Thus, proportional reasoning tests yield gender differences, as do math achievement tests, and tests of reasoning about displaced volume yield gender differences, as do science achievement tests. In contrast, tests such as letter series, controlling variables, classification ability, and combinatorial reasoning fail to yield gender differences.

Male-female differences in cognitive abilities appear well established but small. Methodological and logical issues include specification of the constructs showing differences, magnitude of the effects, and consistency of the effects. We shall review research findings and comment on logical and methodological issues. Although we realize that "vote-counting" methods of summarizing research are biased and can be misleading (for example, Hedges, 1982; Olkin,

1982), we shall combine vote counts with meta-analyses to ensure reporting of recent findings.

Verbal Ability

Differences in verbal ability were reviewed by Maccoby and Jacklin (1974), who found gender differences emerging at age 11 and favoring females in 11 of 27 studies. Both Hyde (1981) and Plomin and Foch (1982) have conducted meta-analyses of these studies which showed that sex accounted for only about 1% of the variance, constituting about one-fourth of a standard deviation. Plomin and Foch indicated that the gender differences in verbal ability seem uniformly distributed across age, in contrast to Maccoby and Jacklin's (1974) suggestion that they emerge in adolescence. Recent findings (see chapter 14, this volume) suggest that males may outperform females on some verbal measures.

More attention has been focused on gender differences in other cognitive abilities. Recent reviews have been conducted by Harris (1978), Maccoby and Jacklin (1974), McGee (1979), Newcombe, Bandura, & Taylor (in press), Parsons (1982), and Petersen, Tobin-Richards, & Crockett (1982).

One difficulty for researchers in this area concerns the measurement of spatial ability in those under age 10. Many commonly employed tests such as mental rotations (Shephard & Metzler, 1971), adapted for groups by Wilson and Vandenberg (1978), or Paper Folding (French, Ekstrom, & Price, 1963) are responded to at the chance level by young children.

Spatial Ability

The construct of spatial ability lacks a uniform definition among researchers. Spatial ability is measured by tests such as mental rotations (Shephard & Metzler, 1971), perception of horizontality (Piagetian Water Level), Hidden Figures (French, Ekstrom, & Price, 1963) and Paper Folding (French, Ekstrom, & Price, 1963). Measures of spatial orientation require subjects to identify matching but reoriented figures. Measures of perception of horizontality (and verticality, such as the rod and frame test) are associated with an aspect of field-dependence/independence (Linn & Kyllonen, 1981; Witkin & Goodenough, 1981). Measures requiring multistep reorganizations of visually presented information such as Paper Folding, Surface Development (French, Ekstrom, & Price, 1963), WISC Block Design, Primary Mental Abilities, Space Subtest (Thurstone & Thurstone, 1941), and DAT Spatial Relations (Bennett, Seashore, & Wesman, 1973) have been referred to as spatial visualization (Guilford, 1967). Measures of cognitive restructuring such as the Hidden Figures Test have been, at times, characterized as Fluid Ability (Snow, Federico, & Montague, 1980), spatial ability (Guilford, 1947), and field-dependence/independence (Witkin & Goodenough, 1981), but are difficult to differentiate from spatial visualization. We refer to three aspects of spatial ability: spatial orientation, horizontality/verticality, and visualization.

An aspect of spatial ability, which might be called spatial memory, differs from the aspects of spatial ability described above. Ability to reconstruct three-dimensional space from memory may favor young males, as may map reading (for example, Newcombe, 1982). These are probably different from the abilities referred to above. Evidence relating these abilities to those typically called spatial ability in older individuals is lacking.

Of the three aspects of spatial ability identified above, sex differences favoring males are most pronounced and consistent for mental rotations and horizontality/verticality and least consistent for spatial visualization. Using these categories, Linn & Petersen (1983) conducted a meta-analysis of studies of gender differences in spatial ability conducted subsequent to Maccoby & Jacklin's (1974) review of gender difference research. Their meta-analysis of 172 effect size estimates reveals that gender differences in spatial ability (1) are not first detected in adolescence and therefore cannot be attributed to pubertal change, and (2) are found on tasks requiring skill in using kinesthetic cues and in speed of mental rotation but not on spatial visualization tasks which require analytic processes to select and apply strategies to complex problems. They found that horizontality/verticality, which is characterized by ability to disembed kinesthetic cues from visual cues, is easier for males than females among those over 18; differences range between one-third and two-thirds of a standard deviation unit, depending on the age of the respondents. Mental rotations, which is characterized by speed of angular rotation of a two or three dimensional figure, is also easier for males than females; differences range from about one-quarter of a standard deviation unit for PMA Space, to almost an entire standard deviation unit for the Vandenberg. Spatial visualization, which is characterized by analytic combination of both visual and non-visual strategies, is about equally difficult for males and females; males on the average have a slight, but not significant, advantage of about one-tenth of a standard deviation unit.

The Linn & Petersen (1983) findings for Horizontality/Verticality are consistent with Hyde's (1981) meta-analysis of the Maccoby and Jacklin's (1974) data showing that 1% of the variance in what they called field-articulation usually measured by RFT was related to gender. The findings for spatial visualization and mental rotations are difficult to compare to Hyde's analysis of Maccoby and Jacklin's data since tests of visualization were combined with tests of mental rotations. Hyde's combined group of tests showed that 5% of the variance and of one standard deviation were associated with gender.

Training and Experience

One possible method of investigating the role of cognitive factors in gender differences is to examine the effects of training and experience related to these factors. In general, training can influence performance on the tests for which it is designed but might not influence school or career performance.

The influences of experience stem from play and other leisure activities. For example, play preferences for spatial-type activities such as building with blocks differ for young males and females and appear to be associated with performance on measures of disembedding (for example, Block, 1981; Connor & Serbin, 1980). Books (Connor & Serbin, 1978), television programs (Sternglanz & Serbin, 1974; Vogel, Broverman, & Gardner, 1970), and toys (Lyon, 1972) for young children reflect sex stereotyping.

During adolescence, males and females differentially engage in a wide range of leisure activities associated with spatial ability (Newcombe, Bandura, & Taylor, in press). These include athletics, musical performance, social activities, and other leisure time pursuits. These activities are far more sex-stereotyped than the small gender differences in cognitive ability would suggest.

When successful, training in spatial ability sometimes favors females more than males (Newcombe, 1982), suggesting the ability of experience to alter cognitive sex differences, but many training procedures enhance performance of all subjects (for example, Pulos, de Benedictis, Linn, Sullivan, & Clement, 1982; Thomas, Jamison, & Hummel, 1973). Connor, Serbin, and Schackman (1977) and Connor, Schackman, and Serbin (1978) succeeded in training both sexes in cognitive restructuring ability; the training reduced the gender differences. In these two studies, however, training was on a measure of cognitive restructuring, which our review of spatial ability suggests infrequently yields gender differences. The transfer of such training to school performance and career performance has not been established.

Conclusions about Cognitive Gender Differences

The lack of research on verbal ability probably reflects bias in selection of research topics; however, those few studies that have been done indicate that small but fairly systematic sex differences on verbal ability measures appear to exist. Aspects of spatial ability referred to as horizontality and mental rotations yield more consistent differences than other measures of cognitive ability. Between 1 and 5% of the variance is typically associated with gender. Inconsistency in findings reflects the small size of the effect.

We purposely referred to "aspects" of verbal and spatial ability, since constructs have not been established. The lack of uniformity in findings reflects this problem. Within the same subject group or subject pool, some measures of the same cognitive ability yield sex differences and others do not. Of 24 multiple measure studies of spatial visualization, Petersen, Tobin-Richards, & Crockett (1982) report that 12 yield inconsistent sex differences across tests, subjects, or ages. Lack of consistency in performance may reflect lack of statistical power to detect small effects, or lack of clear constructs. Furthermore, differences may reflect differential experiences at school (for example, Fennema & Sherman, 1978; Linn & Pulos, 1983a, b).

Causal inference about the role of cognitive abilities in gender differences presents problems, since the constructs are poorly defined. Even when causal relations are established, their nature may be undefined.

Spatial and verbal ability generally yield some gender differences and often have substantial within-gender relationships with achievement or whatever criteria they are intended to explain. Yet, the mechanisms that explain between-gender differences in cognitive ability could be different from the mechanisms that account for the within-group relationships. In fact, researchers sometimes find that dimensions revealing gender differences have similar relationships with criteria for the sexes and do not account for any of the gender-related variance in the criteria (for example, Barnett, King, Howard, & Dino, 1980; Fennema & Sherman, 1978; Linn & Pulos, 1983a, b).

Consider an example. Suppose gender differences on a spatial ability test reflect specific experience with gears and pulleys. Suppose further that gender differences on a criterion such as science problem solving reflect familiarity with concepts such as temperature and acceleration. Insofar as experience with gears and pulleys is correlated with familiarity with temperature and acceleration, then between-gender differences on spatial ability will overlap with between-gender differences on science problem solving. Suppose further that performance on both spatial ability and science problem solving reflects use of analytic ability. Insofar as within-group differences reflect *only* analytic ability, and analytic ability is equally distributed in the sexes, then within-group relationships will be identical for the sexes. Thus, within-group differences could reflect equally available abilities, while between-group differences could reflect unequal experiences.

PSYCHOSOCIAL SEX DIFFERENCES

In this section, we discuss constructs identified by social psychologists, clinical psychologists, and others which affect gender differences in performance in school and career settings. By psychosocial we mean noncognitive personality or social behaviors. Gender differences in what we call psychosocial behavior emerge frequently but tend to resist generalization. The lack of good construct definitions, both theoretical and operational, as well as the inconsistent use of those definitions that are available, contributes to the ambiguity of this research area. Constructs such as aggression and altruism frequently include intent as well as behavior, making measurement more difficult. Five categories of psychosocial behavior have revealed gender differences: (1) confidence/anxiety, (2) conformity or dependency, (3) empathy, (4) aggression, and (5) self-esteem.

Confidence/Anxiety

Lack of self-confidence may be one explanation for women's underrepresentation in many careers. Maccoby and Jacklin (1974) found self-confidence, defined in terms of grade expectancy and success on particular tasks, to be consistently lower in women than in men. Lenny's (1977) review of the literature suggested the role of context: confidence depends on the nature of the task and on the availability of clear and unambiguous information concerning ability. In addition, the presence of social comparisons appears to contribute to lowered confidence in women but not in men (Lenny & Gold, 1982). Petersen, Tobin-Richards, & Crockett (1982) summarized recent literature and found that 60% of recent studies revealed consistent differences in expectancies of success, with males more confident than females.

Sex differences in causal attributions about success and failure probably reflect confidence. Frieze, Whitley, Hanusa, & McHugh (in press) summarized the literature and concluded that women are unlikely to attribute their success to ability. Findings in the recent literature (Petersen, Tobin-Richards, & Crockett) support the notion that people are more likely to attribute successful performance to ability or skill when the successful individual is male. In addition, tasks are judged more difficult when they are successfully accomplished by males, and less so when accomplished by females. Furthermore males, more than females, tend to attribute success to internal factors and failure to external factors.

Women may experience a greater degree of anxiety than men. Although Maccoby and Jacklin (1974) concluded that the findings were too ambiguous and limited to support a conclusion of sex differences in either general anxiety or test anxiety, Block (1976) reported that 58% of the studies reviewed by them showed that anxiety is higher for girls. Block (1981), reviewing recent literature, concluded that females are more fearful, manifest greater anxiety, and have less confidence in themselves and their performance on specific tasks than males. Thus, females appear to display greater anxiety than males, although the reasons are unclear.

Conformity or Dependency

Literature on sex differences in conformity was reviewed recently by Eagly (1978), who concluded that females demonstrate more conformity only in group situations characterized by uncertainty. Cooper's (1979) reanalysis of Maccoby and Jacklin's data pertaining to conformity in group situations confirmed this result. Males conformed significantly less than females only under the surveillance of other group members (Eagly, Wood, & Fishbaugh, 1981). Other context factors shown to be important include sex appropriateness of the activity (Morelock, 1980) and task familiarity (Eagly, 1978; Lockheed, 1976; Stake & Stake, 1979).

Dependency, an aspect of conformity defined as the tendency to seek close contact with attachment objects or their surrogates, does not vary consistently by sex (Maccoby & Jacklin, 1974). Block (1976) came to the same conclusion by reviewing Maccoby and Jacklin's tabled studies. A different finding emerged, however, when she tabled other studies found in Maccoby and Jacklin's annotated bibliography. All of those 13 studies reported females to be more dependent.

Empathy

Hoffman (1977), in a major review of the research, concluded that females do indeed appear to be more empathic than males. He defined empathy as the vicarious affective response to another person's feelings. Hoffman suggested that empathy in females may be part of a prosocial affective orientation that includes the tendency to experience guilt over harming others, and that females may tend, more than males, to imagine themselves in the other's place. In contrast, Maccoby and Jacklin (1974), who included studies of constructs more broadly construed than that of Hoffman, concluded that there is no clear tendency for girls to be more sensitive than boys to social cues. Block (1976) reported that 23% of the studies reviewed by Maccoby and Jacklin indicated sex differences in favor of girls, while 10% favored boys. A review of studies published after 1974 (Petersen, Tobin-Richards, & Crockett, 1982) produced a somewhat more decisive picture in favor of sex differences: of nine recent studies, females expressed greater empathy in four. To conclude, slight evidence of greater empathic response from females than males has emerged.

Sociability, an aspect of empathy, appears to produce mixed results with regard to sex differences, although research on proximity to friends favors girls (Block, 1976; Maccoby & Jacklin, 1974). Several recent studies of infants have found sex differences, with girls initiating more social contact (Gunnar & Donahue, 1980), displaying greater social competence (Klein & Durfee, 1978), and engaging in more positive interactions with their mothers (Clarke-Stewart, 1973). Females more than males maintain proximity to other persons as measured by eye contact, distance, and physical contact (for example, Block, 1973). Block's review as well as other research (for example, Savin-Williams, 1980) has demonstrated that the sexes differ in social behaviors and in the patterns used to relate to others.

Responsiveness to the young is considered one measure of empathy, frequently called nurturance. In a comprehensive review of the literature on sex differences in responsiveness to the young, Berman (1980) found strong contextual effects based on factors such as prior role relationships with the young, social qualities of the situation, cultural expectations, and age of the subjects. Berman found no support for the belief that nurturing behavior reflects physiological conditions such as hormonal levels.

Aggression

Sex differences in aggression seem fairly well established (Maccoby & Jacklin, 1980; Tieger, 1980). Aggression is defined as behavior that hurts another or appears intended to do so. In 55% of the 94 studies reviewed by Maccoby and Jacklin (1974), males were found to aggress more than females. Block (1976) found similar differences. The greater prevalence of aggressive behavior found in males seems to occur across the life span, beginning as early as age 2, and has been measured in a variety of ways including observation (Barrett, 1979; Feshback, 1970; Smith & Green, 1975), ratings, questionnaires, and projective measures (for example, Brissett & Nowicki, 1973). Maccoby and Jacklin (1980) recently reviewed studies of children 6 years old and younger. In 64% of the studies, boys behaved more aggressively than girls. Frodi, Macaulay, and Thome (1977), in a review of the literature on adult aggression, concluded that sex differences appear in self-report measures, but not in continued observational situations. They note that factors that provoke anger in men may provoke anxiety in women.

Possible components of aggression which contribute to the observed differences between males and females include activity level, competitiveness, and dominance. Recent studies of competition-cooperation (Ahlgren & Johnson, 1979; Moely, Skarin, & Weil, 1979) have reported that boys are more competitive than girls under all conditions and have consistently more positive attitudes toward competition. Rocha and Rogers (1976) have found evidence for a relationship between aggression and competition. Higher levels of competition and reward magnitude produced more aggressive behavior than lower levels of these variables in children 5 to 7 years of age.

Block (1976) observed, in a review of the literature on activity level, that boys are more active than girls. Males also appear to be more curious, to engage in more exploratory behavior, to suffer more accidents requiring medical care, and to be more impulsive (Block & Block, 1980; Hult, 1978; Maccoby & Jacklin, 1974; Manheimer & Mellinger, 1967; Willerman, 1979).

Self-esteem

Maccoby and Jacklin (1974) concluded that there was no evidence for sex differences in self-esteem. Block (1976), however, noted that while the findings on self-esteem per se were inconsistent, males clearly exhibited a stronger, more potent self-concept than females.

Males have feelings of greater personal efficacy, power, ambition, energy, potency, instrumentality, and mastery. In contrast, females perceive themselves in terms of interpersonal values, expressiveness, generosity, sensitivity, and nurturance (Bakan, 1966; Bem, 1974; Block, 1973; Dweck, Davidson, Nelson, & Enna, 1978; Spence & Helmreich, 1978).

Training Studies

Training on psychosocial dimensions such as anxiety and confidence has been shown to influence these factors but, as found for cognitive factors, not necessarily to affect school and career activities. For example, courses in Math without Fear reduce reported anxiety associated with mathematics (Kreinberg, 1981).

Summary of Psychosocial Gender Differences

In summary, psychosocial differences between males and females have been documented. Differences in aggression are most pronounced; differences in confidence/anxiety, conformity, empathy, and self-esteem are less strong. All observed psychosocial differences reflect a strong contextual component. Thus, females exhibit more anxiety and less self-confidence in situations requiring mathematics than in those requiring verbal skill.

Taken together, these findings suggest that females are more sensitive to social cues than are males. Females are more able to put themselves in the place of others and also more likely to respond to the opinions of others—including opinions about their lack of ability in subjects such as mathematics or science.

There has been a general tendency to assume that cognitive differences are biologically determined, while psychosocial differences are more often attributed to socialization (Petersen, 1980). In both cases, there has been only minimal attention to the processes by which biological or socialization factors might operate. Whatever processes operate at the individual level, however, they cannot explain the large sex differences observed in educational and occupational attainment in many areas. Situational factors (for example, other roles selected by women) as well as discrimination are clearly important as well.

Gilligan (1982) has argued that females' greater ability to respond to social cues reflects a needed aspect of society. Gilligan's call for the advantage of "a different voice," or a female perspective, reflects concern for pluralism and diversity; clearly, such diversity benefits all members of society. As Gilligan notes, the presence of females in previously traditionally male roles can empower males in the role to behave differently. For example, female medical doctors who display great sorrow at the loss of a patient empower males in the situation to display sorrow more openly. However, insofar as diversity stems from discriminatory socialization patterns or societal expectations, we may achieve diversity at the expense of permitting all to achieve their full potential. Ideally, pluralism must stem from equitable experiences. Diversity, then, will reflect freedom of choice, not cultural determinism.

RELATING BIOLOGICAL, COGNITIVE, AND PSYCHOSOCIAL FACTORS TO SCHOOL ACTIVITIES AND CAREER CHOICES

As the previous sections demonstrated, differences in biological, cognitive, and psychosocial factors that can be attributed to gender are small. In addition, both methodological issues associated with inferring cause and logical issues associated with labeling of the constructs make it difficult to characterize exactly what the differences are and what they stem from. In spite of these difficulties, however, both researchers and popular writers frequently infer that biological, cognitive, and psychosocial factors account for differences between the sexes in school and career activities.

Just as methodological and logical issues make it difficult to infer relationships among biological, cognitive, and psychosocial factors, so do they make it difficult to relate these factors to gender differences in school and career activities. One major methodological problem is the lack of power in the typical correlational analyses that have been used to attempt to investigate these relationships. Our statistical techniques lack power for establishing whether one correlation coefficient is different from another, such as those for males and females. In addition, it is difficult to determine whether observed gender differences in one factor, for example spatial ability, can be used to explain gender differences in another factor, for example mathematics achievement. Thus, it is difficult even to establish relationships, much less to infer cause, due to the lack of power in the techniques available for investigating these relationships.

As we mentioned above, definitions of constructs introduce logical confusion when one attempts to establish the relationships among the various factors thought to contribute to gender differences in biological, cognitive, and psychosocial factors. These problems become even more complex when one attempts to relate individual difference factors to school and career performance. For example, "success" in school could reflect achievement, some form of aptitude, willingness to comply with school rules, or age relative to other students in one's grade.

When we attempt to relate individual difference factors to school and career activities, both sex role stereotypes and prior experience in areas related to school success introduce additional complexities. For example, Newcombe, Bandura, and Taylor (in press) have shown that males more than females have science- and math-related hobbies. Linn (1983) has reported that males visit science museums more than females. The mediating effects of these experiences must be considered when establishing causal relationships. Without this information, causal relationships are difficult to characterize.

Further difficulties are introduced when we note that the classroom experiences of males and females may differ (for example, Becker, 1981; Brophy & Good, 1970; Lockheed, chapter 11, this volume; Stallings & Robertson, 1979) and that parental expectations for males and females may differ, even from birth (for example, Haugh, Hoffman, & Cowan, 1980). Parents provide different experiences for their male and female children and may engender differences in expectations. For example, parents design rooms for females differently from those for males (Rheingold & Cook, 1975), and their expectations influence performance in mathematics (for example, Parsons, 1982).

Evidence for Relationships

Several researchers have attempted to demonstrate the relationship between individual factors and academic performance. In general, a wide range of factors including verbal ability, spatial ability, confidence, and anxiety are related to academic performance for both sexes. Findings demonstrating that these factors differentiate between male and female academic preformance are far less frequent. The lack of power in establishing these relationships undoubtedly contributes to these findings and, of course, also contributes to the inconsistent results. Thus, as mentioned above, a number of researchers have found strong relationships between cognitive abilities and achievement in math and science (for example, Fennema & Sherman, 1978), but many fewer have found that these correlations can be used to explain the gender differences in achievement or career choices (for example, Barnett, King, Howard, & Dino, 1980; Fennema & Sherman, 1978, Linn & Pulos, 1983a, b).

Training on cognitive and psychosocial dimensions, as discussed above, can have an impact on gender differences. Experience appears also to affect these factors and biological characteristics of the sexes. Whether training or experience results in changes in school and career performance remains to be seen. It is important to note, however, that cognitive and psychosocial factors have not been shown to present insurmountable barriers to school and career performance.

Causal relationships are difficult to infer under any circumstances. It seems clear, however, that events that occur prior to other events are more likely to be causal than the reverse. To gain evidence about the order of events in this complex area, longitudinal study is essential. Several longitudinal studies are currently underway. Results relevant to the points we discuss in this chapter are just starting to become available. For example, the subjects in Block and Block's longitudinal study (in progress) are reaching adolescence. The effects of cognitive and psychosocial differences on the sorts of school activities and career choices that these youngsters make will soon be reportable. This sort of evidence will bring us closer to making causal statements concerning cognitive and psychosocial differences between the sexes.

Evidence concerning the effects of socialization practices and sex role stereotypes is also extremely difficult to ascertain. Yet, these factors may mediate the observed relationships between cognitive and psychosocial factors on the one hand and school and career activities on the other. In this important area, relevant studies are also just emerging, primarily from longitudinal studies (for example, Kaurell & Petersen, in press).

Both the preliminary findings of these studies and the reanalyses of previously reported data by other researchers (for example, Linn & Petersen, 1982) suggest that gender differences emerge slowly rather than dramatically during adolescence. The trend toward observing gender differences among younger individuals deserves scrutiny by researchers, for it places greater emphasis on the role of socialization and stereotyping behavior and reduces the importance of the "turbulence" of adolescence as a contributor to gender differences in school and career activities.

IMPLICATIONS

As this review suggests, the answer to "what causes what" is unclear in the area of gender differences in school and career activities. To counteract the notion that such differences reflect biological differences between males and females, more evidence about other possible causes is needed. Additional evidence will also facilitate the design of programs to remedy inequitable opportunities for the sexes in school and career activities.

Male-female differences in achievements probably reflect the interaction of biological, cognitive, psychosocial, and experiential factors. Research reveals small but systematic gender differences in factors considered relatively unresponsive to instruction. Gender differences in factors considered responsive to instruction tend to be larger than differences in factors considered less so. For example, gender differences typically account for 1 to 5% of the variance in spatial visualization (a possible aspect of engineering), yet 92% of undergraduate degrees in engineering in 1979 were awarded to men (*Chronicle of Higher Education*, 1980).

Analysis of gender differences must focus on the strengths of both sexes. Females display reasonably well-established superiority in verbal ability (Maccoby & Jacklin, 1974), interpersonal skill (Gilligan, 1982; Loevinger, 1976), and computational skill (Armstrong, 1979). Observers of career paths (Levinson, 1978) note that the female role of attention to home and family has been adopted by some males to the benefit of society. We need to know which female skills deserve encouragement and could be effectively imitated by males, just as we need to know which male skills can be effectively imitated by females.

Given the many difficulties in establishing the role of biological, cognitive, and psychosocial factors in gender differences in school activities and career choice, why are these factors considered important at all? Focus on these factors certainly stems, at least in part, from a tendency toward reductionism in psychological research. Researchers hope to find the "basis," or underlying factors, which can explain complex performance. No doubt, researchers have pursued biological factors because they can observe some biological differences between the sexes. Similarly, cognitive and psychosocial factors are perceived as basic in psychological research and therefore have been pursued by researchers. The pursuit of these factors has resulted in some interesting findings and has led to further research. Nevertheless, in spite of these advances, one might wonder whether researchers are studying the appropriate factors.

Perhaps the most important implication of the current research is that gender differences have not been shown to limit the possible school and career activities of either males or females. Certainly, the availability of training programs (such as medical school) has had a far more profound impact on access of both males and females to careers than any limitations that might be the result of biological, cognitive, or psychosocial differences between the sexes. Factors that might possibly limit opportunities on the basis of sex appear amenable to instruction and, thus, responsive to environmental influence. There seems to be no reason to restrict access on the basis of sex to school activities or career options.

ULTIMATE OBJECTIVES REVISITED

We indicated that our ultimate objective was to ensure achievement of the full potential of each member of society. The role of biological, cognitive, and psychosocial factors in gender differences in school and career activities must be examined in order to ensure that expectations about the roles of these factors are not roadblocks to ultimate achievements for either males or females. For example, when females choose not to study mathematics, they choose to avoid a large number of careers. If factors such as socialization practices and sex role stereotypes are contributing to these decisions, then ultimately these practices are limiting the accomplishment of full potential for that segment of the population. Achievement of equity means elimination of roadblocks such as these. By examining the role of biological, cognitive, and psychosocial differences in gender differences in school and career activities, we can eliminate erroneous expectations about the role of these factors and ultimately, through intervention programs, enhance the likelihood that all members of our society will achieve their full potential.

REFERENCES

Ahlgren, A., & Johnson, D. W. (1979). Sex differences in cooperative and competitive attitudes from the 2nd through the 12th grades. *Developmental Psychology, 15,* 45–49.

Armstrong, J. M. (1979). *A national assessment of achievement and participation of women in mathematics.* Denver: Education Commission of the States.

Bakan, D. (1966). *The duality of human existence.* Chicago: Rand McNally.

Barnett, M. A., King, L. M., Howard, J. A., & Dino, G. A. (1980). Empathy in young children: Relation to parents' empathy, affection, and emphasis on the feelings of others. *Developmental Psychology, 16,* 243–244.

Barrett, D. E. (1979). A naturalistic study of sex differences in children's aggression. *Merrill-Palmer Quarterly, 25,* 193–204.

Becker, J. R. (1981). Differential treatment of females and males in mathematics classes. *Journal for Research in Mathematics Education, 12*(1), 10–53.

Bem, S. L. (1974). The measurement of psychological androgyny. *Journal of Consulting and Clinical Psychology, 42,* 155–162.

Benbow, C. P., & Stanley, J. C. (1980). Sex differences in mathematical ability: Fact or artifact? *Science, 210,* 1262–1264.

Bennett, G. K., Seashore, A. C., & Wesman, A. G. (1973). *The Differential Aptitude Test.* New York: Psychological Corporation.

Berman, P. W. (1980). Are women more responsive than men to the young? A review of developmental, parental, and situational variables. *Psychological Bulletin, 88,* 668–695.

Block, J. H. (1973). Conceptions of sex role: Some cross-cultural and longitudinal perspectives. *American Psychologist, 28,* 512–526.

Block, J. H. (1976). Issues, problems, and pitfalls in assessing sex differences. *Merrill-Palmer Quarterly, 22,* 283–308.

Block, J. H. (1981). *Personality development in males and females: The influences of differential socialization.* Paper presented at the annual meeting of the American Psychological Association.

Block, J. H., & Block, J. (1980) The role of ego-control and ego-resiliency in the organization of behavior. In W. A. Collins (Ed.), *Minnesota Symposia on Child Psychology* (Vol. 13). Hinsdale, NJ: Erlbaum.

Block, J. H., & Block, J. (in progress). *Cognitive development from childhood to adolescence* (NIMH Grant MH 16080).

Brissett, M., & Nowicki, S. (1973). Internal versus external control of reinforcement and reaction to frustration. *Journal of Personality and Social Psychology, 25,* 35–44.

Brophy, J. E., & Good, T. L. (1970). Teachers' communication of differential expectations for children's classroom performance: Some behavioral data. *Journal of Educational Psychology, 61*(6), 365–374.

Chronicle of Higher Education. (1980, November).

Clarke-Stewart, K. A. (1973). Interactions between mothers and their young children: Characteristics and consequences. *Monographs of the Society for Research in Child Development, 38,*(6–7, Serial No. 153).

Connor, J. M., Schackman, M. E., & Serbin, L. A. (1978). Sex-related differences in response to practice on a visual-spatial test and generalization to a related test. *Child Development, 49,* 24–29.

Connor, J. M., & Serbin, L. A. (1978). Children's responses to stories with male and female characters. *Sex Roles, 4,* 637–645.

Connor, J. M., & Serbin, L. A. (1980). *Mathematics, visual-spatial ability, and sex-roles* (final report). Washington, DC: National Institute of Education.

Connor, J. M., Serbin, L. A., & Schackman, M. (1977). Sex differences in children's response to training on a visual-spatial test. *Developmental Psychology, 3,* 293–294.

Cooper, H. M. (1979). Statistically combining independent studies: A meta-analysis of sex differences in conformity research. *Journal of Personality and Social Psychology, 37,* 131–146.

Cronbach, L. J. (1969). Heredity, environment, and educational policy. *Harvard Educational Review, 39,* 338–347.

de Lacoste-Utamsing, C., & Holloway, R. L. (1982). Sexual dimorphism in the human corpus callosum. *Science, 216,* 1431–1432.

Dweck, C. S., Davidson, W., Nelson, S., & Enna, B. (1978). Sex differences in learned helplessness: II. The contingencies of evaluation feedback in the classroom. III. An experimental analysis. *Developmental Psychology, 14,* 268–276.

Eagly, A. H. (1978). Sex differences in influenceability. *Psychological Bulletin, 85,* 86–116.

Eagly, A. H., Wood, W., & Fishbaugh, L. (1981). Sex differences in conformity: Surveillance by the group as a determinant of male nonconformity. *Journal of Personality and Social Psychology, 40,* 384–394.

Fennema, E., & Sherman, J. (1978). Sex-related differences in mathematics achievement and related factors: A further study. *Journal for Research in Mathematics Education, 9,* 189–203.

Feshback, S. (1970). Aggression. In P. H. Mussen (Ed.), *Carmichael's manual of child psychology.* New York: Wiley.

French, J. W., Ekstrom, R. B., & Price, L. A. (1963). *Manual for kit of reference tests for cognitive factors* (rev. ed.). Princeton, NJ: Educational Testing Service.

Frieze, I. H., Whitley, B. E., Hanusa, B. H., & McHugh, M. C. (in press). Assessing the theoretical model for sex differences in causal attributions for success and failure. *Sex Roles.*

Frisch, R. (1983). Fatness, puberty, and fertility: The effects of nutrition and athletic training on menarche and ovulation. In J. Brooks-Gunn & A. C. Petersen (Eds.),

Puberty in girls: Biological and psychological perspectives (pp. 29–49). New York: Plenum.

Frodi, A., Macaulay, J., & Thome, P. R. (1977). Are women always less aggressive than men? A review of the experimental literature. *Psychological Bulletin,* 1977, *84,* 634–660.

The gender factor in math. (1980, December 15). *Time,* p. 57.

Gilligan, C. (1982). *In a different voice.* Cambridge: Harvard University Press.

Grady, K. E. (1977, April). *The belief in sex differences.* Paper presented at the annual meeting of the Eastern Psychological Association, Boston.

Grant, M. N. (1982, March). The feminization of ob/gyn. *Savvy,* pp. 87, 89–91.

Guilford, J. P. (Ed.). (1947). *Printed classification tests.* Washington, DC: U.S. Government Printing Office.

Guilford, J. P. (1967). *The nature of human intelligence.* New York: McGraw-Hill.

Gunnar, M. R., & Donahue, M. (1980). Sex differences in social responsiveness between six months and twelve months. *Child Development, 51,* 262–265.

Harris, L. J. (1978). Sex differences in spatial ability: Possible environmental, genetic, and neurological factors. In M. Kinsbourne (Ed.), *Asymmetrical functions of the brain.* Cambridge: Cambridge University Press.

Haugh, S. S., Hoffman, C. D., & Cowan, G. (1980). The eye of a very young beholder: Sex typing of infants by young children. *Child Development, 51,* 598–600.

Hedges, L. V. (1982, April). *Synthesis of independent research studies—a review.* In N. L. Gage (Chair), *Statistical aspects of meta-analysis.* Symposium conducted at the annual meeting of the American Educational Research Association, New York.

Henley, N. M. (1977). *Body politics: Power, sex, and nonverbal communication.* Englewood Cliffs, NJ: Prentice-Hall.

Hier, D. B. (1981). Sex differences in brain structure. In A. Ansara, N. Geschwind, A. Galaburda, M. Albert, & N. Gartrell (Eds.), *The significance of sex differences in dyslexia* (pp. 21–30). Towson, MD: Orton Dyslexia Society Press.

Hoffman, M. L. (1977). Sex differences in empathy and related behaviors. *Psychological Bulletin, 84,* 712–722.

Hult, C. (1978). Curiosity in young children. *Science Journal, 6,* 68–71.

Hyde, J. S. (1981). How large are cognitive gender differences? *American Psychologist, 36,* 892–901.

Jacklin, C. N. (1981). Methodological issues in the study of sex-related differences. *Developmental Review, 1,* 266–273.

Kaurell, S. M., & Petersen, A. C. (in press). Patterns of achievement in early adolescence. In M. L. Maehr & M. W. Stein Kamp (Eds.), *Women and science.* Greenwich, CT: JAI Press.

Klein, R. P., & Durfee, J. J. (1978). Effects of sex and birth order on infant social behavior. *Infant Behavior and Development, 1,* 106–117.

Kreinberg, N. (1981). 1000 teachers later: Women, mathematics, and the components of change. *Public Affairs Report, 22.*

Lenny, E. (1977). Women's self-confidence in achievement settings. *Psychological Bulletin, 84,* 1–13.

Lenny, E., & Gold, J. (1982). Sex differences in self-confidence: The effects of task completion and of comparison to competent others. *Personality and Social Psychology Bulletin, 8,* 74–80.

Levinson, P. J. (1978). *The seasons of a man's life.* New York: Knopf.

Linn, M. C. (1983). Evaluation in the museum setting: Focus on expectations. *Educational Evaluation & Policy Analysis, 5,* 119–127.

Linn, M. C., & Kyllonen, P. (1981). The field dependency construct: Some, one, or none. *Journal of Educational Psychology, 73,* 261–273.

Linn, M. C., & Petersen, A. C. (1983). *Emergence and characterization of gender differences in spatial ability: A meta-analysis.* Berkeley: University of California, Adolescent Reasoning Project.

Linn, M. C., & Pulos, S. (1983a). Aptitude and experience influences on proportional reasoning during adolescence: Focus on male-female differences. *Journal of Educational Psychology, 14,* 30–46.

Linn, M. C., & Pulos, S. (1983b). Male-female differences in predicting displaced volume: Strategy usage, aptitude relationships, and experience influences. *Journal of Educational Psychology, 75,* 86–96.

Lockheed, M. E. (1976). *The modification of female leadership behavior in the presence of males* (final report). Princeton, NJ: Educational Testing Service.

Lockheed, M. E., Chapter 11, this volume.

Loevinger, J. (1976). *Ego development: Conceptions and theories.* San Francisco: Jossey-Bass.

Lyon, N. (1972). A report on children's toys and socialization to sex roles. *Ms., 1*(6), 57.

Maccoby, E. E., & Jacklin, C. N. (1974). *The Psychology of Sex Differences.* Palo Alto, CA: Stanford University Press.

Maccoby, E. E., & Jacklin, C. N. (1980). Sex differences in aggression: A rejoinder and reprise. *Child Development, 1980, 51,* 964–980.

Manheimer, D. L., & Mellinger, G. D. (1967). Personality characteristics of the child accident reporter. *Child Development, 38,* 491–513.

McGee, M. G. (1979). Human spatial abilities: Psychometric studies and environmental, genetic, hormonal, and neurological influences. *Psychological Bulletin, 86,* 889–917.

McGlone, J. (1980). Sex differences in human brain asymmetry: A critical survey. *Behavioral and Brain Sciences, 3,* 215–227.

Moely, B. E., Skarin, K., & Weil, S. (1979). Sex differences in competition-cooperation behavior of children at two age levels. *Sex Roles, 5,* 329–342.

Morelock, J. C. (1980). Sex differences in susceptibility to social influence. *Sex Roles, 6,* 537–548.

Newcombe, N. (1982). Sex-related differences in spatial ability problems and gaps in current approaches. In M. Potegal (Ed.), *Spatial orientation: Developmental and physiological bases* (pp. 223–250). New York: Academic Press.

Newcombe, N., Bandura, M. M., & Taylor, D. G. (in press). Sex differences in spatial ability and spatial activities. *Sex Roles.*

Olkin, I. (1982, April). Synthesis of independent research studies—Statistical procedures. In N. L. Gage (Chair), *Statistical aspects of meta-analysis.* Symposium conducted at the annual meeting of the American Educational Research Association, New York.

O'Toole, P. (1982, April). Moving ahead by moving around. *Savvy,* pp. 37–41.

Parsons, J. E. (1982, March). *Sex differences in math achievement and course enrollment.* Paper presented at the annual meeting of the American Educational Research Association, New York.

Petersen, A. C. (1980). Biopsychosocial processes in the development of sex-related differences. In J. Parsons (Ed.), *The psychobiology of sex differences and sex roles* (pp. 31–55). New York: Hemisphere.

Petersen, A. C. (1982, January). *Biological correlates of spatial ability and mathematical performance.* Paper presented at the annual meeting of the American Association for the Advancement of Science, Washington, DC.

Petersen, A. C., & Gitelson, I. B. (in preparation). *Toward understanding sex-related differences in cognitive performance.* New York: Academic Press.

Petersen, A. C., Tobin-Richards, M. H., & Crockett, L. (1982). Sex differences. In H. E. Mitzel (Ed.), *Encyclopedia of educational research* (5th ed.) (pp. 1696–1712). New York: Free Press.

Plomin, R., & Foch, T. T. (1982). Sex differences and individual differences. *Child Development, 52,* 383–385.

Pulos, S., de Benedictis, T., Linn, M. C., Sullivan, P., & Clement, C. (1982). Modification of gender differences in the understanding of displaced volume. *Journal of Early Adolescence, 2,* 61–74.

Rheingold, H. C., & Cook, K. V. (1975). The content of boys' and girls' rooms as an index of parents' behavior. *Child Development, 46,* 459–463.

Rocha, R. E., & Rogers, S. W. (1976). Ares and Babbitt in the classroom: Effects of competition and reward on children's aggression. *Journal of Personality and Social Psychology, 33,* 588–593.

Sachs, J., Liebeman, P., & Erickson, D. (1973). Anatomical and cultural determinants of male and female speech. In R. W. Shay & R. W. Fasold (Eds.), *Language attitudes: Current trends and prospects.* Washington, DC: Georgetown University Press.

Savin-Williams, R. (1980). Dominance hierarchies in groups of middle to late adolescent males. *Journal of Youth and Adolescence, 9,* 75–85.

Shephard, R. N., & Metzler, J. (1971). Mental rotation of three-dimensional objects. *Science, 171,* 701–703.

Sherman, J. (1967). Problem of sex differences in space perception and aspects of intellectual functioning. *Psychological Review, 74,* 290–299.

Sherman, J. (1978). *Sex-related cognitive differences: An essay on theory and evidence.* Springfield, IL: Charles C. Thomas.

Smith, P. K., & Green, M. (1975). Aggressive behavior in English nurseries and play groups: Sex differences and response of adults. *Child Development, 46,* 211–214.

Snow, R. C., Federico, P. A., & Montague, W. (Eds.). (1980). *Aptitude, learning, and instruction: Cognitive process analysis* (Vol. 1). Hillsdale, NJ: Erlbaum.

Spence, J. T., & Helmreich, R. L. (1978). *Masculinity and femininity: Their psychological dimensions, correlates, and antecedents.* Austin, TX: University of Texas Press.

Stake, J. E., & Stake, M. N. (1979). Performance, self-esteem, and dominance behavior in mixed-sex dyads. *Journal of Personality, 47.*

Stallings, J., & Robertson, A. (1979). *Factors influencing women's decision to enroll in advanced mathematics courses* (final report, SRI International Project 7009). Washington, DC: National Institute of Education.

Sternglanz, S. H., & Serbin, L. A. (1974). Sex role stereotyping in children's television programs. *Developmental Psychology, 10,* 710–715.

Thomas, H., Jamison, W., & Hummel, D. D. (1973). Observation is sufficient for discovering that the surface of still water is invariantly horizontal. *Science, 181,* 173–174.

Thurstone, L. L., & Thurstone, T. G. (1941). Factorial studies of intelligence. *Psychometric Monographs,* No. 2.

Tieger, T. (1980). On the biological basis of sex differences in aggression. *Child Development, 51,* 943–963.

Vogel, S., Broverman, I., & Gardner, J. E. (1970). *Sesame Street and Sex-Role Stereotypes.* Pittsburgh: KNOW, Inc.

Waber, D. P. (1976). Sex differences in cognition: A function of maturation rate? *Science, 192,* 572–574.

Waber, D. P. (1977). Sex differences in mental abilities, hemispheric lateralization, and rate of physical growth at adolescence. *Developmental Psychology, 13,* 29–38.

Warren, M. (1983). Hormonal aspects of puberty. In J. Brooks-Gunn & A. C. Petersen (Eds.), *Puberty in girls: Biological and psychological perspectives* (pp. 3–28). New York: Plenum.

Willerman, L. (1979). *The psychology of individual and group differences.* San Francisco: Freeman.

Williams, D. A., & King, P. (1980, December 15). Do males have a math gene? *Newsweek,* p. 73.

Wilson, J. R., & Vandenberg, S. G. (1978). Sex differences in cognition: Evidence from the Hawaii family study. In T. E. McGill, D. A. Dewsbury, & B. D. Sachs (Eds.), *Sex and behavior* (pp. 317–335). New York: Plenum.

Witkin, H. A., & Goodenough, D. R. (1981). *Cognitive styles: Essence and origins.* New York: International Universities Press.

6

Educational Equity and Sex Role Development

Candace Garrett Schau,
with Carol Kehr Tittle

All educational materials and instructional settings in the United States are used with students who typically view at least some aspects of their own roles and adult roles in sex-stereotyped terms. Educational equity materials and settings must overcome these stereotypes and the strong emotional components associated with them in order to assist students in attaining their full individual potential regardless of sex. This chapter presents an introduction to those aspects of sex role development throughout the lifespan that must be understood if we are to achieve educational equity.

DEFINITION OF TERMS

Viewed from a psychological perspective, *sex roles* are constellations of characteristics that various cultures attribute to individuals according to sex. These attributes include those associated with behaviors such as cognitive skills and job choices, personality characteristics, feelings, and attitudes. Sex role beliefs or expectations about these attributes generally are shared by a significant number of people in the cultures; they take on the status of norms. *Sex role stereotypes* involve rigid beliefs in and applications of sex roles to almost all females and males in all cultures—that is, the belief that sex roles are universally true and biologically "natural." The process through which people accept and display the attributes contained in sex roles is called *sex role development*.

Sex role development encompasses several separate but related components: sex role knowledge, attitudes, behaviors, self-concept, and cognitions. Occasionally, some of these terms are used synonymously with the term sex role development, or the same term is used to label different concepts. The result is some confusion regarding these definitions.

Sex role knowledge refers to the content of people's knowledge about cultural sex role stereotypes. *Sex role attitudes* also are called norms, standards, prescriptions, or attributes. They include judgments about how and what sex roles "should" be, and how they may or may not be changed.

Individuals' feelings about their own functioning as measured against their sex role attitudes relate to *sex role self-concepts. Gender identity,* in regard to the self-concept, is the belief in one's biological maleness or femaleness (in one of the cognitive theories of sex role development, this same term means the correct labeling of the self and others for sex). It is the core of the sex role self-concept and is established by about 18 months of age, coinciding with initial language acquisition (Money & Ehrhardt, 1972). A strong and unambiguous gender identity often is assumed to be essential for healthy functioning throughout life. The goal is for children to know and to accept their own biological sex. Once this occurs, cultural influences in conjunction with cognitive skills, past experience, sex role knowledge, and sex role attitudes feed into the sex role self-concept across the life span. All of these aspects interact and affect each other and behavior.

Materials and settings that involve heavy use of sex role stereotypes are called *sex-role stereotyped, sex-stereotyped, sex-typed,* or *sex-biased.* Those that show males and females in both stereotyped and nonstereotyped roles are called *sex-fair.* The role portrayal of individuals who exhibit traits and behaviors that are culturally sex-stereotyped for the opposite sex is called *sex-role reversed,* or *role-reversed. Sex-affirmative* situations and materials emphasize role reversals but also explain the benefits and problems (such as discrimination) associated with role reversals. The term *sex-equitable* includes both sex-fair and sex-affirmative. *Same-sex* includes only members of the same sex as the users of the materials or participants in the settings.

SEX ROLE STEREOTYPES

Role attributes result from the cognitive tendency of individuals to categorize everything on the basis of outstanding characteristics. This categorization process assists people in imposing order on the tremendous amounts of information that they continually experience (Chafetz, 1978). Cultural beliefs about which attributes are most salient in conjunction with this categorizing process form the basis for the stereotypes we have. In addition to sex, many other categories are used to stereotype groups and their appropriate (and inappropriate) roles. Many cultures have role expectations and stereotypes about groups identified by ethnicity, race, age, occupation, and so on.

All known cultures have sex roles and sex role stereotypes that are used in assigning roles to adults and in socializing children for their eventual places in these roles. The sex role stereotypes of the more technically developed cultures, including most of those in the United States, show some similarities. According to the feminine stereotype, females are supposed to be expressive or communal. They should excel in language tasks and want to be wives and mothers. If they work outside the home, they usually are expected to work in traditional jobs for women, such as secretarial and teaching positions, and jobs that involve caring for other people and their possessions, such as nursing, flight attendant positions, and domestic work. They often are expected to be physically weak, helpless, dependent, emotional, and giving. According to the masculine stereotype, males are supposed to be instrumental or agentic. They should excel in mathematics, engineering, and the sciences, and expect to have careers as well as families. They are allowed a greater range of career options but are not supposed to be interested in occupations associated with the feminine sex role stereotype. They usually are expected to be aggressive, smart, strong, and active.

Cross-culturally, especially in cultures that are not technologically developed, the content and importance of sex roles and the stereotypes that accompany them vary greatly. For example, Mead (1935) researched the day-to-day lives of women and men in three tribal cultures in New Guinea. The sex roles and stereotypes she identified were not congruent with the masculine-instrumental and the feminine-expressive ones of technologically developed nations nor with each other. Since sex roles do differ depending upon the culture in which they are found, it is clear that many of the characteristics contained in them are transmitted primarily by the cultures involved, not by biology.

One cross-cultural commonality in sex role stereotypes, however, relates to the home and childrearing. Cross-culturally, males often are expected to be responsible for tasks like hunting and fighting that require them to leave home; females usually are responsible for tasks near home that allow them to take major childcare responsibility (Rosenblatt & Cunningham, 1976).

Although categorizing itself is a basic cognitive process, cultures prescribe the particular categories that will form the basis of group stereotypes. Sex is a poor category choice. In present-day cultures in the United States, sex role stereotypes frequently are not accurate. For example, current data indicate that less than one-fifth of the households in the United States fit sex-stereotyped expectations of the marriage and family roles emphasized for adult men and women: a household in which the husband works, the wife is at home, and there are one or more children at home. The two-wage-earner family has become the most common family form (Eisenstein, 1982).

Of the psychological characteristics contained in sex role stereotypes, the sex differences on the few characteristics that do show reliable (that is, statistically significant) differences are small in a numeric sense (see chapter 5). Training on tasks that do show sex differences may reduce or eliminate them. For example, training on some visual-spatial tasks improves females' scores until they match those of males; the small sex difference disappears (Vandenberg & Kuse, 1979).

Sex-stereotyped skills and school achievement have highly overlapping distributions for men and women; most females and males fall within the same score ranges on them. There is more score variability within each sex than there is between them. No judgment about an individual's skill in a sex-stereotyped area such as mathematics can be made just from knowing that person's sex.

Masculinity and femininity are not opposites along a single self-concept dimension, as the stereotypes suggest. Rather, they form at least two separate dimensions. A person can vary from highly feminine to not feminine, with a similar dimension for that person's masculinity. This bidimensionality forms the basis for two of the most popular sex role inventories, the *Bem Inventory* (Bem, 1978) and the *Personal Attributes Questionnaire* (Spence, Helmreich, & Stapp, 1974). Someone can be highly masculine and highly feminine in their self-concept (androgynous); highly feminine with low masculinity (feminine); highly masculine with low femininity (masculine); or have little femininity and little masculinity (undifferentiated). Various males and females fall into each of these four basic sex role types, although typically there are more females than males in the femininity classification and more males than females in the masculinity classification.

Items on the *Bem Inventory* (Bem, 1978) form clusters that can be identified as a caring-about-others factor, a dominant-assertiveness factor, and an independence factor (Richardson, Merrifield, and Jacobson, 1979). Such descriptions are more meaningful for use in educational settings than is the use of terms such as feminine and masculine. Educators who might find it difficult to encourage girls to be more "masculine" and boys to be more "feminine" would have less difficulty in helping girls to act on their own behalf and in helping boys to share a concern for others. These skills are useful to all students, female and male.

Some aspects of sex role stereotypes are changing, especially for females. For example, at least small numbers of women have been accepted as belonging in professions like law, medicine, and business administration. More and more girls and women are participating in athletics. They also are enrolling in more mathematics and science courses and participating in male-stereotyped vocational programs and college majors. However, sex role stereotypes for males are changing much more slowly. For example, few men have entered occupations such as nursing that are female-stereotyped.

To meet the changing conditions and expectations in the United States, adults need to possess a wide variety of skills and traits found in both the traditional masculine and feminine sex role stereotypes which they can use depending upon environmental demands. Flexibility is a necessity. Without it, problems occur. For example, beliefs in the traditional feminine stereotype about woman's place in relation to the adult roles of homemaker and parent, when combined with forced participation of many women in the labor market, have created tensions for both men and women between the roles of worker, spouse, homemaker, and parent. Dilemmas arise from sheer work overload and the discrepancy between personal needs and desires and cultural stereotypes.

SEX ROLE DEVELOPMENT THEORIES

Traditionally, three general classes of psychological theories have been applied to sex role development. These theories include psychoanalytic, social learning, and cognitive models and focus on how people acquire sex roles as well as on the content of sex roles.

Psychoanalytic theory is the oldest of the three classes. It emphasizes early childhood to age 5 or 6 as the most critical period in sex role development, and identification with the same-sex parent as an important concept. Limitations of the theory for educational equity are the stress on a biological basis of sex role development and lack of detailed mechanisms that could be used to develop or analyze sex-equitable educational materials and settings.

Social learning theory emphasizes three environmentally-based processes in the sex role development process: direct instruction, direct reinforcement, and modeling. Some aspects of sex roles are learned through direct instruction. Children, for example, are taught how to dress and behave in stereotypically sex-appropriate ways and how to avoid dress and behavior that are sex-inappropriate. Even during the preschool years, many boys will not play "dress-up" in women's clothes. In direct reinforcement, individuals often receive rewards for conforming to sex role prescriptions and punishments for violating them. For example, if a high school girl wants to date boys, but they will not associate with her because she wins a prize at her local science fair, she is being punished for violating the sex role stereotype that ascribes high interest and skill in science to males.

Most importantly, this theory posits that the greatest amount of sex role learning, as well as all other kinds of social learning, occurs from observing (modeling or imitating) other people (Mischel, 1970). Observational learning consists of three basic sequential processes: learning, abstraction, and performance. In the learning phase, children observe the behavior of many female and male models; they notice sex differences in the frequency of behaviors in various situations. Girls and boys learn the content of both the masculine and feminine sex roles in this manner. In the abstraction phase, children then abstract and generalize these observations to sex role rules. They use these rules to guide their own behavior. In the performance phase, children perform stereotypically sex-appropriate behaviors because they expect rewards for these behaviors and avoid sex-inappropriate ones because they expect punishment for them. They learn their expectations through vicarious reinforcement, by watching models receive positive consequences for sex-appropriate, and negative consequences for sex-inappropriate, behaviors (Perry & Bussey, 1979).

Cognitive theories stress the cognitive, rather than the environmental, processes involved in sex role development. One type of cognitive theory proposes a developmental progression in sex role development starting with gender identity (the correct labeling of self and others for sex), followed by gender stability (the understanding that sex doesn't change across time), and then gender constancy (the understanding that sex doesn't change with appearance changes) (Slaby & Frey, 1975). According to this theory, once gender constancy is attained, children find sex-appropriate behaviors self-reinforcing (Kohlberg, 1966).

A second type of cognitive theory stresses information-processing constructs as important in sex role development. These theories hypothesize that a cognitive structure called a gender schema guides sex role development. Bem

(1981), for example, proposes that the gender schema provides a cognitive readiness to perceive information in sex-role related ways. People differ in the degree to which they have assimilated their self-concepts into their own gender schemas. People with well-developed gender schemas should be more sex-typed than those with less well-developed schemas.

These sex role development theories, with the exception of gender schema theory, have concentrated primarily on children. However, starting during the 1970s, some developmental psychologists began arguing for a life span approach to development in most areas, including sex roles, that acknowledges change and continuity throughout life (for example, Emmerich, 1973). Although currently there is a great deal of discussion about adult sex role development, the application of sex role developmental theories to adults has been slow.

Rebecca, Hefner, and Oleshansky (1976) have proposed a life span model of sex role development. It is based partially on Kohlberg's theory of moral development and Piaget's theory of cognitive development in which postconventional stages are the highest developmental level. Their theory postulates three stages in the sex role development process: undifferentiated sex roles, polarized sex roles (which characterize the stereotypes of most people), and sex role transcendence (the highest level of sex role development). Individuals who have attained the sex role transcendence stage are flexible and do not stereotype themselves or others on the basis of gender.

Katz (1979) has proposed a descriptive life span model of sex role acquisition. Unlike the previously described theories, it is not based on a general developmental theory but on research findings. Her model postulates three developmental levels in sex role acquisition, each of which includes two or three stages containing different cognitive and social tasks to be mastered. They include learning of appropriate childhood sex roles (birth to 12), preparation for adult sex roles (12 to 19), and development of adult sex roles (20 to death).

Other theorists have started to take adult development models of specific areas such as vocational and career development that have been based on the lives of men and expand them to include women. They do so by adding roles, characteristics, tasks, behaviors, and feelings that are particularly salient to women (for example, Kaufman & Richardson, 1982). Unfortunately, most have not yet been explicitly applied to sex role development in ways that can directly assist educators interested in sex equity concerns. An integration of the adult development theories and the current sex role development theories is necessary.

AGE PATTERNS IN SEX ROLE DEVELOPMENT

A general understanding of the age trends from four areas of sex role development research is most important for attaining sex equity in education. One of these areas, cognitive sex role characteristics, is based on the cognitive theories of sex role development. The other three, including sex role knowledge, attitudes, and behaviors, are based primarily on social learning theory.

Cognitive Sex Role Characteristics

In order to learn sex roles initially, children must be able to sort other people accurately into female and male categories. In order fully to understand, abstract, and apply sex roles, children must realize that sex is a permanent attribute; that is, they must have attained gender constancy, which occurs at about 7 years of age.

Most children can accurately identify their own sex by about 2 years of age and the sexes of others by about 3 (Thompson, 1975). Prior to this, they can mimic information that they have been directly taught, but they cannot apply it or generalize from it. They still think, however, that people can change their sex if they want to or with the passage of time, in the same way that people grow taller over time. They then attain gender stability and drop these notions. Even with the understanding of gender stability, however, children think that people can change sex by changing their appearance, including dress, behavior, and/or name. This is very logical, since children use general appearance to identify people as female or male. They then realize, at about 7, that sex doesn't change with changes in appearance, and so attain gender consistency. The attainment of these three levels of understanding—identification by gender, gender stability, and gender consistency—is called gender constancy (Slaby & Frey, 1975). They finally understand that genital appearance is the major attribute that socially identifies a person's sex; this understanding usually occurs between about 7 and 9 years of age (McConaghy, 1979). Understanding in each of these areas occurs in the following sequence: self, same-sex people, and finally opposite-sex people (Eaton & Von Bargen, 1981).

Research based on the cognitive theory of gender schemas has shown that the degree of sex typing in people is related to the use of sex-related information in cognitive processing; that is, sex-typed people are more likely than androgynous or undifferentiated people to process information based on its sex-related aspects (Bem, 1981). Also, information consistent with gender schemas is more likely to be perceived and processed than is inconsistent information (for example, people may not perceive a male as a nurse, since nursing is sex-typed as a feminine occupation), and people will alter information to fit their gender schemas (for example, people may remember the male nurse as a male doctor). Gender schemas usually are quite powerful in children; they vary in power for adults (Martin & Halverson, 1981).

More cognitively advanced children are better able to perform all three aspects of the sex role learning chain suggested by social learning theory. The attention span of children increases with age, so older children can attend for greater amounts of time to sex role models. Their perceptions are more accurate and their memories are better, so they can remember longer what they have experienced. Their language skills are better, allowing them to understand the verbal parts of modeling more completely and giving them access to a larger variety of verbal symbols for use in coding.

Because older children's skills in inference and generalization are superior, they are better able to abstract sex role principles. Also, they can remember the resulting principles longer.

As children grow older, their advanced cognitive (and physical) skills make them increasingly able to perform accurately the behaviors derived from their cognitive principles. Also, they are able to anticipate consequences of their behaviors and to consider alternatives, which are important motivational aspects in the performance of sex role behaviors. In addition, they are better able to understand and remember sex role labels.

Sex Role Knowledge

In the social learning theory of sex role development, sex role knowledge refers to what is learned. With increased age, and so increased environmental exposure, children's sex role knowledge increases. By about 3 years of age, children have learned those simple aspects of sex roles, related to appearance and behavior, that are needed to identify the sexes. They complete their learning of most sex role knowledge by middle- to late-elementary school age (Emmerich & Shepard, 1982).

Sex Role Attitudes

Most of the research on sex role attitudes has studied roles, traits, activities, occupations, and people's own sex role self-concepts. Unfortunately, these areas have not been studied systematically across age or developmental levels, so that the age trends presented here are tentative. Also, most research has used white, middle-class subjects; generalization to other groups is risky. These age patterns may differ by socioeconomic status, cognitive maturity, and race (Emmerich & Shepard, 1982).

From about 2 years of age until early elementary school, sex role attitudes generally become increasingly sex-typed (Tremaine, Schau, & Busch, 1982). During elementary and early junior high school, sex role attitudes about most areas become increasingly *less* sex-typed (for example, see Garrett, Ein, & Tremaine, 1977; Shepard & Hess, 1975). Then, attitudes about at least some aspects of sex roles become increasingly sex-typed from junior high through high school (Urberg, 1979), although there is comparatively little research with this age group. In adulthood, the sex role attitudes of parents with children at home are most sex-typed, while parents without children at home and older childless people are most androgynous (Abrahams, Feldman, & Nash, 1978; Feldman, Biringen, & Nash, 1981).

Males tend to be more sex-typed than females at all ages, especially in regard to attributing home and childcare roles to women. Also, at least during elementary school, children may exhibit a same-sex preference in addition to, or sometimes rather than, their sex-typed attitudes (Emmerich & Shepard, 1982).

That is, they may attribute positive characteristics to people of their own sex regardless of whether those characteristics are stereotypically associated with that sex.

In young children, knowledge and attitudes usually are closely aligned. Older children and adults know the stereotypes, but their sex role attitudes vary greatly. Also, sex role attitudes may differ when applied to the self and to others.

Sex Role Behaviors

There are many more similarities than differences in sex role behaviors (see chapter 5). Unfortunately, sex role stereotypes lead people to expect more and larger sex differences than actually exist.

SEX DIFFERENCES IN LIFE EXPERIENCES

A very few sex role components, such as pregnancy and some aspects of physical strength, are based on biological sex differences. However, the environment also has an effect: there is an element of choice for most women and men regarding the timing and number of pregnancies and the extent to which they exercise to maximize their physical strength.

Biological differences among people, especially genetic differences, set broad limits on the development of individual females and males, but the environment is the real key in these areas. From birth, females and males have different experiences in many aspects of life.

Most boys are socialized primarily for their future occupational roles, while most girls are socialized primarily for family roles (Hoffman, 1977). Within the United States and across a variety of other societies ranging from mostly nonliterate through highly literate, adults socialize girls for greater nurturance and responsibility and boys for greater self-reliance and achievement (Barry, Bacon, & Child, 1957). For example, boys and girls often are given different names, clothes, and sex-typed toys; these toy differences encourage them to practice different skills and behaviors (for example, girls "mothering" baby dolls, boys behaving aggressively with toy guns). Adults play more roughly with boys and pressure boys to be independent, achieving, and emotionally controlled (Hoffman, 1977). The media continually present a very sex-typed view of reality to children and adults.

Education is sex-typed. Women and men hold different jobs within schools. When students start making course choices, girls and boys are encouraged to enroll in different subject areas (Stockard, 1980).

Job training and jobs differ by sex. Women are clustered in lower-paying occupations such as office staff, teaching, health, and domestic jobs. More women than men work part-time. But even when women perform the same jobs at the same competence levels, they are paid significantly less (Tittle, 1981).

There are sex differences in other life areas also, but the areas discussed here are most important for educational equity concerns.

IMPLICATIONS FOR SEX EQUITY IN EDUCATION

This chapter has presented theories and findings that are important in analyzing the educational settings and materials designed to help achieve educational equity. For example, if children read books in which boys are continually reinforced for active behaviors while girls are continually reinforced for passive behaviors, they learn that girls are expected to be passive and boys active as part of their sex roles. They also gain the expectations that they themselves will be rewarded for active behaviors if they are boys and for passive behaviors if they are girls. These expectations help to motivate some girls to be passive and some boys to be active.

But not all models are equally potent. The most effective models for children are those that are attractive, that have power, and that are examples of the children's own sex role stereotypes. In other words, children tend to ignore people who are performing behaviors that do not match the children's abstracted sex role principles (Perry & Bussey, 1979). This implies that instructional materials presenting a few token males and females engaged in role-reversed and sex-affirmative activities and behaviors will not change children's sex role attitudes, knowledge, behaviors, and schemas. Similarly, single brief intervention attempts will not work. Children must be exposed to a sufficient quantity of sex-equitable materials to allow them to incorporate nontraditional role behaviors and characteristics into their schemas and abstracted principles about sex roles.

Somewhat different strategies are needed for students in different developmental stages. Since children below about mid-elementary school cognitively are quite rigid, are developing potent gender schemas, and are learning about sex role stereotypes, they need to be exposed to as many sex-equitable materials and situations as possible. This is especially important for preschool-aged children, since the content of their stereotypes and their accompanying gender schemas will be based on this environmental information.

Generally, however, most children's experiences will match cultural sex role stereotypes. Because of this, it is important for educators to explicitly point out and discuss the nonstereotyped aspects of materials and situations. This should assist students in accurately perceiving and remembering these aspects. However, educators should not be concerned if young children's attitudes still become sex-stereotyped. Their thinking often is perception-bound, and the overwhelming amount of sex-stereotyped information they experience may result in sex-typed attitudes. This is especially true for areas not included in the sex-equitable settings and materials. Young children usually cannot generalize to new situations.

Although elementary school children's sex role attitudes become increasingly less sex-typed with age, they also need exposure to sex-equitable materials and settings. But they especially need guidance in understanding the sex-affirmative aspects of these settings and materials. They are very interested in fairness. This interest can be useful in discussing the effects of sex role stereotypes.

Students in junior high, high school, and college, as well as adults, need to be exposed to situations and materials that portray sex-fair reality. Boys and girls should not be raised to expect that most women will be homemakers and mothers but will not work outside of the home; this is not reality. Similarly, the lack of attention paid to the male role in parenting and homemaking is misleading and unrealistic. Educational materials are needed that portray men and women realistically in all adult roles and portray options and flexibility in role patterns. Materials need to incorporate consideration of all the major adult roles simultaneously, so that students recognize that changes in values about, or salience of, one or more roles have implications for other roles. The ideas of choice, patterns, and responsibilities in adult roles are not explicit parts of the learning of sex roles. Yet these concepts are critical for sex equity.

CONCLUSIONS

Most educators and psychologists believe that environmental and developmental cognitive effects in conjunction with very small biological potentials contribute to the development of sex differences in roles. The development of sex roles and the tendency to sex-stereotype the behaviors, attitudes, and personality characteristics expected of females and males in our culture have a strong and pervasive influence throughout all of our lives. The positive features of these concepts are in the stability they can lend to individual lives. Their negative features are in a rigidity and unthinking acceptance of the definitions, so that they constitute barriers to the development of individuals to their full potential in all areas of adult life.

We have every expectation that future theories of, and research in, sex role development will further our understanding and our effectiveness in developing sex-equitable strategies in education. We look forward to the time when sex role development truly becomes human development and gender is not related to the types of activities, occupations, and personal attributes that individuals choose.

REFERENCES

Abrahams, B., Feldman, S. S., & Nash, S. C. (1978). Sex-role self-concept and sex-role attitudes: Enduring personality characteristics or adaptations to changing life situations? *Developmental Psychology, 14,* 393–400.
Barry, H., Bacon, M. K., & Child, I. L. (1957). A cross-cultural survey of some sex differences in socialization. *Journal of Abnormal and Social Psychology, 55,* 327–332.
Bem, S. L. (1978). *Bem inventory.* Palo Alto, CA: Consulting Psychologists Press.
Bem, S. L. (1981). Gender schema theory: A cognitive account of sex typing. *Psychological Review, 88,* 354–364.
Chafetz, J. S. (1978). *Masculine, feminine or human?* Itasca, IL: F. E. Peacock.
Eaton, W. O., & Von Bargen, D. (1981). Asynchronous development of gender understanding in preschool children. *Child Development, 52,* 1020–1027.

Eisenstein, Z. R. (1982). The sexual politics of the New Right: Understanding the "Crisis of Liberalism" for the 1980s. *Signs, 7,* 567–588.

Emmerich, W. (1973). Socialization and sex-role development. In P. B. Baltes & K. W. Schaie (Eds.), *Life-span developmental psychology: Personality and socialization* (pp. 123–144). New York: Academic Press.

Emmerich, W., & Shepard, K. (1982). Development of sex-differentiated preferences during late childhood and adolescence. *Developmental Psychology, 18,* 406–417.

Feldman, S. S., Biringen, Z. C., & Nash, S. C. (1981). Fluctuations of sex-related self-attributions as a function of stage of family life cycle. *Developmental Psychology, 17,* 24–35.

Garrett, C. S., Ein, P. L., & Tremaine, L. S. (1977). The development of gender stereotyping of adult occupations in elementary school children. *Child Development, 48,* 507–512.

Hoffman, L. W. (1977). Changes in family roles, socialization, and sex differences *American Psychologist, 32,* 644–657.

Katz, P. A. (1979). The development of female identity. *Sex Roles, 5,* 155–178.

Kaufman, D. R., & Richardson, B. (1982). *Achievement and women: Challenging the assumptions.* New York: Free Press.

Kohlberg, L. (1966). A cognitive-developmental analysis of children's sex-role concepts and attitudes. In E. E. Maccoby (Ed.), *The development of sex differences* (pp. 82–173). Stanford, CA: Stanford University Press.

Martin, C. L., & Halverson, C. F. (1981). A schematic processing model of sex typing and stereotyping in children. *Child Development, 52,* 1119–1134.

McConaghy, M. J. (1979). Gender permanence and the genital basis of gender: Stages in the development of constancy of gender identity. *Child Development, 50,* 1223–1226.

Mead, M. (1935/1963). *Sex and temperament in three primitive societies.* New York: William Morrow.

Mischel, W. (1970). Sex-typing and socialization. In P. H. Mussen (Ed.), *Carmichael's manual of child psychology* (3rd ed.) (Pp. 3–72). New York: Wiley.

Money, J., & Ehrhardt, A. A. (1972). *Man & woman, boy & girl.* Baltimore: Johns Hopkins University Press.

Perry, D. G., & Bussey, K. (1979). The social learning theory of sex differences: Imitation is alive and well. *Journal of Personality and Social Psychology, 37,* 1699–1712.

Rebecca, M., Hefner, R., & Oleshansky, B. (1976). A model of sex-role transcendence. *Journal of Social Issues, 32,* 197–206.

Richardson, M. S., Merrifield, P., & Jacobson, S. (1979, September). *A factor analytic study of the Bem sex-role inventory.* Paper presented at the annual meeting of the American Psychological Association, New York.

Rosenblatt, P. C., & Cunningham, M. R. (1976). Sex differences in cross-cultural perspective. In B. Lloyd & J. Archer (Eds.), *Exploring sex differences* (pp. 71–94). New York: Academic Press.

Shepard, W. O., & Hess, D. T. (1975). Attitudes in four age groups toward sex-role division in adult occupation and activities. *Journal of Vocational Behavior, 6,* 27–39.

Slaby, R. G., & Frey, K. S. (1975). Development of gender constancy and selective attention to same-sex models. *Child Development, 46,* 849–856.

Spence, J. T., Helmreich, R., & Stapp, J. (1974). The personal attributes questionnaire: A measure of sex-role stereotypes and masculinity-femininity. *Journal Supplement Abstract Service Catalog of Selected Documents in Psychology, 4,* 43. (MS. No. 617)

Stockard, J. (1980). Sex inequities in the experiences of students. In J. Stockard, P. A. Schmuck, K. Kempner, P. Williams, S. K. Edson, & M. A. Smith (Eds.), *Sex equity in education* (pp. 11–48). New York: Academic Press.

Thompson, S. K. (1975). Gender labels and early sex-role development. *Child Development, 46,* 339–347.

Tittle, C. K. (1981). *Careers and family: Sex role and adolescent life plans.* Beverly Hills, CA: Sage.

Tremaine, L. S., Schau, C. G., & Busch, J. W. (1982). Children's occupational sex-typing. *Sex Roles, 8,* 691–710.

Urberg, K. A. (1979). Sex-role conceptualizations in adolescents and adults. *Developmental Psychology, 15,* 90–92.

Vandenberg, S. G., & Kuse, A. R. (1979). Spatial ability: A critical review of the sex-linked major gene hypothesis. In M. A. Wittig & A. C. Petersen (Eds.), *Sex-related differences in cognitive functioning: Developmental issues* (pp. 67–95). New York: Academic Press.

PART II
Administrative Strategies for Implementing Sex Equity

Patricia A. Schmuck

This section is about the ways in which mandates regarding sex equity are administratively implemented in educational agencies. All three chapters describe at least one aspect of the process of implementing the federal mandates. Certainly, civil rights advocates have learned that legislative mandates by themselves are no guarantee of changing school practice; the intent of Congress and the subsequent regulations may be ignored, thwarted, or successfully implemented. The strength of a mandate rests in the power of its implementation, and each of these chapters attempts to ferret out those administrative procedures which are likely to result in successful school practices regarding sex equity.

There is a wealth of literature documenting successful and unsuccessful efforts to bring about changes in schools. Studies of curriculum innovations (such as new programs in math or social studies), teacher classroom behaviors (such as the introduction of team teaching or new models of teacher-student interaction), new organizational patterns (such as nongraded schools or schools without walls), and other changes have provided guideposts concerning the most effective strategies for bringing about new school practices.

Strategies for achieving sex equity involve many different approaches to change: they range from formulating new educational policy to the formation of active community pressure groups, from training teachers in methods of changing sex-stereotyped attitudes and behaviors to rewriting curriculum materials, from providing technical assistance to providing information on how to sue. Even though students and employees are guaranteed by law that sex cannot be used as a discriminatory attribute, the literature on school change makes it very clear that individuals or institutions do not change behavior or practice by administrative fiat alone. Even though the regulations specifically prescribe what may and may not be done, the intent of the law will be realized only under certain conditions. The chapters in this section suggest those administrative conditions under which we may presume sex equity is being achieved. Thus, it is from the literature on school change that we can formulate the guidelines for effective or ineffective strategies of implementing sex equity. In the following section I have laid out three such guidelines for assessing the strategies discussed.

1. Does the strategy for equity lead to changes in the social system which alter organizational practice?
2. Does the strategy for equity lead to changes in individual participants?
3. Does the strategy for equity lead to continued and long-lasting changes in institutions and individuals?

CHANGES IN THE SOCIAL SYSTEM

Chapter 7, by Schmuck et al., describes and discusses the formal linkages between federal policy and classroom practice. The evidence about effectiveness cited in this chapter includes three different research efforts: (1) a comparison of Title IX coordinators at the local educational agency level (prescribed by Title IX) and state sex equity coordinators (prescribed by the Vocational Education Amendments); (2) the impact of a coalition of agency partners working with several California school districts; and (3) the evidence gathered by federally funded demonstration centers in five local school districts. The description of internal and external intervention strategies shows that each has certain advantages and disadvantages (Kempner, 1980). The evidence comparing two roles of equity coordinators shows that the internal change agent can create a powerful role that reaches many different levels of a school system under certain conditions. If those conditions are not met, however, the equity coordinator will probably be ineffective. The evidence in the California study shows a major barrier facing intermediary agencies—the necessity of selling the importance of providing sex-fair educational practice. External agencies must be invited into the system and given the power to institute change. In contrast to the internal approach to change, there is no legitimate power invested in the role. Once there is a good match between the goals of the external agency and a school system, however, the process of implementation may be highly successful as shown in the California case.

Chapter 8, by Shakeshaft, states the need for changing social system variables rather than explicating the conditions under which we might expect changes to be implemented. Her chapter details the barriers facing the employment of women as administrators and describes some projects directed at eliminating some of these barriers. Unfortunately, however, the long-range outcomes of these projects are not well documented. One may presume the barriers still exist, since the most current data regarding women's employment as administrators do not yet reflect positive changes. Shakeshaft's extensive reference list and overview of strategies used to achieve greater equity in administration provide a wealth of material for scholars and practitioners. An important unanswered question remains, however. Will a better sex balance in school management have a positive impact on creating sex-fair educational environments?

We don't know. There is some research indicating a strong positive relationship between employment and women's attitudes toward equality (Klein, 1976). There is also some evidence that the greater the proportion of women on a management team, the higher the awareness of sex discriminatory issues (Finigan, 1982). In contrast, there is some evidence that sex alone is not a distinguishing characteristic in a manager's school performance (Charters & Jovick, 1981). While the achievement of sex equity in school administration is a worthy goal per se, it remains unclear whether the increased employment of women administrators will alter the educational system enough to be an effective tool to implement and diffuse other sex equity practices in schools.

In Chapter 9, Sadker and Sadker describe curricular innovations in equity materials for teachers, which have been initiated primarily by individuals in intermediary agencies. They also discuss the changes needed in materials and policies of existing organizations such as professional associations and the National Council for the Accreditation of Teacher Education. While their recommendations clearly outline the administrative strategy needed for integrating sex equity issues into teacher education programs, they do not provide substantive information concerning actual changes made. Their chapter, like Shakeshaft's, is a description of training needs rather than a description of educators' sex equity practices. There is no doubt that the written materials that have been developed as instructional units for college teachers and teacher guides for sex fair classroom practices are a necessary first step in integrating equity concerns into the professional development of teachers. But they are only a first step. Certainly in years to come we need more information on the social system process of making future teachers knowledgeable and skilled in providing equal educational opportunity at the classroom level.

CHANGES IN INDIVIDUAL BEHAVIOR

All the authors present evidence that interventions caused some individuals to change their attitudes and practices regarding sex equity; effective Title IX and vocational education sex equity coordinators did influence individual behaviors and practice. The California Coalition and the Equity Demonstration Projects offer concrete evidence that technical assistance led to some changes in school district personnel, but also suggest that more follow-up work must be done. Sadker and Sadker present percentages and anecdotal evidence indicating that teacher trainees using the equity materials increased their awareness of equity issues, although not all changes were in the desired direction. Shakeshaft discusses changes among women aspirants for administration; clearly the projects she describes have inspired individual women to "pursue and persist," but there is no information about increases in equity among existing administrators or from those having the power to hire and promote. The weakness of evaluation is evident in all the chapters and suggests a future research need. In all fairness, however, it must be pointed out that the magnitude of the projects reported leads to difficulty in precise evaluation. While the outcome data are perhaps the weakest in showing how individuals were affected by the equity interventions, all chapters provide fairly objective and sometimes quantifiable data about successes and failures.

EQUITY INTERVENTIONS AND LONG-TERM CHANGE

We have just celebrated the 12th anniversary of the passage of Title IX. This is a very short time. While all the chapters suggest some of the conditions which may be promising for continued equity activities, none of the authors can yet present data indicating the longevity of such changes. Certainly, this is a crucial area for continued research. But as all the authors indicate, we have barely begun to scratch the surface of understanding what administrative strategies are effective in bringing about equal educational opportunity on the basis of sex. For example, we do not know to what extent the February 1984 Supreme Court decision in *Grove City College v. Bell* limiting the coverage of Title IX to programs and activities (rather than institutions) receiving federal financial assistance will curtail commitments to achieving sex equity.

Recently I had an experience that provided a unique perspective on school change. I had the good fortune to live and work in Belgium for a year, and I interviewed a school principal. She was a nun, the head of a very old and prestigious girls' secondary school, which was an all-boys' school until 1940. She excitedly described a major curriculum innovation in her school; they were adding four hours of physical science to the Latin-Greek program. She exclaimed, "You know, except for the change to an all girls' school, such an innovation has not taken place in this school since the Renaissance!" I hope we do not have to wait several centuries before we can provide data indicating effective administrative strategies for implementing sex equity in our nation's schools. All of these chapters are useful, helpful, and informative about a decade of work. But we have only just begun.

REFERENCES

Charters, W. W., Jr., & Jovick, T. (1981). The gender of principals and principal / teacher relations in elementary schools. In P. A. Schmuck, W. W. Charters, Jr., & R. O. Carlson (Eds.), *Educational policy and management: Sex differentials* (pp. 307–330). New York: Academic Press.

Finigan, M. W. (1982). The effects of token representation on participation in small decision-making groups. *Economic and Industrial Democracy: An International Journal, 3*(4), 531–550.

Kempner, K. (1980). A social psychological analysis of the context for change. In J. Stockard, P. Schmuck, K. Kempner, P. Williams, S. Edson, & M. Smith, *Sex equity in education* (pp. 119–140). New York: Academic Press.

Klein, E. (1976). The rise of the women's movement: A case study in political development. In D. McGuigan (Ed.), *New research on women and sex roles* (pp. 209–220). Ann Arbor: University of Michigan Press.

7

Administrative Strategies for Institutionalizing Sex Equity in Education and the Role of Government

Patricia A. Schmuck, Judith A. Adkison,
Barbara Peterson, Susan Bailey,
Georgia S. Glick, Susan S. Klein,
Scott McDonald, Jane Schubert,
and Stephen L. Tarason

We view the institutionalization of sex equity as both a process and an outcome goal. In this chapter we shall treat the institutionalization of sex equity as a special case of the more general process of adopting educational innovations. We shall discuss evidence that policies, procedures, and strategies designed to eliminate unequal treatment between girls and boys and women and men have become accepted regular features in the operation of some state education agencies and school districts and thus have become institutionalized. That is, changes that were initiated by specially funded projects at the state or district level have now become part of standard educational programs and practices.

Although there are many similarities in implementing sex equity and other educational innovations, there are also differences. Unlike the "Right-to-Read" program, which did not have to garner understanding and support for the notion that every student can and should be able to read, or the rapid adoption of an appealing tangible innovation such as microcomputers, sex equity projects often had to begin by convincing individuals and agencies of the need to provide a sex-fair educational environment for students and staffs. Another difference is that we have had relatively few years to benefit from Title IX, the major federal policy prohibiting sex discrimination in education. Although Title IX was passed in 1972, it did not have implementing regulations until 1975, and it was never accompanied by substantial federal or state financial assistance. Certainly, 12 years is not an adequate period of time in which to institutionalize change; one estimate suggests that at least 50 years is required for adoption of an educational innovation (Mort & Campbell, 1941, cited in Miles, 1964). Similarly, federal financial support and incentives to help educators implement sex equity practices have been almost infinitesimal compared to other Department of Education pro-

The authors would like to thank Dolores Grayson, Robert Lyke, and David Sadker for comments.

grams, and thus cannot be expected to be a tremendous incentive for changing state and local education agency operations.

To investigate the progress made toward the institutionalization of sex equity in education despite these obstacles, we will

1. describe the major federal policies and activities that promote sex equity in education;
2. describe the roles and interrelationships among federal, regional, state, and local efforts toward sex equity;
3. review three studies of effective ways to institutionalize sex equity at the local school district level; and
4. review strategies that have been employed to institutionalize sex equity at all governmental levels.

The chapter will conclude with recommendations for future research and action to quicken the pace of the overall institutionalization of sex equity in all content areas and at all levels of education. Subsequent chapters will address ways of institutionalizing sex equity in more specialized contexts.

Federal Policies and Activities for Institutionalizing Sex Equity in Education

There are federal laws prohibiting sex discrimination in areas ranging from employment to housing. There are also many states with laws and statutes such as broad state equal rights amendments or specific laws prohibiting sex discrimination in education. Title IX, the major federal law that prohibits sex discrimination in education, states: "No person in the United States shall, on the basis of sex, be excluded from participation in, be denied the benefits of, or be subjected to discrimination under any education program or activity receiving Federal financial assistance." Additional key federal laws are designed to provide incentives and assistance to other levels of government, other organizations, and individuals in implementing the letter and spirit of Title IX. The agency with primary enforcement responsibility for civil rights in federally assisted education activities is the Office for Civil Rights, in the U.S. Department of Education. The key federal laws designed to promote sex equity in education are listed in tier A, table 2. The laws that provide positive incentives and assistance for achieving sex equity include Title IV of the Civil Rights Act of 1964 (CRA IV), the Women's Educational Equity Act of 1974 and 1978 (WEEA), the 1976 amendments to the Vocational Education Act of 1963 (VEA), the 1972 law authorizing the National Institute of Education (NIE), the 1957 law creating the U.S. Commission on Civil Rights, the National Science Foundation (NSF) Science and Technology Equal Opportunities Act of Fiscal Year 1981, and the annual congressional and presidential Women's History Week resolutions. Activities at other levels of government for implementing these and other sex equity policies are listed in tiers B, C, and D of table 2.

Title IX.   The 1975 regulations that interpret Title IX specifically prohibit discrimination or the denial of benefits on the basis of sex in admissions, recruitment, educational programs or activities, facilities, course offerings, counseling or appraisal, financial assistance, marital or parental status, athletics, and employment. They also state that recipients of federal financial assistance must designate at least one employee to coordinate Title IX efforts and activities. In 1982, the U.S. Supreme Court ruled that the department had authority to write regulations covering employees as well as students. In 1984, the Supreme Court ruled in *Grove City College v. Bell* that Title IX coverage extended only to programs and activities that received federal financial assistance and not to the entire institution, as many had previously interpreted. In light of this ruling, bills were introduced in Congress to protect the broad coverage under Title IX.

CRA IV.   This law prohibits discrimination on the basis of race, national origin, and sex. Its regulations authorize federal funding for regional assistance centers and state education agencies in order that those agencies may provide free assistance to elementary and secondary schools to ensure students equal educational opportunities. Initially, local school boards and training institutes were included, but these categories were deleted in 1982.

WEEA.   This act authorizes funding at all levels of education for model educational programs of national, statewide, or general significance to overcome sex stereotyping and achieve educational equity for girls and women. It also established the National Advisory Council on Women's Educational Programs to advise the Secretary of Education regarding this program and to make recommendations to federal officials on the improvement of educational equity for women in all federal policies and programs. As a result of the 1978 reauthorization of the act, programs to provide financial assistance to individual educational agencies and institutions for programs of local significance to meet the requirement of Title IX are allowed when funding of the act reaches a specific level.

VEA.   This major funding law requires that states receiving federal vocational education funds develop and carry out activities and programs to eliminate sex bias, stereotyping, and discrimination in vocational education, including homemaking programs, and that states assure equal access to such programs for both women and men. It also permits allocating federal funds to programs for displaced homemakers, single heads of households, homemakers, part-time workers seeking full-time jobs, and persons seeking jobs in areas nontraditional for their sex.

NIE.   The legislation authorizing NIE states that learning how to advance equal educational opportunities is one of the agency's basic principles. This was reemphasized and made one of the institute's mandated funding priorities when the agency was reauthorized in 1976 and 1980.

U.S. Commission on Civil Rights.   The commission has supported studies

Table 2. The Role of Government in Mandating and Implementing Sex Equity in Education

Tier A Major Federal Sex Equity Policies	Tier B Regional or Multistate Activities	Tier C State Government (SEA) Activities and Policies	Tier D Local Government (LEA) Activities and Policies
1. Title IX of the 1972 Education Amendments	1. 10 Office for Civil Rights regional offices to facilitate Title IX compliance	1. Title IX coordinators in SEAs	1. Title IX coordinators in LEAs (and other education institutions receiving federal funds)
2. Title IV of the 1964 Civil Rights Act (CRA IV)	2. CRA IV-funded Sex Desegregation Assistance Centers (SDACs)	2. CRA IV state sex equity grants to SEAs (receive SDAC services)	2. Previous CRA IV awards to LEAs (receive SDAC services)
3. The Women's Educational Equity Act (WEEA) 1974—Created WEEA Program and National Advisory Council on Women's Educational Programs	3. 5 demonstration site contractors funded by WEEA	3. WEEA grants to a few SEAs and sometimes to CCSSO	3. Grants to some LEAs, including demonstration site contractors—many users of WEEA products
4. The 1976 amendments to the Vocational Education Act of 1963 (VEA)		4. State vocational education sex equity coordinators	4. Some SEA and VEA grants and technical assistance to LEAs
5. Annual Women's History Week resolutions by Congress and the President 1982–84		5. Some SEAs prepare curricular materials for Women's History Week	5. Some LEA or school celebrations of Women's History Week
6. The 1957 act creating the U.S. Commission on Civil Rights			

7. The 1972 act creating the National Institute of Education with a charge to conduct research on equal educational opportunity

8. Compliance with state policies and use of state services

9. Local district initiated policies and activities (Shouldn't contradict 1 or 8)

10. Local school initiated policies and activities (Shouldn't contradict 1, 8, or 9)

11. Individual classroom initiated policies and activities (Shouldn't contradict 1, 8, 9, or 10)

8. State Equity Laws and Activities—wide variety of strategies (Shouldn't contradict 1)

7. The 1972 act creating the National Institute of Education with a charge to conduct research on equal educational opportunity

8. The Equal Employment Act of 1972, which broadened the nondiscrimination coverage of Title VII of the 1964 Civil Rights Act to employees of state and local governments and of nonreligious private schools

9. Part B of the National Science Foundation Authorization Act for FY 1981, The Science and Technology Equal Opportunities Act, created the Committee on Equal Opportunities in Science and Technology and authorized several activities for women and minorities such as the Visiting Professorships for Women

Note. The general progression is from Tier A to Tier B, then C, then D; however, there may be a direct connection among activities in any tier or within tiers. Although users in Tiers C and D who receive federal financial assistance are supposed to comply with Title IX, they have a great deal of autonomy in deciding on the extent of use of other sex equity activities and may of course initiate their own policies and activities as long as they don't contradict higher-level policies.

of sex equity in education ranging from bias and fairness in textbooks to analyses of Title IX enforcement.

Women's History Week Congressional Resolutions and Activities. These are an excellent way to remind the nation of women's contributions to society and of sex equity issues as well.

Funding and Executive Department support for CRA IV, WEEA, NIE, and the sex equity aspects of VEA has decreased by about $13 million during the Reagan administration. At its height in 1980, federal funding for sex equity was minuscule, about 0.2% of the Education Department budget (Klein & Dauito, 1982). The Reagan administration has recommended no funding for WEEA or CRA IV programs for Fiscal Years 1982–1985 and has eliminated the Women's Research Team and the Minority and Women's Program in NIE. As a result of grassroots support, Congress has not agreed with the Executive Department's requests to eliminate WEEA and CRA IV legislation. Thus, these and a few other incentive programs such as the Fund for the Improvement of Postsecondary Education, which has traditionally supported some sex equity work, have continued operating. Since 1981 they have provided about $18 million annually for badly needed R&D and for technical assistance to educators and the general public in implementing Title IX and institutionalizing sex equity in education.

Many national organizations, including coalitions of women's groups, individual women's membership organizations, professional education and behavioral science organizations, and foundations have provided a wide array of support activities to help maintain the crucial federal role in promoting sex equity and to supplement these federal efforts.

The Relationship among Federal, Regional, State, and Local Levels of Governance

Federal policy and the subsequent federal programs are designed to bring about change at the local school level and ultimately to improve boys' and girls' educational opportunities at the classroom level. But how can mandates issued by Congress influence the variety of classrooms in our country? How can we presume that federal policies can affect the diversity of educational values, teaching methods, and school organizations in our country? The linkage of policy to practice is a loosely organized system of relationships. Karl Weick (1976) graphically portrays this reality by analogy.

> Imagine that you're either the referee, coach, player, or spectator at an unconventional soccer match: the field for the game is round; there are several goals scattered haphazardly around the circular field; people can enter and leave the game whenever they want to; they can throw balls in whenever they want; they can say "that's my goal" whenever they want to, as many times as they want to, and for as many goals as they want to; the entire game takes place on a sloped field; and the game is played as if it makes sense. . . .
> If you now substitute in that example principals for referees, teachers for

> coaches, students for players, parents for spectators, and schooling for soccer, you have an equally unconventional depiction of school organizations. The beauty of this depiction is that it captures a different set of realities within educational organizations than are caught when these same organizations are viewed through the tenets of bureaucratic theory. (p. 1)

Weick goes on to say:

> An organization does what it does because of plans, intentional selection of means . . . and some of this is accomplished by such rationalized procedures as cost-benefit analysis, division of labor, specified areas of discretion, authority invested in office, job descriptions and a consistent evaluation and reward system. The only problem with this portrait is that it is rare in nature. . . . Parts of some organizations are heavily rationalized, but many parts also prove intractable to analysis. (p. 1)

In other words, some parts of the links between federal policy regarding sex equity and classroom practice are sequential, deliberate, orderly, rational processes carried out by some people. Others are more random. We shall describe some of the rational processes at the regional, state, and local level that are designed to implement sex equity as depicted in table 2's tiers.

The Federal-Regional Relationship in Implementing
Sex Equity in Education (Table 2, Tier B)

In the United States, regional or multistate governance is primarily used by the federal government as a way to provide services and technical assistance to geographical sections of the country. The U.S. Department of Education has used this to help enforce Title IX by working with the 10 regional offices of the Office for Civil Rights, by supporting 12 Sex Desegregation Assistance Centers (SDACs) under CRA IV, and by funding 5 Equity Demonstration Projects under WEEA in diverse regions of the country.

The SDACs assist school districts with consulting services and training to ensure students' equal educational opportunities. Examples include helping elementary and secondary school educators identify and eliminate sex bias in curricular materials, identifying resource materials that describe ways to increase the enrollment of girls in mathematics and science, and establishing non-discriminatory employment practices. In 1982 the centers provided service to 5,104, or less than one-third, of the school districts in the United States. While each SDAC has a similar charge, there are differences among them as to the kinds of assistance and training offered. Some SDACs work closely with state departments of education and cosponsor and share the cost of activities. In other states with no state program or personnel assigned to sex equity activities, the SDACs assume all the burden of providing resources and personnel (Kaser, Sadker, & Sadker, 1983).

The WEEAP national demonstration projects were located in Massachusetts, Arizona, North Carolina, Oregon, and Florida. They were designed to show how school districts can implement sex equity at all grade levels, in all subjects, and by working with educational personnel ranging from custodial staff and bus drivers to district superintendents. They demonstrated their activities to those in their region by sponsoring interns, conducting site visits, and distributing descriptions of their programs and the programs' effects. These national demonstration projects ended in fall 1983 upon completion of their federal contracts.

The Role of State Agencies in the Institutionalization of Sex Equity

The activity of states in regard to sex equity is usually consistent with past state behavior related to civil rights issues and the state's role in implementing federal education mandates. If a state has been active in implementing Title IX, this is probably a continuation of earlier roles. In recent years, more SEAs have competed for and received federal funds (primarily from CRA IV and VEA), and thus have become more viable intermediary agencies in promoting sex equity.

State agencies differ both historically and currently with regard to their relationships with federal and local agencies. Some agencies have a history of regulation of and/or technical assistance to local education agencies, while others have emphasized a more purely administrative role. Some state education agencies have moved voluntarily to monitor local compliance with federal as well as state requirements, but others have strongly rejected any compliance monitoring functions. The sex equity program is influenced by the state agency's general definitions of its role, responsibility, and authority.

No single pattern of relationships between federal, state, and local levels exists today; the roles of each level with regard to financing, establishing standards, and evaluating programs have been undergoing redefinition. It is in this context that the role of the state education agency in the achievement of sex equity must be considered. The constraints imposed by declining funds (and the possible removal of various federal regulations) will not alter the obligations of local and state education agencies to ensure the civil rights of all students. Therefore, the role of state leadership in achieving equitable programs for girls and boys will increase in both significance and prominence. Current sex equity programs and policies at the state level provide instructive examples of the leadership role SEAs can exercise on educational equity issues.

Approaches range from comprehensive state legislation prohibiting sex discrimination in education to providing technical assistance on request to local school districts. While most states have at least a general sex equity policy statement in place, some have passed the kind of detailed policy statements and specific guidelines for action that can be used to guide decision making by personnel at the state education agency. The dissemination of information about these policies is a step in furthering their implementation. The more people that are aware of a policy, the more pressure can be exerted for its effective imple-mentation. These more detailed policy statements reflect a wide range of regional and organizational differences (Bailey, 1982).

State Sex Equity Legislation and Policies.   Strong sex equity laws and/or policies can be considered a first step in achieving sex equity. Laws in Mas-sachusetts, Washington, and Alaska represent examples of state legislation which go beyond the federal Title IX statute, especially in the area of reducing sex role stereotyping. These laws provide a strong base for SEAs to influence the institutionalization of sex equity in districts or agencies that receive state support. In Massachusetts, Chapter 622, passed in 1972, prohibits discrimination on the basis of sex, race, color, religion, or national origin in any public school in the state. The implementing regulation establishes standards for school admissions, admission to courses of study, guidance, curricula, extracurricular activities, facilities, and local compliance procedures. It also requires "active efforts" by local school committees to establish policies, regulations, and procedures and to implement monitoring and evaluation practices that promote affirmative action. Washington's Chapter 28A.25, passed in 1972, and Alaska's Chapter 17, passed in 1981, prohibit sex discrimination in employment, admissions, guidance, cur-riculum, extracurricular activities, and school facilities.

Nebraska and Minnesota have developed procedural policies for facilitat-ing civil rights compliance. Nebraska's 1982 policy focuses on procedural safe-guards to insure redress for any person aggrieved by a violation of the act. It sets forth a detailed complaint procedure and empowers the school board to take any action necessary, including the award of compensatory money damages. It places responsibility for carrying out the general mandate of the law on the local school districts, in contrast to the Alaska and Washington approaches where responsibility is at the state rather than the local level.

Minnesota statute S124.15 directs school districts to file assurances of compliance with state and federal laws prohibiting discrimination and to submit to the state information needed to indicate compliance. To implement this statute and the subsequent State Board of Education Rule, the Minnesota Department of Education has developed MINCRIS (the Minnesota Civil Rights Information System), a comprehensive automated system of civil rights data collection, stor-age, and retrieval. Data collected by MINCRIS are used to ascertain school districts' compliance with state and federal laws prohibiting discrimination, for pre-grant reviews, to investigate complaints filed against specific districts, and to assess the nature of civil rights problems in Minnesota schools. In addition to providing an annual data base for the state's public schools, the system generates information that facilitates the SEA's reporting of all required local data to federal offices, including the Office for Civil Rights and the Equal Employment Opportunity Commission, and provides the LEA information with which it can evaluate its own performance and make necessary improvements. MINCRIS reflects the assumption that equity has measurable components and that accurate information is essential to maintaining the integrity of the equity determination process.

Other states have enacted more narrowly focused legislation or state board policy directed at a single program area. Iowa's 1978 law requiring that all program areas be taught from a multicultural nonsexist perspective is an example of this approach. A long-range plan was developed that recognized that sex or cultural stereotyping may exist in currently used instructional materials. In such instances, the stereotyping must be brought to the attention of the students and supplementary materials used to offset this stereotyping. Each Iowa district must develop a written plan that contains (1) goals and objectives for each curriculum and program area; (2) a description of how the district will train employees over the five-year period; (3) evidence of input in the development of the plan by men and women, persons of diverse racial and ethnic groups, and disabled persons; and (4) strategy for evaluating the implementation of the plan. By the fall of 1981, 430 of the 433 school districts in Iowa had filed plans for integrating multicultural nonsexist concepts into their educational programs. Additionally, 405 districts reported that inservice training sessions were planned to assist staff in using the new multicultural nonsexist materials.

States have also worked on teacher training and employment issues. Oregon focused on teacher preparation and practice and since 1979 has required that *all* educators participate in a workshop on nondiscrimination for teaching and administrative certification.

In New York, the State Department of Education helps local education agencies to recruit and promote women in professional and managerial positions. The department, working with a Statewide Advisory Council and local education agencies, has been operating a statewide candidate pool and administrative job information service, the Job Network Information Service (JNIS), since 1978. Listings of administrative job openings are published and disseminated bimonthly to chief school officers, job information centers in the state library system, SUNY and CUNY college placement centers, selected women's organizations, and approximately 500 women registered in the candidate pool. The service also provides a mechanism for monitoring administrative hiring.

SEA Policies for Providing Sex Equity Technical Assistance to Local Education Agencies (LEAs).   Some states have initiated review procedures for providing technical assistance designed to help local districts move ahead with the development of sex-equitable programs. One of the most successful efforts has been instituted by the California State Department of Education's Title IX Assistance Office. The process, called Observation/Commentary/Visitation (OCV), provides an intensive diagnostic assessment that enables the LEA to increase awareness of sex equity issues and to ensure its compliance with Title IX requirements. OCV has been particularly successful because LEAs request the on-site visitation. The visitation team includes skilled observers, drawn from the department staff and a consultant pool of educators, who are trained to review the policies, practices, and programs of LEAs. The visit is a means of obtaining an accurate assessment of the status of equity efforts in order to facilitate the LEA's planning of further action.

Building on the California OCV model, the Michigan State Department of Education has developed a three-phase on-site needs assessment and planning model to assist LEAs in achieving sex equity. Michigan's On-Site Needs Assessment and Long-Range Planning model (LRP) is a consultive service provided upon request to determine and plan for a school district's sex equity needs.

Internal Activities Initiated by SEAs.   Examples of internal SEA sex equity activities are less easily documented because they do not fall into concise program categories as easily as do externally oriented activities. However, the following initiatives have been undertaken in one or more states: (1) strengthened policy and procedural guarantees of commitment to educational equity, including the development of guidelines for distribution of block grant funds involving equity issues; (2) increased activities for securing external financial support for equity activities, primarily by applying for CRA IV funds; (3) heightened cooperation among equity specialists and, in some cases, a visible program role for the Title IX coordinator, and effective use of the vocational education sex equity coordinator; (4) increased infusion of responsibilities for equity issues throughout each state department bureau or division, and (5) increased outreach involving the educational skills and contributions of equity staff to others both inside and outside the agency, such as the effective relationship between equity staff in the Maryland State Department of Education and the Maryland Women's Commission in producing annual Women's History Week curriculum packages. Formal research on the precise effectiveness of these internal and external SEA strategies or budgets is not available. However, the fact that these activities have been undertaken is evidence of both public and institutional support for sex equity in education. This support is perhaps the most crucial variable in the success of the institutionalization process.

The various examples of SEAs as intermediary intervention units are intended to support the theses that (1) adoption of state policy with specific direction for implementation provides positive support for local action, while not interfering in local change processes; (2) procedures that promote the expanded participation of underrepresented groups (for example, women administrators in New York) or provide direct technical assistance that facilitates the implementation of sex equity process and outcome goals can actually provide a direct link between federal policy and local practice (for example, OCV in California); and (3) internal initiatives on the part of SEAs demonstrate a commitment to provide civil rights guarantees to all students.

Relatively little is known about the amount of financial or other personnel or material resources that states contribute to these and related sex equity efforts out of their own budgets, or how they use federal financial assistance from CRA IV state grants or other federal programs such as WEEA. Most of what is known is due to efforts of the Council of Chief State School Officers Resource Center on Sex Equity (Bailey & Smith, 1982), which has received both federal and private foundation funds for work with state departments of education in institutionalizing sex equity. The Project on Equal Educational Rights (PEER) of the NOW Legal Defense and Educational Fund (1982) developed state-by-state reports on key indicators of Title IX compliance such as vocational education enrollments, numbers of women administrators, and athletic participation.

The Role of Local School Districts in Institutionalizing
Sex Equity (Table 2, Tier D)

Much less general information is known about our 16,000 school districts' sex equity policies or implementation activities than about related state education agency activities. Most of what we know is about those relatively few local districts that have taken a leadership role and secured external funding for a sex equity project, or about districts in states that have systematically collected such information, or from a few national studies of Title IX coordinators or legal actions. With a few exceptions such as the WEEA demonstration contracts and some of the CRA IV local education agency grants, which were discontinued in 1982, most of the very sparse external funding was for the development of WEEA products for specific areas of sex equity rather than for institutionalizing comprehensive sex equity activities in the entire district. The funds for WEEA that were to fund local sex equity implementation activities were not appropriated. On the basis of unsystematic and limited information, we suspect that most LEA efforts are directed at complying with the federal and state civil rights laws that prohibit sex discrimination (on threat of withdrawal of funding or certification). It is likely, however, that the few LEA-initiated policies and activities intended to increase sex equity are found in fairly large districts, most of which received some external funding for sex equity projects. We also suspect that most conscious sex equity activities in local districts are fairly narrow as far as content or number of people involved, and that they are sporadic and unlikely to result in comprehensive institutionalization of sex equity. Examples of promising LEA-oriented sex equity policies and activities include Los Angeles County's Infusion Process Model, which is designed to broaden the base of support and resulting activities within its 95 school districts, and the School District of Philadelphia's Affirmative Action and Equal Educational Opportunity Plan (Council of the Chief State School Officers, 1983).

A REVIEW OF THE FINDINGS FROM STUDIES
OF THE INSTITUTIONALIZATION OF SEX EQUITY
IN EDUCATION

This section will describe three studies that have examined how local school districts have implemented sex-equitable practices. The first is a federally funded state project, the California Coalition for Sex Equity in Education (CCSEE). The second is an analysis of some local school district Title IX coordinators as they are compared to state vocational education sex equity coordinators. The third is of the WEEA demonstration projects.

The California Coalition for Sex Equity in Education (CCSEE)

CCSEE illustrates the operations of a loosely coupled system of translating federal policy into classroom practice. CCSEE was a coalition of the Sex Desegregation Assistance Center for Region IX, the California State Department of Education, the California School Boards Association, and the Association of California Administrators. It was funded by WEEA in 1978.

The purpose of CCSEE was to test a power-based strategy: the key decision makers and staff sex equity advocates in 36 school districts were identified as the major path by which to infuse sex equity issues into classrooms. Through the access provided by these key authorities, workshops, seminars, and technical assistance were provided to the school districts by CCSEE.

A stratified random sample of 36 California school districts was selected to participate and was assigned to a control or an experimental group (McDonald, 1981). Twenty-three experimental group districts received the services of CCSEE; the 13 control group districts did not. A pre- and post-test, Institutional Sex Bias (a measure created by CCSEE), was given. It contained a Steps of Implementation Measure—an interview indicating the sequential steps a district would take to implement sex equity concerns—and a Compliance Measure—an interview to indicate district level compliance with Title IX.

The interviews took place at the school district with teams of district personnel including administrators, unionized and nonunionized teachers, counselors, classified staff, students, and board members. For 33 of the 36 districts the Compliance Measure agreed substantially with written reports on district status, data from observations at site visits, and other independent data sources about the district. The measures on the sequence of steps for implementation, however, provided little information; not one of the scales showed any observable sequential pattern of district implementation. It is impossible to determine whether the fault rests in the scale construction of the instrument or whether the change processes of school districts are as helter-skelter as the results suggest. Thus, only the Compliance Measure was used to assess the effects of CCSEE's year-and-a-half intervention.

After receiving training and technical assistance from CCSEE, the experimental group scores improved to indicate statistically significant differences in the areas "access to courses," "physical education," and "employment," and in the overall total score on Title IX compliance. This is indicated in Table 3.

The lack of gains in "minimal compliance" perhaps stems from the fact that most districts had met nearly all of their minimal compliance requirements, such as appointing a Title IX coordinator, before becoming involved in the project. They had little room to improve in those areas. The only lack of improvement in experimental group compliance was in "non-academic activities" such as participation in cocurricular and extracurricular activities.

Table 3.   Mann-Whitney U-Test for Differences in Gain Scores on the Title IX Compliance Measure between Experimental and Control Groups of School Districts

Title IX Dimensions	Mean Rank		U	Z	2-Tailed p-Value
	Control (N = 12)	Experimental (N = 21)			
Access to courses	10.75	20.57	51.0	−2.807	.005*
Non-academic activities	14.50	18.43	96.0	−1.123	.262
Physical education	11.79	19.98	63.5	−2.339	.019*
Athletics	12.79	19.40	75.5	−1.890	.059
Employment	11.92	19.90	65.0	−2.283	.022*
Minimal compliance	13.79	18.83	87.5	−1.451	.147
Total score (all dimensions)	10.83	20.52	52.0	−2.769	.006*

Was the training related to district gains? Further analysis tested the relationship between the specific CCSEE services provided to districts and their specific areas of score gains in Title IX compliance. Indeed, there was a striking correspondence. Except in the areas of "non-academic activities" and "employment," districts gained in the same dimensions of Title IX that the CCSEE intervention had addressed.

Were some strategies to help the LEAs institutionalize sex equity more effective than others? A comparison showed little difference among strategies ranging from inservice teacher training to the dissemination of sex equity information. The notable exception, however, was the "resource linkage/networking" strategy—an approach that clearly emerged from the pack and demonstrated greater effectiveness.

What difference did experience make? It appears that districts reached a threshold, and additional services to aid compliance yielded diminishing returns.

Which districts made the most gains? A composite sketch of the "high-impact" districts (that is, the districts that tended to make the greatest strides toward Title IX compliance) yielded some differences: high-impact districts were (1) elementary school districts, (2) smaller districts (in terms of number of schools, number of employees, and average daily attendance), (3) non-metropolitan districts, and (4) districts that had not had any prior contact with proequity training and technical assistance programs. With regard to organizational features, high-impact districts (1) had designated the superintendent or the assistant superintendent to be the liaison to CCSEE, (2) had Title IX coordinators with flexible time commitments, (3) had relatively little fiscal trauma, (4) were marked by flexibility rather than by cumbersome bureaucracy and red tape, and (5) had teaching staff with good overall morale.

But what happened in those districts after the CCSEE team withdrew?

Because CCSEE was disbanded, the Region IX Sex Desegregation Assistance Center used a telephone survey to contact the experimental districts to assess the impact of their Title IX reforms since December 1979 (McDonald, 1982). Despite some flaws in the sample, the telephone interview suggested a portrait of stability. For the most part, equity reforms implemented during participation in the project remained in place. Nearly all reporting districts had maintained the programmatic changes initiated with CCSEE. Districts with new initiatives often were completing work already begun and planned (but not yet implemented) in January 1980, as seen in table 4.

In January 1980 three districts reported that enrollment sex ratios had changed; however, only one district continued monitoring after that time. Course enrollments showed an 8% increase of boys in cooking classes, but a 2% decline of girls in auto shop.

Title IX and Sex Equity Coordinators:
A Role Comparison

The creation of a position with sex equity responsibilities in public schools, postsecondary institutions, and state education agencies is a key component of federal legislation to achieve sex equity in education. In this section we will review the evidence comparing the roles of Title IX coordinators in school districts and postsecondary institutions and the sex equity coordinators in state departments required under the 1976 amendments to the Vocational Education Act.

The data reported here include the reports of single state and regional surveys conducted between 1978 and 1982. The reported survey data indicate differences in effectiveness of the roles in three different arenas: clarity of role assignment, personal role orientation, and organizational arrangements. Each one of these will be discussed.

Clarity and Specificity of the Role Assignment in the Laws.   Montjoy and O'Toole (1979) indicate that policy implementation is directly related to both the clarity and specificity of the legal description of expected activities and the availability of new resources. Their model explains many of the differences between the impact of Title IX coordinators in school districts and postsecondary institutions and the vocational education sex equity coordinators at the state department level.

Title IX requires that organizations designate an individual with coordination responsibilities, but the law requires no specific activities and provides no funds to support the Title IX coordinator position. In contrast, the 1976 amendments to the Vocational Education Act delineate ten specific areas of sex equity coordinator responsibility and allocate funds to support sex equity activities in vocational education in state education agencies.

As would be predicted from the Montjoy and O'Toole model, the Title IX coordinator, lacking both job description and new resources, has limited poten-

Table 4.   Program Maintenance by Area of Prior Emphasis with Reporting Districts

Emphasis	Maintained (%)	Reduced (%)	Extended (%)	N
Access to courses	89	11	0	9
Access to non-academic activities	75	17	8	12
Physical education	100	0	0	8
Athletics	91	9	0	11
Employment	86	7	7	14

tial to change organizational routines. However, the state vocational education sex equity coordinator, with a specific and extensive list of responsibilities and funding to implement them, has greater potential to change organizational policies, procedures, and practices. The research evidence summarized below shows that the majority of Title IX coordinators have had a minimal effect on school districts, although under special conditions a few have had greater impact. Conversely, the state-level vocational education sex equity coordinators have undertaken a wide range of activities directed at changing their own and other educational organizations.

In four single-state surveys of district Title IX coordinators (Garcia, 1979; Norton, 1977; "Title IX Action," 1978; Turetzky, 1979), most districts appointed Title IX coordinators, although the speed of their appointment varied. Typically, districts did not consider the responsibility extensive enough to require a full-time position, a job description, or resources. Garcia (1979) reported that the majority of Title IX coordinators spent less than half a day a month on Title IX responsibilities, and about 28% had never attended a workshop on Title IX.

The lack of time reserved for Title IX coordinators was also noted by two multistate surveys. Miller and Associates (1978) and Hill and Rettig (1980) found the Title IX coordinator role to be a set of tasks added on to already existing assignments. Only in the largest districts, where Title IX duties could be assigned along with other civil rights responsibilities, did coordinators spend as much as one-fourth of their time on Title IX.

The surveys provided little information about activities or Title IX coordinator effectiveness. Garcia (1979) reported some correlation of gender and position with level of activity in the role; Title IX coordinators located in the central office were more likely to be active than those with responsibilities in individual schools, and women were more likely than men to receive grievances and believe such grievances should be handled through formal channels.

At the postsecondary level, Hill and Rettig (1980) examined the Title IX role in 12 institutions ranging in size from 1,300 to 30,000 students. Four schools were private, two were community colleges, one a four-year college, and others were institutions with graduate programs. In all cases Title IX responsibilities were added to a larger set of duties.

Vocational education sex equity coordinators were studied by Beuke, Lucas, Brigham, Glick, and Breen (1980) and Glick (1981, 1982). While this body of evidence is less extensive than that on Title IX coordinators, the specific responsibilities assigned led to more extensive work and time spent on coordinating activities as compared to district or postsecondary Title IX coordinators. Glick (1981, 1982) examined state and federal documents and interviewed vocational education sex equity coordinators in 15 states. Every state in her sample had appointed a coordinator by the required year of 1978, and all coordinators were attempting to conduct activities under the 10 functions prescribed in the job description. All coordinators interviewed reported that the explicitness of their functions was instrumental in enabling them to carry out the objectives of the legislation; this explicitness provided guidelines for their own work and was an important key in gaining the cooperation of others in their agencies.

The Individual Title IX or Vocational Education Sex Equity Coordinator's Role Orientation. While the specificity of the job assignment is a crucial variable in determining the level of organizational support, there is variation among Title IX and vocational education sex equity coordinators, depending on the person's orientation to the job. Some Title IX coordinators with less authority and less role specificity than vocational education sex equity coordinators manage to initiate more changes in schools. It depends in part on how individuals define and create their role. Three orientations to the role have been described: the "apologist" is the defender of the institution buffering the organization from external pressure, the "administrator" stresses organizational compliance with the law's formal requirements, and the "advocate" assumes active leadership in the change process (Hill & Rettig, 1980). One sample of 12 school districts showed the administrator orientation to be the most common (Hill & Rettig, 1980). Hill and Rettig went on to show the relationship between district activities and the Title IX coordinator's role orientation. Where coordinators were apologists, district responses were "weak" and the self-evaluation and grievance procedures were "meaningless." Where the coordinators served as administrators, the self-evaluations were conducted but then ignored while the district's grievance procedures were bypassed. Where the coordinators were advocates, centrally planned change efforts, commonly using technical assistance and training strategies, were evident, and the coordinator was the key to change.

In a study of seven school districts, Adkison (1982) found three coordinators with administrator, and four coordinators with advocate, orientations. The administrators had no job descriptions and no resources earmarked for Title IX, and spent little time on compliance activities. No inservice training or other efforts to inform teachers about sex equity had occurred. In contrast, the four advocates actively directed change efforts. They expressed commitment to the spirit of Title IX and promoted changes in curriculum and teacher behavior by offering many district activities. They had clarified their roles and obtained some district resources.

Adkison identified two factors that distinguished advocates from administrators. First, they were entrepreneurs; they expanded the resources of their office by expanding staff, providing additional training activities, and purchasing materials. They also used the services available from state educational agencies and the SDACs to supplement their district's resources. Second, they participated in state and national networks of equity professionals and advocates. Interaction with local, regional, and national experts shaped their understanding of Title IX and educational equity.

When compared with Title IX coordinators in public school districts, Title IX coordinators in higher education tend to be advocates (Hill & Rettig, 1980). They are more likely to be employed full-time as a civil rights or equity specialist and to have a professional role orientation as a civil rights or equity specialist. Many take part in informal and formal organizations of affirmative action/equal opportunity officers in higher education. Some may even plan careers in this field. In contrast, Hill and Rettig showed that Title IX coordinators in school districts, even those holding a complex of civil rights responsibilities, are likely to have risen from the ranks of their organization and intend to move from the equity-related position to another administrative position. They are professional school administrators rather than equity professionals. The impact of this pattern on the institutionalization of sex equity has not been examined.

Although the apologist/administrator/advocate typology has not been applied to the state vocational education sex equity coordinators, Glick's description of their role would indicate most would fall into the advocate role orientation. The difference between the more and less successful advocate, however, seems to be related to other factors within the organizational structure.

Organizational Factors.   Access to authority and to resources seems to be a most critical factor in role effectiveness. Among the state vocational education sex equity coordinators, "insider" status was often noted as a central factor in identifying and channeling resources to sex equity. Insider status and access to the state vocational education director appear related. "Outsiders" tended to be out of the purview of the vocational education division and further removed from the authority of the director. In addition, the states that spent the highest percentage of the set-aside funds were those in which coordinators were hired early, came from within the agency, and remained in the positions continuously. Glick also found that the organizational arrangements and the level of expenditure for the sex equity coordinators affected the comprehensiveness of the state vocational education plans. For FY 1979, the states that submitted the most comprehensive overall plans were those that provided comparatively high levels of financial and organizational support for the coordinator and kept the same coordinator throughout the period.

Whereas in the state vocational education sex equity coordinator's role such organizational arrangements were made easier by the specificity of the job and the additional resources, it is also clear that the most effective Title IX coordinators in school districts or postsecondary institutions were advocates

who, through their own entrepreneurship, created access to authority and gar-
nered funds for their equity purposes.

Preliminary Findings of the WEEA National
Demonstration Projects

The five LEA-based demonstration projects discussed previously were
designed to institutionalize sex equity in a comprehensive fashion on a district-
wide K–12 basis. The three-year project implementation phase began in the fall
of 1980, following a one-year needs assessment and planning phase at each site.
The findings discussed here represent only the first and second implementation
year outcomes (Hergert, 1983; Hutchison, 1983; Schubert, 1981, 1983a,
1983b).

Like the effective Title IX coordinators, state sex equity coordinators, and
high-impact school districts in California, there was an administrative commitment to educational equity at each site. In addition to a full-time project coordinator in the district office, equity advocates were placed in levels of the district
hierarchy, teacher associations, and district committees. Each of the demonstration projects developed community involvement activities and had access to the
full range of WEEA and other sex equity products in inservice training, career
education, physical education, counseling, and early childhood education as well
as in content areas such as math, science, history, and language arts. Thus, these
five demonstrations were uniquely advantaged in having clear authority and
commitment, a budget, and a full array of resources. Evaluations at these demonstration sites addressed questions regarding (1) the use, availability, and adoption
of materials with an equity focus; (2) the training required for classroom teachers
to use, adapt, and develop sex/race-fair classroom practices; (3) the impact on
students; and (4) the overall effectiveness of the demonstration model in helping
other educators to learn about and implement sex equity in their own districts.

Use of Sex Equity Materials.   Each of the five sites independently reached
similar conclusions about the value of individual sex equity resources for classroom implementation. In general, they found that (1) plenty of resources were
available, and except for audio-visual materials, they were relatively inexpensive;
(2) the extent to which the resources were ready to use was highly variable; (3)
self-contained curriculum packages were seldom adopted intact by teachers or
teacher trainers—the tendency was to pick those items or portions that fit into an
existing curriculum plan; (4) resources that contain lessons or activities with stated
objectives for students and well-organized plans were very popular because they
minimized teacher preparation; and (5) fewer resources were available for early
childhood educators than for faculty responsible for upper primary and secondary
students.

Once faculty reviewed and selected gender-fair and gender-affirmative
materials and learned where and how to obtain them, they used and infused the

materials in three ways: (1) adapting lessons or activities as is; (2) expanding or developing an idea found in a resource; and (3) going beyond the resource by developing their own ideas or altering a traditional practice or procedure. Expanding an idea or developing a spinoff activity was required often because of special class needs. It was also common to find teachers of one grade level adapting an idea initially designed for another grade level.

Involvement of Professional Educators and Community Members. A crucial element in any change project is to get the support of the people responsible for the desired actions. All the demonstration projects started by working with school administrators and faculty with the most favorable attitudes toward equity. Although their initial charge was to work with nonprofessional as well as professional school staff, all sites gave highest priority to training classroom teachers. A cadre of educators committed to sex equity, capable of identifying discriminatory practices, and knowledgeable about procedures aimed toward reducing sexism in schools guided the training and inservice programs at each site. They generally did this by working in schools most favorable to goals of making sex equity an integral part of instructional strategies, classroom organization, recreational activities, and other aspects of school life. Additionally, all project directors believed that parent and community involvement was important and reached out to this generally supportive constituency by conducting presentations, publicizing the project through local media, and seeking advice and help from them.

Approximately 250 professional educators received inservice training through the demonstration projects. The nature and type of the inservice experience varied by site: the range of offerings included presentations by prominent sex equity specialists, workshops and seminars that covered topics such as classroom interaction or bias in textbooks, classes for which faculty received credit toward certification or met specified state requirements (for example, learning about Title IX); and conferences away from the district at which educators received intense, specialized sex equity training.

During the first implementation year, much of the inservice activity was directed toward increasing faculty awareness. The next level of development was to build skills in compensating for existing bias and in converting awareness of stereotyping to actions that led to more equitable opportunities for students.

While each site had a project coordinator to initiate activities, there were also many examples of faculty-initiated events designed to inform colleagues and students about the principles of equity. At one site, faculty increased their colleagues' use of the equity resources. At another site, one physical education teacher offered a workshop to introduce teachers from all over the district to recreational activities in which both males and females could comfortably participate. At yet another site three teachers conducted inservice programs and programs for student teachers enrolled at the local university. A promising indicator of teacher commitment is a handbook of equity-based activities for early childhood education written by three kindergarten teachers who identified a gap in the resources and did something about it. At another site, community members created a Women's History Week celebration.

Three sites administered Hawley's *Attitude toward Sex Role Scales,* a measure of faculty attitudes toward equity, and found no significant differences between project and nonproject teachers. However, differences favoring increased awareness of the need for equity and actual changes in the behavior of teachers who participated in the demonstration projects were documented by classroom and workshop observations, teacher interviews, and reports of special faculty projects.

Impact on Students.   Has the use of special sex equity materials and staff involvement activities had any measurable effect on students? From classroom observations, interviews, reviews of the resources, weekly staff reports, participant evaluations of project events, and critical incidents it would seem that the answer is yes, particularly for elementary school students. All five projects administered all or part of the *Who Should* test developed by Project Equality to a selected sample of elementary students. Students in project schools "consistently displayed less stereotypic attitudes toward male and female roles and showed significant growth in equity over the school year as compared with their counterparts in nonproject schools" (Hutchison, 1983). At two sites, students with teachers who were active in the projects scored higher than those whose teachers were less involved. Students of less involved teachers had scores similar to those of control students. At one site, among students in grades 3–6, the post-test data revealed that the proportion of nonproject students who scored stereotyped responses was nearly twice as large as the scores of the project students.

Some sites found that female students had less tendency to stereotype than male students. One site found that some of the male students in project schools became more polarized in their attitudes toward nontraditional careers on the *Your Opinion* questionnaire when they were post-tested and that male students became three times more negative in their responses to the *Secondary Student Questionnaire* than did the female students, who remained neutral.

Among the secondary students, data in advanced math and science courses at one site showed substantially increased enrollments of females in advanced biology, physics, trigonometry, and calculus. At the same site, enrollments in introductory vocational education classes indicated that females comprised 46% of students in a manufacturing/construction class, which represents a gain of 35% over the previous year. In the high school course in Fundamentals of Agriculture, 54% of the students were female, compared with 10% the previous year.

The experience at the demonstration sites has been very encouraging. There are signs of progress toward equity as an integral part of school life. The demonstration projects have not reached their long-term goal of gender-fair environment; they cannot hope to remove all the inequities in an education system. However, these projects are another part of the solution in implementing the chain of events linking federal policy to classroom practice.

STRATEGIES LINKING POLICY
TO IMPLEMENTATION

In the previous sections, we outlined the key roles of various levels of government in making and implementing sex equity policies in education. In this section we shall illustrate the various strategies employed by educational agencies which are designed to achieve sex equity in education. Each of these strategies may be employed by any one of the tiers of government.

Compliance. The U.S. Congress (which enacts laws), the U.S. Department of Education, particularly the Office for Civil Rights (which develops and enforces regulations), state legislatures (which enact state laws), state departments of education (which develop and enforce these regulations), and local education agencies are the primary actors in compliance functions. These are the educational agencies with governmental authority to proclaim, "Thou shalt" or "Thou shalt not." Lack of school district or personal compliance may result in loss of federal funds, state funds, state accreditation, or teacher certification. Enforcement may include legal actions and complaint or grievance procedures.

Monitoring and Evaluation for Compliance. This is the responsibility of the enforcement and related advisory agencies such as the U.S. Department of Education, the U.S. Commission on Civil Rights, state departments of education, and local school districts. Self-evaluations were initially required by Title IX, and a study by Hill and Rettig (1980) recommends that self-evaluations with firm deadlines be widely published and renewed regularly, and that they include suggestions from all interested groups—students, faculty, staff, and community. The report also suggests ways to increase the use of the self-evaluation form in the daily running of a school system. Monitoring and evaluation functions are also used by agencies or citizens as a watch-dog strategy to assure compliance or evaluate progress. The Minnesota Civil Rights Information System and the California and Michigan site visit models provide good examples.

Information Dissemination. This is primarily supported at the federal level by WEEA through the Women's Educational Equity Act Publishing Center at the Education Development Center; the CRA IV regional SDACS; and the NIE-supported ERIC System, particularly the Social Studies Clearinghouse in Boulder, Colorado. Previously, WEEA supported the development of the Women's Educational Equity Communications Network in San Francisco. State and local education agencies often provide and disseminate information such as teacher packets, newsletters, and curricular materials. Private publishers such as the Feminist Press and professional and women's advocacy organizations also disseminate information on sex equity issues and activities.

Technical Assistance. This includes a multitude of direct services to educational agencies, schools, and individuals to help them provide equal educational opportunities to students. Services may include clarifying grievances, providing legal updates and interpretations, on-site visitations, finding resources, consulting, providing information, devising new organizational procedures, evaluating, and advising. Technical assistance is the primary mission of the SDACs, state departments of education, and some intermediate education agencies that serve multiple LEAs within states, as well as the LEAs themselves. Certain WEEA grants also provide some direct assistance. Certainly, universities and the private sector of consultants and nonprofit agencies with expertise in equity issues and Title IX and sex equity coordinators are also sources of technical assistance.

Training.   Training comprises specifically designed workshops, conferences, or meetings for the purpose of increasing the awareness, information, and skill of educational personnel and community members. The content of sex equity training may encompass issues such as hiring practices, recognizing bias in curriculum materials, decreasing bias in teacher-student interactions, or creating new organizational structures. Training is provided by the SDACs, some SEAs, Title IX and vocational education sex equity coordinators, universities, and private consultants or professional organizations. The greater part of the WEEA-and many of the VEA-sponsored materials are designed to be used in training educators to implement equity in their schools. The people trained may include different cross-sections of educational personnel: personnel in a school building, content specialists from a district, or representatives from several districts, as well as community members.

Working through the Leaders.   This is a "power-based" strategy. Much of the research in the equity implementation and change literature suggests that it is important to have the support of administrative leaders. This finding was supported by evidence that the sex equity compliance gains resulting from the CCSEE project that used a power-based model were maintained after the official project activities stopped. It was also judged important by those involved with the WEEA demonstration projects and by the Hill and Rettig (1981) study of civil rights guarantees. The demonstration projects also found that change could be institutionalized even if the educational leader was fairly neutral, if others in the hierarchy cared about equity and knew what to do. Other projects have focused some attention on working with school board members or leaders outside the official educational hierarchy.

Development and Replication.   These functions are usually provided through federal grants. The WEEA program is the primary sponsor of the development of over 200 sex equity products and model programs that are designed for use in multiple settings. The use and effectiveness of many of these are discussed in subsequent chapters and in evaluations of the WEEA program (National Advisory Council on Women's Educational Programs, 1981).

Coalition Formation and Networking.   The formation of coalitions of groups and networks of individuals concerned with sex equity in education has been a popular and promising strategy. A few of these activities, such as CCSEE and some minority women's networking projects, are supported by the WEEA program. Others, such as the Project on the Education and Status of Women at the American Association of Colleges in Washington, D.C., receive some foundation support. Most of these groups, such as the National Coalition of Women and Girls in Education and the National Coalition for Sex Equity in Education, are primarily dependent on the voluntary contributions of member organizations and individuals. Their activities and concerns typically focus on promoting sex equity at all levels of government. Active participation in these groups seems to be an indicator of a successful Title IX coordinator or sex equity coordinator, and networking seemed to be the most effective strategy in the CCSEE project.

Research and Evaluation.   R&E strategies may be used to help institutionalize sex equity at all levels of government and in nongovernmental groups. In addition to the monitoring and evaluation strategy discussed earlier, sex equity R&E helps us understand the crucial issues and potential solutions related to the achievement of sex equity. The value of this strategy in guiding our actions in particular areas of sex equity concern will be apparent throughout this book. Much of the research and evaluation of specific products has been supported by federal funds or as part of individual voluntary scholarly activities. At this point we know we have much more to learn about how to make sex equity policies and their goals a reality.

CONCLUSIONS AND RECOMMENDATIONS FOR HASTENING THE INSTITUTIONALIZATION OF SEX EQUITY IN EDUCATION

The evidence presented here offers encouragement that some students have benefited from policies such as Title IX. There is also reason to believe that these sex equity reforms will remain despite attacks on Title IX and other equity legislation (Klein, 1984). Once rights and privileges are attained, they are difficult to take away. Changing norms in the society regarding roles of women and men will also help sustain equity efforts. Many of today's and tomorrow's parents, most of whom are in the labor force, recognize the need for all children to receive an adequate education in which options are not limited by gender. While many positive strides have been taken toward sex equity in education, the work ahead will not decrease. Assistance and insistence, persistence and patience have been the hallmarks of sex equity advocates in the past. We will continue to need more of the same.

In this final section we have identified three areas of findings and recommendations: policy, increasing beneficial interrelationships among those involved in institutionalizing sex equity in education, and suggestions for research.

Sex Equity Policies

The evidence suggests that equity policies at all levels of government are valuable in starting the chain of action toward institutionalizing sex equity in education. Thus, we recommend:

1.   The passage of federal and state equal rights amendments and maintenance and augmentation of continued enforcement and funding for sex equity laws

such as Title IX, CRA IV, WEEA, and VEA at the federal, state, and local levels of government

2. That new sex equity policies or improvements in current policies include the most effective elements of existing policies, such as:

   a. Clearly articulating goals and tasks, acquiring financial and other resources, and assigning adequate authority and specific functions to individuals with sex equity responsibilities. The comparative data provided in this chapter on the roles of Title IX and state vocational education sex equity coordinators strongly suggest that policy makers at the federal, state, and local levels can shape the behaviors of the legislated sex equity advocate to a significant extent by specifying tasks to be accomplished, providing funds to support the positions, providing access to authority, and supporting national and regional networks of equity advocates. The lack of job specificity of local education agency Title IX coordinators compared to the relatively higher level of role specificity of the vocational education sex equity coordinators explains many of the differences described in these two roles. In many organizations, provisions of law are treated as statements of the minimum action required. While there are limits to the specificity with which policy can be written, a delineation of responsibility clearly affects the organization's responses to the created roles.

   b. Comprehensive and appropriate use of multiple sex equity strategies, ranging from personnel training, to influencing those in power, to networking and R&D. In addition to equity policies covering entire agencies or school districts, specific equity goals for each bureau, division, department of the agency, or school district should be developed and disseminated. The more specifically job-related the goals are, the greater the chance of accomplishment. Specialists in other areas can see themselves as part of the equity effort most clearly when they help develop concrete suggestions related to their ongoing concerns. It is also useful for equity specialists to work within the agency's existing priorities and within other specialists' areas of expertise.

   c. Sufficient budgetary and other types of resource support. The decrease in support for the worthwhile sex equity programs in the U.S. Department of Education should be reversed, and state and local education agencies should consider allocating staff and money to develop and implement valuable sex equity laws and policies. It is also useful to mandate sex equity activities as part of other activities, for example targeting inservice training funds for equity training.

   d. Evaluation criteria and mechanisms to ensure that the policy is being adequately implemented and to identify new concerns. Such data can also provide the kinds of specific information that states and school districts need to demonstrate the effectiveness of their programs. It is also a way to continue to determine which strategies work best in various settings.

Increasing Beneficial Interrelationships among Those
Involved in Institutionalizing Sex Equity

Because links among various governmental and constituent groups concerned with education are not always hierarchical, predictable, or nonoverlapping, individuals must be helped to identify and use multiple sources of governmental support for sex equity. As new agency activities are planned, they should be designed to complement ongoing activities and to avoid establishing conflicting procedures. Specific suggestions for improving these interrelationships include:

1. Identifying and filling gaps in existing policies and services. For example, CRA IV-supported SDACs are limited to serving K–12 institutions; many state and local education agencies do not have active Title IX coordinators; and many educators are confused about the role of state and local agencies in Title IX compliance responsibilities.
2. Networking and forming coalitions of individuals and organizations working with different governmental agencies and nongovernmental groups that support sex equity. The CCSEE study, the demonstration projects, and the study of Title IX and sex equity coordinators showed that networking was an important component for schools, districts, or persons with equity responsibilities. The cross-fertilization of ideas, programs, resources, and people is an enduring and continuing aspect of school improvement.
3. Working cooperatively with equity specialists. Current funding and regulatory patterns have fostered the growth of a cadre of equity specialists at the state and school district level, each of whom works in a single equity area: race, sex, disability, or language differences. The specialists have generally targeted programs toward a specific group of students. In state and local educational agencies a press for coordinated programs may be heightened by a decrease in federal dollars and the block grant concept of program allocation. A coordinated equity program may also help insure that funds such as those available through the federal Chapter 2 Education Consolidation and Improvement Act block grant be spent on equity activities. Districts may also demand that inservice programs and monitoring activities be consolidated into one equity program. Coordination of services among equity specialists may have a very positive effect on the implementation of equity programs. In time, coordinated services could reduce paperwork, lessen the amount of time necessary for assessment and monitoring, and decrease the time spent in attending multiple inservice training activities related to the various equity programs.

Recommendations for Research

This chapter indicates that although we have gained some useful insights into the institutionalization of sex equity in education, some basic questions remain unanswered.

We have little cumulative information on the nature and extent of sex equity activities in education at any level of government and tend to know much less about the 16,000 school districts and the schools and classrooms within them than about federal and state level activities. Thus, we recommend federal funding of a national study to determine how educational agencies are using their own and federal resources to facilitate compliance with both the letter and spirit of Title IX. Such a study could reveal effective procedures that could be disseminated as models for others. Bogart (1983) is developing similar model program information for postsecondary institutions. The study could also identify areas where increased federal and state support are needed to foster action. Complementary roles of equity advocacy groups and private enterprise could also be examined.

In addition to a limited knowledge of what has been or is being done to implement sex equity in education, we have very limited knowledge of how to actually institutionalize sex equity activities to attain specified sex-equitable outcomes over time. The few studies reported in this chapter suggest that it can be done, but we do not know what general strategies or elements will sustain sex equity activities most effectively. At the very least, we suggest that the federal government provide funds for follow-up research on the WEEA demonstration projects, the CCSEE project, and selected success stories from activities of the SDACs, local Title IX and vocational education sex equity coordinators, and state departments of education. We also urge that SEAs and individual researchers initiate their own studies of this specialized change process.

We also need to learn more about the similarities and differences in achieving educational equity as it relates to sex, race, national origin, disability, and economic status so that coordinated equity policies and activities can be developed.

Finally, we urge federal and state support of research to identify which sex equity strategies work best and in what combination in specified environments and as changes occur in educational priorities. For example, is it more cost-effective to work with a power-based strategy that relies on a superintendent's commitment to equity or a bottom-up strategy to provide incentives to empower teachers? To what extent is it advisable to develop comprehensive equity strategies that are tied to the latest educational concerns such as improved educational standards or increased achievement in science and mathematics?

We know that there is a great deal of natural variation across specific content/student age levels, but we are just beginning to learn about the ways that broad strategies to institutionalize sex equity can reinforce the more specific sex equity activities discussed in the following chapters.

REFERENCES

Adkison, J. A. (1982). *Advocates and administrators: Perspectives on the Title IX coordinator's role.* Paper presented at the annual meeting of the American Educational Research Association, New York.

Bailey, S. (1982). *Are the states willing and able to promote sex equity?* Paper presented at the annual meeting of the American Educational Research Association, New York.

Bailey, S., & Smith, R. (1982). *Policies for the future: State policies, regulations, and resources related to the achievement of educational equity for females and males.* Washington, DC: Council of the Chief State School Officers.

Beuke, V. L., Lucas, C. V., Brigham, N., Glick, G. S., & Breen, J. P. (1980). *Implementation of the Education Amendments of 1976: A study of state and local compliance and evaluation practices in vocational education.* Cambridge, MA: Abt Associates.

Bogart, K. (1983, January). *Exemplary programs and policies that promote sex equity in postsecondary education.* Summary report of Advisory Panel meeting, Hood College, Frederick, MD.

Council of the Chief State School Officers. (1983). Strong local policies play a critical role. *Concerns,* No. 8, pp. 1–2.

Garcia, G. F. (1979). *A study of compliance with Title IX of the Education Amendments of 1972 in selected Iowa public school districts.* Unpublished doctoral dissertation, Drake University, Des Moines, IA.

Glick, G. S. (1981). *Implementation of the Education Amendments of 1976: A study of state and local compliance practices of sex equity in vocational education.* Paper presented at the annual meeting of the American Educational Research Association, Los Angeles.

Glick, G. S. (1982). *The implementation of a federal change agent program at the state level: A standardized case study of the Vocational Education Amendments of 1976, sex equity provisions.* Unpublished doctoral dissertation, Boston University.

Hergert, L. F. (1983). *Parent and community involvement in school improvement: The experience of the five sex equity projects.* Paper presented at the annual meeting of the American Educational Research Association, Montreal.

Hill, P. T., & Rettig, R. (1980). *Mechanisms for the implementation of civil rights guarantees by educational institutions.* Santa Monica, CA: Rand Corporation. (ERIC Document Reproduction Service No. ED 190 719)

Hutchison, B. (1983). *Assessing educational equity: Impact on students.* Paper presented at the annual meeting of the American Educational Research Association, Montreal.

Kaser, J., Sadker, D., & Sadker, M. (1983). *Sex Desegregation Assistance Centers (SDACS): A report card.* Washington, DC: American University.

Klein, S. (1984). Education. In S. Pritchard (Ed.), *The Woman's Annual, 1983: The Year in Review.* Boston: G. K. Hall.

Klein, S., & Dauito, K. (1982). *What's left of federal funding for sex equity in education?* Washington, DC: National Advisory Council on Women's Educational Programs.

McDonald, S. C. (1981). *School system response to planned intervention to reduce sex bias.* Paper presented at the annual meeting of the American Educational Research Association, Los Angeles.

McDonald, S. C. (1982). *An inquiry into the resilience of Title IX reforms at the local level.* Paper presented at the annual meeting of the American Educational Research Association, New York.

Miles, M. (1964). *Innovation in Education.* New York: Teachers College Press.

Miller & Associates, Inc. (1978). *The status of Title IX in Region X: An evaluation of models and barriers to implementation of Title IX of the Education Amendments of*

1972 for Region X of the U.S. Department of Health, Education and Welfare. Olympia, WA: author. (ERIC Document Reproduction Service No. ED 177 250)

Montjoy, R. S., & O'Toole, L. J., Jr. (1979). Toward a theory of policy implementation: An organizational perspective. *Public Administration Review, 39*(5), 465–476.

National Advisory Council on Women's Educational Programs. (1981). *FY 1980 evaluation of the Women's Educational Equity Act Program*. Washington, DC: author.

Norton, N. L. (1977). *Implementation of Title IX of the 1972 Education Amendments in selected school districts in Alabama*. Unpublished doctoral dissertation, Auburn University, Auburn, AL.

Project on Equal Educational Rights. (1982). National Silver Snail Award. Washington, DC: NOW Legal Defense and Education Fund.

Schubert, J. G. (1981). *Focus: A national demonstration of educational equity in Tuscon* (Final Report Year One). Palo Alto, CA: American Institutes for Research.

Schubert, J. G. (1983a). *Five national demonstrations of educational equity*. Palo Alto, CA: American Institutes for Research.

Schubert, J. G. (1983b). *An interactive approach to infusing equity: A teacher model*. Paper presented at the annual meeting of the American Educational Research Association, Montreal.

Title IX action limited, Washington State ACLU says. (1978). *Peer Perspective, 4*(3), 1, 5.

Turetzky, J. A. (1979). *Compliance with Title IX by Tennessee public schools during 1975–76*. Unpublished doctoral dissertation, University of Tennessee.

Weick, K. (1976). Educational organizations as loosely coupled systems. *Administrative Science Quarterly, 21*(1), 1.

8
Strategies for Overcoming the Barriers to Women in Educational Administration

Charol Shakeshaft

"A wild patience has taken me this far,"* might well be an appropriate motto for the women who have become school administrators in this country during the past three decades. Until recently, these strong and gifted women have, by and large, waited their turn for leadership positions. Despite its genteel virtues, waiting one's turn, unfortunately, appears not to have increased the ranks of women school administrators; indeed, such action seems to have diminished women's participation in the formal management of schools.

The purpose of this chapter is to review women's representation in school administration, to identify the barriers that have kept women from attaining administrative positions, and to explore some of the strategies and programs that have been developed to overcome these barriers.

ISSUES: THE BARRIERS

Current myth would lead one to believe that the overrepresentation of male school administrators is a thing of the past, as affirmative action and women's raised consciousness combine to assure increased hiring of female school administrators. Being myth, however, this belief is based more upon expediency or self-serving convenience than on fact, since a reading of the numbers tells us that women's presence in school administration, if increasing at all, is doing so at an extremely slow pace. Although the feminist movement had generated a surge of women ready for school administration, declining enrollments, financial crises, and sex discrimination have combined to neutralize that trend.

While some researchers point to statistics that demonstrate a radical decline

Susan Bailey, Thomas Lovia Brown, Grace Butler, Suzanne Howard, Effie Jones, Fannie Lovelady-Dawson, Catherine Marshall, Xenia Montenegro, Joan Shapiro, and Patricia Schmuck assisted in the preparation of this chapter.
*From "Integrity" by Adrienne Rich in *A Wild Patience Has Taken Me This Far* (New York: Norton, 1981).

in the number of women administrators over the past 50 years (for example, Howard, 1980), others such as Charters (1981) caution against overreliance on early counts of female administrators, since they tend to be based upon small, localized, and nongeneralizable samples. Thus, women may have always been underrepresented in school administration, so that current statistics represent a reinforcement of the downward linear trend of women in school administration rather than a reversal of past practice.

Whatever the case may be, recent statistics on women educators tell us that in 1981 women were the majority (66.9%) of all public school instructional personnel (Databank, 1982) and that women were 83% of the elementary teachers and 46% of secondary school teachers (Howard, 1980). In 1979, 28% of all doctoral degrees in educational administration and supervision were granted to women (Howard, 1980). About 18% of elementary school principals (Lovelady-Dawson, 1981) and 7% of secondary school principals are women (Howard, 1980). In 1981, 80.5% of elementary teachers and 95.3% of secondary teachers worked under male principals (Databank, 1982), most (98.2%) district superintendents were male (Jones & Montenegro, 1982), and 28.3% of school board members were female (Underwood, Fortune, & Meyer, 1983, p. 24). In higher education, only 8% of college presidents are women (Howard, 1980), and, as Karen Bogart points out in chapter 24, few women are faculty members in postsecondary institutions.

A comparison between the number of female instructors and the number of female managers illustrates women's underrepresentation in the formal leadership of schools. This imbalance is all the more disquieting when one considers that the woman teacher or administrator is, by and large, more able than the male teacher or administrator (Brown, 1981; Frasher & Frasher, 1979; Tibbets, 1980). These researchers have pointed out that in studies comparing male and female teachers and administrators on selected criteria (teaching evaluations, teacher exam scores, college grade point average, warmth, administrative functioning, and so forth), when there is a difference, females are favored. Thus, one finds that both gender and talent imbalances result when women are passed over for administrative positions (Fishel & Pottker, 1975; Gross & Trask, 1976).

If this is the case, why has it happened? Why the "higher you go, the fewer you see" syndrome for women in educational administration? The barriers to women who desire positions as school administrators have been determined in a number of ways: through self-report questionnaires, in interviews, and in ethnographic studies. Many of the researchers have employed experimental and quasi-experimental research designs. The following section is a discussion of those factors that have been singled out as hindrances to women moving toward school administration.

Poor Self-Image or Lack of Confidence

Schmuck (1976) among others lists lack of confidence and poor self-image as barriers that prevent women from considering school administration. Many women either do not see themselves as school administrators or lack the self-confidence to pursue such an end. While this is related to the next barrier, lack of aspiration or motivation, there is a distinction between the two. Poor self-image and lack of self-confidence do not necessarily inhibit motivation, and one can be unmotivated in particular areas without a poor self-image or lack of self-confidence.

Lack of Aspiration or Motivation

A number of studies (see, for instance, Dias, 1975) suggest that women's lack of success in obtaining administrative positions is due to lowered aspiration or lack of motivation on the part of women. While it is true that women have traditionally applied less often than have men for administrative positions and that women, more often than men, need to be encouraged to enter administration, there is little evidence that women are less aspiring or less motivated than are men. One way to understand women's perceived failure to aspire to higher levels of school service is to rethink the achievement norm inherent in this belief. Studies tell us that most women enter pre-K–12 teaching to teach, while most men enter teaching to administer. Thus, these women teachers are aspiring and achieving that which they are aiming for. Many of these same women do not value administration and the role of administrators, nor do they desire a position that separates them from students. For instance, Baughman (1977) found that women perceived many administrative positions as entailing too much paperwork and not enough educational content and that therefore these jobs were not of interest to many women.

Another approach to understanding women's achievement motivation in educational careers is provided by Kanter (1977). Kanter points out that "opportunity structures shape behavior in such a way that they confirm their own prophecies" (p. 158). Thus, people who have very little opportunity to move up the hierarchy (women teachers) disengage in the form of depressed aspirations, low commitment, or nonresponsibility. Those people who are highly mobile within the hierarchy (men teachers), however, "tend to develop attitudes and values that impel them further along the track: work commitment, high aspirations, and upward orientation" (p. 138). Thus, women's so-called lack of aspiration in administration might more accurately be seen as an expected response to lack of opportunity.

Finally, a seeming lack of aspiration or motivation in women may actually be a realistic reaction in light of home and family responsibilities and job opportunities. Thus, lack of aspiration or motivation seems not to be a real barrier to women in administration but rather a by-product of other obstacles.

Lack of Support, Encouragement, and Counseling

A number of researchers (for instance, Baughman, 1977; Schmuck, 1976) have pointed out that women have traditionally had little support, encouragement, or counseling from family, peers, superordinates, or educational institutions to pursue careers in administration. More often, these women have been given negative cues by family and work groups concerning such an endeavor. The importance of encouragement and support can be seen in light of studies (Shakeshaft, 1979) indicating that of the women who have decided to pursue administrative careers, most have done so because some significant other (husband, mother, father, principal, college professor) encouraged them.

Family and Home Responsibilities

Family and home responsibilities, including the major responsibility for child and home care, were listed as barriers to women's achievement in administration in a number of studies (for instance, see Schmuck, 1976). Concomitantly, lack of reliable childcare and limited pregnancy benefits were listed as obstacles to taking on additional administrative responsibilities. As a result, the profile of the typical woman administrator is of a woman (1) who does not have children, or (2) whose children are grown, or (3) who has private childcare in the form of a full-time housekeeper or, more often, her own mother.

Socialization and Sex Role Stereotyping

Socialization and sex role stereotyping have been cited by several researchers (Poll, 1978; Schmuck, 1976) as explanations of why women themselves, as well as men, do not immediately connect women with administration. Not only have women been socialized in ways that have not made them administratively inclined, but those who hire have been socialized to believe that those qualities frequently associated with females are antithetical to those qualities needed to manage and, conversely, that qualities needed to manage are ones not possessed by women. For instance, assertiveness is a skill that women, by and large, have not been socialized to call their own. Relatedly, women's contributions are often ignored, and women have reported feeling invisible in policy-making groups (Kanter, 1977). Socialization is also partly responsible for the resentment, from both males and females, which women aspirants sometimes find directed at them. Some writers, however, have posited that many stereotypically female qualities are exactly what administrators need. For instance, Frasher and Frasher (1979) believe that women reduce conflict more effectively than do men. Marshall (1981) posits that "organizational socialization processes place aspiring women in a marginal organizational status" (p. 227). Whether individual or organizational, socialization and sex role stereotyping have been potent obstacles to increasing women's participation in the management of schools.

Lack of Preparation or Experience

Traditionally, fewer females than males have participated in certification, doctoral, or internship programs in administration. Several researchers (for instance, Edson, 1981; Schmuck, 1976) have cited both lack of formal preparation and few administrative learning experiences while still a teacher vis-à-vis committees, unions, coaching, discipline duty, or extracurricular responsibilities as areas that render women less experienced or prepared for administration than are men. Recent work (Edson, 1981; Paddock, 1977) indicates that this barrier is being overcome as more women receive internships, administrative certification, and doctoral degrees.

Lack of Finances for Continuing Training

Women, more than men, cite lack of finances as a reason for being unable to continue administrative training (Edson, 1981). Women in the general labor force earn 59 cents for every dollar earned by a man; women in public school teaching and administration also earn less than their male colleagues (Databank, 1982). Women have tended to sacrifice financially for their families, thus cutting short educational opportunities. Additionally, it must be remembered that there is a higher percentage of financially disadvantaged among females than among males and that women teachers earn less than do men teachers. Therefore, women are more likely than men to be financially disadvantaged and, more than men, are expected, and expect, to sacrifice their education or needs so that the resources may be used for family purposes.

Too Few Role Models

The lack of opportunity to see other women in a variety of administrative positions, to hear how these women describe their lives, and to compare themselves with women just one step higher up the hierarchy has been cited as a reason why women have not moved into administrative positions in larger numbers (Schmuck, 1976). The importance of role models in helping both women themselves and men within the system to view women administrators as a normal occurrence rather than an exceptional one cannot be overstated.

Lack of Sponsorship or Mentors

Unlike role models, which generally must be of the same sex and race in order for women to identify with the model, sponsors or mentors may be either male or female. However, a sponsor or a mentor is much more important to the individual woman than is a role model because it is the sponsor or mentor who advises the woman, supports her for jobs, and promotes and helps her. Sponsors and mentors, who have traditionally been white males, have tended to promote other white males. Minority women often suffer doubly in the area of sponsorship—first, because they are female, and second, because of their minority status (Lovelady-Dawson, 1980). While most women have not had either sponsors or mentors, most who have been successful in acquiring administrative titles have sponsors or mentors. Thus, the process of sponsorship or mentoring appears to be important in an administrative career (Poll, 1978).

Lack of a Network

Related to sponsorship is the need to have access to a network that provides one with information on job openings and administrative strategies as well as with visibility and that functions as a support group. Women have traditionally been excluded from these networks and thus have not heard about administrative positions, have not been known by others, and have had few people to approach for counsel (Schmuck, 1976).

Sex Discrimination in Hiring and Promotion

Finally, a number of studies (see, for instance, Baughman, 1977; Fox, 1975; Goldsmith, 1976; Poll, 1978; Robinson, 1978; Schmuck, 1976; Thomas, 1976) document the existence of overt sex discrimination by school boards, boards of trustees, departments of educational administration, and educational administrators which has prevented women from becoming school administrators. Studies tell us that people tend to hire those like themselves. Thus, white males hire white males (Kanter, 1977; Ortiz, 1981). Additionally, a number of researchers (for example, Marshall, 1981) have pointed out that affirmative action policies are often misused—either through hiring a less qualified woman or minority applicant where a more qualified woman or minority applicant exists or by failing to take into account a woman's personal career orientation or interests and, thus, misplacing her in the organization.

Curricular Materials

A number of researchers have commented on the relationship between sexist curricular materials and the dampened career goals of women. A number of studies (Nagle, Gardner, Levine, & Wolf, 1982; Schmuck, Butman, & Person, 1982; Shakeshaft & Hanson, 1982; Tietze, Shakeshaft, & Davis, 1981) have examined the textbooks and journals in the field for gender bias and have found a shocking proportion of sexist content in the research and writing. Thus, an additional barrier for women in administration is the lack of appropriate and positive curricular materials for them to read.

A number of models have been suggested in an effort to understand these barriers. Estler (1975), for instance, believes the lack of women in administration has been explained by writers using the following models: the Women's Place Model, which assumes that women's nonparticipation in administrative careers is based solely on social norms; the Discrimination Model, which "draws on the assumption that institutional patterns are a result of the efforts of one group to exclude participation of another" (p. 369); and the Meritocracy Model, which assumes that the most competent people have been promoted, and thus women are not competent. Estler provides evidence for support of both the Woman's Place and Discrimination Models, but found that the Meritocracy Model did not fit reality.

Adkison (1981) uses competing explanations to account for women's lack of success in entering administration, illustrating that "the same data can be explained equally well by different concepts" (p. 330). Thus, she analyzes women's career barriers in terms of sex role stereotyping, sex role socialization, career socialization, organizational characteristics, and devaluation of women.

An additional framework for examining barriers is to place them within the domains of internal and external barriers. Internal barriers can be overcome by individual change, while external barriers require social and institutional change. Although several models have been conceptualized to understand these barriers, further work needs to be done.

While all the barriers identified do not affect all women, neither are they equally prohibitive at all career levels. Lack of sponsorship may be less a problem at the department chair level than at the superintendency. Conversely, socialization and sex role stereotyping may hinder a woman who has not taken the first step toward becoming an administrator more than it hinders a woman who has served as an administrator. Relatedly, racial and ethnic minority women find that the barriers are compounded by their racial and ethnic identification. Contrary to popular myth, minority women are the most underemployed and underpaid in school administration (Databank, p. 14).

THE ANSWERS: STRATEGIES FOR CHANGE

Strategies for change, whether implemented or imagined, vary depending upon which of the conceptual lenses is used to view barriers. Thus, internal barriers require one sort óf approach; while external obstacles call for quite another. Concomitantly, if one believes that the barriers are primarily the result of social devaluation of women, the strategy for increasing women in educational administration will be quite different than if one is working from the premise that sex role socialization results in too few women administrators. Thus, strategies for change differ according to the barriers targeted. These strategies are not mutually exclusive, and it is their combined effects that are probably necessary to make lasting change.

There have been a number of federally funded projects as well as individual and organizational efforts to increase the representation of women in administration. While the research on the effectiveness of these strategies is limited, and while not all effective strategies have been included here, the remainder of this chapter will be devoted to describing a variety of tactics or programs as well as offering, where available, evidence of the effectiveness of those approaches.

Recruitment of Women into Preparation Programs

In an effort to overcome the initial resistance of women to the nontraditional career of school administrator, a number of methods have been used to reach women teachers and students and to provide them with information that might encourage their entrance into school administration. For instance, personnel from Minnesota's Women in School Administration (WISA); A Project of Internships, Certification Equity-Leadership, and Support (ICES); Female Leaders for Administration and Management in Education (FLAME); and Sex Equity in Education Leadership (SEEL) spoke to education groups in an effort to reach prospective women administrators. Additionally, WISA provided field-based courses in an attempt to recruit women in rural areas and to provide a statewide recruitment and selection pool. In St. Paul, a recruitment program within the school district identified women for a special administrative training program.

Financial Assistance for Women

Once they are made aware of training options, women often confront the problem of lack of financial resources. Thus, one approach to helping women become school administrators is the provision of scholarships and stipends. FLAME interns, for example, were paid a monthly stipend while taking leaves of absence to pursue full-time graduate work; ICES awarded scholarships to women to attend university summer sessions and ICES workshops.

General Administration Courses and Workshops

So that women could gain knowledge about administrative skills and/or acquire certification credentials, programs provided administrative knowledge either via formal university educational administration courses or in the form of skills workshops. FLAME interns, for instance, enrolled in full-time doctoral administration programs, while ICES interns took administration coursework during the summer. WISA offered workshops on conflict management, the study of power and leadership, time management, and grant writing, along with other topics. ICES workshops concentrated on conflict management, business management, and the politics of education. Higher Education Resource Service (HERS), through their program called The Next Move, provides a leadership and management clinic for women in higher education. These general courses, available to both males and females, are essential for women entering school administration. In some states, they are required for administrative certification, while in others they are recommended. Whatever the case, skills courses in administration are invaluable for women desiring to enter administration.

Increasing the Number of Women Professors
of Educational Administration

As women began to take courses in educational administration, they were confronted by the lack of female professors who could serve as role models and advisers, and this was compounded by negative attitudes from some male professors. Thus, one strategy used to provide aspiring women administrators with role models and sponsors at the university is that of increasing the number of women professors of educational administration. WISA provided several courses taught by women, while FLAME was involved in the hiring of women professors by three universities.

Courses and Workshops Concerned with Specific
Barriers to Women in Administration

In addition to the lack of female professors to serve as role models in formal university programs, women also encountered the absence of courses to meet their particular needs as women entering a male-dominated field. Thus, a number of courses and workshops have been provided, supported by universities or federal funding, to address the specific needs of women. SEEL offered yearly conferences and workshops for women, while ICES provided workshops on educational equity issues. WISA's activities included sessions on assertiveness training, sex role stereotyping, socialization, and balancing one's life. Assisting Women to Advance through Resources and Encouragement (AWARE) provided a number of workshops through their six project sites as well as through separate conferences and sessions at annual AASA meetings on such topics as networking, self-concept, résumé writing, how to enlist sponsors, discovering job potential, interviewing techniques, and employment negotiation. Florida State University offered women a program in goal setting, self-knowledge, and awareness of career opportunities in an effort to encourage participation in nontraditional fields. Hofstra University offers a course to women annually as part of the certification program in an effort to confront barriers to women through the teaching of skills related to job searches, assertiveness, networking, résumé preparation, interviewing, recognizing sex discrimination, presentation of self, sponsorship, and the importance of self-confidence. Brayfield developed a workshop in social literacy training to overcome internal factors that inhibit the pursuit of administrative careers by women, while The Next Move included sessions on barriers to women. Women in Leadership Learning (WILL) and the St. Paul school district both provided similar training to women so that they might learn strategies for confronting obstacles to entering school administration.

Curricular Materials

Within both general administrative courses and workshops and those directed specifically at women, a lack of appropriate materials on women's issues, sex role stereotyping, socialization, and barriers and strategies for women in administration was evident. Thus, one approach to the larger problem of women's absence from the administration of educational institutions was the development of awareness and training materials for use in classrooms or at conferences with both women and men. DICEL, for instance, produced four training modules for women on androgyny, assertion, power, and leadership, as well as a videotape on women in administration. ICES developed a 30-minute videotape of five women administrators discussing their careers, a videotape on role-playing, and two videotapes describing their project. SEEL staff published a textbook, *Sex Equity in Education*, prepared a slide show on the issues surrounding women in administration, and provided a quarterly newsletter to inform people about the issues as well as to raise awareness. University Council of Educational Administration (UCEA) in conjunction with teams at six universities developed six multimedia instructional modules for women preparing for educational administration, for professors of educational administration, for policy and decision makers in K–12 systems, for other educators, for male and female trainees, and for policy and decision makers in postsecondary systems in an effort to alter conditions for girls and women in educational institutions (Silver, 1979). WILL developed modules for training in balancing personal and professional life, conflict resolution, competition, cooperation, developing strategies and diagnosing organizations, team building, developing support networks, and understanding maintenance systems. WISA published a hiring procedures manual for school trustees.

Internship

Once women began receiving training or decided to become administrators, it became clear that most lacked actual experience in administrative situations. Thus, many programs implemented internship experiences for the women involved. FLAME provided participants with a variety of internship experiences both in and out of education; ICES interns spent 10 months in a school district; and WISA interns trained in rural and small urban settings.

Support Systems

Once trained, many future women administrators still find a need for a support system that reinforces their aspirations as well as providing a mechanism for ventilation, generating strategies, and providing professional companionship. In an effort to deal with the frequent problem of lack of family support, FLAME instituted a program that reached out to families of interns so that they could understand the program and anticiapte the problems. Additionally, family counseling was made available. FLAME also created an advisory group composed of influential educators to act as sponsors for their interns. The ICES interns identified support teams in their districts with which they could meet regularly, while SEEL formed support groups for women in educational administration in Oregon.

Networks

In addition to a support group for women, there is a need for a system that can compete with the Old Boys' Club. A common vehicle for providing women with both contacts and information is a network. Both SEEL and UCEA offer directories of women in educational administration. AWARE, FLAME, and

Hofstra University have instituted formal networking systems. Additionally, SEEL linked women administrators in Oregon through the Oregon Women in Educational Administration group and then linked this group with existing state and national organizations to expand the network. NECEL and CCEL provide these services in New England. Related to networking is the method of providing a formal and institutionalized vehicle for bringing job information to women's attention as well as bringing women to the attention of employers. SEEL published *A Directory of Administrators,* which included both men and women, in an effort to highlight women candidates. Another approach to visibility was used by both WISA and FLAME, whose interns were sent to districts and other states so that they might be both seen and heard.

Political Clout

Moving from the women themselves to the larger world, many strategists believe that before women will be hired in great numbers, the issue of the underemployment of women administrators must be taken seriously. Therefore, a number of organizations have been formed nationwide to provide political clout to help accomplish federal, state, and local change. SEEL, for instance, has been effective in providing a strong voice that keeps the issue of underrepresentation of women in administration in the public eye.

Legal Remedies and Affirmative Action Programs

The use of the legal system ranges from indirect action such as teaching the intricacies of antidiscrimination laws to women, administrators, and school boards to the more direct approach of forcing districts to comply with those laws. Compliance may be pushed through affirmative action programs or through direct legal action. For instance, the legal battle of two women administrators with the Los Angeles Unified School District resulted in the adoption of a court settlement which will "substantially increase management opportunity for women" (Reigelhaupt, 1980, p. 1). A further strategy within the legal realm involves a change of teacher education competencies in Oregon to include knowledge of antidiscrimination laws and mandates. The impact of legal strategies is largely unknown; no studies are available that chart the relationship between such strategies and increased employment for women in administrative positions.

Consciousness Raising and Technical Assistance to Organizations and People Who Impact on Hiring Policies and Practices

One strategy has been to make organizations and others who hire aware of the bias against women as well as to provide these groups and individuals with technical assistance and materials to help them evaluate and change their own policies and practices. This has been done using a number of approaches. UCEA and WISA developed materials; WISA's was a handbook of hiring procedures for school boards. Other strategies include workshops for policy makers at local, regional, and national meetings. The effectiveness of this strategy has not been determined. While evaluations of the materials and workshop presentations rate them as endeavors of high quality, participation at workshops by the targeted audiences has been low, and actual use of the materials by these same audiences is undetermined.

Creating Jobs

Despite these efforts and in large part because of the effects of declining enrollments in schools, many qualified women are unable to obtain administrative positions. A strategy that FLAME pioneered was teaching interns to create their own jobs by writing and getting funding for new programs in school districts, which they can then administer.

ILLUSTRATIVE PROGRAMS

There are a number of programs which have attempted to remedy the problem of the scarcity of women in formal leadership positions in schools. Although some exemplary approaches have been isolated for discussion here, there are many additional programs that could just as well be substituted for the ones included, had they but come to the author's attention, or were more detailed evaluation information available. The following descriptions are included because they have sufficient evaluation data to make a case for their effectiveness.

The suggestion that the effectiveness of the programs can be measured warrants some discussion of the difficulties of such a task. At this point there is certainly more evidence on the issues than the answers. There are several reasons why this is the case. It is too soon, in many cases, for the evidence to be in; there is a necessary and expected time lag between receipt of administrative certification or training and receipt of an administrative job offer. Additionally, the general decline in enrollment, cutbacks in school budgets and federal financing of education, and the reluctance of many to retire from teaching and administration has made it even more difficult to measure the effects of the programs. Even if this were not the case, methodological weaknesses in the evaluations render assessments difficult: control groups are seldom used; participants are not randomly selected; existing instruments and measures are inadequate to uncover subtleties in attitudes, beliefs, self-concept, and confidence. Concomitantly, more support (funding, institutional, peer) has been provided for documentation of the issues than for developing and testing strategies of change. Finally, it is nearly impossible to separate the programs from their larger context in which social change issues, particularly those concerning sex equity, are debated. Partialing out the effects of larger social movements is not only difficult but probably unwise. It is too soon to determine if there has been the beginning of individual, organizational, and social change that in the long run will shape a world in which women as well as men play substantive roles in all facets of schooling. This is an issue of morality and excellence; deciding who gets credit (or blame) for these changes is the province of politics. Moreover, the ultimate goal is change in the gender imbalance in school leadership—how it occurs is less important than that it happens.

AWARE (Assisting Women to Advance through Resources and Encouragement). The American Association of School Administrators (AASA), through funding from the Ford Foundation, coordinates six project AWARE regional centers (Phoenix; Chapel Hill, North Carolina; Eugene, Oregon; Atlanta; Lincoln, Massachusetts; and Austin, Texas), which attempt to promote women in educational administration (Jones & Montenegro, 1982, p. 10).

Florida State University. A training program to help women overcome the barriers to entering nontraditional careers was given to females from three community or junior colleges in Florida (Thomas, 1979, p. 5).

Women in Administration, Hofstra University. Annually since 1980, Hofstra University has offered within its administrative certification program a three-credit course, team-taught by an assistant superintendent of schools, a secondary school principal, and an assistant professor of educational administration, which confronts a number of barriers which have hindered women from becoming school administrators (Shakeshaft, Gilligan, & Pierce, 1982).

ICES (A Project of Internships, Certification, Equity-Leadership, and Support). ICES was a two-year project funded by the Women's Educational Equity Act Program from 1977 to 1979 to train women in school administration and place them in leadership positions (Adkison, Barley, Schreiner, Sillin, & Warren, n.d.).

SEEL (Sex Equity in Educational Leadership. SEEL was a three-year effort funded by the Women's Educational Equity Act Program from 1977 to 1979 whose primary goal was to build a model to achieve sex equity in Oregon's school management that could be transported to other states (Stockard, 1980).

RECOMMENDATIONS

Although there are a number of unique barriers to women's access to administrative positions, several approaches have been formalized that have proved, in varying degrees, to be successful. How successful each program or strategy has been is still to be determined. The real measure of success will be seen in an increase in the number of women administrators—this change, if it occurs, will take time.

In an attempt to summarize the efforts which have been undertaken, table 5 provides a way of relating strategy to barrier to use. Where available, evaluation outcome is also included.

The essential concept to internalize when examining the strategies used to counter barriers to women in administration is that no one strategy will solve the problem. Unless an approach is used that links equipping women with needed skills and mindsets to changing the structure in which they work, it is unlikely that overall, large-scale change will occur. No matter how qualified, how com-

Table 5. Strategies for Increasing Women's Access to Administrative Positions

Strategy	Barrier(s) Targeted	Outcomes	Examples of Use
Consciousness-raising and recruitment of women into preparation programs	Lack of support, encouragement, counseling Socialization and sex role stereotyping Lack of preparation	WISA: Increased enrollment of women in certification courses from 20 to 80%	WISA ICES } Talks to educational groups, FLAME professional organizations SEEL } WISA: Field-based courses taught whereby professors traveled to rural areas to recruit; statewide recruitment and selection FLAME: Recruited applicants from local educational agencies SEEL: Counseled students St. Paul recruitment model: Recruited 35 women into training program.
Financial assistance	Lack of finances	FLAME: Interns completed training that would have otherwise been impossible without financial assistance	FLAME: Interns were paid a monthly stipend while taking leave of absence to return to graduate school full time ICES: Scholarships were given to women to attend university summer session and ICES workshops
General administration courses and workshops	Lack of preparation/experience	FLAME: Some interns became knowledgeable in previously male-dominated areas ICES: Interns kept high grade point average and impressed administration faculty.	FLAME: Interns enrolled in full-time doctoral programs ICES: Interns took summer administration courses, workshops on conflict management, business management, and politics of education

(continued)

Table 5. (*Continued*)

Strategy	Barrier(s) targeted	Outcomes	Examples of use
		WISA: Evaluated by participants as important activity	The Next Move: Leadership and management clinic for women in higher education
			WISA: Workshops on conflict management, study of power and leadership, time management, and grant writing
Increase number of women professors of educational administration	Too few role models	FLAME: Three women professors of educational administration hired	FLAME: Three women professors of educational administration hired
	Lack of sponsorship	WISA: Courses team-taught by professors and women administrators	WISA: Courses team-taught by professors and female administrators
Courses and workshops concerned with specific barriers to women in administration	Poor self-image/lack of self-confidence	AWARE: Decreased external barriers	AWARE: Workshops at six project sites and at conferences
	Lack of support, encouragement, counseling	Florida State University: Formal evaluation indicates changes in goals, values	Florida State University: Workshops for women to encourage entrance into nontraditional careers
	Socialization and sex role stereotyping	Hofstra University: Formal evaluation indicates changes in self-confidence, goals, and jobs	Hofstra University: Course for women within administrative certification program
	Too few role models		ICES: Workshops on educational equity
	Lack of sponsorship		SEEL: Yearly conferences for women in administration
	Sex discrimination	Social literacy training: Evaluation indicates that those who received training were more likely than those who did not to apply for administrative position	Social literacy training: Training to overcome internal factors that inhibit entrance into administrative careers

	The Next Move: Participants indicated usefulness of program WISA: Evaluated by participants as most helpful training activities	The Next Move: Seminars for women St. Paul recruitment model: 25-hour training program WILL: Conferences and workshops for women WISA: Activities including understanding of assertiveness training, sex role stereotyping, and socialization
Curriculum materials	Poor self-image/lack of self-confidence Lack of support, encouragement, counseling Socialization and sex role stereotyping Lack of preparation Too few role models Lack of network Sex discrimination	DICEL: Videotape/modules ICES: Four videotapes SEEL: Book, slide-tape, newsletters UCEA: Six modules WILL: Modules WISA: Hiring procedures manual
Internship	FLAME: Evaluated by participants as one of the most rewarding activities; most interns were offered jobs at the conclusion of the field experience	FLAME: 12 women in executive-level internships in noneducational and educational settings ICES: 13 women in 10-month internships WISA: 12 interns in seven school districts

(continued)

Table 5. (*Continued*)

Strategy	Barrier(s) targeted	Outcomes	Examples of use
Support systems	Lack of support, encouragement, counseling Family and home responsibilities Lack of sponsorship	FLAME: Majority of interns had support of family	FLAME: Families of interns were invited to retreat workshop so they could understand the program and anticipate problems; family counseling made available; advisory groups of educators acted as sponsors WILL: Human Resources Center established to provide support system ICES: Each intern identified a support team in her district SEEL: Oregon Women in Educational Administration was formed as a support group
Networking	Too few role models Lack of networking	AWARE: Networks increased	SEEL, UCEA: Directories of women in administration SEEL: Oregon Women in Educational Administration; link with national organizations AWARE, FLAME, HOFSTRA: Formal network systems WISA, FLAME: Interns traveled to gain visibility
Political clout	Socialization/sex role stereotyping Sex discrimination		SEEL: Oregon Women in Educational Administration

Legal remedies and affirmative action programs	Sex discrimination	Legal remedies: Little documentation on the number of successful and unsuccessful instances of litigation Affirmative action programs: Effectiveness of affirmative action programs has not been systematically studied	*Szewiola and Jones v. Los Angeles United School District* Oregon: New teaching standards require familiarity with EEO concepts and laws
Consciousness-raising and technical assistance to those who have impact on hiring policies and practices	Sex discrimination Socialization/sex role stereotyping Lack of sponsorship Lack of network	FLAME: Those superintendents who participated were most often supportive of interns SEEL: Internal sponsorship had high attendance; presentations to male groups less successful Judgment analysis: Provides nonsexist evaluation (April, 1975)	WISA: Developed hiring procedures manual for use by school boards; held classes for men and women UCEA: Developed modules for professors of educational administration and policy makers in K–12 and higher education FLAME: School superintendents were asked to participate in workshops and seminars SEEL: Presentations made to male groups Judgment analysis: Technique used to provide nondiscriminatory rating performance
Creating jobs	Sex discrimination	Two FLAME interns created jobs for themselves	FLAME: Interns took courses in grant writing and submitted actual proposals

petent, or how psychologically and emotionally ready women are to assume administrative positions in schools, they are still living and working within a society and school organizational framework that is both sexist and racist. While researchers need to evaluate the effectiveness of the proposed strategies more rigorously, practitioners can still implement the strategies identified to overcome barriers to women in school administrations. However, comprehensive programs that incorporate those strategies directed at the women themselves and those intended to change the workplace and the gate keepers will be most effective for long-term change.

REFERENCES

Adkison, J. A. (1981). Women in school administration: A review of the research. *Review of Educational Research, 51*(3), 311–343.

Adkison, J. A., Barley, J. D., Schreiner, J. O., Sillin, P., & Warren, A. (n.d.). *Project ICES final report.* Washington, DC: U.S. Department of Health, Education, and Welfare.

April, E. A. A. (1975). The use of judgment analysis in determining perceived differences in judging the competence of male and female administrators. *Dissertation Abstracts International, 36,* 4883A. (University Microfilms No. X-03880)

Baughman, M. K. (1977). Attitudes and perceptions of a selected sample of women senior high teachers toward becoming school administrators in Detroit public schools. *Dissertation Abstracts International, 38,* 6420A. (University Microfilms No. 7804644)

Brown, D. J. (1981). The financial penalty of the sex talent inversion in Canadian education. *Interchange, 12*(1), 69–82.

Charters, W. W., Jr. (1981). *Principal sex and sex equity in educational policies and practices.* In P. A. Schmuck, W. W. Charters, Jr., & R. O. Carlson (Eds.), *Educational policy and management: Sex differentials* (pp. 35–54). New York: Academic Press.

Databank. (1982, March 10). *Education Week,* pp. 12–13.

Dias, S. L. (1975). A study of personal, perceptual, and motivational factors influential in predicting the aspiration level of women and men toward the administrative roles in education. *Dissertation Abstracts International, 36,* 1202A. (University Microfilms No. 75–20, 946)

Edson, S. K. (1981). "If they can, I can": Women aspirants to administrative positions in public schools. In P. A. Schmuck, W. W. Charters, Jr., & R. O. Carlson (Eds.), *Educational Policy and Management: Sex Differentials.* New York: Academic Press.

Estler, S. (1975). Women as leaders in public education. *Signs: Journal of Women in Culture and Society, 1*(3), 363–386.

Fischel, J., & Pottker, J. (1975). Performance of women principals: A review of behavioral and attitudinal studies. *Journal of the NAWDAC,* 110–115.

Fox, F. J. (1975). Black women administrators in the Denver public schools. *Dissertation Abstracts International, 36,* 7089A. (University Microfilms No. 76–11, 574).

Frasher, J. M., & Frasher, R. S. (1979). Educational administration: A feminine profession. *Educational Administration Quarterly, 15*(2), 1–13.

Goldsmith, H. B. (1976). The categorical dominance of sex, race, and national origin in the preferences of white, black, Hispanic male and female New York City elementary school teachers for white, black, Hispanic male and female elementary school principal candidates by means of a simulation activity. *Dissertation Abstracts International, 38,* 1148A–1149A. (University Microfilms No. 77–16, 424)

Gross, N., & Trask, A. E. (1976). *The sex factor and the management of schools.* New York: Wiley.

Howard, S. (1980, September). *Fact sheet on women in educational administration.* (Available from author, 402 Tennessee Ave., Alexandria, VA 22305.)

Jones, E. H., & Montenegro, X. P. (1982). *Climbing the career ladder: A research study of women in school administration.* Arlington, VA: American Association of School Administrators.

Kanter, R. M. (1977). *Men and women of the corporation.* New York: Basic Books.

Lovelady-Dawson, F. (1980). Women and minorities in the principalship: Career opportunities and problems. *NASSP Bulletin, 64*(440), 18–28.

Lovelady-Dawson, F. (1981, September). No room at the top. *Principal,* pp. 37–40.

Marshall, C. (1981). Organizational policy and women's socialization in administration. *Urban Education, 16*(2), 205–231.

Nagle, L., Gardner, D. W., Levine, M., & Wolf, S. (1982, March). *Sexist bias in instructional supervision textbooks.* Paper presented at the annual meeting of the American Educational Research Association, New York.

Ortiz, F. I. (1981). *Career patterns in education: Men, women and minorities in public school administration.* New York: Praeger.

Paddock, S. (1977). Women's careers in administration. *Dissertation Abstracts International, 38,* 5834A. (University Microfilms No. 7802552)

Poll, C. (1978). No room at the top: A study of the social processes that contribute to the underrepresentation of women on the administrative levels of the New York City school system. *Dissertation Abstracts International, 39,* 3165A. (University Microfilms No. 7821905)

Rich, A. (1981). *A wild patience has taken me this far.* New York: Norton.

Riegelhaupt, B. (1980, November 16). School board tackling sex discrimination with two pioneering actions. *Valley News,* pp. 1, 14.

Robinson, O. T. (1978). Contributions of Black American academic women to American higher education. *Dissertation Abstracts International, 39,* 2094A. (University Microfilms No. 7816079)

Schmuck, P. A. H. (1976). Sex differentiation in public school administration. *Dissertation Abstracts International, 36,* 5719A. (University Microfilms No. 76–5204)

Schmuck, P. A., Butman, L., & Person, L. R. (1982, March). Analyzing sex bias in *Planning and Changing.* Paper presented at the annual meeting of the American Educational Research Association, New York.

Shakeshaft, C. (1979). Dissertation research on women in educational administration: A synthesis of findings and paradigm for future research. *Dissertation Abstracts International, 40,* 6455A. (University Microfilms No. 80 11994)

Shakeshaft, C., Gilligan, A., & Pierce, D. (1982, March). *Evaluation of a course for women in educational administration.* Paper presented at the annual meeting of the American Educational Research Association, New York.

Shakeshaft, C., & Hanson, M. (1982, March). *Androcentric bias in the* Educational

Administration Quarterly. Paper presented at the annual meeting of the American Educational Research Association, New York.

Silver, P. (1979). *Evaluation report* (Project 565AH61258, Grant No. G007604964). Washington, DC: U.S. Office of Education/Women's Educational Equity Act.

Stockard, J. (1980). *Sex equity in educational leadership: An analysis of a planned social change project.* Washington, DC: U.S. Office of Education.

Thomas, E. J. (1976). Career patterns of black women administrators in historically Negro senior colleges and universities. *Dissertation Abstracts International, 36,* 3459A–3460A. (University Microfilms No. 76-27-763)

Thomas, H. B. (1979, November). *Impact of an education program designed to assist women overcome the deterrents to entering non-traditional occupations.* Paper presented at the fifth annual conference on Research on Women and Education, Cleveland State University.

Tibbetts, S. L. (1980). Women principals: Superior to the male? *Journal of NAWDAC, 43,* 15–18.

Tietze, I. N., Shakeshaft, C., & Davis, B. H. (1981, April). *Sexism in texts in educational administration.* Paper presented at the annual meeting of the American Educational Research Association, Los Angeles.

Underwood, K. E., Fortune, J. C., & Meyer, J. A. (1983, January). Readout: All about who you are. *American School Board Journal,* 23–25.

9
The Treatment of Sex Equity in Teacher Education

David Sadker and Myra Sadker

Each year approximately 175,000 future teachers graduate from colleges and universities. The postsecondary training they receive is integral to the way these prospective teachers are prepared to work with children. Through the curriculum and instruction of their teacher education programs, these teachers can learn about the nature and impact of sex bias in education. They can discuss curricular resources that supplement biased instructional materials and can be trained in instructional skills and approaches that are fair to both female and male students. They can discuss Title IX and its implications for education and can learn about outstanding women, as well as outstanding men, who have contributed to and helped shape the field of education. The organization, structure, and content of teacher preparation programs are crucial if this nation is to attain elementary and secondary curricula and instruction that meet the needs and maximize the potential of all our students.

Unfortunately, teacher education programs do not appear to be meeting these goals. Rather, through omission and stereotyping these programs may be reinforcing or even creating biased teacher attitudes and behaviors. In the following section, we provide evidence to document the low level of attention that sex equity issues receive in teacher education programs. In the remaining sections, we describe some of the major efforts to bring sex equity into the mainstream of teacher education. While our emphasis is on the preservice preparation of future teachers, there is some discussion of inservice preparation for experienced teachers as well. Finally, we make recommendations for future research, policy, and practice.

The authors wish to express their appreciation to Kathryn Girard, Patti Lather, and Susan Klein for their excellent assistance in the conceptualization of and research for this chapter.

THE PROBLEM: A STRUGGLE FOR RECOGNITION

In 1973 Florence Howe reported that 1,200 women's studies courses were offered in the nation's colleges and universities. Fewer than ten of these were taught in schools or departments of education (Howe, 1973, p. xiii). In 1975 Shirley McCune and Martha Matthews surveyed 1,200 teacher education programs and found only 184 courses related to women's issues in 104 institutions. There were approximately 43 times as many women's studies courses taught in other departments of this nation's postsecondary institutions. During this time, the American Association of Colleges for Teacher Education noted that any "exposure of prospective teachers to sex equity issues is often elective and usually occurs outside the school's department of education" (Gollnick, 1979, p. 16). In 1979 Howe surveyed women's studies programs and courses nationally and concluded that schools of education "were among the most resistant to the impact of the women's movement" Recently, Patti Lather (1982) has begun to update the McCune and Matthews listing of women's studies courses and is finding that while there are some few but notable efforts both to infuse existing courses and to create separate courses with sex equity perspectives, such efforts in no way reflect an institutionalized commitment to sex equity in teacher education. Rather, such efforts have depended upon the initiative of individual teacher educators who, as often as not, battle the resistance of students, peers, and administrators in their efforts to bring sex equity into teacher education.

A number of reasons have been advanced to explain the resistance of education departments to sex equity. Tobias (1978) and Howe (1973) point out that women's studies courses are typically established because of the activism of female professors and students who demand such courses. Political activism is less common among students in schools of education than among students in other academic departments (Antonucci, 1980). Lather (1981, p. 3) finds limited resources in the political awareness and aspirations of education students and places the responsibility for promoting sex equity "squarely on the shoulders of teacher education faculty."

Teacher educators have been less responsive to this issue than faculty in many other university departments—which is not to say that other departments have been responsive. Although teacher education students are mainly women, the university-wide pattern of male-oriented staffing is also reflected in schools of education. Approximately one-third of education faculty members are female, but less than 15% of education chairs or deans are women (Gollnick, 1979). Female faculty members are most frequently found in human development and curriculum, and males account for the majority in research, administration, and philosophy. As in the university at large, female faculty members involved in teacher education become even less visible at the higher faculty ranks, and approximately 75% of all tenured education faculty members are male (McCune, Mathews, & Earle, 1978). In terms of leadership positions, females are more likely to be chairs of departments than deans of schools or colleges of education; more likely to lead a teacher education program at a Catholic-affiliated college than at a secular institution; and more likely to lead an education program at a predominantly white institution. Traditionally, schools and departments of education have provided a professional career path for women students. But staffing patterns in teacher education send the message to students from elementary school through graduate study that education is directed, managed, and led by men.

These staffing inequities are compounded by a general lack of awareness among teacher education faculty, male and female, concerning the cost of sex bias in the classroom (Kimmel, 1980). In most schools and departments of education, the overwhelming perception is that sexism is of peripheral concern (Lather, 1981). As a result, little research is conducted on the issue of sex equity and teacher education. Few nonsexist teacher education programs have been developed and implemented. In 1981, Girard and her colleagues conducted a literature search of the ERIC data base to determine research and developments in the area of sex equity and teacher education. They found that between 1978 and 1981 there were 15,782 entries concerned with general teacher education. An additional 6,756 entries were categorized as dealing with inservice education, and 3,754 entries were concerned with perservice teacher education. Of this total of 22,425 teacher education descriptors in ERIC, only 88 concerned sex equity or discrimination or race equity. In short, less than $\frac{1}{2}$ of 1% of the entries on teacher education reflected equity and/or discrimination issues!

Little research and curriculum development is done on sex equity and teacher education. Several special courses have been developed in schools and departments of education on this topic, but it is unlikely that information concerning sex bias and sex equity is integrated in any coherent or systematic manner into the core courses of teacher education—for example, foundations, psychology, and methods of teaching in the various content areas (Lather, 1982).

The structure and content of teacher education texts provide insight into the nature of teacher education training. Not only is the content of these texts an important part of a student's training as a teacher, but textbooks frequently provide professors with direction in developing course syllabi. In short, teacher education texts provide us with valuable data as to which topics, issues, and skills are emphasized, and which are ignored.

In a comprehensive line-by-line analysis of the 24 best-selling teacher education texts published after 1972, Sadker and Sadker (1980) found that 23 of these books gave less than 1% of their space to the issue of sexism. Many of the texts did not treat the issue at all. Following is a more detailed summary of the results of this content analysis.

Twenty-four teacher education texts were analyzed.

- Twenty-three gave less than 1% of their space to the issue of sexism.
- One-third did not mention the issue of sexism at all. Most of the texts guilty of this oversight are in math and science—the areas where girls are most likely to have achievement difficulties.

- Not a single text provided future teachers with curricular resources and instructional strategies to counteract sexism in the classroom and its harmful impact on children.

Four Foundations of Education or Introduction to Education texts were analyzed.

- There was over five times as much content space allocated to males as to females.
- Three of the four books analyzed did not mention Title IX of the Education Amendments of 1972, the legislation that prohibits sex discrimination in educational programs receiving federal financial assistance. The one book that did mention Title IX spent more space on an unnamed 19th-century normal school than on this important current law and its implications for schools across the country.
- Two of the four books did not discuss sexism in education. The most attention any individual book gave to this issue was less than $\frac{1}{2}$ of 1% of the total content.
- One of the four books presents an extended discussion of the advantages and disadvantages of a dual salary scale, one that would pay female teachers less than male teachers.
- Not one of the books told the history of women in American education. It goes unremarked that women were denied access to education (beyond the dame school) for the first half of this country's history.
- If there is any field to which women have contributed—both collectively and individually—it is that of education. But one would not know it from reading these books. All four books described Horace Mann, but not one mentioned Emma Willard. One book discussed Vergerius but did not include Maria Montessori.

Three Psychology of Education texts were analyzed.

- There was an average of five times as much content space allocated to males as to females.
- Two of the three books devoted less than 1% of their content space to the issue of sexism; the third gave 1.7% of its space to this issue.
- All three books discussed the topic of sex differences, but none provided thorough and current analysis of the research in this very complex area.
- All three books were written by men. For every female listed in the indexes of these books, there was an average of more than 20 males cited. On the average, four times more male than female authors were cited in the footnotes and bibliographies. These books tell the beginning teacher that educational psychology is a field conceptualized, studied, recorded, and dominated by men.

Seventeen methods texts in science, math, language arts, reading, and social studies were analyzed.

- In the three science methods texts, an average of seven times more space was given to males than females.
- Results from the National Assessment of Educational Progress (NAEP), the most comprehensive effort to examine achievement on a national basis, show that the science achievement scores of males are higher than those of females at both the elementary and secondary levels. Two of the three science books did not mention this disparity. One did note that girls are more likely than boys to have problems in science. As important as this would seem to be, the book spent far more space on the best buys in bath soaps.
- Not one of the three math methods texts mentioned the issue of sexism.
- The National Assessment of Educational Progress shows that female students fall farther and farther behind their male counterparts in math achievement as they go up through the grades. None of the math methods textbooks mentioned the problem or what teachers should be doing to counteract it.
- In the five reading texts analyzed, an average of more than twice as much space was allocated to males than to females.
- Scores on achievement tests (including the NAEP) show that many more boys than girls have problems in reading. All five of the reading methods texts discussed sex differences in reading achievement and/or interests. The discussion is often stereotypic and inaccurate, according to research reported in our chapters on reading and instructional materials: "Boys show interest in action and aggressiveness in the affairs of the world and therefore prefer adventure, science, hero stories, biography, history and tall tales, while girls still cling to the fanciful stories, myths, stories of chivalry and romance, home life, biography, and accounts of everyday life" (Dallmann et al., 1974, p. 370).
- Three of the five reading texts did not mention the issue of sexism.
- The discussions of sex differences in reading interests in two of the four language arts texts were themselves stereotyped and inaccurate. In one instance, the stereotyping pushed inexorably on to a rationalization for increased discrimination: "For example, it has been found that boys will not read 'girl books,' whereas girls will read 'boy books.' Therefore the ratio of boy books should be about two to one in the classroom library collection" (Rubin, 1975, p. 191).

"Of all the means for implementing change," writes Florence Howe, "I would place priority on the education of teachers, both female and male. . . . When teachers change, so does everything in their classrooms" (Howe, 1973, p. xiv). But as the preceding discussion indicates, teacher education has not provided the scholarship, leadership, direction, or impetus for change toward equity. From staffing patterns to research activities, from bias in textbooks to the lack of women's studies courses, schools and departments of education have generally been impervious to the need for reform. However, there have been a few bright spots. In the following section, we shall describe some of the programs and projects that have exerted leadership in addressing sex equity and teacher education.

THE RESPONSE

Policy and Law

The most widely known legal remedy for sex bias and sex discrimination in education is Title IX of the Education Amendments of 1972. The regulations for implementing this law are discussed in other chapters of this book, and they offer a crucial means of eliminating or reducing certain aspects of sex discrimination in teacher education. However, most teacher educators are neither sufficiently informed of, nor influenced by, the Title IX regulations.

Legal remedies and policy statements at the state level have also fallen far short of eliminating sexism from teacher education programs. In addition to some state laws that are similar to Title IX, a primary vehicle for state influence has been teacher certification standards. A number of states, including Minnesota, Wisconsin, and Iowa, have included sex equity criteria in their accreditation standards. Further, many states encourage and/or require teacher applicants to take the National Teacher Exam (ETS) in order to receive a teaching certificate. This exam now includes several questions on individual educational rights, including sex equity.

At the national level, teacher certification policy is coordinated by two organizations that influence licensing requirements in most states. Organized in 1954 by associations representing state departments of education, the teaching profession, and local boards of education, the National Council for the Accreditation of Teacher Education (NCATE) accredits most teacher education institutions, which prepare over 80% of the nation's teachers. NCATE's goals include the formulation and application of standards to teacher education programs and the encouragement of institutional self-evaluation.

In January 1979, NCATE revised its *Standards for Accreditation of Teacher Education* to include a clear commitment to multicultural education. The standards indicate that sex equity is viewed as part of multicultural education:

> Multicultural education could include but not be limited to experiences which:
> (1) Promote analytical and evaluative abilities to confront issues such as
> participatory democracy, racism and sexism, and the parity of power; (2)
> Develop skills for values clarification including the study of the manifest and
> latent transmission of values; (3) Examine the dynamics of diverse cultures and
> the implications for developing teaching strategies; and (4) Examine linguistic
> variations and diverse learning styles as a basis for the development of
> appropriate teaching strategies. (p. 4)

NCATE applies this standard not only in evaluating the content of the teacher education programs but also in analyzing other aspects of teacher education institutions, including recruitment, faculty development, and long-range planning. Before the inclusion of the word "sexism" in the 1979 standard, there was no mention of sexism or sex equity in any of the NCATE standards. Although the inclusion of this standard represents some progress, its effectiveness in accomplishing real change in teacher education programs appears to have been minimal. There are a number of reasons for this. First, for most educators and noneducators alike, sex equity is not usually considered part of multicultural education. While sex equity is related to multicultural education, most people consider it a distinct issue with special implications for teacher training programs. Further, the standard presents sex equity as an option, stating that sex equity "could" be included. A teacher education program without any reference to sex bias and sex equity but with a strong program in teaching ethnic or racial minorities could pass an evaluation on this standard.

Second, a standard is only as strong as its enforcement. In 1979, the first year of the standard, 67 teacher education institutions were reviewed, and not one of the basic preparation programs was cited for "weakness" in multicultural education. Only one institution was found weak in this area at the advanced (graduate) level (Woolever, 1981). Five schools were cited for their "strength" in multicultural education at the basic level, and four received similar praise for their graduate programs.

The 1980 reviews indicated a toughening of this standard. Of the 64 institutions reviewed that year, two were cited for weaknesses in multicultural education at the basic level, and three were cited at the advanced level. The 1980 NCATE Annual Report summarized these findings as follows:

> Where failure to meet multicultural education standards 2.1.1 and G-2.1.1 was not a factor in the denial of any basic and only one advanced program in 1979, violations of multicultural education standards were cited in 36% of the 1980 denials of basic programs and 25% of denials for advanced programs. We reported in 1979 that the Council apparently was taking a "wait and see" attitude with regard to multicultural education. Apparently the Council has concluded that it has waited and seen enough. (p. 7)

The National Association of State Directors of Teacher Education and Certification (NASDTEC) is the other major interstate reciprocal accrediting agency. In its 1979 standards, NASDTEC had several references concerning teacher sensitivity to cultural, racial, and/or ethnic groups. There was only one reference in the basic standards that appeared related to sex equity concerns. 3.3 Professional Education, standard III, states:

> The program shall provide experiences which will lead the teacher candidate to develop those human qualities that will enhance pupil learnings to include but not be restricted to personal self-esteem and confidence; open attitudes of

evaluating practices which affect social groups; and knowledge, humaneness, and sensitivity which reduce conflict and tension and promote constructive interactions among people of differing economic, social, racial, ethnic and religious backgrounds or sex, language, cultural, and other differences. (p. 17)

There is no reference to sex equity in the advanced standards except for standards for school counselors (4.4.1, standard V), which states:

The program shall assure understanding of family relations, societal forces and cultural changes with particular reference to sex equity and socio-economic, ethnic and racial groups. (p. 96)

In fact, this standard is the only one we found at the advanced level, and it is far stronger than the sex equity criterion stated at the basic or undergraduate level. Programs preparing school superintendents, principals, supervisors, psychologists, social workers, and others have no sex equity standards at all. The limited application of this standard indicates the need for greater attention from NASDTEC to the issue of sex equity in its accreditation criteria.

The success of NCATE and NASDTEC standards in influencing teacher education programs to address sex equity research and training will depend upon the inclusion of sex equity as a distinct and separate requirement and upon the strength of the enforcement. Until this occurs, the NCATE and NASDTEC standards will not have sufficient influence to accomplish major change on the issue of sex equity in education.

Resources: Federal Agencies and Professional Associations

The federal government has supported several programs concerned with sex equity in preservice and inservice teacher education. One of these, the Women's Educational Equity Act (WEEA), was enacted in 1974 and reenacted in 1978 to promote educational equity for girls and women in all areas and at all levels of education. A recent analysis (NACWEP, 1981) indicated that 156 of the 233 WEEA products developed from 1976 to 1980 were intended for teacher education use, three times the number intended for student use. However, these teacher education materials appear to be targeted for inservice use by experienced teachers. Few of these WEEA materials have been developed for the preservice teacher. Consequently, they have been of limited use for teacher educators who wish to train new teachers in skills requisite to the elimination of sex bias in the classroom.

Further, these and the more general sex equity products for education personnel have enjoyed only limited dissemination and for the most part have been distributed to those teacher educators already committed to sex equity. At the preservice level especially, it is very possible that the typical teacher educator is not even aware of the existence of these WEEA materials. WEEA has yet to penetrate the mainstream of teacher education.

Another major federal effort to provide sex equity information and training for teachers is funded under Title IV of the 1964 Civil Rights Act (CRA IV) through training institutes, LEA and SEA grants, and Sex Desegregation Assistance Centers (SDACs), which are responsible for assisting school districts in complying with Title IX and eliminating sex segregation and bias in educational policies, programs, and practices. These CRA IV-sponsored activities have provided sex equity assistance not only for inservice teacher education, but also to a broad range of individuals involved in education, including administrators, counselors, school board members, students, and parents. Their regulations, however, do not allow them to provide assistance to postsecondary institutions, and therefore they give no services to preservice teacher education programs or to teacher education faculties. It is likely that approximately 175,000 preservice teachers certified each year have only limited knowledge of sex bias in education and are taught few if any skills to remedy this problem.

Professional education associations have also recognized the problem of sex bias in teacher education and have undertaken several actions to address the issue. They have sponsored publications concerned with sexism in teacher education, training activities for members, revision of teacher certification standards to reflect the importance of sex equity, and interest groups and task forces committed to promoting sex equity in education.

Since the early 1970s, publications such as the *Journal of Teacher Education, Social Education,* and *Phi Delta Kappan* have communicated research and information concerning sexism in schools. Articles in these journals have recognized the importance of sex equity in education and have introduced the topic to many educators who had been unaware of this issue. For instance, the summer 1975 issue of the *Journal of Teacher Education* was devoted exclusively to this topic.

Organizations ranging from the American Educational Research Association to the National Council for the Social Studies, from the American Association of Colleges for Teacher Education to the National Council of Teachers of Mathematics have built upon this growing awareness and have generated practical training sessions and scholarly research on sex equity in teacher education. Many of these activities have been sponsored by members who form special interest groups within the organizations to promote equity in teacher education. For example, the American Federation of Teachers and the National Education Association have sponsored a number of women's caucuses throughout the nation as well as sex equity inservice teacher education workshops at the state and local levels.

In summary, although professional organizations have made some attempts to respond to problems of sex bias, persistent barriers still remain. Articles published in professional journals do reach the entire membership, but they provide only a basic awareness of the issue to those who choose to read them. Further, conferences and training provided by these associations rarely reach the level of preservice teacher education, so future teachers do not have access to sex equity research and training. To a great extent, then, sex equity continues to be viewed as a special interest topic in these associations and has yet to be recognized as a valid and pressing issue for both preservice and inservice teacher education.

Resources: Instructional Materials

The major WEEA project targeted specifically and directly at preservice teacher education was the Non-Sexist Teacher Education Project (NSTEP) co-directed by Myra and David Sadker and based at American University, Washington, D.C. Consequently, NSTEP will be discussed in some detail. The focus of this project was to develop sex equity materials in those key areas documented as omitted from the most widely used teacher education textbooks. During 1978–1979, NSTEP contracted with authors to develop the following units to address these deficiencies:

Rita Bornstein, "Sexism in American Education." This module examines the nature and impact of sex bias in schools. It 1) presents a brief history of sexism in American education, 2) provides information on the emergence of the increased awareness for sex equity from the civil rights movement to the requirements of Title IX, and 3) focuses on the challenges to education in a time of changing values and norms.

Linda Kerber, "The Impact of Women on American Education." This unit identifies the central themes in the history of women's access to education and the contributions women have made to American educational institutions. Utilizing the information found in diaries, local school records, and the newsletters of teachers' organizations as well as in other primary and secondary sources, the module spans over two hundred years of American educational history.

Joyce Gall and Meredith Gall, "Boys and Girls in School: A Psychological Perspective." This module takes a close look at what the best available research says about sex differences and similarities in six major areas: (1) school achievement in math and science, (2) school achievement in reading and writing, (3) school achievement in social studies and humanities, (4) school grades, (5) exceptional learners (handicapped and gifted), and (6) personality characteristics.

Myra Sadker and David Sadker, "Between Teacher and Student: Overcoming Sex Bias in the Classroom." This module examines the research on sex bias in teacher expectations and interaction patterns. It offers several classroom scenarios and gives readers the opportunity to analyze these vignettes for potential bias in the way teachers treat male and female students. A variety of observation systems are provided so that teacher candidates can assess the nature and degree of sex bias in the real world of the classroom.

Donna Gollnick, Myra Sadker, and David Sadker, "Beyond the Dick and Jane Syndrome: Confronting Sex Bias in Instructional Materials." This module describes six forms of bias that often characterize instructional materials: invisibility, stereotyping, imbalance, unreality, fragmentation, and linguistic bias. A variety of exercises allow teacher candidates to analyze passages from elementary and secondary school texts for sex bias.

Patricia Schmuck and Richard Schmuck, "Promoting Sex Equity in School Organizations." This unit uses three paradigms—biological, psychological, and sociological—to explain sex differences in schools. It explores in some detail a fourth paradigm—one drawn from a social psychological perspective. The authors draw a portrait of the school as a miniature society, a setting that has a unique culture and social structure that may either encourage or inhibit sex equity.

Five of these six modules were field tested during 1979–1980 at 10 teacher education institutions selected for diversity in geographic location, size, nature of the institution, and student population. An independent evaluation (Stake & Stake, 1980) was conducted to assess the impact of the NSTEP curriculum. The Stakes administered pre- and post-trial attitude surveys, made on-site observations, and interviewed instructors and students at each of the sites. In addition, students and instructors at each site kept logs in which they recorded their reactions to the NSTEP materials.

The results showed that students responded positively to the NSTEP sex equity materials. Ten times as many students found the materials "relevant" as found them "not relevant," and five times as many students indicated the equity issues presented in the materials were "timely" as opposed to "out-of-date." In terms of written quality, five times as many students characterized the NSTEP materials as "well written" as opposed to "poorly written," and eight times as many students perceived the equity issues presented in the modules as "clear" as opposed to "confusing."

Through attitude surveys administered at the sites, students reported that sex equity is an important issue, one that should continue to be taught in education courses. Students also indicated that their perception of the importance of sex equity increased after using the NSTEP materials. Following exposure to NSTEP materials, 20 of 27 (or 74%) of the classes in the field trial showed an increase in their rating of sex equity as an important issue, giving it a significant gain in importance over control topics such as teenage drinking and drugs and developing new energy sources. Further, 77% of the students felt that as a result of their readings and discussions they had a better understanding of how teachers can influence the sex stereotyping of students. Thus, it appears that sex equity became a priority among these education students who were exposed to the NSTEP materials.

However, not all teacher education students reported positive attitudes toward topics related to sex equity in education. Sometimes students were not ready or willing to accept the teaching of the NSTEP materials on religious grounds:

> I believe absolutely that women should have equal opportunities. If they're doing the same job and if they can do the same job well enough they should be paid the same. But as far as all the other stuff about women's lib, the woman being the head of the house, anything along that line, I'd be absolutely against it because I am a Born Again Christian and I know the Bible is the Word of God. . . . I wouldn't recommend the materials and I wouldn't want to read more.

There were a variety of other objections. A student from Illinois commented:

> There has to be a reason for men and women to fit into roles. Might be a natural law—it would be the same if we started all over again.

A female student said:

> I think most students were dissatisfied. Some commented that the information and materials were outdated and the idea of sexism overdone. I am left with the impression that the class members have already grown past the content of the materials. The boob tube beat the author to it.

And this from a Houston student:

> After reading one of the modules I felt hostile about it. I think it was kind of attacking me as a teacher. It says you are going to do this and that and I'm saying I don't think that I do that. But even though I did get a negative reaction, I'm glad I read it. (Stake & Stake, 1980)

One of the most interesting findings concerned the large number of students who reported experiencing a critical insight. All educators expect and believe that everyone in a class will gain new understandings as a result of taking the class, but moments of insight rarely occur, even in the best of sessions. The evaluators of the NSTEP curriculum were prepared to acknowledge the teaching of NSTEP materials as successful if even 15% of the students responded that they had experienced "a moment of special insight, something to be remembered for a long time."

The student response during the NSTEP field study far exceeded these expectations. Over 50% of the students who participated in the field trial indicated that they had experienced such an insight while studying NSTEP materials. For example, here's how one student described this insight.

I read it cover to cover. I agreed with it. I wasn't aware of it, but so many times while I was reading it a light went on, and I said, "Yeah, yeah, that's what happens." I wasn't looking for it, sexism, but now I'm aware of it, I heard it, and it was like a slap across the face. I heard it, and it was just like a screech. I was very glad that I had the opportunity to read it [the module]. Next semester, I'll be student-teaching and I know I'll have it as a top priority, something to conquer.

While several WEEA projects have attempted to incorporate sex equity into inservice teacher preparation, the Non-Sexist Teacher Education Project has been the major preservice WEEA endeavor to integrate sex equity content into teacher preparation courses. The material from this and other related teacher education projects has been incorporated into *Sex Equity Handbook for Schools* (Sadker & Sadker, 1982), which is in use in a number of the nation's colleges. Although originally designed for preservice teacher education, the *Handbook* and its accompanying *Guide for Sex Equity Training* provide the material for inservice teacher education programs as well. WEEA has also supported scores of other teacher training projects, most of which are designed for inservice teacher education. Many focus on specific curriculum areas and will be discussed in subsequent chapters.

RECOMMENDATIONS

The following are recommendations for integrating sex equity issues into teacher education programs so that teachers will attain knowledge and skills for effective instruction of both male and female students.

Postsecondary Teacher Education Programs

Step 1: Self-evaluation.   Review education policies and practices to ensure that sex bias and discrimination are not part of ongoing teacher education activities. This institutional self-evaluation should include, but not be limited to, a review and plan to correct any sex bias found in

a. curricular materials, syllabi, and textbooks;
b. recruitment, employment, promotion, and tenure practices;
c. administrative and committee assignments;
d. brochures, policy statements, student-teacher evaluation forms, and so forth;
e. the enrollment of male and female students in graduate and undergraduate programs;
f. institutional compliance with Title IX and other antidiscrimination laws and regulations.

Step 2: Remediation and Integration.   Schools and departments of education should correct any forms of bias found as a result of these self-evaluations.

This remediation can be accomplished through the establishment of revised policies and practices, the actions of standing committees, or the formation of special task forces or ad hoc committees. Selected objectives that should be addressed include

a. ensuring that information concerning Title IX and antidiscrimination legislation is disseminated to education faculty and students;
b. integrating sex equity information into the mainstream of teacher education courses and programs, including a knowledge of the history and contributions of women to education, studies of sex differences, strategies for identifying and revising sex bias in K-12 curricular materials, and so forth;
c. providing inservice training to teacher educators to ensure that they are knowledgeable about and skilled in sex equity issues;
d. developing and implementing specialized courses dealing with sex equity and education and encouraging students to choose these topics for theses, dissertations, and research papers.

Step 3: Skills Training.   Effective teacher education programs are marked by clinical components. Knowledge of effective instructional strategies must be translated into behaviors in order to be successful. Therefore, departments and schools of education should

a. revise methods of teaching, microteaching clinics, and other skills development courses to ensure the inclusion of sex-equitable teaching skills;
b. modify student teaching evaluation forms, seminars, and supervisory sessions to include sex equity concerns;
c. provide inservice training to teacher education faculty members to ensure that their own teaching demonstrates and models sex equity;
d. provide inservice training to inservice teachers and supervisors in local school districts to promote knowledge of and skills in sex equity.

Step 4: Research and Development.   Aside from preparing and retraining teachers, schools and departments of education should provide leadership in developing new frontiers of knowledge related to educational issues. To this end, teacher educators should encourage graduate-level research into the nature and impact of sex bias and sex discrimination, as well as rigorous assessments of the efficacy of proposed treatments.

Teacher Accreditation Agencies

As part of their accreditation function, these agencies should

1. develop and incorporate sex equity knowledge and skills into both basic and advanced teacher certification standards, which should include direct and

substantive sex equity requirements at both the knowledge and the skills level;

2. insure that accreditation review teams include individuals with expertise in the area of combating sexism in education;

3. develop and implement standards to ensure equal opportunity employment in schools/departments of education.

Federal and State Agencies

Federal and state agencies should

1. support the research, development, and implementation of accreditation guidelines and course requirements which are responsive to problems of sex bias and discrimination in education;

2. ensure that federal and state standards, boards, and related educational committees include individuals with expertise in sex equity;

3. support inservice sex equity training for supervisors, teachers, and particularly teacher educators at institutions of higher education;

4. fund and utilize research efforts to explore the nature and impact of sex bias in education, the nature of sex differences, and the development of new strategies and technologies to combat sexism in teacher education;

5. promote procedures for teacher evaluation and tenure decisions which incorporate criteria related to sex equity.

Teacher Education Textbook Publishers

As purveyors of classroom materials, textbook publishers should

1. provide a balanced and accurate portrayal of contributions women have made to education and, when pertinent, to related fields;

2. provide a balanced and accurate portrayal of the barriers that have confronted women in gaining access to and equal treatment in the educational process;

3. provide an analysis of the issue of sexism in its current educational and social context;

4. offer curricular and instructional strategies and resources to help future teachers create sex-fair classrooms;

5. provide an up-to-date, accurate, and comprehensive analysis of the research on sex differences;.

6. integrate information on women, sexism, and related issues throughout the text rather than segregating these issues in separate inserts or sections;

7. provide equitable representation of females and males in illustrative materials;

8. avoid promoting sex bias through use of sexist language;

9. portray characters who exhibit a full range of behaviors, abilities, values,

and roles, and who avoid assumptions and generalizations that reflect sex role stereotypes.

At this point, the integration of sex equity into teacher education is more hope than reality. But it is essential that aspiration be translated into daily practice. As a recent editorial in the *Journal of Teacher Education* (Sadker, Sadker, & Hicks, 1980) stated:

> We cannot afford to prepare another generation of teachers who will be likely to promote rather than eliminate sex bias. The loss of human potential is too great. Sex equity in teacher preparation must be a priority for this decade.

REFERENCES

Antonucci, T. (1980). The need for female role models in education. In S. Bilken & M. Brannigan (Eds.), *Women and educational leadership* (pp. 64–89). Lexington, MA: Lexington Books.

Dallmann, M. et al. (1974). *The teaching of reading* (4th ed., p. 370). New York: Holt, Rinehart, & Winston.

Girard, K. et al. (1981). Unpublished research study, University of Massachusetts.

Gollnick, D. (1979). Comparative study of multicultural teacher education in teacher corps and other institutions. Washington, DC: American Association of Colleges for Teacher Education.

Howe, F. (1973). Introduction: The teacher and the women's movement. In N. Frazier & M. Sadker (Eds.), *Sexism in school and society*. New York: Harper & Row.

Howe, F. (1979). The first decade of women's studies. *Harvard Educational Review, 49,* 413–421.

Kimmel, E. (1980). On empowering women. *Changing times: Sex desegregation and American education* (pp. 17–26). (Monograph). Bloomington: Indiana University, School of Education.

Lather, P. (1981). Reeducating educators: Sex equity in teacher education. *Educational Horizons, 60*(1), 38–40.

Lather, P. (1984). Update on women's studies courses in teacher education. Bloomington: Indiana University, School of Education. In preparation.

McCune, S., & Matthews, M. (1975). Women's studies and teacher education: Actuality and potential, *Journal of Teacher Education, 26,* 340–344.

McCune, S., Matthews, M., & Earle, J. (1978). Teacher education: A new set of goals. In *Taking sexism out of education* (OE 77–01017) (pp. 68–79). Washington, DC: Department of Health, Education, and Welfare.

National Advisory Council on Women's Educational Programs. (1981). *Women's education: The challenge of the 80's* (Sixth Annual Report). Washington, DC: author.

National Association of State Directors of Teacher Education and Certification. (1979). *Standards for State approval of teacher education.* Salt Lake City, UT: author.

National Council for Accreditation of Teacher Education (NCATE). (1979). *Standards for accreditation of teacher education.* Washington DC: author.

National Council for Accreditation of Teacher Education. (1980). *Annual Report* (p. 7). Washington, DC: author.

Rubin, D. (1975). *Teaching elementary language arts.* New York: Holt, Rinehart, & Winston.

Sadker, M., & Sadker, D. (1980). *Beyond pictures and pronouns: Sexism in teacher education textbooks.* Newton, MA: EDC/WEEA Publishing Center.

Sadker, M., & Sadker, D. (1982). *Sex equity handbook for schools.* New York: Longman.

Sadker, M., Sadker, D., & Hicks, T. (1980). Sex equity in teacher preparation: A priority for the eighties. *Journal of Teacher Education, 31*(3), 3.

Stake, B., & Stake, R. (1980). *Non-sexist teacher education project field trial: Evaluation report.* Urbana: University of Illinois, College of Education.

Tobias, S. (1978). Women's studies: Its origins, its organization, and its prospects. *Women's Studies International Quarterly, 1,* 85–97.

Woolever, R. (1981, November 20). *Sex equity in teacher education.* Paper presented at the annual conference of the National Council for the Social Studies, Detroit.

PART III

General Educational Practices for Promoting Sex Equity

Patricia B. Campbell

In education there are a number of general practices that cut across both content area and grade level. These practices are generally seen as the framework on which schooling is built. The three most basic and most important of these areas are educational testing, classroom climate, and instructional materials. The following section takes each of these three areas and examines them, from a research perspective, in terms of how they are affected by both sex-biased and sex-equitable procedures. The chapters also describe how stereotyped and non-stereotyped educational practices influence education and those being educated.

The following assumptions are common to the three chapters composing this section:

1. Structures of the larger society are reproduced in the schools
2. Sex-equitable general educational practices can be created, and
3. Sex-equitable general educational practices have at best positive, and at worst neutral, effects on students

Using a research base, these assumptions are presented and examined in each of the three areas: educational testing, classroom climate, and instructional materials.

In chapter 10, Diamond and Tittle discuss, from a historical perspective, how testing reflected stereotypes about women and men in item content and in the interpretation of test results. They also cover ways that testing has changed due to the influence both of Title IX and of those researchers working to make testing more sex equitable and more accurate.

Lockheed, in chapter 11, discusses sex inequities in coeducational class-room organization and climate and describes efforts to reduce the negative effects of these sex inequities. Like Diamond and Tittle, she shows that the class-room is frequently a microcosm of the larger society with its segregation of the

163

sexes and male preeminence, but that with effort, these patterns can be changed to make the classroom a more equitable place.

In chapter 12, Scott and Schau examine the effects of gender-related characteristics of instructional materials on students. Specifically, they discuss how sex-biased language distorts perceptions of reality and how sex-equitable materials affect students' attitudes about sex roles, motivation to learn, and comprehension.

While the organization of all three chapters is based on the three assumptions listed earlier, there are some major differences as well. Instructional materials was the first major topic area studied in regard to sex stereotyping in education. Many studies were done documenting the preponderance of boys and men in instructional materials and the severe stereotyping of roles. Somewhere over 50 different sets of guidelines were developed by researchers, activists, publishers, and some states to reduce stereotyping in instructional materials. This topic has been paid much attention, has generated much controversy and is based upon much somewhat methodologically unsophisticated descriptive research.

Testing has also been extensively studied in terms of stereotyping and bias, but from a different perspective than instructional materials. The emphasis has been on influences on test scores and on the effects of biased tests on both scores and decision making. Research has, in general, been somewhat technical in nature (for example, comparisons of the effects of dual- versus single-sex norms) and has been somewhat removed from public discussion. Charges about feminist censorship are regularly made about work in instructional materials; rarely is anything said about effects of or efforts to rectify sex bias in testing. As Diamond and Tittle indicate, tremendous changes have occurred in testing in the past 10 years that have made it more equitable and more accurate. These changes, while in all probability more far-reaching than the changes in instructional materials, have occurred without much public knowledge.

The third area, classroom climate, is quite different from the other two. Although it is perhaps the most influential of the general educational practices, little attention has been paid to this area and little research has been done on the effects of stereotyping on classroom climate. No specific legislation has highlighted this area. Title IX regulations specifically cover biased testing and specifically exclude instructional materials. However, legislation in states such as New Jersey, Massachusetts, and California does prohibit sex-biased instructional materials. Although the general wording of Title IX may be interpreted as including nondiscrimination in classroom interactions, no legislation has tried to deal specifically with this general educational practice. The lack of both research and specific legislation means that this area has essentially been ignored. Lockheed has, however, pulled together the small amount of research that has been done and the programs that have been established to demonstrate the importance of this area and the need to pay it the attention it deserves.

While the major emphasis of this section is on the effects of sex-biased and sex-equitable educational practices on students, there is a second emphasis as well. Stereotypes in classroom climate, instructional materials, and, most importantly, educational testing can have a strong biasing effect on research and can lead to inaccurate research results. For example, male superiority in some types of mathematics may be due to test items that favor boys (such as objective items, items with males featured, items dealing with mechanics), a classroom climate where boys receive more opportunities to do mathematics and get more feedback on their efforts, instructional materials that present boys as skilled in mathematics and females as not, or some combination of the above. Yet these variables are rarely considered in research on sex differences. In each of the chapters, the authors bring out a number of findings that may have long-range implications not just for research on sex differences and sex stereotyping but on the design and interpretation of educational research in general.

While the emphasis of this section and, indeed, of the book, is sex equity in education, Scott and Schau remind us in chapter 12 that other areas of bias such as race, ethnicity, age, handicapping condition, and religious preference are of equal importance with sex bias and are usually combined with it. Although these areas are not dealt with in any depth in this section, they are factors in studies of sex bias and need to be considered. As Scott and Schau comment, the issues and answers are frequently very similar across areas of bias. Although they are specifically discussing instructional materials, their comments hold as well in testing and classroom climate, where issues of bias toward and isolation of minorities are critical. Also, it is clear that there can be no real sex equity in education while bias and unequal treatment in education exist based on characteristics such as ethnic background or religion.

In general, the tone of this section is quite positive. Although, as the initial assumptions imply, general educational practices have not been equitable in the past, during the last 12 years there have been many positive changes in all three areas. Although much more research needs to be conducted and changes need to be institutionalized on a long-term basis, preliminary results appear to indicate that these changes are having positive effects on students.

The following chapters are excellent summaries of where we have been and where we may be going. They may depress you or fill you with elation; however, they will inform you and will further your thinking about sex equity in education.

10
Sex Equity in Testing

Esther E. Diamond and Carol Kehr Tittle

Sex equity in education and educational research is not possible unless there is also sex equity in the educational and psychological measurements used to generalize from research findings and to make educational and vocational decisions about women and men. Examples of such uses are admission to particular school programs and to institutions of higher education, and counseling students about their educational and vocational plans.

The regulations for Title IX of the Education Amendments of 1972, which prohibit discrimination on the basis of sex in educational programs or activities supported by federal funds, forbid discrimination in the use of appraisal and counseling materials. Specific prohibitions include use of numerical limitations and biased tests that favor one sex or the other and admission policies that discriminate on the basis of marital or parental status (Department of Health, Education, and Welfare, 1975).

Despite these specific regulations for Title IX, sex bias in testing remains a highly controversial issue far from resolution, largely because we are still learning about its nature and effects. This chapter will deal with sex equity in tests of achievement, developed abilities, and interests because tests in these areas are most common in making educational and vocational decisions. They also represent the areas most commonly criticized for sex bias in testing. And because sex bias in testing has consequences for decisions affecting women to a far greater extent than is true of men, the main emphasis will be on bias affecting women.

The question of bias in tests is raised when two or more groups—for example, females and males—respond differently to the test items. The differences found in most tests of general abilities, aptitudes, and achievement depend largely on the mix of items included in the tests. A word of caution is appropriate when examining studies of sex differences in test performance. As Hyde (1981) points out, "well established" gender differences have come to be equated with "large" or "sizable" gender differences. Hyde applied meta-analysis to the studies cited by Maccoby and Jacklin and found that gender differences accounted for only 1% of the variance in verbal ability and general ability, 4% in visual-spatial ability, and about $2\frac{1}{2}$% in visual-analytic spatial ability. These differences were too small to account for the differences in the occupational distributions of females and males in engineering and comparable fields traditionally dominated by males. In 1978, for example, women accounted for only 1.5% of the total labor force of engineers, and in 1979 women were only 10.8% of the Ph.D. labor force in science and engineering (Vetter, 1981). Hyde also expressed concern about the tendency of many counselors to give undue weight to these differences in the vocational counseling of students.

DEFINING SEX BIAS IN TESTING: ISSUES AND ANSWERS

The terms *bias* and *fairness* have often been used as though they are flip sides of the same coin. Currently, however, the consensus seems to be to view bias as referring to the intrinsic characteristics of a test—content, the construct or constructs the test is supposedly measuring, and the context within which the content is embedded, while *unfairness* refers to ethical questions involving use of the test results. Bias is considered to occur when two individuals of equal ability but from different groups respond differently to a test item and therefore do not have the same probability of success on the item.

Other Definitions

Other definitions of sex bias have been closely tied to the methods of detecting its existence. One such method is judgmental. In one aspect of this method, a test is considered biased if the number of characters or referents of one sex exceeds the number represented by the other sex and if the roles of the characters are presented stereotypically—for example, if girls are consistently portrayed as being passive, timid, and compliant, while boys are adventurous, active, innovative, and good at solving problems. Cole (1981) pointed out the necessity for considering another aspect of judgmental bias detection—judgment involving item content that is irrelevant to the intended construct but that might elicit different responses to items from different groups such as females and males, or minority groups. Still other methods define and detect bias statistically.

Sources of Sex Bias in Testing

Definitions of sex bias (as distinguished from unfairness) cannot be considered apart from the sources of that bias. Anastasi (1973) discussed the role of social expectancy in female-male differences in test performance. Closer identification with the masculine sex role among both men and women is associated with superior problem-solving skill, which is critical in tests of mathematical reasoning. Individuals exhibiting more dependency and social conformity have been shown to be less successful in breaking a set of restructuring elements in problem solving. Traditional female experience and role models, Anastasi reasoned, may have encouraged greater dependency and social conformity among girls in our culture than among boys.

Many of the differences between men and women in test performance have been attributed to differences in the socialization process; exposure to different sets of experiences; different attitudes and expectations on the part of parents, teachers, and other school personnel; encouragement to take certain courses and reject others; and career expectations that follow stereotypical lines. Test content often reflects experiences that traditional social roles have closed to women or discouraged them from exploring. Often the item pool in an area traditionally considered one in which males are dominant tends to be based on male experiences or to use male referents. Many women, for example, have not been exposed to such tasks as blueprint reading or understanding how a carburetor works. Yet, understanding the spatial relations between parts of a pattern may well require skills highly similar to those involved in blueprint reading, and understanding how a sewing machine works may involve the kinds of concepts involved in understanding how a carburetor works.

SEX DIFFERENCES AND SEX EQUITY
IN ACHIEVEMENT TESTS

There is no single piece of evidence that permits test users to decide that a test is sex-fair. Many of the procedures used to evaluate sex-fairness also apply to the study of test bias against minority or ethnic groups. Three of these procedures are described here. The first, most direct procedure examines the test content for instances of sex role stereotyping and for the fair representation of women. The second examines whether females and males performed differently on achievement test items. The third examines the influences on, or variables related to, sex differences in performance. Thus, the first review of items for stereotyping has to do with what may be called the face validity or apparent fairness of the test for females and males. It is also concerned to some extent with the content validity of tests—that women are represented equitably in history, science, literature, and so on. Both the second and third approaches are concerned with the content and construct vadidity of tests—the accuracy of inferences about students on the basis of test scores. To the extent that sex differences appear on test items that are irrelevant to the content or construct to be measured, the validity of the items is in question.

The effect of sex-fairness in the representation of women may or may not be reflected in achievement test performance. Whether content that is biased or unrepresentative in this sense affects performance is irrelevant to the larger issue of fairness of representation. A basic principle of justice holds that test content should be representative and face valid. Efforts to examine item or test bias from a statistical or experimental viewpoint also have an important role in the procedures to eliminate sex bias and provide a sex-fair test. The discussion below and the studies cited are based on standardized, norm-referenced tests. However, the research, issues, and policies are also applicable to criterion- or domain-referenced tests, to minimum competency or basic skills tests, to computer-administered tests, and to tests constructed by teachers for use in the classroom.

Judgments of Stereotyping and Representation

An earlier review of the portrayal of women in educational achievement tests provided this summary:

> Women are portrayed almost exclusively as homemakers or in the pursuit of hobbies (e.g., "Mrs. Jones, the President of the Garden Club . . ."). Young girls carry out "female chores" (e.g., father helps Betty and Tom build a playhouse. When it is completed, "Betty sets out dishes on the table, while Tom carries in the chairs . . ."). (Tittle, McCarthy, & Steckler, 1974, p. 22)

Recent reviews of item pools for standardized tests show that it is difficult to change this image. Although publishers now use guidelines emphasizing representation of women in a wide variety of occupational and family roles, items, particularly in reading passages, may still present women as witches (with no warlocks in evidence) or describe well-known males more frequently than well-known females. Thus, the use of guidelines and review procedures is required every time a test is developed or selected for local use. Category systems for reviewing tests for bias are described in Tittle (1982). Diamond (1980) described the current activities of publishers in attaining sex equity in the representation of women in achievement tests. Selkow (in press) has provided an analysis of sex bias in commonly used intelligence, personality, and special education tests and has suggested guidelines and forms for reviewing tests for sex bias.

Item Content and Performance

While it is not argued here that attaining sex equity in test content alone will affect the performance of females or males on achievement test items, it should be noted that there is some research literature that supports this relationship. (See Donlon, Ekstrom, & Lockheed, 1979; Medley & Quirk, 1974; and Milton, 1959.) Balanced against this evidence, however, are a series of studies that have not identified a relationship between items on which there were different performances by females and males and the apparent sex stereotyping or female/male orientation of the items. (For example, see Plake, Hoover, & Loyd, 1978.)

McCarthy (1975), however, found more systematic differences in performance on test items for which the context or setting was judged to be more familiar to females, males, or equally familiar to each. She used a sample of high school students in grades 10 to 12 and mathematics content. She constructed an item pool, varying the item context and holding the mathematical processes constant. Her results were in line with the general trend in the research literature toward no sex differences in math performance in the early grades and some findings of sex differences in the later, high school grade levels.

The role of the sample and/or item specifications in producing sex-related differences in test performance has been explored by Dwyer (1979), who used as one example the history of sex differences in scores on the verbal and mathematical sections of the Scholastic Aptitude Test. Although experimental evidence for performance differences linked to sex-typing of items is mixed, educational achievement tests equitable to both sexes can and should be developed. This is done by using judges to review test content and by the use of item bias detection techniques. Both the judgmental and statistical procedures are extensively described in a series of papers edited by Berk (1982).

Factors Influencing Performance

This section will briefly examine some of the test-related issues in findings of sex differences in performance on measures in mathematics. These issues are related to the construct validity of tests and the inferences made about differences in performance. A basic assumption in comparing individuals or groups categorized by fixed characteristics such as sex or ethnic or minority group membership is that persons taking the test have had an opportunity to learn the process and content assessed by the test item. Further, there are assumptions that individuals have similar motivation, practice in taking tests, and so on. Thus, if there are differences in performance, this is often interpreted to mean that the differences cannot be changed.

These assumptions have been tested in research and have not been supported. For example, in mathematics sex differences in performance have been shown to be related to number of years of coursework. One such study used a sample of 2,093 students drawn from all Washington State high school juniors taking a precollege test battery in 1973 (de Wolf, 1981). Males took significantly more coursework in three mathematics areas (algebra, geometry, and advanced mathematics) and physics. They also scored higher than females on the six subtests of the test battery studied: four tests of quantitative skills, applied mathematics, and mathematics achievement; a measure of spatial ability, the ability to visualize transformations in three dimensions; and a measure of mechanical reasoning, the ability to understand physical principles as applied to mechanical devices. After controlling for the amount of coursework taken, sex differences disappeared on two of the four quantitative tests and on the test of spatial ability. Although item context was not examined for the other two tests, it was suggested as a possible reason for the remaining differences. Wise (1979) suggests that long-term career outcomes for women are influenced by sex differences in high school math courses taken.

Carlson (described by Cole, 1978) examined items categorized by content on the science achievement test of the International Association for the Evaluation of Educational Achievement (IEA). Sex differences in science achievement were reported: Boys did better on an "understanding" item involving how to put batteries in a flashlight. Girls did better on an "understanding" item about how to place a jar under hot water to get the lid off.

Thus, in both science and mathematics, research suggests that the opportunity to learn through coursework or sex-differentiated activities plays an important role. To the extent that opportunity to learn differs for the sexes out of school, then inferences about sex differences in ability or achievement are inaccurate. Educationally relevant variables—courses taken, attitudes, and motivation, all of which are amenable to intervention—should be related to achievement test scores, not to a fixed characteristic such as gender. To the degree that an educationally irrelevant variable such as gender correlates with test scores, the scores may be biased. We should be able to specify the educational and psychological variables that are of concern to schools. The schools cannot change an individual's gender, but sex equity has as one of its meanings eliminating sex as a predictor variable in educational and psychological research.

A study by Benbow and Stanley (1980) illustrates the problem with identifying gender as a causal variable in sex differences in test scores. Studies of mathematically gifted children have identified more males than females as highly gifted, but little account is taken of the educational and psychological variables that may be relevant—for example, parental attitudes toward gifted boys and girls, opportunities provided by the family and educational institutions, and peer attitudes and socialization pressures. The inference is made that differences based on test scores are fixed or genetic in origin, thus reinforcing common stereotypes of women and their lack of ability to achieve in mathematics. Such inferences are not directly substantiated by genetic evidence, and they impede efforts to educate the gifted of both genders and to understand the process of mathematical achievement. Of greater value would be an analysis of the types of items such highly gifted students pass and fail and development of hypotheses describing psychological variables related to test performance.

Summary

Studies of achievement tests have included judgments of stereotyping and representation of women, item content and sex differences in performance, and factors influencing performance. Almost all major test publishers now try to minimize stereotyping and to examine sex differences in responses to items. Research continues on factors influencing the performance of females and males, particularly on the relationship of experience in activities and opportunities to learn such subjects as mathematics and science.

Critical areas for school review of achievement tests for bias and for future research are identified below.

Recommendations for Use

1. Review standardized, domain-referenced, and minimum competency tests and a sample of locally written (classroom) tests for freedom from sex role

stereotyping and for fair representation of females and males in test items, reading passages, and illustrations.

2. Help teachers and others responsible for classroom materials to write tests that are free of sex role stereotyping and that represent activities and occupations as being open to both sexes. Use guidelines for nonsexist writing.

3. Review achievement test results for sex differences in performance. Do females and males score similarly, on the average? If there are differences, the items can be examined to locate those that have different proportions of females and males answering correctly.

4. At the high school level, there should be a review of score differences in areas such as mathematics and science. Are differences due to a few items that are apparently not sex-fair in context? Or are differences due to fewer females taking mathematics or science courses? School policy should be concerned with achieving sex equity in these areas.

Recommendations for Research

1. Further study is needed of the factors influencing performance of females and males on items in specific content areas. Such studies could include process or think-aloud studies on items or item types where there are substantial or consistent differences.

2. Further study is needed with tests such as the National Assessment of Educational Progress, where unusual item response formats are used (for example, the response "I don't know," which groups, including women, appear to interpret and use differently).

3. Study of the item pools in statewide minimum competency tests is needed, since few reports are available on their freedom from sex role stereotyping, their affirmative representation of women, or the item performance of groups such as boys, girls, blacks, Hispanics, and whites.

SEX DIFFERENCES AND SEX EQUITY IN TESTS OF DEVELOPED ABILITIES

Different issues arise in the construction and use of tests of developed abilities, or aptitude tests, at both the secondary and the postsecondary levels. The discussion is separated for the two levels because of differences in test use.

Aptitude measures are more homogeneous in item content than measures of general ability (intelligence), are assumed to be less linked to defined educational curricula and experiences than are achievement measures, and are designed to predict student performance at the secondary level in specific vocationally related areas such as clerical, mechanical, art, or music. At the postsecondary level they are used to predict success in college (typically, first-year grade-point averages) or success in professional schools, for example law, medicine, or business. A basic assumption is made in using aptitude measures to predict later academic or professional school performance. The assumption is that the experiences of different groups have been to some considerable degree common. In order to make the same inferences from test scores, it is assumed that females and males have had similar opportunities, experiences, activities, and so on. Any differences in performance that occur on aptitude tests are thus a reflection of differences in abilities developed to that point in time. This assumption is clearly untenable for girls in the mechanical area, for example, and sometimes for boys in tests of verbal ability or perceptual speed and accuracy. Research has not been able to separate clearly in any test score for an individual the extent to which experience and "ability" are reflected in test performance.

Secondary Level: Vocational Aptitude Measures

Vocational aptitude measures have two main uses at the secondary level: (1) early in the secondary school years, to select students or to assist students in selecting specific vocational programs such as shop or business; and (2) at any stage in secondary school, to encourage students to explore vocations for which their aptitude scores, interests, and experiences suggest they might be successful. The first use emphasizes the prediction of how well the student will perform in a specific vocational training program or later occupational placement. The second use includes the comparison of the student's scores with those of individuals who have been successful in a training program or occupation. Differential prediction is needed when there is more than one aptitude measure and when two or more vocational or occupational (criterion) groups are considered at the same time. That is, evidence is needed that the aptitude measures discriminate among profiles or scores for successful workers or trainees in different occupations.

Two vocational aptitude tests are frequently used in secondary schools. The most commonly used is the Armed Services Vocational Aptitude Battery (ASVAB); the other is the Differential Aptitude Test (DAT) Battery. The ASVAB yields six composite scores in high school reports: Verbal, Math, Perceptual Speed, Mechanical, Trade Technical, and Academic Ability (Wilfong, 1980). One of the major criticisms of the ASVAB has been that some tests are apparently sex-linked in experience, particularly Shop Information and Automotive Information (which enter into some of the reported score composites). They would thus provide little indication of the ability of girls to learn information in these or related areas and are likely to be misleading if thought of as predictors of performance in vocational courses. (See also the comments by Cronbach, 1978, 1981, on this test).

The DAT provides eight scores: Verbal Reasoning, Numerical Ability, Abstract Reasoning, Clerical Speed and Accuracy, Mechanical Reasoning, Space Relations, Spelling, and Language Usage. The tests show predictive validity with high school course grades, but "the results are somewhat less encouraging with regard to differential prediction. . . . There is evidence of a large general factor underlying performance in all academic work" (Anastasi, 1982, p. 378). Sex differences on the DAT are found for average scores on the Clerical, Spelling, Language Usage, and Mechanical Reasoning tests, with girls obtaining higher scores on the first three and boys obtaining higher scores on the last. The DAT reports separate sex norms for every test in the battery. For tests such as Mechanical Reasoning, girls with a high standing on girls' norms will not have as high a percentile rank on the norms for boys. The provision of two sets of norms can be used by counselors to explore with both girls and boys the relationship between experiences—particularly if individual students appear to have sex-typed activity experiences—and scores on the two sets of norms reported to students. (Similar comments apply to the ASVAB.) Unless the distributions of raw scores are essentially the same for boys and girls, separate sex norms should be available for interpreting test scores. When raw score distributions are the same, combined sex norms (a single norms table) should be used for both females and males.

Given the present set of data on both the ASVAB and the DAT, their best use is in counseling settings where options are not closed off and where students are encouraged to explore new experiences related to some of the tests. Of great concern is the use of aptitude measures to place students in particular vocational courses. Test validity, using a prediction approach, must be established, either from the publisher's data or from local data. Prediction studies should analyze and report data for each sex. Such data are especially needed when tests provide evidence of adverse impact—that is, when the effect of using tests in selection is that proportionally fewer females than males who apply are admitted to particular vocational courses.

Postsecondary Level: Admissions Testing

At the postsecondary level, tests of developed abilities or aptitudes are often used to select students for a particular college or professional school program. Among the better-known admissions tests are the American College Testing Program (ACT) and the Scholastic Aptitude Test (SAT). Since forms are continually developed and changed, with several test administrations each year, it is difficult to review these tests. Earlier versions showed sex stereotyping, but the testing programs have instituted internal review procedures to minimize this source of bias. There is no recent evidence available from outside review of these tests. Lockheed (1982) reviewed the evidence for sex bias in tests used in postsecondary education and concluded that there is little or no support for claims of bias.

Another issue with tests used in selection is whether the selection procedure is fair to both men and women. The regulations for Title IX of the Education Amendments of 1972 include Section 106.21, which prohibits discrimination on the basis of sex in admissions to institutions that receive federal funding. Fewer analyses of college admissions tests have included examination of males and females than of minority groups (Wild & Dwyer, 1980). Angoff (1971) reported higher predictive validity coefficients for women, against criteria of first-year grades. Ekstrom (1972) has suggested that the use of tests is among the institutional ways in which barriers are raised to women's postsecondary education (for example, higher SAT scores are required for women than for men at some institutions). Virtually no systematic data are available to provide evidence for or against this issue.

One of the few recent studies that examined within-group correlations and regression equations for females and males was conducted for the SAT and a "performance" criterion of essay scores (Breland & Griswold, 1981). Correlation patterns were similar for the sexes, and the slopes of the regression lines were parallel. Tests of the coincidence of the lines (the intercepts) tended to differ, however. The practical implication is that if a common regression equation (based on both females and males) is used in the admissions process, female scores on the criterion are underpredicted. That is, their actual scores on the criterion are higher than predicted. Using a common regression line and selection score means that fewer females would be admitted than males, despite their actual performance on the criterion.

The foregoing comments rely on one model—the standard regression line, which systematically over- or underpredicts criterion scores for members of a particular group. If the regression equations are not identical (if there are different intercepts), use of the common regression line to select students with the highest criterion scores is considered unfair. (See Cole, 1981, for a summary of other proposed models.)

Summary

Fewer studies are available of the sex role stereotyping and representation of women (in illustrations, for example) in tests of developed abilities than in achievement tests. Earlier reviews indicate that a major issue is the extent to which the tests are in fact good predictors for women at the high school level or in the armed forces. This is of particular concern for the nontraditional skilled trades areas, where women's experiences may be limited. Use of same-sex norms can assist counselors in exploring with individual clients the usefulness of these scores. Little systematic study of differences in the use of admissions tests with females and males has been done, but the available studies indicate that the effects of such tests should be examined separately for men and women.

Recommendations for Use

1. For aptitude tests, as for achievement tests, test users need evidence that tests are free of sex role stereotypes and represent women fairly, that statistical item bias techniques have been used in test development, and that descriptions of the results of the item bias detection procedures are published.
2. The effects of tests used in counseling and selection for vocational programs and admissions to colleges and professional schools and programs also need to be examined. At a minimum, the proportions of females and males applying to colleges and other programs and the proportions of those admitted should be public information.

3. In the college and professional school admissions process, separate analyses should be presented to show the actual regression equation used and the equations for female and male groups. The separate regression equations should be compared for differences in slope and intercept. Educational institutions should be prepared to respond to requests for these data.

Recommendations for Research

1. A systematic review of the available studies, published and unpublished, on the comparability of regression equations used in college and professional school selection for females and males should be carried out.
2. The effects of using tests of developed abilities in vocational course placement at the high school level, and the predictive validity of these tests for females and males, need study.
3. Where tests of developed abilities show large sex differences, it may be useful to study the process used by females and males in responding to such items. The researcher should consider obtaining estimates from students of the extent to which they can identify experiences or activities that may have helped or hindered them in responding to such items.

SEX DIFFERENCES AND SEX EQUITY IN INTEREST MEASUREMENT

Holland, Magoon, and Spokane (1981) described interest inventories as perhaps the most popular form of vocational assistance. Nevertheless, since the early 1970s interest inventories have been at the heart of a controversy regarding their sex-fairness. Sex bias and sex-fairness in career interest measurement have been dealt with at length in Diamond (1975) and Tittle and Zytowski (1978). Fitzgerald and Crites (1980) described the issue of sex bias in interest measurement as "probably the most complex as well as the most controversial involved in career counseling with women" (p. 50).

Early History of Interest Measurement

The Carnegie Interest Inventory, the first published interest inventory, made its appearance in 1921. By 1939, Buros's *First Mental Measurements Yearbook* included reviews of 15 measures of vocational interest. Today there are approximately 80 interest inventories in use.

Until relatively recently, interest inventories—particularly those with empirically built scales based on the responses of occupational criterion groups—focused mainly on male interests. Women were generally expected to marry and raise families. Those who worked outside the home were employed mainly in low-level, dead-end jobs that non-career-oriented women held until marriage and, often, after their children entered school.

The early work of vocational development theorists such as Ginzberg, Ginsburg, Axelrad, and Herma (1951) and Super et al. (1957) focused almost entirely on the vocational development of males. Not until the early 1970s did

Ginzberg (1972) pay attention to the career development and occupational choices of women and recognize that the male model of preparation and choice did not fit the female prototype; the career development of most women was marked by frequent shifts between home and work. Ginzberg also became aware that both the educational system and the world of work discriminated against women, as well as against minorities. Only recently has the role of interest inventories been perceived as that of a catalyst that can help men and women consider a wider spectrum of occupations, both traditional and nontraditional, and that hopefully will change the inequitable occupational distribution. Inventory results can suggest the wisdom of acquiring some exploratory experience in areas that earlier may have been closed off to the counselee in some way. A woman who has had no experience with scientific and mechanical activities, or even a chance to explore them in a very general way, cannot be expected to score high in those areas. The same would be true for a man with little social service or nurturing experience.

It is apparent from research studies that the stereotyping of occupations is a virulent condition that persists at all age levels, even among preschool and elementary school children, despite concerted efforts to minimize or eliminate it. (See, for example, Marini, 1978; Teglasi, 1981; and chapter 18 in this handbook, "Sex Equity in Career and Vocational Education," by Farmer & Sidney.)

Recent Changes and Current Concerns

The women's movement of the early 1970s caused the development of the National Institute of Education's Guidelines for the Assessment of Sex Bias and Sex-Fairness in Career Interest Measurement (Diamond, 1975), and the following working definition:

> Within the context of career guidance, sex bias is defined as any factor that might influence a person to limit—or might cause others to limit—his or her consideration of a career solely on the basis of gender. (p. xxiii)

These guidelines, together with the work of the Commission on Sex Bias in Measurement of the Association for Measurement and Evaluation in Guidance, led to dramatic changes in some of the most commonly used interest inventories. For example, the pink (for women) and blue (for men) forms of one inventory were combined into a single form with a single item pool. At least two empirically developed inventories began reporting scores on all scales to both sexes, regardless of the norm group on which the scales were developed. Occupational titles were made gender-free in most inventories where they appeared, and language was made gender-neutral. Both the Strong-Campbell Interest Inventory (SCII) and the Kuder Occupational Interest Survey (KOIS) expanded the number of scales normed on women.

Anastasi (1982) described three major changes in career counseling reflected by the more recently developed or revised inventories as (1) increasing emphasis on self-exploration, (2) increasing emphasis on expansion of career options, and (3) concern for sex-fairness of interest inventories.

With the pressures for changes in interest measurement, however, have come a number of controversial areas of concern. These are:

1. Same-Sex, Opposite-Sex, and Combined-Sex Norms. The concern for three ways of constructing and reporting norms stems from the fact that response rates for items in almost all inventories differ for males and females, even when they are in the same occupation. The problem is not identical for empirically developed occupational scales such as those in the SCII and the KOIS, and for homogeneous, internally constructed scales such as those in the Kuder Preference Record—Vocational and the Kuder General Interest Survey, the Self-Directed Search (SDS), and the ACT Interest Inventory. For homogeneous scales, as Prediger (1976) and others have found, both combined-sex norms and opposite-sex norms produce profiles that are widely divergent for males and females, whereas same-sex norms reflect the responses of people who have been subjected to similar socialization experiences. The Title IX regulations advocate scoring all inventories on both same-sex and opposite-sex norms (if scales have justifiably been developed separately by sex), so that respondents can see appropriate comparisons with both sexes and take these into consideration in educational and career exploration.

Attempts to use combined-sex norms with empirical scales work for some occupations, but not for others. For example, Hansen (1976) and Webber and Harmon (1978) experimented with same-sex scales with biased items (those that differentiated between the sexes) either deleted or retained, and with combined-sex scales with biased items either deleted or retained. None of the four methods was clearly superior in predicting across sexes or occupations. Campbell and Hansen (1981), reviewing the studies and adding some applications of their own, concluded that attempts to develop combined-sex scales appear to be premature, and that same-sex scales with biased items retained work best for the SCII.

Reporting scores on opposite-sex-normed occupational scales—particularly when an occupation has been normed on only one sex—seems to be relatively problem-free when the scale is based only on the responses of the criterion, or occupational, group—as in the KOIS. When response differences between the criterion group and a group of males or females in general are used as the basis for scale construction, however, as in the SCII, scores on other-sex norms tend to be inflated on traditional occupations for one's own sex and depressed on occupations that are nontraditional for one's own sex (Johnson, 1978; Laime & Zytowski, 1964). The reason is that members of one sex generally respond differently from a group made up of members of the other sex. For example, women typically endorse items that men in general do not endorse, and vice versa, and so they receive higher scores on scales that try to distinguish males or females in a given occupation from males or females in general. For this reason, Campbell and Hansen (1981) considered use of other-sex norms inadvisable with the SCII. Where this problem does not exist, however, as for example in the KOIS, scores on opposite-sex-normed scales can be ranked separately, and high scores can suggest occupations for which scales might not be available on own-sex norms.

2. Raw Scores versus Normed Scores.   An ongoing controversy about normed scores versus raw scores and the degree to which the latter may be sex-biased has been concerned mainly with the Self-Directed Search (SDS), which uses raw scores. (See Hanson, Noeth, & Prediger, 1978; Gottfredson & Holland, 1978; Prediger, 1981; and Holland, 1982.) Much journal space has been devoted to this issue. A larger concern, however, is whether, given that the Holland codes or scales are based on item endorsements that reflect the existing occupational distribution (with mainly men in, for example, Realistic occupations such as engineering and the skilled trades), the traditional predictive validity model is valid for women today or whether it simply helps perpetuate the existing occupational distribution. A meta-analysis by Prediger (1981) indicated a wide disparity between Holland codes for 1,417 women in a variety of occupations who had taken the SDS and their actual occupations. Fifty-four percent of the women scored higher on the code other than the appropriate one for their occupation. These classification errors were reduced to 31% when normed scores were used. Somewhat similar findings were obtained by Matthews and Walsh (1978), who found high-point Social codes on the SDS for nondegreed working women who had held jobs in Realistic, Investigative, Enterprising, and Conventional, as well as Social, occupations for 3 to 11 years.

3. Sex-balanced Scales.   Hanson and Rayman (1976) and Lunneborg (1980) attempted to develop item pools for the ACT Interest Inventory (ACT II) and the Vocational Interest Inventory, respectively, that elicited similar response rates from females and males, or—when this could not be accomplished—that balanced items favored by each sex within scales. Five of the six sex-balanced ACT II scales showed more than 90% overlap for males and females. However, Lunneborg found that despite the careful item selection based on approximately equal proportions of the sexes endorsing the items, women generally preferred the Service and Artistic areas and men the Technical, Outdoor, and Scientific areas. It should be noted that items in the Vocational Interest Inventory, Holland Vocational Preference Inventory, and Part I of the SCII are occupational titles. Stereotypical conceptions of occupations as "male" or "female" could influence scores on scales that use occupational titles rather than activities.

4. Predictive versus Exploration Validity.   Cole and Hanson (1975) described the two principal rationales that have been used to relate interest measurement to the criterion of job satisfaction: the people-similarity rationale, which links satisfaction to the degree of similarity between an individual's likes and dislikes and those of people in a given occupation, and the activity-similarity rationale, which links satisfaction to the degree of preference for activities similar to those required in an occupation. The people-similarity rationale relies heavily on a stable socialization process closely tied to the past; when the future follows a new direction, the empiricism of interest measurement impedes the path of constructive change. Researchers should be aware, however, that differences in the socialization of males and females raise questions about the activity-similarity rationale. The authors question whether the socialization process for girls predicts their job satisfaction as well as the socialization process for boys predicts theirs.

Tittle (1978) and others have suggested that the concept of "exploration validity" is perhaps more valid for women than is the traditional predictive validity model. That is, to what extent does an interest inventory stimulate the client to explore options that might otherwise not be explored?

5. *Effects of Interest Inventories.*   Concern about the effects of interest inventories is closely related to concerns about predictive and exploration validity. Studies of effects have been summarized by Tittle (1978) and Diamond (1981a). In general, the effects of interest inventories on client career perceptions and exploration behavior have been small and statistically insignificant, although there have been some impressive exceptions. For example, Siebel and Walsh (1977) found that modified SDS instructions, which permitted clients to express preference for activities to which they had had little or no exposure, resulted in significantly higher scores on certain subscales. Females tended to give an increased number of positive responses on traditionally masculine scales (Realistic, Investigative, and Enterprising), and males on traditionally feminine scales (Artistic, Social, and Conventional).

Wilson and Daniel (1981) used a combination of measures, including the Kuder General Interest Survey, Form E, in a middle-school workshop on career options. Pre-post differences on a stereotype survey were highly significant for the experimental group but not for the control group. The experimental group seemed more aware of events in their everyday environment, in which people had preconceptions about male and female roles.

For the most part, though, the impact of interest inventories on course choice and career-related decisions has been difficult to measure. Many variables are involved, most of them difficult to isolate or control—for example, influence of parents, schools, media, and even counselors. As Harmon (1973) pointed out concerning the 1969 revision of the Strong Vocational Interest Blank (SVIB) for Women: "The existence of a revised SVIB for women does not change the social facts. Only insofar as it reflects a wide spectrum of the occupations available and accents potential areas of conflict can it contribute to counseling women about their individual choices" (p. 85).

6. *Dual Interest Patterns.*   As members of each sex go into occupations that have traditionally been the turf of the opposite sex, dual interest patterns— that is, patterns that strongly resemble the traditional interests of both men and women—may well emerge. Rand (1968) found that career-oriented college freshman women scored significantly higher than homemaking-oriented women on 9 of 10 masculine characteristics related to interest, potential, achievement, and competencies; but they also scored higher on a number of feminine variables. Diamond found a similar phenomenon in interpreting KOIS profiles and in

examining criterion group KOIS profiles for score overlap on male-normed and female-normed scales (1981b). If we accept the premise, which is supported by empirical evidence, that people who work in an environment in which the interests of coworkers are congruent with their own will find greater satisfaction in their work (Campbell, 1971; Kuder & Diamond, 1979), dual interest patterns may cease to be an isolated phenomenon. Until now, male skilled workers, for example, generally shared with other males, in addition to on-the-job interests, interests in tradtional male sports and traditional male concerns. Female office workers and sales clerks tended to find their work more satisfying if, in addition to shared interests with other females in on-the-job activities, they also shared non-job-related interests and traditionally feminine concerns about home and family. As segregation of the sexes in the workplace diminishes and social roles change, more similar patterns of interest for females and males should result, representing the relevant interests of both.

   7. *Interest Measurement and Minority Women.*   As Gump and Rivers (1975) pointed out, there is not much in the way of validity data supporting the use of interest inventories with minority women, and there may in fact be a mismatch between the interest structures of minority women and those of the normative or criterion groups used. Thus, minority women may be subject to both sex and ethnic bias in interest inventories. Gump and Rivers suggested use of a measure of cultural exposure level as a moderator variable to enhance validity of interest inventories for minority women.

   8. *Interest Measurement and Handicapped Women.*   Two inventories for mildly retarded adults present a far more limited set of options for females than they do for males; no rationale for this is given. Little research is available on the use of interest inventories with other groups of women such as the gifted, those living in rural areas, and adult women (although see Denker & Tittle, 1976, for the perceived usefulness of an interest inventory with returning women).

Summary

   More changes have been made in interest measurement since the early 1970s, and more research has been done on the question of gender differences in interest inventory responses and the extent to which they contribute to sex inequities in education, than in the 50 years preceding. The problem of sex equity in interest measurement is, in many ways, more complex than in achievement or aptitude measurement. The effects of socialization, as reflected in the inventory results, are more pervasive, and effective interventions appear to be more difficult to design and the intervening variables harder to isolate and control. Moreover, it is difficult to tell to what extent the bias exists in the inventories themselves—the item content and context—and to what extent their results reflect the bias in society, including that of parents, schools, the media, and other societal influences. It may be a long time before the socialization process catches up with the social changes that have taken place at the legal, theoretical, and legislative levels. The recommendations that follow are offered with a view to speeding up that process as much as possible.

Recommendations for Use

1. Users of interest inventories should examine them for the extent to which they conform to Title IX and the NIE guidelines. For example, is the language of the items gender-free? Is the same form used for females and males? Do the items reflect experiences and activities that are familiar to both females and males? Are scores on all scales given to both sexes, regardless of the sex of the norm or criterion group? Are the language and activities in the items also free of bias or offensiveness toward ethnic and minority groups, handicapped groups, and older persons?
2. Users should also be sure that it is possible for members of both sexes to obtain high scores on scales that are nontraditional for their sex.
3. The spectrum of occupations or general interest areas should be broad enough to suggest a variety of feasible options for exploration.
4. The interpretive materials should deal with the subject of sex differences in the occupational distribution and possibly in inventory scores, and should suggest to those who have high scores only on traditional occupations that they might want to try out areas that are unfamiliar to them but in which they think they might be interested.
5. Training of counselors in the recognition of all aspects of sex bias in interest measurement and its interaction with sex role socialization is paramount. Counselors also need to be sensitive to their own biases.
6. Interest inventories should not be used only once—administered and put to rest after counselees have received their profiles. Instead, interest inventories should be part of a long-range, comprehensive educational and vocational intervention program, and should follow adequate orientation on the ways that interests relate to the world of work.
7. Intervention programs designed to broaden the interests of females and males should begin in the very early grades. Children should learn that there are no such things as "men's jobs" and "women's jobs" and that, given the requisite abilities and training, they can become anything they want to be.

Recommendations for Research

1. Further study is needed on the use of same-sex, combined-sex, and opposite-sex norms, for both homogeneous and occupational scales.
2. Research is needed on actual changes in response rates over time for items in sex-balanced scales as well as items in inventories where sex balance has not been achieved—by sex, age, and occupational field and level.
3. Research is needed to determine which differences in response rates between

the sexes are based on general female-male role differences and which are clearly related to what one does in a particular occupation.

4. Research is needed to determine whether removal of items of established validity favored by one sex and substitution of items favored by the other sex or equally endorsed by both might make the inventory more valid or less so. Researchers should consider the valid items as one sample of a behavior for which there should be a universe of possible samples, at least some of which could meet requirements of both validity and sex balance.

5. The implications of equal endorsement of items in homogeneous scales by females and males in a general norm group of students or adults need to be investigated. What happens when these items are administered to females and males in the same occupation? Are endorsement rates maintained?

6. Studies are needed of the long-range effects of sex-fair interest measurement embedded in a well-integrated intervention program, with maximum control and analysis of the multiple variables influencing career decisions.

7. Consideration should be given to the expansion of outcome criteria, as suggested by Tittle (1983), to include examination of other adult roles and developmental tasks as factors contributing to career decisions.

CONCLUSION

A question of social justice has been raised in reference to all educational and psychological measurement. Messick (1980) maintained that not only should tests be evaluated in terms of their measurement properties, but the use of tests should be evaluated in terms of potential social consequences.

As a matter of simple human justice, any aspect of any test that is offensive to members of a group should be eliminated routinely—whether or not it actually affects the way group members respond and whether the test is to be used for selection or other decisions about the respondent, or mainly for the respondent's own information, exploration, and decision making. This does not mean that test use should be exempt from the requirements of validity, but that the whole concept of valid test use in the context of sex equity needs to be reexamined along the lines suggested in this chapter.

REFERENCES

Anastasi, A. (1973). *Common fallacies about heredity, environment, and human behavior* (ACT Research Report No. 58). Iowa City: American College Testing Program.

Anastasi, A. (1982). *Psychological testing* (5th ed.). New York: Macmillan.

Angoff, W. H. (Ed.). (1971). *The College Board Admissions Testing Program: A technical report on research and development activities relating to the Scholastic Aptitude Test and Achievement Tests.* New York: College Entrance Examination Board.

Benbow, C. P., & Stanley, J. C. (1980). Sex differences in mathematical ability: Fact or artifact? *Science, 210,* 1262–1264.

Berk, R. (Ed.). (1982). *Handbook of methods for detecting test bias*. Baltimore: Johns Hopkins University Press.

Breland, H. M., & Griswold, P. A. (1981). *Group comparisons for basic skills measures* (College Board Report No. 81–6). New York: College Entrance Examination Board.

Campbell, D. P. (1971). *Handbook for the Strong Vocational Interest Blank*. Stanford, CA: Stanford University Press.

Campbell, D. P., & Hansen, J. C. (1981). *Manual for the SVIB-SCII* (3rd ed.). Stanford, CA: Stanford University Press.

Cole, N. S. (1978, March). *Approaches to examining bias in achievement test items*. Paper presented at the annual meeting of the American Personnel and Guidance Association, Washington, DC.

Cole, N. S. (1981). Bias in testing. *American Psychologist, 36,* 1067–1077.

Cole, N. S., & Hanson, G. R. (1975). Impact of interest inventories on career choice. In E. E. Diamond (Ed.), *Issues of sex bias and sex fairness in career interest measurement* (pp. 1–17). Washington, DC: National Institute of Education.

Cronbach, L. J. (1978, February 16). Caution urged in use of armed forces battery. *APGA Guidepost*, pp. 1, 10.

Cronbach, L. J. (1981, November 12). ASVAB Update. *APGA Guidepost*, P. 2.

Denker, E. R., & Tittle, C. K. (1976). "Reasonableness" of KOIS results for re-entry women: Implications for test validity. *Educational and Psychological Measurement, 36,* 495–500.

Department of Health, Education, and Welfare. (1975). Nondiscrimination on the basis of sex. *Federal Register, 40,* 24128 24145.

deWolf, V. A. (1981). High school mathematics preparation and sex differences in quantitative abilities. *Psychology of Women Quarterly, 5,* 555–567.

Diamond, E. E. (Ed.). (1975) *Issues of sex bias and sex fairness in career interest measurement*. Washington, DC: National Institute of Education.

Diamond, E. E. (1980). The AMEG Commission report on sex bias in achievement testing. *Measurement and Evaluation in Guidance, 13,* 135–147.

Diamond, E. E. (1981a). Can interest inventories help erode the effects of past socialization? In D. P. Campbell (Chair), *Interest measurement effects studies: Do they tell the whole story?* Symposium presented at the annual meeting of the American Psychological Association, Los Angeles.

Diamond, E. E. (1981b). Sex-typical and sex-atypical interests of Kuder Occupational Interest Survey criterion groups: Implications for counseling. *Journal of Counseling Psychology, 28,* 229–242.

Donlon, T. F., Ekstrom, R. B., & Lockheed, M. E. (1979). The consequences of sex bias in the content of major achievement test batteries. *Measurement and Evaluation in Guidance, 11,* 202–216.

Dwyer, C. A. (1979). The role of tests and their construction in producing apparent sex-related differences. In M. A. Wittig and A. C. Petersen (Eds.), *Sex-related differences in cognitive functioning* (pp. 335–353). New York: Academic Press.

Ekstrom, R. B. (1972, September). *Barriers to women's participation in post-secondary education: A review of the literature*. Paper presented at the annual meeting of the American Psychological Association, Honolulu.

Fitzgerald, L. F., & Crites, J. O. (1980). Toward a career psychology of women: What do we know? What do we need to know? *Journal of Counseling Psychology, 27,* 44–62.

Ginzberg, E. (1972). Toward a theory of occupational choice: A restatement. *Vocational Guidance Quarterly, 20,* 169–176.

Ginzberg, E., Ginsburg, S. W., Axelrad, S., & Herma, J. L. (1951). *Occupational choice: An approach to a general theory.* New York: Columbia University Press.

Gottfredson, G. D., & Holland, J. L. (1978). Toward beneficial resolution of the interest inventory controversy. In C. K. Tittle & D. G. Zytowski (Eds.), *Sex-fair interest measurement: Research and implications* (pp. 43–51). Washington, DC: National Institute of Education.

Gump, J. P., & Rivers, L. W. (1975). A consideration of race in efforts to end sex bias. In E. E. Diamond (Ed.), *Issues of sex bias and sex fairness in career interest measurement* (pp. 123–139). Washington, DC: National Institute of Education.

Hansen, J. C. (1976). Exploring new directions for Strong-Campbell Interest Inventory occupational scale construction. *Journal of Vocational Behavior, 9,* 147–160.

Hanson, G. R., Noeth, R. J., & Prediger, D. J. (1978). The validity of diverse procedures for reporting interest scores: An analysis of longitudinal data. In C. K. Tittle & O. G. Zytowski (Eds.), *Sex-fair interest measurement: Research and implications* (pp. 53–59). Washington, DC: National Institute of Education.

Hanson, G. R., & Rayman, J. (1976). Validity of sex-balanced interest inventory scales. *Journal of Vocational Behavior, 9,* 279–291.

Harmon, L. W. (1973). The 1969 revision of the SVIB for Women. In D. G. Zytowski (Ed.), *Contemporary approaches to interest measurement* (pp. 58–96). Minneapolis: University of Minnesota Press.

Holland, J. L. (1982). The SDS helps both females and males: A comment. *Vocational Guidance Quarterly, 30,* 195–197.

Holland, J. L., Magoon, T. M., & Spokane, A. R. (1981). Counseling psychology: Career interventions, research, and theory. *Annual Review of Psychology, 32,* 279–305.

Hyde, J. S. (1981). How large are cognitive gender differences? A meta-analysis using ω^2 and d. *American Psychologist, 36,* 892–901.

Johnson, R. W. (1978). Relationships between female and male interest scales for the same occupation. In C. K. Tittle & D. G. Zytowski (Eds.), *Sex-fair interest measurement: Research and implications* (pp. 95–101). Washington, DC: National Institute of Education.

Kuder, F., & Diamond, E. E. (1979). *General manual, Kuder Occupational Interest Survey* (2nd ed.). Chicago: Science Research Associates.

Laime, B. F., & Zytowski, D. G. (1964). Women's scores on the M and F forms of the SVIB. *Vocational Guidance Quarterly, 12,* 116–118.

Lockheed, M. E. (1982). Sex bias in aptitude and achievement tests used in higher education. In P. J. Perun (Ed.), *The undergraduate woman: Issues in educational equity* (pp. 99–126). Lexington, MA: Lexington Books.

Lunneborg, P. W. (1980). Reducing sex bias in interest measurement at the item level. *Journal of Vocational Behavior, 16,* 226–234.

Marini, M. M. (1978). Sex differences in the determination of adolescent aspirations: A review of research. *Sex Roles, 4,* 723–753.

Matthews, D. F., & Walsh, W. B. (1978). Concurrent validity of Holland's theory for 114 non-college-degreed working women. *Journal of Vocational Behavior, 12,* 371–379.

McCarthy, K. (1975). *Sex bias in tests of mathematical aptitude.* Unpublished doctoral dissertation, City University of New York.

Medley, D. M., & Quirk, T. J. (1974). The application of a factorial design to the study of cultural bias in the General Culture items in the National Teacher Examination. *Journal of Educational Measurement, 11,* 235–245.

Messick, S. (1980). Test validity and the ethics of assessment. *American Psychologist, 35,* 1012–1027.

Milton, G. A. (1959). Sex differences in problem solving as a function of role appropriateness of the problem content. *Psychological Reports, 5,* 705–708.

Plake, B. S., Hoover, H. D., & Loyd, B. H. (1978, March). *An investigation of differential item performances by sex on the Iowa Tests of Basic Skills.* Paper presented at the annual meeting of the National Council on Measurement in Education, Toronto.

Prediger, D. J. (1976, September 9). Contradictory results predicted. *APGA Guidepost,* p. 2.

Prediger, D. J. (1981). A note on Self-Directed Search validity for females. *Vocational Quarterly, 30,* 117–129.

Rand, L. (1968). Masculinity or femininity? Differentiating career-oriented and homemaking-oriented college freshmen women. *Journal of Counseling Psychology, 15,* 444–450.

Selkow, P. (in press). *Assessing sex bias in testing: A review of the issues and evaluations of 74 psychological tests.* Westport, CT: Greenwood Press.

Siebel, C. E., & Walsh, W. B. (1977). A modification of the instructions to Holland's Self-Directed Search. *Journal of Vocational Behavior, 11,* 282–290.

Super, D. E., Crites, J. O., Hummel, R. C., Moser, H. P., Overstreet, P. L., & Warnath, C. F. (1957). *Vocational development: A framework for research.* New York: Columbia University, Teachers College, Bureau of Publications.

Teglasi, H. (1981). Children's choices and value judgments about sex-typed toys and occupations. *Journal of Vocational Behavior, 18,* 184–195.

Tittle, C. K. (1978). *Sex bias in testing: A review with policy recommendations.* San Francisco: Women's Educational. Equity Communications Network, Far West Laboratory.

Tittle, C. K. (1982). Use of judgmental methods in item bias studies. In R. Berk (Ed.), *Handbook of methods for detecting test bias* (pp. 31–63). Baltimore: Johns Hopkins University Press.

Tittle, C. K. (1983). Studies of the effects of career interest inventories: Expanding outcome criteria to reflect women's experiences. *Journal of Vocational Behavior, 22,* 149–158.

Tittle, C. K., McCarthy, D. A., & Steckler, J. F. (1974). *Women and educational testing: A selective review of the research literature and testing practices.* Princeton, NJ: Educational Testing Service and the Association for Measurement and Evaluation in Guidance.

Tittle, C. K., & Zytowski, D. G (Eds.). (1978). *Sex-fair interest measurement: Research and implications.* Washington, DC: National Institute of Education.

Vetter, B. M. (1981). Women scientists and engineers: Trends in participation. *Science, 214,* 1313–1321.

Webber, P., & Harmon, L. W. (1978). The reliability and concurrent validity of three types of occupational scales for two occupational groups: Some evidence bearing on handling sex differences in interest scale construction. In Tittle, C. K., & Zytowski, D. G. *Sex-fair interest measurement: Research and implications* (pp. 77–82). Washington, DC: National Institute of Education.

Wild, C. L., & Dwyer, C. A. (1980). Sex bias in selection. In L. J. Th. van der Kamp, D.

N. M. de Gruijter, & W. F. Langerak (Eds.), *Psychometrics for educational debates* (pp. 153–168). New York: Wiley.

Wilfong, H. D. (1980). *ASVAB technical supplement to the high school counselor's guide*. Fort Sheridan, IL: Directorate of Testing, United States Military Enlistment Processing Command.

Wilson, J., & Daniel, R. (1981). The effects of a career-options workshop on social and vocational stereotypes. *Vocational Guidance Quarterly, 29,* 341–349.

Wise, L. L. (1979, April). *Long-term consequences of sex differences in high school mathematics education*. Paper presented at the annual meeting of the American Educational Research Association, San Francisco.

11
Sex Equity in Classroom Organization and Climate

Marlaine E. Lockheed,
with Susan S. Klein

School classrooms are minisocieties (Jackson, 1968) that, while self-contained, replicate the larger society (Bourdieu & Passeron, 1977). Sex inequities characteristic of the larger society are found in abundance in coeducational classrooms; the most common of these inequities are sex segregation, male dominance, and interpersonal interactions designed to subtly reinforce sex differences and sex stereotyping. Although coeducational schools were hailed as a major victory for women's educational equity in the late 19th and early 20th centuries, since they provided girls and women access to education previously denied them, they were not intended to prepare girls and boys for similar positions in society. Not only were coeducational schools formally segregated, with separate entrances for girls and boys, but the curriculum was differentiated by sex according to then-current standards: domestic science for girls, "real world" subjects for boys.

Present-day public coeducational schools are generally prohibited by law from providing different services to boys and girls, but subtle inequities remain in coeducational classrooms—inequities that are quite capable of perpetuating a sex-inequitable adult society. The purpose of this chapter is to document the presence of these classroom inequities, to identify methods that have been found effective in reducing or eliminating these inequities, and to make recommendations regarding future research and practice.

DEFINING A SEX-EQUITABLE CLASSROOM ENVIRONMENT

The focus of this chapter is on the interpersonal and structural aspects of the environment. This environment may be influenced by the physical characteristics of the room, such as its location and the size and location of its furniture;

The authors gratefully acknowledge the assistance of Roberta Hall, Barrie Thorne, Raphaela Best, and Abigail Harris, who read and commented on earlier versions of this chapter.

by the pedagogical materials used in class; by verbal and nonverbal messages from the teacher, such as her or his use of praise, eye contact, or the direct content of instruction; by verbal and nonverbal messages from the student's classmates; and by the general organizational context in which the classroom is located, including such characteristics of the school as its staff, rules, or even the playground or special instructional facilities. Each of these environmental characteristics is capable of communicating a message to the student; some messages are part of the overt school curriculum, others are part of the "hidden curriculum" of the school and classroom. Each message treats the student equitably or inequitably.

A sex-equitable classroom environment is one in which both the overt and the hidden curriculum treat boys and girls equitably, so that they receive equal benefits from instruction. Major categories of treatment include role models, teacher-student interaction, peer interactions, school rules, and the physical location of resources. In a sex-equitable classroom environment, role models—in textbook stories or biographies, in pictures in books or on bulletin boards, or on the school staff—show boys and girls or men and women employed in similar occupations, engaged in similar activities, and exhibiting similar characteristics. Furthermore, boys and girls are themselves praised for engaging in the same activities, such as playing with dolls or balls, and for exhibiting the same characteristics, such as curiosity, cooperativeness, assertiveness, or helpfulness. School rules—including those regarding dress, discipline, classroom chores, or lining up for lunch—are the same for boys and girls. Moreover, teachers interact in the same way with boys and girls, not excusing male rowdiness while censuring it in girls, or excusing passive behavior in girls but worrying about it in boys. The physical use of resources provides equal access—both psychologically and physically—to male and female students. For example, a decision to locate a microcomputer in a high school library might encourage more sex-equitable use than a decision to locate it in a math classroom (stereotypically male) or in a typing classroom (stereotypically female). In general, sex equity calls for the provision of identical classroom environments for boys and girls.

To the extent that students entering the classroom exhibit sex differences in behavior, the provision of equal environments for boys and girls may not be sex-equitable; it may only set the conditions for equitable education, not guarantee it. Other elements can intrude to counteract the effects of the equal environment: family, peers, or media, for example. Children themselves may create a learning environment that is neither sex-equal nor sex-equitable. Teachers may need to undertake short-term compensatory actions to intervene against inequities or correct past inequities.

Many aspects of the coeducational classroom environment are more equitable today than they were 10 years ago. They have been changed largely through the concerted efforts of individual teachers who are attempting to be fair to students of both sexes in the graphic materials on display in their classrooms, in the curricular materials they use, in their seating arrangements, in the way they line students up for classroom activities, in the student teams they compose, and in student leaders they themselves select. In these actions toward equity, teachers deal primarily with the physical environment, which is relatively easy to change. What is more difficult to change is the interactional climate of the classroom, including student preferences for sex inequities, particularly since changing these aspects of the classroom requires the teacher to assume a more managerial role than most educators feel comfortable assuming. In fact, substantial and long-term interventions are required if the interactional inequities are to be reduced.

We recognize that the problem of reducing sex stereotyping and eliminating sex discrimination is circular: sex differences in the larger society—possibly due to historical discrimination—lead to stereotypes about individual sex differences that in turn lead to further sex differences in society. The problem is, where to intervene? In the following discussion of classroom organization and climate, we identify several types of interpersonal and structural inequities that teachers have found can be changed in the coeducational classroom; we also raise the question of single-sex education as a short-term alternative to coeducation in creating equitable opportunities and benefits.

ISSUES

Three major types of interpersonal inequities characterize typical coeducational classes: sex segregation, sex inequities in teacher-student interaction, and sex inequities in peer interaction.

Sex Segregation

Sex segregation is rarely viewed as a problem, possibly because it is seen as a natural developmental stage that terminates in late adolescence. Yet, it is a problem. It appears that sex segregation among children may have social consequences that persist into adulthood. Since all-female groups differ from all-male groups (Fennel, Barchas, Cohen, McMahon, & Hildebrand, 1978; Lockheed, 1976) in their interaction patterns, sex segregation may perpetuate these sex differences while inhibiting cross-sex cooperation. Although adult men and women appear to cooperate, there is considerable research evidence that they do not, in fact, interact equally when working together. Following a review of research on mixed-sex discussion groups, Lockheed and Hall (1976) drew three generalizations about behavior in these groups:

1. Men are more verbally active than women; that is, the average man initiates more verbal acts than the average woman.
2. Men are more influential than women; a woman is more likely to yield to a man's opinion than vice versa.
3. Men initiate a higher proportion of their acts than women in task-oriented categories of behavior, whereas women initiate a higher proportion of their acts in social-emotional categories.

These generalizations are consistent with the findings of a recent meta-analysis of research on the dynamics of mixed-sex task groups which concluded that, in general, males assumed the leadership positions in these groups (Lockheed, in press). These sex differences were associated with stereotyped expectations regarding the relative abilities of males and females; when the conditions of the task groups were changed so that the women were expected to be more competent at the task, the men no longer emerged as leaders. Lockheed interpreted these results as indicative of status differences between males and females and as consistent with the characterization of sex as a diffuse status characteristic (Lockheed & Hall, 1976; Meeker & Weitzel-O'Neill, 1977).

Evidence shows that as early as the elementary school years, sex as a status characteristic can be detected in children's cross-sex behavior and attitudes. In a study of second- and fifth-grade mixed-sex problem-solving groups, Zander and Van Egmond (1958) reported that males did significantly more talking than their female peers and were more involved in the influencing process. By the senior high school level, male domination of mixed-sex groups is well documented (Lockheed, 1977; Lockheed & Hall, 1976).

Also during the elementary school years, children's awareness of sex stereotypes increases and their attitudes become more stereotyped. Williams, Bennett, and Best (1975) found that as early as age 5, children had developed an appreciable degree of knowledge of adult stereotypes and that this knowledge increased during the next two years.

Stein and Smithells (1969) also investigated children's awareness and attitudes regarding sex stereotypes. They asked 2nd-, 6th-, and 12th-grade students to label as masculine or feminine certain items from six areas: social, artistic, reading, mathematics, spatial and mechanical, and athletic. In the 2nd-grade group, members of each sex tended to view all items as more appropriate for their own sex; by 12th grade, boys and girls concurred that reading was feminine and athletics were masculine. The 6th-grade responses fell in between. The stereotypes of the 12th-graders were consistent with those held by adults (Broverman, Vogel, Broverman, Clarkson, & Rosenkrantz, 1972). Stein and Smithells and other researchers reviewed in chapter 6 (Educational Equity and Sex Role Development) also suggest that during the school years, children learn increasingly what is stereotypically inappropriate for one's sex rather than what is stereotypically appropriate. This interpretation was supported by Nash's (1975) study of 6th- and 9th-grade boys and girls who were asked to rate "the average male" and "the average female" on 95 different attributes. Nash found that older adolescents attributed more sex stereotypes. More recently, Best (1983) observed that elementary school boys had clearer stereotypes about what girls should do than girls had about what boys should do; both girls' and boys' stereotypes were instrumental in excluding the other sex from their activities.

Thus, the patterns of inequitable behavior that are found in studies of mixed-sex groups of adults seem to have their roots in the elementary years. The sex segregation that occurs during the elementary school years may not represent a "harmless" developmental stage. It coincides with critical growth and changes in children's awareness, attitudes, and behaviors. By allowing boys and girls the option of segregating themselves and not cooperating with each other, and by failing to teach them to cooperate equally, educators and others may be communicating to children a normative acceptance of sex segregation and its consequences, thereby providing children with an environment in which stereotyped attitudes and behaviors can develop unchallenged.

In addition to the social consequences of sex segregation, there may be achievement or achievement-related consequences. On the basis of ethnographic studies of elementary school environments in California, Michigan, and Maryland, Throne (1979) and Best (1983) noted differences in the social organization and patterns of interactions in boys' and girls' groups. They both concluded that sex segregation leads to a loss of valuable learning experiences. For example, Thorne noted that by not playing in team sports, girls forfeit an excellent opportunity to learn complex rules, to increase their mastery of the skills of teamwork, to receive mentoring from older children, and to be trained in settling disputes. Similarly, in the classroom Webb (1982) and Allen (1976) have demonstrated that peer learning is an important factor in student achievement; to the extent that sex segregation limits the opportunities for boys and girls to learn from each other, the achievement of both may fall short of its potential.

Sex segregation is found extensively in preschool and elementary classrooms and persists into junior high school. A summary of studies documenting sex segregation in student friendship choices, peer interactions, seating patterns, work partner preferences, and play is presented in table 6. In general, sex segregation is voluntarily initiated by children, with teachers rarely intervening to encourage sex desegregation.

Children enter school with well-defined sex role stereotypes (Weinraub & Leite, 1977) about appropriate male and female behavior. Since stereotypes can be refuted by contradictory reality, children's stereotypes about substantial differences between the sexes could be reduced by interacting with cross-sex classmates. A highly sex-integrated classroom would provide many opportunities for sex stereotypes to be confronted by contradictory evidence and subsequently minimized; however, the sex-segregated classroom that is typical in elementary grades does not provide such an opportunity.

Sex Inequities in Teacher-Student Interaction

Research on teacher-student interaction has been conducted for the last three decades; some of the more recent studies have attended to sex and ethnic differences in interaction patterns. Unlike conscious or unconscious sex segregation—which is both inherently discriminatory and a powerful means of perpetuating stereotypes—the classroom interaction issue is more complex. If female and male students behave differently in the classroom, it may be appropriate for the teacher to treat them differently if the teacher's objective is ulti-

Table 6.   Recent Studies of Sex Segregation in Schools

Author	Sample	Measure	Results
Berk & Lewis (1977)	22 boys, 22 girls, aged 4–8 years, in 4 school types	Observed social contacts, interchanges	Girls engaged in more same-sex interchanges than boys. The proportion of same- to cross-sex interchanges = 4:1 to 3:1 in 3 schools; progressive schools = 1:3.
Campbell (1979)	~ 250 elementary students in 11 classrooms	Voluntary group composition	78% of students joined same-sex groups.
	11 six-person, cross-race, cross-sex groups	Observed amount of interaction	63% of all interactions were same-sex interactions; 20% of all interactions were cross-sex, cross-race interactions.
		Observed type of interactions	43% of cross-sex, cross-race interactions were negative; 78% of same-sex, same-race interactions were positive.
Damico (1975)	30 students, 8–10 years in university lab school	Ethnography	There was no recorded incidence of spontaneous cross-sex academic helping behavior. Two separate sex-segregated social systems were identified.
Fagot (1977)	106 boys, 101 girls in preschool	Fagot-Patterson observation	Boys who showed cross-gender preference were given more peer criticism and fewer positive reactions. There was no peer criticism of cross-gender girls.
Grant (1982)	6 1st-grade classrooms	Ethnographic observations	There were fewer actual cross-sex interactions than expected (~ 10%

Table 6.   (*Continued*)

Author	Sample	Measure	Results
			fewer in 4 classes, 3% fewer in 1 class, and 22% fewer in 1 class). Cross-sex helping was rare, and cross-sex academic helping was more frequently F → M (> 70% in 3 classes, > 50% in 2; in one class M → F was greater).
Hallinan (1977)	51 classes in grades 5–8	Sociometric	A total separation by sex existed in the cliques in every class.
Hallinan & Tuma (1978)	4th-, 5th-, and 6th-grade students in 18 classrooms	Sociometric of Best Friend, Friend, Not a Friend	77% of Best Friends were same-sex peers.
Lockheed & Harris (1982)	29 4th- and 5th-grade classrooms	Observation of target student verbal interaction	Same-sex responses to target student behavior were twice as frequent as cross-sex responses.
		Sociometric rating	Mean cross-sex ratings were lower than mean same-sex ratings.
Lockheed & Harris (1983)	29 4th- and 5th-grade classrooms	Observation of target students in groups	14% of observations indicated cross-sex groups.
Lockheed, Finkelstein, & Harris (1979)	211 4th-grade boys 266 4th-grade girls	Choice of three work partners	Same-sex choice was made by 72% of boys and 67% of girls.
	234 5th-grade boys 223 5th-grade girls	Choice of three work partners	Same-sex choice was made by 65% of boys and 57% of girls.
Marquis & Cooper (1982)	2 preschool classes	Selection of work partner for self-disciplined work session	Virtual sex segregation in choices of partners was observed on six occasions.
Phillis (1971)	30 boys, 30 girls, aged 5–8 years, in	Sociometric	There were sex differences in choice of

(*continued*)

Table 6. *(Continued)*

Author	Sample	Measure	Results
	laboratory summer school		play partners and leader of physical education team.
Schofield & Sagar (1977)	7th- and 8th-grade students at lunch	Seating patterns at 32 tables in cafeteria	Cross-sex adjacencies were extremely rare.
Serbin, Tonick, & Sternglanz (1977)	2 nursery school classes	Cross-sex cooperative play	Baseline showed low rate of cooperative cross-sex play.
Singleton & Asher (1977)	197 white, 48 black 3rd-grade students	Sociometric	Same-sex peer play and work partner ratings were more positive than cross-sex ratings.
	39 white, 39 black 3rd-grade students	Observation of teacher-student cross-sex and single-sex interaction	77.8% of peer interaction was same-sex peer interaction.
Wilkinson & Subkoviak (1982)	23 boys and girls in four 1st-grade reading groups	Seating charts	Same-sex preference occurred in seating.

Note. The complete citations for these references are available from the senior author on request.

mately to reduce those sex differences. We noted previously that there was little evidence of academic differences between girls and boys in the classroom. There is, however, substantial evidence of behavioral differences: girls are less disruptive than boys and speak out less than boys. Should a teacher seek to lessen male disruptive behavior or to increase female verbal participation in class, the teacher might need to interact differently with the girls and boys in the classroom— calling on girls more than on boys, or selectively ignoring certain male behavior. Equality of treatment would be an inappropriate teacher response to differential student behavior. If student behavior were not sex-differentiated, however, then sex-differentiated teacher response could lead to sex-differentiated student behavior. The matter is further complicated by considering teacher attention as a classroom resource to be evenly distributed to all students. In that case, teachers should attend to all students identically, without regard to student behavior. This suggestion, however, is not likely to be accepted by teachers who are concerned with maintaining control over disruptive students or who are eager to encourage the participation of reticent students.

Research on sex differences in teacher-student interaction has not been consistent in reporting inequities; because this literature is voluminous, in this chapter we touch on it only lightly.

The earliest observational studies of sex differences in teacher-student interaction were motivated by interest in behavior modification through positive and negative reinforcement; these studies focused on the amount of teacher praise and criticism that was directed at girls versus boys in classrooms. Results of these early studies are inconsistent. For example, Meyer and Thompson's (1956) study of children in three sixth grades reported that boys received a larger number of disapproval contacts than girls received, but that there were no sex differences in approval contacts. Meyer and Lindstrom (1969), however, in a study of 13 classes of Head Start children, reported no sex differences in the rates either of received "praise" or "blame." In contrast, Spaulding (1963), in a study of 21 fourth- and sixth grade classrooms, found that boys received both more praise and more criticism than did girls. This was also found more recently by Etaugh and Harlow (1975) for female teachers of fifth- and sixth-grade students, by Wirtenberg (1979), and by Sadker and Sadker (1982) in 102 fourth, sixth, and eighth-grade classes. Finally, Delefes and Jackson (1972) found that fifth- and eighth-grade boys received more praise than their female classmates; no sex differences in criticism received were reported. Other studies, differently motivated, examined sex differences in the opportunities that teachers provided for the girls and boys in their classes. For example, Morrison (1979) found that boys received more direct teacher questions than did girls and that the ideas of boys were more often used in classroom discussions. Sikes (1972) reported that teachers were more likely to seek out boys to check their work and to give them help.

Recognizing that teacher-student interaction was as much a function of student-initiated interaction as a function of teacher-to-student interaction (Klein, 1971), investigators began to study how students behaviors contributed to the reported differences in teacher-student interaction. In general, these studies found greater activity on the part of boys relative to girls. For example, Good, Sikes, and Brophy (1973) studied 16 junior high school classes and found that boys initiated more contacts of all types with teachers. Although the pattern of greater male activity has generally been reported (Good & Findley, in press, contains a review) some exceptions to this pattern have been noted.

At the college level, studies of student-teacher interaction have been confounded by teacher sex and type of subject matter. For example, while Karp and Yoels (1976) reported that in 10 male-taught nonscience classes a higher proportion of teacher interactions occurred with male students than with female students, no such difference was found when sex of teacher and subject matter were controlled (Boersma, Gay, Jones, Morrison, & Remick, 1981). Similarly, in another incomplete design, Sternglanz and Lyberger-Ficek (1977) found that males initiated more contact with the teacher in 16 male-taught science classes and 44 nonscience classes, 33 taught by males, a finding not replicated in the Boersma et al. study in which teacher sex and subject matter were balanced.

Because sex differences in student behavior have been observed, differences in teacher behavior directed at students are not surprising. Praising, criticizing, asking questions, and interacting are all powerful methods of maintaining classroom discipline, as well as of instructing. To determine whether teachers respond inequitably to girls versus boys, it is necessary to identify the student behaviors (or contingencies) that precipitate teacher responses and to hold such student behavior constant while examining teacher response. Most past studies of student-teacher interaction have not controlled precipitating student behavior. Their conclusions about differential teacher responses should not be interpreted as documenting inequitable teacher response (Good et al., 1973; Hillman & Davenport, 1978; Sikes, 1971).

Some studies, however, have sought to address student contingencies. For example, it has been reported that girls have received less praise for correct answers (Brophy & Good, 1970); that praise received by girls occurs randomly, while boys are praised for participation in academic activities (Delefes & Jackson, 1972); that girls receive more negative feedback on the intellectual quality of their work (Dweck, Davidson, Nelson, & Enna, 1978); and that twice the proportion of criticism that girls receive is for "lack of knowledge or skill" (Spaulding, 1963). Because these studies have used the teacher as the unit of observation, there remains the question of how sex differences in the frequency of student-initiated behavior toward the teacher come to effect these teacher responses. That is, if one particular boy initiates many contacts with the teacher, the response to him might not be the same as the teacher's general response to boys. To study sex differences in teacher responses more generally, it is necessary to sample the student behavior of both boys and girls and then observe teacher responses. This was done in a study of 29 fourth- and fifth-grade classrooms in which the behaviors of six randomly selected students, three boys and three girls, were observed during an entire instructional day (Lockheed & Harris, 1982). Different students were observed for each of 8 observation days spread across the school year. Consistent with previous research, more behaviors were recorded for male than female students, and higher proportions of male behaviors were coded as not conforming to the classroom norm, while a higher proportion of female events were coded as normatively appropriate. Few sex differences in teacher responses to student behaviors were found, and no sex differences in teacher responses to student behaviors were found when analyses were conducted separately within nine different subject matter areas, including reading and mathematics.

Another study of 85 children in seven second-grade and four sixth-grade classrooms shows that teachers may respond to female and male students in the same way, even when the behavior initiated by boys and girls is different. Pintrich and Blumenfeld (1982) reported that teachers did not respond differently to boys and girls during recitation, small group work, or seatwork, even though student behavior varied by sex. In small group settings boys talked more, whereas girls sought help more; in seatwork boys engaged in more social comparison than girls. In general, girls seemed more comforming, behaving more appropriately than boys in recitation and small group settings. In transition—that is, moving from one activity to another—however, boys received more negative feedback than girls, and girls were more often targets of teacher commands. The authors note that these results are interesting because although boys' and girls' behavior varied in other settings, it was similar in transitions.

Other teacher behaviors that communicate sex-differentiated expectations have been summarized by Hall (1982). She noted that teachers may devalue the work of female students relative to males and may encourage female helplessness by solving a problem posed by girls, while explaining to boys how to solve the problems. Hall also notes that in interactions with postsecondary or adult students, teachers call on or make eye contact with male students more frequently than with female students, and that female students are more frequently victims of sexual harassment.

In summary, although teachers on the whole treat their female and male students differently, this differential treatment is primarily in response to sex differences in precipitating student behaviors. Recent research has been able to detect this relationship by using sophisticated techniques of observation and analysis to examine sequential interaction patterns. Moreover, it is also likely that after a decade of exposure to Title IX and to the civil rights and women's movements, those teachers who have always wanted to treat their students fairly have become more aware of how to do so. The next step will be to help teachers restructure their classrooms so that female and male students can behave more similarly in desired ways.

Sex Inequities in Peer Interaction

Peer interaction in the classroom occurs throughout the day and for all subject matter areas, whether or not it is intended by the teacher. Lockheed estimates that peer contacts account for 29% of all experiences of a child in a typical classroom (Lockheed, 1982). In addition, some teachers organize their classrooms so that greater peer interaction is encouraged through unstructured small group work. Peer interaction is an important source of sex inequities, although relatively little research has been conducted on unstructured peer interaction in the classroom. Studies of sex segregation, reviewed in the previous discussion of classroom organization, suggest that little cross-sex peer interaction occurs. Yet, these studies of seating arrangements, friendship choices, or even the extent of interaction do not describe the nature of the interaction.

Research on unstructured cross-sex interaction indicates that it is characterized by lack of cooperation and by male dominance. For example, Serbin, Tonick, and Sternglanz (1977) found a low rate of cooperative cross-sex play in two nursery school classes, and Grant (1982) reported that cross-sex helping was rarely observed in first grade. Similarly, Wilkinson and Subkoviak (1982) reported finding low rates of cross-sex requests for information in four first-grade reading groups. In an ethnographic study of one classroom of students aged 8 to

10, Damico (1975) reported "no recorded incidence of spontaneous cross-sex academic helping behavior." Webb (1982) found that girls in homogeneously composed high school mathematics groups responded equally to requests for help from both other girls and boys, but that boys responded virtually only to boys.

Although little research on leadership in classroom peer interaction has been conducted, some laboratory studies—using school-age individuals as subjects—have been done. These studies show that the interaction in mixed-sex groups is typically imbalanced in favor of males (Lockheed, in press). Indicators of imbalance include verbal and nonverbal activity, influence, and perceived leadership. Studies of sex differences in these indicators are summarized in table 7.

Relatively few studies have examined sex differences in leadership interaction in children's task groups. Exceptions are a series of studies conducted by Lockheed and her colleagues and another series of studies conducted by Webb. Lockheed's laboratory studies utilized a common stimulus task, a maze game requiring group collaboration; interaction in the group was videotaped and subsequently coded. No sex differences in either verbal participation or influence were found in groups composed of fourth- and fifth-grade strangers matched on field independence, age, height, and social class (Lockheed, Harris, & Nemceff, 1983), but considerable sex differences were observed in both participation and influence in groups of similar children from ongoing classrooms, with boys generally more active and influential than girls (Lockheed, Finkelstein, & Harris, 1979). Studies of high school students showed no sex differences in task participation when ability was controlled (Webb, 1982) or when cognitive style was field-independent (Lockheed, 1977).

Studies of college-age groups generally report sex differences favoring males. If, however, the females are known to possess a skill that is particularly relevant to the group task (Artz, 1975; Swanson & Tjosvold, 1979) or have been assigned to leadership roles (Jacobson & Effertz, 1974; Maier, 1979), they are more active and influential than the male students. A review of the literature recently completed by Hall (1982) concluded that the quality of cross-sex classroom interaction in higher education may be negative for women, insofar as women students may be ignored by male classmates, may have their contributions discounted, and may be subject to stereotyped language and expectations on the part of other students. Quantitative evidence regarding such inequities is limited and dated, but to the extent that such inequities have existed or are felt now to exist by female students, these types of inequities in interaction constitute problems to be addressed.

Just as sex inequities in society are reflected in classroom climate and organization, so too are inequities related to race, ethnicity, and perceived ability. Thus, studies indicate that minority girls experience a different classroom environment from minority boys or nonminority girls (Grant, 1983; Morrison, 1979; U.S. Commission on Civil Rights, 1973). Similar differences have also been noted for disabled and gifted girls (Leinhardt, Seewald, & Engel, 1979; Parsons, Futterman, Kaczala, & Meece, 1979).

Table 7. Recent Studies of Face-to-Face Cross-Sex Interaction in Small Groups

Author and date	Sample	Task	Dependent variable	Result
Elementary school				
Harris & Lockheed (1982)	38 mixed-sex groups of 4th-grade students	"Lost on the Moon"	Influence over group ranking of items to be saved	n.s.d.
	26 mixed-sex groups of 5th-grade students	"Lost on the Moon"	Influence over group ranking of items to be saved	n.s.d.
Lockheed, Finkelstein, & Harris (1979)	31 four-person (2 male, 2 female) groups of 4th- and 5th-grade students from ongoing classrooms	Kill the Bull: a board game in which group members decide on best path to move token through maze to reach a goal	Modified Bales IPA coded from videotapes; acts initiated and received and actual influence over group decisions	M > F
Lockheed, Harris, & Nemceff (1983)	17 four-person (2 male, 2 female) groups of 4th- and 5th-grade students	Kill the Bull	Modified Bales IPA coded from videotapes; acts initiated and received and actual influence over group decisions	n.s.d.
Raviv (1982)	21 mixed-sex groups of 7th-grade students from "Group Investigation" classes (Israel)	Lego construction task	Verbal cooperation, non-verbal cooperation, competition	F > M verbal coop. n.s.d. nonverbal coop. n.s.d. competition
	26 mixed-sex groups of 7th-grade students from STAD classes (Israel)	Lego construction task	Verbal cooperation, non-verbal cooperation, competition	F > M verbal coop. n.s.d. nonverbal coop. n.s.d. competition

(continued)

Table 7. (*Continued*)

Author and date	Sample	Task	Dependent variable	Result
	18 mixed-sex groups of 7th-grade students from whole-class classes (Israel)	Lego construction task	Verbal cooperation, non-verbal cooperation, competition	F > M verbal coop. F > M nonverbal coop. F > M competition
High School				
Lockheed (1976)	8 four-person (2 male, 2 female) groups of high school students	Kill the Bull	Modified Bales IPA coded from videotapes; acts initiated and received and actual influence over group decisions	M > F
	9 four-person (2 male, 2 female) groups of high school students familiar with task	Kill the Bull	Modified Bales IPA coded from videotapes; acts initiated and received and actual influence over group decisions	n.s.d.
Lockheed (1977)	9 four-person (2 male, 2 female) groups of field-dependent high school students	Kill the Bull	Modified Bales IPA coded from videotapes; acts initiated and received and actual influence over group decisions	M > F
	10 four-person (2 male, 2 female) groups of field-dependent high school students	Kill the Bull	Modified Bales IPA coded from videotapes; acts initiated and received and actual influence over group decisions	n.s.d.
Webb (1982)	33 female and 44 male	Unit on exponents and	Gives explanation, re-	n.s.d.

high school mathematics students, working in groups; groups composed of mixed- or matched-ability students	scientific notation	ceives explanation, receives no explanation	F > M
		Responds to requests for help	
Undergraduate			
Artz (1975)			
23 cross-sex dyads of undergraduates	Creative story writing for men's magazine	Number of individuals' ideas incorporated into dyads' story	M > F
21 cross-sex dyads of undergraduates	Creative story writing	Number of individuals' ideas incorporated into dyads' story	n.s.d.
21 cross-sex dyads of undergraduates	Creative story writing for women's magazine	Number of individuals' ideas incorporated into dyads' story	F > M
22 cross-sex dyads of undergraduates, male with higher "creative writing aptitude"	Creative story writing for men's magazine	Number of individuals' ideas incorporated into dyads' story	M > F
22 cross-sex dyads of undergraduates, female with higher "creative writing aptitude"	Creative story writing for men's magazine	Number of individual's ideas incorporated into dyads' story	M > F
Bartol (1973)			
24 mixed-sex groups of undergraduate business majors	"The Executive Game": a firm making a single product	Peer ranking on "goal achievement" from 4 questions	M > F

(continued)

Table 7. (*Continued*)

Author and date	Sample	Task	Dependent variable	Result
Crosbie (1979)	20 mixed-sex groups of undergraduates	SIMSOC	Peer ratings on within-group participation; peer ratings of power and prestige combined with actual resources controlled (status rank)	M > F
Eskilson & Wiley (1976)	12 groups of undergraduates (4 same- and 8 mixed-sex) with female leaders assigned randomly	Assembling a puzzle consisting of 17 multi-colored geometric felt figures that could be arranged to form five equal-size squares	Bales Interaction Process Analysis scored from videotapes; proportion of group speaking time in "leaderlike" categories	M > F
	12 groups of undergraduates (4 same- and 8 mixed-sex) with female leaders assigned on the basis of "spatial perception ability"	Assembling a puzzle consisting of 17 multi-colored geometric felt figures that could be arranged to form five equal-size squares	Bales Interaction Process Analysis scored from videotapes; proportion of group speaking time in "leaderlike" categories	M > F
Hall (1974)	20 four-person (2 male, 2 female) groups of student teachers	"Johnny Rocco" case discussion	Modified Bales IPA score from videotapes; proportion of group "task acts"; probability of being "most active" in group. Most influential.	M > F
Jacobson & Effertz (1974)	6 three-person (1 female, 2 male) groups of un-	Reproducing a design in dominoes; leader has	Percentage of dominoes correctly placed by	F > M

	dergraduates in which the female was randomly assigned as leader	design and followers have dominoes	followers	
	6 three-person (1 male, 2 female) groups of undergraduates in which the male was randomly assigned as leader	Reproducing a design in dominoes; leader has design and followers have dominoes	Percentage of dominoes correctly placed by followers	M > F
Nemeth, Endicott, & Wachtler (1976)	28 six-person mixed-sex groups of undergraduates from ongoing classes	"Jury" deliberation on murder case	Bales IPA categories; task orientation	M > F
Parker (1973)	207 college students in 10 discussion sections	History and sociology	Verbal participation	M > F
Piliavin & Martin (1978)	46 mixed-sex groups of undergraduates	"Johnny Rocco"; girl discovers roommate using heroin; race relations problem	Bales IPA categories coded from audiotapes; task orientation	M > F
Stake & Stake (1979)	11 cross-sex dyads of undergraduates, matched on high performance self-esteem	Joint decision regarding 10 best ways of reducing crime on campus, after individual decision made	Number of opinions; relative weight given to individual decision in contribution to group decision	n.s.d.
	11 cross-sex dyads of undergraduates, female performance self-esteem higher than male performance self-esteem	Joint decision regarding 10 best ways of reducing crime on campus, after individual decision made	Number of opinions; relative weight given to individual decision in contribution to group decision	F > M

(continued)

Table 7. (*Continued*)

Author and date	Sample	Task	Dependent variable	Result
	11 cross-sex dyads of undergraduates, male performance self-esteem higher than female performance self-esteem	Joint decision regarding ten best ways of reducing crime on campus, after individual decision made	Number of opinions; relative weight given to individual decision in contribution to group decision	M > F
	11 cross-sex dyads of undergraduates matched on low performance self-esteem	Joint decision regarding ten best ways of reducing crime on campus, after individual decision made	Number of opinions; relative weight given to individual decision in contribution to group decision	M > F
Swanson & Tjosvold (1979)	15 cross-sex dyads of undergraduates in which females had greater task competence than males	Identifying hidden figures	Number of figures identified	F > M
	13 cross-sex dyads of undergraduates in which males had greater task competence than females	Identifying hidden figures	Number of figures identified	M > F
Webber (1976)	83 four-person groups from ongoing management classes	Analyzing cases and writing group reports	Peer ratings on task leadership and task contribution	M > F

Note: The complete citations for these references are available from the senior author on request.

SOLUTIONS

Until recently most educators have been unaware that sex segregation, sex-stereotyped teacher-student interaction, and imbalanced cross-sex peer interactions constituted problems of sex inequity. It has been important to draw the attention of practitioners to these problems through the publication of research documenting these phenomena and demonstrating their negative effects on learning and development. At present, some of this research is being incorporated into teacher and administrator training and is being made more widely available through publications such as "The Classroom Climate: A Chilly One for Women," a paper published by the project on the Status and Education of Women of the Association of American Colleges (Hall, 1982), which deals with postsecondary education. Awareness alone, however, is a necessary but insufficient condition for effecting change. Specific strategies for reducing sex segregation and bringing about sex-equitable student-teacher and peer interactions are needed. In this section we shall discuss some strategies; other strategies specific to content or age-group are discussed in other chapters.

Strategies for Reducing Sex Segregation

Strategies reported in this section are derived from research; thus, the research is discussed with the strategy. All have been evaluated and found effective, if only temporarily.

1. Teacher Reinforcement of Cross-sex Play.   Positive evaluation of cross-sex peer interaction by the teacher is an effective way of encouraging such behavior. In a study of two nursery school classes of 4-year-old children, teachers praised, attended to, and publicly acknowledged naturally occurring cooperative cross-sex play (Serbin, Tonick, & Sternglanz, 1977). Reinforcement increased rates of cooperative cross-sex play significantly in both classes, but removal of treatment resulted in a complete reversal to the baseline rate of same-sex play. Had the teacher continued to reinforce cross-sex interaction, the boys and girls might have continued to interact with each other.

2. Teacher-directed Cross-sex Physical Adjacencies.   To inquire about the effects on sex segregation of teacher-required cross-sex seating, lines, or teams seems redundant: if the teacher requires students to integrate, then we should not observe sex segregation. Effective strategies for integrating the classroom, therefore, have rarely been studied alone. It is generally assumed that if teachers use nonsexist procedures for assigning seats or lining up students, then student behavior will reflect sex desegregation. Anecdotal findings suggest, however, that without continued intervention by the teacher, students will return to voluntarily sex-segregated patterns.

3. Teacher Discussion.   Teachers rarely confront their students to determine why they voluntarily segregate themselves. Classroom discussion of sex segregation may be an effective technique for eliminating it. For example, Kevin Karkau, a student teacher, described several teacher-led discussions he had with his fourth-grade class, one of which dealt with cross-sex interaction: "For the second discussion, the goals were to discover reasons why boys and girls interacted so rarely, to make them aware of their behavior and its limiting effects on people, suggest activities where the kids could interact more with POTOS* (such as helping with classwork, integrating the art tables and lines), and, if they seemed ready, initiate a reward system (M & M's) for performance on integrating activities." Students in his class reported that after the discussions they felt more at ease in cross-sex talking, standing in line, sitting, helping, playing at recess, and touching; students also reported less teasing when a boy and girl were observed talking or touching (Karkau, 1973). In her 3-year longitudinal intervention, Raphaela Best (1983) used two types of discussion activities to develop lasting patterns of sex integration among elementary school students. The first discussion strategy was consciously to help the students refute sex stereotypes; the second, to encourage cross-sex peer dialogue on topics of mutual concern, one of which was human sexuality and sexual dimorphism.

4. *Programs of Infusion.*   Few sex equity interventions are specifically directed toward reducing sex segregation, although many multifaceted programs include sex desegregation as an objective. For example, the Lincoln County National Demonstration Project (Hutchison, 1981) used a large number of WEEAP (Women's Educational Equity Act Program) and other products to demonstrate their effectiveness in promoting educational equity. Evaluation of the project activities included interviews with students and teachers. Both groups were asked whether they noticed any ways in which student behavior differed from that of previous years. At the elementary schools, both students and teachers commented on changes in playground behavior. They reported that there were no longer any single-sex games: some boys now joined in jump rope, baton twirling, and games of jacks, and girls were joining boys in tetherball and marbles. In addition, elementary teachers reported that more girls and boys were playing together on teams and choosing each other as partners and that there was a decrease in the number of all-girl and all-boy tables in the cafeteria. Secondary students noticed fewer changes, but they did report more association between the sexes and more inclination to try things traditional to the opposite sex. Secondary teachers reported more girls and boys working together on projects.

Strategies for Promoting Equal Status Peer Interaction

Equal status interaction is a powerful tool for reducing stereotypes about "others" (Cohen, Lockheed, & Lohman, 1976; Cohen & Roper, 1972; Katz & Benjamin, 1960). Most research on equal status interaction has occurred in laboratories, but a few attempts have been made to restructure classrooms to promote such interaction. The most extensively used approach is to utilize structured cooperative, mixed-sex groups as a major instructional strategy. We emphasize that the teacher must build equal status interaction into the structure of

*Persons of the opposite sex

the cooperative groups; failure to structure the groups can result in the confirmation of stereotypes (Lockheed & Harris, 1984). Evidence that structured groups can promote sex equity is provided by several recent studies that are summarized in the following paragraphs.

1. Group Investigation Method. An Israeli experiment conducted by Sharan and his colleagues (1982) compared cross-sex cooperation in small groups composed of students from 33 seventh-grade classrooms randomly assigned to one of three treatment conditions: the Group Investigative (GI) method (Sharan & Hertz-Lazarowitz, 1980); Student-Teams Achievement Divisions (STAD) method (Slavin, 1980); and traditional whole-class instruction. Both the GI and STAD methods use various forms of cooperative peer interaction in small groups. GI stresses a shared academic task, and STAD stresses peer tutoring and between-team competition.

The three different instructional methods were implemented in the classrooms for 3 to 4 months following several months of teacher training. At the end of the year, small cross-sex, cross-ethnic groups were composed and given a shared task to complete. Interactions in these small groups were coded for verbal cooperation, nonverbal cooperation, and competition. Raviv (1982) examined cross-sex cooperation and found statistically significant differences in the amount of cooperation between the three methods, with students from GI classes demonstrating twice as much verbal and nonverbal cross-sex cooperation as students from traditional whole-class instruction classes, but only one-third of the cross-sex competition. Students in groups from STAD classes were similar to whole-class groups in verbal cooperation, similar to GI groups in competition, and between GI and whole-class groups in nonverbal cooperation.

2. Student Teams Achievement Division (STAD). An experiment to test the effectiveness of STAD in increasing cross-sex friendship choices was conducted in eight fourth- and fifth-grade classrooms randomly assigned to control experimental conditions (Hansell, 1982). In the experimental (STAD) condition, students were assigned to four- or five-member cross-sex learning groups. Groups met for two periods each week to study for the twice-weekly quizzes. During this time, students were encouraged to tutor one another, to quiz one another, and generally to help one another learn the academic material. After the group session students were individually quizzed, and their individual score, adjusted for past performance, was summed to form a group score. Control classrooms did not work in groups. STAD increased student liking for all classmates, including liking for cross-sex classmates.

3. Curriculum and Research for Equity (CARE). A quasi-experimental study conducted by Lockheed and her colleagues in five fourth- and fifth-grade units in three elementary schools in New Jersey examined the effects of teacher training in encouraging cross-sex grouping on a variety of student outcomes, including student willingness to work in cross-sex groups and student interaction patterns in small groups. Teachers in two experimental units received 12 hours of in-service teacher training regarding sex stereotypes, cross-sex interaction, and female leadership and participated in a 60-hour summer workshop developing experimental curriculum materials covering each of these topics.

Students of the teachers were surveyed annually, and small task groups composed of students from experimental and control units were videotaped and subsequently coded. Analysis of the survey showed that girls in the experimental units reported more experiences working in mixed-sex groups than did girls in control units; no effect was found for boys (Lockheed & Harris, 1978). Analysis of videotapes of the small mixed-sex task groups showed significant sex by grade by experimental condition effects for verbal activity, actual influence, and perceived leadership. Unexpectedly, the experimental treatment reduced girls' status relative to boys' in the fourth grade, but improved it in the fifth grade (Lockheed & Harris, 1978).

4. *Collaborative Groups.*   A study of 29 fourth- and fifth-grade classrooms in California and Connecticut sheds some light on the relationship between group work and cross-sex prosocial attitudes and behavior (Lockheed & Harris, 1982). Although few opportunities for cross-sex group work were typically provided in these classrooms, a comparison between classrooms in which students expressed a willingness to work in cross-sex groups and actually engaged in such work, and those for which these conditions did not hold, showed that students from the more collaborative classrooms had a less male-biased perception of their classmates' competence (Lockheed & Harris, 1982), and their cross-sex task groups were more productive (Harris & Lockheed, 1982).

Strategies for Promoting
Equitable Teacher-Student Interaction

Strategies in this section are just beginning to emerge and are primarily teacher education strategies such as Intersect, a micro–teaching skills package that helps teachers identify several types of inequitable student-teacher interactions and practice more equitable alternative interaction patterns. Teachers trained with Intersect were found to engage in more equitable interactions than were comparison fourth-, sixth-, and eighth-grade teachers (Sadker, Sadker, Bauchner, & Hergert, 1982). As with much teacher intervention work, the effects on students for this and other interventions are as yet relatively unknown.

Single-Sex Education as a Strategy for Attaining Sex
Equity Goals

Many of the inequities found in coeducational classrooms result from comparisons, made by teacher and students, between males and females. One way to minimize the frequency of such comparisons is to have single-sex classrooms. Single-sex classrooms, however, are not necessarily sex equitable. They can be used to reinforce a variety of sex stereotypes, and—to the extent that resources are greater for single-sex male schools than for single-sex female schools—discrimination against female students may also occur through single-sex education.

At the same time, sex-differentiated instruction under the guise of coeducation is presently the norm rather than the exception in most schools, and single-sex education offers a possible alternative. Statements about the relative effects of coeducation versus single-sex education on student outcomes, however, cannot be made with great certainty due to several research-based factors such as (1) self-selection of students into single-sex or coeducational schools, (2) noncomparable curricula between types of schools, (3) preeminence of parochial single-sex schools, and (4) selectivity of private (single-sex) schools. Notwithstanding these reservations, the results of several studies that compare student achievement and affective outcomes in single-sex versus coeducational schools suggest that single-sex education in some form may be a short-term solution to problems of sex inequities in coeducational classrooms (Husen, 1967; Newby & Scott, 1982).

To suggest sex segregation as a solution to sex inequities in coeducational classrooms raises a number of issues. There is some evidence, however, that single-sex instruction used as an intervention—for example, using single-sex groups for the purpose of introducing new academic material—may have positive effects on subsequent coeducational classroom interaction (Fox, 1976; Lockheed & Harris, 1982). However, this is an area in need of further research before specific recommendations can be formulated. It is likely that the long-term effects of sex segregation will be to perpetuate sex stereotypes present in the larger society rather than to decrease these stereotypes.

RECOMMENDATIONS

In this chapter we have summarized a large body of research regarding sex segregation, peer interaction, and student-teacher interaction. We have identified some strategies that have proven useful in treating the problems identified. Yet much remains to be studied, and the intervention strategies need to be more widely adopted by practitioners.

Research Issues

The following are some research issues that need to be addressed:

1. For what ages and under what conditions do various types of interventions to reduce sex segregation have long-term effects?
2. Are there conditions under which single-sex education is a strategy that can be used to enhance subsequent mixed-sex classroom experiences and equitable outcomes?
3. What can teachers do to promote equal status interaction in their classrooms?
4. What are the most effective strategies that teachers can use to change student behaviors without interacting more frequently with male students?
5. What are the most effective ways to involve teachers in restructuring their classrooms in the direction of equity?

6. What are the similarities and differences between classroom sex inequities
    and inequities due to ethnicity, perceived ability, or other characteristics that
    differentiate students?
7. What are the long-term effects on students' affective and cognitive outcomes
    for restructuring the classroom environment? Are these effects different for
    male and female students?

These research questions suggest the adoption of certain methodological
approaches such as collecting and reporting data separately by sex, ethnicity, and
other student characteristics as appropriate; collecting strings of interaction data
rather than counts of behaviors; conducting field experiments to test hypotheses;
involving students and teachers in the research as active participants; focusing on
behavioral outcomes; collecting data longitudinally; and utilizing both qualitative
and quantitative research methods.

Practitioners

The research summarized in this chapter suggests that educational practitioners should

1. learn about patterns of sex inequities in classrooms and their effects;
2. act as researchers and observers of inequities in their own schools and
    institute remedial and monitoring activities if major inequities are observed;
3. assume a managerial role and actively restructure the classroom to set the
    conditions for equity; and
4. solicit the participation of students in desegregating their classes, creating
    equal status peer interactions, and adopting nonstereotyped behaviors.

The following commonsensical teacher intervention strategies have been
used effectively, and so provide directions for teachers:

1. To reduce sex segregation, teachers should restructure their classrooms to
    utilize cooperative cross-sex learning and discussion groups. Cooperative
    learning methods are described in *Cooperation in Education* (Sharan, Hare,
    Webb, & Hertz-Lazarowitz, 1980).
2. To improve student-teacher interaction, teachers should monitor their own
    behavior to be sure that they praise or reward male and female students for
    engaging in the same activities and exhibiting the same characteristics,
    punish and reprimand students of both sexes in a similar manner, and com-
    municate similar expectations and evaluations to both male and female
    students. Specific behaviors for teachers to self-monitor are described in *A
    Sex Equity Handbook for Schools* (Sadker & Sadker, 1982).
3. To improve the nature of peer interaction, teachers should assign roles to
    students in groups, designating leaders, recorders, and other roles according

to the group task. Methods for assigning roles to students in groups are described in *Describimento/Finding Out* (Cohen & Anthony, 1982) and *Curriculum and Research for Equity (CARE)* (Lockheed, Finkelstein, & Harris, 1983).

Changing classroom organization and climate is not a simple task for either researchers or practitioners. Despite longstanding evidence that group learning approaches are effective for integrating children in the classroom, teachers rarely group students for instruction. It is undoubtedly easier for motivated teachers to warm up the classroom climate than it is to reorganize the structure of instruction. Yet both these changes must take place before the classroom itself becomes a model of sex equity.

REFERENCES

Allen, V. (1976). *Children as teachers*. New York: Academic Press.

Artz, R. O. (1975). *Sex roles and influence in dyadic interaction*. Paper presented at the annual meeting of the American Sociological Association.

Best, R. (1983). *We've all got scars: What boys and girls learn in elementary schools*. Bloomington: Indiana University Press.

Boersma, P. D., Gay, D., Jones, R. A., Morrison, L., & Remick, H. (1981). Sex differences in college student-teacher interactions: Fact or fantasy? *Sex Roles, 7*(8) 775–784.

Bourdieu, P., & Passeron, J. C. (1977). *Reproduction in education, society, and culture*. London: Sage.

Brophy, J. E., & Good, T. L. (1970). Teachers' communication of differential expectations for children's classroom performance: Some behavioral data. *Journal of Educational Psychology, 61*(5), 365–374.

Broverman, I. K., Vogel, S. R., Broverman, D. M., Clarkson, F. E., & Rosenkrantz, P. (1972). Sex-role stereotypes: A current appraisal. *Journal of Social Issues, 28*(2), 59–78.

Cohen, E. G., & Anthony, B. (1982, March). *Expectation states theory and classroom learning*. Paper presented at the annual meeting of the American Educational Research Association, New York.

Cohen, E. G., Lockheed, M. E., & Lohman, M. R. (1976). The center for interracial cooperation: A field experiment. *Sociology of Education, 49*(1), 47–58.

Cohen, E. G., & Roper, S. R. (1972). Modification of interracial interaction. *American Sociological Review, 37*(6), 643–657.

Damico, S. B. (1975). Sexual differences in the responses of elementary pupils to their classroom. *Psychology in the Schools, 12,* 462–467.

Delefes, P., & Jackson, B. (1972). Teacher-pupil interaction as a function of location in the classroom. *Psychology in the Schools, 1972, 9*(2), 119–123.

Dweck, C. S., Davidson, W., Nelson, S., & Enna, B. (1978). Sex differences in learned helplessness: I. The contingencies of evaluative feedback in the classroom and II. An experimental analysis. *Developmental Psychology, 14*(3), 268–276.

Etaugh, C., & Harlow, H. (1975). Behaviors of male and female teachers as related to behaviors and attitudes of elementary school children. *Journal of Genetic Psychology, 127,* 163–170.

Fennel, M., Barchas, P., Cohen, E., McMahon, A., & Hildebrand, P. (1978). An alternative perspective on sex differences in organizational settings: The process of legitimation. *Sex Roles, 4,* 589–604.

Fox, L. (1976). *The effects of sex role socialization on mathematics participation and achievement.* Baltimore: Johns Hopkins University.

Good, T. L., & Findley, M. J. (in press). *Sex role expectations and achievement.* Unpublished manuscript.

Good, T. L., Sikes, J. N., & Brophy, J. E. (1973). Effects of teacher sex and student sex on classroom interaction. *Journal of Educational Psychology, 65*(1), 74–87.

Grant, L. (1982, March). *Sex roles and statuses in peer interactions in elementary schools.* Paper presented at the annual meeting of the American Educational Research Association, New York.

Grant, L. (1983). *Black females' "place" in desegregated classrooms.* Carbondale: Southern Illinois University.

Hall, R. (1982). *The classroom climate: A chilly one for women?* Washington, D.C.: Association of American Colleges, Project on the Status and Education of Women.

Hansell, S. (1982, July). *Cooperative group learning and the racial and sexual integration of peer friendships.* Paper presented at the Second International Conference on Cooperation in Education at Brigham Young University, Provo, Utah.

Harris, A. M., & Lockheed, M. E. (1982, March). *Individual and group scientific problem solving performance for boys and girls.* Paper presented at the annual meeting of the American Educational Research Association, New York.

Hillman, S. B., & Davenport, G. G. (1978). Teacher-student interactions in desegregated schools. *Journal of Educational Psychology, 70,* 545–553.

Husen, T. (1967). *IEEA report: International study of achievement in mathematics.* Stockholm: Almquist and Wiksell.

Hutchison, B. (1981). *Lincoln County National Demonstration Project.* Portland OR: North Western Regional Education Laboratory.

Jackson, P. (1968). *Life in classrooms.* New York: Holt, Rinehart and Winston.

Jacobson, M. S., & Effertz, J. (1974). Sex roles and leadership perceptions of the leaders and the led. *Organizational Behavior and Human Performance, 12,* 383–396.

Karkau, K. (1973). *Sexism in the fourth grade.* Pittsburgh: KNOW, Inc.

Karp, D. A., & Yoels, W. C. (1976). The college classroom: Some observations on the meanings of student participation. *Sociology and Social Research, 60,* 421–439.

Katz, I., & Benjamin, L. (1960). Effects of white authoritarianism in biracial work groups. *Journal of Abnormal and Social Psychology, 61,* 448–556.

Klein, S. S. (1971). Student influence on teacher behavior. *American Educational Research Journal, 8*(3), 403–421.

Leinhardt, G., Seewald, A. M., & Engel, M. (1979). Learning what's taught: Sex differences in instruction. *Journal of Educational Psychology, 71*(4), 432–439.

Lockheed, M. E. (1976). *The modification of female leadership behavior in the presence of males* (Final Report No. PR 76–28). Princeton, NJ: Educational Testing Service.

Lockheed, M. E. (1977). Cognitive style effects on sex status in student work groups. *Journal of Educational Psychology, 69*(2), 158–165.

Lockheed, M. E. (1982, March). *Sex equity in classroom interaction research: An analy-*

sis of behavior chains. Paper presented at the annual meeting of the American Educational Research Association, New York.

Lockheed, M. E. (in press). Sex and social influence: A meta-analysis guided by theory. In J. Berger & M. Zelditch (Eds.), *Status, attributions and rewards*. San Francisco: Jossey-Bass.

Lockheed, M. E., Finkelstein, K. J., & Harris, A. M. (1979). *Curriculum and research for equity (CARE): Model data package*. Princeton, NJ: Educational Testing Service.

Lockheed, M. E., Finkelstein, K. J., & Harris, A. M. (1983). *Curriculum and research for equity (CARE): A training manual for promoting sex equity in the classroom*. Newton, MA: Education Development Center.

Lockheed, M. E., & Hall, K. P. (1976). Conceptualizing sex as a status characteristic: Application to leadership training strategies. *Journal of Social Issues, 32*(3), 111–124.

Lockheed, M. E., & Harris, A. M. (1978). *The effects of equal status cross-sex contact on students' sex stereotyped attitudes and behavior*. Paper presented at the annual meeting of the American Educational Research Association, Toronto.

Lockheed, M. S., & Harris, A. M. (1982). Classroom interaction and opportunities for cross-sex peer learning in science. *Journal of Early Adolescence, 2*(2), 135–143.

Lockheed, M. E., & Harris, A. M. (in press). Cross-sex collaborative learning in elementary classrooms. *American Educational Research Journal*.

Lockheed, M. E., Harris, A. M., & Nemceff, W. P. (1983). Sex and social influence: Does sex function as a status characteristic in mixed-sex groups of children? *Journal of Educational Psychology, 75*, 877–888.

Maier, N. R. F. (1979). Male versus female discussion leaders. *Personnel Psychology, 23*, 455–461.

Meeker, B. F., & Weitzel-O'Neill, P. A. (1977). Sex roles and interpersonal behavior in task-oriented groups. *American Sociological Review, 42*, 91–105.

Meyer, M., & Thompson, G. (1956). Teacher interactions with boys as contrasted with girls. In R. G. Kuhler & G. G. Thompson (Eds.), *Psychological studies of human development*. New York: Appleton-Century-Crofts.

Meyer, W., & Lindstrom, D. (1969). *The distribution of teacher approval and disapproval of Head Start children* (final report). Washington, DC: Office of Economic Opportunity.

Morrison, T. L. (1979). Classroom structure, work involvement, and social climate in elementary school classrooms. *Journal of Educational Psychology, 71*, 471–477.

Nash, S. C. (1975). The relationship among sex-role stereotyping, sex-role preference, and the sex difference in spatial visualization. *Sex Roles, 1*(1), 15–32.

Newby, R. G., & Scott, N. J. (1982, March). *Single-sex schooling and sex-role socialization*. Paper presented at the annual meeting of the American Educational Research Association, New York.

Parsons, J., Futterman, R., Kaczala, C., & Meece, J. (1979). *Attributions and academic choice: Origins and change*. Washington, DC: National Institute of Education.

Pintrich, P. R., & Blumenfeld, P. C. (1982, March). *Teacher and student behavior in different activity structures*. Paper presented at the annual meeting of the American Educational Research Association, New York.

Raviv, S. (1982, July). *The effects of three teaching methods on the cross-sex cooperative and competitive behaviors of students in ethnically-mixed seventh grade classes*. Paper presented at the Second International Conference on Cooperation in Education at Brigham Young University, Provo, Utah.

Sadker, M. P., & Sadker, D. M. (1982). *A sex equity handbook for schools.* New York: Longman.

Sadker, M. P., Sadker, D. M., Bauchner, J., & Hergert, L. (1982). *Year 2: Final report—Promoting effectiveness in classroom instruction.* Andover, MA: The Network.

Serbin, L. A., Tonick, I. J., & Sternglanz, S. H. (1977). Shaping cooperative cross-sex play. *Child Development, 48,* 924–929.

Sharan, S., & Hertz-Lazarowitz, R. (1980). A group investigation method of cooperative learning in the classroom. In S. Sharan, P. Hare, C. D. Webb, & R. Hertz-Lazarowitz (Eds.), *Cooperation in Education* (pp. 14–46). (based on the proceedings of the First International Conference on Cooperation in Education). Provo, UT: Brigham Young University Press.

Sharan, S., Kussell, P., Sharan, Y., Bejerano, Y., Raviv, S., Hertz-Lazarowitz, R., Brosh, T., & Pelag, R. (1982). *Cooperative learning, whole-class instruction, and the academic achievement and social relations of pupils in ethnically-mixed junior high schools in Israel* (final report to the Ford Foundation).

Sikes, J. N. (1972). Differential behavior of male and female teachers with male and female students (Doctoral dissertation, University of Texas at Austin, 1971). *Dissertation Abstracts International, 33*(1), 217A.

Slavin, R. E. (1980). Cooperative learning. *Review of Educational Research, 5*(20), 315–342.

Spaulding, B. L. (1963). *Achievement, creativity, and self-concept correlates of teacher-pupil transactions in elementary schools* (Cooperative Research Project No. 1352). Washington, DC: Office of Education.

Stein, A. H., & Smithells, J. (1969). Age and sex differences in children's sex-role standards about achievement. *Developmental Psychology, 1,* 252–259.

Sternglanz, S. H., & Lyberger-Ficek, S. (1977). Sex differences in student-teacher interactions in the college classroom. *Sex Roles, 3,* 345–352.

Swanson, M. A., & Tjosvold, D. (1979). The effects of unequal competence and sex on achievement and self-presentation. *Sex Roles, 5*(3), 279–285.

Thorne, B. (1979, September). *Claiming verbal space: Women's speech and language in college classrooms.* Paper presented at the Research Conference on Educational Environments and the Undergraduate Woman, Wellesley College, Wellesley, MA.

U. S. Commission on Civil Rights. (1973). *Teachers and students: Report on the Mexican American education study of differences in teacher interaction with Mexican American and Anglo students.* Washington, DC: author.

Webb, N. (1982, March). *Interaction patterns: Powerful predictors of achievement in cooperative small groups.* Paper presented at the annual meeting of the American Educational Research Association, New York.

Weinraub, M., & Leite, J. (1977). *Sex-typed toy preference and knowledge of sex-role stereotypes and two-year-old children.* Paper presented at the annual meeting of the Eastern Psychological Association, Boston.

Wilkinson, C., & Subkoviak, M. (1982). *Sex differences in classroom communication.* Paper presented at the International Interdisciplinary Congress on Women, Haifa, Israel.

Williams, J. E., Bennett, S. M., & Best, D. L. (1975). Awareness and expression of sex stereotypes in young children. *Developmental Psychology, 11*(5), 635–642.

Wirtenberg, T. J. (1979). Expanding girls' occupational potential: A case study of the implementation of Title IX's anti-sex-segregation provision in seventh grade practical arts. *Dissertation Abstracts International, 40,* 176A. (University Microfilms No. 79–15, 609)

Zander, A., & van Egmond, E. (1958). Relationship of intelligence and social power to the interpersonal behavior of children. *Journal of Educational Psychology, 49,* 257–268.

12

Sex Equity and Sex Bias in Instructional Materials

Kathryn P. Scott
and Candace Garrett Schau

Approximately 90% of pupil learning time in schools involves the use of print and nonprint instructional materials, including textbooks, literature, films, filmstrips, records, tapes, television, and computer software. Outside of school, students also spend large amounts of time with the same kinds of materials. These materials, then, have tremendous potential to influence children. And they do.

This chapter presents evidence concerning the effects of gender-related characteristics of instructional materials on students. Research evidence similar to that presented in this chapter is also available on the effects of other characteristics of instructional materials, such as those related to race, ethnicity, age, handicapping condition, and religious preference (for example, Campbell & Wirtenberg, 1980; U.S. Commission on Civil Rights, 1980). These areas of bias, although of equal importance with sex bias and typically intersecting it, are not explicitly discussed due to space limitations. Very frequently the issues and answers in these areas are similar to those that we shall present for sex bias.

Theories of sex role development suggest why instructional materials can greatly influence pupils' learning (see chapter 6, Educational Equity and Sex Role Development). Observational learning (modeling) is a very powerful process in sex role development. Instructional materials present numerous sex role models as well as direct instruction about sex roles, even though their purposes usually are to teach content or process skills to students.

Sex-equitable materials are advocated by educators, publishers, and state policy makers who believe that instructional materials should reflect the reality of the presence of females in the world, their contributions, and the changing roles of both females and males. At one end of a continuum are *sex-fair* materials, which include females and males in numbers proportional to reality and present both traditional and nontraditional roles. Since females constitute approximately 50% of the population, they are portrayed at least 50% of the time wherever possible. Use of male generic language forms is avoided. At the other

218

end of the continuum of sex-equitable materials, *sex-affirmative* ones emphasize females and males in nontraditional roles and explain the benefits of these roles and the difficulties in attaining them, including institutional barriers and discrimination. Because many people behave in nonstereotypical ways (chapter 5, Facts and Assumptions about the Nature of Sex Differences, debunks many of these myths), showing them in nontraditional roles is necessary in order to portray reality accurately. Language that is gender-specific is emphasized.

In contrast, *sex-biased* materials are those in which (1) females appear as main characters and in illustrations far less frequently than males; (2) females and males are overwhelmingly portrayed in sex-stereotypical roles; (3) females appear more often than males in derogatory roles; and/or (4) male generic language is used.

Evidence presented in this chapter highlights six findings about instructional materials of significance to educators: (1) sex-biased language in materials distorts pupils' perceptions of reality; (2) sex-equitable materials expand sex role attitudes and knowledge about sex roles; (3) sex-equitable materials increase motivation to learn; (4) sex-equitable materials influence comprehension; (5) sex-equitable materials influence sex role behavior; and (6) many commonly used materials are sex-biased.

1. Sex-biased Language Distorts Pupils' Perceptions of Reality.   Sex bias in language communicates biased knowledge about society. Firmly rooted in cultural values and traditions, language often reflects the same inequities between the sexes that exist in society. As a number of analyses have documented, language often differs when referring to females in comparison to males (Eakins & Eakins, 1978; Lakoff, 1975; Miller & Swift, 1977; Nilsen, Bosmajian, Gershuny, & Stanley, 1977; Thorne & Henley, 1975). For example, words such as "wizard" and "master," which have positive connotations in describing male behavior, take on quite different meanings when used in their female forms of "witch" and " mistress."

Not only does our language reflect our culture but it also changes as our cultural values and norms change. As the belief that women should be treated on an equal basis with men has gained acceptance in modern society, many forms of gender-linked language are now recognized as unfair or inappropriate. For example, the use of male generic terminology such as "man" and "mankind" is often replaced by more inclusive terminology such as "people" or "humanity."

Educators are concerned about the impact of language on students' learning. Generic nouns and pronouns are frequently used in the English language as referents to general society. Traditionally, *male generic* language refers to people in general or to an individual when the sex of the person is unknown or not relevant. *Gender-unspecified* language eliminates the male referent by substituting another term such as "people" for "man," or by changing to a plural, for example "they" instead of "he." *Gender-specific* language refers to both females and males, as in "women and men" and "he or she."

How does the use of each of the above three language forms enhance or detract from student learning? Research that has compared the impact of gender-unspecified and gender-specific forms with traditional male generic forms clearly shows that the form of language affects students' knowledge and images (for example, Adamsky, 1981; Harrison, 1975; Harrison & Passero, 1975; Jean & Murphy-Berman, 1981; Kidd, 1971; Martyna, 1978; Moulton, Robinson, & Elias, 1978; Schneider & Hacker, 1973; Wilson, 1978).

The findings can be summarized as follows: (1) male generic language produces images and knowledge that are overwhelmingly male, especially for male students; (2) gender-unspecified and gender-specific language elicit more gender-balanced images and understanding than generic language for both males and females; and (3) gender-specific language elicits the most gender-balanced images and understanding, especially for males. These generalizations apply to students of all ages, from primary to college level.

Since over 50% of the U.S. population is female, it is necessary that students have mixed-gender images of the world. Without this imagery and knowledge, students at all educational levels will continue to have male-biased and inaccurate views of humankind. Therefore, the use of gender-unspecified and gender-specific language forms can greatly enhance students' learning.

2. *Sex-Equitable Instructional Materials Broaden Attitudes about Sex Roles.* In general, the gender characteristics of print and nonprint materials, including the behavior of the characters, affect students' attitudes about sex roles. Students are continually exposed to large amounts of sexist instructional materials. Thus, we would not necessarily expect additional sex typing in attitudes from exposure to a few more sex-typed materials. When it does occur, it should happen most often with younger children, since they are in the process of learning about sex roles and developing gender schema. Research supports these ideas. Sometimes exposure to sexist materials increases sex-typed attitudes (Yanico, 1978), especially among children who are under 7 years of age (Jenkins, cited in Nilsen et al., 1977; Knell & Winer, 1979).

Because children are exposed to few sex-equitable instructional materials, we might expect that such exposures would result in attitudes that are less sex-typed. Again, research supports this conclusion. In most cases, exposure to sex-equitable materials and to same-sex nontraditional characters results in moderating sex-typed attitudes. Students from 3 years of age through college have become less sex-typed in their attitudes about roles, traits, activities, and occupations than control students of the same ages who have not been exposed to these materials (Barclay, 1974; Bem & Bem, 1973; Berg-Cross & Berg-Cross, 1978; Costello, 1979; Davidson, Yasuna, & Tower, 1979; Flerx, Fidler, & Rogers, 1976; Franzoni, 1980; Greene, Sullivan, & Beyard-Tyler, 1982; Hurwitz & White, 1977; Johnston, Ettema, & Davidson, 1980; Lutes-Dunckley, 1978; Schau, 1978; Scott & Feldman-Summers, 1979). Only two studies found inconclusive or no effects (Pingree, 1978; Schau, Kahn, & Tremaine, 1976).

As educators, we hope that students will generalize from sex-equitable materials and so become less sex-typed in their attitudes about areas not specifically covered in these materials. Unfortunately, this is not usually the case (Barclay, 1974; Schau, 1978; Scott & Feldman-Summers, 1979). Occasionally studies have found generalization, but only to the same sex (Ashby & Wittmaier, 1978, for girls only; Greene, Sullivan, & Beyard-Tyler, 1982, for boys only), or to some content areas but not others (Flerx, Fidler, & Rogers, 1976; Knell & Winer, 1979).

We would also expect that increasing exposure to sex-equitable materials would yield continually decreasing sex typing in attitudes. The very few studies that have examined this relationship support this conclusion (Johnston, Ettema, & Davidson, 1980; Schau, 1978). Also, increasing exposure to sexist materials, especially with young children, may result in increasing sex-typing (see Jenkins, cited in Nilsen et al., 1977). Correlational research supports the positive relationship between sex-typed attitudes and amount of exposure to television shows containing traditional sex role content for children (Beuf, 1974; McGhee & Frueh, 1980) and for adults (Ross, Anderson, & Wisocki, 1982).

Many studies have found no sex differences in attitude change. Those that have reported sex differences show few consistent patterns (Ashby & Wittmaier, 1978; Bem & Bem, 1973; Costello, 1979; Flerx, Fidler, & Rogers, 1976; Franzoni, 1980; Greene, Sullivan, & Beyard-Tyler, 1982; Johnston, Ettema, & Davidson, 1980; Knell & Winer, 1979). Overall, then, sex-equitable and sex-biased materials tend to affect females' and males' attitudes about equally.

Theories and findings about sex role development might suggest age differences in the effects of sexist and sex-equitable materials on attitudes, due to differences in amount of previous exposure, current sex role attitudes, and cognitive characteristics. Few studies have looked at age differences or have even included subjects of several ages in order to examine age trends. The majority of studies reported that exposure to sex-equitable or to same-sex nontraditional materials resulted in significantly decreased sex-typed attitudes among all ages of students from 3, the youngest age studied, to 22, the oldest age studied.

The findings from the research on both print and nonprint materials can be summarized as follows: (1) exposure to sexist materials may increase sex-typed attitudes, especially among young children; (2) exposure to sex-equitable materials and to same-sex characters results in decreased sex-typed attitudes in students from 3 to at least 22 years of age; (3) the effects of sex-equitable materials do not usually generalize to areas not specifically covered in the materials, especially for preschool and elementary-aged students, although there may be some generalization for older students, especially those who initially are more sex-typed; and (4) attitude change toward equity increases with increased exposure.

These generalizations apply to both female and male students. Thus, it is very clear that use of sex-equitable materials in schools helps students develop more flexible sex role attitudes, which allow them to make educational and career choices based on their own interests rather than on preconceived notions of what is "right" for a female or male.

3. Sex-Equitable Instructional Materials Increase Motivation to Learn.   Interest in particular instructional materials may greatly influence the extent to which pupils are motivated to learn from them. Since we want female and male students to learn and achieve to their maximum potentials, we desire instructional materials with high interest for both sexes.

In previous decades, educators believed that boys had higher comprehension of high-interest materials than of low-interest materials but that girls' comprehension was not affected by interest. However, a recent review of research indicates that this common interpretation is incorrect and that comprehension and interest are similarly linked for both girls and boys (Johnson & Greenbaum, 1982).

Before the 1970s, surveys indicated that boys preferred content about other males, while girls liked to read about both girls and boys (Zimet, 1966). Reading specialists recommended that instructional materials include a higher proportion of male content so that boys would have ample opportunities for interesting reading. Since girls appeared to like stories about males or females, stories with male characters would be suitable for them also.

More recently, these surveys of pupils' preferences have been questioned on several grounds (Tibbetts, 1974). First, boys may express these preferences because of cultural expectations about what is appropriate sex-typed content for them to read rather than inherent interest. Second, the apparent dislike by boys of stories about females may reflect a difference in the quality of "girl" and "boy" stories. For example, in a survey by Women on Words and Images (1972), stories about girls were weak and uninteresting in comparison to those about boys. Therefore, to gain a more complete understanding of pupils' preferences it is necessary to systematically vary both the sex of the main character and the role behaviors while maintaining comparable story quality.

Fortunately, some studies have examined pupil preferences in relation to the sex of the main characters, roles of the main characters, or both. Studies that compare children's preferences on the basis of sex of character with only traditional story content indicate that both girls and boys at all ages prefer stories with same-sex characters (Beyard-Tyler & Sullivan, 1980; Connor & Serbin, 1978; Klein, 1979; Rose, Zimet, & Blom, 1972). This finding is supported by research on sex role development showing that many children exhibit a same-sex preference rather than, or in addition to, sex-typed preferences (see chapter 6). Evidently when girls read stories about traditional roles today, they prefer female characters over male characters, a preference that highlights the importance of including female characters in instructional materials.

Other studies have examined only boys' preferences for either male traditional or nontraditional roles or only girls' preferences for either female traditional or nontraditional roles (Frasher & Frasher, 1978; Jennings, 1975) or both girls' and boys' preferences for female traditional or nontraditional roles (Frasher, 1977; Rakes, Bowman, & Gottfred, 1977). Results indicated no clear preference for either traditional or nontraditional characters.

Three studies examined preferences for both female and male characters in traditional and nontraditional roles. Scott and Feldman-Summers (1979) found no differences. Kaudon-Kropp and Halverson (1983) found preferences for sex-typed story content regardless of the sex of the main character. Klein (1970) found a preference for sex-typed story content for boys and a preference for stories with female main characters regardless of activity for girls.

The evaluation of the sex-affirmative television series *Freestyle* also included interest measures. *Freestyle* was carried by 230 of the 265 Public Broadcasting System (PBS) stations in the United States (about 87%). Its average Nielsen rating was slightly above 2.0, which is the midpoint for children's PBS programs. On the average, about 5.5% of U.S. families containing 6- to 11-year-old children watched this series. Of the families asked to view the series as part of the *Freestyle* evaluation scheme, an average of 32% actually did. The evaluators concluded that the series was quite interesting to the target-age children (Johnston, Ettema, & Davidson, 1980).

Several conclusions can be drawn from the evidence regarding pupils' interest in sex-equitable materials: (1) females seem to show a preference for female main characters, regardless of roles; (2) while boys also show a preference for same-sex characters, evidence exists that boys show their strongest preference for stories with traditional male content, regardless of the sex of the characters; (3) stories featuring main characters in nontraditional roles are not rejected by students and in some cases are preferred over those with sex-typed themes; and (4) one well-produced sex-affirmative television series is evidence that nonprint sex-equitable materials are at least moderately interesting to all children and are at least as interesting as the average sexist nonprint materials.

Hence, the inclusion of female main characters and sex-equitable content in instructional materials can contribute to students' increased interest in instructional materials. When females are presented in nontraditional (that is, traditionally male sex-typed) roles, boys also can be expected to show an interest in the materials.

4. Effects of Sex-Equitable Instructional Materials on Comprehension. Instructional materials are designed to assist students in learning content and skills. Thus, a fourth issue concerns the relationship, if any, between the gender characteristics of instructional materials and students' recall and comprehension. If students are to benefit from instructional materials, it is important that both females and males comprehend and remember what they have read or heard.

A number of studies have investigated this relationship but only for recall, the lowest type of cognitive skill according to Bloom's taxonomy of learning. The findings regarding recall of stories with female and male main characters are not conclusive. There is some evidence that pupils recall more about stories with same-sex rather than opposite-sex main characters when the content is traditional or sex-neutral (Deutsch, 1975; Klein, 1970). Franzoni (1980), however, found no differences in recall related to the sex of the main characters or the sex of the subjects or their interaction.

Other studies have compared pupils' recall for stories with nontraditional and sexist content. The evidence is not conclusive here either. Two stories found that pupils have higher recall for sex-equitable than for sex-biased stories (Frasher & Frasher, 1978; Jennings, 1975). Other studies, however, have found higher recall for traditional role characters (Koblinsky, Cruse, & Sugawara, 1978, for both sexes; Klein, 1970, for girls only; McArthur & Eisen, 1976, for boys only). Finally, Jaudon-Kropp and Halverson (1983) reported no differences in recall of male characters in sexist and sex-equitable roles.

The effects of sex-equitable materials in comparison to sex-biased materials on students' recall needs further investigation. Although a number of studies found significant differences, the studies were at odds in the direction of these differences. Many other factors may affect students' recall, such as their age, their knowledge of sex role concepts, and their degree of sex role stereotyping and gender schema development (see chapter 6).

5. Sex-Equitable Instructional Materials Influence Pupils' Sex Role Behaviors. From social learning theory we can predict that children will imitate actions of others in their environment, including people in school textbooks (Mischel, 1970). Only a few studies have examined the effects of characters in instructional materials on pupils' sex role behaviors, and all of the studies had young children as participants. The results of four studies indicated that sex of character, role of character, or both can have an influence. For example, Fischer and Torney (1976) found that the role behavior of the main character, but not sex of character or sex-typing, influenced behavior. Preschool children who heard a story about dependent behavior were slightly more likely to ask for help on a subsequent task of completing a puzzle than were others, regardless of the sex of the character in the story. Similarly, four-year-olds in Larder's study (1962) were more likely to engage in aggressive play after hearing a story with an aggressive theme than one with a nonaggressive theme.

Further evidence for the impact of instructional materials on children's sex-typed behaviors can be derived from studies of the effects of films and television. Bandura (1965, 1967) found that both female and male preschool children imitated aggression viewed on films when these behaviors were reinforced. An analysis of 10 years of scientific research on the effects of violence on television concluded that violent scenes increase children's aggressiveness, disobedience, and impatience (National Institutes of Mental Health, 1982). Similarly, children can also learn prosocial behaviors from television and generalize that learning to other situations, especially when accompanied by role-play training and verbal labeling (Friedrich & Stein, 1975).

In summary, there is evidence to indicate that young children's behavior is influenced by instructional materials. When children hear stories or see films that contain sex role behaviors, both traditional and nontraditional, they may imitate these behaviors.

6. Many Commonly Used Instructional Materials Are Sex-biased. A host of sex-affirmative supplementary materials, especially ones featuring women, have become available. Some sex-equitable fiction and trade books also are now available. But similar changes in basic textbooks have been slow (Britton & Lumpkin, 1977), and roles for men remain especially sexist. For example, in an analysis of recent reading texts, Scott (1981) found both traditional and nontraditional roles for females but few nontraditional roles for males.

There are at least five reasons why sex-equitable materials are not either widely available or used in schools. First, school districts typically purchase texts in a subject area no more than once every 5 years, so that many old books still are in use. Second, because it is a lengthy and costly process for publishers to develop a new textbook series, a time lag may exist in producing them. Third, sex-biased materials may be purchased by school districts because of inadequate attention to criteria for sex equity by school district review panels or state adoption committees. Fourth, there is resistance in some communities to sex-equitable materials because they do not focus exclusively on traditional roles for females and males. Some people believe that there are many innate differences between the sexes (see chapter 5 for a discussion of this fallacy), that these differences should be reinforced in the school curriculum, and that sex-affirmative materials should be banned from school because they present an inaccurate view of the world. Finally, others have suggested caution in using sex-equitable materials until their effects have been carefully studied (Kingston & Lovelace, 1977-78).

Consequently, the gap between the goal of sex-equitable instruction for students and the reality of sex-biased instructional materials presents a major problem for educators. In the next section we propose solutions to this problem.

PRACTICAL ANSWERS AND RECOMMENDATIONS

It is very clear that the gender characteristics of the language used in instructional materials and of the content of the materials affect students. When sex-biased language is used, pupils gain a distorted view of the world, one that assumes males are dominant in human culture and that females are not important enough to be visible in language. Stereotyped protrayals of females and males in instructional materials restrict pupils' attitudes about who can and who should engage in a wide variety of human activities. As educators we have a responsibility to ensure that what our pupils learn is not biased and that they achieve as a result of their individual talents, not on the basis of whether they were born male or female.

The use of sex-equitable instructional materials, therefore, is essential for improving the quality of pupils' learning and will not result in decreased quality in any area. Female and male students develop more flexible sex role attitudes, acquire more realistic knowledge from sex-equitable materials, and are at least as interested, often more so, in sex-equitable materials. For recall and imitation, sex-equitable and sexist materials appear to be about equivalent in their effects.

As indicated by the research, however, presenting just a few token females and males engaged in nontraditional activities will not influence pupils' sex role attitudes, knowledge, or behavior beyond the examples presented. Pupils need exposure to a sufficient quantity of sex-equitable materials to allow them to incorporate nontraditional role behaviors and attitudes into their cognitive schemas and abstract principles about sex roles.

Recommendations

A. *Publication of Materials.* A large number of publishing companies, states, and professional organizations have developed and issued guidelines for eliminating sexism and other forms of discrimination from publications (see U.S. Commission on Civil Rights, 1979). However, the existence of such guidelines is not necessarily related to the amount of sexism in a particular publisher's materials. Even with the guidelines, many publishing company personnel do not have the commitment or the expertise, especially in subtle forms of discrimination, to deal adequately with equity issues. In addition, many companies feel that their materials are already sex-fair, which to them means equal representation of the sexes, the absence of blatantly stereotyped examples, and some manner (not always sex-fair) of handling third-person singular pronouns. We urge the following:

1. Publishers should sensitize their writers and all personnel so that they fully implement guidelines already in place to eliminate sex bias in materials.
2. Special attention should be given to the publication of sex-affirmative instructional materials in which both males and females are portrayed in nonstereotyped roles and the benefits and problems of these roles are addressed.
3. Professional organizations and state departments of education should monitor the implementation of their guidelines on sex equity to ensure that all publications are sex-fair and that a proportion are sex-affirmative.

B. *Selection of Materials.* Controversy has surrounded the introduction of sex-equitable materials on the publishing market and in the public schools. Cries of censorship accompanied the publication of guidelines for eliminating sex bias in materials (for example, Kingston & Lovelace, 1977). Lawsuits calling for a ban of sex-equitable materials have been filed against schools by right-wing groups; other lawsuits protesting the censorship of specific books have been filed by teachers, parents, and students (American Library Association, 1981; Scott, 1982). Publishers, however, continue to publish a variety of instructional materials, both sex-biased and sex-equitable, and only a relatively few books have been banned from schools as a result of protest. Threats, however, may have influenced policies and discreet removal of some books. We urge the following:

1. All state and local school districts should pass legislation or develop policy statements that prohibit the purchase of sex-biased materials for public

schools (see Resource Center on Sex Equity, 1982, for a number of state plans already in effect).

2. Educators and citizen review panels who recommend purchase of textbooks should be trained in evaluating and selecting sex-equitable materials (see training programs available from Women's Educational Equity Act Program, Education Development Center, 55 Chapel Street, Newton, MA 02160).

3. Before purchasing instructional materials, educators should evaluate the quality and extent of sex-equitable content, using one of a number of review instruments available (see, for example, U.S. Commission on Civil Rights, 1979).

4. Educators should give special consideration to making purchases from publishers that are well known for their sex-affirmative materials (for example, Council on Interracial Books for Children, 1841 Broadway, New York, NY 10023; The Feminist Press, Box 334, Old Westbury, NY 11568; TABS: Aids for Ending Sexism in School, 744 Carroll Street, Brooklyn, NY 11215; Women's Action Alliance, 370 Lexington Avenue, New York, NY 10017; Women's Educational Equity Act Program, Education Development Center, address above. *Fair Textbooks* lists others).

5. School districts should purchase only instructional materials that are sex-fair or sex-affirmative. Characteristics of these materials include (*a*) language that uses gender-unspecified or gender-specific forms rather than male generic terminology, (*b*) females portrayed in numbers proportional to reality, (*c*) nontraditional roles portrayed for both females and males, and (*d*) explanations of the problems and benefits of nonstereotypic roles and activities.

C. *Using Materials.* Realistically, teachers may have little choice but to teach with sex-biased materials. In making decisions about how to use sex-biased as well as sex-equitable material, teachers need to consider the effects of gender-related characteristics as well as the developmental stage of their pupils. We urge teachers to do the following:

1. For all students, attempt to reduce the potentially damaging effects of sex-biased materials by teaching children to evaluate materials for sex bias. By comparing them to reality, children can see the inaccurate pictures shown by the materials. Pupils can revise sex-biased materials by changing names and pronouns and by applying positive qualities to both females and males.

2. For all students, point out and discuss the nonstereotyped aspects of the people and situations portrayed in order to heighten pupils' perceptions and memory. Because pupils have difficulty generalizing from a single example, many nontraditional role models are necessary to counteract the many stereotypes found in instructional materials.

3. For preschool and primary school age children, provide exposure to as many sex-equitable materials, especially pictures, as possible. In these formative

years, the environment has a large impact on the development of gender schema, including those related to sex roles and sex role stereotypes.

4. For elementary age pupils, provide both exposure to sex-equitable materials and guidance in understanding the sex-affirmative aspects of people and situations. Pupils are very concerned with fairness,which can be used as a criterion for evaluating examples of both sex bias and sex equity in materials.

5. For secondary and college students, provide special exposure to and emphasis on the multiple roles found in adulthood and how those roles may be maintained simultaneously, may change over time, and/or may conflict with each other.

D. *Further Research.* A growing body of research literature supports the use of sex-equitable materials in the classroom. Several questions, however, need further investigation:

1. Which of the characteristics of sex-equitable materials are most responsible for change, and how powerful is each characteristic?
2. How much exposure to sex-equitable materials is necessary before they have an impact? Will attitudes continue to change with more and more exposure? And how long do the changes last?
3. How reliable and valid are the instruments being used to measure the effects?
4. Will adolescents and adults, with whom fewer studies have been done to date, be affected in the same ways as children by sex-equitable materials?
5. Will sex-equitable materials on topics other than vocational information, fiction, and social studies have the same effects? (For example, studies using mathematics, biological and physical sciences, and microcomputer materials are needed.)

CONCLUSION

Pupils who are exposed to sex-equitable materials are more likely than others to (1) have gender-balanced knowledge of people in society, (2) develop more flexible attitudes and more accurate sex role knowledge, and (3) imitate role behaviors contained in the materials. Neither interest in materials nor recall seems reduced by their use. The evidence is strong in support of using these materials to improve the learning experiences of both females and males. We urge that educators, publishers, policy makers, and parents take the steps recommended in this chapter to ensure sex equity in instructional materials.

REFERENCES

Adamsky, C. (1981). Changes in pronominal usage in a classroom situation. *Psychology of Women Quarterly, 5,* 773–779.

American Library Association. (1981). *Limiting what students shall read: Books and other learning materials in our public schools: How they are selected and how they are removed.* Chicago: Author.

Ashby, M. S., & Wittmaier, B. C. (1978). Attitude changes in children after exposure to stories about women in traditional or nontraditional occupations. *Journal of Educational Psychology, 70,* 945–949.

Bandura, A. (1965). Influence of models' reinforcement contingencies on the acquisition of imitative responses. *Journal of Personality and Social Psychology, 1,* 589–595.

Bandura, A. (1967). The role of modeling processes in personality development. In W. W. Hartup & N. L. Smothergill (Eds.), *The young child: Reviews of research* (pp. 334–343). Washington, DC: National Association for the Education of Young Children.

Barclay, L. K. (1974). The emergence of vocational expectations in preschool children. *Journal of Vocational Behavior, 4,* 1–14.

Bem, S. L., & Bem, D. J. (1973). Does sex-biased job advertising "aid and abet" sex discrimination? *Journal of Applied Social Psychology, 3,* 6–18.

Berg, Cross, L., & Berg-Cross, G. (1978). Listening to stories may change children's attitudes. *Reading Teacher, 31,* 659–663.

Beuf, A. Doctor, lawyer, household drudge. (1974). *Journal of Communications, 24,* 142–145.

Beyard-Tyler, K. C., & Sullivan, H. J. (1980). Adolescent reading preferences for type of theme and sex of character. *Reading Research Quarterly, 16,* 104–120.

Britton, G. E., & Lumpkin, M. C. (1977). For sale: Subliminal bias in textbooks. *Reading Teacher, 31,* 40–45.

Campbell, P. C., & Wirtenberg, J. (1980). How books influence children: What the research shows. *Interracial Books for Children, 11,* 3–6.

Connor, J. M., & Serbin, L. A. (1978). Children's responses to stories with male and female characters. *Sex Roles, 4,* 637–645.

Costello, E. M. (1979). The impact of language in job advertising on fair practices in hiring: a research note. *Journal of Applied Social Psychology, 9,* 323–325.

Davidson, E. S., Yasuna, A., & Tower, A. (1979). The effects of television cartoons on sex-role stereotyping in young girls. *Child Development, 50,* 597–600.

Deutsch, F. (1975). Effects of sex of subject and story character on preschoolers' perceptions of affective responses and intrapersonal behavior in story sequences. *Developmental Psychology, 11,* 112–113.

Eakins, B. W., & Eakins, R. G. (1978). *Sex differences in human communication.* Boston: Houghton Mifflin.

Fischer, P. L., & Torney, J. V. (1976). Influence of children's stories on dependency, a sex-typed behavior. *Developmental Psychology, 12,* 489–490.

Flerx, V. C., Fidler, D. S., & Rogers, R. W. (1976). Sex role stereotypes: Developmental aspects and early intervention. *Child Development, 47,* 998–1007.

Franzoni, J. B. (1980). *Children's reactions to gender-biased materials in career education.* Paper presented at the annual meeting of the American Psychological Association, Montreal.

Frasher, R. S. (1977). Boys, girls, and *Pippi Longstocking. Reading Teacher, 30,* 860–863.

Frasher, R. S., & Frasher, J. M. (1978). Influence of story characters' roles on comprehension. *Reading Teacher, 32,* 160–164.

Friedrich, L. K., & Stein, A. H. (1975). Prosocial television and young children: The effects of verbal labeling and role playing on learning and behavior. *Child Development, 46,* 27–38.

Greene, A. L., Sullivan, H. J., & Beyard-Tyler, K. (1982). Attitudinal effects of the use of role models in information about sex-typed careers. *Journal of Educational Psychology, 74,* 393–398.

Harrison, L. (1975). Cro-Magnon women—In eclipse. *Science Teacher, 42,* 8–11.

Harrison, L., & Passero, R. (1975). Sexism in the language of elementary school textbooks. *Science and Children, 12,* 22–25.

Hurwitz, R. E., & White, M. A. (1977). Effect of sex-linked vocational information on reported occupational choices of high school juniors. *Psychology of Women Quarterly, 2,* 149–156.

Jaudon-Kropp, J., & Halverson, C. F. (1983). Preschool children's preferences and recall for sex-appropriate and sex-inappropriate stories. *Sex Roles, 9,* 261–272.

Jean, P., & Murphy-Berman, V. (1981). *Children's perception of "gender neutral" words: A case of sexism in language processings.* Unpublished manuscript, University of Nebraska-Lincoln.

Jennings, S. A. (1975). Effects of sex typing in children's stories on preference and recall. *Child Development, 46,* 220–223.

Johnson, C. S., & Greenbaum, G. R. (1982). Girls' and boys' reading interests: A review of the research. In E. Sheridan (Ed.), *Sex stereotypes and reading: Research and strategies* (pp. 35–48). Newark, DE: International Reading Association.

Johnston, J., Ettema, J., & Davidson, T. (1980). *An evaluation of* Freestyle: *A television series to reduce sex-role stereotypes.* Ann Arbor: University of Michigan, Institute for Social Research.

Kidd, V. (1971). A study of the images produced through the use of male pronoun as the generic. *Moments in Contemporary Rhetoric and Communication, 1,* 25–30.

Kingston, A. J., & Lovelace, T. L. (1977). Guidelines for authors: A new form of censorship. *Journal of Reading Behavior, 9,* 89–93.

Kingston, A. J., & Lovelace, T. L. (1977–78). Sexism and reading: A critical review of the literature. *Reading Research Quarterly, 13,* 133–161.

Klein, H. A. (1970). Interest and comprehension in sex-typed materials. In J. H. Catterson (Ed.), *Children and literature.* Newark, DE: International Reading Association.

Klein, H. A. (1979). What effect does nonsexist content have on the reading of boys and girls? *Reading Improvement, 16,* 134–138.

Knell, S., & Winer, G. A. (1979). Effects of reading content on occupational sex role stereotypes. *Journal of Vocational Behavior, 14,* 78–87.

Koblinsky, S. G., Cruse, D. F., & Sugawara, A. I. (1978). Sex role stereotypes and children's memory for story content. *Child Development, 49,* 452–458.

Lakoff, R. (1975). *Language and woman's place.* New York: Harper & Row.

Larder, D. L. (1962). Effect of aggressive story content on nonverbal play behavior. *Psychological Reports, 11,* 14.

Lutes-Dunckley, C. J. (1978). Sex-role preferences as a function of sex of storyteller and story content. *Journal of Psychology, 100,* 151–158.

Martyna, W. (1978). What does "he" mean? Use of generic masculine. *Journal of Communication, 28,* 131–138.

McArthur, L. Z., & Eisen, S. V. (1976). Achievements of male and female storybook characters as determinants of achievement behavior by boys and girls. *Journal of Personality and Social Psychology, 33,* 467–473.

McGhee, P. E., & Frueh, T. (1980). Television viewing and the learning of sex-role stereotypes. *Sex Roles, 6,* 179–188.

Miller, C., & Swift, K. (1977). *Words and women.* Garden City, N.Y.: Anchor Books.

Mischel, W. (1970). Sex-typing and socialization. In P. H. Mussen (Ed.), *Carmichael's manual of child psychology* (pp. 3–60) (3rd ed.). NY: Wiley.

Moulton, J., Robinson, G. M., & Elias, C. (1978). Sex bias in language use: "Neutral" pronouns that aren't. *American Psychologist, 33,* 1032–1036.

National Institutes of Mental Health. (1982). *Television and behavior.* Bethesda, MD: Author.

Nilsen, A. P., Bosmajian, H., Gershuny, H. L., & Stanley, J. P. (Eds.). (1977). *Sexism and language.* Urbana, IL: National Council of Teachers of English.

Pingree, S. (1978). The effects of nonsexist television commercials and perceptions of reality on children's attitudes about women. *Psychology of Women Quarterly, 2,* 262–277.

Rakes, T. A., Bowman, H. L., & Gottfred, S. (1977). Reader preference as related to female aggressiveness and stereotyped character roles. *Reading Improvement, 14,* 30–35.

Resource Center on Sex Equity. (1982). *Policies for the future: State policies, regulations, and resources related to the achievement of educational equity for females and males.* Washington, DC: Council of Chief State School Officers.

Rose, C., Zimet, S. G., & Blom, G. E. (1972). Content counts: Children have preferences in reading textbook stories. *Elementary English, 49,* 14–19.

Ross, L., Anderson, D. R., & Wisocki, P. A. (1982). Television viewing and adult sex-role attitudes. *Sex Roles, 8,* 589–592.

Schau, C. G. (1978). *Evaluating the use of sex-role-reversed stories for changing children's stereotypes.* Paper presented at the annual meeting of the American Educational Research Association, Toronto.

Schau, C. G., Kahn, L., & Tremaine, L. (1976). *Effects of stories on elementary school children's gender-stereotyped attitudes toward adult occupations.* Unpublished manuscript, University of New Mexico, Albuquerque.

Schneider, J. W., & Hacker, S. L. (1973). Sex-role imagery and use of the generic "man" in introductory texts: A case in the sociology of sociology. *American Sociologist, 8,* 12–18.

Scott, J. A. (1982). Book banning in the high schools, 1975–81. *Social Education, 46,* 257–262.

Scott, K. P. (1981). Whatever happened to Jane and Dick: Sexism in texts re-examined. *Peabody Journal of Education, 58,* 135–140.

Scott, K. P., & Feldman-Summers, S. (1979). Children's reactions to textbook stories in which females are portrayed in traditionally male roles. *Journal of Educational Psychology, 71,* 396–402.

Thorne, B., & Henley, N. (Eds.). (1975). *Language and sex: Difference and dominance.* Rowley, MA: Newbury House.

Tibbetts, S. L. (1974). Sex differences in children's reading preferences. *Reading Teacher, 28,* 279–281.

U.S. Commission on Civil Rights. (1979). *Fair textbooks: A resource guide.* Washington, DC: U.S. Government Printing Office.

U.S. Commission on Civil Rights. (1980). *Characters in textbooks: A review of the literature.* Washington, DC: U.S. Government Printing Office.

Wilson, L. C. (1978). Teachers' inclusion of males and females in generic nouns. *Research in the Teaching of English, 12,* 155–161.

Women on Words and Images. (1972). *Dick and Jane as victims: Sex stereotyping in children's readers.* Princeton, NJ: Author.

Yanico, B. J. (1978). Sex bias in career information: Effects of language on attitudes. *Journal of Vocational Behavior, 13,* 26–34.

Zimet, S. G. (1966). Children's interest and story preferences: A critical review of the literature. *Elementary School Journal, 67,* 122–130.

PART IV

Sex Equity Strategies in the Content Areas

Peggy J. Blackwell and Lillian N. Russo

This section is about achieving sex equity through the content of education offered in the schools. The six chapters, which discuss mathematics, science, and engineering; communication skills; social studies; visual arts education; physical education and athletics; and career and vocational education, cover a variety of approaches to sex equity within the curriculum of education. Of necessity, these chapters reflect only a sampling of the possible content areas, but were chosen to present a sample of sufficient breadth and depth to represent six critical aspects of sex equity achievements in the content domain. The focus on strategies in the content areas builds, in particular, on the previous section on general educational practices for promoting sex equity.

The authors describe the key needs and issues involved in their content areas, the strategies and sex-fair programs that have been developed to respond to the needs and issues, the outcomes that have occurred in implementation of the strategies and programs, and recommendations for future research and policy. As might be expected, some content areas have substantial and well-documented evidence of successes and failures in achieving equity, while others are just in the beginning stages. This is probably due to equity concerns in federal laws such as Title IX and the Career and Vocational Education Acts, which have aided the progress of work in sex equity in some content areas, such as mathematics and science, more than in others such as the arts or business, where sex equity in education has not been mentioned.

An overall state-of-the-art description and a documentation of the processes involved in achieving that state are provided by the authors. Their reports indicate that the effective approaches for achieving sex equity are as many and as complex as the constraints hindering their fulfillment. The outcomes documented are generally positive, although not always even or consistent. But the research reported demonstrates that sex equity can be taught, that it can be taught as an integral part of the content, and that quality control of the process is possible.

In chapter 13, Stage, Kreinberg, Parsons, and Becker address the progress made over the past 15 years for women in science, mathematics, and engineering. Two key issues are identified. First, mathematics is a critical filter for women in making a career choice in any of the three general fields; thus, there has been a systematic attempt in public and higher education to influence girls and women to enroll in mathematics and science courses. Second, this field has suffered from a history of inadequate role models, confused career development planning, and poor teaching, which is often confounded by differential teacher interactions with female and male students. A model for other educational content areas is presented, however, by the close relationship between sex equity research and development in these three fields. This relationship has been a significantly synergistic one, with research findings leading to program development and the results from implementation of programs feeding back into research.

Chapter 14, by Scott, Dwyer, and Lieb-Brilhart, looks at sex differences in language-related areas and examines educational approaches that are effective in promoting sex equity. Although females are typically presented as superior to males in reading and language, the authors point out that on measures taken after puberty, females do not score consistently higher on complex verbal skills than do males. They also provide evidence indicating that small sex differences appear in gifted populations, that larger sex differences are associated with disadvantaged and lower-ability students, and that different measuring instruments result in different patterns of apparent sex differences. Not surprisingly, the authors conclude that more and better role models are needed in reading for boys and in more complex verbal skill areas for girls and that nonstereotyped reading materials are necessary.

In chapter 15, Hahn and Bernard-Powers examine the field of social studies and indicate that the practitioners in the field do not, in fact, practice what they teach—that there is equality and justice for all in the content and inequity in practice in staffing patterns and in curriculum and media presentation. Issues identified include textbooks, where females are generally underrepresented and presented in stereotypic fashion; gender differences in knowledge and attitude; and the cultural impact of knowledge about and attitudes toward women when some students have unrealistic information about the economic position of women. Research in the field has shown that gender stereotyping decreases when students are exposed to instruction specifically directed at that goal, and the authors recommend that such instruction be made a part of the curriculum.

In chapter 16, Sandell, Collins, and Sherman address the professional and content issues in visual arts education. They point out that in the art world the female population is large, but the field is dominated by males. Women tend to be perceived as less serious and less committed. Sex inequities in visual arts are not always apparent, and the anomaly arises that in a field heavily populated by women, there are few role models available for them. Men are perceived as the "artists," and art education has been relegated to second-class status because it is viewed as feminine. Perhaps in part due to this, strategies for equity have been developed and implemented at the higher education level, but to a much lesser extent at the public elementary and secondary school levels. The authors recommend the development of a discipline-specific model for sex equity efforts in art education.

The topic of Chapter 17, by Geadelmann, is physical education and athletics. This chapter presents the concept of fairness and fair play as the basis of American athletics and physical education and makes the point that although women have had separate and different worlds in these fields, their worlds have not been separate and equal. The perpetuation of sex stereotypes, different expectations and treatments, and the loss of leadership opportunities for women have compounded this problem. Positive changes have occurred with the recognition of the physical capabilities of females and with public support and promotion of sport experience for females. Unfortunately, the exclusion and limited access of women have long been a standard part of physical education and athletics. Females have been deprived of options for full development, and the result has been a negative self-image. The author recommends research directed toward a conceptual framework that can provide for the full development of males and females alike.

Career and vocational education are the subject of chapter 18, by Farmer and Sidney. A focus of this chapter is the shifting roles of men and women and the need to increase the options available to young people. One issue presented is the influence of sex-related occupational and homemaking stereotypes on the life choices made by students. Another is differences in self-concept: females tend not to see themselves in terms of work and aggression, while males identify less with home and relationships. The authors discuss the inequalities in analytic and decision-making skills related to choosing a career and the inadequate training of counselors. In addition, they present information related to the inequalities in vocational education. The authors identify several programs with demonstrated effectiveness for high school students and survey promising programs that have the potential of being field-tested. Key recommendations are that research be undertaken to compare different approaches to achieving sex equity goals, that longitudinal studies be conducted, and that emphasis be placed on the curriculum from elementary level to adult education.

As one reads the chapters in this section, common themes are evident. Perhaps the key theme is the question of sex differences or gender superiority. Investigation into potential sex differences (for example, male superiority in many areas) predates the systematic sex equity research and development currently prevalent. And, as pointed out in the chapters, conflicting results from the new scholarship on sex equity have challenged the findings of previous investigations. One conclusion is that sex differences are related more to the research design of the studies than to gender itself and thus might be referred to as gender-demonstrated (related to the design) rather than gender-induced (caused by gender). The sex differences issue, nevertheless, prevails in the chapters as a gender-induced concern instead of a research design question, although the authors generally conclude that almost all sex differences are learned rather than inherited.

A second theme of the chapters is the nature of instruction itself. All chapter authors report appreciable gains in information levels and skills development and positive changes in values and attitudes about sex equity issues and concerns. Instruction can and does make a positive (or a negative) difference and, in reality, cannot be addressed apart from the content areas. A major issue of instruction yet to be resolved is the question of separate- or same-sex groupings or classes. While some authors report that same-gender groupings facilitate and enhance instruction, for example in mathematics, others report that same-gender groups inhibit the primary objectives of the program or course, for example in physical education. It would seem that this is not an either-or issue, but one in which trade-offs between balance and priorities must be made.

A third key issue is the development of a positive self-image. The authors make clear that there is abundant evidence that the role expectations of parents, teachers, the media, and the general culture, as well as role models, are the key sources of one's self-concept. They also make clear that gender-free expectations and positive role models lead to positive ego-image development and that a positive self-image is a primary condition of successful personal growth and development, for both females and males. A significant outgrowth of these findings is increased emphasis on the affective dimensions of learning. Special attention is given to support activities and networks that focus on reducing subject-related anxiety, increasing confidence, and providing assertiveness training, even though the primary focus is on the academic area. It is these kinds of growth in understanding and responding to learner needs within the content areas that could never have occurred without the research and development work provided by sex equity specialists.

13

Increasing the Participation and Achievement of Girls and Women in Mathematics, Science, and Engineering

Elizabeth K. Stage, Nancy Kreinberg,
Jacquelynne Eccles (Parsons),
and Joanne Rossi Becker,
with Michele Aldrich, Kriston Anton,
M. Joan Callanan, Patricia Casserly,
Claudia E. Cohen, Nancy Cook,
Yolanda Scott George, Shelia M. Humphreys,
Judith Jacobs, Alma Lantz,
Shirley Malcom, Sheila M. Pfafflin,
Diane Resek, Carol M. Shaw,
Walter S. Smith, Henrie Turner,
Betty Vetter, and Iris Weiss

Women have made substantial inroads in the last 15 years into the fields of mathematics, science, and engineering. The proportion of women earning doctorates in science and engineering, for example, has risen from 7% in 1965 to 25% in 1980 (National Research Council, 1980). As figure 2 shows, however, most of this increase is attributable to large proportions of women in the social and life sciences; women are still at or below 12% of the Ph.D.'s in mathematics, the physical sciences, and engineering. At the undergraduate level, the proportion of women planning majors in science and engineering also has been increasing (Cooperative Institutional Research Program, 1974–1982). The greatest percentage increase has been in the field of engineering, in which there were 358 women who earned bachelor's degrees in 1970, representing 0.8% of the graduating class, and 5,680 women in 1980, representing 9.7% of the graduating class. With a projection for 1984 of 14%, it is clear that there have been impressive inroads in the area of engineering. Yet, at this rate of 1% per year, it will be 2020 before there are equal numbers of women and men earning engineering degrees!

A similarly mixed picture appears when the employment of women scien-

Reviewers for this chapter were Peggy Blackwell, Elizabeth Fennema, Sheila Humphreys, Susan Klein, Lillian Russo, and Carol Tittle.

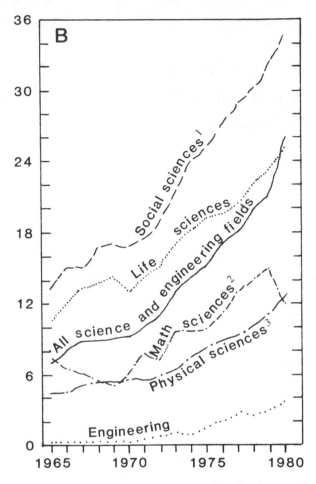

Figure 2.   Women as a percentage of total science and engineering doctorate recipients by field: 1965–80.
(*Source:* National Research Council. From "Women Scientists and Engineers: Trends in Participation" by B. M. Vetter, *Science, 214,* pp. 1313–1321, 18 December 1981. © 1981 by the AAAS.)
[1]Includes psychology.
[2]Includes computer sciences.
[3]Includes environmental sciences (earth sciences, oceanography, and atmospheric sciences).

tists and engineers is surveyed. Female degree holders have higher unemployment rates than male degree holders, are less likely to be employed in science and engineering jobs, and are paid less. In academic settings, for example, 62.5% of the men with doctorates had tenure in their fields in 1979, compared to only 35.2% of the women with doctorates (Vetter, 1981).

Examination of participation and achievement of young women in mathematics and science, relative to young men, indicates that the message is also inconsistent. Some national enrollment surveys have found parity in election of mathematics courses in high school (Armstrong, 1981), except at the highest level of calculus, though investigation from state to state shows that there are still substantial differences at the intermediate level of Algebra II (California Basic Educational Data System, 1981). Some researchers are not finding sex-related differences in achievement in areas in which they used to find them consistently (for example, spatial visualization; see discussion below). The National Assessment of Educational Progress, however, continues to find sex-related differences in science and mathematics achievement that increase from age 9 to age 13 to age 17 (Fennema & Carpenter, 1981).

The progress of women in science is, of course, due to a number of factors. In this chapter, however, we will concentrate on educational research and educational program development, and their interrelationship, as major contributors to this progress. It is our contention that the close relationship between research and development activities related to women's participation in math-related fields is an important catalyst for advancement in both research and development. A good example is the research of the Berkeley sociologist Lucy Sells, who investigated the persistence of women and minorities in different doctoral fields (Sells, 1975). She found that mathematics training in secondary schools was a "critical filter" for these groups, keeping many students from studying various scientific fields as undergraduate or graduate students. Her personal enthusiasm prompted the founding of the Math/Science Network, now a group of 1,000 scientists, educators, and community people who work together to promote the participation of women in math-related and nontraditional fields. Several Network programs are described in later sections in this chapter. The popularization of the "critical filter" idea (Ernest, 1976) caused many educators to take an interest in secondary school mathematics course enrollments.

At about the same time, Maccoby and Jacklin (1974) published their landmark review of the published and unpublished literature on psychological sex differences. While they cast serious doubt on many long-held myths, they allowed to stand as "fairly well established" the belief that "boys excel in mathematical ability" (p. 352). They noted that males and females are similar in mathematical skills through elementary school, but that at about ages 12–13 boys' mathematical skills increase faster than girls'. They also indicated that the rate of improvement was not entirely a function of the number of mathematics courses taken, although that question had not been extensively studied at that time. Shortly thereafter, however, the work of Fennema and Sherman (1977) showed that among students whose mathematics backgrounds were similar, sex-related differences in mathematics achievement were found inconsistently, were small, and were related to affective factors such as confidence, perceived usefulness of mathematics, and perceptions of significant others.

The emerging emphasis on enrollment in elective mathematics classes led to two parallel movements. The desire to understand the causes of lower enrollment among females prompted the National Institute of Education (NIE) to commission papers to assist them in planning their research agenda for 1978 and 1979 (Fox, Fennema, & Sherman, 1977). A concerted research program was launched, in which researchers with various perspectives and methodologies set out to investigate the participation and achievement of women in mathematics. These studies are some of the classics to be reviewed in the following section. (A forthcoming book, *Women and Mathematics: Balancing the Equation* [Chipman, Brush, & Wilson, in press] synthesizes this work.) The desire to influence girls and women to enroll in mathematics and science courses and programs and to increase their success once enrolled prompted a number of educators to step up their activity in programs for women in science and mathematics education. There have been interaction and cooperation between the researchers and the developers, and many individuals have participated. For purposes of examining the impact of these activities, however, it is helpful first to summarize the issues raised by the research, then to detail the ways in which these issues have been addressed by intervention programs and changes in the educational system. Research issues in mathematics will be considered before the other sciences because of its status as a prerequisite for success in science and engineering.

ISSUES IDENTIFIED BY THE RESEARCH ON WOMEN IN MATHEMATICS

Sex-related Differences in Mathematics

Sex Differences on Tests of Quantitative Skills.   The following results are fairly consistent across studies using a variety of achievement tests: (1) high school boys perform a little better than high school girls on tests of mathematical reasoning (primarily solving word problems); (2) boys and girls perform similarly on tests of algebra and basic mathematical knowledge; and (3) girls occasionally outperform boys on tests of computational skills (Armstrong, 1981; Burnett, Lane, & Dratt, 1979; Connor & Serbin, 1980; E.T.S., 1979; Fennema & Sherman, 1977, 1978; Hyde, 1981; Schratz, 1978; Sherman, 1980, 1981; Starr, 1979; Steel & Wise, 1979; Wittig & Petersen, 1979). Among normal populations, achievement differences favoring boys do not emerge with any consistency prior to the 10th grade, are typically not very large, and are not universally found, even in advanced high school populations. There is some evidence, however, that the general pattern of sex differences may emerge somewhat earlier among gifted and talented students (Benbow & Stanley, 1980; E.T.S., 1979).

Sex Differences in Spatial Skills.   The findings regarding sex differences in spatial skills are also fairly consistent, though not universal, and do not emerge prior to about the 10th grade. Among these older adolescents, boys outperform girls on some measures of spatial skills, but the magnitude of the sex difference varies depending on body type (Petersen, 1979), on personality characteristics associated with masculinity and femininity (Nash, 1979), on previous experience with spatial activities (Burnett & Lane, 1980; Connor, Schackman, &

Serbin, 1978; Connor, Serbin, & Schackman, 1977), on ethnic background, parental styles, and socioeconomic status (Fennema & Sherman, 1977; Nash, 1979; Schratz, 1978), on maturational rate (Waber, 1979), and on the particular test given (Connor & Serbin, 1980). In fact, in a recent national survey study of 3,240 junior and senior high school students, 13-year-old girls did better on a test of spatial skill than 13-year-old boys; 12th-grade boys and girls did equally well (Armstrong, 1981). Thus, as Connor and Serbin conclude, "Junior and senior high school males . . . perform better than females on some visual-spatial measures, some of the time" (p. 36).

Relation of Spatial Skills to Mathematics Achievement.   Several studies have demonstrated a strong positive correlation between spatial skills and a variety of mathematical achievement test scores (Armstrong, 1981; Burnett et al., 1979; Connor & Serbin, 1980; Fennema & Sherman, 1977, 1978; Sherman, 1980; Steel & Wise, 1979). But verbal abilities also correlate quite highly with mathematical performance; not all measures of spatial skills correlate significantly with all measures of mathematical achievement; and the patterns of these relations vary across grade level, sex, and study (Armstrong, 1981; Burnett et al., 1979; Connor & Serbin, 1980; Fennema & Sherman, 1977, 1978; Hyde, Geiringer, & Yen, 1975; Sherman, 1980; Steel & Wise, 1979). Further, in a recent factor analytic study, Connor and Serbin (1980) found that the tests of spatial skills factor together and independently of measures of mathematical achievement. Thus, the relation between spatial skills and mathematical achievement is not clear. Furthermore, whether or not the sex difference in spatial skills contributes to the sex difference in mathematical achievement is even less clear. While some findings are consistent with this hypothesis (for example, Burnett et al., 1979; Fennema & Sherman, 1977; and Hyde et al., 1975), others are not (for example, Connor & Serbin, 1980; Steel & Wise, 1979).

Whether the sex differences in either mathematical ability or spatial skills contribute to the sex differences in course participation rates is even more debatable. The pattern of results is quite mixed. For example, in a study by Sherman (1981), spatial skills predicted girls' but not boys' participation. In contrast, in Steel and Wise's study (1979), spatial skills predicted for boys only. Participation is also predicted by scores on vocabulary tests (Sherman, 1981), by past math achievements (Armstrong, 1981; Dunteman, Wisenbaker, & Taylor, 1978; Eccles, Adler, & Meece, 1984; Steel & Wise, 1979), by interest in mathematics and career plans (for example, Eccles (Parsons) et al., 1983; Steel & Wise, 1979), and by a variety of attitudinal and social factors which will be reviewed in the next section. In addition, it must be noted that spatial visualization skills can be trained (Burnett & Lane, 1980; Connor et al., 1977, 1978; Goldstein & Chance, 1965).

Socialization Factors

Modeling Effects.   Several studies have found that adult females are both less likely to be engaged in math activities and more likely to express doubts about their math abilities than are adult males. For example, after sixth grade, fathers are more likely to help their children with their math homework than are mothers (Ernest, 1976); advanced math courses are more likely to be taught by men (Fox et al., 1977); female elementary preservice teachers have lower estimates of their math ability and openly admit they are less comfortable teaching math than their male peers (Aiken, 1970); and finally, mothers hold a more negative view of their math abilities and interest than do fathers (Parsons, Adler, & Kaczala, 1982). This underrepresentation of appropriate female role models could discourage some girls from engaging in activities involving mathematics during the high school years. The success of several recent intervention programs designed to increase female math participation through exposure to female models supports this line of reasoning (for example, Brody & Fox, 1980; Tobin & Fox, 1980).

Socializers' Expectations and Related Behaviors.   The expectations parents and teachers hold for children are another possible source of influence on children's math involvement. Several studies indicate that parents and teachers have higher educational expectancies for high school and college age males than for comparable females (Good, Sikes, & Brophy, 1973; Hilton & Berglun, 1974; Sears, Maccoby, & Levin, 1957). Only a few studies have directly measured the expectancies that parents and teachers hold for math achievement. While these studies have yielded a mixed pattern of results, when differences emerge, they favor boys. For example, in some studies both parents and teachers believe boys are better at math than girls (Casserly, 1975; Ernest, 1976; Haven, 1971; Luchins, 1976). Similarly, parents rate math as more difficult for daughters than for sons and feel that girls have to work harder than boys in order to do well in math courses (Parsons, Adler, & Kaczala, 1982). Other studies, however, yield either inconsistent or nonsignificant sex effects (for example, Ernest, 1976, Parsons, Adler, & Kaczala, 1982; Parsons, Kaczala, & Meece, 1982). For example, in the 1982 studies by Parsons and her associates, neither parents nor teachers had lower expectations for their girls' math performance than for their boys'. Thus, it appears that the sex stereotypes held by parents and teachers are small and perhaps diminishing, but favor boys when they are present.

Do these stereotypes affect students' attitudes, and if so, how? Parents, teachers, and counselors have all been found to provide boys more explicit rewards, encouragement, and reinforcements for learning math and for considering math-related careers than girls (Cooperative Institutional Research Program, 1974; Casserly, 1975; Haven, 1971; Luchins, 1976; Parsons, Adler, & Kaczala, 1982; Parsons, Kaczala, & Meece, 1982). In one study the counselors openly admitted discouraging girls from taking these courses, citing reasons that reflected their stereotyped views of appropriate adult roles and math abilities. In addition, based on extensive observations in classrooms, several investigators have concluded that the quantity and type of teacher instruction sometimes varies according to the sex of the student and the subject matter being taught. Some, but not all, teachers interact more with, provide more praise to, and provide more formal instruction to boys than girls, especially in mathematics and science classes (Bean, 1976; Becker, 1981; Brophy & Good, 1974; Leinhardt, Seewald, & Engel, 1979; Eccles, Kaczala, & Meece, 1982); Stallings, 1979). These differences in teacher behavior, when found, are most extreme among students with high math ability.

While the pattern of results associated with differential treatment is fairly consistent, studies that have attempted to assess the causal influence of these differences on course enrollment or career aspirations have yielded a much less definitive picture. Both Heller and Parsons (1981) and Eccles, Kaczala, & Meece, 1982) tested the relation of student-teacher interaction patterns both to students' attitudes toward math and to their plans to continue taking math. While both studies found a significant relation between teachers' expectations for a student (as provided by the teacher on a written questionnaire) and student attitudes even after the effects of the students' past grades in mathematics had been partialed out, both studies found very few significant relations between actual teacher behaviors and student attitudes—and those that did emerge were quite small. Other studies, focusing more on the impact of a single salient teacher, suggest that teachers can have a big impact on girls' attitudes. But the teachers must provide *active* encouragement to the girls in the form of (1) exposure to role models, (2) sincere praise for high ability and high performance, and (3) explicit advice regarding the value of math and its potential utility for high-paying, prestigious jobs (Casserly, 1975, 1979).

Studies demonstrating the causal influence of parents in shaping sex differences in math participation are virtually nonexistent. For example, Parsons and her colleagues have demonstrated that parents' sex-stereotyped beliefs are related to girls' more negative attitudes toward math. It is not clear, however, whether the parents' stereotyping fostered the daughters' negative attitudes or the daughters' negative attitudes fostered the parents' stereotyping (Parsons, Adler, & Kaczala, 1982).

Differential Experiences.   In addition to the more direct socialization effects discussed thus far, parents and teachers also influence children's achievement behaviors and values through the experiences they provide or encourage. Exposure to different toys and recreational activities has been linked to sex differences in both spatial skill and attitudes toward math and science (Astin, 1974; Connor et al., 1978; Hilton & Berglund, 1974).

Early independence training has also been suggested as a cause of sex differences in math involvement (Ferguson & Maccoby, 1966; Hoffman, 1972; Stein & Bailey, 1973). Since independence training facilitates math achievement (Bing, 1963; Ferguson & Maccoby, 1966), and since girls may get less independence training than boys, the sex difference in math involvement may result from these differential socialization practices. This hypothesis has yet to be tested directly.

Summary.   The studies reviewed in this section provide strong support for the hypothesis that socializers treat boys and girls differently in a variety of ways that might be linked to math achievement and course selection. But only a few studies have assessed the causal impact of these socialization experiences on students' math attitudes, math achievement, and course selection. The results of these few studies suggest that sex differences in math behaviors and course selection may result from the differential treatment accorded girls and boys. For example, encouragement from parents has emerged in several studies as an important factor in girls' decisions to elect advanced mathematics courses in high school (for example, Armstrong, 1981; Haven, 1971; Luchins, 1976; Parsons, Adler, & Kaczala, 1982). The effects hold up longitudinally and are significant even when the effects of the children's past performance in mathematics are partialed out (Eccles [Parsons] et al., 1983). Thus, it seems likely that parents and teachers are having a negative impact on some girls' decisions to take math courses.

Attitudinal Factors

Confidence in One's Math Ability.   The pattern of findings regarding confidence in one's math ability and related attitudes are quite consistent. While sex differences are typically not present among elementary school children, by junior high school boys are more confident of their math abilities than girls (for example, Armstrong & Kahl, 1980; Brush, 1980; Eccles [Parsons] et al., 1983; Ernest, 1976; Fennema & Sherman, 1977; Fox, Brody, & Tobin, 1980; Kaminski, Erickson, Ross, & Bradfield, 1976; Sherman, 1980). This sex difference, however, is not reflected in students' expectations for their performance in the courses in which they are currently enrolled (Eccles [Parsons] et al., 1983; Heller & Parsons, 1981). Rather, the sex difference emerges on measures reflecting students' more general rating of confidence in their math abilities and their expectations for future courses.

Although sex differences in confidence have been established, only a few studies have tested the link between confidence in one's math ability and course selection. These studies have yielded consistent findings of a positive relation between confidence and enrollment patterns (Armstrong, 1981; Eccles [Parsons] et al., 1983; Kaminski et al., 1976; Sherman, 1980; Sherman & Fennema, 1977). More studies, however, are needed to clarify the causal significance of this relationship.

Sex Typing of Mathematics.   Although numerous studies have shown that when high school students sex-type mathematics they classify it as a male achievement domain (Armstrong & Kahl, 1980; Eccles [Parsons] et al., 1983; Ernest, 1976; Stein & Smithells, 1969), the implication of this fact for math enrollment is not clear for several reasons. First, math is neither always stereotyped as masculine (for example, Eccles [Parsons] et al., 1983; Stein & Smithells, 1969), nor is it even one of the most likely subject areas to be stereotyped; mechanical arts courses and athletics are both more likely to be classified as masculine (Stein & Smithells, 1969). Second, boys are more likely to stereotype math as masculine than are girls (for example, Brush, 1980; Eccles

[Parsons] et al., 1983; Fennema & Sherman, 1977; Sherman, 1980). Third, studies that have attempted to assess the relation of sex-typing of math to actual math achievement and course plans have yielded mixed results. Furthermore, the variations in results do not follow a consistent pattern (Boswell, 1979; Dwyer, 1974; Eccles, Kaczala, & Meece, 1982; Fennema & Sherman, 1977; Nash, 1975, 1979; Sherman, 1980). Thus, the relation between the sex-typing of mathematics and students' achievements and course plans in mathematics is not clear at present.

Perceived Value of Math.   Ratings of the utility value of math also vary by sex. Several studies indicate that boys, as early as the seventh and eighth grades, rate math as more useful than do girls (Brush, 1980; Eccles [Parsons] et al., 1983; Fennema & Sherman, 1977; Fox, Tobin, & Brody, 1979; Haven, 1971; Hilton & Berglund, 1974; Wise, Steel, & MacDonald, 1979). These results, however, are not entirely consistent across age groups and schools (Fennema & Sherman, 1977; Sherman, 1980).

Perceived value of math and math-related career plans emerge as significant predictors of both achievement and course plans in most studies (for example, Armstrong, 1981; Brush, 1980; Eccles [Parsons] et al., 1983; Eccles [Parsons], Adler, & Meece, 1984; Fennema & Sherman, 1977; Fox et al., 1980; Fox & Denham, 1974; Lantz & Smith, 1981; Wise et al., 1979). Furthermore, while Brush (1980) found that the perceived usefulness of math was a relatively weak predictor of course participation in comparison to other predictors such as ability level, socioeconomic status, and general feelings toward math, other investigators have found that interest in math and perceived utility value are two of the most important mediators of the sex differences in math involvement.

Affective Factors

In recent years math anxiety has emerged as yet another explanation for the sex difference in math involvement (Lazarus, 1974; Tobias, 1978; Tobias & Weissbrod, 1980). Although there are only a few empirical studies that have tested for sex differences in "math anxiety," and these are not entirely consistent, there is some support for the hypothesis that in high school and beyond girls have more negative affective response to math than boys (Brush, 1978, 1980; Dreger & Aiken, 1957; Meece, 1981; Suinn & Richardson, 1972). These studies, however, have not controlled for the possibility that boys may be less willing to admit to feelings of anxiety, especially since they regard mathematics as a male domain.

The few studies that have tested for the causal impact of anxiety on course taking suggest that anxiety does not have a large direct effect on course plans. Instead, it appears to have its most important effect on other variables related to students' course selection, such as how much they expect to like the course and how well they expect to do (Brush, 1980; Meece, 1981; Eccles, Adler, & Meece, 1984). In two of these studies, girls' attitudes were affected more by their anxiety levels than boys'. Thus, it is likely that anxiety is having a more negative effect on girls' math involvement than on boys'.

Summary of Past Research

We have reviewed several explanations for the sex difference in math involvement. Not surprisingly, no one cause has emerged with unequivocal support. Because aptitude differences appear to be quite small and difficult to assess, and because the majority of the researchers have been interested in identifying *modifiable* determinants of sex differences in participation, much of the recent research has focused on social and experiential factors. Evidence from these studies suggests that socializers have a powerful influence on students' academic choices. There is also fairly strong evidence suggesting that students themselves, through their attitudes, self-perceptions, and feelings about mathematics, are a major source of the sex differences in both math achievement and course enrollment patterns. Of these variables, confidence in one's ability and the perceived value of math appear to play the most critical roles.

RELATIONSHIP OF THE RESEARCH ON WOMEN IN SCIENCE AND ENGINEERING TO THAT IN MATHEMATICS

The research on women in science and engineering begins with the prerequisite abilities in mathematics, but the differences in mathematical ability and achievement described above cannot completely account for the differences in achievement and participation in science and engineering. This section considers the extent to which the research issues above are also relevant for science, and considers the additional factors in science and engineering.

The quantitative and spatial skills associated with high achievement in mathematics are also associated with high achievement in science, though the importance of spatial ability for science achievement is similarly uncertain. There is some evidence that spatial ability may be more important for some areas of science, particularly physical sciences and engineering, than it is for others, namely the life sciences (Kelly, 1975). Again, because differential experience with spatial activities is confounded with spatial ability, most science educators believe that the spatial ability deficit, if it exists, is modifiable through educational experiences.

The socialization factors discussed above are involved in science as well. Some factors, such as modeling, may be magnified with respect to science because there are fewer women to serve as role models, especially in engineering and physics. It has even been suggested that the most effective strategy for addressing the low participation of women in science is to reclaim the women who have science training and are not currently active as scientists. This would enlarge the proportion of active women scientists and alleviate the lack of role models and the sense of isolation that many female scientists feel (Lantz, 1979).

The sex-typing of science as masculine has been found as early as first and second grade, but recent research indicates that this stereotyping may be limited now to the physical sciences (Vockell & Lobonc, 1981). Similarly, analyzing the National Assessment of Educational Progress survey information on students' science experiences, investigators found that females were somewhat more likely than males to report experience with living plants and animals, but substantially less likely to report experience with magnets and electricity (Kahle & Lakes, 1983). These experiential differences increase with age, as do achievement differences in science.

Additional research that goes beyond the factors identified for mathematics has been done in science education. It has focused primarily on career development issues and has been hampered in two important ways. First, theories and literature in career development, especially in the sciences, are models that have been developed on male samples. A good example of this is a longitudinal study, using the Project TALENT data bank, in which the prediction equation for factors in high school that predicted subsequent scientific careers had to be based on the male sample because too few women in the sample of 23,700 1960 high school students became scientists by 1975 (Gilmartin, McLaughlin, Wise, & Rossi, 1976). Second, and closely related to the first point, retrospective studies of women who have succeeded in scientific careers have found that they are extremely capable individuals who probably could have succeeded in almost any field, so that their lives do not yield particular insights into women in science per se (for example, Kundsin, 1974). More extensive treatment of women's career development is given in chapter 18, Sex Equity in Career and Vocational Education.

INTERVENTION PROGRAMS DESIGNED TO INCREASE GIRLS' AND WOMEN'S PARTICIPATION AND ACHIEVEMENT IN MATHEMATICS, SCIENCE, AND ENGINEERING

Two years ago, the American Association for the Advancement of Science (AAAS) prepared an inventory of programs for women and girls in mathematics, science, and engineering (Aldrich & Hall, 1980). It covered projects started in the United States since 1966 and ended data collection in 1978. While such an inventory can never be complete, it included 315 projects. Observing that only half of the directors of NSF-funded career days for college women had completed the requested summaries, one of the authors has estimated that there may easily have been twice as many programs in all of the categories (Aldrich, 1982). Realizing that it is impossible to do justice to as many as 600 programs, in this section we will first summarize the characteristics of programs in the directory, then turn to descriptions of model programs.

Of the 315 projects in the AAAS directory, more than a third covered six or more fields of science, nearly all of which included mathematics. Of those projects that covered five or fewer fields, engineering (the focus of half) was the most popular. Approximately one-fifth of the program concentrated exclusively on mathematics. The projects were distributed throughout the educational system in almost a normal curve with respect to age—that is, a few at the elementary level, more in junior high and high schools, and the largest number at the undergraduate level, with a tapering off at the graduate and faculty development levels. The projects were also distributed widely around the country, and nearly all of them (84%) were university-based. There was variability in the participation of boys and men, and no project director reported the exclusion of men. The rate of involvement of minority and disabled women was requested from the project directors, but many did not have accurate data on their presence.

Model programs were selected by virtue of the availability of program descriptions and evaluation data, as well as judgments about the likelihood of replication and impact elsewhere. The presentation of the model programs will be organized by educational strategy (curriculum, conferences, and so forth) rather than by the problem that they set out to solve, because most of the programs had a number of complementary goals.

Due to space limitations, several important areas of concern have not been covered in depth in the program descriptions. Programs for minority women can' be investigated through the Minority Women in Science Network (Paula Quick Hall, Office for Opportunities in Science, AAAS, 1776 Massachusetts Avenue, Washington, DC 20036), and the Minorities and Mathematics Network (Westina Matthews, c/o Chicago Associates for Social Research, 410 South Michigan Avenue, Suite 525, Chicago, IL 60605). Activities sponsored or facilitated by campus women's centers provide support to students and faculty (for example, Humphreys, 1981). Outside the United States there are programs such as a major national study in Canada (see Ferguson, 1982) and an "action research project" in England (Small, Whyte, & Kelly, 1982). The emerging area of women and technology has also been neglected in this chapter (Zimmerman, 1981), although intervention strategies have been developed for equal access to computer technology (Kreinberg & Stage, 1983).

Special Classes for Women

Colleges for women such as Smith and Wellesley were founded in order to offer women an education comparable to that offered to men in institutions that did not admit women. Now, of course, women are admitted to all of the prestigious colleges and universities in the United States. Comparison of the female graduates of coeducational colleges and universities with graduates of women's colleges has shown that graduates of women's colleges are more likely to obtain Ph.D.'s, not only in the humanities, but in the physical, life, and social sciences (Tidball & Kistiakowsky, 1976). High selectivity and student interest in attending a women's college make it impossible to attribute the finding to the experience of attending a women's college per se, but there is some sentiment that achievement for women is easier in an all-female environment. With respect to a traditionally male-dominated field like science, the sense of being out of place is alleviated by the presence of other women.

With the advent of Title IX, it became more difficult to conduct sex-segregated classes in public institutions. In private institutions that receive public funding, the picture is less clear. Several projects have experimented with all-female environments, indicating that there may be some advantage to female students from spending some of their instructional time in single-sex settings. All of the projects described below, however, used several strategies in conjunction with the exclusion of males, so that they cannot be said to test a single-sex setting per se.

Math for Girls.   In 1973, the Lawrence Hall of Science (University of California, Berkeley), which offers after-school classes in mathematics, computer science, and the sciences, found that fewer than 25% of the participants were girls. To attract girls to the Hall and to inform them and their parents that mathematics is an appropriate topic for girls to study, a "Math for Girls" course was established. The course, which aims to increase positive attitudes toward mathematics and to increase problem-solving skills, has four problem-solving strands: (1) logic, strategies, and patterns; (2) breaking set; (3) creative thinking, estimating, and observing; and (4) spatial visualization. The eight $1\frac{1}{2}$–2-hour sessions are taught by a young woman who uses mathematics in her studies (often a University of California science major) or in her career, who establishes a cooperative, recreational atmosphere.

The course is supported by tuition and has not had the resources to conduct a formal evaluation. The original goal, to increase young women's participation in Hall course offerings, has been met in part, as female enrollment in other courses has increased from 25% to 40%. The role of the Math for Girls course in influencing this progress cannot be disentangled from several other Lawrence Hall of Science outreach efforts, however. The course does remain popular, though, and a handbook that gives a detailed curriculum guide for the course has sold 2,500 copies (Downie, Slesnick, & Stenmark, 1981).

An Acceleration Program for Mathematically Gifted Girls.   The Johns Hopkins University Study of Mathematically Precocious Youth (SMPY) was established in 1971 to identify mathematically precocious youth and to encourage their talent by tailoring educational experiences to their needs. After identifying mathematically talented students by superior performance on the Scholastic Aptitude Test, SMPY conducted a fast-paced mathematics class for students as young as 10 years old that taught them high school mathematics. The program was far more successful in identifying and accelerating the progress of boys than of girls (Fox, 1976), so that an experimental program was started just for girls.

The program and its evaluation are described in Fox (1976) and Brody and Fox (1980). Designed to counter the formal, competitive, and theoretical conditions that observation and interviews indicated were factors diminishing the girls' success in the coeducational class, the girls' class was taught in an informal, cooperative style by three women. The relevance of mathematics to social problems was stressed through rewritten mathematics problems and speakers who described interesting fields, such as operations research, in which mathematics is used to solve social problems. Female role models also discussed their combination of interesting mathematics-related careers with raising families.

The all-girls' class was more successful in attracting girls to the accelerated class than the coeducational class had been, and the completion rate was similar to the females' rate in the coeducational classes. Eighteen of the 27 girls completed the experimental class, meaning that they had learned Algebra I over a 3-month summer period, meeting about 4 hours a week. Their performance on a ninth grade-normed Algebra I test was at the 89th percentile, significantly higher than that of control boys and girls who had been matched from the SMPY sample for SAT scores.

Attempts to place these girls in Algebra II when they were eighth graders met administrative barriers, so that only 11 girls were able to accelerate. Follow-up studies were conducted annually, and they revealed that the control boys had accelerated in mathematics on their own, while few of the control girls had done so. By the end of the 1976–77 school year, 42% of the experimental girls, 46% of the control boys, and 8% of the control girls had accelerated.

An Experiment at the College Level.   A special section of a mathematics course for women has also been tried successfully at the college level. In 1974–75, the University of Missouri-Kansas City conducted an NSF-funded project that offered a special section of the introductory mathematics sequence (Mac-Donald, 1980). This section enrolled 33 students in the first semester and 22 in the second semester, compared with 55–60 students in the regular sections. Taught by a female professor and a female advanced graduate student, the class was preceded by a one-hour optional tutoring session in which students worked in small groups in a social, informal atmosphere. Other supplemental activities included discussions of the socialization of women, services available to students on campus, social and cultural issues, and personal experiences. Students were given take-home review tests and had the chance to take each test a second time, counting the second score if better, or the average if not. A comparison of participants in the special course with women in the regular sections showed that they had higher grades and a better completion rate. While the retaking of tests may have contributed to higher grades, the women in the special section had been selected because of weaker backgrounds. Women in the special section also reported greater satisfaction with the course than those in the regular sections, and they reported that they had spent more time studying mathematics. It is not possible to determine which of the many differences contributed to success, but 56% of the participants went on to enroll in another mathematics course, compared with 17% of the women in other sections.

Retention of Women in the Science Disciplines.   A program at Purdue University combined intensive counseling, a course that offered students the opportunity to meet women scientists, and special laboratory projects for freshman students in an effort to increase the retention of women in undergraduate science majors; it was found that the effects of these interventions were cumulative (Brown, 1976). In the special projects, students were assigned to small laboratory groups to work on projects directly with professors, an experience not usually given to freshmen. Although no female reported experiencing discrimination in the laboratory situation, it was found that the greatest percentage of female students who completed the project and reported the greatest personal satisfaction were participants in either all-female groups or groups in which females were at least half of the group membership. The sex composition of the group did not have a similar effect on the male students. The author pointed out that the small numbers involved (120 women in the entire project) and the voluntary character of the sample (after random selection, participation was not required) limit it the reliability and the generalizability of the findings.

Women in Engineering.   Another program at Purdue, in its engineering department, was designed to meet the special needs of freshman engineering women, particularly to address their lack of "hands-on," technical experience compared with males' childhood experience gained through hobbies and educational experiences. The course combined laboratory experiences (with hand tools, power tools, engines, plumbing, and metals) and lectures from a variety of male and female role models. Students were randomly selected from those who had expressed interest, yielding one section that was predominantly female (85%) and one section that was balanced. Pre- and post-test comparisons showed that male and female participants in the special course gained in technical knowledge and self-confidence when compared with the control groups. The progress of the women in the two sections was similar, so that the gap between the experimental women and men was substantially narrowed during the one-semester course (Heckert et al., 1978).

Reentry Programs for Women in Science.   Surveys have shown that as many as 40% of all female scientists drop out of the labor force at some time (Burks & Connolly, 1977). To reclaim this underutilized segment of the labor force, reentry programs have been developed to bring these women back into the sciences, updating their competency so that they can be full participants. A successful group of reentry programs was funded by the Women in Science Program of the National Science Foundation (NSF), all of which emphasized a strong academic component, although they included confidence building, study skills, and other nonacademic components. The NSF-supported programs concentrated on updating a woman's knowledge in an area in which she already had a bachelor's degree, facilitating a change of major (for example, from mathematics to electrical engineering), or both. The goal of accomplishing this transformation in approximately one academic or calendar year has encouraged creative approaches to curricula. In addition, most programs have included skills for success, counseling, and assistance with child care. Linking the academic program with industry helps students gain internship experiences and assists with placement upon graduation.

One of the most successful of these NSF-sponsored programs is that directed by Carol M. Shaw at the University of Dayton; it provides a mechanism for career change from science to chemical and electrical engineering. The program offers traditional lecture courses (15 weeks), sequential short courses (7 weeks), and self-paced instruction over an 11½-month period. With an initial group of 71 students, 60% of whom were unemployed or underemployed, 63 students completed the program, 61 of whom are employed and one of whom is in graduate school. The students received an average of three job offers each (Shaw & Bulkin, 1981).

Special Classes to Address Problems Faced by Women

A thin line separates the courses described above, which were explicitly designed to attract women and in some cases are restricted to female enrollment, and the courses that will be described in this section, which were designed to address the issues in mathematics and science instruction that have been identified as particularly important for women. As indicated previously, Title IX restricts schools from providing educational opportunities on the basis of sex, so that caution must be exercised in creating courses that would segregate students by sex. In addition, it can be argued that special courses for girls and women reinforce the idea that females have deficiencies that need to be remedied, and therefore contribute to the problem they are trying to solve.

The "Math Anxiety"/"Math without Fear" Continuum. In the mid-1970s, a number of people in institutions of higher education became aware that existing mathematics curricula did not meet the needs of students who were unprepared to take calculus. When women undergraduates in particular sought fields of study and work that required quantitative skills, they found that there were no appropriate courses to address their lack of confidence and/or competence in mathematics. There were a number of factors in these students' elementary and secondary education that were identified as probable causes of this situation, clustering around the idea that mathematics is often taught in such a way that it creates strong negative feelings that are increasingly hard to overcome. Two major approaches have been used in higher education settings to assist students who lack confidence in their mathematical ability and skills— attempts to decrease math anxiety and attempts to teach mathematics in an environment that will increase confidence. While these approaches are usually combined in most interventions, they will first be described separately for purposes of discussion.

The "math anxiety" approach was popularized by Sheila Tobias (1978), who coined the phrase that captured the frustration and difficulty faced by many students when confronted with failure in mathematics. Working with professional psychologists and mathematicians, she set up the Math Anxiety Clinic at Wesleyan University, where she was associate provost; the clinic provided counseling for students to assist them in overcoming negative feelings about themselves as learners of mathematics. The success of the clinic in enabling students to conquer their math anxiety so that they could take courses and graduate school entrance examinations that had been precluded before led to considerable replication of this approach. Tobias has catalogued the programs and resources regarding math anxiety; the listing is available from the Institute for the Study of Anxiety in Learning that she established in Washington, D.C. (Tobias, 1980).

Investigations of the math anxiety construct have found that anxiety can be broken down into two components—math test anxiety and numerical anxiety (Hendel, 1981). This finding points out one of the subtleties in research and program development in this area—that the observed anxiety comes from more than one source. While some of the anxiety is associated with the subject matter per se, another source of anxiety may be the typical environment of mathematics courses, which includes more frequent assessment than other courses and a more prevalent message that there is just one right answer (Brush, 1980).

An alternative approach to conquering math anxiety, then, has been to change the classroom environment in which mathematics is taught so as to reduce the feelings of anxiety that some students have reported feeling in traditional classes. One example of this approach is the "Math without Fear" course established by Diane Resek at San Francisco State University in 1975 (Resek & Rupley, 1980). Resek's premise is that a great deal of the discomfort that many students experience in mathematics courses comes from the strategy they have used to learn mathematics. Having tried to memorize a set of rules or procedures for solving problems rather than understanding mathematical concepts, they have no fallback strategy when their memories fail them. The course tries to convert these "rule-oriented" students to a conceptual approach to mathematics that will enable them to solve problems for which they have no set algorithm to follow (Davis & Stage, 1980). Techniques used to improve students' problem solving include guessing, using physical materials to build abstract concepts, using visual representations to solve problems, small group and recreational activities, and explicit recognition of difficulties. The "Math without Fear" course has been successful in moving 70 to 80% of its students to a conceptual approach in one semester (Resek & Rupley, 1980). A Center for Mathematics Literacy has been established at San Francisco State that has added "Statistics without Fear" and "Computers without Fear" courses in order to increase access to these quantitative fields for the students, primarily women and minorities, who arrive at the university without adequate preparation for the standard entry-level courses.

A sister course to the one at San Francisco State was started by Ruth Afflack at California State University, Long Beach. It was more formally evaluated by external evaluators (Davis & Stage, 1980), who found that students' attitudes toward mathematics and problem solving were improved, that their mathematics skills improved, and that their performance in subsequent mathematics courses exceeded their performance in courses they had attempted prior to taking "Math without Fear."

Combined Approach.   As indicated above, most programs for adults with low mathematics confidence combine anxiety reduction with mathematics instruction. Some have criticized the "math anxiety" approach as an example of "blaming the victim," since it identifies the problem as pathology within the student rather than the educational and social systems that influenced her. Not all math anxiety programs teach mathematics, but many do (Tobias & Weissbrod, 1980). Conversely, not all programs for building math confidence deal explicitly with the psychological barriers to success in mathematics (Davis & Stage, 1980), but most of them do. There are, however, courses that have explicitly adopted components of both models, one of which is offered at Humboldt State University.

The "Building Math Confidence in Women" course at Humboldt (which is open to men as well) is a two-quarter sequence described by Gale, Frances, Friel, and Gruber (1978). The first quarter prepares the student psychologically for a regular college mathematics course and provides intensive tutoring in basic math skills. The second quarter provides psychological and mathematics tutoring support while the student is enrolled in a regular college mathematics course at the level of algebra or higher. The psychology instruction includes relaxation training, anxiety control, acquiring a positive self-image, and acquiring assertiveness in the mathematics classroom. The mathematics instruction emphasizes logical thinking. Evaluation showed significant gains in arithmetic skills, improvement on the Math Anxiety Rating Scale, and acceptable performance in regular mathematics courses.

Curricula Designed to Address Special Needs of Women

A thin line also separates the special courses described above from the curriculum development efforts that have tried to increase females' achievement and interest in mathematics and science. As with the courses, some curricula have focused on a particular issue such as the usefulness of mathematics for future careers, while others have taken a more global approach and have tried to influence many areas. In this section, one general program and two specifically targeted approaches will be described.

Solving Problems of Access to Careers in Engineering and Science (SPACES). The SPACES project at the Lawrence Hall of Science took a broad mandate, to develop a set of 30 enrichment activities for grades 3 to 10 that would provide career awareness and certain mathematical skills that are important for problem solving. The career awareness activities emphasize the variety of employment options available to people with a good mathematics background, including nontraditional areas for women such as construction and the trades in addition to the sciences and engineering. The mathematical skills that are emphasized are problem solving, particularly the gathering and organizing of data, and spatial visualization.

Trial versions of the activities were used in 100 classrooms in 1980–81 and were evaluated by pre- and post-testing students on six major objectives. Significant improvement was found, above the improvement observed in the comparison group, in five of the six areas tested. While attitudes toward mathematics did not change, the SPACES students improved in career awareness (career interest, career knowledge, and identification of tools) and in mathematical skills (word problem solving and spatial visualization). The program was developed to assist girls in areas in which they have traditionally not been strong, but it was effective for boys and girls who used the materials, which are available from the Lawrence Hall of Science (Fraser, 1982).

Career-Oriented Modules for Exploring Topics in Science (COM-ETS). The COMETS project at the University of Kansas is a parallel in science to SPACES in math, but it has focused on the particular strategy of using role models to encourage science career interest. Each of the 24 modules described science activities that role models, called community resource people, can use to arouse interest in a science concept that is being studied by the students and is used in the person's career. Following an introductory activity, such as conducting a perc test with a geologist, the geologist can go on to describe his/her own testing of soils for various characteristics. The resource person is then asked to talk about the career and how she or he prepared for it and how it relates to other parts of her or his life, such as family roles. The materials are produced so that the introductory activities can be conducted by the classroom teacher in preparation for the resource person's visit; they provide teachers with additional information about women's contributions to science, including biographical and language arts materials. Materials, revised on the basis of field testing and evaluation, are available at cost for national trial from the developer, Walter S. Smith, University of Kansas (Smith, Molitor, Nelson, & Matthew, 1982).

Multiplying Options and Subtracting Bias. The set of videotapes *Multiplying Options and Subtracting Bias* focuses on the decision to take elective mathematics courses by addressing issues and concerns of four specific groups: junior and senior high students, mathematics and science teachers, parents, and counselors. The program aims to increase knowledge about sex-related differences in mathematics and to improve attitudes toward females as learners of mathematics held by females, their male peers, and the adults who influence them. The tapes provide specific information about the amount of mathematics required for various careers and discuss stereotyping and differential treatment of males and females with regard to mathematics and counseling. A facilitator's guide accompanies the tapes to provide an outline for each workshop, including information and points for discussion to be held in conjunction with viewing the tapes. It is recommended by the authors (Fennema, Becker, Wolleat, & Pedro, 1980) that the tapes be used in a full intervention—that is, with each of the target groups in a school or school system, since the attitudes of young women are influenced by these other groups and, in some cases, are less in need of intervention than those of significant others.

An evaluation of the videotapes alone (that is, without the workshops) in nine high schools in Minnesota and Wisconsin (Fennema, Wolleat, Pedro, & Becker, 1981), using a pre- and post-test, control group design, found that the tapes were more successful with students than with the adults. Although males' increase in plans to take mathematics in high school was not as great as females' increase, males and females in the experimental group made similar gains in plans to take mathematics after high school and in their knowledge of sex-related differences in mathematics. Few changes were observed in teachers and counselors.

The videotapes are distributed by the National Council of Teachers of Mathematics, 1906 Association Dr., Reston, VA 22091, but they also can be rented from "Women and Mathematics Education," c/o Judith Jacobs, George Mason University, 4400 University Drive, Fairfax, VA 22030.

Teacher Education Programs

As indicated above, the attitudes and knowledge of teachers are important influences on students' attitudes and achievement, and several programs have been developed to address the particular issues of concern in mathematics. With regard to elementary teachers, the observation has been made that their own avoidance of mathematics may be perpetuated in their subsequent teaching, so that elementary programs have tried to improve the attitudes and skills of the teachers themselves to begin to break the cycle. Two such programs, one concentrating on attitudes and one empasizing spatial visualization, will be described below. Then, an inservice program that works to change the school and classroom climate will be detailed.

Teacher Education and Mathematics (TEAM).   The TEAM program was designed to help prospective teachers at Queens College develop positive attitudes toward and deal effectively with mathematics (Chapline, Newman, Denker, & Title, 1980). Four mathematics content modules and four attitudinal modules constitute a course to be taken prior to the math methods course, or can be used as supplementary materials in other preservice courses. Although based on small samples, comparison of postcourse measures of attitudes, math anxiety, and mathematical concepts indicated that TEAM students benefited from the program. In addition, they were able to suggest ways to counteract sex role bias in mathematics education, and more of them volunteered to teach mathematics than did a comparison group of student teachers.

Improving Teachers' Ability to Visualize Mathematics.   A course was developed at the University of Washington by Nancy Cook and Betty Kersh that had three goals: to improve elementary teachers' spatial skills, problem-solving skills, and attitudes toward mathematics. The 30-hour course focused on three aspects of spatial ability: visual imagery, mental rotation, and mental transformation. The course moved sequentially from the spatial tasks to the materials used to the strategy of instruction. The tasks proceeded from those requiring no movement of the image to movement of the complete image to movement of different parts of the image; from two dimensions to three dimensions; and from concrete representations to pictures. The instructional strategies moved from free exploration to structured analysis. All work was done in pairs, and students were encouraged to discuss their ideas so that they would become aware of their own thinking and of individual differences in frames of reference. Significant improvement was found in three classes of teachers on three spatial tests, a college-level algebra word problem-solving test, and five attitude scales (Cook & Kersh, 1980).

EQUALS.   The EQUALS program is an inservice program for teachers, administrators, and counselors, grades K–12, to assist educators in using materials and activities to promote the participation and achievement of women and minorities in mathematics. Educators attend 10- or 30-hour inservice workshops during the school year. They collect and analyze research findings on sex differences in mathematics participation and career aspirations, explore math-related fields of work and study, participate in activities that promote improved student attitudes and understanding of mathematics, develop problem-solving skills, and plan inservice presentations to disseminate EQUALS to other educators.

The evaluation of the EQUALS program has examined its impact on several levels. The most directly affected participants, the educators who attend the workshops, keep journals and report their activities at the subsequent workshops. Nearly all of the activities and teaching strategies are used by a majority of the teachers, with an average implementation level for each activity of over 70%. A follow-up survey conducted in 1981 of all participants since 1977 found that the majority were still using EQUALS materials.

The effect of the materials on students has been investigated by a pre- and post-test, control group design using a career awareness survey and a mathematics attitude scale for older students and pictures of bears in various occupations for younger students. Over the years of evaluation the results have varied, but they have indicated modest improvement in attitudes toward mathematics and increased interest in math-related fields. An additional measure of effectiveness has been student enrollment in elective mathematics classes. While there are many factors influencing student enrollment, including availability of qualified teachers and changes in state requirements, there is indication that increased participation of girls has been associated with EQUALS activity by teachers in some schools (Kreinberg, 1981b).

In addition to the regular program, which is held at the Lawrence Hall of Science, EQUALS staff members have conducted workshops for school districts throughout California and in 25 other states. Staff development personnel from 14 states have attended training seminars at the Lawrence Hall of Science to enable them to design workshops for their states or districts. Workshops have also been conducted for 300 educational leaders (administrators, school board members, community leaders) to inform them of the efforts of teachers and to assist in their support of the teachers in their areas. A handbook has been produced by the program (Kaseberg, Kreinberg, & Downie, 1980) that has allowed others to conduct EQUALS workshops without direct assistance from the program.

Efforts of School Districts

Many school districts have surveyed their mathematics enrollments and have discovered the low participation of females at the higher levels. A number of them have designed programs to increase females' participation, or all students' participation, in mathematics and science courses. In the San Francisco Bay area, several spinoffs from the EQUALS program have evolved, including projects in Emeryville, Napa, Novato, Santa Cruz, and San Francisco. There are also projects in Arizona, Kansas, Montana, North Dakota, Oregon, and Pennsylvania. These programs, while adapted to local characteristics, are similar to EQUALS in their emphasis on awareness of the importance of mathematics achievement for all students, problem solving and building competence in mathematics, and the relationship between mathematics and career opportunities.

In Minneapolis, the public schools' 1976 finding of only 25 to 35% female enrollment in highest-level mathematics courses prompted a major emphasis on increasing female enrollment in college preparatory mathematics courses. The goals were discussed at teacher inservice workshops, department head meetings, and in communications with teachers. Activities included use of the "Multiplying Options and Subtracting Bias" videotapes (discussed above), participation in the Visiting Women in Science Program (discussed below), bringing in speakers from local corporations, and conducting workshops on mathematics anxiety for teachers. To inform students about the importance of mathematics to their future educational and career opportunities, a series of six career information brochures called "Don't Knock It, Unlock It with Math," listing careers that demand knowledge of the material in algebra, geometry, trigonometry, advanced algebra, probability and statistics, and has increased in the advanced courses to between 43 and 57%, a substantial improvement in a short period of time (Taylor, 1979). While other factors may have helped these enrollment figures, they are nevertheless encouraging.

Extracurricular Activities for Women

The preceding sections have described a variety of programs that have attempted to change the educational experiences of girls and women in educational institutions, either by developing special classes or curricula, or by changing the outlook or behavior of teachers and counselors. A complementary approach to these interventions has been seen in the development of a variety of extracurricular or cocurricular activities that attempt to enhance the effect of the regular school offerings, including visiting programs, conferences, and support networks.

The Visiting Women Scientists Program.   The idea of inviting a woman scientist or mathematician to speak to a group of secondary students about her career has been tried by a variety of groups. For several years, the Women and Mathematics Program of the Mathematical Association of America has arranged for women mathematicians to visit schools (Dr. Carole B. Lacampagne, National

Director, Department of Mathematics, Bergen Community College, Paramus NJ 07652). In 1977, a large-scale demonstration program was contracted by NSF to the Research Triangle Institute to design and implement a pilot Visiting Women Scientists program, the purpose of which was to motivate female high school students to consider careers in science, including engineering, mathematics, the social sciences and the biological and physical sciences.

The program included visits by 40 women scientists to 110 high schools across the United States. Approximately 40% of a national sample of high schools accepted the offer to participate in the pilot program, and they were randomly assigned to experimental and control groups. The visit of the woman scientist to the participating high schools included some combination of the following: large and small group meetings with female students, sessions with individual coeducational classes, and meetings with school staff members. Scientists talked about their jobs, their educational and personal backgrounds, and ways of resolving problems associated with combining a career in science with a full family life.

A major goal of the program was to encourage high school girls to seek more information about scientific careers (Weiss, Pace, & Conaway, 1978). Students in both experimental and control schools were given postcards for requesting further information, and the return rate from experimental schools was significantly greater than from control schools (21 versus 6%). A survey of school staff with career guidance responsibility found that 57% of the experimental schools versus 38% of the control schools reported that more than the usual number of female students had sought information about scientific careers.

A Manual on Program Operations is available from ERIC; a Women Scientists Roster is available from the National Science Teachers Association.

Expanding Your Horizons in Science and Mathematics Conferences. Beginning with two conferences in the San Francisco Bay area in 1976, there were 43 Expanding Your Horizons conferences sponsored by the Math/Science Network in 1982, half of which were outside California and three of which were outside the United States. The Math/Science Network is a group of over 1,000 scientists, educators, and community people who work together to increase girls' and women's participation in math-related and nontraditional fields, and their sponsorship of these conferences is one of their most extensive efforts. The purposes of the conferences, which are held in the spring on college campuses, are to increase students' interest in science and mathematics, to foster awareness of career opportunities in math and science-related fields, and to provide students with an opportunity to meet and form personal contacts with women working in traditionally male fields.

While individual conference committees plan and conduct their own programs, the Network provides guidance and technical assistance (Koltnow, 1979). Features common to the conferences are panel presentations, "hands-on" workshops, and career workshops with women in nontraditional, math- and science-related fields. Evaluation includes surveys on the day of the conference and follow-up surveys six to nine months after the conference. Students have increased the number of math, science, and computer classes they plan to take in high school and have learned more about these career fields. Six months after the conference, they actually enrolled in as many or more mathematics courses as they had indicated that they planned at the conclusion of the conference, and they had taken a number of other actions to further their knowledge of and experience related to these careers. A report on the longitudinal study and a kit for evaluating interventions like this are available from the Math/Science Resource Center, Mills College, Oakland, CA 94613 (Sheila Humphreys, Principal Investigator).

NSF Science Career Workshops. One of the major activities of the NSF Women in Science Program was the support of one- or two-day Science Career Workshops, designed to provide factual information and practical advice regarding careers in science to prospective female scientists and engineers. During the six years of the program, a total of 135 workshops were conducted in 37 states, the District of Columbia, and Puerto Rico by 107 different institutions, the majority of which were universities. From 1976 to 1979, the workshops were directed at undergraduate and graduate students. In 1980–81, at least a third of the participants were expected to be women with at least a bachelor's degree in science who were unemployed or underemployed in science.

Evaluations of these programs took several forms. Summer interns in the Women in Science Program office analyzed final technical reports in 1978 and 1979 and concluded that the majority of the workshops were extremely effective and valuable and that personal feelings of enthusiasm and warmth from the conferences translated into increased confidence and motivation of the participants. As evaluation methods were not prescribed by NSF, it is not possible to generalize about effects, but two sample evaluations are presented here as examples. (More information about the conferences and suggestions for conducting them are contained in a handbook, *Ideas for Developing and Conducting a Women in Science Career Workshop,* Kreinberg, 1981a; it is available without charge from NSF.)

Rutgers' Science Career Workshop. Freshman and sophomore women from colleges in New Jersey attended a one-day workshop where 12 scientists spoke about their work and personal backgrounds and then led informal discussions for each of the science disciplines represented. The students who attended the workshop filled out a questionnaire six months later, in which they reported that the workshop stimulated their thinking (90%), that they had learned useful information about job requirements and salaries (85%), and that it was possible to combine a science career with a family (75%) (Cohen & Elgart, 1981). The following proportions of career-related actions were taken by the participants and attributed to the workshop: enrolled in a science course (96% took action, 14% of whom attributed it to the workshop); engaged in research (24%, 44%); joined science-related organization (29%, 30%); sought contacts with women scientists (29%, 60%); sought information in books or magazines (71%, 67%); sent for science career pamphlets (26%, 62%); and watched scientific television programs (79%, 28%). The discrimination in their attributions to the workshop—

low for actions they were likely to pursue, such as coursework; high for actions they learned about at the workshop, such as the willingness of female scientists to speak with them about their careers—gives confidence that the workshop probably did bring about some additional career-related activity on the part of the students.

Women Moving Up Conferences.   A total of five conferences were conducted by the Math/Science Network at the University of California, Berkeley, and Mills College for women with undergraduate degrees in the sciences to provide them with information and resources for advancing their careers or for reentering the labor force after an absence. Keynote panel discussions by government, industry, and academic leaders in science were followed by workshop sessions on job advancement, education, company profiles, employment outlooks, and career development strategies. A *Women Moving Up Directory* (Cremer, 1980) gave additional information and career resource lists to participants. Follow-up surveys, conducted six to nine months after the conferences, found that over 75% of the participants had taken some action to advance their careers, and at least a third had taken a course in math, science, or computer science. A similar proportion of the participants had interviewed for a new job since the time of the conference.

SUMMARY AND CONCLUSIONS

The programs reviewed in this chapter share several elements that provide guidance for future efforts to increase women's participation and achievement in mathematics, science; and engineering. Three general features are present in nearly all of the successful programs: strong academic emphases, multiple strategies, and systems approaches.

Strong Academic Emphasis

The causes and mechanisms of the sex-related differences in science and mathematics achievement are not clearly understood, but program planners have acknowledged their existence by designing curricula that address the specific skills identified by research as potential causes. Thus, tools for developing spatial ability, problem solving ability, and mechanical sophistication are present in many programs. A commitment to extending competence by enrolling in advanced courses and acquiring marketable skills is presented as an essential goal for young women in science. By defining such specific and measurable goals, the programs can evaluate their efforts and demonstrate measurable gains to others. The presence of evaluation and the link to research strengthens both program development and dissemination.

Multiple Strategies

Most successful programs have made use of more than one strategy for increasing women's participation in science. They have tried to influence the environment in which mathematics and science are taught—to make these fields accessible to women and to present them as viable options for women. Role models of women in math- and science-related fields are highly motivational for students because they also deliver information and strategies for achieving in science activities. Hands-on experiences, particularly in all-female groups, promote confidence as well as skills that can be relied on in subsequent courses. Combined goals of confidence and competence enhance each other, as do the complementary attitudes of enjoying and appreciating the usefulness of quantitative activities. Given the complex origins of the low participation of women in science, it makes sense that multiple strategies are needed to solve the problem; in practice, it is not only sensible but effective to use several strategies.

Systems Approach

As indicated more prominently in the research section of this chapter than in the program descriptions, the problems for women in science are not theirs alone. The expectations and sex stereotyped practices of parents and teachers, their lack of awareness of the importance of mathematics and science proficiency for all students, and their lack of experience in problem solving and spatial skills, which they fail to develop in females, all contribute to women's difficulties. Some of the programs described above, notably *Multiplying Options and Subtracting Bias,* have developed materials for several target groups, and others are extending their efforts to include parents, administrators, teachers, and students.

Final Thought

These elements—strong academic emphasis, multiple strategies, and systems approaches—represent the strengths of programs for increasing women's participation and achievement in math, science, and engineering, but they also represent sound educational practice. One might argue that girls and women are more susceptible than are boys and men to poor educational practices such as learning mathematics as a collection of rules or science as a set of formulae. But as long as so few women reach their potential in the sciences, specific strategies that address the reasons for their low participation and achievement must be designed, implemented, and evaluated.

REFERENCES

Aiken, L. (1970). Attitudes toward mathematics. *Review of Educational Research, 40,* 551–596.

Aldrich, M. L. (1982, March). *Women and mathematics: Recent programs.* Paper presented at the annual meeting of the American Educational Research Association, New York.

Aldrich, M. L., & Hall, P. W. (1980). *Programs in science, mathematics, and engineering for women and girls in the United States: 1976–1978.* Washington, DC: American Association for the Advancement of Science.

Armstrong, J. M. (1981). Achievement and participation of women in mathematics. *Journal for Research in Mathematics Education, 12,* 356–372.

Armstrong, J., & Kahl, S. (1980). *A national assessment of performance and participation of women in mathematics* (final report). Washington, DC: National Institute of Education.

Astin, H. S. (1974). Sex differences in mathematical and scientific precocity. In J. C. Stanley, D. P. Keating, & L. Fox (Eds.), *Mathematical talent: Discovery, description, and development* (pp. 70–86). Baltimore: Johns Hopkins University Press.

Bean, J. P. (1976). *What's happening in mathematics and science classrooms: Student-teacher interactions.* Paper presented at the annual meeting of the American Educational Research Association, San Francisco.

Becker, J. R. (1981). Differential treatment of females and males in mathematics classes. *Journal for Research in Mathematics Education, 12,* 40–53.

Benbow, C. P., & Stanley, J. C. (1980). Sex differences in mathematical ability: Fact or artifact? *Science, 210,* 1262–1264.

Bing, E. (1963). Effect of childrearing practices on development of differential cognitive abilities. *Child Development, 34,* 631–648.

Boswell, S. (1979). *Nice girls don't study mathematics: The perspective from elementary school.* Symposium paper presented at the annual meeting of the American Educational Research Association, San Francisco.

Brody, L., & Fox, L. H. (1980). An accelerative intervention program for mathematically gifted girls. In L. H. Fox, L. Brody, & D. Tobin (Eds.), *Women and the mathematical mystique* (pp. 164–178). Baltimore. Johns Hopkins University Press.

Brophy, J. E., & Good, T. (1974). *Teacher-student relationships: Causes and consequences.* New York: Holt, Rinehart & Winston.

Brown, L. H. (1976). *The retention of women in the science disciplines* (final report 1973–1975, Fund for Improvement of Post Secondary Education). West Lafayette, IN: Purdue University.

Brush, L. (1978). A validation study of the mathematics anxiety rating scale (MARS). *Educational and Psychological Measurement, 38,* 485–490.

Brush, L. R. (1980). *Encouraging girls in mathematics: The problem and the solution.* Boston: Abt Associates.

Burks, E. L., & Connolly, T. (1977). Women in science and engineering: Characteristics and experiences of established professionals. *Engineering Education,* December, 234–240.

Burnett, S. A., & Lane, D. M. (1980). Effects of academic instruction on spatial visualization. *Intelligence, 4,* 233–242.

Burnett, S. A., Lane, D. M., & Dratt, L. M. (1979). Spatial visualization and sex differences in quantitative ability. *Intelligence, 3,* 345–354.

California Basic Educational Data System. (1981). *Student enrollment by subject in California public schools for 1980–1981.* Sacramento: California State Department of Education.

Casserly, P. L. (1975). *An assessment of factors affecting female participation in advanced placement programs in mathematics, chemistry, and physics* (Report). Washington, DC: National Science Foundation.

Casserly, P. L. (1979). *The advanced placement teacher as the critical factor in high school women's decisions to persist in the study of mathematics.* Paper presented at the annual meeting of the American Educational Research Association, San Francisco.

Chapline, R., Newman, C., Denker, E., & Tittle, C. K. (1980). *Final report: Teacher education and mathematics project.* New York: Queens College, City University of New York.

Chipman, S., Brush, L., & Wilson, D. (Eds.). (in press.) *Women of mathematics: Balancing the equation.* Hillsdale, NJ: Erlbaum.

Cohen, C. E., & Elgart, C. K. (1981). *Promoting the entry of women into science careers: Report on a career workshop for college women.* Unpublished manuscript, Douglass College, Rutgers University, New Brunswick, NJ.

Connor, J. M., Schachman, M. E., & Serbin, L. A. (1978). Sex-related differences in response to practice on a visual-spatial test and generalization to a related test. *Child Development, 49,* 24–29.

Connor, J. M., & Serbin, L. A. (1980). *Mathematics, visual-spatial ability, and sex roles* (final report). Washington, DC: National Institute of Education.

Connor, J. M., Serbin, L. A., & Schachman, M. (1977). Sex differences in children's response to training on a visual-spatial test. *Developmental Psychology, 3,* 293–294.

Cook, N., & Kersh, M. E. (1980). Improving teachers' ability to visualize mathematics. In R. Karplus (Ed.), *Proceedings of the fourth international conference for the psychology of mathematics education* (pp. 377–383). Berkeley: University of California, Lawrence Hall of Science.

Cooperative Institutional Research Program. (1974–1982). *The American freshman: National norms for fall 1971–1980.* Los Angeles: UCLA, Graduate School of Education.

Cremer, C. (1980). *Women moving up directory.* Berkeley: University of California, Lawrence Hall of Science.

Davis, B. G., & Stage, E. K. (1980). *Evaluation report for a math learning center with microcomputers.* Berkeley: University of California.

Dreger, R. M., & Aiken, L. R. (1957). Identification of number anxiety. *Journal of Educational Psychology, 47* 344–351.

Downie, D., Slesnick, T., & Stenmark, J. K. (1981). *Math for girls and other problem solvers.* Berkeley: University of California, Lawrence Hall of Science.

Dunteman, G. H., Wisenbaker, J., & Taylor, M. E. (1978). *Race and sex differences in college science program participation* (report prepared for the National Science Foundation). Research Triangle Park NC: Research Triangle Institute.

Dwyer, C. A. (1974). Influence of children's sex-role standards on reading and arithmetic. *Journal of Educational Psychology, 66,* 811–816.

Eccles (Parsons), J., Adler, T. F., Futterman, R., Goff, S. B., Kaczala, C. M., Meece, J. L., & Midgley, C. (1983). Expectations, values, and academic behaviors. In J. T. Spence (Ed.), *Perspective on achievement and achievement motivation.* San Francisco: W. H. Freeman.

Eccles, J., Adler, T., & Meece, J. L. (1984). Sex differences in achievement: A test of alternate theories. *Journal of Personality and Social Psychology, 46,* 26–43.

E.T.S. (Educational Testing Service). (1979). *National college-bound seniors.* Princeton, NJ: College Entrance Examination Board.

Ernest, J. (1976). *Mathematics and sex.* Santa Barbara: University of California, Department of Mathematics.

Fennema, E., Becker, A. D., Wolleat, P. L., & Pedro, J. D. (1980). *Multiplying options and subtracting bias.* Reston, VA: National Council of Teachers of Mathematics.

Fennema, E., & Carpenter, T. (1981). Sex-related differences in mathematics: Results from the National Assessment. *Mathematics Teacher, 74*(7), 554–559.

Fennema, E., & Sherman, J. (1977). Sex-related differences in mathematics achievement, spatial visualization, and affective factors. *American Educational Research Journal, 14,* 51–71.

Fennema, E., & Sherman, J. (1978). Sex-related differences in mathematical achievement and related factors: A further study. *Journal for Research in Mathematics Education, 9,* 189–203.

Fennema, E., Wolleat, P. L., Pedro, J. D., & Becker, A. D. (1981). Increasing women's participation in mathematics: An intervention study. *Journal for Research in Mathematics Education, 12*(1), 3–14.

Ferguson, J. (1982). *Who turns the wheel?* Ottawa: Science Council of Canada.

Ferguson, L., & Maccoby, E. (1966). Interpersonal correlates of differential abilities. *Child Development, 37,* 549–571.

Fox, L. H. (1976). Sex differences in mathematical precocity: Bridging the gap. In D. P. Keating (Ed.), *Intellectual talent: Research and development* (pp. 183–214). Baltimore: Johns Hopkins University Press.

Fox, L. H., Brody, L., & Tobin, D. (Eds.). (1980). *Women and the mathematical mystique.* Baltimore: Johns Hopkins University Press.

Fox, L. H., & Denham, S. A. (1974). Values and career interests of mathematically and scientifically precocious youth. In J. C. Stanley, D. P. Keating, & L. H. Fox (Eds.), *Mathematical talent: Discovery, description and development* (pp. 140–175). Baltimore: Johns Hopkins University Press.

Fox, L. H., Fennema, E., & Sherman, J. (1977). *Women and mathematics: Research perspectives for change.* Washington, DC: National Institute of Education.

Fox, L. H., Tobin, D., & Brody, L. (1979). Sex-role socialization and achievement in mathematics. In M. S. Wittig & A. C. Petersen (Eds.), *Sex-related differences in cognitive functioning: Developmental issues* (pp. 303–332). New York: Academic Press.

Fraser, S. (1982). *SPACES: Solving problems of access to careers in engineering and science.* Berkeley: University of California, Lawrence Hall of Science.

Gale, D., Frances, S., Friel, M., & Gruber, M. (1978). *Building math confidence in women* (report of 1977–78 innovative grant). Humboldt, CA: Humboldt State University, Department of Mathematics.

Gilmartin, K. J., McLaughlin, D. H., Wise, L. L., & Rossi, R. J. (1976). *The development of scientific careers: The high school years.* Palo Alto, CA: American Institutes for Research.

Goldstein, A. G., & Chance, J. E. (1965). Effects of practice on sex-related differences in performance on embedded figures. *Psychonomic Science, 3,* 361–362.

Good, T., Sikes, J. N., & Brophy, J. E. (1973). Effects of teacher sex and student sex on classroom interaction. *Journal of Educational Psychology, 65,* 74–87.

Haven, E. W. (1971). Factors associated with the selection of advanced academic mathematics courses by girls in high school. *Dissertation Abstracts International, 32,* 1747A. (University of Microfilms No. 71–26027)

Heckert, B. L., LeBold, W. K., Butler, B., Knigga, M., Smith, C. D., Blalock, M., & Hoover, E. (1978, March). *A model research program to provide equity for women entering engineering.* Paper presented at the annual meeting of the American Educational Research Association, Toronto.

Heller, K. A., & Parsons, J. E. (1981). Sex differences in teachers' evaluative feedback and students' expectancies for success in mathematics. *Child Development, 52,* 1015–1019.

Hendel, D. D. (1981, April). *The effects on adult women and men of participating in a math anxiety program.* Paper presented at the annual meeting of the American Educational Research Association, Los Angeles.

Hilton, T. L., & Berglund, G. W. (1974). Sex differences in mathematics achievement: A longitudinal study. *Journal of Educational Research, 67,* 231–237.

Hoffman, L. W. (1972). Early childhood experiences and women's achievement motives. *Journal of Social Issues, 28,* 129–155.

Humphreys, S. (1981). Catalyst for change at Berkeley: The U.C. Women's Center. *Public Affairs Report,* 1981, *22*(6), 1–7.

Hyde, J. S. (1981). How large are cognitive gender differences? A meta-analysis using ω^2 and d. *American Psychologist, 36,* 892–901.

Hyde, J. S., Geiringer, E. P., & Yen, W. M. (1975). On the empirical relation between spatial ability and sex differences in other aspects of cognitive performance. *Multivariate Behavioral Research, 10,* 289–309.

Kahle, J. B., & Lakes, M. K. (1983). The myth of equality in science classrooms. *Journal for Research in Science Teaching, 20,* 131–140.

Kaminski, D., Erickson, E., Ross, M., & Bradfield, L. (1976, August). *Why females don't like mathematics: The effect of parental expectations.* Paper presented at the annual meeting of the American Sociological Association, New York.

Kaseberg, A., Kreinberg, N., & Downie, D. (1980). *Use EQUALS to promote the participation of women in mathematics.* Berkeley: University of California, Lawrence Hall of Science.

Kelly, A. (1975). *Girls and science education—Cause for concern?* England: Chelsea College, Centre for Science Education.

Koltnow, J. (1979). *Expanding your horizons: Conferences for young women interested in new career options.* Washington, DC: U. S. Department of Education.

Kreinberg, N. (1981a). *Ideas for developing and conducting a women in science career workshop.* Washington, DC: National Science Foundation.

Kreinberg, N. (1981b). 1,000 teachers later: Women, mathematics, and the components of change. *Public Affairs Report, 22*(4), 1–7.

Kreinberg, N., & Stage, E. (1983). EQUALS in computer technology. In J. Zimmerman (Ed.), *The technological woman: Interfacing with tomorrow* (pp. 251–259). New York: Praeger.

Kundsin, R. B. (Ed.). (1974). *Women & Success: The anatomy of achievement.* New York: Morrow.

Lantz, A. (1979). Strategies to increase the number of women in science: Comment on Vol. 4, No. 1. *Signs, 5*(1), 186–189.

Lantz, A. E., & Smith, G. P. (1981). Factors influencing the choice of nonrequired mathematics courses. *Journal of Educational Psychology, 73,* 825–837.

Lazarus, M. (1974). Mathophobia: Some personal speculations. *The Principal, 53*(2), 16–22.

Leinhardt, G., Seewald, A. M., & Engel, M. (1979). Learning what's taught: Sex differences in instruction. *Journal of Educational Psychology, 71,* 432–439.

Luchins, E. (1976, February). *Women mathematicians: A contemporary appraisal.* Paper presented at the annual meeting of the American Association for the Advancement of Science, Boston.

Maccoby, E. E., & Jacklin, C. N. (1974). *The psychology of sex differences.* Stanford, CA: Stanford University Press.

MacDonald, C. T. (1980). An experiment in mathematics education at the college level.

In L. H. Fox, L. Brody, & D. Tobin (Eds.), *Women and the mathematical mystique* (pp. 115–137). Baltimore: Johns Hopkins University Press.

Meece, J. L. (1981). *Sex differences in achievement-related affect.* Paper presented at the annual meeting of the American Educational Research Association, Los Angeles.

Nash, S. C. (1975). The relationship among sex-role stereotyping, sex-role preference, and sex differences on spatial visualization. *Sex Roles, 1,* 15–32.

Nash, S. C. (1979). Sex role as a mediator of intellectual functioning. In M. A. Wittig & A. C. Petersen (Eds.), *Sex-related differences in cognitive functioning: Developmental issues* (pp. 263–302). New York: Academic Press.

National Research Council. (1974, 1976, 1978, 1980). *Science and engineering doctorates in the United States, 1973 profile* and *Science and engineering doctorates in the United States, 1975 profile: Employment status of doctoral scientists and engineers 1973 and 1975; Science, engineering, and humanities doctorates in the United States, 1979 profile.* Washington, DC: National Academy of Sciences.

Parsons, J. E., Adler, T. F., & Kaczala, C. (1982). Socialization of achievement attitudes and beliefs: Parental influences. *Child Development, 53,* 310–321.

Parsons, J. E., Kaczala, C., & Meece, J. (1982). Socialization of achievement attitudes and beliefs: Classroom influences. *Child Development, 53,* 322–339.

Petersen, A. G. (1979). Hormones and cognitive functioning in normal development. In M. A. Wittig & A. C. Petersen (Eds.), *Sex-related differences in cognitive functioning* (pp. 189–214). New York: Academic Press.

Resek, D., & Rupley, W. H. (1980). Combatting "mathophobia" with a conceptual approach to mathematics. *Educational Studies in Mathematics, 11,* 423–441.

Schratz, M. (1978). A developmental investigation of sex differences in spatial visual-analytic and mathematical skills in three ethnic groups. *Developmental Psychology, 14,* 263–267.

Sears, R. R., Maccoby, E. E., & Levin, H. (1957). *Patterns of child rearing.* Evanston, IL: Row & Peterson.

Sells, L. (1975). *Sex, ethnic, and field differences in doctoral outcomes.* Unpublished doctoral dissertation, University of California, Berkeley.

Shaw, C. M., & Bulkin, B. J. (1981). *Reentry programs: Their design and impact.* Unpublished manuscript, University of Dayton, Dayton, OH.

Sherman, J. (1980). Mathematics, spatial visualization, and related factors: Changes in girls and boys, grades 8–11. *Journal of Educational Psychology, 72,* 476–482.

Sherman, J. (1981). Girls' and boys' enrollment in theoretical math courses: A longitudinal study. *Psychology of Women Quarterly, 5,* 681–689.

Sherman, J., & Fennema, E. (1977). The study of mathematics by high school girls and boys: Related variables. *American Educational Research Journal, 14,* 159–168.

Small, B., Whyte, J., & Kelly, A. (1982). Girls into science and technology: The first two years. *School Science Review, 63,* 620–630.

Smith, W. S., Molitor, L. L., Nelson, B. J., Matthew, C. E. (1982). *Career oriented modules to explore topics in science.* Lawrence: University of Kansas, School of Education, Department of Curriculum and Instruction.

Stallings, J. A. (1979, September). *Comparison of men's and women's behaviors in high school math classes.* Paper presented at the annual meeting of the American Psychological Association, New York.

Starr, B. S. (1979). Sex differences among personality correlates of mathematical ability in high school seniors. *Psychology of Women Quarterly, 4,* 212–220.

Steel, L., & Wise, L. (1979). *Origins of sex differences in high school math achievement and participation.* Paper presented at the annual meeting of the American Educational Research Association, San Francisco.

Stein, A. H., & Bailey, M. M. (1973). The socialization of achievement orientation in females. *Psychological Bulletin, 80,* 345–366.

Stein, A. H., & Smithells, J. (1969). Age and sex differences in children's sex-role standards about achievement. *Developmental Psychology, 1,* 252–259.

Suinn, R., & Richardson, F. (1972). The mathematics anxiety scale: Psychometric data. *Journal of Counseling Psychology, 19,* 551–554.

Taylor, R. (1979). Female enrollment in mathematics approaches level of equality. *Minneapolis Public Schools Women's Studies Newsletter, 4.*

Tidball, M. E., & Kistiakowsky, V. (1976). Baccalaureate origins of American scientists and scholars. *Science, 193,* 646–652.

Tobias, S. (1978). *Overcoming math anxiety.* New York: Norton.

Tobias, S. (1980). *Paths to programs for intervention: Math anxiety, math avoidance, and reentry mathematics.* Washington, DC: Institute for the Study of Anxiety in Learning.

Tobias, S., & Weissbrod, C. (1980). Anxiety and mathematics: An update. *Harvard Educational Review, 50,* 63–70.

Tobin, D., & Fox, L. H. (1980). Career interests and career education: A key to change. In L. H. Fox, L. Brody, and D. Tobin (Eds.), *Women and the mathematical mystique* (pp. 179–191). Baltimore: Johns Hopkins University Press.

Vetter, B. (1981). Women in science and engineering: Trends in participation. *Science, 214,* 1313–1321.

Vockell, E. L., & Lobonc, S. (1981). Sex-role stereotyping by high school females in science. *Journal of Research in Science Teaching, 18,* 209–219.

Waber, D. P. (1979). Cognitive abilities and sex-related variations in the maturation of cerebral cortical functions. In M. S. Wittig & A. C. Petersen (Eds.), *Sex-related differences in cognitive functioning* (pp. 161–186). New York: Academic Press.

Weiss, I., Pace, C., & Conaway, L. E. (1978). The visiting woman scientists pilot program 1978. *Highlights Report.* Research Triangle Park, NC: Research Triangle Institute.

Wise, L., Steel, L., & MacDonald, C. (1979). *Origins and career consequences of sex differences in high school mathematics achievement* (final report). Washington, DC: National Institute of Education.

Wittig, M. A., & Petersen, A. C. (1979). *Sex-related differences in cognitive functioning: Developmental issue.* New York: Academic Press.

Zimmerman, J. (Ed.). (1981). *Future, technology, and woman.* San Diego: San Diego State University, Women's Studies Department.

14
Sex Equity in Reading and Communication Skills

Kathryn P. Scott, Carol Anne Dwyer,
and Barbara Lieb-Brilhart

The purpose of this chapter is to explore the research on sex differences in language-related areas and to examine educational approaches that are effective in promoting sex equity. School success in reading, language arts, and English has traditionally been associated with girls more than boys. The cultural stereotypes maintain that verbal ability is the forte of females. In contrast, however, as adults, women often encounter more difficulties than men in achievement in reading, effectiveness in communication, and success in literary fields.

Two common myths are dispelled in this chapter. The first asserts that females are consistently superior to males in all reading skills. The second claims that females outperform males in both oral and written language expression. After a discussion of the research that refutes these myths, we suggest implications for educational practice and derive recommendations for educators.

ISSUES

Research on Sex Differences in Reading and Related Skills

It is commonly thought, among professionals as well as the general public, that sex differences in verbal and quantitative skills represent two sides of a coin: girls excel in verbal skills; boys, in quantitative skills. As is true of most human phenomena, reality is considerably more complex than these simple statements would make it seem. Patterns of verbal ability, including reading, shift with age, culture, general ability level, and the particular skill being studied; the same factors influence quantitative skills.

Recent analytical treatments of this topic support the following basic conclusions:

We would like to thank Barrie Thorne for her helpful suggestions on an earlier draft of this chapter.

1. Verbal abilities are not unitary. Female and male achievement patterns in beginning reading comprehension differ from those for higher-level inferential skills. Further, performance on reading tests is an issue distinct from identification and placement of problem readers.

2. Mean sex differences in most verbal abilities are very small, and male and female distributions greatly overlap (Hyde, 1981; Maccoby & Jacklin, 1974).

3. Sex differences in verbal skills seldom appear in studies of children up to about age 10; after this age, females as a group tend to surpass males on many measures. However, males perform better on vocabulary tests (Dwyer, 1976, 1979) and on some tests of complex higher-level verbal skills such as the verbal sections of the Scholastic Aptitude Test (Educational Testing Service, 1981).

4. Young American males are identified by elementary schools as problem readers far more often than are females. This finding does not hold up in many other countries (Johnson, 1973–74; Murphy, 1977; Preston, 1962).

The following summary of trends in the research on sex differences may be helpful in understanding the background and implications of the general conclusions just outlined.

From the turn of the century to the present, considerable data related to sex differences in reading have been accumulated. In 1974, Maccoby and Jacklin summarized the results of over 100 of the more representative and well-designed studies in this area, but many more now exist in the psychological and educational literature. Then as now, however, the great preponderance of these data have treated sex as a control or matching variable, peripheral to the central purposes of the study. Moreover, there has been a bias toward reporting significant differences; instances of no sex differences are less likely to be reported. Few studies have attempted to study the interrelations of reading and sex role development.

Maccoby and Jacklin concluded from an analysis of a wide range of reports covering a long time span and diverse populations that before the age of 10 or 11 there are no sex differences in verbal abilities, and after the age of 10 or 11 girls' verbal skills begin to increase relative to those of boys. Unfortunately, Maccoby and Jacklin did not examine various verbal subskills separately, so their conclusions are not completely pertinent to reading comprehension, the main reading activity of interest to educators.

Some important contradictory evidence has arisen since the Maccoby and Jacklin review. As the time of their report, they did not have available to them the information about recent Scholastic Aptitude Test (SAT) trends, which indicate an advantage for males on the verbal section of the SAT, a section largely composed of reading questions (Educational Testing Service, 1981). Until the early 1970s, females consistently scored higher than males on this verbal section. (The SAT is taken almost exclusively by high school students.) Another important issue not addressed by Maccoby and Jacklin in their otherwise comprehensive analysis is the fact that reading tests at the lower educational and age levels rely more heavily on vocabulary questions than on reading comprehension questions. This situation reverses itself in the upper grades. Thus, comparisons across levels are necessarily imprecise.

Despite the promise of the new research directions in this area, new descriptive studies have not added a great deal to Maccoby and Jacklin's basic findings; however, two points seem particularly salient:

1. The largest, most consistent, and most easily studied sex differences in reading are related to girls' and boys' diagnosed reading failures, not to the relative reading progress of "normal" students; as mentioned earlier, young American boys are more often identified as problem readers.
2. Average and proficient pupils are now being more widely studied, particularly with an emphasis on broader aspects of cognitive development, student-teacher interactions, and possible educational interventions.

After Maccoby and Jacklin's sophisticated analysis, descriptive studies of sex differences seemed no longer to be considered important topics of research in and of themselves. From the early 1970s to the present, more attention has been given to the causes and ramifications of sex-related differences and similarities. More recent research on sex differences in reading has emphasized the search for causal factors and potential interventions for skill deficiencies in reading (for example, Leinhart, Seewald, & Engel, 1979; Stockard, Schmuck, Kempner, Williams, Edson, & Smith, 1980). We believe that there are three primary variables that must be considered when interpreting these apparent sex differences in reading (Dwyer, 1979):

1. *Age.* Patterns of sex differences in verbal skills in general, as well as in reading comprehension in particular, seem to change at puberty. Older studies reported that females drew ahead at puberty. Some later data, such as those mentioned earlier on the SAT, are now reporting that males score higher on measures of complex verbal skills. These measures are typically taken after puberty.
2. *Ability level.* Smaller population sex differences in reading and other academic areas are associated with gifted individuals. Larger sex differences are associated with lower-ability students.
3. *Instruments.* Reading achievement is measured in a wide variety of ways: reading comprehension passages with associated questions, vocabulary recognition, and teacher judgment. Each of these measures of student reading achievement seems to result in different patterns of apparent sex differences or similarities.

Much research on the causes of sex differences has failed to consider these three variables or to control for them in a systematic or easily interpreted way. Many appear to have focused on the somewhat limited area of verbal skills, in which girls' skills clearly surpass boys', and have sought explanations (or in some instances, cures) for this situation.

Explanations for Differences in Reading.   A great many explanations have been advanced to account for girls' assumed advantage in reading comprehension. These explanations may be broadly classified into five categories:

1. *Physical maturity.* It has been suggested that girls, being more developmentally advanced in more areas than boys, may simply acquire language proficiency earlier, although boys catch up with them at puberty. This explanation does not, however, account for the fact that sex differences in other academic achievement areas favor males during the same time period and that cross-cultural studies do not support the results of research with American subjects.

2. *Inappropriate reading materials.* It has been suggested that classroom reading materials are not interesting or challenging to young males and do not appeal to their interests. However, the large number of studies which have demonstrated that the content of readers, trade books, and curricular materials is predominantly male-oriented refute this claim.

3. *Negative treatment.* It has been suggested that schools are a predominantly feminine environment, and that as a consequence teachers may consider boys to be disruptive and may give preferential treatment to girls. Again, however, this does not account for boys' superiority in other areas. An important factor to remember in analyzing such studies is that the sex of the teacher is not the relevant variable in investigating preferential treatment. Teachers of both sexes appear to act in similar ways toward boys and girls.

4. *Differential treatment.* Many recent explanations of sex differences in reading focus on ways in which teachers may interact differentially with boys and girls. It is important to note that this is currently distinguished from negative treatment as described above. Rather, differential treatment refers to a situation that may or may not lead to negative outcomes for one sex or the other. Some types of differential treatment that have been explored are differences in teaching styles and differential reinforcement of student responses during reading instruction.

5. *Cultural factors.* It has been suggested that in the mainstream American culture, reading, as well as many other intellectual activities, is perceived as being primarily a passive occupation more appropriate to the female sex role. Teachers may inadvertently be perpetuating a negative valuation of reading for males.

It is important to note that some of the most productive research related to understanding sex differences in reading has been in the area of differential teacher behaviors and cultural expectations (for example, Mokros & Koff, 1978) rather than pupil traits or behaviors.

Conclusions.   For those who are interested in the practical implications of these data and analyses, we offer a few research-based and value-oriented conclusions:

1. Group sex differences are certainly too small to be used in predicting an individual girl's or boy's reading or other verbal skills and are probably too small to be of use even in group educational policy decisions.
2. Better reading role models for young boys are needed, as is more intensive skills instruction for many boys in the early grades. Boys in other countries (for example, Japan, England, Germany) are not "problem readers." American boys do not need to be "problems" either.
3. Better intellectual role models are needed for adolescent girls, as is instruction in strategies for coping with complex and inferential reading materials. There is no need for teenage girls' skills to deteriorate with more difficult tasks.

Research on Sex Differences in Communication

To what extent do males and females differ in the ways in which they communicate? Although Maccoby and Jacklin (1974) found that girls tend to be superior to boys in verbal ability, there is little evidence to support the notion of differences in communication that are linked to innate sex differences. Much of the empirical evidence on sex differences in language acquisition and language use contains flaws that exaggerate the extent of reported differences (Klann-Delius, 1981; Thorne, Kramarae, & Henley, 1983). The differences that have been found tend to be due to differing cultural expectations for boys and girls as a result of sex stereotyping and extensive sex segregation among children. A summary of the findings for oral language, written language, and nonverbal expression follows.

Kagan (1964) found that children tend to associate male communication with aggression, dominance, and independence and female communication with passivity, nurturance, and emotionality. Studies of adults indicate that females in comparison to males employ distinct patterns of intonation, more correct pronunciation, direct rather than indirect forms of expressing emotions, and indirect rather than direct forms of expressing requests (Edelsky, 1977). However, in reviewing the cumulative research on actual sex differences in speech patterns, Thorne (1978) noted that "empirical findings of difference (for example, in syntactic and phonetic usage, word choice, or conversational style) are fewer than stereotyped dichotomies of female and male language" (p. 4).

By filming infants and children, Birdwhistell (1970) concluded that the body language (posture, pelvic tilt, and so forth) associated with gender is established by the second year of life. It is highly likely, however, that such behaviors are the result of early expectations rather than innate biological characteristics. Wood (1981) supports the idea of cultural impact on gender cues by stating that "further study of the body language of gender communication may reveal a shift in children's communication from traditional gender cues to a more modern set of cues" (p. 183).

Analyses of children's writing reveal both similarities and differences between females and males. Price and Graves (1980) found that there were no differences in syntactic maturity or sophistication of sentence construction in the writing of eighth-grade pupils. However, girls showed a stronger adherence to grammatically correct usage than did boys. In a study of 7-year-olds, topics chosen by girls differed greatly from those of boys in accordance with stereotyped roles (Graves, 1973). While girls' thematic choices were those associated with "primary territory" (for example, home, school, and self), boys chose topics in more "extended territories" (for example, current events, occupations). Girls, however, were more likely than boys to write objectively, vividly, and with the use of the first person.

Edelsky (1977) studied the extent to which there is agreement by adults and children about how men and women talk. She found that there are definite stereotypes about language and sex in our culture and that adults show agreement on many of the particulars concerning the stereotypes. Children showed a gradual progression in their acquisition of the adults' norms from first to sixth grade. In Edelsky's studies, first-graders used form more than topic to identify sex of speaker for various sentences. For example, a sentence about a hammer with the phrase, "pretty please" was rated as female. But at the third-grade level, children also considered topic as an indicator of the sex of the speaker, so that the preceding example was rated either male because of the topic (hammer) or female because of the form (pretty please).

Adults, too, associate profanity with males and words like "divine" and "oh, dear" with females. However, there is often a discrepancy between performance and belief, as was demonstrated when a male subject said that men would not use "oh, dear" because it was passive, but later, when unable to think of a response to another question, said, "Oh, dear, I'm just going to run the tape down" (Edelsky, 1977).

Montgomery and Norton (1981) reviewed the literature on communication style, which suggested that males appear more dominant than females in communication, while women appear more attentive than men. Males appear to be more relaxed than females in their communication styles, while females appear to be more animated (as indicated by eye contact, gesture, facial expressions, and body movements). Their study found that males report being more precise, and females report being more animated, in their communication behaviors.

In a similar vein, Bate (1976) reported that female students are more uncomfortable than male students in asserting themselves in various interpersonal situations and that females report more fear in speaking before groups. Eakins and Eakins (1978), in reviewing findings on men's and women's communication, reported that women tend to speak less frequently than men in mixed groups and dyads and are less likely to initiate topics of discussion, while men interrupt more than women. According to Bate, men may be rewarded for dogmatic or authoritative responses in conflict situations; they may worry about being "real men" if they express warmth or reveal personal emotions.

Instructional materials also reinforce cultural stereotypes about sex differences in communication. In an analysis of textbooks, Sprague (1975) found that (1) most model speeches featured speeches by men; (2) many hypothetical applications of communication skills in textbooks perpetuated role stereotypes— for example, a man arguing a case in court and a woman making an announcement at a PTA meeting; and (3) audience analysis sections of texts usually emphasize that women are more persuasible and less logical than men and that sex of your audience is an important variable to know because it will make a difference in how you adapt your content.

ANSWERS

Sex-Equitable Reading Instruction and Learning

Based on the research evidence presented earlier, we find several promising approaches for increasing sex equity in reading instruction and learning. Since the best explanations to date for the poorer performance of young boys focus on teacher instructional patterns and cultural factors, it is in these two areas that solutions are to be found. When boys' reading instruction and reinforcement for reading behaviors are increased, their reading performance improves (Leinhart, Seewald, & Engel, 1979). Other approaches, such as all-male reading classes, are not necessarily helpful and may have harmful effects as well (Brophy & Good, 1974).

Another unsuccessful approach that has been advocated over the years is to increase the male characters and content of reading materials. However, instructional materials for reading are already heavily male-oriented, and their use may reduce reading interest for girls (see chapter 12, "Sex Equity and Sex Bias in Instructional Materials"). More positive images of males as readers are needed, however, to counter the stereotype that reading is a female activity. Such images can be provided by characters in reading books or through direct classroom investigation of sex-typing in reading. One basal series has approached this issue and other equity concerns. *Embers,* developed by the Council on Interracial Books for Children with Women's Educational Equity Act Program funds, presents content that illustrates concepts of sex, race, and disability equity as well as critical reading skills.

At the secondary level, we need better intellectual role models for adolescent girls and more intensive instruction for young women in coping with complex and inferential reading materials. Preventing the deterioration of adolescent females' skills is a goal. Here, reading instruction in the content areas, such as science and social studies, is of critical importance. In addition, both females and males can benefit from a sex-equitable literature curriculum (see, for example, Cornillon, 1974; National Council of Teachers of English, 1976; Rosenfelt, 1976; Showalter, 1974).

Sex-Equitable Language Instruction and Learning

In language arts, two kinds of instructional programs are sought: those that teach about sex-linked differences in language, including oral, written, and nonverbal language; and those that decrease pupils' gender-salient communication styles—for example, that increase the assertive communication of females and the emotional expression of males.

Two instructional programs are available that address these needs for sex-equitable language arts instruction and learning. For middle school students, *Decisions about Language* (see Women's Educational Equity Act Program, 1983) examines sex-biased language and communication differences as well as the impact of pupils' self-concept on communication style (Scott, 1982). Pupils who received this text and sex-equity instruction in five other subject areas as part of a school equity program made significant gains in achievement, sex role flexibility, and attitudes about participation in making decisions. They also understood more about the relationship between sex differences in language and self-concept, had less sex-biased attitudes about language, and were more supportive of language change than a control group of pupils.

For senior high and college students, *Changing Words in a Changing World* (Nilsen, 1979) focuses on language and language change in a social context, especially on the way language is used differently either by or about females and males. All students who participated in the validation of this text increased their knowledge about language and sociolinguistics. Students with positive attitudes about language change prior to instruction were even more positive about language change at the conclusion of the program.

Finally, Friedman (1981) reported on promising approaches to increasing opportunities for women and men to communicate with each other. The following topics are addressed in these programs:

1. *Self-concept:* How have cultural and familial sex-role stereotypes shaped students' views of themselves and what they are able to do? Do females believe in their own ability to think logically, to organize, and to articulate their ideas?
2. *Interaction conditioning:* What are the unspoken "rules" of interaction between males and females? How are distinctions made between what is denigrated as "aggressive" and what is admired as determined or forceful?
3. *Disclosure:* What are the differences between what females and males share within same-sex groups and what is disclosed to members of the opposite sex? What fears are perpetuated by these limitations, and what misunderstandings occur as a result of the distorted impressions each receives?
4. *Assertiveness/receptivity:* How can females learn to affirm their beliefs, concerns, rights, preferences, etc., without muffling or minimizing (or imposing) them? How can they best handle the conflicts that may arise when old patterns of interaction are first broken? (p. 142)

RECOMMENDATIONS

Sex equity in reading, writing, and communication instruction will enhance the competence of males as well as females. We recommend the following guidelines:

1. Reading instruction for young children should focus on the difficulties and strengths of individual students, male or female, without perpetuating sex stereotypes.
2. As pupils progress beyond basic reading proficiencies, instruction in high-level reading skills is needed, especially for adolescent females.
3. Reading materials that portray females and males in nonstereotypical situations need to be developed to strengthen the image of reading as something males can do and high level-thinking as something females can do.
4. Language instruction and materials that address sex-linked differences in language and communication expectations should be provided for students at all age levels.
5. Instruction in listening, interacting with others, disclosure, and assertiveness should be provided to all students to promote sex-equitable communication patterns.
6. Teachers need to be knowledgeable about sex-stereotyped patterns of classroom interaction (between and among both teachers and students) and trained to use intervention strategies (see chapter 11, Sex Equity in Classroom Organization and Climate).
7. Teacher training programs and materials need to dispel myths about sex differences in reading and communication. Effective strategies for promoting sex-equitable outcomes in learning should be part of every pre- and inservice education program.

REFERENCES

Bate, B. (1976). Assertive speaking: An approach to communication education for the future. *Communication Education, 25,* 53–59.
Birdwhistell, R. L. (1970). *Kinesics and context: Essays in body motion communication.* Philadelphia: University of Pennsylvania Press.
Brophy, J. E., & Good, T. L. (1974). *Teacher-student relationships: Causes and consequences.* New York: Holt.
Cornillon, S. K. (Ed.). (1974). *Images of women in fiction: Feminist perspectives.* Bowling Green, OH: Bowling Green University Press.
Dwyer, C. A. (1976). Test content and sex differences in reading. *Reading Teacher, 29,* 753–757.
Dwyer, C. A. (1979). The role of tests and their construction in producing apparent sex-

related differences. In M. A. Wittig and A. C. Petersen (Eds.), *Sex-related differences in cognitive functioning* (pp. 335–353). New York: Academic Press.

Eakins, B. & Eakins, G. R. (1978). *Sex differences in human communication.* Boston: Houghton-Mifflin.

Edelsky, C. (1977). Acquisition of an aspect of communicative competence: Learning what it means to talk like a lady. In S. E. Tripp & C. Mitchell-Kernan (Eds.), *Child discourse* (pp. 225–243). New York: Academic Press.

Educational Testing Service. (1981). *National Report on College-Bound Seniors, 1981.* Princeton, NJ: Author.

Friedman, P. (1981). Special needs of handicapped, reticent, gifted, bilingual, and female students. In G. W. Friedman (Ed.), *Education in the '80's: Speech Communication* (pp. 131–144). Washington, DC: National Education Association.

Graves, D. H. (1973). Sex differences in children's writing. *Elementary English, 50,* 1101–1106.

Hyde, J. S. (1981). How large are cognitive gender differences? A meta-analysis using ω^2 and d. *American Psychologist, 36,* 892–901.

Johnson, D. D. (1973–74). Sex differences in reading across cultures. *Reading Research Quarterly, 9,* 67–86.

Kagan, J. (1964). Acquisition and significance of sex-typing and sex-role identity. In M. L. Hoffman and L. W. Hoffman (Eds.), *Review of Child Development Research* (Vol. 1) (pp. 137–167). New York: Russell Sage Foundation.

Klann-Delius, G. (1981). Sex and language acquisition—Is there any influence? *Journal of Pragmatics, 5,* 1–25.

Leinhart, G., Seewald, A. M., & Engel, M. (1979). Learning what's taught: Sex differences in instruction. *Journal of Educational Psychology, 71,* 432–439.

Maccoby, E. E., & Jacklin, C. N. (1974). *The psychology of sex differences.* Palo Alto, CA: Stanford University Press.

Mokros, J. R., & Koff, E. (1978). Sex stereotyping of children's success in mathematics and reading. *Psychological Reports, 42,* 1287–1293.

Montgomery, B. M., & Norton, R. W. (1981). Sex differences and similarities in communicator style. *Communication Monographs, 48,* 121–132.

Murphy, Roger J. L. (1977, July). *Sex differences in examination performance: Do these reflect differences in ability or sex-role stereotypes?* Paper presented at the International Conference on Sex-Role Stereotyping, Cardiff, Wales.

National Council of Teachers of English. (1976). *Responses to sexism: Class practices in teaching English, 1976–77.* Urbana, IL: NCTE.

Nilsen, A. P. (1979). *Changing words in a changing world.* Newton, MA: Education Development Center.

Preston, R. C. (1962). Reading achievement of German and American children. *School and Society, 90,* 350–354.

Price, G. B., & Graves, R. L. (1980). Sex differences in syntax and usage in oral and written language. *Research in the Teaching of English, 14,* 147–153.

Rosenfelt, D. S. (Ed.). (1976). *Strong women.* Old Westbury, NY: Feminist Press.

Scott, K. P. (1982). Teaching about sex differences in language. *Clearing House, 55,* 410–413.

Showalter, E. (Ed.). (1974). *Women's liberation and literature.* NY: Harcourt Brace Jovanovich.

Sprague, J. (1975). The reduction of sexism in speech communication education. *Speech Teacher, 24,* 37–45.

Stockard, J., Schmuck, P. A., Kempner, K., Williams, P., Edson, S. K., and Smith, M. A. (1980). *Sex equity in education.* New York: Academic Press.

Thorne, B. (1978). *Gender . . . how it is best conceptualized.* Paper delivered at the annual meeting of the American Sociological Association.

Thorne, B., Kramarae, C., & Henley, N. (1983). *Language, gender, and society.* Rowley, MA: Newbury House.

Women's Educational Equity Act Program. (1983). *Fair play: Developing self-concept and decision-making skills in the middle school.* Newton, MA: Education Development Center.

Wood, B. S. (1981). *Children and communication: Verbal and nonverbal language development* (2nd ed.). Englewood Cliffs, NJ: Prentice-Hall.

15

Sex Equity in Social Studies

Carole L. Hahn and Jane Bernard-Powers,
with Lisa Hunter, Susan Groves,
Molly MacGregor, and Kathryn P. Scott

Social studies is the area of the curriculum that has traditionally been expected to instill in youth respect for our democratic heritage. It is the social studies teacher who teaches that the nation was founded on the principle of equality and justice for all. However in the social studies class, as in all other aspects of schooling, sex equity often does not exist.

Research over the past 20 years has documented inequities in student achievement, staffing patterns, and the curriculum. The need for change has been made clear, and a number of critical issues have been raised. This chapter will describe those issues and some of the exemplary sex-fair programs that address them. It will also recommend specific approaches for policy makers, curriculum developers, and users of the new materials.

THE ISSUES: FINDINGS FROM RESEARCH

Inadequate Textbooks

The most extensively documented inequity in social studies is the under-representation and stereotyping of females in social studies textbooks. Studies have concluded that females appear far less frequently than males in elementary school textbooks. When women or girls do appear, they are often portrayed in passive roles and/or stereotyped occupations (O'Donnell, 1973; Scardina, 1972; Sheridan, 1975; Zimmerman, 1975).

At the secondary level, similar generalizations apply to United States history, government, world history, and economics textbooks. Males dominate photographs, quotations, examples, and case studies (Arlow & Froschl, 1976; Blankenship & Hahn, 1982; Burr, Dunn, & Farquhar, 1973; Hahn & Blankenship, 1983; Julian, 1979; MacLeod & Silverman, 1973; Smith, 1977;

280

Trecker, 1971; Weinbaum, 1979). This may partially explain why females are less interested in social studies than are males (McTeer, 1975) and why all students learn less about famous women in history than about men (Lockheed & Harris, 1978).

In the 1970s, several publishers adopted guidelines to encourage authors to eliminate sexist bias from their materials. As a result, in the newer books sexist language occurs less frequently, a few more famous women appear, and photos show women in a greater variety of roles. Still, many social studies textbooks retain their sexist bias (Blankenship & Hahn, 1982). Publishers also responded to the new demand for sex-fair materials from educators, which emerged in the seventies. Supplementary materials were produced—mostly paperback books or audiovisual kits—that focused on the changing role of women and women's issues. The extent of the dissemination of these supplementary materials is unclear, however. Extensive reports by the National Science Foundation on the status of social studies have concluded that the traditional textbook continues to dominate classroom instruction and homework (Shaver, Helburn, & Davis, 1979).

Gender Differences in Knowledge and Attitudes

A second line of research on sex equity in social studies has focused on gender differences in student knowledge and attitudes. The National Assessment of Educational Progress (NAEP) found that males consistently outperformed females on measures of political knowledge (Education Commission of the States, 1971, 1973, 1974, 1978). In addition, NAEP found attitudinal differences between males and females. Females were slightly more willing to associate with persons of different races, and they were more involved as good citizens within families.

Sex differences have also emerged in political socialization research. It has been found that as early as the fifth grade, females tend to demonstrate less political knowledge than males; at both the elementary and secondary levels, females hold different political attitudes than males. Females are more likely to say they would vote for candidates who are peace-oriented, honest, and sincere, while over twice as many males as females say they would choose the candidate whose ideas would contribute to the country's economic growth (Iglitzin, 1974).

Until very recently, most studies of economic knowledge concluded that males did better than females on tests of economic knowledge (Soper, 1979). However, economics was previously an elective that many females did not choose. Studies done in the past 3 years have found no gender differences in economics learning (Hahn, 1982; Jackstadt, 1980; McCullough, 1980). This shows that when all students are required to take a course in economics for high school graduation, as they are in many states today, females acquire the same economic knowledge as males.

Student Knowledge of and Attitudes toward Women in Society

A third line of social studies research has examined students' attitudes toward and knowledge of women's changing roles in society. One study found that most high school students still have unrealistic information about the current economic position of women (Davis, 1976). Most students, however, do support egalitarian statements about the economic status of women—equal pay for equal work and equal access to jobs. The students holding the most egalitarian attitudes are those who have the most realistic information, earn the highest grades, plan to go to college, and aspire to high-status jobs. In general, female students tend to hold attitudes more supportive of equality than do male students (Davis, 1976).

In an international study of female and male students' political attitudes, youth in the United States were found to be less supportive of women as political leaders than were students in the other nine nations studied (Torney, Oppenheim, & Farnen, 1975). Other studies also have found that students in the United States do not support the idea of women holding political office (Iglitzin, 1974).

It is possible that students do not have realistic information about women in the economy and do not believe that women ought to be political leaders because the social studies curriculum has not shown women to be active in the economic and political spheres. Unfortunately, equity programs have not focused on the teaching of economics and political science.

The Hidden Curriculum

A fourth line of research has identified needs in the "hidden curriculum" of social studies. The hidden curriculum consists of the collection of messages transmitted to young people about the status and character of individuals and social groups (Byrne, 1978; Frazier & Sadker, 1973; Lockheed, 1985). The hidden curriculum in social studies works through organizational patterns in schools, colleges, publishing houses, and professional organizations.

According to the National Science Foundation, 62% of social studies teachers in grades 7–9, and 75% of social studies teachers in grades 10–12, are men (Directorate for Science Education, 1980). Similar data were obtained as recently as 1983 (Hahn, 1984). The dearth of female role models may suggest to students that social studies is a male domain.

This point is further reinforced for the few women social studies teachers who might aspire to advance in the profession. A study of the secondary school systems in one large state found that 90% of the social studies department heads were male (Carney, 1980). Most authors of social studies methods books and most social studies researchers are males (Hahn, 1980). Furthermore, most social studies supervisors are men, and most officers in the National Council for the Social Studies have been men.

Other aspects of the hidden curriculum that may influence social studies learning are student leadership (if student body presidents are most often males), sex-segregated classes (if electives in psychology and sociology draw mostly females, while economics electives draw mostly males), and classroom interaction patterns (if males take more risks in initiating responses). Unfortunately, there has not been sufficient research into the effects of these informal processes. The issues associated with the formal curriculum, rather than those associated with the hidden one, have received the most attention to date.

THE ANSWERS

Developing Curricula to Compensate for Inadequate Elementary and Secondary Social Studies Textbooks

In response to the first issue—the underrepresentation and stereotyping of females in social studies textbooks—several programs and individuals have developed student materials and teacher guides to supplement traditional materials and courses. Several claims can be made about these materials and their effects:

1. Materials are available for students of all ages that teach more about women in history than textbooks have traditionally taught.
2. Materials are available that teach students about women from diverse ethnic backgrounds and that teach students about the lives of average or typical women as well as about the contributions of great women.
3. Students of all ages enjoy learning about women in history.
4. Teachers enjoy teaching about women in history, regardless of the ages of their students.
5. Discriminatory attitudes based on sex are reduced in both female and male students at the elementary, middle school, and secondary levels when students study about gender roles, stereotyping, and the status and achievements of women throughout history.
6. Sex-stereotyped behaviors by both boys and girls are reduced when primary grade instruction includes units designed specifically to counter stereotypes.
7. Self-esteem increases for both female and male students when secondary social studies instruction includes women's history; changes are particularly evident among female students.
8. Federal funding that focuses on women and history and on overcoming gender stereotypes has been effective in stimulating curriculum development at both elementary and secondary school levels.

The preceding claims have been documented by the various projects listed in table 8. These and similar programs developed by local school systems around the country have focused on overcoming traditional stereotypes of female and male behavior as they were traditionally presented in social studies courses. These programs have also attempted to compensate for the traditional omission

Table 8. Sex Equity Curriculum Projects in Social Studies

Title/developer	Grade	Format	Content	Evaluation	Availability
Elementary Curriculum, Women's Studies Program, Berkeley Unified Schools. Susan Gross, Berkeley Unified Schools, Berkeley, CA	1–3, 4–6	Series of lessons	1–3: overcoming stereotypes; 4–6: Nontraditional careers, women in history, and development of nonstereotyped skills like carpentry, bike repair, and dance	Field-tested in varied SES schools and pre-post tests used. Primary students showed less stereotyped behaviors and greater cooperation after instruction. 4–6 showed decreases in stereotyped attitudes in experimental group as compared to control. No effect on students' stereotyped career aspirations	Women's Studies Program, Berkeley Unified Schools, Berkeley, CA
Upper Midwest Women's History Center for Teachers: Elementary Curriculum. St. Louis Park, MN	K–6	6 units contain sections for primary, intermediate, and teachers	Immigration, westward movement, reformers, geography, writing skills	Field-tested in varied SES schools. Teachers liked materials and planned to use again	Upper MW Women's History Center for Teachers, 6300 Walker St., St. Louis Park, MN 55416
Winning Justice for All. Council on Interracial Books for Children	5–6	Student workbook, teacher handbook, 3 filmstrips with cassette tapes	Inquiry approach to studying current and historic sex and race discrimination	Field-tested in 9 varied SES schools. Pupils in experimental classes made knowledge gains and had less	Council on Interracial Books for Children, Racism/Sexism Resource Center, 1841 Broadway, New

284

(continued)

				stereotyped attitudes as compared to pupils in control classes	York, NY 10023
Decisions and You, Decisions about Roles, From "Fair Play: Developing Self-Concept and Decision-Making Skill." Byron Massialas and Kathryn Scott, Florida State University, Tallahassee, FL	6–8	Student texts, teacher guides, and an implementation guide	Teaches concepts related to sex equity and helps students explore their own self-concepts through topics usually taught in social studies. Other units available for language arts, math, science, and PE	Field-tested in 3 schools. Pupils in experimental classes made significant gains in achievement, sex role flexibility, and decision making as compared to students in control classes	Education Development Center, 55 Chapel Street, Newton, MA 02160
In Search of Our Past. Susan Groves, Berkeley Unified Schools, Berkeley, CA	8–12	6 units in two books supplement American and world history textbooks	Events, time periods, and concepts of importance to various ethnic groups. Students gather oral history	Pilot-tested in varied SES schools. Teachers and students had favorable reactions to material	Education Development Center, 55 Chapel Street, Newton, MA 02160
Women in World Area Studies. Marjorie Bigham and Susan Gross, St. Louis Park Schools, St. Louis Park, MN	9–12	9 student booklets and teacher guides, filmstrips, and tapes. Supplemental to world cultures courses	Women in Soviet Union, Israel, Islam, India, China, ancient Greece and Rome, Africa, Latin America	Tested in 11th-grade suburban classes. Significant learning gains for experimental classes as compared to control. Favorable reactions from teachers and students	GEM Publications, Inc., 411 Mallallien Dr., Hudson, WI 54016

Table 8. (Continued)

Title/developer	Grade	Format	Content	Evaluation	Availability
Women's Roots. June Stephenson	9–12	A world history textbook	Surveys prehistoric to modern times. Attention to religious, political, social, and economic influences on gender roles. Women's achievements	In experimental conditions, students who read text had reduced discriminatory attitudes and increased self-esteem as compared to control group. Self-esteem of female students increased more than that of male students	
Sources of Strength: Women and Culture. Lisa Hunter, Far West Laboratory, San Francisco, CA	9–12	Teachers' guide and annotated bibliography to be used in world history, cultures, women's studies, or sociology courses	Cultural comparisons of Nigerian, Chinese, Afro-American, and Asian-American women. Oral history. Decision making in students' lives	Field-tested in varied SES schools. Experimental group had clear gains on the oral history test as compared to control. Males and females affected equally. Students had favorable reaction to program	Education Development Center, 55 Chapel Street, Newton, MA 02160

	Grade level	Materials	Purpose	Field test	Source
Women's Lives/ Women's Work. The Feminist Press	9–12	12 books to supplement English and social studies curricula	Historical approach: uses diaries, letters, biographies, oral histories, poems, and essays	Extensive national field test in varied SES schools. Books on Third World women especially effective with Blacks and Hispanic students. Some males reacted with hostility	The Feminist Press, Box 334, Old Westbury, NY 11568
National Women's History Week Project	K–12	1 printed guide for teachers and 1 for community organizers.	To promote celebrations of Women's History Week in March. Recommends speakers, activities, and resources	Spread from 1 school system to a national celebration in 3 years	National Women's History Week, Box 3716, Santa Rosa, CA 95402
We the People: Sex Bias in American History. Patricia Campbell, Georgia State University	Teachers of K–12	Module containing audio cassette tape and written materials	To help teachers amend their U.S. history instruction to better represent women in history	Field-tested in social studies methods courses.	Education Development Center, 55 Chapel Street, Newton, MA 02160

Note. Data were contributed by Susan Gross, Susan Groves, Lisa Hunter, Molly MacGregor, Kathryn Scott, The Feminist Press, and the Upper Midwest Women's History Center.

of women from history and world culture textbooks. Most of the projects contain materials for student use as well as teachers' guides. These materials are generally used as supplementary lessons in social studies and occasionally in language arts courses. Other sex equity materials that are appropriate for students in social studies classes are described in chapters 11, 14, and 18, on classroom organization and climate, reading and communication skills, and career and vocational education. The other issues identified in the first part of this chapter have not received the same amount of attention. As mentioned earlier, recent research has indicated that when economics is required in secondary schools, female students learn as much as male students (McCullough, 1980; Hahn, 1982). However, no programs were identified that confront the issue of the low level of political knowledge among females as compared to males. Similarly, none were found that address the basis of the different political attitudes found among female and male youth in the United States or the negative attitudes of American students compared to students in other parts of the world with regard to the role of women as political leaders. Finally, no programs were found that teach students about women's rights legislation or that consciously help students counter the effects of the hidden curriculum—either on student learning or on attitudes related to social studies.

Teacher Education

The success of a sex-fair social studies curriculum depends to a great extent on helping teachers to identify and challenge sex bias in their own attitudes, in their classroom practices, and in curricular material. Furthermore, teacher education must provide teachers with positive examples of sex-equitable alternatives. The ideal social studies teacher should have a thorough understanding of sex role socialization and sex role stereotyping, the role of women in history, the history of the family, the role of women in the economy from both a historical and a contemporary legal and political perspective, and the interrelationships between gender, class, and race issues. In addition, the ideally educated social studies teacher should know how to analyze all types of media and curricular materials for general bias as well as sex bias. Knowledge of and access to sex-fair social studies materials, both for reference and for classroom use, are another facet of this ideal teacher makeup. These characteristics represent the objectives and challenges that have been presented to social studies professionals who are involved in teacher training at both the preservice and inservice levels.

The following discussion provides a view of what is being done in social studies teacher education to realize the goals. The information available on the topic is uneven; moreover, evaluative data are scarce. It is nonetheless important to chronicle the responses of teacher educators in social studies; to discuss what has been effective where there is evidence to support claims of effectiveness; and to suggest future directions for teacher education in the social studies. Together the variety of programs and approaches demonstrate four major points:

1. Introductory courses in history and the social sciences have been revised at many colleges to incorporate feminist scholarship.
2. Financial incentives to institutions and to individual faculty members have been effective in stimulating curriculum revision to include feminist scholarship.
3. A few preservice social studies methods courses have been revised to draw attention to the need for sex equity in instruction and to introduce beginning teachers to resources for teaching about women.
4. Inservice summer institutes are an effective means of retraining experienced teachers when they include lectures and seminars on feminist scholarship and on the development of curricular materials by teachers for use in their own teaching.

Preservice Teacher Education. In social studies, preservice teacher education consists of college-level coursework in the social sciences and courses in curriculum and instructional methods for social studies. Social science coursework falls in the domain of preservice education because the specific knowledge and world view implicit in course content form the basis for future social studies teaching in schools. There is a trickle-down effect from college-level courses that must be acknowledged. Thus, efforts by college educators to integrate feminist scholarship into social science courses are relevant to a discussion of preservice education.

The following four institutions provide examples of what can be done in attempting to achieve sex equity in the social studies curriculum:

Wheaton College in Massachusetts, with funding from the Department of Education's Fund for the Improvement of Post-Secondary Education, undertook a 3-year project to revise introductory courses in several disciplines to include feminist perspectives. This project has been described as a model for curriculum reform and has been characterized as a successful project by college officials who report that over half of Wheaton's faculty members have taken part in the program including many who were not previously involved in research on women (Hook, 1981; Merrill, 1982).

Stanford University's approach centers on the revival and revision of an undergraduate course sequence called Western Civilization so that it reflects feminist theory and thought. This approach represents one viable method of curriculum revision for undergraduates: the return to a core sequence of required courses that presents the comparable and different experiences of men and women from a feminist perspective, "noting the incompleteness of the record on women, [and] examining the power relations in the past which caused the incompleteness" (Lougee, 1981).

Wellesley College awarded 35 fellowships to faculty members in universities across the United States to enable them to conduct research on women "that would lead to a 'balancing of views of men and women' in the college curriculum" (Hook, 1981). This program was based on the premise that college faculty are willing to avail themselves of feminist thought and research, but that the reeducation process takes time, and release time is a critical factor. Fellowships provide both the time and incentive for faculty participation (Hook, 1981).

Utah State University, in a project directed by Judith Gappa and Judith Pearce and funded by the Women's Educational Equity Act Program, developed a series of course syllabi entitled "Sex and Gender in the Social Sciences: Reassessing the Introductory Course" (Gappa & Pearce, 1980). Course guides for introductory microeconomics, psychology, and sociology were written by the project staff based on the premise that women are underrepresented in basic social science curricula because faculty do not have time to revise their courses. Having experts provide course outlines that include feminist thought and scholarship is a reasonable solution to the problem. An important part of the project was faculty participation in the evaluation and revision of course guidelines.

Periodically, networks of educators meet to discuss bringing sex-equitable materials into undergraduate education. At the 1981 Wingspread Conference, women's studies scholars and college administrators gathered to discuss strategies for integrating scholarship about women into the liberal arts curriculum. Representatives from Wellesley College reported that there were 49 projects under way around the United States that were designed to bring about changes in core undergraduate curricula, including the social sciences (McIntosh, 1982). Although research that assesses the effects of these projects is not available, it would be accurate to say that the focus on sex equity in colleges and universities has led to both an awareness of the problem of a male-centered curriculum and the generation of positive solutions in the form of faculty development and curriculum revision. The next critical phase of the process is a comprehensive evaluation to examine the effects of curriculum revision on faculty, students, and, ultimately, future social studies teachers.

Another facet of preservice teacher training that merits consideration here is coursework in education. Because in chapter 9 Myra and David Sadker have dealt with general courses in education such as educational psychology and the history of education, discussion here is confined to courses in curriculum and instruction in social studies.

Definitive statements about what is taught and the degree to which sex equity issues are addressed would be presumptions given the lack of data, but there are some indications of both the need for change and change. For example, one study of 18 social studies methods textbooks published between 1975 and 1979 found that only five books discussed sex bias as a problem social studies teachers should confront (Hahn, 1980). However, informal reports at meetings of the National Council for Social Studies (NCSS) and the NCSS Special Interest Group for Sex Equity in the Social Studies have indicated that sex bias and sex equity are regularly addressed in the methods courses of some instructors today (Bernard-Powers, 1981). For example, teacher interns in Stanford University's

Secondary Teacher Education Program have been required to analyze materials for sex bias. They have also been introduced to available resources for integrating women into the social studies curriculum, and they have regularly discussed the importance of including women's history and social history in the curriculum. Further evidence is found in a recent study of sex equity in teacher education; the researcher found that five institutions reported the inclusion of sex-fair curriculum resources and instructional methods in their social studies methods courses (Lather, 1983).

The studies of methods textbooks and the informal reporting discussed above indicate that some future social studies teachers are being exposed to sex equity issues and concerns. Nevertheless, there is a dire need for more comprehensive and extensive evaluation of the extent to which sex equity topics are addressed in social studies methods courses. Such research should document how many, to what extent, and by what means social studies methods courses and instructors address sex equity issues. It should also include both short-term and long-term assessments of the impact of sex equity training on preservice teachers, their students, and their colleagues.

In summary, preservice teacher training is a critical link in the process of creating sex-equitable social studies curricula and instruction. College-level social science courses that reflect current research and scholarship constitute an important part of future social studies teachers' preservice training. The programs designed to integrate feminist perspectives and gender research into the mainstream curricula through faculty training and development and curriculum revision will play a significant role in the education of future social studies teachers. The initiation of the 49 programs referred to earlier in this section is evidence of the positive impact of concern for sex equity. Similarly, informal reporting from a limited number of people suggests that some methods courses have changed to include issues, strategies, and resoues relevant to sex equity. In the future, more reliable and systematic reporting and evaluation in this area are needed.

Inservice Teacher Education. Training those who are already in the classroom is potentially more important than preservice training. Given a maturing teaching population—the average numbers of years of teaching experience, according to a 1979 National Science Foundation survey of math, science, and social studies teachers, was 11.9 years—we cannot rely on younger teachers to carry the burden of reform (National Science Foundation, 1980). Reform in social studies curricula greatly depends on retraining teachers currently in the field.

There are numerous settings and forums in which inservice education in social studies currently takes place. Professional associations such as the National Council for the Social Studies, teacher centers, school systems, and privately funded organizations offer inservice training workshops that vary considerably in duration and format. The summer institute is a popular format that enjoys considerable advantage over the "one-shot" or short-term inservice program. It affords the time necessary to learn new content and/or new theoretical frameworks. The Sarah Lawrence Summer Institute in Women's History and the Stanford Summer Institute in Women's History are excellent examples of such an approach.

The Sarah Lawrence Summer Institute in Women's History was a 3-week program for high school teachers that was designed to facilitate the integration of women's history into secondary courses. It was cosponsored by the American Historical Association and Sarah Lawrence College. Participants heard lectures in women's history, critiqued classroom materials currently used, and developed curricular materials. The two basic objectives of the institute were, first, to have participants share their new knowledge, enthusiasm, and curriculum with personnel in their school districts; and second, to create a summer institute model that would be replicable.

The curricular materials that were designed during the workshop were field-tested by participants throughout the following year and subsequently revised. A year after the institute, participants reported that they had been able to share the content and curriculum with colleagues, administrators, and people in the community. In the summary report the evaluators concluded that "the Sarah Lawrence Summer Institute in Women's History has fulfilled its objectives in a highly successful manner. It trained students in women's history; it produced learning packets for use in teaching women's history; it encouraged the development of a support network; and it has provided a valuable experience which should serve as a model for future institutes" (Sammons & Kolb, 1978).

There were two spin-offs from this institute that deserve mention. One was the subsequent development by the women's studies department at Sarah Lawrence of an inservice course for high school teachers on integrating women's history into the high school curriculum. The second was the development of the Stanford Summer Institute in Women's History, modeled after the Sarah Lawrence institute.

The Upper Midwest Women's History Center provides another example of inservice education focused on sex equity in social studies. The 5-day program was divided between lecture/discussions that concentrated on historical periods and topics, and the presentation of bibliographies and curricular materials for classroom use.

These inservice summer institutes for social studies teachers were successful in changing the behavior and perceptions of teachers. The majority of teachers indicated that they had learned new ideas and strategies as a result of the workshop experience and that they intended to use them in their classrooms and to disseminate them to others in the school and community.

Developments in inservice education have provided the most positive evidence of the impact of sex-equitable policies, programs, and practices. The success of the summer institutes described in this report suggests that the models generated should be replicated elsewhere. Inservice education may be the most potent tool for influencing the greatest number of social studies teachers. As is true in other areas, there is a need for more comprehensive evaluation and research to assess the comparative effectiveness of inservice programs in attracting participants, retraining teachers, providing for dissemination of materials and expertise in local districts, and ultimately affecting students.

In reflecting on the need for sex equity training for social studies educators, we note that no programs or policies have been identified that attempt to increase the number or status of women within the profession. Rather, the purpose of programs for adults has been to influence both male and female social studies teachers to teach more intelligently about women.

RECOMMENDATIONS

In a wide variety of organizations and institutions, action has been taken to foster research, develop curricula, and support teacher training that ultimately contributes to sex equity in social studies. The work that has been done and the progress that has been realized, as well as the work that needs to be done, suggest the following recommendations.

An impressive array of curricular materials has been developed to supplement classroom instruction and materials. The continued dissemination of these materials is a critical step toward sex-equitable social studies. At the same time, publishers of textbooks for social studies at all levels need continued encouragement to revise their old texts and publish new ones that are sex-fair and include recent feminist scholarship in the social sciences.

While it has been demonstrated that students in government and economics courses learn less about women than they do about men, we have not identified any programs that attempt to rectify the inequity. Because government/civics and economics courses are required for high school graduation in most states, it is particularly important that curriculum development be undertaken in those areas. In the 1970s, federal funding was an impetus that helped bring about curriculum revision. In the future, local school systems, state education agencies, and private foundations will need to act as additional catalysts for curricular change.

Gender stereotyping does decline when students are exposed to instruction specifically directed at that goal. Such instruction should be part of the curriculum in all elementary and middle schools. Social studies, language arts, and career exploration objectives can thus be approached in an integrated unit of study.

Authors of social studies methods books and professors of social studies methods should give both preservice and inservice teachers guidance in how to eliminate sexism from social studies curricula and instruction. Numerous articles published by the National Council for the Social Studies and its state affiliates are available to support these efforts.

State social studies organizations, teachers' centers, and universities should offer inservice courses to enable teachers to learn how new scholarship on women may influence the teaching of history, psychology, and the social sciences. Directors of the programs can benefit from the experiences of others who have conducted similar institutes. This approach is desperately needed because teachers—no matter how well-intentioned—are themselves products of the traditional, sex-biased curriculum. In order to break the cycle, they must have the opportunity and encouragement to learn feminist history and social science. At the same time, beginning teachers must have the opportunity to take women's studies courses or sex-fair history and social science courses in their undergraduate programs.

Finally, more research is needed in several areas that touch on social studies. What are the effects of the sex-fair materials and programs on student learning and attitudes? (Both locally and nationally developed programs need to be evaluated in the particular setting in which they are used.) To what extent have sex equity programs been disseminated, and what are the inhibitors and facilitators of effective adoption and implementation? Do female and male students learn equally well from the various strategies employed in social studies, such as role playing or competitive games, and how can research on the effects of status in the classroom inform social studies teaching? In reading and science, teacher expectations have been found to affect student achievement. Do social studies teachers hold different expectations for females than males in particular courses such as foreign policy and economics as opposed to sociology, and do those different expectations affect student achievement?

There is some evidence that females display fewer assertive behaviors than males in secondary school social studies classes (Hedrick & Chance, 1977). More research is needed to determine the extent to which this occurs, its possible effect on achievement, and whether teacher training or student education can change the pattern.

Research on career choices and on political socialization suggests that classroom instruction has a greater influence on knowledge than on attitudes— with the notable exception that positive attitudes develop when the climate of the classroom and of the school reflects the goals that are evoked (Dodson, 1973; Ehman, 1980; Grant, 1977; Pope, 1971; Sullivan, 1975; Vetter & Sethney, 1972). This suggests that a sex-fair curriculum needs to be reinforced by a hidden curriculum in which sex equity is practiced. Then, attitudinal changes as well as knowledge gains may result. Research is needed to test this hypothesis.

These are just a few examples of the questions we cannot yet answer. There are others to which we now have responses. For example, we know that instruction can increase students' knowledge of women's history. But whether that finding is put to widespread use or not remains to be seen. The realization of sex equity in social studies depends on the cooperation of local school districts, which can support and encourage the use of available materials; teacher centers, teacher training institutions, and professional organizations that can support and encourage preservice and inservice training that addresses sex equity issues; individual researchers and their institutional support systems who can explore the unanswered questions; and the publishing concerns, special agencies, and textbook authors who produce the classroom materials from which our students learn. Working in concert, these individuals, agencies, and institutions can meet the challenge of providing sex-equitable social studies education.

REFERENCES

Arlow, P., & Froschl, M. (1976). Women in the high school curriculum: A review of U.S. history and English literature texts. In Florence Howe (Ed.), *High school feminist studies* (pp. vi–xvii). Old Westbury, NY: Feminist Press.

Bernard-Powers, J. (1981). *Sex equity and the social studies.* Paper presented at the annual meeting of the College and University Faculty Assembly of the National Council for the Social Studies, Detroit.

Blankenship, G., & Hahn, C. L. (1982). Sex bias in Georgia high school economics textbooks. *Georgia Social Science Journal, 13,* 1–3.

Burr, E., Dunn, S., & Farquhar, N. (1972). Women and the language of inequality. *Social Education, 36,* 841–845.

Byrne, E. M. (1978). *Women and education.* London: Tavistock.

Carney, L. (1980). Responses to sexism: Two steps forward and one back? *Racism and sexism: Responding to the challenge* Washington, DC: National Council for the Social Studies.

Davis, L. C. (1976, November). *The information and perceptions of twelfth-grade students about the economic and political roles of women.* Paper presented at the annual meeting of the College and University Faculty Assembly of the National Council for the Social Studies, Washington, DC.

Directorate for Science Education. (1980). *Science education databook.* Washington, DC: National Science Foundation.

Dodson, E. A. (1973). *Effects of female role models on occupational exploration and attitudes of adolescents.* Unpublished doctoral dissertation, Michigan State University, East Lansing.

Education Commission of the States. (1971, July). *1969–1970 citizenship: Group results for sex, region, and size of community* (National Assessment of Educational Progress Report No. 16). Washington D.C.: U.S. Government Printing Office.

Education Commission of the States. (1973, December). *Political knowledge and attitudes.* (National Assessment of Educational Progress). Washington, DC: U. S. Government Printing Office.

Education Commission of the States. (1974, June). *The first social studies assessment: An overview.* (National Assessment of Educational Progress). Washington, DC: U.S. Government Printing Office.

Education Commission of the States. (1978). *Changes in social studies performance, 1972–1976. Changes in political knowledge and attitudes, 1969–1976. Citizenship: An overview, 1975–1976.* (National Assessment of Educational Progress). Denver: Education Commission of the States.

Ehman, L. H. (1980). The American school in the political socialization process. *Review of Educational Research, 50,* 99–120.

Frazier, N., & Sadker, M. (1973). *Sexism in school and society*. New York: Harper & Row.

Gappa, J. M., & Pearce, J. (1980, December). *Sex and gender in the social sciences: Reassessing the introductory course Principles in Microeconomics* (produced under the auspices of the Women's Educational Equity Act). Washington, DC: Department of Education.

Grant, E. (1977). The effect of a two-week women's study course on student attitudes toward women. *Journal of Social Studies Research, 1,* 36–41.

Hahn, C. L. (1980). Social studies with equality and justice for all: Toward the elimination of sexism. *Journal of Research and Development in Education, 13,* 103–112.

Hahn, C. L. (1982). Are there gender differences in high school economics in the eighties? *Journal of Economic Education, 13,* 57–65.

Hahn, C. L. (1984). The status of the social studies. *Social Education.*

Hahn, C. L., & Blankenship, G. (1983). Women and economics textbooks. *Theory and Research in Social Education, 11*(3), 67–76.

Hedrick, T. E., & Chance, J. E. (1977). Sex differences in assertive achievement patterns. *Sex Roles, 3,* 129–139.

Hook, J. (1981, November 4). Scholars wage compaign to integrate research on women into standard liberal arts courses. *Chronicle of Higher Education,* p. 8.

Iglitzin, L. B. (1974). The making of the apolitical woman: Femininity and sex stereotyping. In J. S. Jaquette (Ed.), *Women in politics.* New York: Wiley.

Jackstadt, S. L. (1980). *A study of the relationship between economic knowledge and attitudes of high school students.* Unpublished doctoral dissertation, Indiana University, Bloomington.

Julian, N. B. (1979). *An analysis of treatment of women in selected junior and senior high school United States history textbooks.* Unpublished doctoral dissertation, New Mexico State University, University Park.

Lather, P. (1983, April). *Struggling mightily: Teacher education and curriculum change.* Paper presented at the annual meeting of the American Educational Research Association, Montreal.

Lockheed, M. E. (1985). Sex equity in classroom organization and climate. Chapter 11, this volume.

Lockheed, M. E., & Harris, A. M. (1978, March). *The effects of equal status cross-sex contact on students' sex-stereotyped attitudes and behavior.* Paper presented at the annual meeting of the American Educational Research Association, Toronto.

Lougee, C. (1981). Women, history and the humanities: An argument in favor of the general studies curriculum. *Women's Studies Quarterly, 10,* 4–7.

MacLeod, F. S., & Silverman, S. T. (1973). *You won't do: What textbooks on U.S. government teach high school girls.* Pittsburgh: KNOW, Inc.

McCullough, C. (1980). *Sex differences in achievement in social studies.* Unpublished project for diploma for advanced studies in teaching, Emory University, Atlanta.

McIntosh, P. (1982). Warning: the new scholarship on women may be hazardous to your ego. *Women's Studies Quarterly, 10,* 29–31.

McTeer, J. H. (1975). The relationship of sex to students' interest in social studies. *Social Studies, 46,* 167–169.

Merrill, K. (1982). Wheaton College: Integrating the study of women into the liberal arts. *Women's Studies Quarterly, 10,* 24–25.

National Science Foundation. (1980). *What are the needs in precollege science, mathe-*

matics, and social science education? Views from the field. Washington, DC: U.S. Government Printing Office.

O'Donnell, R. W. (1973). Sex bias in primary social studies textbooks. *Educational Leadership, 31,* 137–141.

Pope, S. K. (1971). *Effects of female career role models on occupational aspirations, attitude, and personalities of high school seniors.* Unpublished doctoral dissertation, University of Missouri, Columbia.

Sammons, J., & Kolb, F. (1978, November 10). *Sarah Lawrence Summer Institute in Women's History, Final Evaluation: July 15, 1977.* Unpublished report. Sarah Lawrence College, Bronxville, NY.

Scardina, F. (1972). *Sexism in textbooks in Pittsburgh public schools, grades K–5.* Pittsburgh: KNOW, Inc.

Shaver, J. P., Helburn, S., & Davis, O. L., Jr. (1979). The status of social studies education: Impressions from three NSF studies. *Social Education, 43,* 150–153.

Sheridan, E. M. (1975). *Analysis of sex stereotypes in textbooks used in South Bend, Indiana schools* (report of the education committee of the South Bend Mayor's Commission on the Status of Women).

Smith, J. W. (1977). *An appraisal of the treatment of females in United States high school history textbooks from 1959 until 1976.* Unpublished doctoral dissertation, Indiana University, Bloomington.

Soper, J. C. (1979). *Test of economic literacy: Discussion guide and rationale.* New York Joint Council on Economic Education.

Sullivan, K. A. (1975). *Changes in girls' perceptions of the appropriateness of occupations for females through films which counter sex stereotyping.* Unpublished doctoral dissertation, Fordham University, New York.

Torney, J. G., Oppenheim, A. N., & Farnen, R. F. (1975). *Civic education in ten countries.* New York: Wiley.

Trecker, J. L. (1971). Women in U.S. history high school textbooks. *Social Education, 35,* 248–260.

Vetter, L., & Sethney, B. J. (1972). Women in the work force: Development and field testing of curriculum materials. Columbus: Ohio State University Center for Vocational and Technical Education.

Weinbaum, S. (1979). Women in high school history texts: Where are the changes? *Women's Studies Newsletter, 7*(2), 4–7.

Zimmerman, R. (1975). Social studies textbooks still neglect racial minorities, women, and shortchange children. *Negro Educational Review, 26,* 116–123.

16
Sex Equity in Visual Arts Education

Renee Sandell, Georgia C. Collins,
and Ann Sherman

Artists, art historians, and art critics have begun to identify and move against the inequitable effects of sexism in the professional art world. In education, the campaign for sex equity has brought about revisions in the teaching of many subjects. Yet, art educators have only recently paid serious attention to the issues raised and actions taken by feminists in the parent fields of art and education. The purpose of this chapter is to review these emerging sex equity issues and initiatives in art education and, in light of these, to make recommendations for future sex equity research and practice in the discipline. The field of art education includes a broad spectrum of concerns and occupations: preschool, elementary, and secondary public and private school art teaching and administration; undergraduate art teacher education and certification; graduate studies in art education; museum education, art therapy, and nonacademic art teaching; and art education research and development. Where possible, attention will be given to the unique problems and opportunities for sex equity in these various realms of art education.

SEX EQUITY ISSUES IN ART EDUCATION

The identification and analysis of sexism, as well as prescriptions for its remedy, continue to be debated among those concerned with sex equity issues in art. The significant discrepancies between female and male participation, conditions of work, achievement, and rewards that have been documented by feminist artists, art historians, critics, and educators indicate inequities in the areas of professional art production, history, criticism, and higher education in art and art

The authors gratefully acknowledge the assistance of Marylou Kuhn and John Mahlman, who reviewed this chapter. This chapter is largely based upon material in *Women, Art, and Education,* coauthored by Georgia Collins and Renee Sandell (Reston, VA: National Art Education Association, 1984).

298

education. Furthermore, inequitable educational patterns in higher education have their counterparts in the public school art classroom. That sex inequities exist in art and art education and that reforms are needed to bring about increased sex equity in art and society are, however, matters of general agreement. As a goal for art education, sex equity would mean equal female and male participation in all art-related activities, under equal conditions, with commensurate achievement and reward. In order for women to be able to participate equally in the world of art, they must have equal representation in the establishment of criteria for achievement in the application of these criteria, and in the determination and distribution of the benefits and rewards for artistic merit. It is further assumed that the conditions for participation and achievement in art will require equal effort and bring equal satisfaction for individuals of either sex.

In summarizing the problem of sex inequity in art and art education, three key issues emerge. These involve questions surrounding the status of women in art and art education, sex-fair and sex-affirmative content and practice in art education, and curricular equity for art in public schools.

The Status of Women in Art and Art Education

Women within the fields of art and art education are often treated and/or view themselves as second-class citizens. Although females tend to equal or outnumber male students at entry levels of art education, males have dominated art education and art world hierarchies. Fewer women than men are represented in prestigious exhibitions and museum collections (Baker, 1971; Lippard, 1971; Wayne, 1972). Fewer women artists have received coverage and recognition by art critics and art historians (Nemser, 1973; Nochlin, 1971; Petersen and Wilson, 1976). Historical and critical evaluations of women's art have often been sexist in effect if not intent (Chicago, 1975; Nemser, 1972a, 1972b). In terms of positions, ranks, and salaries, women have not achieved parity with men in educational institutions, from elementary schools through colleges and universities (Hall, 1973; Harris, 1972; Lovano-Kerr, Semler, & Zimmerman, 1977; Michael, 1977; Packard, 1977; White & White, 1973; Whitesel, 1975a). While young men might be discouraged from entering art-related fields because of art's popular feminine identification (Wayne, 1974), once they have entered they not only receive disproportionately more recognition and reward (Lippard, 1971; Nemser, 1973), they will also have had more exposure to same-sex role models.

Although anecdotal reports of discrimination against women in art persist, blatant discrimination with regard to selection, admission, treatment, condition, and reward has diminished in response to consciousness raising, political protest, and legal confrontation (Glueck, 1980). In addition to a residue of intentional discrimination, other, more subtle inequities may be partly responsible for women's lower status in art. It has been suggested, for example, that women begin to fail the informal tests of seriousness, commitment, and belief in their own abilities as they go on to higher education in art or enter art-related professions (Whitesel, 1975b).

The relationship between the status of women in art and the education of female and male students in art has not been adequately researched. Indeed, sex inequities in art education at the public school level, which might foreshadow women's lesser status in the art world, are not immediately apparent. Girls elect to take art as often as boys do, and if there are inequities of achievement related to sex, the nature of art and art education makes their identification and measurement difficult. While art educators often value creativity, self-expression, and craftsmanship, there is no firm consensus as to the particular skills, attitudes, and concepts that are essential for achievement. Furthermore, preparation for careers in art is often not a primary concern of art educators who, along with many school systems, view art as a life enrichment or developmental experience.

In addition, chapter 5, "Facts and Assumptions about the Nature of Sex Differences," reports several sex differences that would seem to preclude or make difficult female achievement in an art world that puts a premium on self-directed and risk-taking behavior. Among these are differences in verbal and spatial abilities, confidence, conformity, dependency, empathy, cooperation, aggression, self-esteem, self-concept, media depictions, and life experiences such as parental expectations. A recent review of this literature selects those reported sex differences potentially related to art performance and suggests that art educators begin to inquire into the role of such differences in art achievement (Sherman, 1982). One key sex equity need in the field is to test and evaluate art-related sex differences as possible variables in the determination of women's status in art and possible sources of sex inequity in art education.

Sex-Fair and Sex-Affirmative Content and Practice in Art Education

The content and practice of art education in some ways is outdated as well as sexist in orientation. Much art content that is taught is based on the white, Western, male viewpoint of art history and criticism (Vogel, 1974; Nochlin, 1974). The women's art movement has raised aesthetic, ethical, and pedagogic issues that challenge the sexist content and practice of art teaching. These issues include the exclusion of the female artist from Western art history; the image of women in fine and commercial art; the sexist implications of the fine arts and crafts hierarchy; art criticism that assumes or reinforces notions of female artistic inferiority; the social and psychological values of art; careerism and dilettantism; and new modes of historiography of art. Attention to these issues promises not only revisions in content and practice that are sex-fair and sex-affirmative but also the enlargement of the personal and cultural relevance of art education for all individuals. In particular, collective experience and reports of common practices suggest the following five areas where these issues affect art education:

1. *Interpretation of interest in art.* Female interest in art is likely to be perceived as different in type and/or degree from male interest. In other words, the traits of seriousness, commitment, and belief in one's own abilities are

ascribed to boys who express an interest in art, while it is assumed that girls' interest in art is probably a personal desire for pursuing gender-appropriate accomplishments. Boys might need assurance that noncareer values are to be found in art for males as well as for females, and girls might need assurance that a career interest in art is appropriate for women as well as for men. Actual or potential conflict between art career goals, personal values, and sex roles should be a matter of serious study (Acuff and Packard, 1974); Collins, 1977, 1978; Packard, 1974; Snyder-Ott, 1974; Whitesel, 1975a).

2. *Provision of role models.* If same-sex role models are important as sources of motivation and self-evaluation in art, the female art student is at a disadvantage (Bastian, 1975; Whitesel, 1977). Feminist revisions of art history and the productivity of contemporary women artists are beginning to correct this problem, but the slides of art work introduced in public school art classes are usually of the familiar male "greats." In addition, the art values in female work that is close at hand, such as a grandmother's quilts or a classroom teacher's bulletin boards, are often denigrated by the art teacher. The female art student is also frequently deprived of a strong female role model in that art teachers often lack the confidence to perceive themselves as viable artists.

3. *Uncritical acceptance of traditional art and education values.* Although there are exceptions, a hierarchy of art forms, media, processes, subject matter, and even colors is assumed by many art teachers. Those materials and processes that have become associated with women tend to have the lowest value in this hierarchy; those associated with male artists, the highest. Thus watercolors, embroidery, and small-scale work are presented as less serious endeavors than larger-scale oil paintings or sculptures on themes such as war. In addition, current problem-solving models for creativity have tended to place high values on male-associated personality characteristics such as field-independence, risk taking, internalized goals, and the willingness to view both the natural and the human environment in terms of instrumentalities (Helson, 1974). Uncritical acceptance of low valuations of female-dominated art forms and feminine personality characteristics reinforces notions of female inferiority in art and effectively reduces the pool of credible female role models and/or options for individual expression of art (Loeb, 1975).

4. *Art criticism that ignores social and psychological values.* Adhering to formal analyses of artists' and students' work, most teachers generally allow stereotypic images of women in fine and commercial art to be presented without serious question or comment. Art that challenges these images, such as contemporary women's art exploring female life and body experiences, is likely to be denied serious formal analysis and dismissed as political or propagandistic work. If it is correct to assume that visual images have the power to enlighten or deceive as well as to give aesthetic pleasure, then images of the female and male, of femininity and masculinity, in both their

fine and commercial forms need to be examined for their impact on sex equity in this society and its public school art programs (Berger, 1974; Chalmers, 1977; De Bretteville, 1974; Dobbs, 1975; Goffman, 1979; Janeway, 1974; Lippard, 1976; Sandell, 1980).

5. *Classroom practices and interactions.* Since art courses often do not use textbook and lecture/test approaches, classroom practices and student-teacher interactions related to studio activity become major components of course content (Feinberg, 1977; Majewski, 1978). The general significance of classroom interactions has been addressed in chapter 11, "Sex Equity in Classroom Organization and Climate," and has particular relevance to teaching art in public schools. Many practices in the typical art class thoughtlessly reinforce sex-stereotyped behaviors and are of no value for the study of art (Belotti, 1978; Kuhn, 1980; Ricks & Pyke, 1973). Boys are asked to lift heavy equipment; girls, to clean the brushes. Moreover, gender-related life experiences that might relate both positively and negatively to student art work are not discussed.

The cumulative effects of sex bias in content and practice in art education have been experienced but not measured. While research is needed to give direction and credibility to revisions in content and practice, a heightened awareness of sex bias in teaching art should bring about substantial efforts to develop sex-fair and sex-affirmative curricula and instruction in art education.

Curricular Equity for Art in the Public Schools

The inequity of art as a discipline in school and society is an issue strongly tied to sex equity, since art, along with nursing and home economics, has been assigned a feminine identification in our culture. The fact that art is viewed as an educational frill with low curricular and budgetary status in public schools is closely related to this identification. The fact that certain art forms, media, processes, and content are viewed as more feminine and of lower status within the art world reinforces this relationship. As a consequence, most individuals in society have been denied a high-quality art education, in part because of biased and sexist attitudes toward art in general and toward certain art forms in particular.

Evidence for the feminine identification of art in this society and its schools is abundant. It exists in mythological, analogical, and personifying beliefs about the nature and value of art (Garrard, 1976; Wayne, 1974). Reinforcement of these popular notions is found in the visible association of women and art at local levels and by psychologists who use an expressed interest in art as an indicator of femininity on personality tests (Helson, 1966; Tyler, 1947). In addition, the adjectives used to describe art and women fulfilling their stereotypical roles are disconcertingly similar: ornamental, sensuous, intuitive, nonintellectual, and consoling. Although "serious" art study and careers take on masculine-identified values and purposes within the art world, men who work at these levels are often stereotyped as feminine, and art in the public schools is viewed as performing a feminine function with regard to the articulation and catharsis of emotion.

While the marginal status of art in the public schools may not be viewed as a sex equity issue by some, this status makes sustained sex equity effort at that level very difficult. The feminine identification of art also tends to obscure the need for such effort. The continuing possibility that the marginal status of art is itself a result of cultural and educational sex bias (Collins, 1979) makes the explication of this relationship a key sex equity issue in art education for the public school art and teacher education levels.

Although many issues remain unresolved for the feminist in art and art education, sex equity efforts have not waited upon their resolution. The remaining sections of this chapter review the different approaches that have been taken in answer to sex equity issues in art education and conclude with recommendations for future sex equity efforts.

SEX EQUITY EFFORTS IN VISUAL ARTS EDUCATION

The Women's Art Movement as an Educational Force

The women's art movement of the 1970s was carried out primarily by women artists and art historians engaged in bringing about sexual political reform in the established art world and in promoting a revisionist approach that reexamined art history and traditional aesthetics from a feminist perspective (Nochlin, 1971; Orenstein, 1975; Schwartz, 1973). While the focus of the movement was mainly on the problematic issues regarding the making (production) and the marketing of women's art, its influence as an educational force has contributed to the increased visibility, interest in, and value of women's art and education during the past decade (Sandell, 1979).

The women's art movement can be described in terms of the educational model it provides. The process of education occurs through (a) self-, (b) informal, and (c) formal educational routes (see figure 3). Descriptions of these areas and sex equity efforts made in them follows.

Self-education. This involves a personal dialogue—the sharing and developing of an ideology which can establish personal and professional support and build toward eventual nonsexist changes in the art world as well as society. The self-education route begins with increased awareness of discrimination and women's weak position in the art making and teaching labor markets (Harris, 1972, 1973; White & White, 1973) as well as in the art making and selling product markets (that is, women's low representation in museums, art publications, and so forth) (Baker, 1971; Lippard, 1971; Wayne, 1972). Provoked by sexist conditions that limited women's visibility in museums and galleries, women artists began to organize in 1969 to establish new support systems for professional women in the arts (Alloway, 1976; Nemser, 1974). Women's art groups first emerged on both the East and West coasts, and later spread nationally and

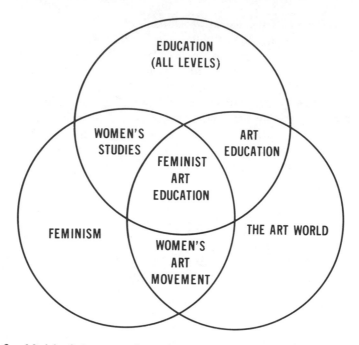

Figure 3. Model of the women's art movement as an educational force. (*Source:* Adapted from "Feminist Art Education: An Analysis of the Women's Art Movement as an Educational Force" by Renee Sandell, *Studies in Art Education, 20*(2), Winter 1979, published by the National Art Education Association, and from *Women, Art, and Education* by Georgia Collins and Renee Sandell, Reston, VA: National Art Education Association, 1984.)

internationally. The process of self-identification and education for women in arts occurs in and through the following: (1) organizations and cooperatives for women artists; (2) exhibitions of women's art; (3) diverse publications to disseminate information to and about women in the arts; (4) programs for women to participate in, such as slide registries and directories of women's art, women's art workshops, and special sessions at professional meetings; and (5) professional development and in-service education for artist/teachers (for specific examples see Sandell, 1979, p. 23). The self-education route is a self-constructed path by which women artists, art historians, art critics, educators, and students can strengthen their individual and collective professional identities and can then enter, transcend, and transform the existing art market.

Informal Education.   Beyond their developing personal dialogue, members of the women's movement educate *other women and men through informal means*—that is, outside of the traditional formal classroom. Their target is members of the established art world and the general public. The education process includes visual and verbal dialogues that tend to threaten existing aesthetic and social attitudes. A visual dialogue that confronts the public and the art world is conducted through the special exhibitions of women's art in museums and art galleries as well as by the content of the art works themselves. These works, which claimed to share female aesthetic views or sensibilities, parallel other current directions in contemporary art but establish a separate, categorical importance by their segregated mode of presentation. Feminist art includes these trends: political art, autobiographical art, a conscious search for archetypal imagery, exploration of female sexuality, and a return to crafts and decorative arts that are historically associated with women (Nemser, 1976). A written dialogue accompanies the visual dialogue. It is carried on by and between art critics and art historians strongly identified with the women's art movement (such as Nochlin, Lippard, Nemser, Orenstein, and Alloway), and verbally articulate artists and art educators (such as Chicago, Schapiro, and Wayne). The written dialogue has resulted in an extensive body of literature found in subject-specific journals and articles, books, and monographs. This literature surveys the work of women artists, exhibition catalogues, bibliographies, and newsletters, all of which deal with the subject of women and art and a variety of aesthetic and political issues of the past and present. In addition to the specialized art publications, the mass media have covered events and ideas surrounding the women artists' efforts to inform the general public (Davis, 1973; Glueck, 1977; Hess, 1977; Hughes, 1972, 1977).

In specific relation to the teaching of art, the Women's Caucus for Art and the Women's Caucus of the National Art Education Association have been forces in self- and informal education at the national and state levels. The Women's Caucus for Art (WCA), a professional organization formed in 1972 that consists of women art historians, curators, artists, and college art teachers, provides an organizational structure of support for women art educators in higher education (especially women teaching fine arts as opposed to art education). Its newsletter contains comprehensive source material (books, films, and so forth) on women artists, historians, and curators which is useful for art teachers who wish to develop nonsexist art education programs. The WCA sponsored the first surveys of college art and art history departments to establish the facts of discrimination; it has also compiled course syllabi on women in art and a collection of slides by women artists. These activities have helped to promote sex equity activities in art at the university level.

Since its formation in 1974, the Women's Caucus of the National Art Education Association (NAEA) has been instrumental in the professional development of women art educators and in the promotion of sex equity activities in art education. Unlike the Women's Caucus for Art, the NAEA Women's Caucus consists primarily of university and public school art education teachers. The caucus publishes a quarterly newsletter announcing job openings, research on women artists and nonsexist art education, and reference material pertinent to sex equity in arts education. The organization has been effective in advancing women art educators' professional participation and recognition through its annual awards for excellence as well as through its support of publications and slide-sharing sessions of women art educators' art work.

Although the NAEA Women's Caucus is presently working on developing inservice education, neither this group nor the WCA has yet conducted inservice education related to sex equity in art education. There have been, however, some scattered inservice projects pertinent to these issues. For example, the Midwest Center for Race and Sex Desegregation, located in Manhattan, Kansas, has conducted a few inservice workshops on nonsexist and nonracist art education, which focus primarily on consciousness-raising discussion groups for public school teachers. In addition, summer institutes and conferences that provide inservice education on sex equity in art education have begun to be offered on university campuses. For example, the Mid-Atlantic Center for Sex Equity held a one-day conference entitled "Nonsexist Approaches to Teaching Visual and Performing Arts," the first of its kind on the East Coast, at American University in Washington, D.C., in March 1983.

Formal Education at the Higher Education Level. Beyond self- and informal educational routes for the enlightenment of the art world and the general public, the women's art movement has had an impact on formal education at the higher education level. It has affected the contents of university art galleries as well as studio art and art history curricula. College art departments have expanded their slide collections to include women's artistic contributions and have offered special seminars on women's art. These attempts have fostered greater awareness of the history of women's art as well as of current personal and professional needs of women (White, 1976). Since the 1970s, courses in fine arts and art history have been offered by university art departments and women's studies programs around the country. The courses deal with various issues raised by the women's art movement in academic settings. The courses fall into three main categories: studio courses for women art students; art history courses on women artists and/or the image of women in art; and socially-oriented courses on the role and fate of women in the art world (Spear & Gellman, 1975). These courses and their derivative exhibitions and research projects constitute feminist art education (see figure 4), which is ongoing and influences the potential art community as well as supportive aesthetic consumers.

The goals of feminist art education correspond to those of women's studies programs in the fine arts (White, 1976). These include research into the history of past and present women artists, rediscovering and reinterpreting their work as well as reinforcing the image of women in art; compensatory education—filling in the gaps in knowledge about women as creators and as subjects in art; consciousness-raising about the barriers that have prevented women from producing the quality and quantity of art that men have; and changing the status of women in the art world. An analysis of feminist art education based on a sample of 50 syllabi from courses offered in the United States from 1970 to 1978 noted the curricula and instruction of women's studies courses in studio art, art history, and women's issues in the arts (Sandell, 1978). The three kinds of courses are briefly described in the paragraphs that follow.

Women's studies courses in studio art are designed to develop women's

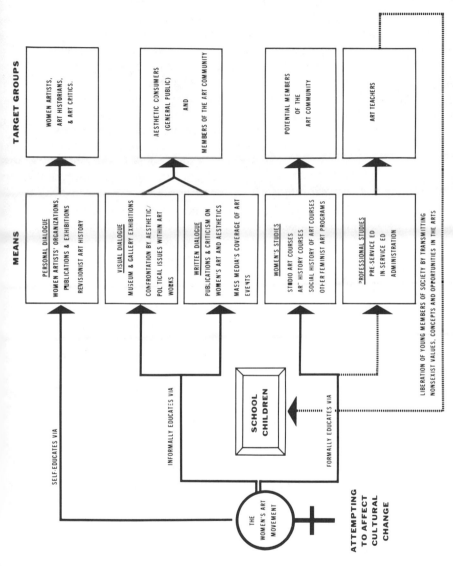

Figure 4. Feminist art education: Location within the universes of feminism, education, and the art world. (*Source:* Adapted from "Feminist Art Education: An Analysis of the Women's Art Movement as an Educational Force" by Renee Sandell, *Studies in Art Education,* 20(2), Winter 1979, published by the National Art Education Association, and from *Women, Art, and Education* by Georgia Collins and Renee Sandell, Reston, VA: National Art Education Association, 1984.)

artistic skills further by utilizing traditionally "masculine" materials and processes such as power tools or large-scale projects. They also attempt to develop authentic imagery and survival skills that would make women's art training more practical and professional. An important course goal is to furnish women students with a support system (that is, a community of women artists who share ideas, sensibilities, and problems) in order to avoid the traditional isolation of women artists, while strengthening their own professional commitment. In several cases, collective student works have culminated in public presentations and exhibitions around feminist themes such as "Womanhouse" and "The Wedding" (Wilding, 1977). Some courses incorporate practical survival skills for women training to become professional artists: employment procedures, setting up a studio, making slides of one's work and presenting them to art dealers, maximizing tax deductions, and coordinating family responsibilities with studio work. These topics, along with the experience of working with less traditional media, tools, and processes to which access has generally been restricted for women, are a kind of remedial instruction.

Courses in revisionist art history focus on women artists' contributions to the history of art. Serving as a reversal of sexist surveys and filling in the great gaps in traditional art history books, which never mention women's art, these courses also examine the social biases affecting the iconographic role of women in works of art. Women have generally been portrayed in service to men, either as temptress/whore or as venerated madonna, mother, or muse. Since much of the information on women and art of the past has been unavailable, unknown, or misrepresented in art history writings and textbooks, an overriding goal of these courses is to fill the great need for scholarly research and enlarge the historical perspective of art. Involving students in original research on women's art works and with the subject of historiography itself partially fulfills the continuing need for basic instructional materials such as slides, visual illustrations, and texts. Exhibitions of women's art and women's art festivals are frequently coordinated with course offerings, reinforcing in an immediate sense the ideas and concepts covered in class.

While the goals of women's studies courses on women's issues in the arts tend to combine those of feminist art courses in studio art and art history, these courses focus upon the contemporary art world from sociological, feminist, and aesthetic perspectives. The primary goal of these courses is, therefore, awareness and comprehension of sexual-political issues for the contemporary woman artist, art historian, and critic, as well as common themes and problems of women in the arts as expressed in art products. Diverse topics broaden the scope of the different courses to include female imagery and female aesthetics; the education of the woman artist; identity and the woman artist; imagery of artists—male versus female; standards and women's art/art criticism; artistic hierarchies (for example, crafts versus fine arts); art and economics; collecting, curatorship, and gallery directing; and alternative modes of exhibiting art.

Finally, there have been a few recent attempts, including those of the authors, to develop and teach women's studies courses on women and art education/nonsexist art education. These courses are designed to have direct impact upon art teachers at the preservice and graduate study levels. The relative nonexistence of this kind of nonsexist programming at the pre- and inservice levels of art education accounts in part for the virtual absence of sex equity activities at the elementary and secondary art education levels (see next section).

In sum, feminist art education, in addressing key sex equity needs in art education, has had the following positive outcomes for individual women students and teachers of art:

1. Providing compensatory education for women students' personal and professional development in art
2. Raising the status and participation of women in art academia and the art world via art exhibitions and journal coverage
3. Raising the status of art as a "feminine" subject, while demystifying the role of the artist
4. Breaking down hierarchies in the academic study of art, while providing new paradigms for art study
5. Revising and reappraising the content in studio art and art history and broadening its scope to include current issues
6. Increasing research efforts on women's art, roles, and iconography as well as on the historiography of art
7. Increasing curricular changes that reinforce and further the previous outcomes, such as expanding slide collections to include women's art works, broadening mainstream courses in art to include women's contributions, and revising general textbooks, such as H. W. Janson's *History of Art,* to include women's work.

Formal Education at the Elementary and Secondary Levels. Although the women's art movement has functioned in education by addressing the need for improving the status of women in the visual arts and establishing sex-fair and sex-affirmative content and practice in art and art education at the higher levels, it has had little impact on the field of art education as it affects grades K–12 via pre- and inservice art education. As shown in figure 3, the educational efforts of artists, art historians, and art critics who compose the women's art movement have for the most part ignored art teachers and have bypassed school-age children. These populations have not been part of the educational process. Despite advances made by feminists in art, only minute, indirect portions of their efforts have been directed toward the formal, non-artist-oriented art education that takes place in the schools. It is unfortunate that members of the movement have paid little attention to the potential role that the field of art education might play in helping to eradicate earlier and perhaps more pervasive sexist influences in art and education (Sandell, 1979).

Although there are anecdotal reports of spontaneous sex equity activities in public school elementary and secondary art programs, these scattered efforts remain undocumented, and to date, evaluations of their success have not been published. Similarly, nonsexist instructional materials for classroom use are few in number, and for those available, there is no information on their actual usage or effectiveness. Nevertheless, the existence of such materials and the reports of individual sex equity efforts in elementary and secondary art education may be taken as important, if small, signs of sex equity progress in the field.

One type of nonsexist material related to visual arts education in the elementary school is the critique of pictorial content in texts and readers. Both the Council on Interracial Books for Children (1978) and the Racism and Sexism Resource Center for Educators (1976) provide materials of this genre. While they suggest methods for examining pictorial materials in books in terms of representational and narrative content that might be sexist, they do not provide tools for in-depth analyses, nor do they avoid reinforcing stereotypes of artists and art activity. A second type of material is exemplified by a children's book on an Indian woman artist (Nelson, 1971). Although it is a good example of how a minority artist strives to illuminate her cultural heritage through art, no attention is given to her particular struggles as a woman. This type of material, therefore, provides indirect and supplementary support for sex equity in elementary art education.

Understandably, reports of sex equity efforts at this level generally involve the individual in the design and preparation of instructional materials. For example, Enid Zimmerman (personal communication, April 15, 1982), who teaches art education at Indiana University, has developed two sets of slide/discussion materials which she has subsequently tested with elementary classroom teachers, art teachers, and elementary students in her region. Both sets take an art historical approach and involve the pairing of art works by male and female artists. According to Zimmerman, "Women Make Art: An Androgynous Point of View" was most successful making the point that art objects themselves have no sex when she encouraged the children to review the images and discuss them fully.

Although materials for sex equity in secondary school art courses generally come in textbook form, there are two sets of materials which include slides or transparencies. There is a 25-minute audiotape with accompanying visual and written materials entitled "Repainting the Sexist Picture: Stereotyping in the Fine Arts" (Campbell, 1979). Information on women artists is provided, along with discussion questions on the problem of sex stereotyping in the arts. Issues raised include differential abilities, fine arts as crafts, and hindrances to opportunities. Another resource, *Women Artists* (Wilson & Petersen, 1976), contains slides and notes on more than 200 women artists. The four programs include "An Historical Survey"; "The Twentieth Century"; "Third World"; and "Images—Themes and Dreams." Among the available textbooks, several strive for equal treatment of women artists or focus entirely on women. These are *Art/Design: Communicating Visually* (Clark & Zimmerman, 1978) and *In Her Own Image:*

Women Working in the Arts (Hedges & Wendt, 1981), which includes some information on women artists. The Clark and Zimmerman text is exemplary in its inclusion of nonsexist art education content and values. Nonsexist language is used, works by male and female artists are paired, and feminine-identified art forms often serve as illustrations of art principles. The Hedges and Wendt text focuses on both professional and "home" women artists and emphasizes the art process.

Sex equity efforts at the secondary level also involve the individual teacher in the design and preparation of instructional materials. For example, Barbara Arnold, a secondary school art teacher in Lexington, Kentucky, has developed several nonsexist slide shows to use in her studio and art history teaching. She incorporates art by women and women's images with popular music as background. Arnold finds that presenting these shows without comment stirs up discussion among her high school art students and is an effective consciousness-raiser (personal communication, March 8, 1979).

If progress is to be made toward sex equity in public school art classes and art teacher education, efforts at these levels need to be documented, evaluated, and disseminated. Strategies that have proved successful at higher levels of art and education need to be adapted for classroom use, and those instructional materials already available need to be assessed for their effectiveness. In addition, new sex equity materials of greater depth, breadth, and relevance need to be devised for studio teaching and career education in the schools. It has been the purpose of this review to clarify sex equity needs and to review such progress as has been made toward the goal of sex equity in art and art education.

RECOMMENDATIONS

Sex equity efforts that have taken place in the world of practicing artists, art critics, and art historians have been energetic and effective. Sex equity efforts that have taken place in other subject areas of teacher and public school education have been systematic and well documented. As we look toward the future, sex equity progress in fields closely related to those reviewed will provide standards of comparison and serve as inspiration for similar achievement in art education. We cannot expect, however, that the models of sex equity effort which have been effective for professional artists or for public school math teachers will automatically be applicable to art education. An adequate model for sex equity effort in art education will need to be discipline-specific. Such a model will need to account for and counter sex bias found in both the world of art and the world of education. If the teaching of art to young children is a feminine-identified occupation of low status among artists, then sex equity efforts in the art world which have not attended to the possible sex bias inherent in this assignment of status would not be adequate. Similarly, if art is of low curricular status in the public school, then educational sex equity efforts that have not attended to the relationship between the feminine identification of certain subjects and their marginal curricular status would not be entirely adequate. Beyond the challenge all art educators face as they try to reconcile disparate values in the art and educational establishments, the feminist art educator must address both the low status of art in education and the low status of education in art if these are not to undermine sex equity efforts in the future.

A discipline-specific model for sex equity efforts in art education will also need to evaluate different approaches to the achievement of sex equity that have been used in art and education. Sex equity efforts in masculine-identified or sex-neutral subject areas have often involved an emphasis on mainstreaming, or an integrationist approach. In the art world, in addition to integrationist sex equity efforts, a distinct separatist approach has encouraged women artists to segregate themselves to search for their lost art heritage and to engage in an extensive critique of art structures and values which assume and reward masculine behaviors (Chicago, 1975). Feminist psychology and philosophy also suggest pluralistic or androgynous approaches for sex equity efforts in art education (Heilbrun, 1974; Helson, 1966; Painter, 1975; Trebilcot, 1977). Although each approach poses particular problems, each can make valuable contributions toward bringing about sex equity in art and art education (Collins, 1981). For example, if the integrationist provision of female role models who have successfully negotiated art careers in the male-dominated mainstream can enhance the female art student's self-confidence and aspirations, then the separatist discussion of female values and reevaluation of female-identified art activities such as quilting might also increase the female student's sense of a unique heritage and artistic identity. In effect, integrationist approaches to sex equity promise to prepare female students to compete in the existing art world; pluralistic approaches promise to help both female and male students to accept and develop both masculine and feminine characteristics as they realize the potential art value of each. We do not advocate mindless eclecticism with regard to the employment of these alternative approaches to increasing sex equity in art education, but rather an understanding of the assumptions and goals of each and the need to make these explicit at the outset of any sex equity effort so that the effectiveness of such efforts can be meaningfully evaluated.

Our review of sex equity issues and answers as well as the discussion of a discipline-specific model for sex equity efforts in art education suggest many possibilities for application in art teacher education and public school art programs. We present the following suggestions as they might relate to an individual interest or position. They are neither inclusive nor ranked in terms of priorities but are intended only to stimulate creative thinking in the realm of positive sex equity efforts in the field.

All Art Educators

All art educators concerned with bringing about an increase of sex equity in the field need to find ways to increase their knowledge and awareness of sex equity issues in art education. Possibilities include (1) taking women's studies courses in art, education, and art education and reading related literature; (2) identifying and discussing sex inequities experienced in one's own education; and (3) raising questions relevant to one's own situation at state and national meetings.

All art educators need to look for ways to identify and implement effective sex equity strategies in art education. Three possibilities are: (1) reviewing existing sex equity materials and modifying these for use in art education; (2) developing and testing nonsexist art instructional materials and sharing findings; and (3) initiating cooperative efforts to secure support for the implementation, evaluation, and dissemination of effective sex equity strategies in art education.

Art Educators as Researchers

Researchers can look for ways to increase their knowledge and awareness of sex inequity in art teacher education and public school art programs. Possibilities include (1) studying art-related sex differences in student input and learner outcomes; (2) developing materials for teacher use in the identification and evaluation of art-related sex differences; and (3) studying and documenting sex bias in the art content, classroom practice, and curricular status of art teachers and public school art programs.

The elimination of sex inequities in awarding funds for research and in the art education occupational hierarchy is another domain of concern to researchers. Possibilities include (1) helping art administrators and public school art education; (2) preparing research reviews and presentations for audiences of public school art teachers and administrators; and (3) monitoring and reporting sex inequities in publication and the awarding of grants for art education research.

Art Educators as Public School Teachers

Finding ways to identify and evaluate art-related sex differences among their students is an important area of inquiry for teachers. Two possibilities are: (1) monitoring sex differences in the acquisition of skills, attitudes, and concepts essential to participation and achievement in art; and (2) preparing and testing remedial and compensatory instruction and documenting the results.

Teachers can also look for ways to eliminate sex bias in their art curriculum content and instruction. Possibilities include (1) keeping a journal on classroom practices and interactions that reinforce or mitigate the stereotype that art is feminine, and that the feminine is of low value; (2) increasing the number of slides of women's art and introducing female and male models for all sorts and levels of art occupations; (3) comparing the social and psychological impact of the women's and black art movements; (4) preparing a slide show on women's and men's leisure time art activity; (5) developing a visual literacy unit on gender and racial stereotypes in commercial art and mass media; (6) working with school counselors on career education in art that eliminates sex bias in the interpretation of student interests, aptitudes, and aspirations; and (7) volunteering to review textbook illustrations and visual materials used in other subjects for their effectiveness or possible sex bias.

Art Educators as Artists

Artists can promote their own and other art educators' growth as artists, art critics, and/or historians. Possibilities are (1) forming an art educators' support and critique group; (2) exhibiting with other art educators; (3) developing a slide collection of art teachers' art work; (4) speaking to art classes and community groups about the art work of art educators; (5) making known success as an artist independent of classroom work; and (6) investigating and preparing a unit on great artists who have also been art teachers.

Artists also can look for ways to promote the development and recognition of women artists. Methods for accomplishing this include (1) forming a women's art support and critique group; (2) studying women's art history and the contemporary women's art movement; (3) developing a slide show-lecture on local women's art work and inviting women artists to speak on the relationship of their work and their work habits to gender experiences; (4) encouraging local women's organizations to promote women's art; and (5) participating in the NAEA Women's Caucus's slide-sharing sessions and initiating similar sessions at state meetings.

Art Educators as Teacher Educators

Teacher educators should look for ways to identify and eliminate sex bias in their art teacher education programs. This can be achieved by (1) reviewing levels and types of art and teaching interest in their students for possible sex differences; (2) investigating possible sex bias in their students' required art studio and art history courses; (3) developing nonsexist career counseling materials for use by art education, art, and education advisers; (4) preparing and teaching women's studies courses in art education; and (5) developing sex-equitable art education materials for use in their own teaching, the public school classroom, and inservice workshops.

Increasing the status of art in education and the status of education in art should be a goal of teacher educators. Possibilities for accomplishing this include (1) investigating whether art education students are receiving equal treatment in art courses, student exhibitions, and general education courses; (2) speaking to faculty in art and education departments on the feminine identification and marginal status of art education and how this affects the quality of public school art programs and art teacher education; and (3) working with public school art teachers and administrators to develop mutual support systems, art education scholarships, nonsexist art career packets, and cooperative exhibitions.

Art Educators as Supervisors and Administrators

Supervisors and administrators can identify ways of building awareness and increasing the status of women in art teaching and administration. Possibilities include (1) documenting sex differences in position, tenure, salary, promotion, and job satisfaction in their area; (2) identifying and working to eliminate institutional structures, practices, and values that effectively discriminate against women; (3) conducting leadership workshops for women in art education; (4) establishing a support network and grievance system for women art teachers; (5) working on developing nonsexist curricula and career education in art; (6) speaking to public school art classes about art administration as a career and the achievements of women in the field; and (7) working with public school art teachers and teacher educators to increase community and governmental support for public school art programs and sex equity efforts in art education.

Increasing sex equity in art education will require both individual initiative and cooperative group effort in the realms of theory and practice. If we are to learn from our mistakes and take heart from our achievements, each of us must take the time to clarify our goals and assumptions and to document and share the results of those efforts. As sex equity programs in art education are implemented, continued dialogue and inquiry will be needed to ensure both their educational effectiveness and their artistic relevance.

REFERENCES

Acuff, B., & Packard, S. (1974). Women's views. *Art Education, 27*(9), 24–25.
Alloway, L. (1976). Women's art of the '70s. *Art in America, 64*(3), 64–72.
Baker, E. C. (1971). Sexual art-politics. *Art News, 69*(9), 47–48, 60–62.
Bastian, L. (1975). Women as artists and teachers. *Art Education, 28*(7), 12–15.
Belotti, E. G. 1978). *What are little girls made of?* New York: Schocken.
Berger, J. (Producer). (1974). *Ways of seeing: Painting nudes and women* [Film]. New York: Time-Life Films.
Campbell, P. (1979). *Repainting the sexist picture: Stereotyping in the fine arts* (Audio tape and print materials from an inservice teacher training program, "Sex Stereotyping in Education"). Newton, MA: Education Development Center.
Chalmers, G. (1977). Women as art viewers: Sex differences and aesthetic preferences. *Studies in Art Education, 18*(2), 49–53.
Chicago, J. (1975). *Through the flower, my struggle as a woman artist.* New York: Doubleday.
Clark, G., & Zimmerman, E. (1978). *Art/design: Communicating visually.* New York: Art Education, Inc. (includes teacher's guide).
Collins, G. C. (1977). Considering an androgynous model for art education. *Studies in Art Education, 18*(2), 54–62.
Collins, G. C. (1978). Reflections on the head of Medusa. *Studies in Art Education, 19*(2), 10–18.
Collins, G. C. (1979). Women and art: The problem of status. *Studies in Art Education, 21*(1), 57–64.
Collins, G. C. (1981). Feminist approaches to art education. *Journal of Aesthetic Education, 15*(2), 83–94.
Collins, G. C., & Sandell, R. (1984). *Women, art, and education.* Reston, VA: National Art Education Association.

Council on Interracial Books for Children. (1978). *Racism and Sexism in Children's Books* [Pamphlets, film strip, & cassette tapes]. New York: author.

Davis, D. (1973, January 29). Women, women, women. *Newsweek*, p. 77.

De Bretteville, S. C. (1974). A reexamination of some aspects of the design arts from the perspective of a woman designer. *Arts in Society, 2*(1), 114–123.

Dobbs, S. (1975). Women in the arts: An optimistic forecast. *Art Education, 28*(7), 24–26.

Feinberg, S. G. (1977). Conceptual content and spatial characteristics in boys' and girls' drawing of fighting and helping. *Studies in Art Education, 18*(2), 63–71.

Garrard, M. P. (1976). Of men, women, and art. *Art Journal, 35*(4), 324–329.

Glueck, G. (1977, September 25). The woman as artist—rediscovering 400 years of masterworks. *New York Times Magazine*, pp. 48–68.

Glueck, G. (1980). Women artists '80. *Art News, 79*(8), 58–63.

Goffman, E. (1979). *Gender advertisements*. New York: Harper & Row.

Hall, L. (1973). In the university. In T. B. Hess & E. C. Baker (Eds.), *Art and sexual politics* (pp. 130–146). New York: Collier Books.

Harris, A. S. (1972). The second sex in academe, fine art division. *Art in America, 60*(3), 18–19.

Harris, A. S. (1973). Women in college art departments and museums. *Art Journal, 32*(4), 417–419.

Hedges, E., & Wendt, I. (1981). *In her own image: Women working in the arts*. New York: Feminist Press. (includes teacher's guide)

Heilbrun, C. G. (1974). *Toward a recognition of androgyny*. New York: Harper & Row.

Helson, R. (1966). Personality of women with imaginative and artistic interests: The role of masculinity, originality, and other characteristics in their creativity. *Journal of Personality, 34*(1), 1–25.

Helson, R. (1974). Inner reality of women. *Art in Society, 2*(1), 25–36.

Hess, T. B. (1977, October 17). Women's work. *New York*, pp. 90–93.

Hughes, R. (1972, March 20). Myths of "sensibility." *Time*, pp. 72–77.

Hughes, R. (1977, January 10). Rediscovered—women painters. *Time*, pp. 60–63.

Janeway, E. (1974). Images of women. *Art in Society, 2*(1), 8–18.

Kuhn, M. (1980). The ninth decade: Women, work, and cultural equity in the art world. In F. Mills & D. Irwing (Eds.), *The visual arts in the ninth decade*. National Council of Art Administration.

Lippard, L. R. (1971). Sexual politics, art style. *Art in America, 59*(5), 19–20.

Lippard, L. R. (1976). The pains and pleasures of rebirth: Women's body art. *Art in America, 64*(3), 73–81.

Loeb, J. (1975). Our women artist/teachers need our help: On changing language, finding cultural heritage, and building self-image. *Art Education, 28*(7), 9–11.

Lovano-Kerr, J., Semler, V., & Zimmerman, E. (1977). A profile of art educators in higher education: Male/female comparative data. *Studies in Art Education, 18*(2), 21–37.

Majewski, M. (1978, March). *The relationship between the drawing characteristics of children and their gender*. Paper presented at annual meeting of the National Art Education Association, Houston.

Michael, J. A.(1977). Women/men in leadership roles in art education. *Studies in Art Education, 18*(2), 7–20.

Nelson, M. (1971). *Pablita Verarde: The story of an American Indian*. Minneapolis: Dillon Press.

Nemser, C. (1972a, March). Art criticism and gender prejudice. *Arts Magazine*, pp. 44–46.

Nemser, C. (1972b). Stereotypes and women artists. *Feminist Art Journal, 1*(1), 1, 22–23.

Nemser, C. (1973). Art criticism and women artists. *Journal of Aesthetic Education, 7*(3), 73–83.

Nemser, C. (1974). The women's art movement. *Feminist Art Journal, 2*(4), 8–10.

Nemser, C. (1976). Towards a feminist sensibility: Contemporary trends in women's art. *Feminist Art Journal, 5*(2), 19–23.

Nochlin, L. (1971). Why have there been no great women artists? *Art News, 69*(9), 22–39, 67–70.

Nochlin, L. (1974). How feminism in the arts can implement cultural change. *Art in Society, 2*(1), 80–89.

Orenstein, G. F. (1975). Art history. *Signs, 1*(1), 505–525.

Packard, S. (1974). A personal statement on discrimination. *Art Education, 27*(9), 25.

Packard, S. (1977). An analysis of current statistics and trends as they influence the status and future for women in the art academe. *Studies in Art Education, 18*(2), 38–48.

Painter, C. (1975). Psychic bisexuality. In M. J. Moffat & C. Painter, (Eds.), *Revelations: Diaries of women* (pp. 392–404). New York: Vintage.

Petersen, K., & Wilson, J. J. (1976). *Women artists: Recognition and reappraisal from the early middle ages to the 20th century*. New York: Harper.

Racism and Sexism Resource Center for Educators. (1976). *Sexism and racism in popular basal readers, 1964–76*. New York: Author.

Ricks, F., & Pyke, S. (1973). Teacher perceptions and attitudes that foster or maintain sex role differences. *Interchange, 4*, 26–33.

Sandell, R. (1979). Feminist art education: An analysis of the women's art movement as an educational force. *Studies in Art Education, 20*(2), 18–28.

Sandell, R. (1980). Female aesthetics: The women's art movement and its aesthetic split. *Journal of Aesthetic Education, 14*(4), 106–110.

Schwartz, T. (1973). They built women a bad art history. *Feminist Art Journal, 2*(3), 10–11, 22.

Sherman, A. L. (1982). Questions that those concerned with non-sexist art education should pose. *Art Education, 35*(3), 26–29.

Snyder-Ott, J. (1974). The female experience and artistic creativity. *Art Education, 27*(6), 15–18.

Spear, A. T., & Gellman, L. (1975). *Women's studies in art and art history* (2nd ed.). New York: Women's Caucus for Art.

Trebilcot, J. (1977). Two forms of androgynism. In M. Vetterling-Braggin, F. A. Elliston, & J. English (Eds.), *Feminism and philosophy*. Totowa, NJ: Littlefield, Adams.

Tyler, L. E. (1947). *The psychology of human differences*. New York: Appleton-Century-Crofts.

Vogel, L. (1974). Fine arts and feminism: The awakening consciousness. *Feminist Studies, 2*(3), 3–37.

Wayne, J. (Ed.). (1972). *Sex differentials in art exhibition reviews: A statistical study*. Los Angeles: Tamarind Lithography Workshop.

Wayne, J. (1974). The male artist as stereotypical female. *Arts in Society, 2*(1), 107–113.

White, B. E. (1976). A 1974 perspective: Why women's studies in art and art history? *Art Journal, 35*(4), 340–344.

White, B. E., & White, L. S. (1973). Survey on the status of women in college art departments. *Art Journal, 32,* 420–422.

Whitesel, L. S. (1975a). Women as art students, teachers, and artists. *Art Education, 28*(3), 21–26.

Whitesel, L. S. (1975b). Scale construction for the measurement of women art students' career commitments. *Studies in Art Education, 17*(1), 47–53.

Whitesel, L. S. (1977). Attitudes of women art students. *Art Education, 30*(1), 25–27.

Wilding, F. (1977). *By our own hands: The women artists' movement, southern California, 1970–76.* Santa Monica: Double X.

Wilson, J., & Petersen, K. (1976). *Women artists* [Slide program and notes]. New York: Harper & Row.

17

Sex Equity in Physical Education and Athletics

Patricia L. Geadelmann,
with Judy Bischoff, Mary Hoferek,
and Dorothy B. McKnight

The concepts of fairness and fair play constitute the very essence of physical education and athletics. They are fundamental to the integrity of a game or contest and are critical to successful participation. Fairness operates from a base of a common set of rules which are clearly established for, understood by, and evenly applied to all participants. The concept of fairness has never been in question, but the application of fairness principles for those seeking to enter the physical activity world has been very uneven. Separate, different, and unequal standards have been applied to participants in physical activity on the basis of sex. Such differential treatment can be traced to historical patterns, beliefs, and expectations for females which have differed from those for males. The results have been exclusion from or limited access to the outcomes that are possible through physical education and athletics, that is, development of one's physical self; acquisition to physical skills; participation in competitive experiences; internalization of the concomitant social values that follow from team play; prestige and recognition; and job opportunities in the field. From separate and different worlds, then, inequities, and thus unfairness, have been perpetuated.

Inequities have persisted from worlds which have purported to be separate and equal. Girls and women have found, as did blacks with their "separate but equal" schools, that in fact equal opportunities, resources, and support services have not been equally provided in separate programs. Fewer teams, fewer and less qualified coaches, limited equipment and fewer available facilities, and smaller budgets have been among the discrepancies.

Even the application of a same-world, same-treatment approach to boys and girls in physical education and athletic programs has produced inequities. These have been manifested in the perpetuation of sex stereotypes in the different expectations and treatment accorded females as compared to males, the loss of

The authors wish to acknowledge the assistance of Patt Dodds, Patricia Griffin, Joan Hult, Barbara Thalacker, and Ann Uhlir in the preparation of this chapter.

319

leadership opportunities for women as programs have been submerged under the guise of merger, and fewer opportunities for girls or women to compete in cases where separate teams have been abandoned for a single team open to all.

Attaining a state of sex equity in physical education and athletics requires that a long historical tradition of differential role expectations and differential societal values for females and males be addressed and overcome. Bridging the gap between what were two very separate and different worlds and what now are sometimes separate, sometimes the same, but always striving to be comparable or equal worlds, creates confusion and difficulty for many. Philosophical differences must be reconciled, stereotypes countered, myths combated, attitudes changed, and discrimination corrected. Positive changes would include (1) recognition of the physical capabilities of females and provision for the realization of these capabilities for all age groups, (2) recognition of the acceptability of participation in the entire spectrum of activities, (3) public support and promotion of sport experiences for girls and women, and (4) the provision of nothing less than equity in programs of physical education and athletics.

Attempting to bridge the gap is an ongoing and difficult process. What follows is a discussion of the history of the movement toward equity in activity programs and of the ways in which fairness or lack of fairness have existed in the worlds of separateness and sameness.

ISSUES

Historical Philosophical Differences

As early as Plato's *Republic*, differential views have been held about the appropriateness of physical activity for women. Plato, in fact, made a bold statement when he advocated the same education for women as for men, including training in gymnastics. He specified in *The Laws,* however, that the education should be in a separate setting for separate purposes: the men were to be trained to fight afield and the women to defend themselves while the men were away. Rousseau (cited in Gerber, 1971, p. 81) also distinguished purposes for providing physical training for females and males: the object for the boys was to bring out strength, while the women were to gain "enough strength to act gracefully." From colonial days in the United States, the feeling was that it was "unwise, impractical, . . . [and] immoral" to have boys and girls in physical activity together (Oberteuffer & Ulrich, 1962, p. 383). The controversies surrounding physical activity for girls and women have centered on which activities were appropriate in terms of women's physical capabilities, what performance level could be expected from women, and which activities were appropriate for joint participation by men and women.

It is important to note that while women were limited in the nature and scope of participation, the sources of these limitations included societal attitudes and expectations, male protection of a "turf" in sport, and sometimes women themselves. At the beginning of the 20th century, women physical educators instructed their female students to compete in sport only for the sheer joy of the game and for their health. They were cautioned never to be competitive or try to win; they were told not to be "too sporty."

Criticisms leveled against men's intercollegiate athletics, as well as a fear that women might lose control of their own programs, precipitated what Ellen Gerber (1974, p. 48) termed "a relatively unified, controlled pattern . . . governed by women physical educators with no external interference." The teacher preparation programs were all conducted within separate departments for men and women. The sex-segregated programs for female and male physical education majors differed significantly throughout the first half of the 20th century. The emphasis for women remained on a broad spectrum of instructional and intramural programs; the men placed emphasis on team sports and varsity-level sports.

In the world of interscholastic athletics, the women physical educators moved slowly from play day to sports day to varsity sports for girls. Where programs were offered for girls, they differed greatly from the boys' programs and rarely contained more than gymnastics, calisthenics, or dance until the 1950s. Exceptions included girls' basketball programs in Iowa and field hockey teams in the East. Programs were then developed for girls which included team sports, some individual sports, exercise programs, track and field, and dance activities. In the more affluent school systems, girls were exposed to many of the "sex-appropriate sports" such as golf, tennis, swimming, winter sports, and gymnastics. Even in these programs, however, the girls were given inferior facilities, less time in activity, and inadequate opportunity for intramurals or club activity. Almost universally, the facilities were inferior for the girls; they were small gyms suitable for conducting "small" programs.

A review of the literature of the period 1900–1950 has identified five major beliefs within women's sports: (1) the concept of "a sport for every girl and every girl for a sport" was in keeping with the democratic social goals of the greatest good for the greatest number (thus, physical education and intramurals should be a part of the education of girls); (2) vigorous sport was unfeminine and, in fact, led to the development of masculine traits, which were undesirable in women (thus, masculinity was synonymous with participation in sports); (3) highly competitive athletics were harmful to the female athlete and would interfere with the childbearing (thus, femininity was synonymous with noncompetition); (4) the evils of the men's athletic programs were evidence of conflicts and commercialization, all of which led to exploitation of the athletes; and (5) women should control women's athletics (Hult, 1979; Hult & Park, 1981).

The period since the 1960s has seen each of the above beliefs questioned. The expansion of what constitutes appropriate sex role behavior for both males and females has led to an increasing acceptance of women in the full range of activities. While traditional male bastions remain, we are now seeing women's rugby teams and a few girls breaking the barriers to participate in football, ice hockey, and wrestling.

An increasing concern by the general public about the positive role of exercise in maintaining both mental and physical health has resulted in extensive promotion of physical activity for everyone. Concern about health may have superseded the concern about role designations. Hence, recent medical research reports discount the myths about the negative effects of exercise on childbearing. The American Medical Association (1975) has strongly affirmed the benefits of vigorous activity and exercise for all. This has had a positive effect on assessments of physical differences between females and males and the accompanying implications for participation in physical activity.

Physical Differences

Safrit, Baumgartner, Jackson, and Stamm (1980) discussed gender differences in motor performance. The greater part of the research in this area has focused on isolating and quantifying gender differences. These can be classified as physical performance differences, body structure and composition differences, and differences in cardiorespiratory function. Safrit et al. go on to say that considerable recent evidence reaffirms the existence of mean differences between male and female students on many measures of physical performance. These differences can be attributed to biological and cultural influences.

Wilmore (1974) found that when leg strength is normalized for lean body weight, gender differences in leg strength disappear. Differences in arm strength are not due to differences in lean body weight. Men's shoulders are larger than women's, which documents gender differences in body structure. Hoffman, Stauffer, and Jackson (1979) suggested that gender differences in arm strength may be due to both structural and body composition differences.

Astrand and Rodehl (1970) reported that prior to puberty the aerobic capacity of men and women is similar. After puberty, the average aerobic capacity of women is about 75% of the average man's. Several studies have documented these gender differences in aerobic powers. The unanswered question, however, concerns the reason for the differences.

Safrit et al. (1980) indicated that at this stage insufficient evidence is available to recommend scientifically valid criterion-referenced standards for boys and girls. In the absence of scientific evidence, they made the following suggestions: (1) focus research efforts on the nature of gender differences; (2) eliminate sex bias from testing whenever possible (for example, by expressing maximal oxygen uptake and strength per unit of lean body weight rather than per total body weight); and (3) on those tests which have consistently shown gender differences, it may be prudent to assume that the differences are predominantly biological in nature; thus, separate standards would be more appropriate.

At the United States Military and Air Force academies, studies were conducted to determine the capabilities of women to perform physically vigorous assignments. The subjects of the study at the United States Military Academy were 30 men and women randomly selected from the entering cadets who participated in 8 weeks of summer basic training. At the start of training the men had considerably greater mean height, weight, lean body weight, muscular strength, power, and absolute and relative maximum oxygen uptake; the women had more actual, and a higher percentage of, body fat. A similar pattern of sex differences existed at the end of basic training (with the exception that men and women were comparable on the Astrand-Rhyming submaximal bicycle ergometer test of maximum oxygen uptake), but the data indicated that some closing of the performance gap between the sexes occurred (Stauffer, 1976). Comparison of women's with men's performance at the end of 1 year of training at the Air Force Academy showed the following results: pushups, 43% of men's; standing long jump, 80% of men's; 600-yard run, 85% of men's; and 2-minute situps, 86% of men's (Thomas & Riding, 1979). The most dramatic improvement by the women was in the 600-yard run, where the initial performance was only 60% of that of men.

The world records of males are 7 to 13% above those of females in all areas except the English Channel swim. The gap has closed considerably, however, because there has been an increase both in emphasis and in the number of opportunities for competition by women (Plowman, 1974). Increased opportunities, then, whether in same world or in separate worlds, have led to improved physical performance.

While studies tend to highlight differences, there are many areas of similarity for females and males. Furthermore, the differences approach examines differences between means for each of the sexes. In reality, the mean scores are only points on distributions for males and females. Many scores for females overlap with many scores for males. In fact, some scholars have suggested that it may be more accurate to research similarities than differences.

Equitable Athletic Programs and Policies

The great growth of participation by girls and women in the 1960s and 1970s paralleled legal mandates and liberalized societal attitudes. The legislation that has been a moving force for equity in both physical education and athletic programs is Title IX of the Education Amendments of 1972. Title IX prohibits discrimination on the basis of sex in education programs and activities receiving federal financial assistance. The most direct implication for physical education has been the prohibition of single-sex classes. In athletics, however, separate but equal teams have been advocated. State legislation and court cases have provided variously for both separate but equal teams and unitary teams. The implications of equal rights amendments for mixed athletic teams are yet to be formulated.

Opportunities for elementary school girls in particular have increased as a result of social and community pressures upon city recreation and other sponsoring agencies to provide equitable opportunities for all. It is not uncommon to observe girls participating in flag football, soccer leagues, softball teams, and even wrestling.

At the secondary school level, growth in athletic programs for girls has been nothing short of dramatic since the inception of Title IX. Statistics kept by the National Federation of State High School Associations reflect more than a quadrupling of programs for girls. Thirty-six percent of high school interscholastic athletes now are female. This is a sixfold increase in the last 10 years. Iowa leads the nation, with girls constituting 51% of the athletes, while Mississippi trails at a mere 23% (Vrean, 1983).

Title IX, despite the criticisms leveled at its lack of clarity and the lack of its enforcement, has been directly responsible for major growth in women's intercollegiate athletics. Cornell University is a striking case in point. Prior to Title IX, it sponsored three sports for women (basketball, field hockey, and fencing) with a budget of $12,000. In 1980, Cornell had 16 sports for women with a budget of $343,000. Cornell athletic director Dick Schultz had this to say: "Title IX is a real plus. Without it, we'd have difficulty going to the administration for additional funds just on the merits of building a better women's sports program. It's always easier when they *have* to do it. Title IX supplies the impetus" (DeCrow, 1980, p. 18).

The growth in both participation and budget shown at Cornell is typical of that across the country. The number of colleges offering athletics to women grew from 280 in 1971 to 971 in 1980–81. Sixty schools offered athletic scholarships to women in 1974; over 500 offered them in 1980, according to the Association for Intercollegiate Athletics for Women's (AIAW) National Office records. Despite gains, however, athletic programs for women generally still fall short of the requirements specified by Title IX. The average number of sports for men at NCAA institutions is 9.3, while for women it is 6.7. Budgets for women constitute an average of only 16% of the athletic dollars, at least 10% less than that required to meet the comparability standards according to numbers of participants. In 1979, the number of male participants in intercollegiate athletics was still double that of females (Lopiano, 1980).

The budget gap between men's and women's intercollegiate sports closed from a difference of 22 times in 1973–74 to a difference of five times in 1980. The average per capita spent on the male athlete in 1978–79 was $5,257, compared to $2,156 for females. While the number of sports offered women has increased 100% since 1973–74, the number available for men still remains 50% higher, on the average. A common complaint has been that in order to provide increased opportunities for women, men's budgets would have to be cut. Statistics show, however, that men's athletic budgets have continued to grow since 1973–74 at a 20 to 30% rate (Association of American Colleges, 1980a).

Athletics Leadership and Governance

During the growth period in participation and budget, there simultaneously occurred a reduction in leadership and coaching opportunities for women. The AIAW was founded in 1971 to provide an organizational structure for the conduct of intercollegiate athletics for women. Leadership was provided by a group of women physical educators committed to the development of an athletic model grounded in education. The aim was to avoid the problems commonly associated with the contemporary male athletic model (excesses in recruiting, overcommercialization, and exploitation of the student-athlete).

In the early 1970s, 96% of the women's athletic programs were administered by women. By 1979, that figure had dropped to less than 36%. The reduction occurred primarily due to campus mergers of men's and women's programs into a single administrative unit. In virtually every case, the new head has been a male (Lopiano, 1980, pp. 23–25). The effect was that over the decade women had less and less direct authority for the operation of their programs at the institutional level and consequently at the national organization level.

There came increasing pressures from the AIAW's institutional members to have a common set of regulations which governed both men's and women's athletics for administrative efficiency and to ensure equity in the application of rules to both sexes. At the same time, a group within the AIAW attempted to resist such changes in order to preserve the integrity of what had been purposely created "separate and different" as an alternative model. Gradually rule changes were effected, however, and the AIAW rules became more similar to those of the NCAA.

Throughout the decade there were sporadic attempts at discussions about cooperative working arrangements between the NCAA and the AIAW, but these were never able to produce any agreements. During the early years the NCAA showed no interest in the fledgling women's programs. In 1975, however, there was for the first time a serious proposal for the NCAA to begin sponsoring championships for women. The measure was not approved, but from that time the NCAA took additional measures to involve women on committees and develop plans for the operation of women's athletics. In January 1981, the NCAA annual convention voted to establish a governance system and championships for women in all divisions. Provisions for women on the NCAA Council called for 4 positions out of 22. Committee representation was also minimally provided for, and economic attractions were provided to the institutions: free membership, reimbursed travel, and television coverage. This effectively led to the demise of the AIAW, which ceased its operations in 1982.

The loss of opportunities for women to coach the ever-expanding number of teams has been great. A study by Holmen and Parkhouse (1981) found that between 1974 and 1979 the total number of male coaches (heads and assistants) in AIAW institutions increased 182%, while the number of females declined by 20%. The number of male assistant coaches increased by 368% compared to an increase of 174% for females (Association of American Colleges, 1980b). A study by Lehr (1980) revealed similar statistics and noted that overall 39% of the women's teams were coached by males in 1979–80. Lehr also noted the increasingly common practice of a male coaching both the men's and women's teams. Rarely was a woman found coaching a male team.

Officiating is still another area in which there has been declining opportunity for women. Originally all officials for women's sports were women, certified through the National Association for Girls and Women in Sports. Men increasingly have become certified and hired through male athletic directors. By contrast, there have been virtually no women hired to officiate for men's teams.

The one area in which there has been growth for women is athletic training. In 1972 there were only 5 women certified in athletic training. That figure has grown to 250 and promises to continue to grow (Moyer, 1980).

Equity in Coeducational Physical Education Classes

Activity Offerings.   A general movement toward greater emphasis on lifetime and carry-over sports activities paralleled the Title IX mandate for coeducational physical education, with separation only during contact sports (football, basketball, wrestling, ice hockey, boxing, and rugby). Even in contact sports, students are required to be together during the instructional/skills work phases of the activity. Prior to this time period, the girls' physical education curricula at the secondary school level as well as the women's physical education major curricula at the collegiate level typically were broader in the scope of offerings than those of the boys and men. This change, then, affected the boys and men more because they were accustomed to team sports. Girls and women did benefit with the addition of some new activities heralded as appropriate for coeducational classes, such as frisbee, rappelling (descending from a height via a rope), and orienteering (use of a compass to follow a course over time).

Geadelmann (1978/1979) found that some activities were eliminated from high school curricula due to the coeducational mandate. Team sports generally received less emphasis because many felt that the girls weren't capable of competing and because the skill differences were too great. Other activities formerly traditional for only one sex, such as modern (interpretative) dance and wrestling, were eliminated because the teachers or the administrators couldn't envision the members of the other sex participating in them. The reduction of team sport opportunities in some schools is particularly limiting for girls who traditionally have not had the opportunity to experience and develop important values of cooperation and sportsmanship associated with team play. The same is also true of wrestling, where girls have had few experiences in physical contact or pitting their bodies against the force of others. Boys lost the opportunity to know the experience of body awareness, control, expression, and creativity that comes from modern dance. The absence of these activities perpetuates the myth that certain activities are only appropriate for one sex. Furthermore, the removal of team sports may serve to raise the antagonism of boys toward girls, who are blamed for the deprival.

A number of schools (Geadelmann, 1978/1979) have adopted rules or altered the nature of games, particularly in team sports, in an attempt to equalize the opportunities. While the best of intentions may have motivated such changes, the results are potentially damaging for members of both sexes. Typical changes include requiring that a girl hit the volleyball at least once on each side of the net, allowing only girls to receive passes in flag football, awarding girls three points for a basket to two for the boys, and making the boys hit with the nondominant hand in softball. As a result of these practices, the images and the expectations of girls' capabilities are lowered in the eyes of both sexes. Girls are made to feel they aren't good enough to play the regular game and need special help. Boys often feel resentful for not getting to play "the real game."

Elective physical activity programs have become increasingly common at both the secondary and collegiate levels. High school programs have gestured toward honoring the interests and desires of the students, often by offering choices along very traditional sex role lines—for example, modern dance or wrestling. This does nothing to broaden the exposure of all students to the full range of activities or to counter the stereotypes that have long been so pervasive.

Requirements for physical education majors at the collegiate level have provided more options for students to specialize in activity clusters (team sports, individual sports, dance, aquatics, and so forth). While a certain number of activity courses are usually required, and while distribution requirements may exist in some programs, there still commonly remains latitude for choice. Given human nature, few major or professional students venture into activities in which they have had little or no experience or into activities with a traditional opposite-sex role association. Geadelmann (1981c) has suggested that there may be an increasing necessity for colleges to establish more broad-based activity requirements that expose majors to a wide variety of activities. Broader preparation should contribute to broader program offerings.

Grouping Patterns.   The Title IX regulations provide for grouping students on the basis of ability, as long as some measure is applied other than sex. Concern exists that physical educators have arbitrarily separated girls and boys under the guise of ability. It has not been uncommon for students to be scheduled in coeducational groups with a single class list and then to be separated by sex for the actual activity. There have also been reports of concern about ability grouping that results in a sizably disproportionate distribution of males and females. Typical is the response, "How is the low-skilled male going to feel in a group of girls?" While direct research data are lacking, there seems to be a parallel between teacher attitudes and teacher leadership within the situation and the desirability of the learning atmosphere. Boys who self-selected a low-ability volleyball class and were a minority expressed satisfaction at being able to learn without undue pressure or ridicule for mistakes (Geadelmann, personal experience). Similarly, girls in a high-ability group welcomed the challenge to go all-out, even though they were in a numerical minority.

Bischoff (1982), in a study of coeducational volleyball at the junior high school level, found that the males who participated on teams with more females and on teams with an equal number of males and females selected more females as future teammates than did males who participated on male-dominated teams.

The males gave as one of their reasons for selecting the females "their ability." This seems to indicate that those males who had the opportunity to play on the same team with girls and observe their play were more aware of the ability of the females. Conversely, it could be concluded that without that opportunity to observe females' play, and in response to the sex stereotyping prevalent in the gym, males would most frequently choose another male regardless of ability. The common thread that ties this information together is that both peers and teachers expect females to be less skilled and react accordingly.

Bunker (1980) investigated the impact of single-sex versus coeducational groupings on performance. It was found that males performed the same in both groupings, but that the females showed a significant improvement in the coeducational groups. The social influences on performance can be very great, and the findings of Bunker have implications for optimizing the performance potential of girls in particular. Also important are the available role models and what is viewed by each sex to be appropriate behavior.

Teacher Attitudes. Merely placing boys and girls together in the same class provides no guarantee of an improved learning situation. In fact, without some specific efforts and planning on the part of the teacher, along with a positive attitude toward and support for the coeducational situation, the setting may well be worse for boys and girls alike, or better for some at the expense of others.

Hoferek (1978) found a relationship between sex role prescriptions and attitudes of physical educators. Her study showed a relationship between the degree of liberality in attitudes toward the role of women in society and (1) favorable attitudes toward the participation of females in various activities and (2) high performance expectations for girls and women in the least traditional activities. The findings reinforce the need for professional preparation programs that address attitudes toward sex roles.

In physical activity, the stereotype of the male as more active and the female as less active is prevalent, and teachers subtly support that sex role stereotype. How a teacher organizes class groups or teams, which students are chosen as leaders or skill demonstrators, or how a teacher addresses inequitable student participation in games are all indicators of the status of sex equity in a particular class (Griffin, 1981).

Geadelmann (1983) studied attitudes of high school students toward coeducational physical education classes. Fifty-two percent of the students (53% of the boys and 51% of the girls) felt that their physical education teachers expected more from the boys than from the girls. Solomons (1976), in her study of elementary school physical education classes, revealed that girls tended to be left out of game interactions even when they were more highly skilled than boys. In addition, she found that teachers had different expectations of boys than of girls and applied higher performance standards to boys without regard to the skill level of the girls. Expectation levels affect aspiration levels, and aspiration levels in turn determine performance levels. The goal of providing a setting in which all students can work to their potential cannot be achieved in settings with differential expectations, be they real or perceived.

Teacher-Student Interactions.   Griffin (1980) identified four categories related to sex equity: (1) class organization and strategies, (2) teacher-student interactions, (3) teacher language, and (4) teacher role modeling. Observations of 50 coeducational physical education class situations at the elementary, junior, and senior high school levels produced the following results: (1) teachers used the command style of teaching almost exclusively, (2) teachers devoted a large proportion of activity time to full-game play, (3) teachers interacted more frequently with boys in practically all the behavior categories observed, and (4) boys were almost always selected as class leaders and demonstrators. Uhlir and her codevelopers (1981) also reported that teachers called males by their last names and females by their first names. Other sex differences in interaction patterns were reported.

Role Models and Relationship of Performance to Perceived Sex Role.   DuQuin (1977) compared the physical activity role models to which boys and girls are exposed via their school textbooks. The study found that vigorously active men were shown 13 times more often than vigorously active women. Throughout the textbooks, boys and men were portrayed in sports and athletics, whereas girls were shown at times only in active play (not sports). DuQuin concluded that according to socialization theory, "Such female models may contribute to young girls restricting their vision of possible future occupations, activities (especially sport activities), and areas of interest in which to move" (p. 292).

Social Effects.   Geadelmann (1978/1979) found from interviews with high school principals and physical education teachers (male and female) that the greatest positive value from coeducational classes was improved male-female relationships. Students concurred, saying that they had come to be friends and to respect each other as individuals apart from dating and sexual pressures. While these benefits are not to be minimized or discounted, concern must be expressed about an apparent emphasis on social outcomes, as opposed to correcting the teacher and learning inequities in terms of skills.

While junior high and high school girls have expressed positive feelings about coeducational classes and have stated that they feel their skills have improved more than in single-sex classes, more than half (54%) have also expressed feelings of less confidence (inferiority) in these same coeducational classes (Geadelmann, 1983). This has a bearing on self-concept, and it is an area worthy of further research. The girls in the same study expressed displeasure at the jeering and belittling remarks that they felt subjected to by the boys during competitive games.

Leadership and Governance.   Although the Title IX regulations did not require single administrative structures, the movement to merge men's and women's physical education departments accompanied the curricular, facility, and schedule changes needed to comply. Ninety percent of the college departments in the Midwest had so joined by 1977 (Ball, 1980). Burke (1979) related that in many cases the merger happened too fast and with little warning or support. Men headed departments in 80% of the cases and in many instances were arbitrarily appointed. Others found in the pooling of professional personnel advantages such as eliminating both conflicts and replication of efforts as well as allowing for greater specialization in teaching. Ball feels that as a result of the implementation, "Physical education programs are emerging with broader political bases, stronger programmatic thrusts and larger and more resourceful faculties" (p. 16). There is a deep concern, however, about the loss of leadership positions for women and the accompanying decline of female models available (Hoferek, 1980).

ANSWERS

The issues identified in the preceding pages are varied and complex. No single approach has remedied the problems, but a number of strategies have been proposed.

Enforcement of Laws

Laws mandating nondiscrimination on the basis of sex are clearly established, but they have been unevenly implemented by schools and colleges across the country. The Office for Civil Rights has been severely criticized for its failure to vigorously enforce Title IX in particular. Equality in provision of coaches, budgets, facilities, schedules, travel, and promotion is still greatly lacking. That enforcement of the law is not enough, however, is shown in the above delineation of the problems related to behavioral practices and attitudes.

Confrontation of Stereotyping in Attitudes of Students

The findings of Geadelmann (1981a) provide an optimistic note in documenting changes in sex role stereotyping in attitudes of students toward participation in sports activities. In a longitudinal study with data collected in 1974, 1977, and 1980, a majority in 1974 responding favorably toward the male in terms of both acceptability of participation and superiority of performance significantly changed to a majority in 1980 responding that either sex might appropriately participate and that either might have a superior performance. Geadelmann has reported the use of direct intervention in class teaching when sexist comments are made by students. When such a direct intervention was used, students' use of sexist comments declined, and their awareness of the inappropriateness of such comments increased.

Project A.C.T.I.V.E. (All Children Totally Involved Via Equity; Arnett, 1979) resulted in reduced sex role stereotyping among fourth- and fifth-grade students over an 8-week period after participation in the project.

Development of Teacher Education Modules
for Addressing Stereotyping

Physical Educators for Educational Equity at Eastern Kentucky University (Uhlir, 1981) developed both preservice and inservice training programs for addressing knowledge and attitudes about sex role stereotyping. Application of the programs resulted in significant changes in both knowledge and attitude scores for both students and teachers. In addition, it was found that the scores of women teachers were considerably less sex-stereotyped than those of the men and changed significantly more than the men's. Further, the youngest age group, 19–24 years, showed the greatest change and changed significantly more than the 25–34-year group. These findings show the importance of addressing stereotyping during the college years and may have implications for the development of special or additional components for men and for older age groups.

Project TEAM (Griffin & Dodds, 1981) at the University of Massachusetts was designed to provide inservice and preservice physical education teacher training centered upon fair and equitable treatment of students of both sexes and of all races. The preservice component consisted of a one-semester, three-credit elective course for juniors prior to student teaching, which addressed awareness, teaching strategies, and equity guidelines for curriculum development. In the post-test, students demonstrated significantly increased awareness and knowledge of sexism and racism; but in observations of the application of teacher behaviors and equity strategies, few differences were found between the student teachers who took the course and those who did not. The increased awareness and stated commitment did not translate into action in student teaching. The findings may have implications for the development of training modules which combine teacher education and student classroom application components.

Professional preparation programs that require a broad range of activity classes for all majors can reduce the traditional stereotyping which emerges out of a lack of exposure or experience. Participation and acquisition of skills in previously nontraditional activity areas can give teachers the confidence necessary to initiate these courses in school programs.

Provision of Role Models

The importance of role models was cited earlier in the work by DuQuin. These can be orchestrated in a variety of ways: invitation of guest teachers or demonstrators; utilization of films, newspaper and magazine articles, and television programs; field trips; or discussions. Individuals in nontraditional careers can serve as role models that have implications for physical education. Jobs which have been nontraditional for females have frequently involved strong physical competency and have traditionally been reserved for men. Women have, however, demonstrated that they can succeed in such fields. For example, females who have completed training programs at the Air Force Academy, become pilots, and served aboard naval ships are all examples, in addition to police officers and firefighters, of competence in physically demanding jobs (Hoferek, 1982; Thomas, 1978).

Men who are relieved of the "macho" burden of sport may seek nontraditional employment areas. While few studies have been conducted, one could speculate that greater social sensitivity in men might lead to nontraditional career choices.

Sensitivity to Grouping Patterns

Evidence indicates that females particularly benefit in skill development from coeducational groupings (Bunker, 1980). Grouping by ability or physical characteristics (height, weight) removes the arbitrariness that occurs when grouping is done by sex and also reduces the tendencies to stereotype on the basis of sex. The results of coeducational classes in physical education cited earlier indicate that much more needs to be done to ensure that the treatment of students within the coeducational setting is in fact equitable. The use of objective measures for grouping students is one step in addressing these needs.

Provision of Special Support to Those in Nontraditional Settings

The self-concepts and confidence levels of students in physical activity groups or situations which have not been traditional or in which they are a minority need to be monitored, protected, and supported. Special encouragement may be necessary, either by establishing a formal group or network or by providing ongoing informal support. It is not enough to simply announce that it is "all right" to engage in the activity; students need to be helped to feel acceptability within themselves and for others.

Establishment of Guarantees for Equality in Leadership Opportunities

The decline in leadership opportunities for women in both physical education and athletics is alarming. Deliberate and specific provisions must be made to ensure full participation of women at all levels of governance. The example of the American Alliance for Health, Physical Education, Recreation, and Dance in alternating the presidency between a man and a woman is one that should be considered for adoption by many groups. The need for affirmative action goals and the persistent pursuit of these goals is compelling.

Utilization of Technical Assistance Programs and Projects

Technical assistance to schools attempting to take positive steps toward equal opportunity has proved invaluable in several instances. Surveys following a variety of interventions revealed that the most critical elements in changes leading to sex equity were the availability of experts in sex equity to provide technical assistance and supportive administrators who contributed to a positive school climate for equity. These held true regardless of school size or socioeconomic level of district (Thalacker, 1979/1980).

Sources of technical assistance for physical education and athletic programs include educational equity divisions in state departments of education, regional sex desegregation assistance centers, the National Association for Girls and Women in Sport (1900 Association Drive, Reston, VA 22091, and Project SPRINT (805 15th St., N.W., Suite 822, Washington, DC 20005). In addition, many women's organizations at the national level carefully monitor sex equity in physical education and athletics, including the National Organization for Women, the American Association of University Women, and the National Women's Political Caucus.

SUMMARY AND RECOMMENDATIONS

Achieving equity in physical education and athletic programs involves some unique factors not present or relevant to most other educational programs. While all have to deal with historically stereotyped roles and attitudes and with traditional expectations, no other has to address physiological differences in such a direct way. A variety of approaches has been attempted via separate and different treatments, separate and equal treatments, and identical treatments. In each case, there are significant shortcomings.

We recognize, on the one hand, that prominent differences in strength, speed, and power make competition between adult males and females generally unfair at this time. Thus, for athletic competition, separate-sex teams have been accepted by legal definition and by the general public as the most equitable approach. The problems with this approach arise in the differences in treatment accorded the boys'/men's teams and the girls'/women's teams. The norm has been greater promotion and greater support of the male teams, and only in rare instances have the female teams been operated on a par with those of the male.

It should further be recognized, however, that the limitations imposed by tradition and stereotype have prevented the full development or realization of physical potential in most girls and women. The reality is that we do not have an accurate sense of what the true physical differences are. The problems are compounded when attitudes reflecting stereotyping are attached to the physical performance aspect. Hence, such factors as confidence, esteem, and aspiration are affected. While one may advocate separate worlds for fairness at the physical level, the separation may serve to perpetuate lack of fairness via accompanying attitudes that separate is "different" and thereby "inferior"; that is, girls aren't good enough to be with boys. Additionally, separation often precludes the opportunity to bring out the best in oneself by going against the best, by being challenged to the utmost. Can the highly skilled girl/woman be fully challenged if confined to competition among members of her own sex if most are less skilled?

The "same worlds" approach has resulted in other problems, perhaps most dramatically related to loss of opportunities for leadership and governance. Not to be overlooked, however, are the expressions of feelings of inferiority and depressed levels of self-confidence from girls in coeducational physical education classes at the secondary level. One might quite legitimately ask why separation is protected in athletics for students in junior high school and beyond and yet prohibited in physical education in these same grades when both arenas are grounded in the acquisition and performance of physical skills. It might even be that girls who develop low regard for their physical abilities in coeducational classes are discouraged from ever pursuing participation on athletic teams, even though these are in separate-sex settings. Studies directed at these factors are recommended.

The case for separation to foster leadership development is well documented historically in physical education and athletics prior to the program mergers. The positive values that can accrue from separation are further explained by the greater prevalence of women in leadership positions at women's colleges than in coeducational institutions.

There is an additional question of how and when one does integrate the separate worlds and how that transition is facilitated. Is "separate" something we should continue for a period of time for "catch-up"? Or is separate something that will always have a place, if only as an alternative as opposed to a norm? Are we as willing to acknowledge that legitimate reasons may exist for males as well as females to need the option of separation? If not, what is the underlying message in that statement? If there is indeed a desirable time for integration as well as for separation, how is the appropriateness of those times to be decided? Are we willing to admit that separate might indeed be better for the whole and accept differences, as opposed to forcing change or integration for the benefit or convenience of a select few? If so, what does this mean for girls who want to play football or baseball, or wrestle?

We might take as an example the studies of the performances of women in the military. The training programs originated in integrated settings, with supplementary programs provided for those with special needs, regardless of sex. After 5 years, however, the army concluded that the same training programs could best be conducted in separate-sex settings, with integration to follow. This change in approach, the performances, the transition process, and the effects of eventual integration are all worthy of careful study and review. What might be the implication of this for physical education? At the elementary school level, there is no physiological basis for separation. By the age of 12, however, significant physical differences appear. Might it be advantageous to do some selective separation in activities which require major efforts of strength, speed, power, and endurance? Under what circumstances? For how long? These questions directly confront the issue of making a decision solely on the basis of sex, a matter that has been adamantly opposed in all other matters of sex equity.

Further study and effort are needed to conceptualize a framework that can indeed provide for the full development of physical skills in females and males alike, foster healthy attitudes of respect for individual skills and differences among individuals apart from sex, and enable all to have equal access to participation in programs as well as to leadership. For too long, the separation of girls/women in physical activity has been based on their being seen as both different and inferior. Since the 1970s in particular, however, significant changes in attitude have occurred toward the roles and capabilities of women and men alike. Those who have fought the separation and the accompanying discrimination will be reluctant to agree to new divisions based on separation, and perhaps even adamant in opposition. At the same time, though, care must be taken not to be blind to the resultant effects of complete integration.

The basic question remains, what is fair? Is it fair for members of one sex to be able to try out for a team of the opposite sex but not vice versa? How can physical differences be fairly addressed concurrently with goals for participation, skill development, and leadership? The rules of the fairness game for sex equity in physical education and athletics are not always clear, and until basic differences can be distinguished from perceived differences or stereotypes, the likelihood of the cry "foul" will persist.

In the interim, research attention must be given to the identification of physical sex differences and similarities; the barriers to the development of full physical potential in girls/women and boys/men; the role and influence of separate-sex versus integrated groupings on skill acquisition, performance, and self-concept, including self-confidence and leadership skills; and the effects of cultural/societal attitudes on participation, performance, and support of girls/women in physical activity. The issues are complex, and our commitment to equity must allow for full study of alternative strategies to achieve the goal.

REFERENCES

American Medical Association Committee on the Medical Aspects of Sports. (1975). Female athletics. *Journal of Physical Education and Recreation, 46*(1), 45–46.

Arnett, C. (1979). *Project A.C.T.I.V.E.* (All Children Totally Involved Via Equity) (DHEW Project No. 565AH700CB). Newton, MA: Education Development Center.

Association of American Colleges. (1980a). Civil rights commission documents sports inequities. *On Campus with Women*, p. 4.

Association of American Colleges. (1980b). Women coaches falling behind. *On Campus with Women*, p. 5.

Astrand, P. O., & Rodehl, K. (1970). *Textbook of work physiology*. New York: McGraw-Hill.

Ball, J. R. (1980). Emerging physical education collegiate departments. *Thresholds in Education, 8*(4), 14–16.

Bischoff, J. A. (1982). Equal opportunity, satisfaction and success? An exploratory study on coed volleyball. *Journal of Teaching in Physical Education, 2*(1), 3–12.

Bunker, L. K. (1980, June). Nature-nurture and the future of coed sports. *National*

Association for Physical Education in Higher Education Annual Conference Proceedings (Vol. 2, pp. 177–194). Champaign, IL: Human Kinetics.

Burke, N. P. (1979, January). *Staffing needs and dilemmas.* Paper presented at the AIAW Athletic Directors Conference, Los Angeles.

DeCrow, K. (1980). Hardlining Title IX: Who's off-side now? *Perspectives: The Civil Rights Quarterly, 12*(2), 16–23.

DuQuinn, M. E. (1977). Differential sex role socialization toward amplitude appropriation. *Research Quarterly, 48*(2), 288–292.

Geadelmann, P. L. (1979). Sex equality in physical education programs of selected NCA accredited Iowa high schools. *Dissertation Abstracts International, 39*, 7221A. (University Microfilms No. 7913048)

Geadelmann, P. L. (1981a). *Changes in sex role stereotyping in attitudes of students toward participation in sports activities.* Unpublished manuscript, University of Northern Iowa, Cedar Falls.

Geadelmann, P. L. (1981b). Coeducational physical education: For better or for worse? *NASSP Bulletin, 65*(443), 91–95.

Geadelmann, P. L. (1981c, March). *Combating sex role stereotyping in professional preparation programs in physical education.* Paper presented at the Central District Convention of the American Alliance for Health, Physical Education, Recreation, and Dance, Minneapolis.

Geadelmann, P. L. (1983, April). *Fairness in coeducational classes.* Paper presented at the National Convention of the American Alliance for Health, Physical Education, Research, and Dance, Minneapolis.

Gerber, E. W. (1971). *Innovators and institutions in physical education.* Philadelphia: Lea & Febiger.

Gerber, E. W. (1974). Collegiate sport. In E. W. Gerber, E. J. Felshin, P. Berlin, & W. Wyrick (Eds.), *The American woman in sport* (pp. 48–85). Reading, MA: Addison-Wesley.

Griffin, P. S. (1980). *Developing a systematic observation instrument to identify sex-role dependent and sex-role independent behavior among physical education teachers.* Unpublished doctoral dissertation, University of Massachusetts, Amherst.

Griffin, P. S. (1981). One small step for personkind: Observations and suggestions for sex equity in coeducational physical education classes. *Journal of Teaching in Physical Education, 1*(1), 12–18.

Griffin, P. S., & Dodds, P. (1981). *Project TEAM: Evaluating a preservice sex and race equity experimental class.* Unpublished manuscript, University of Amherst.

Hoferek, M. J. (1978). Sex-role prescriptions and attitudes of physical educators. *Dissertation Abstracts International, 39*, 183A. (University Microfilms No. 7806428)

Hoferek, M. J. (1980). At the Crossroad: Merger or ———? *Quest, 32*(1), 95–102.

Hoferek, M. J. (1982). Sex-roles and physical activity: Evolving trends. *Quest, 34*(1), 72–81.

Hoffman, T., Stauffer, R., and Jackson, A. (1979). Sex differences in strength. *American Journal of Sports Medicine, 7*, 265–267.

Holmen, M. G., & Parkhouse, B. (1981). Trends in the selection of coaches for female athletes: A demographic inquiry. *Research Quarterly for Exercise and Sports, 52*(1), 9–18.

Hult, J. S. (1979). Different AIAW/NCAA eligibility rules: Tip of the iceberg? *Athletic Purchasing and Facilities, 3*, 12–16.

Hult, J. S., and Park, R. (1981). The role of women in sports. In W. Baker & J. M. Carroll (Eds.), *Sports in modern America* (pp. 115–128). St. Louis: River City Limited.

Lehr, C. (1980). *Sex of coaches in women's intercollegiate athletics, 1973–1980.* Unpublished manuscript, University of Georgia, Athens.

Lopiano, D. A. (1980). Modern athletics: Directions and problems. *Thresholds in Education, 8*(4), 8–13.

Moyer, L. J. (1980). Title IX: Have things really changed? *Thresholds in Education, 8*(4), 17–22.

Oberteuffer, D., & Ulrich, C. (1962). *Physical education.* New York: Harper & Row.

Plowman, S. (1974). Physiological characteristics of female athletes. *Research Quarterly, 45*(4), 349–362.

Safrit, M. J., Baumgartner, T. A., Jackson, A. S., & Stamm, C. L. (1980). Issues in setting motor performance standards. *Quest, 32*(2), 152–162.

Solomons, H. (1976). *Sex-role-mediated achievement behaviors and interpersonal dynamics of fifth-grade coeducational physical education classes.* Unpublished doctoral dissertation, Bryn Mawr College, Bryn Mawr, PA.

Stauffer, R. (1976). *Comparison of United States Military Academy men and women on selected physical performance measures.* West Point, NY: Office of United States Military Academy, Physical Education.

Thalacker, B. (1980). *A study of the common elements of existing exemplary sex-equitable programs in secondary schools in Arizona. Dissertation Abstracts International, 40,* 4944A. (University Microfilms No. 8004778)

Thomas, J. C., & Riding, D. E. (1978, June). Physical performance standards for women. *Proceedings of the NAPECW/NCPEAM National Conference* (pp. 232–239).

Thomas, P. J. (1978, October). New roles for military women. In *The female naval officer: What is her role?* Symposium conducted at the annual meeting of the American Psychological Association, Toronto.

Uhlir, A. (1981). *Physical educators for equity: Teacher education modules for reduction of sex bias in coeducational instruction and program operation of physical education.* Newton, MA: Education Development Center.

Vrean, L. (1983). Title IX: Teetering on the brink. *School Product News, 22*(12), 21–23.

Wilmore, J. H. (1974). Alternations in strength, body composition, and anthropometric measurements consequent to a 10-week weight training program. *Medicine and Science in Sports, 6,* 133–138.

18
Sex Equity in Career and Vocational Education

Helen S. Farmer and Joan Seliger Sidney,
with Barbara A. Bitters and Martine G. Brizius

Roles for men and women continue to change and to expand in contemporary America. While women are shifting from homemaker to homemaker and paid worker, men are shifting from primary wage earner to worker and homemaker. The combining of work and family roles challenges young people today. Through career and vocational education, teachers, counselors, and parents are preparing children for these changes.

This chapter is about options. In order to achieve sex equity in career and vocational education, we must increase the options available to young people in all areas of their lives.

Career, in its broadest sense, means "life path" and thus includes all the roles a person plays throughout life (Super, 1980). Career choice is, therefore, a lifelong pursuit. There is no one career choice; rather, there are multiple choices along the way. These choices are based on what people learn and on the experiences they have. The best choices are those that give satisfaction and pleasure to each person and, at the same time, allow the individual to make a contribution to society. Ideally, every person should match her/his job choice with his/her talents and interests, consistent with economic opportunities and role priorities, and then strive to achieve her/his career goals.

Vocational education is distinguished from career education by a focus on a narrower range of occupations. It covers instruction for all occupations that do not require a B.A. or higher degree. Seven major educational areas are included: agriculture, distributive, occupational home economics, office, health, technical, and industrial.

This chapter limits itself to addressing career education and counseling programs in schools from kindergarten through the senior year in high school

The authors were assisted by Penny Cylo, Jackie Fields, Delores Glanton, Sunny L. Hansen, Laurie R. Harrison, Susan Klein, Ruth Licht, Marie Mayor, Harriet Medaris, Ann T. Meyerson, Beverly M. Postlewaite, Amy Rubin, Stuart Jay Sidney, and Jeana Wirtenberg.

(K–12) and vocational education programs from grade 7 through a 2-year Associate of Arts degree. Some programs related to sex equity in career and vocational education are not addressed because they are covered in greater depth elsewhere in this volume (see chapter 13 for programs in math and science and chapter 22 for programs for adult women).

In this chapter we shall discuss the key sex equity issues for career and vocational education. Identification of the key problem areas are based in part on the reviews of sex differences and of sex roles presented in chapters 5 and 6, and in part on research and theory related to career development and on research evidence of sex discrimination in employment. All of these sources agree that most critical is the effect of sex-related occupational and homemaking stereotypes on the life choices students make. A second concern, inequalities in self-concept, deals with females viewing themselves as more dependent and less competent in relation to work than males, and males viewing themselves as less competent in relation to parenting and helping roles than females. A third concern is inequality in analytical and decision-making skills related to making career choices, with girls less competent than boys, but with boys also unskilled in making life choices based on a consideration of work and family roles and their interrelationships. A fourth problem area relates to the inequalities in vocational education, especially the higher enrollment of females in training for the lower-paying occupations, and the low enrollment of males in training for parenting and homemaking. The fifth and last problem is the inadequate training with respect to sex equity of administrators, counselors, and educators who provide career and vocational education in the schools.

THE NEED TO DECREASE SEX STEREOTYPING AND DISCRIMINATION IN CAREER AND LIFE CHOICES (ISSUES 1–3)

The first three concerns, which deal with sex-stereotyped occupational perceptions and sex differences in self-concepts and decision-making ability related to career and life choices, are interrelated. Their importance and unique effects at certain age levels are explained in good measure by the sex-equitable career development theories of the last decade (Farmer, 1978; Fitzgerald & Crites, 1980; Gottfredson, 1981; Hansen, 1978; Harmon, 1978; Richardson, 1979; Super, 1980; and Tittle, 1981). Although several theoretical viewpoints could be taken regarding career development, we have adopted a developmental view because it encompasses contributions from other theoretical perspectives and at the same time addresses change in persons over time. Developmental theory is based on a view of learning which assumes that persons grow and develop through their interaction with the environment. This view is consistent with the assumptions outlined in chapter 6 and avoids the twin pitfalls of a purely psychological theory, which would locate development within the individual, or a purely sociological approach, which would find the major determinants of development in the environment.

We selected Gottfredson's (1981) theoretical model from among develop-mental theories because it pinpoints particular career development tasks at the elementary, secondary, and, in the case of vocational education, post-secondary levels which are relevant to sex equity. Gottfredson's review presented evidence that sex role socialization occurs early (ages 6–8) and that, by implication, programs to expand options should begin early in the elementary school, with a focus on preoccupational experiences and skill building.

Gottfredson traced the development of occupational stereotypes in young children through adulthood. Preschool children, she found, view occupations as adult roles with which they rarely identify. By age 6, however, children are already socialized to develop an awareness of the gender appropriateness of behaviors in general, and of occupations in particular. Traditional occupations of females span a narrower range than those for males and are less well paid (see also chapter 6). Later, in grades 4 to 8, children develop an awareness of their appropriate level or social class bounds. This awareness is based on a combina-tion of their experiences with family, friends, and community persons and their own estimates of their ability.

Between ages 9 and 12, children become highly sensitive to evaluation by peers and later to more general social group expectation and values (Van den Daele, 1968). They begin to recognize prestige differences among jobs that are valued by society. They may not be able to verbalize social class distinctions, but they can tell how important a person is, for example, by the kind of house s/he lives in and the level of salary earned. Children's own preferences for the kind of work they would like to do are influenced by these values and expectations, their social class, and their ability. Research by Goldstein and Oldham (1979) indi-cates that by grade 8, students recognize the links between education, work, money, and social class. Whereas prestige differences appear irrelevant to the first grader (for example, firefighter and doctor may both be options for the same child), by fourth grade prestige differences do influence students' career choices.

In chapter 6, Schau describes sex role development theories in greater detail and notes that during the middle school years sex role stereotypes are less fixed than previously and less fixed than they will be in adolescence. This is, therefore, a period during which educators may have a greater impact on chang-ing sex role perceptions of students.

Schau also notes that the effect of role models on students is mediated by the power and attractiveness of the model. They point out that parents are replaced as models for children's developing self-concepts during preadoles-cence by the more normative behaviors of persons in the media and their popular peers.

In high school, the student's concern is not primarily with the level of an occupation or its sex appropriateness, but rather with choosing a particular field, for example, health, agriculture, or business. At that time, young people begin to be aware of the appropriateness of a particular occupational field for them. This knowledge develops out of their increasing awareness of their own interests, values, and aptitudes (Rosenberg, 1979). In high school, adolescents are also motivated to make choices about what occupation(s) they might enter and about the kind of future life they want as they become aware of more internally based and abstract concepts of self and the drive for internal direction, autonomy, and coherence (Van den Daele, 1968). They are involved in identifying their uniqueness, in contrast to earlier years when they were involved in coming to terms with the expectations of others. Their concerns include understanding the person they are and would like to be, as well as making life plans and choices related to family, leisure, and work (Rosenberg & Rosenberg, 1982). A positive self-concept is important at this time also, since it has been related to career choices that are most consistent with a person's potential (Fitzgerald & Crites, 1980). Toward the end of high school, some students, particularly those in vocational education programs, are involved in job training and job hunting, a process of compromise. They must adjust their ideal career choice to the realities of training opportunities and employment in that field. The extent to which training is equally accessible to males and females during this period is crucial to achieving sex equity in work.

Although the integration of work and family roles is a task for the adult, a formative stage for this integration takes place in adolescence. Interestingly, on the average, adolescent females and males aspire to similar levels of occupations (Card, Steel, & Abeles, 1980; Farmer, 1983; Tittle, 1981). In fact, some researchers (Farmer, 1983) find that adolescent females aspire to significantly higher levels of occupations than do males. But later, when employed, significant sex differences appear in the occupational level reached, with females at increasingly lower levels than males (Card, Steel, & Abeles, 1980).

Gottfredson's review suggests that when it comes time to make career choices in high school and afterwards, a person's occupational sex stereotypes take priority over his/her perception of what level or what field of occupation to enter. It is all the more critical, therefore, that occupational stereotypes be reduced early, in order to increase the likelihood that young people will consider the appropriate level of occupations and the fields that will use their full potential. In the developmental stage when the bounds of occupational level are being set (grades 4–8), social class values related to family and work roles are also being internalized. During the early school years, these values can be explored and broadened so that in high school and afterwards females and males will choose life plans based more on their own unique interests and aptitudes than on gender. The goal is to increase the likelihood that students will regard all fields of occupations as potential options for them, provided they have the necessary aptitudes. School personnel must work to reduce occupational and homemaking sex role stereotypes. They should also work to reduce social class restrictions on occupational options. Coeducational home economics and industrial arts courses should be required for both sexes, and nontraditional training options should be explored.

There is a need to facilitate the development of a positive self-concept so that students feel good about themselves and feel competent about school work and making decisions. People with positive self-concepts are more likely to increase the level and range of options considered. There is also a need to enhance the problem-solving and career decision-making skills of students. This task involves somewhat different skills for girls than for boys because values related to life choices tend to differ by sex. In life planning, these differences need to be taken into account in order to increase the options considered.

The description of career development issues in this section applies to both career education and vocational education. However, some special equity needs have been identified for vocational education, and these are described next.

SEX DISCRIMINATION AND SEX SEGREGATION IN VOCATIONAL EDUCATION (ISSUE 4)

In spite of the requirements of Title IX, sex segregation in vocational education remains high (Wells, 1983). Data for 1980 indicate that females represent 91% of students in training as nursing assistants, 87% of those in training as community health workers, and 92% of those in cosmetology and in secretarial training. For males these data indicate that they represented 95% in electrical technology, 90% in electronics, 94% in appliance repair, 96% in auto mechanics, 96% in carpentry, 95% in welding, and 96% in small engine repair. In addition to sex segregation, Wells reported that a study of four states (California, Colorado, Florida, and Illinois) showed that males were concentrated in fields with high-paying job opportunities, whereas females were concentrated in fields with low-paying job opportunities.

The reasons for this continued sex segregation were attributed in another study, conducted in Idaho, Iowa, Wisconsin, Pennsylvania, and Massachusetts, to a a lack of active commitment to sex equity on the part of educational officials and school personnel (Wells). These educators did not actively recruit students for nontraditional fields, they frequently maintained sex-segregated high schools in large urban areas, and they did little to assure the nontraditional student's comfort and well-being in classes where they were a minority.

Manifestations of sex bias in the teaching and learning environment create unequal educational opportunities for students. Even in coeducational classrooms, sex bias is visible in vocational texts and instructional materials that not only reflect but exaggerate traditional stereotyped roles and the division of labor; in a curriculum geared to the interests and needs of only one sex; in instructional practices that divide students into single-sex groups; in evaluations that use different criteria for grading males and females; in teacher expectations that differentiate between male and female students; in unequal funding for equipment, labs, and student projects in female-intensive vocational programs; and in a higher ratio of students to teachers in female intensive vocational programs (Wells).

The goal is to increase the enrollment of females and males in vocational education fields formerly dominated by the opposite sex: for females especially those fields with higher salary expectations, and for males those fields that prepare them for increased competence as parents. This goal requires more than equal access. It also requires active recruitment, support services, and sex-fair curricula. Also critical to achieving this goal is the need for a cadre of equity-trained and dedicated educators, counselors, and administrators. These needs are discussed next.

THE INADEQUATE SEX EQUITY TRAINING
OF EDUCATORS (ISSUE 5)

Many school administrators, counselors, and educators continue to view occupations stereotypically (Farris, 1982; Tanney & Birk, 1976). Attitudes of educators, students, parents, and employers reflect outdated and inaccurate information about female labor force participation and a clear belief that there are "men's" jobs and "women's" jobs. These attitudes limit students' career aspirations and occupational choices. Frequently, traditional attitudes about sex-appropriate jobs and about the abilities of students in vocational education contribute to a hostile learning environment for females and males who have made nontraditional vocational choices (Farris, 1982). More recently, sexual harassment of young women in vocational classrooms and labs nontraditional for their sex is being recognized as an additional issue to be addressed (Wells, 1983). Prior to Title IX, counseling practices, materials, and assessment tools reflected traditional sex role stereotypes, with different scales used to measure interests and aptitudes of females and males. Research with vocational educators and students indicated that adolescent males were aware of a greater number of occupations and expected to achieve them, whereas adolescent females were aware of a more limited number of occupations and had low expectations for their achievements in these vocational fields (Farris, 1982). These low expectations for female achievement contrast with the high female career aspiration level reported earlier in this chapter (Farmer, 1983).

Lack of support services in the educational setting acts as a barrier to student participation in nontraditional vocational education. Some needed support services include nontraditional role models, support groups for nontraditional students, and prevocational classes. "Sex-stereotyped attitudes, expectations, and behaviors on the part of parents, teachers, and counselors . . . all need to be reckoned with to overcome the cultural forces that have for so long placed limits on the occupational attainment of women, channeling them into traditionally female occupations and away from traditionally male occupations" (Wirtenberg, 1979).

People have attempted to address the issues described above by creating educational policies and laws and by developing sex-equitable curricula.

MAJOR POLICIES THAT ATTEMPT TO CREATE
SEX-EQUITABLE CAREER AND
VOCATIONAL EDUCATION

The general role of laws and other policies in creating equity is discussed in chapter 7. Following are specific ways that these laws and policies have helped bring about equity in career and vocational education.

Title IX of the Education Amendments of 1972 is the major federal law that prohibits sex discrimination in education. Its enabling regulations specify several ways that discrimination in career and vocational education should be eliminated directly. They include provisions against sex discrimination in admissions to schools, courses, and occupational training and specifically say that a recipient of federal funds may not provide industrial, business, vocational, technical, or home economics courses or educational activities separately on the basis of sex. They also prohibit a recipient's use of sex-discriminatory appraisal and counseling materials or methods.

The Vocational Education Act was amended in 1976 to add specific provisions for eliminating sex bias, stereotyping, and discrimination in vocational education, including homemaking programs. In 1979 the Office for Civil Rights (OCR) issued guidelines that require state education departments to establish a civil rights compliance program to monitor and provide technical assistance in order to ensure nondiscrimination in vocational education programs.

The Vocational Education Act is particularly valuable for establishing affirmative provisions to help educators provide sex equity through federal and state financial assistance. It does this by establishing full-time sex equity coordinators in each state with a minimum $50,000 budget each and by providing funding at both the national and state levels for sex equity programs and curricula, including programs for persons seeking jobs in areas nontraditional for their sex.

The Career Incentive Education Act of 1977, which is now part of the Education Consolidation and Improvement Act of 1981, also contains in chapter 2 specific language requiring that assistance be provided to educational agencies and institutions in eliminating sex bias and stereotyping in career education programs and in promoting equal opportunity in students' career choices.

The Women's Educational Equity Act (WEEA) of 1974, Title IV of the Civil Rights Act of 1964, and state laws and policies have also been used to help support the development and use of sex equity programs and activities in career and vocational education.

Programs, most of which have been supported by federal funds mandated by the previously discussed laws, have been developed to promote sex equity in career and vocational education at the elementary, middle, and high school levels. Evidence from some of these programs shows that they have succeeded in addressing our five sex equity issues.

In examining this evidence we will apply Johnston and Ettema's (1982) distinction between three types of stereotypes: beliefs, attitudes, and interests.

(See also chapter 6 for similar distinctions.) Beliefs mean that which is believed to be true about an object, for example, "Girls are lousy mechanics and boys aren't very nurturant." Attitudes, however, pertain to values. A person may say, for example, "I think it is a good idea for girls to engage in mechanical activities," or "I think it is a good idea for boys to engage in homemaking activities." Interests, in contrast to these more normative beliefs and attitudes, refer to what people themselves would or would not like to do. A person may have stereotyped interests—that is, those commonly held by her/his gender—or may develop interests based on his/her unique aptitudes. Changes in interests, directly bring about changes in behavior but need to be evaluated differently from beliefs and attitudes, since interests are expected to be unique for each person and to be consistent with the things s/he enjoys doing.

Specific Curricula That Appear Effective in Promoting Sex Equity

Elementary School Career Education Programs and Products. There have been several hundred programs developed that attempt to reduce sex role stereotyping of beliefs, attitudes, and interests related to both occupations and homemaking (issue 1). The best of these programs use a variety of methods to reduce stereotyping, but very few have used evaluation techniques adequate to the task of providing evidence that participating students endorsed significantly less stereotypic beliefs and attitudes toward various role behaviors by the end of the program than they did initially (American Institutes for Research, 1978). Four of these programs—Freestyle, Opening the Doors, HEAR, and Equality—have met the Department of Education, Joint Dissemination Review Panel criteria of effectiveness and generalizability. The reference list contains information on where these projects were conducted. Summary findings related to the effectiveness of these programs in reducing sex-stereotyped beliefs and attitudes are provided in table 9.

Freestyle materials consist of 13 half-hour TV video cassettes, divided into twenty-six 15-minute segments for classroom use (grades 3–6). The programs portray a multiethnic group of young teenagers and their families engaging in nonstereotypic activities both at home and at work. Viewers learn about the changing role of men and women in occupations and in family living through the settings and plots of the dramas. Accompanying the programs are a teacher's guide, student comic book/activity book, and a calendar for parents.

Freestyle successfully changed the attitudes of both boys and girls toward several nontraditional role behaviors (Johnston & Ettema, 1982). Girls' attitudes changed positively and significantly toward boys in helping roles, more men in female jobs, and husbands doing more female-stereotyped housework. Boys' attitudes changed positively and significantly toward girls in athletics, girls in mechanical activities, girls as leaders, girls being independent, and more women in traditionally male jobs. Girls also changed attitudes positively and signifi-

Table 9.   Summary Evidence, Using Effect Size,[a] for Elementary School Career Education Programs

| Project by grade in school[b] | Less stereotypic beliefs | | | More positive attitudes; nontraditional role behaviors | n[c] | | Random assignment of subjects | Replicated study | Representative sample[d] |
	M	F	T[e]	T	E	C			
K. Opening Doors	ns		.57		18	24	×	×	×
K. Equality					20	41			
1. Equality				.98	38	166			
1. Opening Doors	ns	*	1.25		17	22	×	×	×
2. Equality				1.42	41	156			
2. Opening Doors	ns	*	.86		54	36	×	×	×
3. Equality				1.32	49	196			
3. Opening Doors	*	*	.64		45	43	×		×
3. Freestyle[f,g]	.39	.48					×	×	×
4. Equality				.89	33	177			
4. Freestyle	.39	.48					×	×	×
4. HEAR			.49		116	42	×	×	×
5. Equality				.73	73	194			
5. Freestyle	.39	.48					×	×	×
6. Equality				.63	47	115			
6. Freestyle	.39	.48					×	×	×

[a]Effect size. In evaluating effect size, Cohen (1977) suggested that a value of .2 is considered a minimum for a meaningful gain; .2 to .5 are small; .5 to .8 are moderate; while those greater than .8 are large. [b]These four projects are approved by the Joint Dissemination Review Panel (Tallmadge, 1977). [c]n = Number of subjects, E = experimental, C = control. [d]Representative of minority and white students and of a range of social classes. [e]M = male, F = female, T = total group. [f]The effect for grade in school was negligible, and therefore data were combined across grades for each of the measures. [g]This study used students in grades 4 through 6, but the results were not reported by grade; total n for experimental group = 686, that for the control group = 264.

*Significant, but data not available. ns = nonsignificant.

cantly toward girls being independent, more women in male jobs, and more wives doing more male-stereotyped housework. Boys' attitudes changed positively and significantly toward boys in helping roles, more men in female-stereotyped jobs, and husbands doing more traditionally female-stereotyped housework.

Girls demonstrated large gains in interest in athletics; moderately increased interests in "realistic" careers, that is, ones that include technical trades and engineering; and small but significant increases in mechanical activities and in business-related careers. Boys demonstrated small but significant gains in interest in "helping" behaviors and in people-related, helping occupations (Johnston & Ettema, 1982). The Freestyle TV series appears to be effective in changing attitudes and beliefs about nontraditional activities both at work and at home.

Project Opening the Doors (grades K–3) and Project HEAR (grades 4–6) attempt to expand students' beliefs about occupations suitable for females and males, but do not address homemaking stereotypes. Opening the Doors and HEAR were designed by the same persons. Table 9 indicates that although both programs were successful in achieving their first goal—reducing stereotypic beliefs about occupations—the effect size for change became increasingly smaller from grades 1 to 4. The range was from 1.25 to .49. Opening the Doors was found to be more effective for females than males in reducing stereotypic occupational beliefs as well as in increasing and maintaining interest in nontraditional occupations.

Project Equality materials include five occupational simulation packets, each of which features a hands-on career education activity. Packets are also designed to help teachers and students expand their awareness of sex role stereotyping and to broaden their view of the roles men and women can fill at home and on the job. The materials were effective in reducing occupational and homemaking stereotypes for grades K–6.

Other programs with potential for reducing stereotypes in elementary schools were identified. The Girl Scouts of America, with federal funding, has developed sex equity career education materials for use by Brownies and Junior Scouts, grades 2 through 6. These materials, *Careers to Explore,* help scouts examine their values, interests, and activities; explore a wide assortment of careers, consider future career possibilities for themselves; and develop positive attitudes toward career choices for women. Although there has not been an evaluation of their effectiveness, these materials have been field-tested and received a "superior" rating from the National Education Association. Other curricular materials, developed with funding support from the Women's Educational Equity Act (WEEA), are described in a catalogue published by the WEEA Publishing Center (1982). One resource for the elementary level, *People and Places, U.S.A.,* is a series of stories encouraging nontraditional career exploration. Another, *Trabahamos: A Bilingual/Multicultural Career Awareness and Language Enrichment Program,* presents 12 nontraditional occupations.

In summary, this section has reviewed programs and materials aimed at increasing the likelihood that elementary students will regard all occupational fields as potential options for them, provided they have the necessary aptitudes. Although four programs effectively reduced sex-stereotyped beliefs and attitudes, none of the programs demonstrated changes in behaviors. While Freestyle and Equality reduced stereotypes related to both family and work roles, Opening Doors and HEAR focused only on reducing occupational stereotypes.

Middle School Programs and Products. Middle school programs and products address issues 1–4. Middle school (junior high), grades 7–9, is a particularly important period for career and vocational education. It is the beginning of the exploration stage of career development (Super, 1980) and thus is an important time to provide young people with information and experiences about the range of career options. At this age students are less stereotypic in outlook, compared to the elementary school years immediately behind them and the adolescent years immediately ahead. It is also during these years when classes in industrial arts and in home economics are provided in the public school system. Positive experiences in these courses for students of both sexes could lead to less stereotypic attitudes, beliefs, and behaviors and to more vocational education students choosing programs nontraditional for their sex in high school.

Curricular changes to enhance sex equity in vocational exploration in junior high can be simple and extremely cost-effective. An especially successful model (AIR, 1979) is a series of coed miniclasses which expose each student to many courses ranging from cooking to welding, as opposed to only those courses traditional for each sex. This entails designing introductory classes where none exist or shortening existing classes so that incoming students can take all or most of them. This approach has the additional benefit of allowing students to share equally in any initial uneasiness about nontraditional classes, thus reducing social pressure to conform to sex stereotypes in choosing a career path.

HEAR (grades 7–9) was designed to increase students' knowledge of occupations and to encourage students to consider all occupations as potential choices for them. Gottfredson (1981) found that students in this age range restrict the level of occupation they view as acceptable based in part on their social class background. One way to combat this tendency may be to increase students' occupational knowledge, exposing them to acceptable role models in a wider range of occupations than their family background has done.

The HEAR curriculum focuses on the occupational fields of health and government and on 18 occupations within those fields that are projected to expand over the next 10 years, with 18 additional slides of people in nontraditional occupations. These units divide into three sections: learning about oneself, the world of work, and decisions. HEAR, part of a larger articulated program for elementary and high school students (K–12), is effective in reducing occupational sex stereotypes for occupations chosen by students in grades 7–9. Expressed interest in an occupation is evidence of desirable behavioral change.

The importance of the Title IX prohibition of sex-segregated home economics and industrial arts courses was supported by the research of Wirtenberg (1979). She compared seventh-grade girls and boys who were required to take coeducational home economics and industrial arts courses (called practical arts) with girls who were required to take sex-segregated (girls only) home economics and with boys who were required to take sex-segregated (boys only) industrial arts. Results indicated that females in the coed practical arts courses increased their sense of competence in a wide variety of traditionally male activities and skills, attributed more traditionally male personality characteristics to themselves (for example, being logical), and indicated a greater interest in activities and occupations in nontraditional areas, compared to the girls who took only home economics. Results were analogous for the boys on measures assessing changes in traditionally male and female personality characteristics, interests, and competencies.

The surprising part of these results, however, was that the differences between the two groups were already evident within two weeks of the school year, and overall differences could almost entirely be attributed to the beginning year differences that resulted merely from being placed in these separate tracks. Although there were still more differences at the end of the year, the potential additional benefits that could have ensued from the actual course content itself were never manifested (Wirtenberg, 1979).

When Wirtenberg looked for possible explanations of these findings, she found considerable evidence of sex role stereotyping within the coed classes, which may have mitigated the impact of the course. Wirtenberg concluded that while there are significant benefits from legislating and enforcing the sex desegregation of home economics and practical arts, it is not enough merely to open up previously all-boys' industrial arts classes to girls, or open up previously all-girls' home economics classes to boys.

The Practical Arts Program was identified by Harrison (1980) as one with potential for enhancing males' and females' sense of competence in relation to nontraditional roles. This program provides coeducational classes in both home economics and industrial arts at the eighth-grade level. One of its goals is to enhance females' self-sufficiency around the home by teaching them skills in repairing electrical equipment, plumbing, and carpentry, in addition to home economics. Another goal is to enhance males' self-sufficiency around the home by teaching them skills in child care, sewing, laundry, nutrition, and cooking, in addition to industrial arts. Teachers for these courses are a coeducational team committed to sex equity, who model nontraditional behaviors.

Curricular materials developed with funding support from the Women's Educational Equity Act are also available for middle school. One such package is *Connections: Women and Work Skills for Good Jobs*, containing activities organized around career preparation for nontraditional jobs.

High School Programs and Products. The first four sex equity issues are relevant for high school students: (1) to decrease occupational and homemaking stereotypes, (2) to facilitate the development of a positive self-concept, (3) to enhance problem-solving and decision-making skills relating to career choice, and (4) to increase student enrollment in vocational courses nontraditional for their sex.

We found only one high school program focused primarily on reducing sex role stereotyping (issue 1) with supporting evidence that it worked: *Women in Nontraditional Careers (WINC)* (Northwest Regional Educational Laboratory, 1980). WINC was conducted in high schools in Portland, Oregon during the years 1979–1980 for 120 young women. The one-semester program successfully increased participants' understanding of the way sex role stereotyping limits women's career planning and preparation. Participants also had more flexible career and life plans when they finished the program compared to the control group. The program's final report contains useful recommendations and excellent qualitative descriptions potentially useful to persons interested in establishing similar programs that could be expanded to include men.

Harrison (1980) identified the Career Internship Program from West Nyack, New York, as a program that enhanced adolescents' sense of competence and independence (issue 2) and that also focused on life-planning skills (issue 3). On a voluntary basis, 8th-, 11th-, and 12th-grade students signed up for a career internship, which involved working in 1 of approximately 25 local nontraditional work sites. Student evaluations of their work experience indicated that a majority acquired an increased sense of competence in the field of work entered. To the extent that adolescents gain experience in high school in nontraditional fields, experience that enhances their sense of competence as well as their life planning skills, this program contributes to advancing sex equity.

Among federally funded and JDRP-approved career education programs, the *Experience-based Career Education* programs (EBCE) for vocational education students in high school provide effective work experience to students who might otherwise not have obtained such training. These programs practice sex-fairness by encouraging both females and males to train in nontraditional work places, by teaching decision-making and life-planning skills, and by facilitating development of a positive self-concept (issues 2, 3, and 4). Anderson (1978) has provided a useful description of increases in sex-fairness for EBCE projects in Nebraska, the state of Washington, Illinois, Virginia, Michigan, and North Carolina.

The Girl Scouts of America have developed sex equity career education materials for Senior Scouts, grades 7 through 12. Their program, *From Dreams to Reality,* helps adolescents develop their skills and abilities in order to make effective career choices. The four-part program includes an activity book, a deck of career cards, a leader's guide, and a council guide. These materials have been rated "superior" by the National Education Association.

Curricular materials were created for high school students with funding support from the Women's Educational Equity Act (WEAA Publishing Center, 1982). One example, *Options: A Curriculum Development Program for Rural High School Students,* develops career and life-planning skills. Students who used these materials made more gains in knowledge and skills associated with effective career planning and chose significantly more nontraditional careers than control group students using the regular home economics curriculum.

Tittle (1981) has added a new dimension to career education and counseling that offers promise for enhancing life-planning skills for female adolescents. To the set of work values identified by Katz (1973) she added marriage and parenthood values. These values are potentially useful in career education programs for adolescents because they permit educators and counselors to identify students' sex-traditional and -nontraditional occupational values, then relate these to developmental needs. Females with sex-traditional occupational values, Tittle suggested, can be assisted in differentiating the value "helping others" as it applies to marriage, family, and work settings. Females with nontraditional occupational values, Tittle found, have surprisingly traditional values related to marriage. She suggested that educators and counselors explore with students whether their values are based on others' expectations or on their own.

Farmer et al. (1981) have developed a product for high school students whose purpose is to increase the likelihood that adolescents consider their home-related values and commitments when they engage in career planning. Students who use the materials are led to consider the role of cooperation as well as competition in achievement and the effect of success in a career on relationships with others. The product was developed over a 5-year period with more than 4,000 adolescents, representative of rural, urban, and inner city locations, in the state of Illinois. The materials were found to be valid for students in that they accurately identified home- and career-related values and interests that influenced students' career motivation.

Changes in student enrollment in vocational courses nontraditional for their sex arc scldom the result of only one program strategy; more often, they are the result of many. The impact of each strategy on the final results—enrollment and eventual placement in employment—is difficult to weigh. A study of Florida secondary schools examined program elements in 21 schools that had been most successful in achieving nontraditional enrollments and in 21 that had been least successful (Becker & Cole, 1980). Six elements were identified that were present in the schools most successful at reducing sex stereotyping in classes: (1) textbooks and teaching materials that were revised to eliminate sex bias, (2) student handbooks that were revised to eliminate sex bias, (3) facilities that were adapted to both sexes, (4) course recruitment activities, (5) unbiased teaching, and (6) vocational student organizations that were an important part of the curriculum.

FACET/FACIT (Female Access to Careers in Engineering/Industrial Technology), at Trident Technical College, South Carolina, addressed the need for both recruitment activities and support services in order to encourage more women to earn an associate degree in engineering or industrial technology (AIR, 1979). Designed originally for high school girls, the program was expanded to include an aggressive recruitment campaign to attract both girls and women to special courses introducing the technical fields. The major recruitment strategy used throughout the community involved showing films depicting women of all ages as technology students, engineers, technicians, and other nontraditional workers. Brochure illustrations also featured women in these roles. Graduates of the courses were encouraged to apply to the regular introductory technology programs at the college. Support services for those who did enroll included counseling, tutoring in English and math, extra help from faculty, and monthly "nurture groups" for discussions with women from the faculty and from industry.

During the summers of 1978, 1979, and 1980, approximately 180 high school girls participated in the free Introduction to Engineering Technology course at Trident Technical College. Those who needed to also took a refresher course in mathematics or algebra. Of this group, approximately 70% indicated they would probably continue their education in engineering or engineering technology. Female enrollment in the industrial programs rose from 2% in 1977 to 6% in 1980. In the 1-year engineering technology programs, the enrollment increased from 7% in 1977 to 20% in 1980. Graduates of these technology programs generally can expect to earn far more than the graduates of typically female-oriented programs in business and allied health.

Programs described in this section provide evidence of success in addressing issues 1–4 in high schools and community colleges. Most programs addressed issue 1 by providing opportunities to reduce stereotypes through experience with sex-fair counseling and nontraditional training. Project WINC provided evidence of gains for females who increased their work-related skills, learned decision-making strategies to help them plan for combining home and work roles, and obtained work experience in nontraditional work settings. EBCE programs in five states were found to have increased work-related and decision-making skills for females. Increases in enrollments in nontraditional courses were found in high schools and community colleges where there was a concerted effort to recruit, provide support services, and adapt facilities. We turn now to a discussion of evidence of changes in educators and related personnel in their attitudes and practices (issue 5).

Educator and Community Programs and Products (issue 5). BORN FREE is a program for teachers, counselors, and administrators designed to help them examine the influence of sex role stereotyping on their own career and the ways it inhibits career opportunities for both sexes. Among the major BORN FREE products are three field-tested training packets for educators at the elementary, secondary, and postsecondary/higher education levels. Designed for use by those who accept the seriousness of the sex role stereotyping problem, the packets consist of a variety of cognitive and experiential learning activities, including simulation, role plays, readings and discussions, videotapes and films, self-evaluations, and introspective exercises. Some packets are built around nine 30-minute videotapes; others focus on institutional change. These packets include a summary review of the literature, a fact pack, selected resources, guidelines for workshop leaders, and extensive references, all of which make them self-contained and convenient to use in workshops lasting from a half-day to 2 weeks. The strategies and packets have been validated through field testing, and many of the learning experiences have gone through two or three revisions (Warsett, 1978).

Other products for educators, such as Equals, and Multiplying Options and Subtracting Bias (both described in chapter 13), help teachers and counselors, K–12, develop awareness of mathematics avoidance among females and realize the importance of mathematics in broadening career options.

Employer-based Career Education programs (Ronald Bucknam, personal communication, May 1982) have focused sex equity efforts on inservice training for vocational education teachers. Their goal is to increase teacher awareness of sex equity issues in career development in order to make teachers' attitudes more sex-fair and to increase teachers' sex equity behaviors.

State coordinators for sex equity in vocational education have been appointed throughout the United States since the Vocational Education Act was revised in 1976. Most have spent the $50,000 set-aside monies for this position and for the conduct of 10 related responsibilities. The primary activity of the state coordinators for vocational education has been to conduct workshops and inservice training for administrators, counselors, and teachers (U.S. Department of Education, 1981). Several states have trained regional sex equity trainers who are then available to local school district staff for technical assistance in their sex equity efforts. They have used some of the products and programs developed primarily for teachers, counselors, and administrators to help prepare them for conducting sex-equitable career and vocational education training sessions.

Project MOVE (Maximize Options in Vocational Education), a statewide graduate course in New York focusing on secondary-level staff attitudes, knowledge, and behaviors related to sex equity, includes a preassessment of those factors (Farris, 1983). The course provides educators with up-to-date information about changes in the work force and the family and trains them to help adolescents develop realistic expectations of these two future roles. During training, the educators develop, carry out, and evaluate a variety of activities and projects designed to eliminate sex discrimination and stereotyping within their professional settings. Classroom teaching behaviors, as reported by students of the participant teachers, became significantly more sex-fair. On follow-up surveys, participants reported not only observable increases in their schools' attention to sex equity policies and practices but also increases in nontraditional enrollment in their particular subject area. Students in coed classes rated their teachers as more sex-fair than teachers of all-male or all-female classes. Changing sex-segregated classes to coed classes increased sex-fair teacher behavior.

Other recommended curricular materials for educators, counselors, and administrators developed with funding support from the Women's Educational Equity Act are It's Her Future, for parents; New Pioneers: A Program to Expand Sex-Role Expectation in Elementary and Secondary Education, for teachers and counselors; Freedom for Individual Development: Vocational Education, for teachers; and Freedom for Individual Development: Counseling and Guidance, for counselors.

Revision of counseling procedures and practices has been initiated in many schools. This involves the use of new sex-fair materials and tests (see chapter 10), new counseling strategies such as peer counseling, and actively promoting consideration of nontraditional careers. Vocational educators are working more closely with counseling staff and taking more responsibility for encouraging or recruiting nontraditional students. The need to develop support services (for example, day care, prevocational classes, job development, special counseling, and remedial instruction) to assist nontraditional students and to meet the special needs of certain students is also being met in some schools.

The Vocational Education Equity Study by the American Institutes for Research looked at promising programs and strategies for achieving sex equity in vocational education (AIR, 1979). The study noted that an essential feature of all such programs was a realization that simply stating that all occupational training areas were open to both sexes was not enough. Actual involvement in these programs and direct support of nontraditional enrollees was needed in order to achieve equity.

In summary, the programs described in this section provide important training for educational personnel in sex equity related to career development and changing family roles, and provide information on the response to issue 5. Most programs or activities focused on increasing awareness of educators, counselors, and administrators with respect to sex equity in career development and vocational education. Some programs, for example, Project MOVE, also included awareness training related to changing family roles. MOVE reported changes in teacher behavior in the classroom as a result of training and experience with coed classes, formerly sex-segregated. Counselors' use of sex-fair career development tests and materials in the schools is becoming more the norm as a result of combined sex equity efforts.

POLICY RECOMMENDATIONS

1. There should be increased efforts to make the public aware of the provisions of the Title IX regulations which are directly relevant to career and vocational education and to enforce these regulations. For example, many were not aware of the extensive sex segregation of the New York City vocational high schools before the FARE Coalition study (Wells, 1983) or that it was illegal for a school district in Pennsylvania to require girls to take 9 weeks of shop and 27 weeks of home economics while the boys were required to take 9 weeks of home economics and 27 weeks of shop (Wells).

2. The recommendations of the National Coalition for Women and Girls in Education on strengthening the federal and state roles in overcoming sex discrimination and sex stereotyping in all vocational education programs (Wells) should be incorporated in the planned revision of the Vocational Education Act. In summary they include:
    —Retaining the objectives to overcome sex discrimination and sex stereotyping, the provision of at least $50,000 per year of federal support to employ someone to work full time promoting sex equity in vocational education, data collection by race and sex, and requirements for appropriate representation of women and minorities on state advisory councils.
    —Requiring states to use federal vocational education funds for fewer purposes than in the past but particularly to enhance opportunities for women in vocational education, including the preparation for nontraditional careers, desirable support services, and needed R&D.

3. We recommend that states and accrediting institutions establish policies that mandate sex equity training and competence for all educators involved in counseling and in career and vocational education. Teachers and counselors should be expected to change their behaviors as well as their perceptions, attitudes, and interests as they relate to sex stereotyping.

4. We recommend that federal funding be provided for R&D to promote sex equity in career and vocational education activities and that implementation

funds be provided school districts to be used to evaluate the effectiveness of their sex equity activities in these areas.

Recommendations for Schools

1. At the elementary school level, emphasis on reducing occupational and homemaking stereotypes should be continued (issue 1). The evidence presented indicates that sex-equitable programs can change students' beliefs and attitudes, but little evidence has been provided that indicates changes in their personal interests in nontraditional behaviors and skills. We recommend support for coed programs which provide students with experience in nontraditional behaviors and skills. These experiences may provide the basis for personal interest in these behaviors and for more gender-free career choices at a later age.

2. At the middle school level, we recommend that educators take advantage of the fluid quality of this developmental stage and require both boys and girls to take coeducational and sex-equitable home economics and industrial arts classes. During this period, exploration of a wide range of work- and home-related experiences is desirable. Such experiences provide the basis for a sense of competence and self-esteem (issue 2) necessary for making wise choices in high school and beyond.

3. At the high school level we recommend that all students take a required course in career and life planning (issue 3). This course would not only teach decision-making skills but would also provide the basis for planning ahead to combine home and work roles.

4. For vocational education students in high school, we recommend provision of the support services necessary for increased enrollments in nontraditional classes (issue 4). Such support services include orientation of students to nontraditional training options, as well as supportive behaviors by teachers and students of the opposite sex toward students who represent a minority within these classes. Special attention to increasing enrollment of females in industrial and technical training courses should be given, since gains for females have been weakest here. Special attention should also be given to increasing enrollment of males in occupational home economics for the same reason.

5. With a curriculum that encourages boys and girls to learn more about nontraditional occupations and behaviors, teachers and counselors should be careful not to discourage students from choosing the more traditional occupations and behaviors. To truly expand life options is to increase students' freedom to choose based on interest rather than on gender or social class.

6. An additional concern for educators should be whether the career education materials are representative of a broad range of social classes and minorities. Materials are frequently focused on white middle-class students, to the exclusion of poor and minority students. Increasing life options for all students may require a different curriculum for the person growing up in

poverty or coming from an environment with different values and customs.

7. In line with our focus on sex equity as it relates to human development, we urge educators to choose activities for their students that are most appropriate to their stage of development and that incorporate both life/home and career planning. Curricula for older students should logically build on earlier content. Some programs reviewed included a focus on decision-making during the middle school years. Super (1980) found that most students were not ready to make career choices before their senior year in high school, and many college-bound students were not ready then. Decision-making skills can be taught from elementary school on, but curricula should avoid pressure to choose a particular occupation.

Research Recommendations

1. Research should be designed to compare different approaches to achieving sex equity goals. We need to know, for example, whether programs offered for one semester are as effective in reducing stereotypes as those offered for a full year or longer. Are programs that combine discussion with experiential learning more or less effective in reducing stereotypes than either approach used alone (issue 1)? When and how can student interests and behaviors related to careers be most influenced? What kinds of role models are most effective for increasing interest in nontraditional work and family behaviors? Is single-sex instruction in career and vocational education ever desirable?

2. We need research that focuses on the generalizability of findings; for example, whether or not students who take nontraditional courses in high school choose nontraditional careers later on (issue 4). It would also be interesting, in this regard, to separate high school students participating in nontraditional courses into two groups: those with special aptitude for these courses compared to those with average or less aptitude. These groups could then be followed up to see if a greater proportion of those with high aptitude choose nontraditional careers, compared to those with average or less aptitude. Such a comparison would permit a more precise evaluation of the effect of experience in nontraditional training on equity.

3. It may be argued, as Johnston and Ettema (1982) do, that changes in interests may be desirable mainly for persons who have aptitudes for certain activities but have formerly avoided them because they viewed these behaviors as inappropriate for their sex—for example, mechanical activities for girls, nurturant activities for boys. Researchers are encouraged to follow Johnston and Ettema's suggestion and evaluate change in interests for persons with relevant aptitudes.

4. As changes are introduced into the school system, research must monitor the desired sex equity outcomes such as those outlined in our five issues. We need longitudinal studies to assess the progress of students who have been

exposed to various degrees of sex-equitable education, after they leave the school system and enter the labor market.

5. Gottfredson's theory of career development outlined at the beginning of this chapter formed the basis for our view of goal setting in career and vocational education. This theory itself needs reexamination of its adequacy in describing the career development of succeeding generations. In our world of rapidly changing environments, personal values, and needs, we require a dynamic view of theory, one that evolves with changing environments and needs. What is true in one decade may not describe the situation in the next.

In this concluding section on research, recommendations have emphasized the need for studies that assess the effects of equity changes on the adult roles and life satisfactions of the participants. This is a particularly relevant emphasis for a chapter on career and vocational education, a field that prepares children and young persons for their adult roles in the workplace.

REFERENCES

American Institutes for Research. (1978). *Career education effectiveness* (report written for U.S. Office of Education, Office of Career Education). Palo Alto, CA: Author.

American Institutes for Research. (1979). *The vocational education equity study, Vol. 3: Case studies and promising approaches* (report written for U.S. Office of Education). Palo Alto, CA: Author.

Anderson, N. (1978). *Past and future directions: Northwest Regional Educational Laboratory's 1978 Experience-based Career Education Conference.* Portland: Northwest Regional Educational Laboratory.

Becker, W. J., & Cole, J. M. (1980). *Reduction of sex stereotyping in vocational education programs* (final report, July 1, 1979–June 30, 1980). Gainesville, FL: University of Florida.

Card, J., Steel, L., & Abeles, R. (1980). Sex differences in realization of individual potential for achievement. *Journal of Vocational Behavior, 17,* 1–21.

Cohen, J. (1977). *Statistical power analysis for the behavioral sciences* (2nd ed.). New York: Academic Press.

Farmer, H. (1978). What inhibits achievement and career motivation in women? In L. Harmon, L. Fitzgerald, J. Birk, & M. Tanney (Eds.), *Counseling Women* (pp. 159–172). Monterey, CA: Brooks Cole.

Farmer, H. (1983). Career and homemaking for high school youth. *Journal of Counseling Psychology, 30,* 40–45.

Farmer, H., with Keane, J., Rooney, G., Vispoel, W., Harmon, L., Lerner, B., Linn, R., & Maehr, M. (1981). *Career motivation achievement planning: C-MAP.* (A measure and administrator's manual available from the first author at the University of Illinois, Department of Educational Psychology, 1310 South Sixth St., Champaign, IL, 61820.)

Farris, C. (1982). *Sex fair knowledge, attitudes, and behaviors of vocational educators: A research report.* Utica: SUNY College of Technology.

Fitzgerald, L., & Crites, J. (1980). Toward a career psychology of women: What do we know? What do we need to know? *Journal of Counseling Psychology, 27,* 44–62.

Goldstein, B., & Oldham, J. (1979). *Children and work: A study of socialization.* New Brunswick, NJ: Transaction Books.

Gottfredson, L. (1981). Circumscription and compromise: A developmental theory of occupational aspirations. *Journal of Counseling Psychology, 28,* 545–579.

Hansen, L. S. (1978). Promoting female growth through a career development curriculum. In L. S. Hansen & R. S. Rapoza (Eds.), *Career development and counseling of women* (pp. 425–442). Springfield, IL: Charles C. Thomas.

Harmon, L. W. (1978). Career counseling for women. In L. S. Hansen & R. S. Rapoza (Eds.), *Career development and counseling of women* (pp. 443–453). Springfield, IL: Charles C. Thomas.

Harrison, L. (1980). Sex-stereotyping programs. In American Institutes for Research (Ed.), *Programs to combat stereotyping in career choice.* Washington, DC: U.S. Office of Education.

Johnston, J., & Ettema, J. (1982). *Positive images: Breaking stereotypes with children's television.* Beverly Hills: Sage.

Katz, M. (1973). Career decision making: A computer-based system of interactive guidance and information (SIGI). *Proceedings of the 1973 ERS Invitational Conference.* Princeton, NJ: Educational Testing Service.

Northwest Regional Educational Laboratory. (1980). *Women in nontraditional careers* (WINC) (final report). Portland: author. Project Equality. (1979). Highline School District, 15675 Ambaum Blvd., Seattle, WA 98166.

Project Freestyle. (1978). Los Angeles County Education Center, 9300 East Imperial Highway, Los Angeles, CA 90242.

Project HEAR. (1980). Cogent Associates, 306 Alexander St., Princeton, NJ 08540.

Project Opening the Doors. (1979). Cogent Associates, 306 Alexander St., Princeton, NJ 08540.

Richardson, M. S. (1979). Toward an expanded view of careers. *Counseling Psychologist, 8,* 34–35.

Rosenberg, M. (1979). *Conceiving the self.* New York: Basic Books.

Rosenberg, M., & Rosenberg, F. (1982). The occupational self: A developmental study. In M. Lynch, A. Norem-Hebeisen, & K. J. Gergen (Eds.), *Self-concept research.* New York: Ballinger.

Super, D. (1980). A life-span, life-space approach to career development. *Journal of Vocational Behavior, 16,* 282–298.

Tallmadge, G. K. (1977). *The Joint Dissemination Review Panel ideabook.* Washington, DC: U.S. Government Printing Office.

Tanney, F., & Birk, J. (1976). Women counselors for women clients: A review of the research. *Counseling Psychologist, 6,* 28–32.

Tittle, C. (1981). *Careers and family: Sex roles and adolescent life plans.* Beverly Hills, CA: Sage.

U.S. Department of Education. (1981). *The Vocational Education Study* (final report, Pub. No. 8). Washington, DC: National Institute of Education.

Van den Daele, L. (1968). A developmental study of the ego-ideal. *Genetic Psychology Monographs, 78,* 191–256.

Warsett, S. (1978). Evaluation report on BORN FREE videotapes, training packets, and selected workshops (Tech. Rep. 9). Minneapolis, MN: University of Minnesota, Project BORN FREE.

Wells, J. (1983). *Statement of the National Coalition for Women and Girls in Education.* Washington, DC: National Coalition for Women and Girls in Education.

Wirtenberg, T. J. (1979). *Expanding girls' occupational potential: A case study of the implementation of Title IX's anti-sex-segregation provision in seventh grade practical arts.* Unpublished doctoral dissertation, University of California, Los Angeles.

Women's Educational Equity Act Publishing Center. (1982). *Resources for educational equity: 1981–1982 catalog.* Newton, MA: Education Development Center.

PART V

Sex Equity Strategies
for Specific Populations

Saundra Rice Murray

Previous sections examined sex equity in education primarily from the perspective of gender-based variation. The chapters in this part have a different focus: important characteristics that distinguish populations of women and girls. There is a host of such characteristics—from age to disability to religion to economic status. We will, however, examine issues and answers for special populations whose sex equity needs have been highlighted in recent years: minority women, rural women, gifted women, and adult women.

For these populations, descriptions of issues and answers should include data on each of the elements in the conceptual framework for this book. Our knowledge of women and girls in special populations is so limited, however, that a comprehensive approach is unrealistic. For example, hundreds of studies on the education of the minority child have been conducted (see Weinberg, 1977). but the bulk have involved only black-white comparisons. Sex differences have often been ignored and, when found, may be inconsistent across studies. Studies of women and girls in Hispanic, Asian-American, Pacific American, and Native American populations are extremely few in number.

Moreover, scholars and educational practitioners have criticized much of the research for its (1) inattention to the historical, cultural, and current environmental contexts of special populations; (2) inappropriate comparisons to values and norms of middle-class whites (and, in the case of white girls and women, inappropriate comparisons to white men and boys); (3) failure to consider variation within special populations; (4) inappropriate application of instruments; and (5) premature reliance on quantitative approaches to research. The reader may wish to examine critiques of research on adult women (for example, Barnett & Baruch, 1981; Safilios-Rothschild, 1979); on minority women (Lightfoot, 1977; Lott, 1980); and overviews of issues concerning disability, sex, and race (Odintz & Ellis, 1982); Council of Chief State School Officers, 1983).

Much remains to be accomplished in developing an adequate base of information on special populations. As the chapters in this section will show, however, progress has been made in identifying and documenting problems and possible solutions.

In the chapter on minority women, Lewis and her coauthors view sex inequity in education as an extension of the inequity that minorities experience in all American institutions. This pervasive inequity is reflected in negative stereotyping, wherein the stereotypes associated with gender are compounded by stereotypes of race or ethnicity, a view of minority women as a monolithic population with equally monolithic concerns and needs, and the relatively low educational attainment and earnings of subgroups of minority women. Consequently, the authors advocate a multidimensional approach to the achievement of parity. The approach includes a recognition of the different characteristics of the groups that are labeled "minority" women (that is, Asian- and Pacific American, Hispanic, Afro-American, and Indian) as well as an emphasis on priorities common to each group, such as (1) delineation of issues regarding sex equity in education, using historical and theoretical contexts appropriate to the group in question; and (2) the development of a data base of research on minority women.

Gordon and Addison's chapter on gifted women traces the history of the definition of gifted females from Terman's study of intellectual genius, conducted in 1919, to recent studies that have both defined giftedness in many domains and suggested that mechanisms other than standardized tests could be appropriately used to identify gifted students. Most considerations of the gifted, however, focus on academic and intellectual activities and the processes through which gifted students are identified and developed. As the authors point out, the identification process may result in inequitable treatment and outcomes for gifted boys and girls, but there is little research on sex differences relative to teacher nomination, use of multiple assessments, and other procedures. Data pertaining to educational programs, career education, and guidance for the gifted girl are more extensive and suggest specific strategies that should be considered by teachers, counselors, and other educators.

Rosenfeld's chapter discusses rural women and girls, a population whose educational needs received little attention in the literature until the mid-1970s. Rosenfeld notes that a unique set of conditions must be considered in discussions about ways to promote equity for this population. Among them are conservatism concerning family roles, religion, and work; low population density; and geographic and social isolation. While such conditions contribute to inequities in education (isolation, for example, reduces women's access to economic and educational opportunities), special circumstances can provide advantages. Thus, the relatively small enrollments of rural schools may have contributed to the greater participation of rural girls, when compared to urban girls, in athletics.

Ekstrom and Marvel discuss four subgroups of adult women: reentry women, displaced homemakers, employed women, and older/retired women. Each of these subgroups faces barriers in its efforts to upgrade skills and status through education. Among them are institutional barriers such as admissions practices and instructor-student interactions that reflect age and sex stereotypes; situational barriers, including geographic location and race; and personal barriers, such as poor self-esteem and conflict over sex roles. Educational programs for adult women, however, have been geared primarily to reentry women and displaced homemakers. Such programs are extremely diverse; they range from Continuing Education for Women (CEW) programs, which have explored ways to make existing educational services accessible and inviting to general populations of adult women, to special programs emphasizing service for women facing crises in their lives, or experiences (such as internships) that prepare women for specific jobs or careers. The authors provide rich descriptions of the full array of programs and note that program evaluations and an increased focus on career preparation are critical needs for the future.

Despite the considerable variation in emphasis and content among the chapters in this section, common themes occur. For example, access to educational opportunities, long-term consequences of inequity, and extent of sex stereotyping are salient issues for each of the special populations considered here.

Employment is also a central concern. As the authors of the chapters on rural, minority, and adult women point out, women in these populations are often concentrated in occupations that are of low remuneration and low prestige. Also, when compared to other groups of women and to men, women in special populations are often found at the bottom of the income ladder. The remedies for sex inequity reflect concerns about this dismal picture, and many programs attempt to upgrade skills, expand participants' knowledge about labor market conditions and options, and channel women into nontraditional occupations. For gifted girls, the emphasis is future-oriented and pertains to ways of assuring access to programs that are math- and science-based.

These and other topics presented in the next four chapters suggest the complexity of the problem for special populations associated with achieving sex equity in and through education. Adequate discussion of concerns and practices for the groups we consider here—and other groups that deserve recognition— would require many volumes and encompass such issues as the low priority given to women in special populations when resources for research and programs are scarce; the application of sex-equitable strategies to the needs of males in special populations; and the problems and conflicts teachers face as they attempt to respond equitably to students with diverse special needs. This section is intended as a basis for further exploration of key issues and programs.

REFERENCES

Barnett, R. C., & Baruch, G. K. (1981). Women in the middle years: A critique of research and theory. In S. Cox (Ed.), *Female psychology: The emerging self* (pp. 283–291). New York: St. Martin's.

Council of Chief State School Officers, Resource Center on Sex Equity. (1983). A concern about . . . sex equitable education for disabled students. *Concerns*, No. 9.

Lightfoot, S. L. (1977). Socialization and education of young black girls in schools. In *Conference on the Educational and Occupational Needs of Black Women: Compendium* (Vol. 2, pp. 3–29). (National Institute of Education). Washington, DC: U.S. Government Printing Office.

Lott, J. T. (1980). Some thoughts on the social research of social minorities: Pacific and Asian-American women and education. In *Conference on the Educational and Occupational Needs of Asian-Pacific-American Women: August 24 and 25, 1976* (pp. 9–16). Washington, DC: National Institute of Education.

Safilios-Rothschild, C. (1979). *Sex role socialization and sex discrimination: A synthesis and critique of the literature.* Washington, DC: National Institute of Education.

Odintz, M. F., & Ellis, D. E. (1982). *Disability, sex, and race issues in educational equity: A review of current literature.* Washington, DC: Disability Rights Education and Defense Fund.

Weinberg, M. (1977). *Minority students: A research appraisal.* Washington, DC: National Institute of Education.

19
Achieving Sex Equity
for Minority Women

Shelby Lewis,
with Owanah Anderson, Lucie Cheng,
Arlene Fong Craig, Njeri Jackson,
Isabella Jenkins, Barbara Jones,
Saundra Rice Murray, Marge Rosensweig,
Patricia Bell Scott, and Bonnie Wallace

Educational systems reflect the values and practices of the larger society. If the larger society is sexist, racist, and based on economic, cultural, and historical inequities, it is unrealistic to expect educational systems to be devoid of these inequities. Educational systems, after all, are the formal, institutionalized, systematized vehicles through which the larger society socializes youth to the values held by the dominant or ruling group.

These dominant values are reinforced by the electronic and print media, the economic, political, and religious systems, and the cultural and historical milieu within which society's members live. As a consequence, individuals and groups are constantly presented with messages that applaud, rationalize, legitimize, justify, and reward racism, sexism, and economic bias (Lewis, 1977; Anderson, 1982). When all of these formal and informal systems are taken together, one finds that education is a process that permeates all aspects of an individual's life. Therefore, defining the very narrow dimension of the formal educational system as the arena within which a struggle for equity is concentrated raises strategic as well as theoretical questions.

We will suggest in this chapter that alternative theoretical constructs must be developed for measuring, evaluating, and linking the causes, relationships, and consequences of inequity in the various dimensions of society. A multidimensional rather than a unidimensional approach to the problem of equity seems appropriate. In order to achieve total equity, strategies needed to bring about equity in one dimension (for example, sex equity in education) must be coordinated with strategies for ending inequity in other dimensions of society. Clearly, mirrors of society such as educational institutions will continue to reflect the attitudes and values held by the larger society. An integrated and coordinated

The authors gratefully acknowledge the assistance of Maria Elena Pynn and Pauline Tsui.

365

struggle against those interlinked inequities that oppress us all would seem to be an appropriate response to multidimensional inequity.

The perspective and approach of this chapter come from a consideration of educational and sex equity priorities of minority women. Although such priorities often differ from those of majority women and sometimes differ among the various groups of minority women, the educational priorities of most minority women are similar. These priorities tend to be broad-based; they link the goal of sex equity with the goals of liberation, survival, and equity for the total target group and sometimes for oppressed people on a global scale. Moreover, minority women tend to consider various forms of inequity when attempting to achieve equity in a given arena; they do not readily isolate racial, ethnic, cultural, economic, or sex inequity (Stone, 1979; Hull, Scott, & Smith, 1982). Sex inequity is viewed by minority women as part of and a logical consequence of the inequitable nature of American society (Stone, 1979; Lewis, 1980; Lindsay, 1979).

It is important to provide a theoretical and historical context for viewing the multidimensional approach to achieving sex equity in education. We do this in this chapter by first examining statistically and analytically the characteristics of Asian-American, Native American, African-American, and Hispanic-American women in order to determine their similarities and differences. We then review the literature on minority women to determine the issues that are important to them. From an analysis of how they confront these issues we extract and discuss their priorities among different kinds of equity. The discussion of priorities leads to an exploration of minority women's approaches to achieving sex equity in education. Finally, we offer suggestions and recommendations geared toward achieving greater awareness and understanding of the multidimensional needs and priorities of minority women.

DIFFERENTIAL CHARACTERISTICS
OF MINORITY WOMEN

A widespread and erroneous notion is that minority women form a cohesive, relatively homogeneous subgroup in the American population. The data presented in this section should dispel that notion and provide a framework for a multidimensional approach to sex equity for minority women.

Cultural Background

Minority women come from a variety of backgrounds. They represent all continents, come in all colors, shapes, and sizes, and speak a multitude of languages. Within the broad subgroupings discussed in this chapter there are significant differences, which may range as widely as differences in origin, language, geographical location, race, ideology, ethnicity, and cultural background. Scholars, educators, and activists have frequently pointed out that it is grossly misleading to think of Asian-Americans as an ethnically homogeneous group (U.S. Commission on Civil Rights, 1979). However, due to their numbers and geographic area of origin, various groups continue to be identified together as Asian-Americans. While such an identity has historical and social roots and is often a political necessity, there is also a tendency to mask the tremendous variations in culture, economic status, and generational differences among the many ethnic groups from Asia. The more recent immigrant Asian groups such as the Filipinos, the Koreans, the Indians, and the Vietnamese are often short-changed by virtue of being lumped together with the Chinese and the Japanese— groups that themselves are quite different from each other and that have developed through the years adaptive mechanisms and institutions as well as political experience.

The situation is further complicated by the fact that some older groups, notably the Chinese, are characterized by significant waves of immigration (pre-World War I, post-1945, and post-1965), each having distinctive social features including differences in language, economic status, and political persuasion. Therefore, to discuss sex equity in education for Asian-American women we must first recognize the diversity that exists among them.

Hispanic-American women are of different races, religions, and countries of origin. They come from South America, Puerto Rico, Cuba, Central America, the Caribbean, and Mexico. They represent different classes, educational levels, and ideologies. Some are recent immigrants, and others have histories in this country that are older than the founding of the United States. The Hispanic language is not sufficient to bridge the gap between Mexican-Americans from California, Cuban-Americans from Florida, and Puerto Ricans from New York. The Hispanic-American label masks differences that have consequences for sex equity in education for women in this subgroup of minority women (Joseph, 1980; Geoffrey, 1976).

Variations among African-American women are also significant. Some are Hispanic; others, like Haitian women, are French-speaking; and some come from other Caribbean islands with still different cultures. Some are southern daughters of slaves, and some are from urban environments in the north. They represent different classes, different educational and political perspectives, and different religions. Some African-American women are from families that trace their lineage back to a period well before the Mayflower, and some are recent immigrants from the African continent. These differences between and among African-American women determine in many ways the priorities of various subgroups and significantly affect the effectiveness of sex equity in education programs (Rodgers-Rose, 1980).

It might be incorrect to label Native Americans as a single ethnic group. The Sioux, Apache, Iroquois, and so forth represent historical nations of people with distinct ethnic, political, linguistic, and social differences. Over 400 separate nations lived in this country hundreds of years before it was known as the United States, and before the media, folklore, music, and literature depicted them as an undifferentiated ethnic group. Diet, language, territory, political institutions, physical appearance, family systems, values, and belief systems of the various "Indian" nations are overlooked when these populations are treated as a homogeneous subgroup (Farb, 1968; Butterfield, 1980; Green, 1980). The differences that exist among Native American women must be considered when designing sex equity programs for them.

Size and Geographical Distribution

As shown in table 10, minorities are distributed throughout the United States, but different groups are concentrated in different regions. Blacks, the largest minority group, are concentrated in the South. Fifty-three percent of the 26.4 million blacks lived in the South in 1980. Outside the South, blacks are found in urban areas of other regions. The second largest minority group, Hispanics, comprises 14.6 million persons from various racial groupings. Almost 60% of them are Mexicans who live in the five southwestern states of Arizona, California, Colorado, New Mexico, and Texas. The next largest group, Puerto Ricans, is concentrated in the New York-New Jersey area, and most of the 800,000 Cubans are in Florida.

With the exception of Asian Indians who are spread fairly evenly across the four major regions of the country, the Asian groups (Chinese, Filipinos, Japanese, Koreans, Vietnamese, and others), as well as Native Americans, are concentrated in the West. With the exception of the Vietnamese, these minorities are underrepresented in the South.

Educational Attainment

Levels of schooling vary among and within minority groups. Native Americans have the lowest proportion of their female population completing high school and, with the Puerto Ricans, have the lowest proportion completing college (8 and 4%, respectively). At the other extreme, 99% of Japanese-American women finish high school, and 51% of Filipino women complete college. Table 11 contains a more complete presentation of high school and college completion rates among minority women.

Although Asian and Pacific Asian women have high average levels of schooling, there are subpopulations with very different educational experiences. pan-Asian wives of U.S. servicemen and Indochinese refugees have a median educational level of only 8 years, compared to 12.7 for the total pan-Asian female population (Cooney, 1979). The variation in education among the Hispanic groups is well known. In 1974, over 50% of Cuban women over 25 had high school diplomas, compared with only 25% of Mexican, and 20% of Puerto Rican, women.

The variations in educational attainment discussed in this section are reflected in the employment characteristics and incomes of women from different minority groups.

Table 10.   Distribution of Racial/Ethnic Populations by Regions, United States, 1980

Racial/ethnic group	Population	U.S.	North-east	North Central	South	West
Total population	226,506	100.0	21.7	26.0	33.2	19.0
Total nonwhite	38,165	100.0	17.8	17.5	43.0	21.7
Black	26,488	100.0	18.3	20.1	53.0	8.5
American Indian[a]	1,418	100.0	5.5	17.5	26.2	50.7
Chinese	806	100.0	27.0	9.0	11.2	52.7
Filipinos	775	100.0	9.7	10.3	10.7	69.3
Japanese	701	100.0	6.7	6.3	6.4	80.6
Asian Indian	362	100.0	33.4	23.5	23.1	20.0
Korean	355	100.0	19.2	17.5	19.8	43.4
Vietnamese	262	100.0	9.5	14.0	30.6	45.8
All other nonwhite races	6,998	100.0	19.0	10.0	22.0	49.0
Whites	188,341	100.0	22.5	27.7	31.3	18.5
Spanish Origin[b,c]	14,606	100.0	17.8	8.7	30.6	42.8
Mexican	7,932	100.0	N.A.	N.A.	N.A.	N.A.
Cuban	831	100.0	N.A.	N.A.	N.A.	N.A.
Puerto Rican	1,823	100.0	N.A.	N.A.	N.A.	N.A.
Central or South American	1,022	100.0	N.A.	N.A.	N.A.	N.A.
Other Spanish	1,635	100.0	N.A.	N.A.	N.A.	N.A.

[a]Includes Aleuts and Eskimos.
[b]The regional distribution of persons of Spanish origin is not available; however, the Women's Bureau, *Women of Spanish Origin* (1976) reports that nearly 6 of 10 Spanish-origin women lived in five Southwestern states in March 1974: Arizona, California, Colorado, New Mexico, and Texas. Nine of 10 of them were of Mexican origin. Persons of Puerto Rican origin were concentrated in the New York-New Jersey area, and those of Cuban origin were in Florida. *Source of data: Statistical Abstract of the United States, 1981*, p. 32.
[c]The data for persons of Spanish origin are from a different data set and are not totally consistent with the other data in the table.

Employment Characteristics

Labor market experiences, like education, vary greatly among women from different minority groups. Asian women—Filipinos, Chinese, and Japanese—have the highest labor force participation rates (Cooney, 1979) and the lowest unemployment rates. The unemployment rate for each of these groups was lower than that of white women in 1976. The lowest labor force participation rates in 1970 were among Puerto Ricans and Native Americans. Different from the rate of any other major ethnic group, the rate for Puerto Rican women actually declined between 1950 and 1970.

Labor force participation rates are positively related to earnings and thus to education (Jones, 1976); therefore, it is not surprising that the minority groups

Table 11. Education Patterns for Racial/Ethnic Populations by Sex, 1976

Racial/ethnic group	High school nonattendance[a]	High school completion[b]	College completion[c]
Females	%	%	%
Native Amer./Alaskan Native	15	58	4
Blacks	6	74	11
Mexican-Americans	14	58	5
Japanese-Americans	1	99	35
Chinese-Americans	NA	90	44
Filipino-Americans	10	78	51[d]
Puerto Ricans	16	60	4
Majority	6	86	22
Males			
Native Amer./Alaskan Native	14	70	8
Blacks	7	74	11
Mexican-Americans	11	64	11
Japanese-Americans	2	98	53
Chinese-Americans	NA	88	60
Filipino-Americans	6	81	34
Puerto Ricans	5	68	6
Majority	5	87	34

[a]The percentage of 15-, 16-, and 17-year-olds who were not enrolled in school on April 1.
[b]The percentage of persons from 20 to 24 years of age who have completed 12 or more years of school.
[c]The percentage of persons from 25 to 29 years of age who have completed at least 4 years of college.
[d]The total Filipino population is very small, and pan-Asian scholars suggest that high educational attainment figures result from selective Filipino migration patterns.

Source of data: U.S. Commission on Civil Rights, *Social Indicators of Equality for Minorities and Women* (1978), pp. 10, 12, 14.

with the highest average education among women—Japanese, Chinese, and Filipinos—have the highest labor force participation rates. Those with the lowest average years of schooling—Native Americans, Puerto Ricans, and Mexicans—have the lowest work rates.

Labor force participation, particularly among females, is also related to unemployment rates. And, with the exception of blacks, the groups with the highest unemployment rates had the lowest labor force participation rates. Black women, however, had high work rates in spite of their unemployment rates, which were second only to those of Puerto Rican women in 1976.

Another aspect of employment that varies with education and among minority group women is type of occupation. Minority women workers are less likely than whites to be employed as professionals or managers, the two occupational categories with the greatest prestige and the highest earnings. They are more likely to be employed as service workers; but again, there are variations among groups. About one-third of Hispanic women workers are employed as operatives, compared with only 12% of the total female work force and 16% of black women. Over one-fourth of black and Hispanic women are clerical workers. Unfortunately, the occupational breakdown on nonblack, non-Hispanic minority women is not available for the late 1970s, but another occupational measure, developed by Temme (1975), suggests that Japanese, Chinese, and Filipino women have an occupational distribution that looks more like that of white women (Lott & Pian, 1979). In fact, the occupational prestige rating of Filipino women exceeds that of whites, while that of the Chinese is about the same, and that of the Japanese, somewhat lower (Bureau of the Census, 1978). However, many scholars have pointed out that in spite of the high prestige rating of occupations of Asian-American women, there is an acute problem of underemployment among immigrant Asian groups. In her study of Chinese women employed in six occupations where they are concentrated, Sung (1975) found that a significant percentage of them had some college education. Immigrant Asian professionals such as physicians, pharmacists, and nurses often cannot practice their professions because a lack of proficiency in English prevents them from getting licensed or certified, even though there is a critical need for bilingual and bicultural health professionals. It is not uncommon to find Asian doctors working as medical assistants, registered nurses as aides, and pharmacists and dentists as technicians (NIE, 1980).

Income and Earnings

The economic well-being of families and individuals is closely tied to income, which is strongly related to earnings. Over 80% of family income comes from wages and salaries (Bureau of the Census, 1978). Thus, the labor market experiences of males and females and family structure are important variables that determine standards of living.

The economic well-being of minorities varies greatly among minority groups. While the per capita income of Japanese-Americans is significantly higher than that of whites, the figures for blacks, Native Americans, Mexicans, and Puerto Ricans are significantly lower. About one-fourth of all minority families have incomes below the poverty level, but this is true for only 6% of Filipinos and 7% of Japanese-Americans. The poverty level for families with no husband present is high: almost half of all minority families so constituted, other than Asians, have incomes below the poverty line. The proportion of Asian female-headed families living in poverty is slightly below the 22% for white families (U.S. Commission on Civil Rights, 1978). To these data should be added the fact that only 9% of Asian families are headed by women, compared to one-third of Puerto Rican, one-sixth of Mexican, and 40% of black, families (U.S. Department of Labor, 1976; Bureau of the Census, 1978). The high poverty rate among black families headed by women, together with the high proportion of black families in this category, has serious implications for the economic well-being of the black population. The relatively low poverty rate among Japanese families headed by women and the extremely small proportion of these families means that the existence of female-headed households does not have the same effect on the economic well-being of Japanese-Americans.

As the high poverty level among minority families with female heads implies, the earnings of minority women are significantly lower than those of their male counterparts. This is true for every racial/ethnic group; however, there are variations in female earnings among these groups.

None of the groups of minority women fare well when compared with white males or with males from their own ethnic group. Black women have the highest earnings relative to their male counterparts, followed closely by Chinese women—66 and 65%, respectively.

A caveat is in order. Caution should be used when interpreting the earnings data for minority women in comparison with those for white women. More information is needed about part-time versus full-time employment, years of work experience, and similar variables that influence earnings before valid conclusions can be drawn about equality in earnings.

The income inequality between minority populations and whites is more a reflection of the differences in earnings among males than among females. However, women from larger ethnic minorities have average earnings below those of white women, and their per capita incomes display even greater inequality. The per capita income figures reflect the low male earnings, the high incidence of female-headed households, and high unemployment. Again, there are exceptions. The incidence of poverty is lower among Asian-Americans than the national average, and Asian-American women earn more, on the average, than white women. However, the most salient fact about the earnings of minority women is that none have earnings equal to their male counterparts or approach the earnings of white males.

Summary

Minority women are a disparate group. They are concentrated in different regions of the country: blacks in the South, Asians in the West, Hispanics in the Southwest, and Native Americans in the Northwest and Southwest. The levels of educational attainment range from extraordinarily high levels among Asian-Americans to extremely low levels among Hispanics and Native Americans. Educational attainment affects labor market activity, and thus income. The higher the level of attainment, the higher the labor force participation rates, the lower the level of unemployment, and the higher the earnings.

These differential characteristics of minority women lead to different priorities and different approaches to sex equity. Thus, a monolithic or a unidimensional approach to the problems and concerns of sex equity for minority women would of necessity ignore many of the subtle and overt aspects of their status in American society.

An attempt will be made in the following section to discuss major educational and sex equity issues facing minority women as a means of isolating educational and sex equity priorities of minority women in the United States.

MAJOR EQUITY ISSUES FOR MINORITY WOMEN

A review of the literature on sex equity programs for minority women tends to confirm the views of Women's Educational Equity Act program directors who attended a priority area workshop for minority women and girls in 1982. They concluded that while many of the strategies and approaches used to achieve sex equity for minority women are unique, some overlapping concerns can be identified. These emerge as major issues to be addressed if adequate programs, strategies, and benefits of the sex equity movement are to be shared between minority and majority women in American society (Women's Educational Equity Act Program, 1982). These issues will be discussed in this section: (1) the myths of the female and minority monoliths, (2) reinforced negative stereotyping of minorities, and (3) unidimensional approaches to sex equity. The issues will be discussed separately.

The Myth of the Monolith

The underlying assumption of sex equity programs is that discrimination based on gender affects all females and remedying sex inequities benefits all females. The assumption is valid as far as it goes, but the problem is its superficiality. Not all women are affected in the same way and to the same degree by sex discrimination, and not all women benefit in the same way and to the same degree when inequities are remedied.

The fact that American women constitute a population varied in race, class, educational status, economic condition, cultural background, legal status, and so forth means that they are differentially affected by individual, group, institutional, and state attitudes and behavior. When a minority woman is denied a promotion, it is difficult to determine whether that denial stems from racial, cultural, sexual, or regional biases. It is also difficult to determine which of these biases is more fundamental to her problem than the others. By the same token, it is difficult to determine whether textbook stereotypes of females are more damaging to the image of minority women than are textbook stereotypes of minorities. All the women are not white and all the minorities are not male: some of both groups are minority women who are discriminated against because they are members of both categories (Hull, Scott, & Smith, 1982). Both are ascribed characteristics; the acquired characteristics of economic status, educational status, and so forth are related to the ascribed characteristics because being born female and nonwhite adds additional restrictions on social mobility in American society.

The myth of the monolith also fosters competition among minority women for funds and causes infighting over program directives. It facilitates the exclusion of minority women from all but set-aside programs and funds and thus limits the scope and depth of projects focused on minority women (Women's Educational Equity Act Program, 1982). Researchers, policy makers, minorities, and other Americans who accept the monolithic approach to minority women fail to understand the need for and make provisions for differential projects, goals, programs, and strategies for distinct subcategories of women.

Reinforced Negative Stereotyping

Stereotyping of groups results in myths, warped perceptions, inaccuracies, and neglect of specifics that would make null the original misconceptions that led to the stereotype. In this as well as in other societies around the world, it is common to label particular groups based on a few observed, if misunderstood, characteristics of representatives of the larger group. These generalizations often develop into stigmatizing labels that become self-fulfilling prophecies, since policies and practices based on the stereotypes force populations to fit the label (Lewis, 1981; Jackson, 1982).

Minority women are negatively stereotyped in two ways: as minorities and as women. It is imperative to explore—and explode—assumptions and misconceptions about minority women in order to increase their opportunities for achieving equity in this society.

Three common themes or concerns emerge from an examination of the stereotyped labels appended to minority women in America: (1) the image or stereotype is one of powerlessness; (2) the image is pathological, that is, the victim is blamed for her victimization; and (3) the image is based on the absence of information or on distorted information. Images and stereotypes vary from one group to another, but the basic denigration of minorities and women holds constant. Specific examples of double negative stereotyping of minority women are discussed in this section.

Native Americans. Views of Native Americans have been distorted since the day Columbus stepped ashore on one of the Bahamas under the assumption that his voyage had brought him to the shores of India. Misconceptions have thrived ever since and are broadly based on lack of public awareness and/or lack of public response to historical diversity within the population, the uniqueness of American Indians in relation to all the rest of the national population, continuing negative stereotyping of American Indian women, and contemporary priorities within the growing Native American population (Butterfield, 1980; Foreman, 1954).

This void in public awareness diminishes all Indian cultures. At a time when we at least talk of equal rights under the Constitution, Americans remain ignorant of the historical leadership roles accorded Indian women and of the achievements of contemporary American Indian women (Foreman, 1954).

The image of the American Indian women is based on the squaw stereotype. The drudge, the bearer of burdens, dutifully walking 10 paces behind the male, whose image is that of the lithe child of the wilderness or savage warrior, is how we see American Indian women today (Deloria, 1969; McNickel, 1973). Life for Indians who live on the reservations and for those who live in urban areas is seldom contrasted in media or textbook images of Indians, nor are the differences among lifestyles of Indian women from one reservation to another or among different age groups, educational levels, geographical locations, and so forth presented to the American public. The various nations and the women of those nations of Native Americans are stereotyped as marginal, powerless, pathological beings.

Asian-Americans.   A number of stereotypes of Asian women have been identified by various scholars. Summarizing the studies on stereotypes, Sue and Kitano (1973) suggest that the "Suzy Wong" stereotype of the slim, sexy, feminine, and charming Chinese female fits well within the American stereotype of femininity, but is extremely limiting in terms of job access and occupational choice (Lott & Pian, 1979). Restrictive sex role characteristics are ascribed to Asian-American women both by their own societies and by the dominant American society. They are seen, for example, as industrious and excelling in the home, but are not viewed as involved in intellectual endeavors. They are portrayed as passive, submissive, and self-effacing, and above all, not assertive (Lott & Pian, 1979).

The recent interest in Asian martial arts such as Kung Fu, which has led to a spurt of exploitation films and television series, has further exacerbated the negative images of Asian-American women. In these films, Asian women are rarely seen, and when they are, they are generally depicted as totally submissive, traditional Orientals or pseudo-modern Suzy Wongs. Asian populations are viewed as harsh, traditional, inscrutable, and subtly negative. The Asian woman is thus subjected to double negative stereotyping.

African-Americans.   King (1977) describes three prevailing stereotyped images of black females in America. The first combines negative opposites: the tough, hard-working matriarch in the home and the appropriately submissive individual in the white-dominated world outside the home. This defeminizing image of black females permits exploitation of black women's labor, subjection to harsh and unsafe social and working conditions, and political neglect of the needs of this population. The second stereotype of the black female is the depreciated or valueless sex object. This image serves to insulate white males (and some black males) against momentary passion, compassion, or compunction that might result from their sexual contact with black females. Thus, black females are seen as sex objects not to be considered for meaningful relationships, especially not marriage. The third stereotype is of black females as losers. This image is specifically aimed at destroying the self-esteem, self-respect, and aspirations of black females. Coupled with the image of black people as lazy, ignorant, dishonest, and powerless, the images of black females depict powerless, pathological losers constrained and limited by biological and historical factors (King, 1977).

Hispanic-Americans. One of the major assumptions about Hispanic women is that they focus only on home and family. As a result of the imposition of the values of the dominant class in America, the values of Hispanic families and peoples are viewed as backward and encumbering. The image of dutiful daughters, wives, and mothers among Hispanic women is a negative one in this society because the sense of duty is linked to subservience and dependency. Hispanic women are seen as content with being sex objects and decorative figures who are required to obtain less education than their male counterparts because they are less capable of using it (Marin, 1977). Further, the image of ultrareligious women who depend on the church and God for change while the rest of the population sleeps and drinks is very common when Hispanic women (especially Mexican women) are depicted in American films. These negative images of the group and of the women lead to the stereotyping of Hispanic-American women as powerless, pathological, prayerful, and dutiful family members.

Summary

All of these stereotypes of minority women are negative. As women and as minorities they are depicted as deserving the contempt of, and exploitation by, minority males as well as the ridicule of males and females in the dominant American culture. Textbooks, films, television, newspapers, advertisements, jokes, the economic system, the political system, and unfounded "sayings" form part of the educational mechanism through which these negative stereotypes are spread and perpetuated from generation to generation. The schools alone are not responsible for popularizing the negative images of minority females. Other agents in society create and reinforce stereotypes; thus, all of these agents must be confronted—along with the educational system—if eradication of the negative images and resulting opportunities for change are to be expected for minority women.

The Unidimensional Approach to Sex Equity

Many of the problems experienced by minority women are also experienced by minority men. Yet, programs and materials are not always developed for both. For example, math anxiety in minority males is very similar to math anxiety in females of all races. Materials and programs for one group should be made available for use by other groups with the same experiences (Women's Educational Equity Act Program, 1982).

Programs for achieving sex equity which assume that sexism is the only or even the major obstacle to equity for women fail to take into account the varied forms of oppression visited upon minority women. Certainly racial, ethnic, and cultural oppression are well known and have been well documented over the past two decades (National Advisory Commission on Civil Disorder, 1968; U.S. Commission on Civil Rights, 1978). However, there is still a tendency in this society to assume that patriarchy affects all women the same way, regardless of racial, class, or ethnic background. Thus, the argument goes, we can approach the attainment of sex equity for women with one strategy. This perspective reflects the dominance of whites of western European origin in the American women's movement. They have attempted to determine issues, strategies, and goals for all women in American society.

Class and regional biases as well as educational differences affect minority men and women alike, though not to the same degree. The percentage of minority women with inadequate education, low economic status, and ghettoized residences is much greater than for majority women. And, since race, sex, and socioeconomic status are all interrelated, the impact of all these factors is obviously significant in determining how minority women view themselves, how others view them, and what their status is in American society. It would seem to follow that sex equity projects that aim at eliminating negative female images from textbooks and elsewhere in the educational system touch only a fraction of the problem facing minority women. A unidimensional approach to sex equity means that progress made by minority women in this area is measurably less than that made by majority women (Hull, Scott, & Smith, 1982; Lewis, 1982).

Sex equity programs exhibit ethnic, cultural, class, and racial biases. Thus, programs designed to promote sex equity sometimes foster inequity in other arenas. The sex equity move to have women defined as minorities so they could obtain set-aside contracts in the Department of Transportation fostered inequity for ethnic minority women who did not have brothers, money, and relatives' firms behind them and who had no other avenue into the contractual world save set-aside or joint venture programs. Further, sex equity programs that concentrate, as many early programs did, on reentry women and women in higher education clearly exhibit class as well as racist tendencies, since "housewives" returning to school or the work force are overwhelmingly white and middle class. Clearly, the unidimensional or single-minded approach to sex equity in education lends itself readily to discriminatory approaches to educational and societal change (Jackson, 1972; King, 1977).

Having identified and briefly discussed the major issues confronting minority women, we now wish to delineate some of the sex equity priorities of minority women in the United States.

EQUITY PRIORITIES OF MINORITY WOMEN

Given the differential characteristics of minority women, it is difficult to identify a set of priorities that holds true for all women in the minority category. Nevertheless, it is possible to determine generally agreed-upon priorities. The most common appear to be (1) contextual: the need to place sex equity in education for minority women in a proper theoretical and historical context; (2) a data base: the need for resource materials on minority women (a need that is linked to the need for research on minority women, by minority women, that is sensitive to the needs of minority women); (3) communication: the need to develop networking and formal communications linkages through print and electronic media sources; (4) career development: the need to provide continuing education and skill development for minority adult women so that negative self-images and skills deficiencies, which most often stem from racial and class inequities, can be overcome.

The Need for a Context

Since the focus of most Third World cultures is on the family and/or group, while the focus of European-based cultures is on the individual, minority women (who are in fact Third World women in terms of status and orientation) relate differently to educational programs and strategies. They are also treated differently by educators and educational programs because of the multidimensional nature of their oppression.

Before we can place sex equity in education for minority women within a proper theoretical and empirical context, we need to discuss some of the specific concerns of women of the various minority groups.

Hispanic Women.   A significant problem that many Hispanic women face is their location in a nether world between two cultures. They are no longer an integral part of the culture from which they came, yet they have not yet become a part of the culture in which they now find themselves.

In this nether world they are torn by conflicting demands. The roles and behaviors appropriate to the traditional environment are sometimes contradictory to those expected in the new environment. If, for example, they adopt Anglo values and attitudes, conflict arises within themselves, between themselves and Hispanic males who tend to prefer the traditionally assigned roles, and between themselves and Anglo society, which generally endorses and perpetuates the myths and stereotypes of Hispanic women. This problem is not limited to Hispanic women. All racial and ethnic minorities are victims of mythmaking and stereotyping.

Native American Women.   The Native American woman is a special case. Unlike other racial and ethnic groups in America, Native Americans view civil/equity rights in terms of special rights bought and paid for with land. Neither the majority nor any other minority has that kind of legal relationship or unique treaty/trust relationship with the government of the United States.

Priorities in Native American communities are basically within the framework of tribal sovereignty and the implications of treaty obligations. As the nation's most deprived citizens, Native Americans hold the dubious distinction of having the shortest lifespan, greatest infant mortality, highest suicide rate, least educational attainment, highest unemployment, and lowest income level in America. However, white Americans do not want to admit that Indians survived attempted genocide. While events of the past dozen years forced the nation to acknowledge shameful chapters in the treatment of Indians, a devastating backlash continues and the life conditions of Indians are still viewed outside the historical context that gave rise to them (Prucha, 1977).

Asian-American Women.   Until public agencies and professional communities place the subject of Asian-American women on their agenda, little change can be expected. The ultimate inequity is the denial of their existence. Reminding policy makers of the diversity among Asian-American women is also important, and the time to start dealing with it is long overdue. One of the things that needs to be done is to collect and report information on each of the Asian groups separately so that we know what the facts are before we give prescriptions.

Linguistic diversity among Asian-American women and barriers between educated and uneducated women make the development of culturally sensitive sex equity materials a necessity. Among both the highly educated and poorly educated are sizable numbers of immigrants. Therefore, the demand for more opportunities to learn English has become most salient. Poorly educated Asian women require knowledge of the language to secure a minimal livelihood, and college graduates need communications skills in English to obtain comparable employment. These concerns will not be addressed unless and until Asian-American women are placed in a proper historical and social context.

African-American Women.   Any discussion of the contemporary educational needs of African-American women must provide at least a glimpse of the historical fabric from which the present emerges. Though historical records are sparse, the evidence suggests that attempts by black women and girls to gain quality education in this society have been thwarted by dominant American mores and values, prejudice against women, racial discrimination, and the American legal system (Lerner, 1972).

Most African-American women are descendants of slaves. For this reason it is inappropriate, inaccurate, and restricting for them to be viewed in the same manner as other ethnic groups are viewed. No other group has had slave origins and has suffered the subsequent stigma, lack of opportunity, legal barriers such as Jim Crow laws, or the cultural and physical rape that African-American women have experienced.

During slavery, education for blacks was viewed as dangerous for both the ruling class and the slaves. It was generally believed that reading and writing would encourage discontent and "ruin a good slave." For this reason severe punishment was meted out to slaves found to be literate and to persons found teaching the enslaved (Franklin, 1947).

This historical context suggests a milieu wherein access to education for black men and women has always been discouraged. It is against this sociocultural and historical backdrop that the contemporary picture emerges. Add to this context the fact that black women form a visible target for inequitable treatment. Color, hair texture, features, mannerisms, and so forth differentiate black women from others, and these factors can neither be hidden or taken lightly. These biological, cultural, and historical constraints on educational equity for black women are serious. When the social, political, and economic structures fail to confer equal status on black women, the educational structure reflects the same inequities. Sex equity programs and materials must be informed by and sensitive to these constraints if black women are to gain sex equity in this society.

The Need for a Data Base

One of the major obstacles confronting researchers and educators attempting to design and implement sex equity programs for minorities is the lack of identifiable, readily accessible sources of data. The authors of a recent bibliography on American women of color note that a cursory examination of the bibliography will reveal the problematic and inadequate nature of existing sources. There is a significantly imbalanced distribution of citations on women of different ethnic backgrounds, and a significant number of sources focus on "minorities and women," making the not-so-subtle suggestion that "all the women are white, all the blacks are men, but some of us are brave" (Hull, Scott, & Smith, 1982). In addition, a large number of the available empirical studies on women of color have focused on issues that make them vulnerable as potential objects of manipulation and social control (for example, fertility studies) (Stineman, Loeb, & Walton, 1979).

Trends in research and publication usually reflect public interest and societal attitudes, and while women have generally been victims of scholarly neglect, minority women have received even less scholarly consideration. The demand for information on minority women has preceded the development of adequate research materials and tools (Sims-Woods, 1980).

Minority women are justifiably committed to uncovering existing data about themselves and building upon it. However, the paucity of thorough, scholarly, sensitive, and relevant works that are readily available suggests the need for minority women to begin creating new data that focus systematic attention on the issues and conditions of specific subgroups of minority women. These data could be utilized in a number of ways. They could provide background and historical contexts for self-definition; aid in determining directions for future research; form the basis of new methodologies for research and teaching about minority women; and provide the empirical data and theories to undergird strategies for achieving sex equity in and through education.

The absence of adequate research data on minority women is a measure of the absence of educational equity, and it is also an indication of the need to place building resources and a data base high on the list of educational priorities of minority women. An important dimension of this priority is the need for this research to be done by minority women themselves. And while we recognize that this does not ensure an adequate contextual and dimensional approach to minority women, it does lessen the possibility that insensitive, irrelevant works will be heralded as representative of the thinking and needs of minority women.

The usefulness of what is known about minority women is very much a function of the kinds of questions that have been asked. In turn, it is also a function of who asks the questions and why. Sociology, anthropology, and psychology have provided most of the disciplinary work on minority women. Yet, much of the work coming out of these disciplines is shaped by frameworks and assumptions that display little or no sensitivity to the conditions that have defined the lives of minority women (Ladner, 1971; Lewis, 1981; Lindsay, 1979). The Moynihan Report is a good example of the type of study that exhibits these faults.

Other disciplines (such as history) address more directly the problems that minority women face (for example, property rights and suffrage), but they fail to provide a framework for discussion about the status of women in society and the alteration of that status through social transformation. They generally reduce solutions to the problems that women face to a simple matter of institutional face lifting, which passes off surface alterations in the status of minority women as essential change. This is a means of trivializing the importance of sexual, class, and racial oppression. Further, minority women's embrace of the meager accommodations offered further trivializes the "woman question." The accommodations do not provide the kind of information necessary to answer such fundamental questions as these: Is there a minority women's world view? Is there a minority women's culture? What are the priorities of minority women?

In order for a data base to be developed, funders must encourage and reward minority women researchers. Even those minority women who do not research topics relating to the priorities of minority women serve as role models for future minority women researchers. A larger share of research dollars must be consciously channeled to minority women, and educational institutions must assist minority women in applying for and obtaining research grants.

Publication is crucial to the establishment of a good data base for and on minority women, because the publication of findings on minority women acts to swell the data base and to encourage minority women researchers. However, assistance in entering the publishing network is necessary if the results of the research are to be widely disseminated.

It is important to emphasize that accurate and informed data as well as good scholarship on minority women would go a long way toward dispelling the myths and stereotypes that serve as barriers to educational equity for minority women. Research and a data base that are accessible, reliable, respected, and adequate are certainly keys to achieving sex equity for minority women.

The Need for Communication

Minority women have serious problems with current communications/media projections of themselves. Related to this is the dearth of minority women in communications. Minority women who do not attend college are especially victimized by media stereotypes. Few popular publications, even fewer scholarly periodicals, and practically no radio or television programs offer positive images of minority women (King, 1977).

Added to the problems with formal communications media is the fact that means of communication between women of the various minority groups are not adequately developed. Networks within specific ethnic groups exist, but few of these are cross-ethnic. Examples are the National Black Women's Hook-Up, the Asian Women's Association, and Ohoyo (for Native-Americans). Even the networks and organizations of women that are theoretically open to all groups—for example, the National Organization for Women—do not provide the setting and climate conducive to cross-ethnic networking. Inadequate networking between and within subgroups is also a problem. Geographical location, group size, language, class, interests, and information flow limit minority women's networks. On the state and national levels the constraints are compounded. Individuals interested in communicating with a cross-section of minority women would have difficulty locating a diverse group in one setting or finding publications that address cross-ethnic or cross-sectional groups. Therefore, one of the priorities of minority women in the United States is to improve cross-cultural/cross-ethnic networking as a strategy for achieving sex equity.

Needs in Career Development: Skills and Employment

A look at most sex equity programs designed by minority women reveals the perceived importance of linking sex equity in education with the development of occupational skills and employment opportunities for minority women. This focus suggests that minority women take a pragmatic approach to sex equity in education. While they understand and support the principles and theory of sex equity, they cannot afford to ignore the possible use of sex equity in education to improve the quality of their economic lives. Job training programs, human relations workshops, apprenticeships, career counseling, and the development of employment networks are usually part of the package of sex equity proposals written by minority women.

Because years of schooling for minority women do not automatically translate into improved economic status, it is essential to link specialized schooling and training to career development. This priority must be viewed in relationship to other priorities to be clearly understood, for it seems obvious that multidimensional needs born of multidimensional oppression require (1) a theoretical context for equity, (2) more research and an adequate data base, (3) more and better communication with and about minority women, and (4) better skills and employment opportunities. All of these culminate in improvements in the quality of life for minority women.

Bilingual and bicultural programs are critical. Educational programs that provide occupational and career development training are also needed. Employment networks, proposal writing workshops, briefing sessions on governmental and private programs and agencies that fund projects related to minority women, and a variety of programs that train women for nontraditional occupations are among the vital needs of minority women. The basic need is for educational programs that combine career counseling, occupational training, and sex consciousness.

MULTIDIMENSIONAL APPROACHES TO SEX EQUITY
IN EDUCATION: ALTERNATIVE ANSWERS

The role of majority women in perpetuating inequities for minority women is not the subject of this chapter, but the cultural pressure to view women's problems from the perspective of the dominant majority does constitute one of the problems that minority women face in their efforts to achieve sex equity in education. Minority women view the integration of strategies for eliminating inequity as basic to any program for achieving sex equity in education. Most of their sex equity projects proceed from this multidimensional perspective.

The following examples of sex equity programs indicate how different are the priorities, strategies, and populations of minority women. They also indicate how these women have managed to cope with and change conceptualizations of themselves. Finally, the programs described in this section illustrate how diverse groups of minority women design educational programs that reflect their basic needs and priorities. Occupational training and career development, communication and networking, expanding research and building a data base, and an integrative approach to sex equity in education are evident in the examples which follow.

Asian-American Women: Two Models. To respond to the needs of immigrant women in the nonprofessional sector, the Organization of Chinese-American Women developed a series of Job Advancement Workshops. These workshops, held from June 20 to July 2, 1981, were organized to help recent immigrant Chinese women develop basic problem-solving skills and attain the self-confidence needed to advance in the working world. Objectives of the workshops included (1) encouraging and preparing Chinese-Americans to seek and hold better-paying jobs; (2) informing Chinese-American women of the wide range of occupational and career choices, especially nontraditional ones, available to them; and (3) encouraging them to seek occupations suitable to their personal interests and abilities rather than those prescribed by stereotyped vocational tracking or cultural expectations.

Workshop topics included cultural differences and women working in the United States, skills assessment and goal setting, expanding job options and résumé writing, job-hunting skills and filling out job applications, interviewing techniques and follow-up activities, and job maintenance skills and the employee's responsibility and fringe benefits. Due to the overwhelming response to the workshops, attendance was limited to the first 45 applicants, 35 of whom attended all seven workshops. Their ages ranged from 25 to 60 years, and their educational background ranged from sixth grade to college, including graduate studies. Most were homemakers or unskilled blue collar workers, but some had been either highly skilled workers or in the professions in their native countries.

Asian, Inc. and Asian Women United administered a sex equity program entitled Education for Occupational Choice: Creating Awareness of Alternatives for Asian-American Women and Girls. The program was based on the assumption that increased education alone does not yield significant increases in earnings for Asian-American women. Although Asian-American women have higher than average labor force participation rates, they are in a narrow range of occupations in a limited number of industries.

Phase one of the program developed information about how Asian-American girls and women make educational and job choices, whom they turn to for help on these issues, what their aspirations and expectations are, how they perceive what choices are open to them, and how they cope with discrimination. The project surveyed students from junior high school through college, parents, teachers, counselors, employers, and community agencies in California.

Phase two was devoted to developing media and print materials to expand awareness of career and educational alternatives and provide assistance in coping with the barriers identified in phase one.

Native-American Women: Two Models. In 1981–82, the Minnesota Chippewa tribe developed a curricular project entitled The Contemporary American Indian Woman: Careers and Contributions. Information that depicts the career choices, life styles, family relationships, tribal relationships, achievements, and contributions of contemporary Indians was seen as important, especially for young Indian women who are unaware of the variety of careers and opportunities available to them.

The materials produced from the project present views of careers in a curriculum unit in book form and in an audiovisual/slide-tape unit. The careers and contributions of Indian women in areas such as business, education, medicine and health-related fields, mathematics, science, law, tribal government and services, politics, social service, sports, the communications media, environment and natural resources, and the performing arts are included in the curriculum unit. The units are geared to students aged 12 to 15 and are designed to provide accurate information about American Indian women and to provide career education information for Indian youth.

Blackfeet Community College established a Blackfeet Women's Resource Center in 1981 to serve the needs of Native American women on campus and on the Blackfeet Reservation. The center provides counseling services for women students, education and training programs to increase opportunities for unemployed and underemployed reservation women, and technical assistance to local school personnel in implementing Title IX for Blackfeet girls and women.

The center also developed an information resource center that collects and disseminates information on Native American women's roles, both traditional and modern, and today's opportunities and expectations for Native American women. Materials on women's rights, legal services, employment opportunities, consumer issues, and other important concerns are also collected and disseminated by the Women's Resource Center.

African-American Women: Two Models. In 1979, the National Council of Negro Women established a Career Exploration Project in two community areas in Montgomery County, Maryland. It was designed to help black female students in the county's secondary schools set career goals and plan realistically to attain these goals by overcoming the barriers of sex and race.

The students participated in the weekly two-hour core program, visited job sites, listened to speakers discuss career opportunities in various fields, and attended social functions. The students and their parents also participated in special workshops and seminars, some of which were open to the public. The curriculum, as well as all programs and activities, was based upon four objectives: career exploration and awareness, academic skill building, social and leadership skills development, and parent involvement.

The Career Exploration Project produced two handbooks, which explain how to develop and implement a community-based career project and provide the curriculum and many of the programs and activities developed in the pilot project.

The Women's Institute of the Southeast of the Atlanta University Center initiated a Transitional Black Women's Project in 1981. The project was a model program for improving the status of transitional black women in the Southeastern region of the United States. Transitional black women were identified as generally poor, undereducated migrants from southern rural areas to urban areas of the Southeast. Educational research, human relations training, occupational counseling and training, high school equivalency training, and on-the-job training were provided for the women as a means of assisting them in obtaining educational equity and the subsequent economic and social improvements that usually accompany such equity. The primary goal of the project was to mount a sequential attack on two problem areas, dysfunctional images and inadequate occupational skills.

Human relations training was provided for employers and social service representatives who interact with transitional black women, and both human relations and occupational training were provided for offspring of transitional women as a means of arresting the generational cycle of poor images and inadequate skills. In addition, three handbooks and a research report were developed.

Hispanic-American Women: Two Models.   The New Mexico Commission on the Status of Women developed the Mature Woman/Diverse Cultures Employment Awareness/Urban/Rural Project as a model for assisting the entry and reentry of mature women (aged 25–60) into the work force by providing a course on employment awareness. An instructor's manual in English and Spanish was developed and tested. Short training sessions on how to use the manual were provided for instructors. County agricultural extension networks were used over the four-state area of New Mexico, Utah, Arizona, and Colorado for adopting and testing the manual among diverse cultures and among rural and urban women.

The Association for Cross-Cultural Education and Social Studies (ACCESS, Inc.) designed, planned, and conducted a three-week residential program entitled "The Summer Leadership Institute" in 1980–81. By using a formal curriculum composed of four learning modules, combined with counseling, hands-on learning, and the development of individualized support systems, AC-CESS provided motivation and skills that would stimulate women to enter and complete programs in higher education and would encourage professional and leadership development for the 35 Hispanic women, aged 15–22, who participated.

SUMMARY AND RECOMMENDATIONS

Summary

In the foregoing discussion on achieving sex equity in education for minority women, we attempted to illustrate that viewing women as a monolithic group distorts the actual differences in race, culture, class, language, economic status, political ideology, educational status, and social status between minority and majority women, and among the various subgroupings of minority women.

In addition, we indicated that none of the minority groupings addressed in this chapter—Asian-Americans, African-Americans, Hispanic-Americans, and Native Americans—is a homogeneous subgroup. The variety of historical, cultural, linguistic, economic, educational, and social differences within each subgroup is significant. Thus, uncritical acceptance of the minority monolith is also viewed by minority women as detrimental to their well-being. Both the myth of monolithic women and the myth of monolithic minorities should be exploded.

What this implies is that characteristics that differentiate among minority and majority women, among subgroupings of minority women, and within subgroupings of minority women lead to differential priorities and a variety of approaches to equity problems.

A constant theme running through this chapter is that the multidimensional nature of minority women's oppression dictates multidimensional approaches to obtaining equity. Forms of exploitation based on race, sex, class, and culture are inextricably interwoven in the fabric of this nation, and minority women who are victims of all of these forms of exploitation must conceptualize theories and strategies that embrace the various dimensions of their oppression. Thus, a multidimensional approach to achieving sex equity in education is a logical, rational, and necessary response to the conditions that minority women face in American society.

The major sex equity issues that were identified centered around dispelling myths and negative images that make it difficult to conceive and implement policies and programs to meet the needs of minority women. The uncritical utilization of a unidimensional approach to sex equity issues was also viewed as a fundamental problem facing minority women in their struggle to obtain educational equity.

Based on an analysis of the strategies and programs used by minority women to confront and resolve equity issues identified as significant to them, a list of priorities for achieving sex equity in education was delineated. It includes (1) developing a theoretical and empirical context; (2) developing a data base; (3) improving communication, and (4) career development. These priorities will be explicated below, and the recommendations for educational change emerging from these priorities will be outlined.

The recommendations will be listed under the priority area that is most appropriate. However, it should be noted that all of the recommendations are complementary, and categorizing them under specific priority areas is not intended to assign weights to them. All of the recommendations are designed to achieve greater sensitivity to and consciousness of the nature and scope of the multidimensional equity problems facing minority women, and to indicate courses of action that are likely to lead to both immediate and long-range benefits for minority women and for society as a whole. The recommendations are also designed to encourage and support research and teaching on and by minority women, as well as to promote improvements in local, state, federal, institutional, and private financing, institutionalization, and implementation of programs and policies for research and teaching on minority women. Ultimately, it is hoped that implementing the recommendations will aid minority women in achieving sex equity in education and in attaining full equity in all dimensions of American life, and will serve as a basis for total liberation of all oppressed persons.

Recommendations

A. *Contextual:* Recommendations in this category address the need to place sex equity in education in a theoretical and historical context that reflects the actual conditions of minority women. They include:

1. Development of a national task force on the status of minority women in American society
2. Development of a team of minority women to monitor and evaluate sex equity programs to ensure that the goals and content of the programs promote nonsexist, nonracist, and non-class-biased activities and positions
3. Procurement of financial and technical support for the publication of materials that focus on the history, theory, and life conditions of minority women
4. Establishment of minority women's studies programs in minority-controlled colleges and universities in the United States
5. Establishment of a scholarship/fellowship program to promote research on minority women by minority women

B. *Development of a Data Base:* This category of recommendations addresses the need for resource materials on minority women and the need for reliable and accessible data centers on minority women. It includes:

1. Establishment of regional minority women's educational equity resource centers

2. Funding for the collection, preservation, and organization of archival materials on minority women
3. Development of a policy-oriented or applied research center that focuses on issues related to the needs of minority women

C. *Communications:* The recommendations listed under this category of priorities reflect the need to develop informal networks, organizational networks, and formal media (both electronic and print) programs to promote the exchange of information and ideas and to serve as support systems and resources for improving the conditions of minority women. They include:

1. Creation of a minority women's communications agency for projecting positive images of minority women via electronic and print media sources
2. Underwriting of a scholarly minority women's journal
3. Development of a clearinghouse or cross-ethnic network to facilitate exchanges between and among ethnic women's networks in the United States

D. *Career Development:* Recommendations in this category focus on the need to provide continuing education and skills development programs for economically exploited women. The need for career counseling and training for minority girls as one means of arresting the generational cycle of unemployment, inadequate skills, and economic deprivation among minority women in America is also reflected in this set of recommendations. They include:

1. Establishment of nontraditional job training programs for minority women as part of continuing education programs in minority colleges and universities
2. Recruitment of minority women faculty and students in science, law, medicine, and engineering programs
3. Development of permanent programs that provide specialized career guidance and counseling to minority girls in the public schools of the nation
4. Development of apprenticeship and on-the-job training model centers for minority women in the four regions of the nation
5. Development of materials, textbooks, and teaching units that provide positive images and encouragement to minority girls in the public schools and undergraduate colleges of America
6. Establishment of women's studies programs that focus on the lives, history, conditions, contributions, and needs of minority women.

REFERENCES

Anderson, O. (1982). *Why Indian women are different: A perspective.* Unpublished manuscript.

Bureau of the Census. (1978). *A Statistical Portrait of Women in the United States: 1978 (Current Population Reports,* Special Studies, Series P-23, No. 100). Washington, DC: author.

Bureau of the Census. (1981). *Statistical Abstract of the United States, 1981.* Washington, DC: author.

Butterfield, N. (1980). Transcending the stereotype: American Indian women embody modern and traditional characteristics. OHOYO.

Cooney, R. S. (1979). Intercity variations in Puerto Rican female participation. *Journal of Human Resources, 14*(2), 222–235.

Deloria, V., Jr. (1969). *Custer died for your sins: An Indian manifesto.* New York: Avoh.

Farb, P. (1968). *Man's rise to civilization.* New York: Dutton.

Foreman, C. T. (1954). *Indian women chiefs.* Muskogee, OK: Hoffman.

Franklin, J. (1947). *From slavery to freedom: A history of Negro Americans.* New York: Knopf.

Geoffrey, C. (1976). Returns to education for Blacks, Anglos, and five Hispanic groups. *Journal of Human Resources, 11*(2), 172–184.

Green, R. (1980). Review: Native American women. *SIGNS: Journal of Women in Culture and Society, 6*(2), 248–267.

Hull, G., Scott, P., & Smith, B. (1982). *All the women are white, all the blacks are men, but some of us are brave: Black women's studies.* Old Westbury, NJ: Feminist Press.

Jackson, J. (1972). Black women in a racist society. In C. Willis (Ed.), *Racism and mental health* (pp. 185–268). Pittsburgh: University of Pittsburgh Press.

Jackson, N. (1982). *Statement on the assumptions and misconceptions about black women.* Unpublished manuscript.

Jones, B. (1976). Factors which determine the labor force participation rates of black wives. *Proceedings of the 29th Annual Meeting of the Industrial Relations Research Association.*

Joseph, G. (1980). Caribbean women: The impact of race, sex, and class. In B. Lindsay (Ed.), *Comparative perspectives of Third World women* (pp. 143–161). New York: Praeger.

King, M. C. (1977). The political role of the stereotyped image of the black woman in America. In S. Lewis (Ed.), *Black political scientists and black survival.* Detroit: Balamp.

Ladner, J. (1971). *Tomorrow's tomorrow: The black woman.* Garden City, NY: Anchor.

Lerner, G. (1972). *Black women in white America: A documentary history.* New York: Vintage.

Lewis, S. (Ed.). (1977). *Black political scientists and black survival.* Detroit: Balamp.

Lewis, S. (1980). African women and national development. In B. Lindsay (Ed.), *Comparative perspectives of Third World women* (pp. 31–54). New York: Praeger.

Lewis, S. (1981). *A theoretical framework for viewing black women in the American political system.* Paper presented at the National Research Conference on Black Women, Washington, DC.

Lewis, S. (1982). *Minority women: Approaches to sex equity.* Presentation to the Director's Meeting of the Women's Educational Equity Act Program, Washington, DC.

Lindsay, B., et al. (1979). Minority women in America. In E. Snyder (Ed.), *The study of women: Enlarging perspectives of social reality.* New York: Harper & Row.

Lott, J. T., & Pian, C. (1979). *Beyond stereotypes and statistics: Emergence of Asian and Pacific American women.* Pamphlet.

Marin, R. (1977). The Puerto Rican woman. *LALUZ, 6.*

McNickle, D'A. (1973). *Native American tribalism.* New York: Oxford University Press.

National Advisory Commission on Civil Disorder. (1968). *Report of the National Advisory Commission on Civil Disorder.* Washington, DC: U.S. Government Printing Office.

National Institute of Education. (1980). *Conference on the Educational and Occupational Needs of Asian-Pacific-American Women.* Washington, DC: U.S. Government Printing Office.

Prucha, F. P. (1977). *A bibliographical guide to the history of Indian-White relations in the United States.* Chicago: University of Chicago Press.

Rodgers-Rose, LaF. (1980). *The black woman.* Beverly Hills: Sage.

Sims-Woods, J. (1980). *The progress of Afro-American women: A selected bibliography and resource guide.* Westport, CT: Greenwood Press.

Stineman, E., Loeb, C., & Walton, W. (1979, September 1). Recent sources for the study of the culture of women of color. *Concerns, 9*(3).

Stone, P. (1979). Feminist consciousness and black women. In J. Freeman (Ed.), *Women: A feminist perspective* (pp. 575–588). Palo Alto: Mayfield.

Sue, S., & Kitano, H. (1973). Stereotypes as a measure of success. *Journal of Social Issues, 29*(2), 83–98.

Sung, B. L. (1975). *Chinese American manpower and employment.* Washington, DC: U.S. Department of Labor, Manpower Administration.

Temme, L. V. (1975). *Occupation: Meanings and measures.* Washington, DC: Bureau of Social Science Research.

U.S. Commission on Civil Rights. (1978). *Social indicators of equality for minorities and women.* Washington, DC: U.S. Government Printing Office.

U.S. Commission on Civil Rights. (1979). *Civil rights issues of Asian and Pacific Americans: Myths and realities.* Washington, DC: U.S. Government Printing Office.

U.S. Department of Labor, Women's Bureau. (1976). *Women of Spanish origin.* Washington, DC: author.

Women's Educational Equity Act Program. (1982). *Director's meeting priority group report.* Unpublished Report, Washington, DC: author.

20
Gifted Girls and Women in Education

Barbara J. A. Gordon and Linda Addison

Equal educational opportunity for our country's gifted and talented women is of utmost importance. The major issue in the area of education for gifted women has always been the potential loss for society if these persons were not identified and provided the opportunities for developing their abilities. Kaley (1971) indicated that unless educators change their perceptions of programs for gifted women, "society will continue to suffer tremendous loss of women's potential contribution."

In addition to this traditional reason for identifying and appropriately educating gifted females, during the past decade another compelling reason has gained prominence. Gifted females need to be identified, not only for the sake of society, but for their own benefit. They deserve the opportunity to develop to their fullest potential in a society which has affirmed via the passage of sex equity laws that it believes in equality of educational opportunity.

In this chapter, we shall be stressing the fact that gifted women have made significant educational gains, particularly in the past decade; however, we shall also demonstrate that in the areas of research, curricular resources, and training, further work is needed. Our discussion will focus on four issues: the definition of giftedness as applied to girls and women; the identification of gifted girls; the adequacy of educational intervention programs, counseling, and career guidance; and pre- and inservice training for education personnel in the area of education for the gifted female.

During the 1970s, equity for girls and women was affirmed as a priority by the passage of laws such as Title IX of the Education Amendments of 1972, the 1976 Amendments to the Vocational Education Act, and the Women's Educational Equity Act. Other education legislation passed during this period has the potential for effecting change in programs for the gifted female. One such law is

The authors wish to express their appreciation to Lynn Fox and Ruth D. Handel, who shared their research on gifted women.

the Gifted and Talented Children's Act of 1978. The regulations accompanying such laws do not contain specific provisions regarding treatment of the gifted female. Laws tend to spur people to action, however, and because of them some progress has been made in the area of educational equality and advocacy for the gifted female. This progress probably would not have been as significant without legislation and, in some cases, fiscal appropriations for implementation. For example, funding from the Women's Educational Equity Act enabled Fleming to develop Project Choice for gifted females (1979), and monies from the Gifted and Talented Children's Act have funded the Equity Institute's Professional Development Project to Encourage the Potential of the Gifted Girl (Addison, 1982).

DEFINITIONS OF GIFTED FEMALES

Have the perceptions of giftedness during the 20th century helped or hampered society's perception of the gifted female? Are we on the way to a more sophisticated approach to defining giftedness? The concept of giftedness has expanded greatly over the past century. Giftedness is culturally defined by what is valued by a society, so the increasing complexity of society is reflected in our broadened definition of gifts. Around the turn of the century, the literature on the gifted tended to focus on the hereditary genius. This idea of a genius is a very limited one within the categories of giftedness. The modern-day genius would be portrayed as a short, skinny boy with thick glasses, glued to a computer, clumsy, unathletic, a loner, and socially awkward. The original research on geniuses was done with men of eminence, and the psychological traits depicted for this group tended to reinforce this stereotypic notion. In the past, the idea of gifted women was extremely limited, since few women had attained positions of eminence.

Lewis Terman's study of genius has had a major influence on the definition of giftedness and the study of gifted education in the 20th century, and probably has also influenced the overall societal perception of women's abilities. As a result of the establishment of a research fellowship for the study of gifted children at Stanford University in 1919, Terman completed a study of 121 students with IQs "for the most part over 140 and for whom considerable supplementary data had been secured" (Terman, 1925, p. 4). Some of the results of this study are important for our present topic. If there are stereotypic concepts of giftedness in females, and if research validates some of these concepts, even though they may have been caused by bias, they tend to be reinforced. It is interesting to note that Terman's first conclusion was that "there is probably a somewhat higher incidence of intellectual superiority among boys than among girls." Furthermore, he stated: "Heredity is superior. Fifty percent of the fathers belong to the professional groups; not one to the unskilled group" (Terman, 1925, p. 4). Mothers are not mentioned in these conclusions.

The idea of sex stereotyping or bias in education was not considered in early investigations of gifted students. Heredity was all-encompassing; therefore, educational intervention was not considered. It is important to note that earlier studies of genius rarely even considered women. Terman not only included women but also to some extent acknowledged sex differences. However, he continued the earlier notion that differences in sex ratios could be explained in terms of heredity; environment was not considered.

In 1921, Terman initiated his *Genetic Studies of Genius*. This was a longitudinal study of 1,444 children between the ages of 2 and 13 who scored between 130 and 200 on the Stanford-Binet test; median IQs tended to be in the upper 140s to lower 150s. Gifted boys in this study outnumbered gifted girls 831 (57.5%) to 613 (42.5%). Terman addressed this sex ratio and considered such possibilities as biased selection, which he dismissed. "It is possible that the method of selection may have favored the boys, although in view of the fact that nominations on the basis of estimated intelligence were in the vast majority of cases made by women teachers, one would hardly expect this to be the case" (p. 50). He also dismissed the fact that the Stanford-Binet test was possibly more favorable to boys than girls by explaining that some of the bias was due to the sex ratio in families of the gifted.

> At the time the material on sex ratio was tabulated, data were available for 502 of the total 578 families which produced the main experimental group of 643 children. These 502 families yielded 317 gifted boys and 274 gifted girls. . . . It appears, therefore, that the fact which operates to give an excess of boys among the gifted affects no less strongly the siblings of the gifted. It has been suggested that superior vigor or vitality of parents favors maleness of offspring, and that this factor might at the same time exert a favorable influence upon the nervous structure and mental development of the offspring. . . . superior vigor of fathers would result in an excess of male births.

However, Terman's mental test data bearing on sex variability were so inconsistent that it would be hard to say which way the weight of evidence inclined. Terman indicated, "On the hypothesis of sex difference in variability one would expect to find the highest intelligence scores in our gifted group earned by boys. This however, is not the case in all groups. In the main experimental group the three highest IQs were earned by girls . . . the means for the sexes are almost identical."

Terman concluded his section on sex ratio by noting: "The true cause of the sex ratio cannot be determined from our data. It may be either variability or the differential death rate of embryos. Both of these factors may be involved and possibly others. Biased selection due to the method of nomination and testing is probably not responsible." It must be added that Terman should be given credit for considering the reasons for the disproportionate representation of girls and boys in his study; in many studies done in the early 20th century, that would not have been considered an important factor. (In addition, although one rarely sees the fact noted, there were several women researchers involved in this study.) Terman did not, however, comment on the racial and class bias of his sample:

most of the subjects were white and middle class. Only 0.1% were black, 0.1% were American Indian, and 0.6% were Japanese (based on racial origin of grandparents).

One of the main conclusions from the earliest phases of the *Genetic Study of Genius* was that the subjects presented a picture of all-around better-adjusted individuals than was previously thought. "His results disproved the folk tales in terms of averages, with the gifted surpassing the unselected children in almost all respects" (Sears, 1979, p. 76). The results of this study broadened the conception of giftedness because Terman used an education environment rather than taking a strictly psychological approach, thus allowing the consideration of females.

The next upsurge of interest in gifted education occurred after the Soviet launching of Sputnik in 1957. This event created a national crisis of confidence in our technological expertise and, hence, in our educational system. Now it seemed urgent to seek out the brightest and educate them—especially those with high ability in science and mathematics, thus adding a new dimension to the definition of gifted and talented. This new dimension, however, seems to have been applied primarily to the identification of gifted males. Project Talent (Flanagan, Shaycoft, Richards, & Claudy, 1971) data indicate that gifted high school women did not choose or were not chosen to participate in these programs. For example, 12th-grade female participants' choices of college majors in mathematics and science were low, with 0.3% choosing engineering, 2.2% choosing physical science, and 3.0% choosing mathematics. This is compared to 12th-grade males' choices of college majors: 23.1%, engineering; 8%, physical science; and 4.2%, mathematics.

The mid-1960s and early 1970s brought a concern for equity. Many of the traditional educational assessment instruments, such as intelligence and achievement tests, came under fire for inadequately and unfairly evaluating the abilities of minority and disadvantaged students. This movement also opened up the investigation of sex bias in intelligence tests, the same notion earlier dismissed by Terman. These instruments had been the primary means for identifying gifted students, so these criticisms provided opportunities to broaden attempts to properly identify gifted girls and boys in all racial and economic groups. This, coupled with an additional concern about strict homogeneous grouping on the basis of achievement practiced in many school districts (declared illegal in some districts by the courts, for example, *Hobson v. District of Columbia Public Schools*), led to more public awareness of and concern for the gifted, culminating in a congressionally mandated study, *Education of the Gifted and Talented: Report to the Congress of the United States* (Marland, 1972).

The central theme of the Marland study was that it "confirmed our impression of inadequate provisions for these students and widespread misunderstanding about their needs" (p. 2). One of the major outcomes of the Marland report was the development of a broadened definition of gifted and talented, which subsequently become a part of the Gifted and Talented Children's Act. "Gifted and talented children are those identified by professionally qualified persons, who by virtue of outstanding abilities are capable of high performance. These are children who require differentiated educational programs and/or services beyond those normally provided by the regular school program in order to realize their contribution to self and society" (p. 2). Children capable of high performance included those with demonstrated achievement and/or potential ability in any of the following areas, singly or in combination: general intellectual ability, specific academic aptitude, creative or productive thinking, leadership ability, the visual and performing arts, and psychomotor ability (this area was dropped by the 1978 legislative revision). It should be noted that this report did not specifically address the treatment of gifted girls.

This definition has major implications for schools. First, it recognizes that giftedness is culturally defined. While academic ability is of prime importance in the schools, other talents are rewarded by society. The definition gives credence to the role that schools could play in providing an education appropriate to all of these talent areas, thus providing more avenues for women to demonstrate talent and establishing a rationale for sex equity emphasis in education. Additionally, the definition points out that the gifted should be identified by professionally qualified individuals. This moves identification away from strict reliance on standardized instruments such as the IQ test, thus allowing for broadened, more appropriate identification procedures, which should help single out gifted girls. Taken as a whole, this definition has had a significant impact on the expansion of the concept of giftedness and the role of education in this process, although research findings are not yet available on its effectiveness in identifying gifted females. However, based on research regarding the sex-differentiated development of creativity and motivation, identification procedures such as those recommended by Renzulli (1979) should be examined for sex equity. Renzulli has proposed, as a result of reviewing biographical information on eminent persons, that there are three determining factors in giftedness: above-average ability, creativity, and task commitment. It is the combination or intersection of these three factors, rather than the possession of only one, which makes for giftedness. Renzulli also states that these three components could be brought to bear on any of the talent areas, thus reinforcing the expanded definition that appears in the Gifted and Talented Children's Act.

These contemporary definitions have moved the concept of giftedness far from the narrow idea of the genius. However, most of the growth in research and educational programming for the gifted has taken place in the areas of general intellectual ability or specific academic aptitude, and this emphasis is likely to remain. Reasons for this concentration, despite attempts to broaden the definition of giftedness, include public attitudes regarding the role of schools and difficulty in identifying other types of giftedness. Many want schools to help learners develop competencies in basic academic subjects more than in leadership or creativity in the visual and performing arts. For this reason, the intellectual and academic areas are the foci of this chapter, although it is critical to note that identification of and programming for students in creative or productive thinking, leadership, and the visual and performing arts should be a part of future research agendas if the needs of all gifted students are to be met.

IDENTIFICATION OF GIFTED STUDENTS

Gifted students typically are identified through a three-stage process: nomination, screening, and placement. Schools aim to set up an identification process that is both effective and efficient. It should be effective in the sense that it selects all students who possess high ability and require differentiated educational services; it should be efficient to the extent that the number nominated is close to the number placed, since the identification process is costly in terms of money, time, and people. Both concerns have implications for gifted females.

Nomination.   The nomination stage of the identification process is critical for gifted females because it determines which students will be selected for appropriate services. Students may be placed in the pool of nominees on the basis of a standardized test score or, more frequently, by teacher nomination. While teacher nomination has frequently been used, the method has been examined critically in several studies. Earlier researchers cautioned against using the opinion of teachers because they tend both to overnominate and to overlook. Teachers tend to have a middle-class point of view that may cause them unconsciously to favor middle-class students. Thus, teachers' biased notion of giftedness may cause the nomination process to be unreliable.

Often, teacher nomination procedures have not provided the teacher with a definition of giftedness, thus causing teachers to rely on their own perceptions. Therefore, Wilson (1963) hypothesized that classroom teachers could effectively determine who the gifted students were if some training were given regarding characteristics gifted children exhibit in the classroom; however, his experimental study showed that such training did not increase the accuracy with which teachers nominated gifted students. Jacobs (1971) sought to investigate further the accuracy of teacher nomination of gifted students. His results indicated that teachers tended to overnominate students who were average in intelligence. Observers found that these students were verbally adept children who were very cooperative and appeared to elicit teacher approval by their actions. This would seem to support one frequent criticism of teacher nomination of gifted students, which centers around the teacher's misconception that the gifted student is the "good lesson learner" or "good student" (Gallagher, 1975).

Taken as a whole, the findings on teacher nomination seem to indicate that teachers consistently overlook half of the gifted students while overnominating students who are actually of average ability. While the research on teacher nomination has not been analyzed according to sex, some implications can be drawn by considering the literature in light of research on gifted girls. Brophy and Good (1974) indicated that teachers tend to reward students who exhibit appropriate sex role characteristics. For girls in elementary school, appropriate behavior fits with the "good student" image of conforming, passive behavior. These are the students the teacher is likely to nominate as gifted. However, research on the personality traits of gifted girls points to a profile that might cause the teacher to overlook many gifted girls. The gifted girl tends to have a more androgynous personality profile, exhibiting both feminine and masculine characteristics. She also displays an interest in many nontraditional areas which are considered more masculine-oriented (Wolleat, 1979). Therefore, if the gifted girl is acting on her abilities, the behaviors she displays are not likely to fit with the teacher's conception of the ideal student. Reliance on teacher nomination with its stereotypic biases may be preventing the identification of gifted girls.

Screening and Placement. The screening process of the identification procedure has been broadened to include multiple assessment procedures, using a variety of instruments and sources of information. There is not complete agreement on the accuracy of these multiple assessments, some of which may contribute differentially to the identification of gifted girls and boys.

One element of multiple assessment is the teacher behavioral rating scale such as that developed by Renzulli, Hartman, & Callahan (1981). In some cases up to half of the information considered for placement may rely on teacher opinion. As research on teacher nomination indicates, teacher judgment may be biased and unreliable. To the extent that teacher rating is a part of the screening procedure, the gifted girl who displays nonstereotypic sex role behaviors may be placed at a serious disadvantage in the identification process.

Other components of the screening procedure usually include standardized tests related to intelligence, achievement, creativity, or critical thinking, depending on the focus of the program. There is almost no research on sex bias and the scores of gifted girls on these instruments. It may be theorized that bias in testing may not be nearly as important to this population as is the ineffectiveness in measuring ability and achievement at the upper extremes. However, extrapolation of other research would seem to indicate that there is a need to explore bias in this area (see chapter 10) as well as a need to understand the meaning of IQ scores in light of the differential socialization and life experiences of males and females. One study of sex differences in IQ of intellectually gifted students found that there was more variability in IQ in adolescent gifted girls than boys, with a greater number of girls showing a decrease over time in IQ. This study also found that gifted girls' grades do not correlate with IQ, thus affecting multiple assessment procedures that include grades as a component and also influencing teacher ratings (Hall, 1980).

Placement decisions are usually made by a school committee and are based on a review of the data gathered. While some school districts place students on the basis of a cut-off score obtained from the multiple assessment procedures, there is also room for consideration of individual differences and needs. Thus, final placement of the gifted girl usually relies on scores and/or subjective opinion.

EDUCATIONAL PROGRAMS FOR GIFTED STUDENTS

The recent upsurge of interest in the education of the gifted has resulted in a variety of programs for these students. Kaplan (1974) has classified these into three major categories: enrichment, acceleration, and guidance. Little research has been conducted on the efficacy of these models for gifted students in general, and there is even less information available on the appropriateness of these models to the specific needs of gifted females. In this section we shall discuss the first two of these three categories.

Enrichment. Enrichment programs are the most common model, particularly at the elementary level, yet there is little research on the effects of these part-time programs. One specific enrichment model calls for revolving students into a special class where they may work toward the completion of an advanced-level product (Reis & Renzulli, 1982). A study of sex differences found that a higher proportion of females took part than males, but there were no significant differences in the quality of products completed by males and females (Reis, 1981). The impact of enrichment programs, which typically have objectives related to developing critical thinking, problem solving, creative thinking, self-concept, and research and product development skills, remains largely uninvestigated with regard to gifted girls.

Acceleration. Most of the research on sex differences in programs for the gifted has focused on acceleration. A study of early admission to school (Birch, 1981), one accelerative option, indicated that the overwhelming majority of the children admitted early to first grade were making satisfactory school adjustments in all areas: academic, social, emotional, and physical. It is important to note that girls outnumbered boys in this sample. Fox (1981) stated that it is unfortunate, especially for girls, that there is not a focus on early admission to first grade: "Studies from twenty or more years ago found these programs were effective in promoting achievement of both boys and girls and more girls than boys were identified for them. The current lack of special academic programs for the gifted student in the early years may be especially problematic for girls because gifted boys are more likely than the girls to move ahead in school on their own in the high school years" (p. 10).

Recent studies of willingness of girls to participate in accelerative opportunities present a mixed picture, especially in the junior and senior high school years. Fox (1981), reporting on the Study of Mathematically Precocious Youth (SMPY) at the Johns Hopkins University, noted that far more boys than girls have participated in this study, although in the verbal programs for the gifted at Hopkins, especially in the writing seminars, girls have outnumbered boys. Fox pointed out, however, that even though girls are still significantly outnumbered by boys, changes have occurred in the attitudes of and benefits for girls in the SMPY program.

Although efforts to help mathematically gifted students in the early 1970s at the Johns Hopkins University were more successful with boys than girls, a recent study of the impact of special programs for mathematically gifted students upon the mathematical interests and achievements of girls found two encouraging results. First, the attitudes of gifted seventh grade girls in 1978 were more positive and more similar to those of gifted boys with respect to course-taking and acceleration than were the attitudes and behaviors of gifted girls who were seventh graders in 1973. Second, girls who had access to special programs seemed to reap some benefits from those experiences. Girls who participated in accelerated programs in their school systems achieved as well as the boys in terms of test performance and were expecting to accelerate their study of mathematics as much as were the boys. Girls who participated in programs in which exposure to female role models was a key component had higher educational aspirations and greater career commitments than did girls in programs without such a component or girls who did not participate in any special program. (p. 10)

Although separate schools or self-contained programs within schools for gifted high school students seem to be on the increase, educational programming for senior high gifted students most often takes the form of advanced courses which are either enriched or presented earlier than the normal sequence (for example, algebra in the eighth grade rather than the ninth). This is a form of selected acceleration, and it moves students toward courses during the last one or two years of high school which can be applied toward college credit. The Educational Testing Service administers a program of Advanced Placement (AP) examinations once per year. The scores students receive on these examinations determine whether or not college credit will be granted and also determines the amount of credit in many cases. The College Entrance Examination Board (CEEB) does not have separate median scores for females and males for these tests; however, the CEEB does keep data on numbers taking the examination, by sex. For example, table 12 shows that even though females were still underrepresented in AP exams in mathematics and physics in 1982, the change in their representation from 1971 to 1982 was positive (CEEB, 1982). Note that the overall participation rate for students taking calculus AB and BC increased approximately 220%, whereas female participation increased over 300%. The trend was the same in chemistry. In physics, where females made up only 8.3% of those taking the test in 1971, there was a 659% increase. Despite this dramatic change, females still made up less than 15% of those taking the physics AP examinations.

Did the incidence of male-female AP test taking change in other subject areas? In the 1982 AP English examinations, the total of 7,463 students who took the language and composition tests consisted of 44.4% males and 55.6% females. In the composition and literature English AP, 41.5% were males and 58.5% were females. The divergence overall was not nearly as great as in the mathematics and science areas.

Male-female differences in scores on the Scholastic Aptitude Test (SAT) remained relatively constant between 1973 and 1981. Median scores on the

Table 12. Participation, by Sex, in Advanced Placement Examinations Administered through the College Entrance Examination Board (Mathematics and Science)

Advanced Placement Test	Participation, 1971						Participation, 1982					
	Female		Male		Total		Female		Male		Total	
	No.	%	No.	%	No.	%	No.	%	No.	%	No.	%
Calculus AB	2613	24.7	7979	75.3	10592	100	9302	39	14523	61	23825	100
Calculus BC	731	17.3	3483	82.7	4214	100	2303	28.5	5790	72.5	8093	100
Chemistry	594	14.8	3411	85.2	4005	100	2532	26.7	6944	73.3	9476	100
Physics B	84	8.3	931	91.7	1015	100	554	21.2	2063	78.8	2617	100
Physics C (1971)	61	6.9	825	93.1	886	100	Not administered in 1982					
1982: Physics C (Mechanics)	Not administered in 1971						361	14.9	2055	85.1	2416	100
Physics C (Elect. & Magnet.)	Not administered in 1971						256	14.5	1515	85.5	1771	100

Source: College Entrance Examination Board (1971 and 1982).

verbal subtest were relatively similar, but the median score on the mathematics subtest for males tended to be approximately 50 points higher than that for females. What occurred at the higher score intervals, where we can infer that gifted students would achieve? Table 13 indicates percentages of males and females in the 600 to 699 and the 700 to 800 score intervals. The incidence for males and females at 700 and above on the verbal subtest was the same and remained constant through the 8-year period. At the 600 to 699 interval, there was a slight downward trend in the percentage of students scoring at that level, but a fairly constant 0 to 2% difference between male and female incidence, favoring the males, remained. In the upper intervals of the mathematics test, the incidence of males was consistently higher in both the 700 to 800 and the 600 to 699 categories. In the 600 to 699 category, there were consistently 7 to 8% fewer females than males. Does this difference end in high school? The results of the Graduate Record Examination shown in table 14 indicate that the gap between males and females in the quantitative area widened and from 1978 to 1981 was a fairly consistent 77 to 79 points lower for females. Verbal median scores for males and females were fairly constant and similar (there was only a two-point difference in favor of females). A relatively common cut-off score for admittance to many graduate programs is a combined GRE score of 1000, and financial aid is often partially based on graduate admissions test scores. The lower scores for women in the quantitative area conceivably could make the difference between being admitted or not admitted to a graduate program. If we theorize that many of the persons who pursue graduate work are gifted, then we can imagine the handicap that lack of a quantitative background is for women.

How can educators best work with gifted females to motivate them in the areas of mathematics and physical science? Casserly (1979) compared school systems that were successful in getting girls to participate in advanced placement mathematics and science courses to those schools having relatively few girls participating. She made the following recommendations based on the differences:

1. Schools should be encouraged to offer AP courses in mathematics, chemistry, and physics, and girls should be actively sought out. Recruitment strategies should be deliberately thought through and begun at the junior high level.
2. Teachers of the AP courses should be used in recruitment efforts.
3. Schools should encourage and enable AP teachers to obtain appropriate materials for conducting college and career counseling within these courses, including information on financial, academic, and professional opportunities open to women.
4. Counselors should become sensitized to their own attitudes toward mathematics and the physical sciences and toward professional women in these fields, and should recognize their responsibility for keeping options open for students and encouraging enrollment of all eligible girls.

Table 13.   Scholastic Aptitude Test Score Incidence Over 600 for Males and Females, 1973–1981

Year Score	1973		1974		1975		1976		1977		1978		1979		1980		1981	
	M	F	M	F	M	F	M	F	M	F	M	F	M	F	M	F	M	F
							Verbal: Percentage in Interval											
700–800	1	1	1	1	1	1	1	1	1	1	1	1	1	1	1	1	1	1
600–699	9	8	9	8	7	6	7	7	7	7	7	6	7	6	7	6	7	6
							Mathematics: Percentage in Interval											
700–800	4	1	6	1	6	1	6	1	6	1	6	1	5	1	4	1	4	1
600–699	17	9	17	10	16	9	17	9	16	9	16	9	16	8	16	9	16	8

Source: College Entrance Examination Board (1982).

5.   Girls from AP classes or girls who have taken these courses should be invited to participate in science or mathematics demonstrations and discussions with younger girls as a way to recruit students.

While AP courses are not designed specifically for gifted students, they are very often the only programming option available for the gifted at the secondary level. They also serve to condense the amount of time the student will need to spend on basic subjects in college. Gifted girls should be encouraged to take advantage of these courses as a way both to accelerate their studies and to provide time for broadening their knowledge.

Other programs to help gifted females participate more fully in and excel in courses such as mathematics and physical sciences are described in chapter 13. Although these programs are not specifically for gifted females, they have many segments that can be replicated or adapted for their use. In addition, the research by Brody and Fox (1980) on gifted girls in the Johns Hopkins SMPY program is current, longitudinal, and readily available. Since it is a unique program for the gifted, results need to be evaluated for inclusion into policies and programs on the local school level. Shorter-term programs such as *Math for Gifted Girls* (Cook, 1980), which was designed "to increase gifted girls' awareness of the usefulness of mathematics in relation to career choice, . . . to increase gifted girls' confidence in their ability to do mathematics, and to increase their mathematics ability," present possibilities for intervening in curricula.

Skipping grades is not as viable an option today as it was several decades ago, even though reviews of research on acceleration indicate that there were no sex differences in the results and that acceleration, on the whole, produced beneficial results (Flesher & Pressey, 1955). Given general reluctance to permit grade skipping and the reluctance of girls (particularly in adolescence) to accelerate even within subject areas, the appropriateness of this programming option for girls should be reexamined and gifted girls should be encouraged to move ahead.

Table 14.   Graduate Record Examination Mean Score by Sex, 1978/79–1980/81*

Graduate Record Examination subtest	Mean score, female			Mean score, male		
	1978/79	1979/80	1980/81	1978/79	1979/80	1980/81
Total taking test	114,558	112,218	109,125	102,580	97,182	92,717
Verbal	489	488	486	487	486	484
Quantitative	478	480	484	555	558	563

*Based on data from Wild (1980, 1981) and Goodison (1982).

Brandt (1981) quoted Stanley in an interview in which he cited examples of students from the Johns Hopkins SMPY program who were radically accelerated and indicated that it is necessary for the good of the individual and the country to have these students complete formal schooling as soon as possible in order that they put their exceptional talent to work: "The average age of the Ph.D. recipients in science or mathematics in this country is 30. Most have been attending school all that time—25 years or so. That is much too long; it prolongs the training period unnecessarily and it is a tragic waste of a rare national resource. . . . at least half the young people we identify will get Ph.D.'s from excellent universities by the time they're in their early twenties, or even their teens" (p. 101). Research on the effects of role models on gifted girls also has implications for programs such as independent study or internships/mentorships. For example, Stake and Granger (1978), who did not specifically use a gifted student sample, found that same-sex teachers had a powerful effect in both encouraging and discouraging commitment to a career in science. A correlation was found between greater career commitment and same-sex teachers only for students who had had large amounts of individual teacher contact through project work and who wanted to emulate the teacher. Fox and Richmond (1979) also emphasized the importance of contact with a female role model for sustaining nontraditional interests in mathematically gifted adolescent girls. Callahan (1979) pointed out the need for more research on mentorships, particularly with regard to the sex of the mentor. Studies on the effect of sex of teacher on achievement of students are inconclusive (Brophy and Good, 1974), making it impossible to draw conclusions with regard to possible effects on the appropriateness of independent study or internships/mentorships for development of potential in gifted girls.

CAREER EDUCATION AND GUIDANCE
OF THE GIFTED GIRL

Since World War II, guidance and career education have been used to help students plan their educational and occupational goals. In its early stages, guidance was mainly vocational. Its goals were broadened in the ensuing decades to include an emphasis on educational and personal-social components. Rarely was the counseling of young girls and women a separate topic in either courses or textbooks for counselors. When the topic was included, it was full of bias and stereotypes as well as the overt acceptance of discrimination. *Counseling Adolescents* (Hamrin & Paulson, 1951) was a popular text used in counselor training. It contained a section on "Girls' Special Problems," which perhaps can serve as a partial explanation of why even gifted girls did not bother to take career planning seriously.

> Most girls who wish to make homemaking their career do not go directly from school into that vocation; they must find some other employment for the interval. Often girls take any kind of job, thinking of it merely as a stopgap between school and the altar. Others make actual vocational plans in spite of the fact that their true interests lie in homemaking rather than in business or the professions. Frequently this deep interest is not expressed because most girls are reluctant to voice their true desires. For some reason, if a girl does voice the desire to marry and then fails to do so, she is apt to feel great chagrin.
> . . . In spite of the fact that most girls, whether they marry or not, eventually become homemakers, much of the effort made to prepare them for vocations is expended in training them to be secretaries and teachers rather than to be homemakers. This makes a vocational choice more difficult for those girls who prefer homemaking to working outside the home. They must choose their vocations without much help and without acknowledging their real desires.
> The girls who genuinely desire to make careers for themselves outside the home must be prepared to enter a work world which is dominated by men. While they must be ready to do the work often done by men, in many businesses at present they must be willing to accept sex discrimination in salary, position, and advancement. (pp. 51–52)

Since the 1950s, when that text was popular, more women have entered fields nontraditional for their sex and an increased percentage have pursued advanced graduate work (see table 15), especially since the 1950s. Along with these changes, counselor education and texts have changed. More attention has been focused on the counseling needs of the gifted female in the past decade. This represents an earnest effort to recognize that gifted students can benefit from counseling just as can the regular student. "It also recognizes that counselors may need preservice and inservice training to be able to play a central role in schools to ensure that attitudes of teachers, administrators, parents, students— and indeed counselors themselves—grow to eliminate sexism in schools for gifted students" (Colangelo & Zaffrann, 1979). Studies in the area of career education and guidance of females can be divided into those concerning special counseling needs of women and girls (see chapter 18) and those specifically concerning the guidance of the gifted woman student. Fox and Richmond (1979) indicated that counselors must turn to research in order to meet the needs of gifted young women. In discussing the results of the Intellectually Gifted Child Study Group at the Johns Hopkins University, they noted three major factors

Table 15. Number and Percentage of Doctoral Degrees Granted to Women, by Field and Decade, 1920–1981

	Decade														
	1920–29		1930–39		1940–49		1950–59		1960–69		1970–79		1980–81		1920–81	
	No.	%	No.	%	No.	%	No.	%	No.	%	No.	%	No.	%	No.	%
Physical Sciences	247	7.6	442	6.6	406	5.0	685	3.7	1,577	4.6	3,946	8.2	1,004	12.1	8,805	6.8
Math	51	14.5	115	14.8	89	10.7	113	5.0	364	5.7	1,092	10.1	207	14.1	2,031	8.9
Physics & Astronomy	39	5.9	51	3.8	62	4.2	98	2.0	213	2.2	532	3.9	140	7.0	1,135	3.4
Chemistry	141	7.3	254	6.4	223	4.2	443	4.4	931	6.4	1,888	10.4	490	15.6	4,370	7.6
Earth & Environ. Sciences	16	4.8	22	3.5	32	5.7	31	1.9	69	2.0	348	5.8	120	9.9	638	4.6
Computer Sciences											38	11.5	47	10.4	85	10.9
Engineering	2	.9	6	.7	7	.5	20	.3	77	.4	424	1.4	189	3.8	725	1.1

(*continued*)

Table 15. *(Continued)*

| | Decade | | | | | | | | | | | | | | | |
| | 1920–29 | | 1930–39 | | 1940–49 | | 1950–59 | | 1960–69 | | 1970–79 | | 1980–81 | | 1920–81 | |
	No.	%	No.	%	No.	%	No.	%	No.	%	No.	%	No.	%	No.	%
Life Sciences	378	15.9	765	15.1	738	12.7	1,318	9.1	3,078	11.6	8,921	18.1	2,785	25.8	17,978	15.8
Biological	341	19.5	698	17.8	699	15.7	1,174	11.8	2,739	15.1	7,068	21.6	1,941	28.5	14,660	18.9
Agricultural	8	2.2	11	1.6	5	.6	36	1.1	80	1.4	496	5.0	256	11.5	892	3.6
Medical	29	10.9	56	12.4	34	6.9	108	8.1	259	9.5	1,303	21.2	588	33.5	2,377	18.1
Social Sciences	325	17.1	562	15.8	580	14.5	1,510	11.0	3,604	14.3	14,641	24.5	4,480	35.1	24,287	20.1
Anthropology	8	22.2	28	22.4	22	15.2	90	19.3	218	21.5	1,450	42.6	326	44.2	2,142	36.1
Sociology	32	15.4	89	19.9	99	17.2	221	14.2	442	17.5	1,808	28.9	473	39.3	3,164	24.6
Economics	52	8.5	71	6.4	83	7.1	125	4.2	245	4.6	734	8.8	201	12.9	1,512	7.1
Pol. Sci. & Pub. Adm.	26	9.0	45	8.5	45	7.8	87	5.4	257	8.2	1,043	14.8	257	20.7	1,787	12.3
Psychology	189	29.4	290	26.0	302	24.1	911	14.8	2,264	20.7	8,361	32.2	2,782	43.1	15,099	28.7
Arts & Humanities	619	25.7	1,291	24.5	1,182	22.9	1,758	15.5	4,423	19.5	14,625	31.4	3,075	40.4	26,973	27.5

Field																
History	143	21.6	277	19.3	237	16.6	327	10.4	638	11.3	1,662	15.9	570	33.7	2,276	9.2
Eng. & Am. Lit.	159	30.8	385	28.4	385	26.8	548	17.8	1,515	23.9	4,669	38.9	920	47.5	8,650	32.4
Modern Foreign Lang.	101	29.8	287	27.0	284	29.2	396	22.9	1,032	31.2	3,336	46.8	571	61.3	4,994	32.3
Professional Fields	38	6.9	78	7.7	113	9.6	249	9.2	798	12.3	2,387	16.9	799	29.2	4,462	15.5
Business Admin.	—	—	2	1.0	14	6.3	32	3.4	77	2.6	355	5.0	181	14.4	661	5.1
Law Jurisprudence	9	3.9	14	4.7	7	6.3	14	4.7	6	2.2	15	5.4	2	4.1	67	1.5
Library Sciences	—	—	8	33.3	15	34.1	18	28.6	43	27.0	233	40.7	76	59.8	393	39.7
Social Work	—	—	1	50.0	3	50.0	26	41.3	180	36.7	506	88.3	191	49.4	907	39.7
Education	209	18.1	615	19.7	1,086	22.8	2,431	18.0	5,367	19.5	21,258	30.2	6,909	45.9	37,875	27.9
Total All Fields	1,826	15.3	3,784	14.8	4,115	13.5	7,972	9.9	18,964	11.7	66,269	20.7	19,259	30.9	122,199	17.7

Source: Doctorate Records file, Office of Science and Engineering Personnel, National Research Council, National Academy of Sciences, Washington, DC (1982).

related to sex differences in the achievement of these gifted students, particularly in the area of mathematics: differential career interests and expectations, encouragement from significant others, and early identification of gifted students. Each of these factors has implications for sound counseling practices. To substantiate these factors, Fox and Richmond cite the Fox, Pasternak, and Peiser (1976) study, which, using the Strong-Campbell Interest Inventory, found that gifted females showed much stronger interest in mathematics and science than a random sample of males and female adolescents, but lower interest than gifted male students. The importance of the significant other in influencing the gifted female student to take mathematics courses, to remain in these courses, and to choose careers in which they can apply these subjects is prominent in studies by Astin, Casserly, Earnest, and Helson.

New Voices in Counseling the Gifted, edited by Colangelo and Zaffrann (1979), contains a major section on counseling gifted females. Besides brief summaries of the research in the area, there are strategies that can assist counselors in their work with the gifted. Wolleat presents research on sex role stereotyping, the career development process, and gifted females; Casserly provides research and strategies on career education for the gifted female; Rodenstein and Glickauf-Hughes discuss their research findings about the factors that influence gifted women to become homemakers, to choose careers, or to combine the two, and the implications of their research for counseling; and Bruch discusses the model she has devised to assist counselors in understanding the counseling needs of the creatively gifted woman. Project Choice (Fleming, 1979) is a career development program designed especially for the talented adolescent female. This 14-session diagnostic-prescriptive program was funded by WEEA. Project Choice was designed to "broaden the career options of talented intellectual adolescent women through identifying those personal and cultural barriers that may interfere with the realization of their great potential and then engaging these students in activities designed to overcome the particular impediments to fulfillment" (p. 3). One of the major problems with this program is its length. It may be difficult for a secondary school counselor to work a 14-session career program for talented female adolescents into a fixed secondary school schedule. Many schools could, however, integrate or adapt part of Project Choice into an existing group guidance program, an extracurricular activity, or an existing, related class.

TEACHER TRAINING

The teacher who interacts with the gifted girl is an important element in the success of educational efforts. Renzulli (1981) surveyed 21 experts in an attempt to identify the key features of successful programs for the gifted. According to the ratings of these experts, the selection and training of the teacher was the most important feature of a successful program, followed by the curriculum designed for these students. Yet there is some evidence in both the general teacher education literature and the research on gifted students that there may be sex differences in teachers' interactions with gifted students. An early study on class-room interactions was conducted by Gallagher, Aschner, and Jenne (1967). The study sought to determine, among other things, whether there was a significant relationship between the teacher's cognitive performance and variation in students' thought processes as assessed by Guilford's Structure of Intellect, and whether there were significant differences among various subgroups of gifted students. They found that there was a close relationship between the type of teacher questions asked and the pattern of thought expression observed in student responses. This relationship existed across a wide range of secondary subject areas and teachers. Sex differences were found, with boys showing more expressiveness in all categories of thought processes. After finding no sex differences in written assessments of thought processes, the authors hypothesized that sex role expectations were the determining factor in differences in classroom expression. Further study of gifted junior high students (Gallagher et al., 1967) found that males received a higher percentage than females of abstract, process questions relative to factual or product questions. Other differences in classroom interaction patterns are described in chapter 11.

General classroom research suggests that teacher interaction with students plays an important role in communicating expectations, encouraging thinking and problem-solving skills, and developing independence and initiative in students. The little research available specifically on the gifted seems to indicate that teacher behaviors in general are not enhancing the intellectual and emotional development of the gifted girl in the same way as such behaviors enhance those of the gifted boy. As Gallagher et al. (1967) conclude, the observed differences in classroom performance are "apparently related more strongly to attitudinal and motivational factors than to basic cognitive differences" (p. 75). This research on the impact of just one component of teacher behavior points out the need to help teachers become aware of the abilities, needs, and interests of gifted girls and to help them acquire the strategies necessary for developing the potential of these girls. As pointed out earlier in this chapter, teachers have expectations and stereotypes of gifted students. Such attitudes are strongly held. The erroneous idea of the gifted student as a conforming, "good" student may directly conflict with the androgynous nature of the gifted girl and her need for direct achievement. Awareness and skill training will be necessary at both the preservice and inservice levels in order to bring about changes in teacher behavior.

Progress has been made in addressing the special needs of gifted females in the teacher and counselor training process. For example, several of the more recent textbooks on the gifted contain specific sections on the gifted female (Clark, 1979; Gallagher, 1975; Gowan, Khatena, and Torrance, 1981; Khatena, 1982; Passow, 1979; and Colangelo and Zaffrann, 1979). While these textbooks are used mainly in graduate training programs and in inservice rather than preservice training, they are attempts, at least, to heighten teachers' awareness of the special needs of gifted students. Course syllabi on the graduate level also frequently include sections on the gifted female as part of a discussion of special populations. Journal articles have begun to appear on the gifted female over the past several years, and one issue of a professional journal of gifted education focused on gifted girls ("Gifted Female," 1980). Sessions specifically on the gifted girl may also be found at national conferences on the gifted and talented and may include specific reference to competencies needed in working with gifted females. A recent inservice program on writing secondary curricula for the gifted included information on gifted females and guidelines for sex-fair curriculum standards. Training materials have been developed at the Equity Institute (Addison, 1983) though funding from the federal Office of the Gifted and Talented. Materials from this project, Professional Development Project to Encourage the Potential of the Gifted Girl, include self-training guides to be used by teachers, counselors, parents, and community group leaders as they interact with secondary-level gifted girls. The objectives of these materials are (1) to help these individuals become aware of the needs of gifted girls and of possibly important factors that might have a negative impact, and (2) to provide them with information and skills that will support the gifted girl in the development of her potential. An Inservice Resource Handbook is also included to provide information and direction for a coordinated local plan to encourage development the gifted girl's potential. All of these examples reflect attempts to reach a professional audience and to train teachers, both directly and indirectly, to meet the specific needs of the gifted girl. Most teacher training programs have occurred at the inservice level, as the majority of these examples illustrate. There remains a need to include training on the gifted in general, and the gifted girl in particular, at the preservice level, in addition to broadening the scope of inservice training on the gifted girl.

RECOMMENDATIONS

Our survey of the research has indicated that there are some positive trends in the education of gifted women; these trends can be seen in the increasing diversity in the careers chosen and entered by gifted women, the upward surge in the number of first professional degrees and other graduate degrees earned, and the incidence of gifted women in programs designed for them. Females tend now (as indicated in the 1980 Elementary and Secondary Civil Rights Survey) to be participating in gifted and talented educational programs at a somewhat higher rate than males: in that survey, their participation rate per thousand students was 27.4, whereas for males it was 24.2. Research is needed to determine, however, whether this participant is truly the gifted female or if she is the "good lesson learner."

Research is also needed to determine the extent of minority females' participation in gifted and talented education. Again, there is evidence that minority students overall are underrepresented in programs for the gifted and talented: their participation rate per thousand in 1980 was 17.3 compared to the white student rate of 28.8. This survey did not, however, break down sex within race, so it is difficult to ascertain with certainty the actual minority female/male participation. When analyzing the 1980 statistics for specific minority groups, it can be noted that the American Indian, Hispanic, and Black minority groups are underrepresented in the gifted and talented programs when compared to their incidence in the population, whereas Asians tend to have higher representation. In addition to obtaining better basic information on representation of minority females in programs for the gifted and talented, it should also be a priority to identify gifted minority women and to assess their special needs in programs for the gifted and talented.

Our review of the research and our gathering of data, particularly on national testing programs, does indicate an increased concern in the United States, particularly at the elementary and secondary levels, for identifying and providing appropriate educational programs for gifted students. There also is some evidence that educators, parents, and gifted females themselves are becoming increasingly aware of the special problems faced by the talented woman in our society. Nevertheless, stereotypes still remain—vestiges of the earlier research on the gifted and talented and of earlier textbook and societal perceptions of the value and "place" of females. Therefore, we have developed some specific recommendations for further research that focuses on the gifted female. Some of this research requires sophisticated techniques and sampling procedures; other suggestions can be carried out in the local setting with a minimum expenditure of resources.

The definition of academic giftedness has been broadened in the past decade; however, future research agendas must address definitions, identification, and educational programs for students gifted in creative or productive thinking, leadership, and the visual and performing arts if the needs of all gifted females are to be met. In addition, emerging definitions should also be evaluated for sex bias.

The identification of gifted females must be of prime importance; rarely will a female who has not been selected by this process receive special services for her talents. Several areas need to be addressed. Nomination forms and behavioral rating scales used in the screening process are based on the results of research that was not analyzed in terms of sex differences. Because much of the earlier research on the gifted included only gifted males, many of those working in the field believe that there are no differences between males and females. The possibilities for bias in the matrix procedure and the possible influence of stereotypic expectations on the part of placement committee members need further investigation. There is evidence that sex bias and stereotypes exist in standardized testing instruments; however, this influence on the assessment of abilities must be more thoroughly investigated before the impact of possible sex discrimination on the identification of gifted girls can be determined.

There is a need for further research on educational programs for the gifted female. What programs really are significant educationally for the gifted female?

Does acceleration, enrichment, separate programming, or a combination produce the best development of potential? Are there environmental motivations that can encourage or discourage the participation of females in programs for the gifted? Research on educational programs should try to determine what effect significant others, such as parents and peers, have on the participation and educational treatment of gifted females. Does research focus too much on the cognitive aspects of giftedness? The literature alludes to the influence of self-concept, socialization, and stereotyping on the development of talent. Researchers do look at the affective domain in some studies; however, many times they tend not to include sex differences as an important part of this area.

We must recognize the importance of mathematics and physical science in expanding the number of careers open to gifted females. Research in this area tends to be limited to a few programs. To add to our research base in this area, other programs designed to increase the participation and retention of gifted students in mathematics (such as *Equals* and *Multiplying Options and Subtracting Bias*) need to be evaluated for use with gifted females. Research is needed on the type of mathematics courses females are taking. Are gifted females participating in higher-level mathematics at an expected rate? For example, advanced placement examination data could be analyzed for score differentials by sex and by minority group with very little effort. If gifted females are not participating, what are the barriers to their participation? What strategies can be used to increase their participation and retention?

Counseling and career guidance are extremely important in all phases of the education of the gifted female. Research is needed to determine the most effective counseling and career education techniques: for example, what are the effects of mentoring, role modeling, and intern programs on the gifted female's course and career selection? Counselor self-monitoring is needed in regard to the incidence and type of counseling of gifted girls. Do counselors tend to subscribe to the old adage that the gifted female will "come out all right" without counseling and career guidance? Are counselors aware of her special counseling needs? Do they use the special counseling programs available for counseling the gifted? Is there early counseling in course selection, especially at the sixth-grade level when sequencing of courses becomes important?

There are several recommendations for teacher training in gifted and talented education. Teachers are the key to delivering bias-free services to the gifted female. Both preservice and inservice education should include a component related to the delivery of this bias-free education for gifted females. Although there has been research on classroom interaction, for example, few generalizable studies exist on teacher interaction with gifted girls, either in programs for the gifted or in regular placement. In addition, textbooks are one of the main tools of undergraduate and graduate education; they need to include resources and research on sex differences between gifted male and female students, acknowledging what exists and eliminating the myths about gifted females. We also need more research on the effect of the sex of the teacher on the student in gifted education; for example, what is the influence of the male science teacher on the education, motivation, and career aspirations of the gifted female?

Until there is a significant body of research on the education of gifted females, this type of research and evaluation should be a priority. We know that there is a dearth of research on the gifted which is analyzed and presented on the basis of sex. The data either need to be collected or need to be reanalyzed. There is also a problem of generalizability from the research that is available on gifted females. The sampling techniques usually lack both adequacy in numbers and randomness in design. Finally, school districts that have programs for the gifted and talented should build into their programming design inexpensive methods of evaluation that also consider differential effects of the program on females and males. A significant amount of information on the value of various curricular strategies for gifted females is lost because of the lack of this type of local school evaluation.

REFERENCES

Addison, L. (1983). *The gifted girl—helping her be the best she can be.* Bethesda, MD: Equity Institute.

Astin, H. S. (1968). Career development of girls during the high school years. *Consulting Psychology 15*(6), 536–540.

Birch, J. W. (1981). Early school admission for mentally advanced children. In W. B. Barbe & J. S. Renzulli (Eds.), *Psychology and education of the gifted* (3rd ed., pp. 303–307). New York: Irvington.

Brandt, R. (1981, November). On mathematically talented youth: A conversation with Julian Stanley. *Educational Leadership,* pp. 101–106.

Brody, L. & Fox, L. H. (1980). An accelerative program for mathematically gifted girls. In L. H. Fox, L. Brody, & D. Tobin (Eds.), *Women and the mathematical mystique* (pp. 164–178). Baltimore: Johns Hopkins University Press.

Brophy, J. E., & Good, T. L. (1974). *Teacher-student relationships: Causes and consequences.* New York: Holt, Rinehart and Winston.

Callahan, C. M. (1979). The gifted and talented woman. In A. H. Passow (Ed.), *The gifted and talented: Their education and development* (pp. 401–423). Chicago: National Society for the Study of Education.

Casserly, P. L. (1979). Helping able young women take math and science seriously in school. In N. Colangelo & R. T. Zaffrann (Eds.), *New voices in counseling the gifted* (pp. 346–369). Dubuque, IA: Kendall/Hunt.

Clark, B. (1979). *Growing up gifted.* Columbus, OH: Merrill.

Colangelo, N., & Zaffrann, R. T. (Eds.). (1979). *New voices in counseling the gifted.* Dubuque, IA: Kendall/Hunt.

College Entrance Examination Board. (1982). *Summary of data from admissions testing programs for achievement, scholastic aptitude tests, and student questionnaires 1973–1981.* Unpublished manuscript. Princeton, NJ: Educational Testing Service.

College Entrance Examination Board, Advanced Placement Program. (1971 and 1982).

State summary reports. Unpublished manuscript. Princeton, NJ: Educational Testing Service.

Cook, N. (1980). *Math for gifted girls.* St. Paul, MN: Northwest Area Foundation.

Ernest, J. (1976). *Mathematics and sex.* Santa Barbara: University of California.

Flanagan, J. C., Shaycoft, M. F., Richards, J. M., & Claudy, J. G. (1971). *Project talent* (final report). Pittsburgh: American Institutes for Research and University of Pittsburgh.

Fleming, E. S., Hollinger, C. L., Plax, E. C., Kahn, D. G., Hervatin, R. M., Parran, M., George, V., & Moore, J. (1979). *Project choice: Creating her options in career exploration.* Newton, MA: Education Development Center.

Flesher, M. A., & Pressey, S. L. (1955). War-time accelerates ten years after. *Journal of Educational Psychology, 46,* 228–238.

Fox, L. H. (1981). Preparing girls for future leadership roles. *G/C/T, 17,* 7–11.

Fox, L. H., Pasternak, S. R., & Peiser, N. L. (1976). Career-related interests of adolescent boys and girls. In D. P. Keating (Ed.), *Intellectual talent: Research and development* (pp. 242–261). Baltimore: Johns Hopkins University Press.

Fox, L. H., & Richmond, L. J. (1979). Gifted females: Are we meeting their counseling needs? *Personnel and Guidance Journal, 57*(5), 256–259.

Gallagher, J. J. (1975). *Teaching the gifted child* (2nd ed.). Boston: Allyn & Bacon.

Gallagher, J. J., Aschner, M. J., & Jenne, W. (1967). *Productive thinking of gifted children in classroom interaction* (research monograph). Reston, VA: Council for Exceptional Children.

The gifted female. (1980). *Roeper Review, 2*(3).

Goodison, M. B. (1982). A summary of data collected from Graduate Record Examination test takers during 1980–81. Princeton, NJ: Educational Testing Service.

Gowan, J. C., Khatena, J., & Torrance, E. P. (1981). *Creativity: Its educational implications* (2nd ed.). Itasca, IL: Peacock.

Hall, E. G. (1980). Sex differences in IQ development for intellectually gifted students. *Roeper Review, 2*(3), 25–28.

Hamrin, S. A., & Paulson, B. B. (1951). *Counseling adolescents.* Chicago: Science Research Associates.

Helson, R. (1971). Women mathematicians and the creative personality. *Journal of Counseling and Clinical Psychology, 36*(2), 210–220.

Jacobs, J. C. (1971). Effectiveness of teacher and parent identification of gifted children as a function of school level. *Psychology in the Schools, 8,* 140–142.

Kaley, M. M. (1971). Attitudes toward the dual role of the married professional woman. *American Psychologist, 26,* 301–306.

Kaplan, S. N. (1974). *Providing programs for gifted and talented.* Reston, VA: Council for Exceptional Children.

Khatena, J. (1982). *Educational psychology of the gifted.* New York: Wiley.

Marland, S. (1972). *Education of the gifted and talented* (Report to the Subcommittee on Education, Committee on Labor and Public Welfare, U.S. Senate). Washington, DC.

Passow, A. l., Ed. (1979). *The gifted and talented: Their education and development.* Chicago: University of Chicago Press.

Reis, S. M. (1981). *An analysis of the productivity of gifted students participating in programs using the Revolving Door Identification Model.* Unpublished doctoral dissertation, University of Connecticut, Storrs.

Reis, S. M., & Renzulli, J. S. (1982). A case for a broadened conception of giftedness. *Phi Delta Kappan, 63*, 619–620.

Renzulli, J. S. (1981). Identifying key features in programs for the gifted. In W. B. Barbe & J. S. Renzulli (Eds.), *Psychology and education of the gifted* (3rd ed., pp. 214–219). New York: Irvington.

Renzulli, J. S. (1979). *What makes giftedness? A reexamination of the definition of the gifted and talented.* Ventura, CA: Ventura County Superintendent of Schools Office.

Renzulli, J. S., Hartman, R. K., & Callahan, C. M. (1981). Scale for rating the behavioral characteristics of superior students. In W. S. Barbe & J. S. Renzulli (Eds.), *Psychology and education of the gifted* (3rd ed., pp. 157–164). New York: Irvington.

Renzulli, J. S., & Stoddard, E. P. (1980). *Under one cover: Gifted and talented education in perspective.* Reston, VA: ERIC Clearinghouse on Handicapped and Gifted Children at the Council for Exceptional Children.

Sears, P. S. (1979). The Terman genetic studies of genius, 1923–1972. In A. H. Passow (Ed.), *The gifted and talented: Their education and development* (pp. 75–96). Chicago: University of Chicago Press.

Stake, J. E., & Granger, C. R. (1978). Same-sex and opposite-sex teacher model influences on science career commitments among high school students. *Journal of Educational Psychology, 70*, 180–186.

Terman, L. M. (1925). *Genetic studies of genius* (Vol. 1). Stanford, CA: Stanford University Press.

U.S. Office for Civil Rights. (1982). *Fall 1980 civil rights survey.* Unpublished manuscript. Washington, DC: U.S. Department of Education.

Walberg, H. J. (1969). Physics, femininity, and creativity. *Developmental Psychology 1,* 47–54.

Wild, C. (1980). *A summary of data collected from Graduate Record Examination test-takers during 1978–79.* Princeton, NJ: Educational Testing Service.

Wild, C. (1981). *A summary of data collected from Graduate Record Examination test-takers during 1979–80.* Princeton, NJ: Educational Testing Service.

Wilson, C. D. (1963). Using test results and teacher evaluation in identifying gifted pupils. *Personnel and Guidance Journal, 41,* 720–721.

Wolleat, P. L. (1979). Guiding the career development of gifted females. In N. Colangelo and R. T. Zaffran (Eds.), *New voices in counseling the gifted.* Dubuque, IA: Kendall/ Hunt.

21
Rural Women and Girls

Stuart A. Rosenfeld,
with Ingrid Fabbe Bauer,
Mary Eldridge, Allie Corbin Hixson,
Mary Ann Luciano, and Gail Parks

> When the girls, as well as the boys, are taught that it is just as honorable, and just as necessary, that they should learn something whereby a sure and honest living can be secured as it is for their brothers, much of the unhappiness of life will have vanished, and many would not, as now, be obliged to marry solely for the sake of being taken care of. (*Journal of the Proceedings,* 1885, p. 132)

When a speaker at the 19th Annual Meeting of the National Grange, in 1885, proposed educating women for careers, there was apparently no debate; it was a natural educational goal for the Grange. Farming was, and still is, a family enterprise; and because women played crucial roles in building agricultural economies and in improving rural education, their contribution to rural economic and political life was valued. Perhaps women did not participate in quite the same way as men, but nonetheless their roles were, on the average, more important economically than the roles of women in cities. Thus it is not surprising that from the first, women in the Grange, one of the oldest and largest of rural organizations, had full membership rights. The Grange, during its more feisty period following the Civil War, advocated opening "all avenues of education and employment to either sex" (*Journal of the Proceedings,* 1885, p. 132).

Unfortunately, that dream of educating all women for work as well as for homemaking was never really realized in rural America. The first federal cooperative extension and vocational education policies in fact helped establish homemaking, rather than farmwork, as the proper goal of public education for girls in rural areas. In 1916, during the congressional debates over the Smith-Hughes Act, which authorized the first federal aid for vocational education, the argument one senator gave for including home economics was that "under present conditions the girls' education is more directed to the making of school-teachers or

Patsy Caswell, Margaret Dunkle, Virginia Foxx, Charley Nell Llewellyn, and Mary Thompson assisted in providing information for this chapter.

shopgirls than to the making of homemakers." Instead, he went on, "every girl should be fitted for homemaking and for mothering. No matter what might be the intermediate means of livelihood, it is as wife and mother that she will attain her fullest development and fulfill her manifest destiny" (*Congressional Record,* 1916).

Today, industrialization pervades most rural areas, and only a small fraction of our rural population farm for a living. The mass media and mass transportation have undeniably had homogenizing effects on rural life. Yet most sociologists agree that many urban-rural differences still persist. Lower population density, isolation, and the remnants of an agricultural tradition create conditions that distinguish rural from urban life.

Rural communities tend to be more culturally homogeneous, politically conservative, religious, and family-oriented (Dewey, 1960; Haer, 1952). These conditions affect women differently than they do men (Chu, 1980), and they create obstacles to achieving sex equity. In rural communities, job opportunities for women are more limited; everyday life is more demanding of women's time; and a rural gemeinschaft and conservatism lead to greater pressures for women and girls to conform to traditional roles and values.

Rural schools and school boards, mirroring their communities, are also generally conservative. Therefore, it is not difficult to find examples of school boards keeping "undesirable" courses and ideas out of their schools or taking such "offensive" materials as *Ms.* magazine or Judy Blume books off their library shelves, or firing teachers who adopt a too "independent" lifestyle. Today, the progress of women toward the kind of education needed for equal opportunities in the labor market is, if anything, slower in rural areas than in cities.

In spite of the lag in progress for rural women, there has been little recognition of special issues in the education of rural women and girls, and there was virtually nothing in the literature about the problems of rural women until the mid-1970s. It was not until the causal link between women's economic opportunities and their educational opportunities was brought to the attention of the public, and until the reverse migration from the cities to rural areas caught the imagination of sociologists and politicians, that "rural" became a special population in need of help. In 1976 the National Advisory Council on Women's Educational Programs conducted on investigation of the educational needs of rural women and girls. They found, among other things, that "with respect to the educational needs, little attention is being directed to rural girls and women—by either rural educators and advocates for rural development, or women's education advocates and providers" (Clarenbach, 1977).

It is not enough, however, to identify women's needs in rural areas. Success depends on finding ways to overcome those rural conditions that limit women's educational opportunities. Moreover, the lessons of the past suggest that some rural conditions can support sex equity as well as hinder it. Small schools and the historical importance of women in rural life present unique opportunities. The key to improving girls' and women's options lies in finding ways of exploiting the opportunities as well as eliminating the barriers. In trying to find strategies for helping women and girls in rural education, and trying to find ways to convince rural communities that sex equity is a rural tradition that predates discrimination, perhaps we can build on whatever advantages rural conditions and traditions have to offer.

RURAL CONDITIONS AND RURAL WOMEN

Rural women are not unacquainted with work. They have worked in the fields, taken care of the livestock, managed the books, and marketed the produce. Yet their vocational education has been different from that of men; there has been one "appropriate" vocational program for boys and another for girls. In rural schools, that has meant vocational agriculture for boys and home economics for girls. It wasn't until 1969 that the first woman was allowed to join the Future Farmers of America (FFA) in her high school. And even now, the girl in FFA is likely to be enrolled in a horticulture program rather than a production agriculture program.

Much has changed in rural areas in the past two decades; urban habits have seeped into the towns and villages via the mass media and urban expatriates who have moved to the country. Still, conditions in rural school districts are different enough to cause Title VI, Title IX, and the Vocational Education Act to be viewed differently in Prairie View, Kansas than in Peoria or Los Angeles. They demand different strategies for overcoming sex biases. Many of the differences identified constrain rather than enhance opportunities for women and girls, but others offer special opportunities to advance equity.

Rural Values

At the heart of the issue of sex equity in rural schools are the values and traditions that are imbedded deeply in rural life. Rural people are more conservative—sometimes to the point of being fundamentalist—than urban dwellers. Their deep-rooted traditions affect the ways rural people perceive their family roles, their work, and their community.

Residents of rural and small communities, for example, tend to be more religious, more family-oriented, more community-oriented and less likely to move, and more morally conservative than residents of cities or suburbs. Fights over the teaching of creationism, the banning of certain books, or opposition to sex education are much more likely to occur in rural school districts than in cities.

Rural women are more likely to marry sooner, stay married longer, have more children, and stay home during their child-rearing years than their urban counterparts (Dunne, 1979; Flora & Johnson, 1978). Even while working side by side with their husbands, "the majority of rural women still conform to the traditional norms concerning woman's proper place: in the home, with the children, and supporting of her spouse's endeavors" (Flora & Johnson, 1978, p. 179). When "housewife" is the occupational choice of girls, however, it is more often an expectation than an aspiration (Cosby & Charner, 1978). In a survey of southern adolescent females, 29% expected to be housewives, but only 3% desired it. Among the high school girls interviewed by Dunne (1979), nearly everyone planned on managing a home with little or no help as well as having to work.

The size and intimacy of small towns can also inhibit a teacher from trying to encourage nontraditional behaviors or even to stimulate new ideas about sex roles. In the small rural school district, the teacher is truly a part of the community, and taking an unpopular position can have serious personal repercussions. The resistance and isolation that Carol Kennicott faced trying to make small social and cultural changes in Sinclair Lewis's fictional town of Gopher Prairie (Lewis, 1920) at the turn of the century still exist today. When I asked a home economics teacher in Mazzepa, Minnesota, why there were no boys in her class despite the intent of the vocational education legislation to eliminate sex bias, her answer was direct and simple: because the parents don't want boys in the class. Another home economics teacher in Cabot, Vermont, told me that having boys in her class just slowed her down.

In spite of a recent populist surge in rural areas regarding economic issues, the women's movement and the ERA are still less popular than in cities. One researcher argues that this is not necessarily opposition to equal rights, but it is due to the perceptions of rural women that they already have equality and therefore don't need to have it legislated (Larson, 1978). It is the activism and politicizing they seem to object to more than the concept.

Yet conservative mores do dominate rural towns, and the strength of local values and traditions in rural communities present dilemmas for rural women. The traditional family orientation is increasingly in conflict with the growing desire for self-fulfillment through a career and with the need to supplement the family income. Because these problems are often deeply ingrained and sometimes quite subtle, they are all the more difficult to solve.

One contributing factor is that the trend of rural men—and women—to "let" women work is tempered by the demands made on the time of rural women. While women may be allowed to plow the fields or work in the town hardware store, they still are expected to do the housework and cooking and to look after the children. As a farm woman wrote recently: "I realized in a flash of recognition that Mae and I were asking to be taught the farming jobs, mowing, using tractors, driving teams, combing, baling, spreading manure. But George and Hal weren't asking to be included more in making cheese, housework, laundry, spending days with Andrew or canning and freezing" (Oberst, 1982). Therefore, equality can seem within reach but in reality be unattainable. There has not been the same pressure for men to do work that has traditionally been women's as there has been for women to do work that has traditionally been done by men. Though not only a rural phenomenon by any means, it is more pronounced in rural areas because housework may be more demanding.

Women in Rural Labor Markets

The ultimate test of equality of educational opportunity is equality of economic opportunity. Sex bias in the schools is inextricably linked to sex bias in the workplace. Although problems of women attributed to rural life exist elsewhere, rural economies are different from urban economies; the structure of their respective labor markets is different, and consequently so are the roles of women.

Rural economies still are generally simple, with only one or two major industries; the nonagricultural businesses tend to be concentrated in extraction industries, nondurable manufacturing, or tourism (Teal, 1981). Much of the production is seasonal and/or highly dependent on unskilled or semiskilled labor. Farming, which used to characterize most of rural life, is the primary occupation of only about 10% of the rural work force. In 1981, however, for the first time in recent years, the number of commercial farms increased, though the currently bleak economic conditions may have already caused a reversal. Moreover, many rural residents depend on farming for supplemental income.

Furthermore, most farmers have to depend on the off-farm income of women to make ends meet. Rural economies may include many very small businesses that provide off-season work or supplementary family income. Thus, there are thousands of microbusinesses or cottage industries in rural America, many of which are run by women.

Women in nonmetropolitan areas increased their participation in the labor force by nearly 60% between 1960 and 1980, even faster than women in metropolitan areas; almost half of all nonmetro women now work. In 1978, about 60% of nonmetro women who completed college were employed as teachers or in clerical occupations, and about 50% of nonmetro women with only high school diplomas were in clerical or service occupations. The most common occupation for a nonmetro woman without a high school education was as an operative in a manufacturing plant. In the South, this is frequently in low-paying textile or food processing industries—which, not coincidentally, are extensions of women's traditional work. The increasing proportion of women in the labor force is attributable to economic necessity brought on by inflation and declining farm prices, to the increased demand for their labor with the growth of rural industrialization, and, not insignificantly, to the desire for personal fulfillment.

There are some unique features of rural women's work that have implications for education. One is the propensity of rural women toward self-employment. In 1979 there were almost 2 million rural women who were reported as being self-employed, and the actual number was undoubtedly higher because only self-employment as a primary occupation was counted. Other entrepreneurial activities were not included. A second feature is that women on farms and in family businesses are often uncounted in the labor market and their activities not recognized as labor. Their contributions are understated in the literature (Bescher-Donnelly & Smith, 1981; O'Leary, 1978). A third feature is that even more than in the cities, women in rural areas tend to be concentrated in low-paying, unskilled work (Haney, 1982). It should not be surprising, then, that girls' career choices tend to be similarly limited.

The less formalized but very real work of many rural women influences girls' attitudes toward work. While they observe women working, they are less likely to know women with "careers." Even among female entrepreneurs or farmers, the role of homemaker appears stronger than the role of wage earner. The rural girl thus has fewer role models for nontraditional work. In a city, even if opportunities are scarce, there are usually some role models for girls; they probably have a friend whose mother goes off to work in the morning. This particularly affects girls when faced with choosing a vocational education program.

Isolation

The very distances that set the rural community apart from other communities cause both social and geographic isolation and thus psychological and physical obstacles to sex equity. The psychological is the more difficult obstacle to overcome. It takes a great deal of strength and courage to break with traditional sex roles in tightly knit communities, which many small towns are. Rural women are often isolated from the kinds of support groups and organizations that urban women can take for granted. Throughout the 1970s, the women's movement had an urban middle-class character, and consequently it made little headway in most rural areas.

Exposing women to nontraditional role models and alternative life styles through the media, though important, is only a first step toward encouraging breaks with old stereotypes. Women need to meet other women who are also making the transition into new fields and new roles. Peer support from friends and neighbors is essential in small communities.

The physical and geographic isolation that reduces women's economic and educational opportunities works in two ways. First, the school district is isolated from the state agency and is thus effectively outside the reach of education regulations. Even though the laws prohibiting discrimination may exist for all schools, monitoring and enforcement of programs by state education officials are virtually impossible. Officials in Nebraska, Illinois, and Texas have over one thousand school districts in each state to worry about.

Second, just as the school is isolated from the state agency, the rural woman may be quite isolated from the education institutions and thus excluded from participating in programs. The rural woman cannot simply hop on a bus or hail a taxi to get to a class at the vocational center or the consolidated high school. Bad roads, inclement weather, or exorbitant gasoline costs can make even a car trip prohibitive. Then there is the problem of children: day care is not readily available in small communities. Finally, the rural woman faces isolation within her peer group if she advances too far beyond it. Providers must be sensitive to the need of the rural woman to maintain her support system.

Some of these problems were addressed in the 1976 amendments to the Vocational Education Act of 1963, which made provisions for day care, support systems for women, programs for displaced homemakers, and grants for over-coming sex bias. Despite the encouragement provided by the amendments, few states spent any significant portions of their federal or state funds on these provisions (Rosenfeld, 1981). Further, based on a survey of school districts in 10 states, rural districts were far less likely to spend funds on sex equity (1 in 10 rural districts) than were urban districts (more than half the cities) (Benson & Hoachlander, 1981).

The Bright Side: Advantages of Rural Conditions

At the same time that isolation, small scale, and tradition operate to con-strain women's opportunities, they also, paradoxically, offer unique advantages. The size of rural schools, for example, may make it imperative that boys and girls be mixed in classes. Just as small schools may not be able to field a baseball team without including both girls and boys, the small school may not be able to justify some courses without offering and even encouraging both boys and girls to enroll. Advanced algebra, for instance, would probably be impossible to offer in a small high school without both boys and girls enrolling.

Analysis of data from the U.S. Education Department's national longitudi-nal survey of high school students in order to compare the participation rates of both males and females in large and small schools in urban and rural districts confirms the greater participation of rural girls. Girls in small rural schools participated more in athletics (45%) and journalism (49%) than girls in large rural schools (30 and 19%, respectively) or in large urban schools (26 and 16%, respectively) (Linsay, 1982).

Moreover, courses in rural schools tend to be less specialized and take on more generic titles, and thus the content may appear more neutral and more acceptable to boys, girls, and parents. This has in fact been recommended as one means of reducing sex stereotyping in vocational education programs (Dunkle, 1981). Although enrollments in consumer and homemaking education and in industrial arts remain unbalanced, many other occupational programs such as vocational agriculture, distributive education, and trade and industrial education have made significant advances in reducing sex bias. By merging fields that are traditionally male with those that are traditionally female, the content can be designed so that males and females gain experience in both fields (Dunne, 1981).

Although rural women are less likely to have professional careers than urban women, they take a more active role in local decision making. The rural woman participates more in local politics and is more likely to hold an office in her own community than is a city woman (Glasgow, 1979). It is true, unfortunately, that women are likely to be in a position subordinate to men and that rural women have not been nearly as successful in capturing state offices. Yet the rural woman, though overburdened, is not entirely disempowered. This is in part because rural officeholders are often voluntary or part-time rather than professionals. Nevertheless, this gives rural women some voice in local education policies and practices.

Finally, rural women have the advantage of their traditional partnership role on the farm and in home-based industries, which predates the discrimination that came about with specialization and industrialization. Rural organizations such as the Grange were concerned with equality; from the beginning, women took on leadership responsibilities. In their early drive for agricultural education, such organizations fully expected girls as well as boys to be taught occupational skills. And with good reason.

As late as the first quarter of this century, farm women provided about 80% of the cash needed for daily living by selling what they produced (Vanek, 1980). As public education became institutionalized, urban and industrial values took hold, and the differences between education for boys and for girls became progressively greater. Yet despite the lack of appropriate education, farm women had to learn agricultural management skills. A 1980 survey of more than 2,500 farm women revealed that nearly half felt quite sure that they could operate their farms without help from their husbands. On three-fifths of the farms, women already were regularly keeping the books, paying the bills, doing the taxes, and playing a substantial role in decision making (Jones & Rosenfeld, 1981). As has been pointed out, roots run deep in rural areas, and tradition can work to women's advantage as well as disadvantage.

THE EDUCATIONAL ATTAINMENT AND ECONOMIC STATUS OF RURAL WOMEN

On the basis of traditional measures of educational attainment, rural girls generally fare better than rural boys. Their average scholastic rankings are higher. According to one study, 33% of the rural high school girls were ranked in the upper quartile of their class, while only about 17% of the boys were so ranked (Schwartzweller, 1976). Women attend school for more years than men when race and place of residence are held constant (Fratoe, 1979). Nonmetro people have completed fewer years of school than metro people; blacks and Hispanics have completed fewer years of education than non-Hispanic whites; and farm residents have completed fewer years of schooling than nonfarm residents. In 1975, in each instance nonmetro women attended school longer than nonmetro men. Black nonmetro women, for example, completed, on the average, 8.9 years of school, while black nonmetro men completed an average of 7.8 years. White farm women completed an average of 12.2 years compared to 11.4 years for white nonfarm women (Fratoe).

These differences between men and women show up in the rates of functional illiteracy and the rates of secondary school completion; the latter are shown in table 16. One plausible explanation for the low years of schooling of men is that the physical labor of boys has been needed earlier than that of girls. One researcher concludes, however, that rural high schools have been more effective in dealing with girls than with boys—to which he attributes the higher aggregate scholastic standing of girls (Schwartzweller, 1976).

This advantage for women, however, ends in the high school classroom. Despite the apparent early educational advantage of women, they are less likely to go on to higher education, and their earnings relative to men are even lower than in metro areas. In 1978, nonmetro women earned only $0.54 for every dollar a nonmetro man earned and $0.81 for every dollar a metro woman earned (Bescher-Donnelly & Smith, 1981).

It is obvious from the data that rural females do as well or better than rural males in educational attainment and scholastic rankings up to the end of high school. This doesn't seem to help them much in postsecondary attainment or in earnings. Since ability is obviously not the reason, some of the disadvantage would appear to be due to the ways in which they are educated and counseled— by the schools as well as by their parents—and to the purposes for which they are educated. This does not show up in the Census Bureau's simple education statistics.

ANSWERS

With the stimuli of the sex equity language in federal education legislation and with the help of some active and progressive state and local educators, progress is being made in rural schools and communities. Some rural education agencies and state agencies have developed programs aimed at overcoming problems of sex bias and discrimination in schools.

Taking Education to the Individual

One solution to the problem of geographic isolation is to take the education to the individual instead of trying to get the individual to a classroom setting. The state of Vermont has an extensive year-round home tutoring program in both basic and preoccupational skills, using full-time and volunteer home tutors. In 1979 about two-thirds of the students in adult basic education were served in the home, in individual instruction or "kitchen seminars" (Eberly & Robinson, 1980). One woman in her late 50s, with 12 children and a home without running water or indoor plumbing, is learning office skills as well as functional literacy. The program put an electric typewriter in her home and provides instruction right there.

In San Juan County, Washington, which is made up entirely of islands, travel is even more difficult than in Vermont in mud season. A community college in an adjoining county holds classes on the local ferry for San Juan residents and is investigating the use of closed circuit television.

Table 16.   Measures of Educational Attainment by Place of Residence and Sex, 1975

Group and residence	Median school years completed, persons over 24		Percentage completing high school, persons over 24	
	Male	Female	Male	Female
White, non-Hispanic				
Metro	12.6	12.4	69.5	67.1
Central cities	12.5	12.3	66.2	61.9
Suburbs	12.6	12.5	71.5	70.5
Nonmetro	12.2	12.2	56.0	58.1
Nonfarm	12.2	12.2	57.3	58.0
Farm	11.4	12.2	46.9	58.8
Black				
Metro	11.6	11.8	47.2	48.5
Central cities	11.5	11.7	46.3	47.7
Suburbs	12.0	12.0	50.5	51.5
Nonmetro	7.8	8.9	23.7	26.1
Nonfarm	8.1	8.9	25.3	27.0
Farm	5.9	7.8	9.4	16.6
Hispanic				
Metro	10.6	9.8	42.5	38.3
Central cities	9.7	9.0	37.9	33.9
Suburbs	11.8	11.2	48.9	45.5
Nonmetro	7.3	7.7	25.2	28.0
Nonfarm	7.4	7.7	26.3	27.5
Farm	n.a.	n.a.	n.a.	n.a.

Source: Fratoe (1979).

Using the Media and Community Resources

Despite the work that women do and have always done on the farm, vocational agriculture has almost exclusively been the domain of men. Although female enrollment has increased in the last few years, most rural programs, which provide training for agribusiness as well as for farming, are virtually all male. School districts in southwest Minnesota used vocational education funds to develop a program called *G*rowth in *A*griculture *T*hrough *E*quality (GATE) to try to get women interested in the programs (Dondelinger & Klein, 1980). They used local newspapers, slide shows, and local meetings to make women aware of the opportunities in agribusiness. One part of their program was to bring women who were employed in agribusiness in the state to speak to students and parents.

In Alabama, the Federation of Southern Cooperatives has developed a guidebook for increasing the participation of rural minority women in nontraditional jobs and in the education programs related to those jobs (Paris & Woolridge, 1979). Their book focuses on ways of utilizing the media and local communications networks and suggests ways to work through existing local organizations and schools.

Sometimes something as simple as child care can made the difference between a rural woman's enrolling in classes or not. The school system in Hardin County, Kentucky, has an outreach program that offers courses for women and girls in remote rural schools in subjects ranging from basic skills to bookkeeping and investments. They provide complete babysitting and recreation for the children while their mothers are in class (C. N. Llewellyn, personal communication, April 20, 1982).

Getting the State to Help

The state of Alaska discovered that "despite the fact that one of the goals of elementary and secondary education is to prepare men and women for equal participation in the work force . . . vocational education has done little to eliminate occupational discrimination," and that occupational discrimination "is mirrored in vocational education enrollments" (*Guidelines*, 1978, p. 2). Thus, they produced and distributed *Guidelines for Developing Sex Bias Free Vocational Education Programs in Small Secondary Schools in Alaska*. Developed by a nine-member task force, the guidelines are a checklist of changes necessary for overcoming sex bias; they also include ways of involving the community and local employers.

Women's Programs in Votech Centers

The state of Wisconsin has established women's centers in its Vocational, Technical, and Adult Education (VTAE) centers to provide skills development, information, and a supportive environment for women, in order to expand their opportunities. Through self-assessment workshops and assertiveness training, and through courses such as small business development, legal issues, and how to reenter the labor market, they help provide the skills needed for new careers.

Though these centers are set up in both urban and rural areas, the rural centers adapt themselves to their conditions. The center in Morain Park, for example, "reaches out rather than pulls in" and uses community resources such as libraries, schools, restaurants, and churches as meeting places (Grengg, 1979). The Nicolet center tries to help women overcome a common winter problem in isolated areas with their "Cabin Fever Specials," which offer cultural activities, shows, and films addressing sex equity issues (Grengg, 1979).

Peer Counseling

In Fennimore, Wisconsin, the Southwest Wisconsin Vocational, Technical, and Adult Education Center began a program targeted specifically at rural displaced homemakers. PIVOT (*Persons Involved in Vocational Orientation and Training*) includes outreach workers who identify the women and a van to get services to the women and women to programs. A key ingredient of the program, however, is the "chum," a woman who works with the homemaker one-on-one, acting as listener, adviser, friend, and supporter (Grengg & Thompson, 1981).

Using Cooperative Extension Programs

Though no organized program was identified in the U.S. Department of Agriculture's Cooperative Extension Program, in rural areas the county agent is in an ideal position to educate women for new roles in the work force. The agent is nonthreatening, trusted by men as well as women. In Vermont, for example, one home economics consultant for the extension service is actively involved in increasing women's awareness of educational and economic opportunities (M. A. Luciano, personal communication, April 1, 1982). In Washington, Oregon, Idaho, and Nevada, Cooperative Extension is developing a leadership training program for rural women through the homemakers' clubs, using volunteers.

Unfortunately, however, all extension agents are not progressive. In other states, educators report that the networks of homemakers' clubs sponsored by the extension service perpetuate the image of the girl as principally a homemaker. Furthermore, a national survey indicates that those women who might benefit the most—the least educated and poorest—are least likely to go to the county agent for assistance. Still, the extension service has the potential to be a valuable resource in rural areas if the agents recognize the educational and economic needs of the girls and women.

SOME FINAL OBSERVATIONS

This quick survey of a sample of states has identified new ideas to bring about sex equity that are being tried in rural communities. Most rely on community resources and emphasize outreach. Few are what one would consider a radical departure from rural traditions. Perhaps given the characteristics of rural America, programs requiring dramatic changes would be unacceptable. Instead, the surveys shows that most efforts build on local institutions. They include systematic programs for educating school administrators, staff, and communities, to ensure that those women who are home-bound due to distances and lack of transportation have educational opportunities and programs open to them. Some programs help women enter nontraditional areas of study and jobs, and these women will themselves become the role models necessary for opening new areas to younger girls in the future.

Another observation is that most programs focus on women and teenagers rather than girls in elementary or junior high schools. This does not mean that there are no efforts in rural schools to achieve sex equity; however, few are designed specifically to overcome or to exploit rural conditions.

Being rural and female creates a double bind for girls growing up and going to school in the country. Isolation and rural fundamentalism exacerbate the traditional barriers to equal educational opportunities. Technology may prove to solve at least one aspect of the problem of isolation—limited access to education—by bringing a wider range of educational opportunities to the rural woman. While there is considerable research concerning the use of technology in rural schools, there is little on the use of technology for isolated rural women. One recommendation, then, is to investigate the use of technology to reach isolated rural women (for example, using Control Data Corporation's Small Farm Project to offer educational programs to women who live on farms).

The problem of rural conservatism is more solidly entrenched and can be best addressed not by outsiders but by rural women themselves. Organizations such as WIFE (Women Involved in Farm Economics) and RAW (Rural American Women) are already working to make women aware of educational and economic options. Rural activist organizations, however, are more difficult to coalesce because they are so geographically dispersed, and even meetings carry a high cost. A recommendation, then, is for foundations and government programs to support rural women's organizations that are working to inform women about expanded educational and economic opportunities and particularly to support efforts for self-education.

Research has neglected rural women's issues. Unfortunately, policy analysts are rarely able to consider either the effect of rural life on girls' educational experiences or the effect of rural labor markets on women's economic opportunities; rural conditions are lost in the aggregate statistics. This leads to three final recommendations, not for a research agenda, but for adequate research designs. (1) If sampling procedures are used to research women's educational issues, rural areas ought to be oversampled to ensure statistical validity and to allow disaggregation by size of community. This is already frequently done for racial and ethnic minorities. (2) Similarly, the work women do in rural areas ought to be examined separately from work women generally do, particularly with regard to entrepreneurial activities of rural women and their role in family business management. (3) Most of the assumptions about the effects of rural life on girls' education are based on small numbers of interviews or illustrative case studies, and we have little information with which to measure the extent of the problems rural women face or regional differences among rural areas. Here, new research would provide information needed to design policies.

The goals of sex equity in rural communities are modest; nevertheless, if we are persistent enough we can bring about lasting changes in rural communities that are inherently resistant to change.

REFERENCES

Benson, C. S., & Hoachlander, E. G. (1981). *The distribution of federal funds under the Vocational Education Act: Interstate and intrastate allocations* (NIE Contract No. 400–78–0039). Berkeley: University of California, Department of Education.

Bescher-Donnelly, L., & Smith, L. W. (1981). The changing roles and status of rural women. In R. T. Coward & W. M. Smith (Eds.), *The family in rural society* (pp. 167–186). New York: Westview.

Chu, L. (1980). *Education for rural women: A global perspective.* Las Cruces, NM: Educational Resource Information Center, ERIC/CRESS.

Clarenbach, K. F. (1977). *Educational needs of rural women and girls.* Washington, DC: National Advisory Council on Women's Educational Programs.

Congressional Record. (1916, December 22), p. 717.

Cosby, A. G., & Charner, I. (1978). *Education and work in rural America: The social context of early career decisions and achievements.* Houston: Stafford-Lowden.

Dewey, R. (1960). "The rural-urban continuum: Real but relatively unimportant." *American Journal of Sociology, 6,* 60 66.

Dondelinger, C. L., & Klein, B. C. (1980). *Growth in agriculture through equality* (Project No. 94–482/1/05–SB–136, Minnesota Department of Education). Canby, MN: School District #891, CATVI.

Dunkle, M. C. (1981). *Options for equity: Federal policies affecting educational opportunities for rural women and girls.* In S. Rosenfeld (Ed.), *Brake shoes, backhoes, and balance sheets: The changing vocational education of rural women* (pp. 127–145). Washington, DC: Rural American Women.

Dunne, F. (1979, May). *Traditional values/contemporary pressures: The conflicting needs of America's rural women.* Paper presented at the Rural Education Seminar, College Park, MD.

Dunne, F. (1981). They'd never hire a girl: Vocational education in rural secondary schools. In S. Rosenfeld (Ed.), *Brake shoes, backhoes, and balance sheets: The changing vocational education of rural women* (pp. 93–126). Washington, DC: Rural American Women.

Eberly, A., & Robinson, S. (1980). *The adult illiterate speaks out: Personal perspectives.* Washington, DC: National Institute of Education.

Flora, C., & Johnson, S. (1978). Discarding the distaff: New roles for rural women. In T. Ford (Ed.), *Rural U.S.A.: Persistence and change* (pp. 168–181). Ames: Iowa State University Press.

Fratoe, F. (1979, August). *Rural women and education.* Paper presented at the annual meeting of the Rural Sociological Society, Burlington, VT.

Glasgow, N. (1979, August). *An evaluation of the political roles on rural women.* Paper presented at the annual meeting of the Rural Sociological Society, Burlington, VT.

Grengg, D. A. (1979). *New horizons: Women's centers in the VTAE system.* Madison: Wisconsin Board of Vocational, Technical, and Adult Education.

Grengg, D. A., & Thompson, M. B. (1981). *Promoting sex equity in the Wisconsin VTAE system.* Madison: Wisconsin Board of Vocational, Technical, and Adult Education.

Guidelines for developing sex bias free vocational education programs in small secondary schools in Alaska (ERIC/CRESS ED167789). (1978). Juneau: Alaska State Department of Education.

Haer, J. L. (1952). Conservatism-radicalism and the rural-urban continuum. *Rural Sociology, 17,* 43–47.

Haney, W. G. (1982). Women. In D. A. Dillman & D. J. Hobbs (Eds.), *Rural society in the U.S.: Issues for the eighties* (pp. 124–135). Boulder, CO: Westview.

Jones, C., & Rosenfeld, R. A. (1981). *American farm women: Findings from a national survey* (Report No. 130). Chicago: National Opinion Research Center.

Journal of the Proceedings of the Nineteenth Session of the National Grange and the Patrons of Husbandry, Boston, MA 1885. Elmira, NY: Husbandmen.

Larson, O. F. (1978). Values and beliefs of rural people. In T. Ford (Ed.), *Rural U.S.A.: Persistence and change*. Ames: Iowa State University Press.

Lewis, S. (1920). *Main Street*. New York: Harcourt, Brace & World.

Linsay, P. (1982). The effect of high school size on student participation, satisfaction, and attendance. *Educational Evaluation and Policy Analysis, 4*, 57–65.

Oberst, S. S. (1982). Teachers and learners: Reflections on women and farming. *ruralamerica 7*, 32.

O'Leary, J. (1978). *The changing role of women in the rural economy*. Unpublished manuscript, U.S. Department of Agriculture, Economics, Statistics and Cooperative Services.

Paris, A., & Woolridge, S. (1979). *Placing rural minority women in training situations for non-traditional jobs*. Washington, DC: U.S. Office of Education.

Rosenfeld, S. (1981). Recollections and realities. In S. Rosenfeld (Ed.), *Brake shoes, backhoes, and balance sheets: The changing vocational education of rural women*. Washington, DC: Rural American Women.

Schwartzweller, H. K. (1976). Scholastic performance, sex differentials, and the structuring of educational ambition among rural youth in three societies. *Rural Sociology, 41*, 194–216.

Teal, P. (1981). Women in the rural economy: Employment and self-employment. In S. Rosenfeld (Ed.), *Brake shoes, backhoes, and balance sheets: The changing vocational education of rural women* (pp. 27–65). Washington, DC: Rural American Women.

Vanek, J. (1980). Work, leisure, and family roles: Farm households in the United States. *Journal of Family History, 5*, 422–431.

22

Educational Programs
for Adult Women

Ruth B. Ekstrom and Marjory G. Marvel,
with Jean M. Swenson

In the past, educational programs prepared individuals for a role they were expected to fill for their entire adult lives. Women were expected to be homemakers, wives, and mothers; men, the family breadwinners. This assumption of unchanging lifelong roles was probably always overly simplistic, but it has become increasingly inappropriate in recent years.

Today change has become the one constant in every adult's life. Some of these changes are the result of personal decisions, while other changes are imposed by external forces. As change in life has become increasingly frequent, educational programs have tried to help adults meet this challenge.

The relationship between change and education has been highlighted in *Americans in Transition: Life Changes As Reasons for Adult Learning* (Aslanian & Brickell, 1980). Interviews with almost 2,000 adults aged 25 and older showed they had gone back to school or decided to study on their own in order to cope with changes in their lives.

Changes have had an especially strong impact on adult women during the past decade. Many more women, especially women with children, are now working for pay outside of the home. In 1979, 41% of women with children under the age of 3 were in the labor force, as were 52% of mothers of children between the ages of 3 and 5, and 62% of women with children aged 6 to 13. It is not surprising, therefore, to find a National Center for Educational Brokering survey showing that adult women were more than half of the clients seeking counseling and information about educational and career opportunities. These women were divided between those wishing to reenter the work force (48%) and those who were changing jobs (46%).

Because change is so much a part of adult women's lives, educational planning for them needs to be viewed from the perspective of adult development.

The authors wish to thank Jean Campbell, Mariam Chamberlain, Carol Eliason, and Barbara Richardson for their assistance.

For women, midlife often means a new opportunity for education, employment, and community service. More research is needed to understand female development through the life cycle and to determine how discontinuous education and work histories affect the lives of adult women.

One of the important outcomes of adult women's participation in education is improved confidence and self-esteem. Education thus becomes an empowering force, enabling women to cope with the changes in their lives and to create change where it is needed.

This chapter begins with a description of adult women and educational programs for them. Next, we discuss the increasing importance of education for adult women and how institutional, situational, and personal barriers can limit women's opportunity to obtain this education. Programs that deal with these barriers are then described. The chapter concludes with our views of future needs in educational programming for adult women and with our recommendations.

ADULT WOMEN AND THE PROGRAMS
THAT SERVE THEM

In this chapter we define adult women as females aged 25 or older. We choose this age for both conceptual and practical reasons. Most women who have had a continuous educational history are at or near its completion by age 25. Also, federal statisticians often use this age as a breakpoint when gathering data on educational participation.

Adult women are a diverse population. We will discuss four main subgroups: reentry women, displaced homemakers, employed women, and older/retired women. However, these groups should not be thought of as discrete; there is considerable overlap. Educators designing programs should avoid relying on stereotypic views of any group.

The term "reentry women" describes women who are resuming education after a hiatus, usually involving homemaking. They may be seeking education as an end in itself or as an avenue to employment. The term "displaced homemaker" describes adult women who are being catapulated into the labor force by a change in life circumstances; most have been recently widowed, divorced, or left in other circumstances forcing them to become financially responsible for themselves and, often, for their children.

Characteristics of Adult Women Learners.   Although there are a number of studies which purport to describe the special characteristics of adult women learners, most should be viewed with caution because variations between subpopulations have not been taken into consideration. Cross (1979, p. 103) points out that the "highly consistent research finding" that women are more interested in hobbies and personal development and men are more interested in job-oriented education fails to take into consideration the fact that some women but almost no men are full-time homemakers. She adds that there is evidence that differences in interests between women in the labor force and those who are homemakers are greater than those between men and women.

One consistent finding, however, is that adult women are more academically and intellectually oriented than younger women (Esperson, 1975), have more positive attitudes toward education and are more effective academically (Clements, 1974), and achieve higher grade-point averages than other groups of students (Beausang, 1976). In short, adult women make good students.

Needs of Adult Women Learners. Adult learners have a variety of special needs. Chief among these, according to Cross (1979), are schedules set at times when adults are free to participate, courses that are offered in convenient locations, teaching methods other than classroom lectures, and information and counseling services. Mangano and Corrado (1978) found that the availability of evening and weekend classes and registration, credit for life experiences, and vocabulary- and mathematics-skill improvement courses are high-priority needs for adult students, both female and male. Adult women also expressed the need for remedial and support services, encouragment and reassurance, and academic skills improvement courses. Supportive learning environments for adult women have been shown to make a significant difference in educational outcomes (Berman, Gelsco, Greenfeig, & Hirsch, 1977). Adult women students report that their biggest problem is finding time both for their studies and for their home/job responsibilities (Esperson, 1975).

Types of Educational Programs for Adult Women. There is a wide variety of educational programs serving adult women students. These include both formal and informal education at the elementary, secondary, and postsecondary levels, in both credit and noncredit classes, part-time and full-time. Although we discuss the informal and noncredit courses offered by community organizations, employers, and unions, our emphasis in this chapter is on postsecondary programs that offer credit because, in our credential-oriented society, these programs appear to offer greater potential for creating sex equity than does nonformal education. Nearly half (45%) of all adult students are enrolled in credit courses leading to a high school certificate (3.9%), a trade or professional certificate or license (9.4%), a 2- or 4-year college degree (13.2%), or a graduate or professional degree (10.0%).

One problem that has limited the acceptance of nonformal learning is the difficulty in monitoring the quality of learning in nonschool settings. Nevertheless, noncredit and nonformal educational programs involve the largest group of adult learners. In 1975, more than half (55%) of all adult learners were in noncredit courses. Methods have been developed to help adults receive college credit for many kinds of noncredit education and training programs (American Council on Education, 1980; University of the State of New York, 1977).

Discussions of educational programs for adults are often complicated by the use of similar terms describing different types of programs, especially adult education, adult basic education, continuing education, and continuing education for women. "Adult education" describes the formal learning activities of adults who are not enrolled full-time in a secondary school or college. In 1981, more than 21 million adults were involved in some type of adult education (National Center for Education Statistics, 1983). Of these about 11.8 million, or 55%, were women. About a quarter of all adult education courses are offered by community colleges or vocational-technical institutes; another quarter are provided by noncollegiate organizations such as businesses, industries, private and community organizations, unions, and government agencies; and 4-year colleges offer about 20%. About 60% of adult education courses are related to the learners' jobs. The probability of individuals' participating in adult education increases with their educational attainment (U.S. Bureau of the Census, 1980). More than 70% of all adult education students are high school graduates, and over 40% have completed four years of college.

"Adult basic education," which should not be confused with adult education, provides instruction for adults at the elementary and secondary levels. Many of these adults are seeking a high school equivalency certificate (GED) or are in programs to learn English as a second language. More than half (55%) of the participants in these programs in 1976 were women, and more than half (55%) were members of minority groups (U.S. Bureau of the Census, 1980). Thus, these programs are important avenues to race and sex equity.

The term "continuing education" is used to describe the lifelong learning activities of adults. It includes both nondegree programs in adult education, such as self-improvement courses, and continuing professional education programs, which help employed adults remain aware of changing knowledge and techniques in their field. Many institutions award a continuing education unit (CEU) to indicate that adults have participated in noncredit continuing education programs.

The term "Continuing Education for Women" (CEW) was originally used to describe programs to provide degree-oriented postsecondary education for adult women in a more flexible manner than traditional postsecondary programs. In recent years this term has come to include both credit and noncredit programs serving adult women.

WHY ARE ADULT WOMEN AN IMPORTANT EDUCATIONAL GROUP?

During the 1970s, adult women were the most rapidly increasing group in postsecondary education. Recent data (National Center for Education Statistics, 1982) show that between 1970 and 1980 the number of women enrolled in college increased from 3,537,000 to 6,223,000. The biggest increase was in part-time adult women students aged 25 to 34 in 2-year and 4-year colleges; part-time adult women students aged 35 and older also increased dramatically.

Projections are that by 1988, the enrollment of adult women in formal postsecondary education will further increase, except for full-time women students aged 35 or older (National Center for Education Statistics, 1980). If these projections are accurate, adult women will be 22% of all postsecondary students by 1988.

A Changing Profile?   There is some indication that the characteristics of adult women seeking formal education may be changing. Data from the University of Michigan CEW program show a leveling-off in the number of program participants (Campbell, 1981). The percentage of married women participants declined from 81% in 1964 to 35.1% in 1980. The proportion of divorced women more than doubled to 18%. The most dramatic increase, however, was in single women, who, at 42.2% made up the largest group of program participants. The average age of program participants also dropped from 37.5 in the 1960s to about 30. According to Campbell, more than half of the Michigan program participants in 1980 had no children, contrasted with 12% in 1965. The other dramatic change in the Michigan participant profile reflects the change in women's employment outside of the home. In 1965, fewer than 25% of the participants were employed; by 1980 the proportion of employed women was 56%. In 1965, about half of the program participants were primarily homemakers; this had decreased to 23% by 1980.

These population changes mean program changes. Campbell (1981, p. 9) has pointed out that employed women are not concerned with "making the initial move from homemaking to paid employment or a return to school, but rather selecting a more appropriate, satisfying or promising career path." Such women may be considering a return to school for a different or higher degree, but the decision is couched in the overall framework of immediate and long-range employment, a distinct difference from the decisions about returning to work made by women 20 years ago. For many women today, a return to school may mean giving up current employment; for those who have no other source of support, such a decision must be weighed carefully in terms of the probable long-term payoff.

A special strength of the Michigan program is that it integrates service, advocacy, and research. This allows the program staff to identify demographic and attitudinal changes in the women coming to them and to modify the program to meet these changing needs.

WHAT ARE THE EDUCATIONAL BARRIERS FACING ADULT WOMEN?

This section uses the conceptual framework of institutional, situational, and personal barriers that has been used in other discussions of adult women's education (for example, Ekstrom, 1972; Tittle & Denker, 1980). Institutional barriers include admissions and financial aid practices, regulations, curricula, services, and faculty and staff attitudes that create special problems for adult women. Situational barriers include the sociological, financial, family, health, and residential circumstances that may limit the educational participation of adult women. Personal barriers include the psychological and societal factors that affect adult women, such as attitudes, expectations, fears, self-concept, sex role conflicts, sex stereotypes, and work values.

Institutional Barriers.   Barriers to formal, for-credit postsecondary education are discussed in chapter 24. We emphasize here those that create special problems for adult women. This discussion applies primarily to undergraduate education for credit.

The application process is often the first barrier for the adult woman returning to school. Adults are often required to present the same credentials as the traditional 18-year-old applicant. Requiring out-of-date high school transcripts and test scores fails to acknowledge that changes have taken place in an individual's knowledge, skills, and motivation during the intervening years. Taking an admissions test after many years away from formal education is a frightening experience for many adults. Women who have been away from school for a number of years frequently need to practice and renew their mathematical skills. Many institutions make no provisions for any test preparation or mathematics refresher courses. Lack of these creates a special obstacle for the entrance of adult women into science and technology programs.

With rising tuition costs, financial aid has become increasingly necessary for many adult students—particularly for women who may feel that they are in competition with their own children for family educational funds. However, financial aid requirements still favor the younger student attending school full time. The publication *Better Late Than Never* (Women's Equity Action League, 1982) identifies financial aid sources for adult women.

Institutional regulations also create barriers for adult women. Chief among these is the failure to provide credit for learning from prior experience. This is an especially serious obstacle for displaced homemakers and for employed women. Another common problem is institutional regulations that place time limits on the recognition or transfer of credits for courses previously taken. Scheduling of courses at inconvenient times and locations also affects adult women students.

Educational programming for adult women needs to give more attention to alternative forms of course presentation such as the use of telecommunications, radio, videodisks, and other technology that will enable adult learners to receive instruction regardless of limitations of time and place. This is particularly important for rural women and for handicapped women.

Adult women students need counseling that is timely and appropriate for their needs. A study of adult women students at the University of Minnesota (Lutter, 1982) found that "women aged 37–45 experienced a great deal of dissonance between old expectations and new desires. Although most still have children at home, a significant number are working full or part time. Frustrations and problems arise because they rarely have placed personal desires first. The research indicates that this group needs special support; they were torn between what they 'should not do and be' in the traditional sense, and what they 'could do or be' as articulated by younger women" (n.p.). If counselors are not aware of this dilemma, attrition is likely to occur. This is not to say that every educational institution must provide all the types of counseling and support services that may be needed by adult women. Counselors must be aware of and able to refer women to appropriate community services, especially if the hours that counseling, library, child care, and other services are available on-campus do not coincide with the schedules of adult women students. Many faculty members and counselors have a limited knowledge of the educational and career opportunities now available to adult women. As a consequence, too many adult women are being given outdated information about their educational and career options.

A more subtle form of institutional barrier occurs in the classroom interactions between faculty members and adult women students. As Sandler and her colleagues (Hall, 1982) have pointed out, "Older women often suffer the results of compounded stereotypes . . . and find it extremely difficult to be taken seriously as students. Frequently, they are devalued not only because of their sex, but also because of their age and part-time status. Too often, they are viewed as bored, middle-aged women who are returning to school because they have nothing better to do" (p. 12). The lack of women faculty members who are themselves reentry women undoubtedly contributes to this problem.

Finally, adult women students need to have contact with other students, especially those like themselves. Yet, women's centers or centers for adult students are not always available.

Situational Barriers.   Among the major situational factors that may act as educational barriers for adult women are socioeconomic status and ethnic or racial group membership. In the past, middle-class white women were the predominant group in many educational programs for adult women. There is now more socioeconomic and racial diversity in both formal and informal educational settings.

A second major group of situational barriers are those related to the family. Several studies have found family needs and responsibilities to be the most serious obstacle to adult women's education. For married women, husbands' attitudes about education play an important role. For displaced homemakers and other single parents, head-of-household responsibilities constitute a serious obstacle. "The problems of these women are indeed severe. Often trapped in low-paying jobs owing to factors such as lack of education or sex discrimination, they cannot afford the additional schooling they need to lift them out of their predicament" (Ekstrom, 1972, p. 47). Childcare responsibilities are also a special problem for many adult women students, especially for working mothers. Other adult women have responsibilities caring for ill or elderly parents or spouses.

Time conflicts and stress are a major result of these situational barriers. Lack of time, whether real or perceived, often prevents adult women from enrolling in school or from participating in informal learning opportunities. Those who do enroll frequently find themselves overwhelmed by conflicting demands on their time. Greater flexibility in educational institutions could alleviate some of this strain. Also, many women are not aware that innovative programs, such as those that grant external degrees, can provide more flexibility by allowing them to study outside of the usual classroom structure.

Geographic location and lack of mobility are also special problems for many adult women students. While younger students may be able to travel away from home for postsecondary education, this is not a common option for adult women. Location presents rural women with special problems in obtaining additional education. Women with a physical handicap or health problems are especially concerned with barriers that arise from their limited mobility.

Personal Barriers.   Adult women returning to education may have considerable ambivalence about this decision. Three personal factors that inhibit women's aspirations have been identified by DiSabatino (1976). These are sex role conflicts, poor self-esteem, and fear of failure. A woman's perception of her role in society affects her decision about continuing her education. As Adler (1976) pointed out, "Men have been raised to assume they will have a career; the nature of their choice is *which* career. Women, in contrast, are generally taught to place work secondary to family; they should have a career until marriage or to fall back on if necessary, but it should not interfere with their marriage opportunities. Thus, many women engage in 'contingency planning' and leave their options open until they find whom they will marry" (p. 202). Adult women may be under pressure from their parents, their husbands, or others to adopt what these individuals believe to be an appropriate role, forgoing education for unpaid work in the home and in volunteer organizations. In recent years, however, younger women have been questioning previous perceptions of women's roles and may experience fewer conflicts.

The psychological literature shows that, in general, females have a poorer self-concept than males. This is especially true for adult women and for lower socioeconomic status women. Turner (1977) has discussed how gender and age stereotypes intersect and the effects of this on middle-aged and older women. Fear of failure has kept many adult women from returning to school and, when they do return, contributes to their selecting educational choices from a narrow range of programs, either because the program draws on familiar skills or because it is a traditionally female field.

Dependence and learned helplessness have often been cited as personal characteristics affecting adult women's educational participation. The willingness of many adult women to achieve vicariously, through the accomplishments of children or husband, rather than directly, through personal accomplishment, has also been cited as contributing to their ambivalence about additional formal education.

WHAT KINDS OF EDUCATIONAL PROGRAMS WORK FOR ADULT WOMEN?

Most existing formal educational programs for adult women focus on serving reentry women and displaced homemakers. This section will, therefore, concentrate on these populations. It will also, however, include material about programs for women without a high school diploma, programs emphasizing experiential learning, programs to encourage women to enter nontraditional occupations, programs for employed women, and programs for older women. The emphasis on programs for reentry women and displaced homemakers should not be taken as an indication that other adult women do not have special needs. Instead, it is an indicator that the educational needs of these other groups must have greater attention.

Reentry Women.   The earliest special programs for adult women students seeking to return to college were the Continuing Education for Women (CEW) programs, which began in the 1960s. As Astin (1976) described them, these experiments did not seek to create, nor did they propose, an alternative system; rather, they aimed at opening the existing system so that the riches could be enjoyed by adult women without struggle, without eternal requests for exceptions to rules, and also without conformity to structures and timing meant for young, unmarried, unemployed students. The common purpose of these CEW programs was to explore every possible way of making higher education available—part time, full time, and recurrently—throughout a woman's life, whenever she had a reason and a desire for it. Women's continuing education identified, and sometimes created, curricular avenues and flexibilities of timing, location, admission, and financial aid that would bring such goals within reach.

The unique creation of CEW was the provision of preadmission academic information and referral for adults, using techniques that differed from traditional student counseling. This preadmission academic advice included choices based on individual goals, existing commitments, and levels of competence rather than on the hospitality of the institution providing the counseling.

The number of programs based on the CEW idea increased rapidly. According to Hersh (1980), there were 20 programs by 1963, 100 by 1966, 376 by 1973, and 500 by 1976. However, many of these later programs differed considerably from the original CEW concept. Astin noted that a number of the programs developed by the mid-1960s were not campus-based, and others had very tenuous connections with the degree-granting parent institutions. A summary describing reentry programs for mature women can be found in Cirksena and Hereth (1977). A review of the research on returning women students has been prepared by Scott (1980).

There are several major features that should be present in programs for reentry women and that can be used in evaluating these programs (Tittle & Denker, 1980). These include institutional flexibility in course scheduling and location, providing credit for experiential learning, providing orientation programs, providing child care facilities or financial support for child care, counseling, presence of a women's center or support group, career development opportunities, job placement, funding from the institutional operating budget and commitment to a full-time professional staff, organizational placement of the program that reflects the institution's commitment and responsibility, and program evaluation.

The National Science Foundation (NSF) Women in Science Program, like most of the early CEW programs, can be viewed as emphasizing previous education. The NSF program, described in *Reentry Women Scientists* (Lantz, Houghton-Alico, & Eaton, 1980), was designed for women who already have college degrees in science and who are unemployed or underemployed. The objective is to prepare the participants for graduate school or for scientific employment. This program has been most useful in helping women who had experience in science teaching find jobs in industry.

Another source of program models for reentry women is the materials that have been developed under grants from the Women's Educational Equity Act Program. (Unless otherwise indicated, they are available from the Education Development Center, 55 Chapel Street, Newton, MA 02160) These materials include *Continuing Education for Women: Administrator's Handbook; Second Wind: A Program for Returning Women Students,* and *New Directions for Rural Women: A Workshop Leader's Manual.* Another program, *Re-Entry Women,* is available from the Project on the Status and Education of Women, Association of American Colleges, 1818 R Street, NW, Washington, DC 20009.

Catalyst (14 East 60th Street, New York, NY 10022) and Wider Opportunities for Women (1325 G Street, NW, Washington, DC 20005) are two national organizations that have pioneered in the development of counseling programs and materials for reentry women. Catalyst has produced several excellent publications for adult women returning to the paid work force. They include *What to Do with the Rest of Your Life* and *How to Go to Work When Your Husband Is Against It, Your Children Aren't Old Enough, and There's Nothing You Can Do Anyhow.*

In the 1960s, reentry women were primarily interested in completing their college education. Today they are becoming more interested in education that leads to paid employment. This change is bringing programs for reentry women closer to programs for displaced homemakers.

Programs for Displaced Homemakers. Educational programs for displaced homemakers differ from those for reentry women in emphasizing the development of job-related and job-finding skills and in providing counseling to help women meet a sudden change in their lives. The rationale for this design lies in counseling theory (Farmer & Becker, 1977), which points out the inappropriateness of stressing self-fulfillment or other internal needs when economic and security needs have not been met. A detailed description of the history of the efforts to develop programs for displaced homemakers can be found in Shields (1981).

Displaced homemakers need education and related counseling that will provide them with marketable skills as quickly as possible. The National Advisory Council on Women's Educational Programs reviewed the educational needs of displaced homemakers and concluded that these women need training for well-paying jobs that offer advancement opportunities. Displaced homemakers also need to remedy their ignorance of such economic realities as money management, credit, insurance, and banking. They need access to financial aid for tuition, childcare, transportation, clothing, and, frequently, living expenses (Eliason, 1978).

The Displaced Homemakers Network Program Policy Statement describes how these needs can be met through outreach, orientation, counseling, assessment, life skill development, skill training, employment preparation, supportive services, referrals, and job placement. The Displaced Homemakers Network, 1010 Vermont Ave., NW, (Suite 817) Washington, DC 20005, exchanges information about and among these programs. A handbook, *Displaced Homemakers: Program Options* (Marano, 1978), describes the approaches used to start these programs and gives advice on how to serve special groups of displaced homemakers, such as rural and minority women.

Some of the strongest displaced homemaker programs can be found on the campuses of junior and community colleges or at county vocational and technical institutes. These programs go beyond providing counseling about career options and train women in job skills. Materials describing displaced homemaker programs that emphasize vocational education, created by the Education Development Center, include *Vocational Counseling for Displaced Homemakers: A Manual* and *Resource Guide for Vocational Educators and Planners: Helping Displaced Homemakers Move from Housework to Paid Work through Vocational Training*.

The Women's Educational Equity Act Program has developed a variety of materials that are designed for both reentry women and displaced homemakers who are entering the labor force. They include *Becoming; Business Management Training for Rural Women; The Career Shopper's Guide; Displaced Homemakers: Vo-Tech Workshop Guide; How Women Find Jobs: A Guide for Workshop Leaders; Life Skills for Women in Transition;* and *Placing Rural Minority Women in Training Situations for Nontraditional Jobs*. (These are available from the Education Development Center.) Another program, *Homemaking and Volunteer Experience Skills*, was prepared by Educational Testing Service and is obtainable from Order Fulfillment Services, ETS, Princeton, NJ 08541.

Programs for Women without a High School Diploma.   Many adult women never contact postsecondary programs because they have not completed secondary school and because they do not know that it is possible to receive a high school equivalency certificate without returning to high school classes. In addition to the GED, available through a testing program offered by the American Council on Education, adult women can often obtain a high school diploma through programs at community colleges or vo-tech institutes. One model program, operated by the Waukeshau (Wisconsin) County Technical Institute, provides adults the opportunity to earn a high school diploma by demonstrating skills learned through life experiences.

Programs Emphasizing Experiential Learning.   The emphasis on experience is especially important in programs for adult women. Experience is the one quality that every adult women has more of than younger women. Capitalizing on prior learning experiences is an effective way of enabling adult women to build on their nonformal learning, especially their unpaid work in the home and the community.

There are two basic types of experiential learning: sponsored learning and learning from prior experience. Sponsored learning usually occurs under the auspices of an educational institution where the student is enrolled. Four kinds of sponsored experiential learning are described in *Internships for Women*

(Mulligan, 1980): programs for reentry women, programs for low-income women, programs to prepare women for specific professional careers, and programs for undergraduate and graduate women.

Experiential reentry programs generally include workshops covering skill identification, résumé writing, and job interviewing. Each woman is then placed in an internship on the basis of her long-range goals. One program, Project Re-Entry, operated by the Civic Center and Clearing House in Boston, states that "the quality of supervision is the most critical variable in determining the success or failure of an internship and supervision by a female mentor is extremely important" (Project Re-Entry, 1977, p. 16).

The programs for low-income women include both displaced homemaker programs and programs for training women currently employed in low-wage occupations to enter well-paying, traditionally male occupations. Many of the experiential programs for low-income women were funded by CETA in the 1970s and early 1980s. Stipended internships are especially important for low-income women, as well as financial support during the skill training and counseling period prior to the internship placement. Program models such as Women in Non-Traditional Jobs (Women's Bureau, 1978) emphasize the importance of skill training, either in the classroom or in a work-while-learning situation.

Internship programs to provide women with preparation for specific careers in which they are underrepresented (such as business management or educational administration) have met with more difficulty than other types of internships, probably because they are aimed at helping women function successfully in positions that have been traditional sources of male power and influence. Thus, these programs may require change in the participating organization, instead of or in addition to change for the participating individual (which is the focus of programs for reentry and low-income women). At the professional level, internships also provide an important way for women to achieve sex equity. A model program for women in educational administration is described in *The Administrative Intern* (Adkison & Warren, 1980).

Despite their advantages, internships or other types of sponsored experiential learning may present problems for employed women or for displaced homemakers. Financial pressures often will not permit women to accept a semester or a year working for little or no salary. An alternative form of sponsored experiential learning, the work/study program, appears to be a better solution for these women. Work/study programs often use job sharing or flexitime so that there is little or no loss of salary while the woman obtains her education. The typical work/study or cooperative education program tries to integrate classroom experience with work experience; a specified amount of time on the job and successful job performance are often part of the college degree requirement.

The *Women's Studies Service Learning Handbook: From the Classroom to the Community* (Fisher & Reuben, 1981) emphasizes how sponsored experiential learning relates voluntary action and education, bringing together the community and the campus, social action and research. Since one goal of service learning programs is to teach women how to work for change, these programs have great potential for increasing sex equity. They have also been an effective link between women's studies and feminist activism.

The other form of experiential learning that is of importance to adult women is assessment or evaluation of learning from prior experience. These programs identify the knowledge, skills, and abilities that adult women have acquired outside of the classroom and use this information either to award academic credit or to provide educational and career guidance, or both. They provide an avenue through which nonformal education can become accepted within formal education programs. Most programs for awarding credit for prior learning are at the postsecondary level.

There are three major ways in which prior learning has been evaluated for college credit: (1) credit recommendations for courses offered by business, industry, and volunteer organizations; (2) standardized tests, most frequently used to assess independent study; and (3) individualized assessments, using demonstrations, interviews, or portfolios that show what an individual has learned and is able to do. Any one of these can be used to assess what adult women have learned from experience. Each has its advantages and its disadvantages, as described in Ekstrom and Eliason (1978).

Some colleges have been reluctant to provide credit for adult women's experience in the home, the community, or in volunteer work because of sex stereotypes or beliefs about the low value of unpaid work. One of the earliest efforts to identify the educational relevance of women's unpaid work experience resulted in the development of the "I Can" competency lists by Educational Testing Service and the Council of National Organizations for Adult Education. These lists are included in *How to Get College Credit for What You Have Learned as a Homemaker and Volunteer* (Ekstrom, Harris, & Lockheed, 1977). A 12-step process to award credit for what women have learned from experience has also been developed (Ekstrom, 1980). A more recent publication, *Making Experience Count in Vocational Education* (Ekstrom, 1981c) helps vocational educators identify and provide recognition for adult women who have relevant prior learning.

Prior experience has also been used as the basis of counseling for women reentering the labor force, since the choice of unpaid work activities is an indicator of the woman's interests as well as an opportunity to acquire skills. The interrelationship between unpaid work and occupational groups is shown in the HAVE Skills workbooks and guides (Ekstrom, 1981a). The relationship between unpaid work experience and selected jobs was also explored in Project ACCESS and is described in *Making Experience Count in Sex Equity Programs* (Ekstrom, 1981b).

The best source of information about college credit for prior experience is the Council for the Advancement of Experiential Learning (CAEL), 10598 Marble Faun Court, Columbia, MD 21045. CAEL has a five-volume directory, *Wherever You Learned It* (McIntyre, 1981), describing experiential learning programs at over 530 colleges. Stanley (1980) has prepared an excellent review of the processes and problems involved in gaining credit for prior learning.

Programs to Encourage Women to Enter Nontraditional Occupations. A number of programs for both reentry women and displaced homemakers have encouraged entrance into nontraditional occupations because these occupations usually pay higher wages and often provide better opportunities than those with a high proportion of females. There has been some question about the effectiveness of these programs with adult women. In a recent review of the factors affecting community college women in nontraditional programs, Young (1981) reported that there is inconclusive and conflicting evidence about whether older women are more or less likely to enter nontraditional careers than younger women.

An early program to encourage mature adult women to enter occupational programs in community colleges was developed by Chitayat and Hymer (1976). This program provided preadmission counseling and developed a peer counseling program that would function as a postadmission service. Although the majority of the women who completed the program enrolled in occupational programs, fields like secretarial science and nursing attracted the largest numbers of students.

Part of adult women's low interest in nontraditional occupations is probably based on the sex stereotypes that they hold. Additionally, because some nontraditional occupations are blue collar jobs, they may be viewed as inappropriate by middle-class women. Another factor affecting many adult women's interest in these occupational programs may be lack of experience in activities related to nontraditional jobs. A survey of adult reentry women's experiential learning (Ekstrom, Beier, Davis, & Gruenberg, 1981) found that adult women tended to develop their interpersonal skills and verbal ability above their physical and mechanical skills and their mathematical and reasoning ability. Although the most commonly found skills were those used in traditionally female jobs, nevertheless significant numbers of adult women acquired skills in areas such as carpentry and auto repair.

The reader should not conclude, therefore, that no adult women will enter nontraditional employment. There are a number of excellent programs that have prepared women for nontraditional occupations. Some of these are described in the publications, *The Nuts and Bolts of NTO: A Handbook of Recruitment, Training, Support Services, and Placement of Women in Nontraditional Occupations* and *Time for a Change! A Woman's Guide to Nontraditional Occupations,* prepared by the Technical Education Research Centers (8 Eliot Street, Cambridge, MA 02138). Another publication, aimed at encouraging women receiving Aid to Families with Dependent Children to enter nontraditional jobs, is *Earning a Breadwinner's Wage,* developed by Women's Enterprises of Boston, 739 Boylston St., Boston, MA 02116.

Programs for Employed Women. There are relatively few programs designed to serve the educational needs of currently employed adult women. Descriptions of prototypical programs for women employees, a literature review, and a bibliography on this topic have been prepared by Vetter and her colleagues (Vetter, Winkfield, Ransom, & Lawrey, 1977).

Two analyses (Harrison, 1979; Wilder, 1980) of the education and training needs of working women focused on the needs of the 80% of working women in jobs that are not professional or managerial. Harrison concluded that "lack of money, lack of time, lack of adequate child care facilities, inadequate or non-existent counseling, few benefits, lack of on-the-job training, failure to acknowledge experience in lieu of degrees, discrimination, lack of job opportunity, negative attitudes—all these obstacles prevent blue and pink collar working women from obtaining the education and job training they need" (p. 25).

Harrison reported that several women "took exception to the idea that further education represents a fruitful course for working women." One woman said "education and training is often used as a byway"; another pointed out that "women's educational attainment does not translate into job status and pay as men's does" (p. 28). We believe that this is a critical issue in achieving sex equity for women. More research is needed to identify the reasons why education has a lower payoff for women than for men.

The belief that education has a limited payoff for women may be partially refuted by a recent analysis (Applebaum, 1981) of the experience of white women aged 30–44 who were part of the National Longitudinal Survey. This showed that adult women's ability to make a successful return to the labor force was enhanced by years of schooling, choice of college major, and participation in training programs. Applebaum's data also showed, however, that length of schooling did not have an effect on growth in wages after women returned to the labor force. Completing a training program in a nonclerical area or obtaining a certificate had a significant effect on wage increases, but going back to school for additional courses, a degree, or a diploma did not affect employed women's wages.

Many working women are intermittently employed or are employed in part-time jobs. This usually results in their being locked into the low-wage sector of the economy. Moreover, they are often ineligible for industry-sponsored education and training programs. Shaw (1979) concluded that the problems of such women "come not from a lack of any recent work experience but from low skills and irregular employment" (p. 18). Programs that meet the needs of these women are not available.

The Fund for the Improvement of Postsecondary Education (FIPSE) has been a leader in encouraging the development of educational programs for employed women. One of the earliest, the Women's Career Program at Northwestern University (Rich, 1977), worked with employers to identify predicted job vacancies and the skills needed in these jobs. The program then developed a personal competency profile for its participants, including both unemployed women and employed women interested in upgrading their skills, to determine the matches and gaps between the jobs and the women. Specific courses were provided to enable the women to learn any missing skills. A similar project, the Women's Management Program at Goucher College, is described in detail in the WEEA publication *Developing Women's Management Programs* (Zubin, 1982).

Another FIPSE-supported project, conducted by the National Commission on Working Women, provides career counseling for women clerical workers. The project also provides industry seminars aimed at increasing the awareness of corporations, unions, and educational leaders of the problems, needs, and aspirations of working women.

Several projects have concentrated their efforts on the special needs of employed women from minority groups. These include the National Council of Negro Women's project to help black women in low-paying jobs earn an associate's degree and enter jobs in administration, management, and sales. Materials for counseling employed minority women, developed by Women's Educational Equity Act projects, include *Career Planning for Minority Women, Management Basics for Minority Women,* the *Minority Women's Survival Kit,* and *Everywoman's Rights.* All are available from the Education Development Center.

One problem largely untouched by educational planners is the multiple roles required of working women, especially working mothers. *How About a Little Strategy?,* a WEEA publication, describes ways of coping with situations commonly encountered by mothers who return to school or to work.

Older Women.   Women aged 65 and over are a group that has, until recently, been virtually ignored by educational planners. This group is significant, however, because it is one that will grow rapidly in the future, both because of increasing life expectancy and because of population demographics. According to King and Marvel (1982), the population of women over 65 will grow to 19 million by the year 2000, and 1 in every 14 Americans will be an older woman.

Due to increased longevity and relatively good health, many older women choose to remain in the work force for their own satisfaction or to enable them to earn an adequate retirement income. Many of these women have had discontinuous work patterns and low salaries and would benefit from on-the-job training as a means of upgrading their skills and enabling them to obtain more highly paid positions.

The majority of older women are widows; however, increasing numbers of older women are being divorced after long marriages. Many of these women find that they *must* work in order to survive financially and are frequently faced with the urgent need to gain marketable skills while simultaneously learning how to cope with living alone—often for the first time in their lives. Community colleges have assisted many of these women by offering courses on financial planning, skills assessment, and job interviewing techniques. Paid internships would be particularly beneficial to these women.

Older women who are not employed often are eager to explore topics that interested them when they were young but which they did not have time to study. According to Cross (1979), "They are learning because it is enjoyable and personally satisfying. Their major subject matter interests are hobbies and crafts, nutrition and health, and other topics that have practical relevance in their lives" (p. 85). Elderhostel, an educational program for women and men over 60, provides university-level noncredit courses at colleges and universities around the country. In 1981, there were 37,000 participants, two-thirds of whom were women. A 1978 survey by the Academy for Educational Development showed that about one-third of all colleges were providing some type of "learning opportunity" for older adults. Twenty-eight states have passed legislation enabling older students to enroll in regularly scheduled classes in public colleges at lower tuition or at no charge.

Innovative programs designed specifically for older women are urgently needed. The participation of these women in all phases of the educational planning process would be an important first step. By sharing the vast accumulation of knowledge they have acquired over a lifetime, they could provide ideas for new directions in both teaching and learning. Their talents might also be utilized in counseling younger women and in teaching; thus, they would serve as role models for students and faculty.

WHAT IS THE EDUCATIONAL FUTURE FOR ADULT WOMEN?

We believe that educational programs for adult women will continue to grow in the 1980s, though they may take a different form from those that were developed and offered during the 1970s. The changing demographic characteristics of the population, including more employed women, women taking less time away from the labor force for child rearing, and increased longevity, suggest that there will be

1. More emphasis on educational programs for employed women
2. More educational programs provided in the workplace, either by employers, unions, or professional organizations or by postsecondary educational institutions working with these groups
3. New programs that help adults consider a wider range of career development options and that emphasize the transfer of skills to new occupations
4. More programs stressing updating of skills either for job advancement or for coping with job loss, and probably emphasizing new technology and changing practices in the workplace
5. A continued need for programs that emphasize handling multiple roles and coping with life changes and transitions
6. More educational programs using new technology to reach women who are not currently participating in educational programs
7. More programs for older and retired women as this group becomes a larger part of the population

Implications for Educational Practitioners.   These changes suggest that there may be fewer adult women enrolled in 4-year degree programs than in the past, especially in full-time credit programs. They also suggest an increase in enrollments in nondegree areas, including certificate programs, continuing education programs, and noncredit programs that focus on the development or updating of occupationally relevant skills. It will become increasingly important for colleges to conduct needs surveys of all adults in their geographic area to identify the populations that can be served and to cooperate with employers in providing programs for employed women. Programs need to be targeted to the needs of various subpopulations (Eliason, 1981).

Research Needs.   One serious problem has been the lack of research on educational programs for adult women. There is little information beyond program descriptions. Although some provide descriptive statistics about the participants and whether they enjoyed the program, evaluative data about long-term effectiveness and impact are almost nonexistent.

McGraw (1982) reviewed programs for reentry women and stated that "experimental research is needed to investigate the efficacy of the many programs" (p. 471). She pointed out that the limited scope of research to date has led to programs that assume "homogeneity of the participants' needs, psychological conditions, and goals" (p. 472). This assumption may not be based on facts. As McGraw noted, women who have not sought counseling or assistance have had little impact on the design of programs.

Research is necessary if educational programs for adult women are to continue to thrive (Rice, 1979). Rice proposed three levels of research: (1) systematic user records for reports and for demonstrating accountability, (2) program evaluations that will show the interaction between such variables as age, race, and marital status and the outcomes and effectiveness of techniques used, so that in a time of diminishing resources the individuals who will most benefit from a program or technique can be assured access to it; and (3) applied research that will document predictive relationships, make comparisons between adult men and women learners in terms of learning approaches, determine the market value of adult women's educational investment, analyze the changing family dynamics that occur when adult women take on new roles, and analyze the kinds of educational-occupational transitions that work best for adult women. We strongly support these recommendations.

These kinds of information would make it possible to develop new and improved programs that would meet the needs of all adults, both female and male, whether employed or engaged in unpaid work, regardless of age, race, income, or geographic location. The educational programs described in this chapter can serve as models for this effort and can bring about improved educational equity for all adults.

RECOMMENDATIONS

Above all else, we recommend that individuals seeking to achieve sex equity in educational programs and services for adult women be aware of the interdependency of educational practice, research, and policy. Each program for adult women should combine service, research, and advocacy. By combining services for adult women with research on these women's needs and on the effectiveness of program models in meeting these needs, information can be developed to inform policy decisions and to support advocacy of approaches that will improve educational equity and reduce stereotypes based on age and gender.

When designing programs and services, conducting research, or developing policy, it is important to remember that adult women are a diverse population. Therefore, we recommend that all programs for women conduct educational needs analyses, both with the women they currently serve and also with populations of women that are not being reached and served. Needs analyses should be related to characteristics of subgroups, such as reentry women, displaced homemakers, underemployed women, professional and managerial women, and older and retired women. Aggregation of information across diverse groups creates confusion and can lead to programs or policies that serve no one well.

We recommend that practitioners also identify demographic and attitudinal changes in the groups of women coming to them and, if possible, in groups that they might also serve. Programs should be modified to meet these demographic and attitudinal changes.

We recommend more programs and services for employed women, especially programs offered in cooperation with employers, unions, or professional organizations. We also recommend working with community groups and volunteer organizations, both as a way of increasing outreach and as a means of delivering services.

New program models need to be developed. Among those that appear to have the highest demand are the following:

1. Review and refresher courses in mathematics and science to help adult women prepare for admissions tests, entrance into technical education, or entrance into technical careers.
2. Programs to assist adult women in coping with life changes and transitions. With more women in the labor force, programs to help women cope with job loss or to make job transitions will become more important. In the future, the need for preretirement education and counseling for women will increase and may become as important as reentry programs have been.
3. Programs that combine education for adult women with counseling about handling multiple roles as wives, mothers, workers, and learners. Many adult women feel conflict between what they find that they must do and what they would like to do. Information and counseling about changing roles and opportunities for women should be incorporated into all programs.

Program delivery also needs to be improved. Practitioners need to continue their efforts to remove institutional and structural barriers to women by providing, if they do not already do so, courses at convenient times and locations, instruction by modes other than classroom lectures, childcare, counseling/information services, and credit for prior learning experiences. We especially recommend that courses for adult women be offered in a more flexible manner, using communications technology such as television, videodisks, and videocassettes, so that learning can take place at the convenience of the individual rather than at the convenience of the institution. More flexible programming is especially important in order to reach older women, rural women, handicapped women, and employed women.

We also recommend that practitioners avoid using the term "continuing education" in describing programs for adult women, since this term has multiple meanings that are easily confused. Clear statements about program goals and the methods by which they will be achieved are important in targeting programs toward specific groups and in ensuring that participant expectations about the program are realistic. These statements also facilitate program evaluation research.

We recommend that research on educational programs for adult women be increased. This should include the following:

1. Evaluations of the long-term effectiveness of programs and analyses of the relationship between program components, participant characteristics, and outcomes so that when resources are limited, services can be provided to those who will benefit the most.
2. Learning more about the educational needs of older adult women and about the best ways to teach them.
3. Developing new methods and materials for assessing adult women's prior learning experiences. Special attention needs to be given to determining how learning in noncredit courses and learning from unpaid work in the community and the home relates to the learning in traditional formal education.
4. Conducting research on the market value of women's educational investment and on the kinds of education-to-employment transitions that work best for adult women.

Finally, we recommend that practitioners and researchers work to disseminate information about effective educational programs and services for adult women to decision makers so that informed educational policies can be developed and educational equity for adult women achieved.

REFERENCES

Adkison, J. A., & Warren, A. (Eds.). (1980). *The administrative internship*. Lawrence: University of Kansas.
Adler, N. E. (1976). Women students. In J. Katz & R. T. Hartnett (Eds.), *Scholars in the*

making: The development of graduate and professional students (pp. 197–225). Cambridge, MA: Ballinger.

American Council on Education. (1980). *The national guide to educational credits for training programs*. Washington, DC: author.

Appelbaum, E. (1981). *Back to work: Determinants of women's successful re-entry*. Boston: Auburn House.

Aslanian, C. B., & Brickell, H. M. (1980). *Americans in transition: Life changes as reasons for adult learning*. New York: College Board.

Astin, H. S. (Ed). (1976). *Some action of her own: The adult woman and higher education*. Lexington, MA: Heath.

Beausang, K. R. (1976). *The increasing enrollment of returning women students and their achievement as measured by their mean GPA*. Moline, IL: Black Hawk College.

Berman, M. R., Gelsco, C. J., Greenfeig, B. R., & Hirsch, R. (1977). The efficacy of supportive learning environments for returning women. *Journal of Counseling Psychology, 24*(4), 324–331.

Campbell, J. W. (1981, December). *The integration of service, advocacy, and research in a university women's center*. Paper presented at the International Interdisciplinary Congress on Women, Haifa, Israel.

Chitayat, D.,& Hymer, S. (1976). *The new occupational student: The mature adult women* (CASE Report No. 35–76). New York: City University of New York, Graduate School and University Center.

Cirkesena, K., & Hereth, F. (Comps.). (1977). *Continuing education: Re-entry and the mature woman. Annotated selected references and resources* (Bibliography Series No. 2). San Francisco: Women's Educational Equity Communications Network.

Clements, K. (1974, April). *Emotional characteristics of mature women students in education*. Paper presented at the annual meeting of the American Educational Research Association, Chicago.

Cross, K. P. (1979). Adult learners: Characteristics, needs, and interests. In R. E. Peterson (Ed.), *Lifelong learning in America* (pp. 75–141). San Francisco: Jossey-Bass.

DiSabatino, M. (1976). Psychological factors inhibiting women's occupational aspirations and vocational choices. *Vocational Guidance Quarterly, 25*, 43–48.

Ekstrom, R. B. (1972). *Barriers to women's participation in post-secondary education: A review of the literature* (RB–72–49). Princeton, NJ: Educational Testing Service.

Ekstrom, R. B. (1980). Evaluating women's volunteer work and homemaking experiences. *Alternative Higher Education, 4*(3), 201–211.

Ekstrom, R. B. (1981a). *HAVE (Homemaking And Volunteer Experience) skills: Women's workbook, counselor's guide, and employer's guide*. Princeton, NJ: Educational Testing Service.

Ekstrom, R. B. (1981b). *Making experience count in sex equity programs*. Princeton, NJ: Educational Testing Service.

Ekstrom, R. B. (1981c). *Making experience count in vocational education*. Princeton, NJ: Educational Testing Service.

Ekstrom, R. B., Beier, J. J., Davis, E. L., & Gruenberg, C. B. (1981). Career and educational counseling implications of women's life experience learning. *Personnel and Guidance Journal, 60*, 97–101.

Ekstrom, R. B., & Eliason, N. C. (1978). *The transferability of women's life experience competencies to employment and to vocational education: A state-of-the-art review* (project report, Task Al, Credentialing Women's Life Experiences). Princeton, NJ: Educational Testing Service. (ERIC Document Reproduction Service No. ED 189 335)

Ekstrom, R. B., Harris, A. M., & Lockheed, M. E. (1977). *How to get college credit for what you have learned as a homemaker and volunteer.* Princeton, NJ: Educational Testing Service.

Eliason, N. C. (1978). *Neglected women: The educational needs of displaced home-makers, single mothers, and older women.* Washington, DC: National Advisory Council on Women's Educational Programs.

Eliason, N. C. (1981). New directions for women's studies and support services. *New Directions for Community Colleges, 34,* 33–42.

Esperson, M. A. (1975). *The mature woman student returning to higher education in a liberal arts college for adults.* Unpublished doctoral dissertation, Columbia University.

Farmer, H. S., & Becker, T. E. (1977). *New career options for women: A counselor's sourcebook.* New York: Human Sciences.

Fisher, J., & Reuben, E. (1981). *The women's studies service learning handbook.* College Park, MD: National Women's Studies Association.

Hall, R. A. (1982). *The classroom climate: A chilly one for women?* Washington, DC: Association of American Colleges, Project on the Status and Education of Women.

Harrison, C. (1979). *Working women speak: Education, training, counseling needs.* Washington, DC: National Advisory Council on Women's Educational Programs.

Hersh, B. G. (1980). *Re-entry women involved in women's studies.* Washington, DC: National Institute of Education.

King, N. R., & Marvel, M. G. (1982). *Issues, policies, and programs for midlife and older women.* Washington, DC: Center for Women Policy Studies.

Lantz, A., Houghton-Alico, D., & Eaton, V. L. (Eds.). (1980). *Reentry women scientists.* Denver: Denver Research Institute.

Lutter, J. M. (1982, March). *Coulds and shoulds: The dilemma.* Paper presented at the annual meeting of the American Educational Research Association, New York.

Mangano, J. A., & Corrado, T. J. (1978). *Meeting academic success needs of re-entry adults.* Albany: State University of New York, Two Year College Development Center.

Marano, C. (Ed.). (1978). *Displaced homemakers: Program options.* Oakland, CA: Older Women's League Educational Fund.

McGraw, L. K. (1982). A selective review of programs and counseling interventions for the reentry woman. *Personnel and Guidance Journal, 60,* 469–472.

McIntyre, V. (1981). *Wherever you learned it: A directory of opportunities for educational credit.* Columbia, MD: Council for the Advancement of Experiential Learning.

Mulligan, K. L. (1980). *Internship programs for women.* Washington, DC: National Society for Internships and Experiential Education.

National Center for Education Statistics. (1980). *Projections of Education Statistics to 1988–89.* Washington, DC: author.

National Center for Education Statistics. (1982). *The condition of education: 1982 edition.* Washington, DC: author.

National Center for Education Statistics. (1983). *The condition of education: 1983 edition.* Washington, DC: Author.

Project Re-Entry: A career education internship for women. (1977). Boston: Civic Center and Clearinghouse.

Rice, J. (1979, October). Continuing education for women: A clarion. *Lifelong Learning: The Adult Years*, pp. 16–19, 25.

Rich, L. (1977). 24 women: 24 managers. *Worklife*, 2(11), 24–26.

Scott, N. A. (1980). *Returning women students: A review of research and descriptive studies*. Washington, DC: National Association of Women Deans, Administrators, and Counselors.

Shaw, L. B. (1979). *A profile of women potentially eligible for the Displaced Homemaker Program under the Comprehensive Employment and Training Act of 1978*. Columbus: Ohio State University, Center for Human Resource Research.

Shields, L. (1981). *Displaced homemakers: Organizing for a new life*. New York: McGraw-Hill.

Stanley, E. (1980). *Credit for prior experience learning*. Columbus: Ohio State University, ERIC Clearinghouse on Adult, Career, and Vocational Education.

Tittle, C. K., & Denker, E. R. (1980). *Returning women students in higher education: Defining policy issues*. New York: Praeger.

Turner, B. F. (1977, August). The self-concepts of older women. In *Socialization to become an old woman*. Symposium conducted at the American Psychological Association annual meeting, San Francisco.

University of the State of New York. (1977). *A guide to education programs in noncollegiate organizations*. Albany: author.

U.S. Bureau of the Census. (1980). *Social indicators III*. Washington, DC: author.

Vetter, L., Winkfield, P. W., Ransom, R. M., & Lowrey, C. M. (1977). *Career planning programs for women employees: Prototype programs*. Columbus: Ohio State University, Center for Vocational Education.

Wilder, D. (1980). *Issues in education and training for working women*. Washington, DC: National Institute for Work and Learning.

Women's Bureau, U.S. Department of Labor. (1978). *Women in nontraditional jobs: a program model*. Washington, DC: author.

Women's Equity Action League. (1982). *Better late than never: Financial aid for older women seeking education and training*. Washington, DC: author.

Young, C. D. (1981, April). *A critical review of factors affecting community college women in nontraditional programs*. Paper presented at the annual meeting of the American Educational Research Association.

Zubin, J. (1982). *Developing women's management programs: A guide to professional job reentry for women*. Towson, MD: Goucher College.

PART VI

Sex Equity from Early through Postsecondary Education

Carol Anne Dwyer

It is all too easy to forget that educational equity issues are important to women and girls of all ages and are present, in various forms, at every level of education from preschool through postsecondary. Many of the basic issues touched on in the two chapters that constitute part VI have been raised throughout this book: the nature of equity; sex-related differences in development, values, and achievement; the role of society and educational institutions in transmitting sex-related expectations and influencing outcomes. The centrality of these issues is undeniable, and thus they recur in these two chapters; yet there are other, perhaps more specific, issues pertaining to the education of the very young and to advanced education that must be explored in greater depth if we are to appreciate fully the significance of these two phases of the process of education. In chapter 23, *Educational Equity in Early Education Environments,* Selma Greenberg argues persuasively that early childhood education experiences set the tone and direction for later personal and professional development. In a similar manner, in chapter 24, *Improving Sex Equity in Postsecondary Education,* Karen Bogart is effective in highlighting the importance of postsecondary education experiences, not only to the individual directly, but indirectly through institutional change and through molding the profession of education. Thus, in an almost organic cycle, we see the seeds of change in the profession of education being sown in individual preschool experiences, as our future professionals are shaped in their attitudes toward life and education, while at the same time postsecondary experiences are shaping the content of the next generation's early education.

23

Educational Equity
in Early Education Environments

Selma Greenberg

The belief in the critical consequences of the early childhood years for subsequent development is one of the most universally cherished psychological insights of the 20th century. Debates related to this issue center not on whether the early childhood years influence subsequent development but rather to what extent "the child is father of the man"—or mother of the woman. The evidence that sociocultural factors, rather than organic deficits, are responsible for 75 to 80% of the children diagnosed as mildly retarded (IQ's 55 to 69) is dramatic proof, if such proof is needed, of the crucial impact of the early years on future development (Edgerton, 1979).

Gender identity, the consistent identification of self as female or male, is one aspect of early childhood learning. It is learning that is achieved early and with absolute consistency. "As early as 2 years of age children know their gender identity. They are either a boy or a girl and they are not likely to forget it ever!" (Brooks-Gunn & Schnapp-Matthews, 1979). For the young child learning the meanings, attitudes, and behaviors—in short, the sex role—attached to being female or male in a particular society is more complex, more significant learning than the simple knowledge that one is female or male. It is learning the prescribed sex role rather than learning of one's gender identity that often has limiting and damaging effects on subsequent development. When society rigidly dichotomizes female and male sex roles, rigorously enforces prescribed sex role behaviors, and regularly punishes breaches of the sex role standard, then beginning at about age 3 children will be vigilant in avoiding actions, activities, and events they believe "inappropriate" for their own sex simply because it is "appropriate" for the other. This will be particularly true in the case of boys, who are likely to conform to what they believe to be behavior appropriate for their

Merle Froschl, Jeanne Kohl, Michael Kean, and Candace Schau provided assistance in the development of this chapter.

own sex. Moreover, young children monitor each other's behaviors to ensure that peers conform to sex role standards (Blomberg, 1981). Young children are also aware that peers monitor the appropriateness of sex role behaviors. Thus, children conform more diligently to the sex role standard when under the observation of a peer than when alone (Serbin, Connor, & Lipman, 1977). When children are unsure of whether they may participate in any activity, action, or event without fear of humiliation, they simply ask the nearest adult, "Can a girl do that?" or, "Is that all right for a boy to do?" These and other questions having to do with all aspects of what constitutes "appropriate" or "inappropriate" sex role attitudes, behaviors, and knowledge form the content of much of the dialogue young children have with their parents and teachers.

Another crucial area of sex role behavior which the child is already exploring at ages 3, 4, and 5 is the "What Can I Be When I Grow Up?" or the aspiration issue. For young children the world of work is divided between the work men do and the work women do. Typically, they associate a job with only one sex. Moreover, young children expect that little girls will grow up to do the jobs that they believe only women now do, and they expect that little boys will grow up to do the jobs that they believe only men now do (Greenberg & Peck, 1973). Thus, young children appear to believe that the future will repeat the past.

As discussed in more detail in chapter 6, "Educational Equity and Sex Role Development," by the time children reach kindergarten they have spent several years conforming to sex role expectations that often track girls into one set of behaviors, attitudes, knowledge, and expectations and boys into another (Block, 1979). If we add to the limiting behaviors children impose upon themselves the narrowed opportunities available to them due to societal sex role stereotypes, one can appreciate the need for strategies to reduce and/or eliminate these barriers to learning. If we accept the verdict of both lay and professional persons that the early childhood years are not only important in themselves but that their effects have lifelong impact, we must view seriously what children do during these years and perhaps view even more seriously what they do not do or avoid doing.

ISSUES: SOME MYTHS ABOUT SEX EQUITY IN EARLY CHILDHOOD EDUCATION ENVIRONMENTS

Myth 1: Children Need to Learn the Same Things That Their Same-Sex Parents Learned, in Much the Same Way.   Children between the ages of 2 and 5 today will live virtually their entire adult lives in the 21st century. Chapters in part I of this handbook have documented how sex roles in our society are less differentiated now than in past generations. If children are to cope with this changed world, they need sex-equitable home and school environments that encourage participation in and access to learning across the widest spectrum of skills, abilities, and knowledge; effective and flexible skills in self-management; a firm sense of self-worth and confidence in one's ability to learn; the ability to gain satisfaction and reward from participation in and commitment to the world of work; the ability to work with and for others to achieve mutually agreed-upon goals; and the ability to give and receive care, love, and affection.

Early education environments have also been changing. Today's middle-class child experiences a much different life style than did middle-class children of generations past. Parental separation or divorce is an all-too-common experience for the very young. More common still is the family with both parents employed outside the home. While in 1980 54% of mothers of young children were employed outside the home, by 1990 it is anticipated that the number will be closer to 70%. Thus, each year more and more children spend more of their early childhood years in some kind of group setting: nursery schools, day care centers, and, most often, family day care arrangements (Hofferth, 1979). In summary, children need to learn that their roles in society will be much less constrained by their sex than their parents' lives have been, and educators must remember that young children spend increasingly more time in group settings outside their homes.

Myth 2: Girls and Boys Benefit Equally from Toys.   Early childhood educators have long understood that play is the vehicle through which children learn. Toys thus represent one important kind of specialized learning tool. In the early 1960s the British novelist C. P. Snow wrote an essay entitled "The Two Cultures" (Snow, 1964), deploring the fact that Britain's most intellectual citizens were ignorant of science. Because the education of Britons was traditionally either completely scientific or completely classical and literary, two cultures had been created that were unable to communicate with or understand each other. One reason that this is a lesser problem in America, Snow indicated, is that American children receive a scientific orientation from their toys. Americans, too, live in two different cultures. Ours, however, are based on gender. The toys Snow so clearly understood to be teaching aids for early mathematics and science education are not the toys of all young Americans. They are the toys of half of America's children: they are boys' toys (Block, 1978).

Myth 3:   Girls and Boys Enter Kindergarten with Quite Similar Abilities, Experiences, and Accomplishments.   Not only do girls and boys have different sets of accomplishments by kindergarten but, in a corollary fashion, a different set of educational needs. The differing learning profile of the young girl from that of the young boy can be constructed from the following list of 16 initial learning attributes:

1. Young girls' opportunities for varied verbal experiences exceed those of young boys (Moss, 1967).
2. Young boys' opportunities for varied spatial experiences exceed those of young girls (Saegert & Hart, 1978).
3. Young girls' opportunities for varied small muscle experiences exceed those of young boys (Medrich, Roisen, Rubin, & Buckley, 1982).

4. Young boys' opportunities for varied large muscle experiences exceed those of young girls (Medrich et al., 1982).
5. Young girls' opportunities for varied repetitive experiences exceed those of young boys (Block, 1979).
6. Young boys' opportunities for varied inventive experiences exceed those of young girls (Block, 1979).
7. Young girls' opportunities for varied nurturing experiences exceed those of young boys (Block, 1979).
8. Young boys' opportunities for varied managing (directing) experiences exceed those of young girls (Block, 1979).
9. Young girls' opportunities for varied one-to-one (intimate) relationships exceed those of young boys (Medrich et al., 1982).
10. Young boys' opportunities for varied group relationships exceed those of young girls (Medrich et al., 1982).
11. Young girls' opportunities for role rehearsal experiences exceed those of young boys (Woodruff, 1974).
12. Young boys' opportunities for experimenting with a wide range of future career and life options exceed those of girls (Papalia & Tennent, 1975).
13. Young girls' opportunities to learn from adult models exceed those of young boys (Lynn, 1972).
14. Young boys' opportunities to learn from direct instruction exceed those of young girls (National Project on Women, 1977).
15. Young girls exceed boys in gaining early impulse control (Maccoby & Jacklin, 1974).
16. Young boys exceed girls in experiences that confirm their self-worth and value (Williams, Bennett, & Best, 1975).

Myth 4: Early Education Environments Meet the Needs of Girls Better than Boys. It has long been observed that the early years of schooling have a differential impact on boys and girls. This observation has often led to the conclusion that schools are "good for girls" and "bad for boys" (Sexton, 1969). The observation that early education environments stress those activities, behaviors, and knowledge at which girls already excel and boys appear deficient is an excellent one. That this observation leads logically to the conclusion that schools favor girls by continually engaging them in behaviors at which they are already accomplished is a highly questionable one. Consider the issue of impulse management, which might be viewed as a metaphor for the education establishment's response to the problems of females and males. Boys as a group, if they have an impulse management problem, tend to require more structures for impulse management, for they suffer from undercontrol. Girls as a group, if they have an impulse management problem, tend to require fewer structures for impulse management, for they suffer from overcontrol. However, when boys' undercontrol is declared "bad" and girls' overcontrol is declared "good," it is arguable whether this has a positive effect on girls. The consequence of this labeling is that attempts are made to remedy the control problems that afflict boys, while girls' control problems remain unobserved and thus go untreated.

A very different learning profile emerges for the typical young girl and typical young boy learner with their equally distinct sets of educational needs. By stressing the knowledge, skills, and abilities that girls already possess and in which boys are deficient, schools in general from early childhood settings on meet the needs of boys but fail to meet those of girls. While clearly not always providing for all learning that would remedy boys' experiential deficits, it is the typical girl who has suffered by far the greatest systematic educational neglect. Consider the usual early childhood environment into which the young child is placed. It is typical in that environment that the educational needs of the young boy are met. Thus, verbal activities (circle time, show and tell, singing games, songs, and stories), opportunities for small muscle development (cutting, painting, sorting, stringing beads, peg play, table games, and cooking), and assistance in gaining impulse control (rule setting and enforcement) are all structured into the early childhood day. These are the activities that the youngsters are strongly encouraged to do each day. These are the activities that the typical early childhood environments promote on a regular basis. If we consult the list of 16 initial learning attributes, we can easily see how crucial these activities are in remedying the learning deficits of the young boy. The educational needs associated with young girls are not systematically addressed. By leaving to chance or choice spatial activities (opportunities for building with blocks, exploring the outdoors, and creating one's own spatial boundaries in indoor and outdoor play), large motor activities (running, jumping, throwing, catching, lifting, pulling, dodging, dancing, exercise, and gymnastics), and investigatory and experimental activities (the use of scales, weights, magnets, instruments, tools, and so forth), the activities necessary to remedy the educational deficits of young girls find no regular place in the curriculum. It is a distinct possibility that a young girl may spend a year or two in an early childhood setting and have few or no experiences with spatial activities, large-motor activities, and investigatory and experimental activities. These form no part of the regular curriculum because they are most frequently consigned to that place in the curriculum designated as "free play."

The early childhood day is typically divided between structured and free play activities. Structured activities may be thought of as required activities in which all children are expected to (and generally do) participate. To those unfamiliar with early childhood environments, it may come as a surprise that nap time, snack time, and toilet time are generally programmed rather than "free" activities. Other structured activities include verbal activities, small-muscle activities, and impulse-control training. Free play is that time of the day when children are free to choose and, perhaps more importantly, free to avoid activities. Free play is generally composed of certain indoor or outdoor activities from which children are free to make selections: doll play and playing house; block play and play with other building materials; carpentry; play with balls, trucks, swings, and doll carriages; investigatory and exploratory activities; and a selection of table games which are generally aids to developing prereading or premathematics skills. But just how free is "free play"? If we consider the list of activities that constitute the array from which the children may choose, we find the list comprises the most highly sex-linked activities: conscious that they are surrounded by peers who monitor their behavior, how many children will freely choose what they have been taught is the "wrong" activity? Thus, the educational needs of young girls are largely unmet; and perhaps more sad still, the young girls themselves are held responsible for choosing limiting, sex-typed activities. Teachers and parents can point to all the opportunities that the girls had to choose exploration, building, or experimenting but left unexplored.

For example, large-muscle development is important for all children but is a particular educational need of the typical young girl, despite the fact that the average girl's physical development proceeds at least at the same pace as young boys' and often more quickly. Except for play with very large blocks, which is usually an all-boy activity, and for dancing, an activity infrequently scheduled, large-muscle development activities take place only during gym and outdoors. Since gym classes are typically not scheduled for young children, it is to outdoor play that we must look to observe how girls' educational needs are served. It comes as no surprise that the children sitting on the swings, pushing the doll carriages, sifting sand, and talking to the teacher are often female, while the children running in a disorganized fashion, using the climbing and balancing equipment, and playing with the balls, trucks, and tricycles are most often male. Here, then, is another example of girls' and boys' choosing activities that they have been taught are appropriate for members of their own sex. But here, too, we see an example of how sex role expectations continue to develop and deepen and further hamper children's learning.

In addition to having fewer of their unique needs addressed than the boys do, the girls also receive less teacher attention than the boys, unless the girls stay physically close to the teacher and lose needed opportunities for inventive and independent experiences.

The finding that boys receive attention whether they stay near to or far from the teacher is closely connected to another finding frequently reported by classroom investigators: the greater salience (visibility, importance, presence) of boys in the classroom. This heightened salience is indicated by the greater number of instructions, questions, comments, and responses directed to boys by the teacher (Sadker & Sadker, 1982). It is important to note that not all researchers report more teacher-male interaction than teacher-female interaction. Galeis and Hegland (1982), for example, report greater teacher-female interaction; however, their work does support other research documenting the different patterns of verbal behavior that exist between teachers and their students of both sexes. Boys, more practiced than girls in receiving instructions, exceed girls in their ability to learn from instruction—first in oral, then in written, form (Lynn, 1972). Boys' greater classroom saliency, however, does not always have a positive effect on their learning. Boys receive the overwhelming majority of negative classroom comments. Boys' "bad" behavior is a common focus of teachers' negative comments. While girls are frequently ignored or their presence discounted in the classroom, boys are frequently singled out for verbal abuse; thus, boys' greater classroom salience seems often to be as negative for them as it is for the girls.

The greater salience of boys in early childhood environments is not simply the result of teacher behavior. Teacher behavior is itself the result of a society in which the male is more visible than the female. The greater visibility of males in society appears in even the earliest school environments, and in many ways in addition to the speech and behavior of teachers. Studies of young children's books reveal that these books both focus on males and posit females as different from males in attitudes, behavior, and knowledge. Classroom teaching materials and aids convey the same messages (Women on Words and Images, 1975). Recent analyses of our language usage patterns have indicated the male bias of the English language (O'Donnell, 1973). Very young children are less able even than adults to understand the concept of generic usage. Thus, the generic use of "man" for "person," or "he" for both "she" and "he," is simply beyond the young child's language power. Additionally, for many the early childhood environment may be the first time the young child has ever been exposed to this kind of language.

The male bias of classroom language, the overwhelming male presence and systematic sex role tracking even in young children's books and teaching materials, the greater salience of the male child, a curriculum more likely to remedy the learning deficits young boys experience, all make it unlikely that early childhood environments will maximize girls' educational opportunities.

STRATEGIES FOR CREATING SEX-EQUITABLE
EARLY EDUCATION ENVIRONMENTS

Comprehensive Sex Equity Programs for Young Children.   Often, even in the most advantaged of early childhood settings, children's learning opportunities are limited by their teachers' conscious or (more often) unconscious sex role channeling. Unfortunately, with few notable exceptions, the needs of these teachers and the children in their charge have largely been overlooked, even by those who have undertaken the task of developing sex-equitable education. For example, only 4.5% of all projects funded by the Women's Educational Equity Act Program (WEEAP) address the educational needs of the early childhood years (National Advisory Council on Women's Educational Programs, 1980). A major focus of this 4.5% has been on working with teachers of young children in workshops to help them become aware of the need to provide nonsexist early childhood environments for young children. It is intended that as a result of this awareness training teachers will become more sensitive to the need to modify their own verbal and nonverbal behavior, to introduce sex-fair and sex-affirmative materials into the classroom, and to encourage all children to make use of all curricular activities. Whether the reliance on teacher influence is sufficient to guarantee early childhood equity, or whether more significant redesign of the curriculum is required, is a subject upon which there is still debate. There is, however, little debate concerning the necessity of promoting teacher awareness as a first step toward improving children's educational equity. Fortunately, the development of general teacher awareness materials has been a particular focus of WEEAP. Between 1976 and 1980, awareness projects accounted for nearly 40% of all funded projects. Additionally, books such as *Equal Their Chances: Children's Activities for Non-Sexist Learning* (Shapiro, Kramer, & Hunerberg, 1981); *Growing Up Free: Raising Your Child in the 80's* (Pogrebin, 1980); and *Right from the Start: A Guide to Non-Sexist Child Rearing* (Greenberg, 1978) offer guidance to parents and the teachers of young children. Of particular interest to the teachers is the manual of Project T.R.E.E. (Training Resources for Educational Equity) entitled *Maximizing Young Children's Potential* (1980).

Strategies for Involving Children in Activities Unusual for Their Sex. Fortunately, there are some strategies that have already been proven to result in involvement of children in activities they might otherwise avoid. Some of the most interesting investigatory and experimental work on teacher behavior in the early childhood environment has been done by Serbin, Connor, and Citron (1978) and has shown how influential the actions of teachers are, particularly for young girls. For example, young girls tend to congregate near the teacher; thus, if teachers simply position themselves near activities that girls typically avoid, the girls' behavior changes. In order to remain close to the teacher, girls will begin engaging in activities they had previously avoided. For those teachers who prefer to discourage girls' proximal behavior rather than to capitalize on it, another technique is available. Teachers must be quick to reinforce girls when they move away. Moreover, teachers must encourage girls to return to activities they have left. Serbin found that teachers are much more likely to encourage boys than girls to continue abandoned efforts. If a child experiences an injury or problem and seeks help from the teacher, the teacher will typically respond similarly to requests for help from boys and girls. The behavior that follows, however, will be different: the teacher is more likely to return the boy to his original activity. The teacher is less likely to do this with a girl, and thus the girl remains by the teacher, her original activity abandoned.

Strategies that Increase Teacher and Student Involvement in Large-Muscle and Spatial Activities. Almost all teachers of young children are female, and they are often those who most easily fit the expected female role. Thus, it is not uncommon that the teacher herself did not have much experience as a child in spatial exploration, large-muscle development, or investigative and experimental activities. These activities are, therefore, less likely to draw the teacher than are art, music, verbal, and small-muscle activities. The teacher literally positions herself closer to those classroom activities with which she is comfortable, and on the playground is often most comfortable just standing still. Classroom experimenters, who are quick to note that the great majority of teachers in early childhood environments is female, have attempted to produce change by introducing male teachers into those environments. In a study by Koblinsky and Sugawara (1979), the experimental group of children in a male-directed nonsexist early childhood environment demonstrated the most movement toward nonstereotypic thinking as compared to the other groups. The findings based on one male and two female teachers are necessarily tentative, but the investigators speculated that the "presence of an adult male in a traditionally female occupation enhances children's awareness of the multiple options available to both sexes" (p. 406). Although this may be accurate, it is important to note that researchers almost universally conclude that fathers are more likely to demand sex role conformity than are mothers. It is unlikely, however, that a male who seeks to work with young children would be a person who enforces rigid sex role expectations. Those who hope early childhood environments may become less stereotypic through the growth of a large cadre of male teachers are likely to be disappointed. The staff of family day care (day care in the home) is even more overwhelmingly female than the larger, more traditional, in-school early childhood environments. This could, of course, change if female-male couples actually became family day care providers; presently this is not the case. Family day care is presently structured as the care by women of the children of families other than their own.

Strategies for Decreasing Children's Sex-Stereotyped Behaviors. In coming to understand the processes by which objects or activites become associated with only one sex, an experiment by Serbin, Connor, and Lipman (1977) is illuminating. In the first step of this experiment, the teacher made the association of an object or activity with only one sex. Second, the teacher assisted the child in making a personal or private single-sex association. Third, the teacher chose a child of that sex to demonstrate the object's use or the activity. Thus, a teacher would hold up a sewing or lace-up card and say (step 1), "This is a sewing card. Many mommies sew"; (step 2), "Have you ever watched your mother sew?" (step 3), "Sally, do you think you could come up here and show us how to sew this card?" This kind of introduction was sufficient to signal the children that sewing is appropriate for girls but off-limits for boys. Teachers were most often likely to stress this process when introducing objects or activities that have societal associations with males. Serbin went on, however, to demonstrate that sex linking is neither natural nor inevitable. Serbin gave an experimental group of teachers sewing cards to introduce to their classes, along with a script to use when first introducing the activity to the class. The script was designed both to avoid sex linkage and to encourage use by all children. The three-step process described above was used again, but with changes. Thus, a teacher would hold up the card and say (step 1), "This is a lace-up card. Many shoes have laces"; (step 2), "Who in this class has shoes on with laces today?" (step 3), "Sally and Steven, do you think you could come up here and show us how to lace up this card?" When teachers introduced toys without linking them for use by only one sex, all children made use of them.

Strategies for Decreasing Young Children's Sex-Stereotyped Knowledge and Attitudes. Sex-fair and sex-affirmative curricular strategies developed for early childhood environments have often centered on working to broaden children's perceptions of adult sex role possibilities and their own aspirations. Several of these projects have reported success in having children increase the number of activities they see as appropriate for both female and male adults. Three of the research studies reporting success with such curricular strategies are Project Equality in the Highline School District in Seattle, a project undertaken by Guttentag and Bray (1976), and one directed by Koblinsky and Sugawara (1979). Koblinsky and Sugawara found that both boys and girls participating in their experimental curriculum demonstrated broadened notions of adult sex role opportunities, particularly when the group was led by a male teacher. These findings differ from those of other researchers, who generally have reported greater change in the responses of young girls (Guttentag & Bray, 1976). Koblinsky and Sugawara were more effective in broadening children's perceptions of appropriate adult activities than they were in broadening children's perceptions of their own activities.

RECOMMENDATIONS FOR CREATING EDUCATIONAL EQUITY IN EARLY EDUCATION ENVIRONMENTS

Recommendations for Parents and Teachers

Parents and teachers can perform many critical functions in debunking the myths about what young girls and boys experience and need by creating sex-equitable early education environments.
Strategies that should be provided for all children:

1. Avoid assigning activities to all children that remedy the problems typical of boys, while permitting all activities that remedy the problems typical of young girls to be a matter of the young child's choice
2. Provide only those activities and materials that all children can use and enjoy and that are sex-fair or sex-affirmative in content
3. Develop verbal and physical interaction patterns that make all children equal participants in non-sex-segregated activities
4. Develop non-sex-biased linguistic and other communication patterns that have a positive impact on both self-management skills and cognition for all children
5. Create opportunities for nurturing and caring activities that are in a problem-solving mode and that invite all children's involvement
6. Use strategies such as teacher proximity and structured play time to involve children in activities they may otherwise avoid

Strategies that should be available to all children, but directed particularly to girls:

7. Provide activities that require spatial exploration
8. Provide activities for practice in large-muscle coordination and development of large-motor skills (increase structured gym activities)
9. Provide equipment that enhances investigatory activity
10. Provide activities that permit learning from following directions
11. Provide tasks that require cooperative groups of three or more children for their accomplishment
12. Encourage distance from adults
13. Provide opportunities for experimenting with a wide range of future career options

Strategies that should be available to all children, but directed particularly to boys:

14. Provide activities that encourage listening, speaking, and conversing
15. Provide activities for small-muscle coordination
16. Provide opportunities to learn from modeling
17. Provide opportunities that encourage responsibility for and to others
18. Help boys to develop flexible, effective self-management skills
19. Provide opportunities for nurturing activities, including family role rehearsal in housekeeping or doll corners

Recommendations for Educational Policy Makers

1. Provide increased federal financial support to continue the past practice of convening annual national meetings of researchers and educational practitioners on equal early education environments
2. Provide increased information to the public and organizations of parents and teachers about practices that promote sex equity in early education environments and that dispel the current myths
3. Encourage males to become teachers of young children because this decreases sex segregation, even though it is unlikely that either male or female teachers will behave in nonstereotyped ways

Recommendations for Research and Development

1. Provide increased federal financial support for developing and evaluating more comprehensive equity-oriented early childhood instructional materials and programs which are based on knowledge gained from research on effective strategies to decrease sex role stereotypes and which expose children to learning opportunities that they need but might not choose
2. Study the impact of training on teachers' ability to modify their cognitive, affective, and managerial classroom behavior to ensure all children's equal participation
3. Conduct short-term studies (a) of changes in children's free time toy and school material selection following planned exposures to sex-stereotypical

items; (b) of girls' ability to distance themselves physically from teachers following a program of appropriate reinforcement; (c) of changes in girl-boy play partner selection when materials and activities are non-stereotypic; and (d) of changes in pattern of pupil classroom participation when assertive as well as conforming behavior is appropriately reinforced

4. Study the long-term effects on academic achievement and occupational choices of students who have had planned remedial spatial exploration experiences and the long-term effects on the social and emotional adjustment of students who have had opportunities to develop assertive as well as conforming behaviors.

REFERENCES

Block, J. H. (1978). Another look at sex differentiation in the socialization behaviors of mothers and fathers. In J. Sherman and F. Denmark (Eds.), *The psychology of women: Future directions for research* (pp. 29–87). New York: Psychological Dimensions.

Block, J. H. (1979). *Personality development in males and females: The influence of differential socialization.* Paper based on a talk given in the Master Lecture Series at the annual meeting of the American Psychological Association, New York.

Blomberg, J. (1981). *Sex-typed channeling behavior in the pre-school peer group: A study of toy choice in same-sex and cross-sex play.* Unpublished doctoral dissertation, University of California, Berkeley.

Brooks-Gunn, J., & Schnapp-Matthews, W. (1979). *He and she: How children develop their sex-role identity.* Englewood Cliffs, NJ: Prentice-Hall.

Edgerton, R. B. (1979). *Mental retardation.* Cambridge: Harvard University Press.

Galeis, I., & Hegland, S. (1982). Teacher-child interactions and children's locus of control tendencies. *American Educational Research Journal, 19,* 293–302.

Greenberg, S. (1978). *Right from the start: A guide to non-sexist child rearing.* Boston: Houghton Mifflin.

Greenberg, S., & Peck, L. (1973). *An experimental curriculum designed to modify children's sex-role perceptions and aspiration levels.* Paper presented at the annual meeting of the American Educational Research Association, New Orleans.

Guttentag, M., & Bray, H. (1976). *Undoing sex stereotypes: Research and resources for educators.* New York: McGraw-Hill.

Hofferth, S. (1979). Day care in the next decade, 1980–1990. *Journal of Marriage and the Family, 41,* 649–656.

Koblinsky, S. A., & Sugawara, A. L. (1979). Effects of non-sexist curriculum intervention on children's sex role learning. *Home Economics Research, 7,* 399–406.

Lynn, D. (1972). Determinants of intellectual growth in women. *School Review, 80,* 241–260.

Maccoby, E. E., & Jacklin, C. N. (1974). *The psychology of sex differences.* Stanford, CA: Stanford University Press.

Medrich, E., Roisen, J., Rubin, V., & Buckley, S. (1982). *The serious business of growing up: A study of children's lives outside of school.* Berkeley and Los Angeles: University of California Press.

Moss, H. A. (1967). Sex, age, and state as determinants of mother-infant interaction. *Merrill-Palmer Quarterly, 13,* 19–36.

National Advisory Council on Women's Educational Programs. (1980). *Women's Educational Equity Act program, evaluation report FY 1980.* Washington, DC: author.

National Project on Women. (1977). *Taking sexism out of education* (Publication No. [OE] 77-01017). Washington, DC: Department of Health, Education and Welfare.

O'Donnell, H. S. (1973). Sexism in language. *Elementary English, 50,* 1067–1072.

Papalia, D. E., & Tennent, S. S. (1975). Vocational aspirations in preschoolers: A manifestation of early sex-role stereotyping. *Sex Roles, 1*(2), 197–199.

Pogrebin, L. C. (1980). *Growing up free: Raising your child in the 80's.* New York: McGraw-Hill.

Project T.R.E.E. (1980). *Maximizing young children's potential: A non-sexist manual for early childhood trainers.* Newton, MA: Education Development Center.

Sadker, M. P., & Sadker, D. M. (1982). *Sex equity handbook for schools.* New York: Longman.

Saegert, S., & Hart, R. (1978). The development of environmental competence in girls and boys. In M. Salter (Ed.), *Play: An anthropological perspective* (pp. 157–175). West Point, NY: Leisure Press.

Serbin, L., Connor, J., & Citron, C. (1978). Environmental control of independent and dependent behaviors in preschool boys and girls: A model for early independence training. *Sex Roles, 1*(6), 867–875.

Serbin, L., Connor, J., & Lipman, I. (1977). Sex stereotyping and non-stereotyped introduction of new toys in the preschool classroom: An observational study of teacher behavior and its effects. *Psychology of Women Quarterly, 4*(2), 261–265.

Sexton, P. (1969). *The feminized male.* New York: Random House.

Shapiro, J., Kramer, S., & Hunerberg, C. (1981). *Equal their chances: Children's activities for non-sexist learning.* Englewood Cliffs, NJ: Prentice-Hall.

Snow, C. P. (1964). *The two cultures and a second look* (2nd ed.). Cambridge: Cambridge University Press.

Williams, J. E., Bennett, S. M., & Best, D. L. (1975). Awareness and expression of sex stereotypes in young children. *Developmental Psychology, 11*(5), 635–642.

Women on Words and Images. (1975). *Dick and Jane as victims: Sex stereotyping in children's readers* (2nd ed.). Princeton, NJ: author.

Woodruff, G. (1974). *The sex-role concepts of the kindergarten, first-, and second-grade child as a function of their home environment.* Unpublished doctoral dissertation, Boston College.

24

Improving Sex Equity
in Postsecondary Education

Karen Bogart,
with Kathleen Wells and Mary Spencer

Over the past few years, there has been an increased emphasis on efforts to expand the opportunities and elevate the status of women in postsecondary institutions. Numerous laws, such as Title IX of the Education Amendments of 1972, have been passed to guarantee equity for women and to develop and promote programs to achieve it.

An examination of recent trends in the education of women by postsecondary institutions suggests that these changes in law and practice have had positive effects. Women students are now in the majority on college and university campuses, many on a part-time and reentry basis. They earn half the bachelor's and master's degrees awarded each year, as well as 25% of the professional degrees and 30% of the doctoral degrees (National Center for Education Statistics, 1980, 1981a). Between 1971 and 1980, women increased by more than 25% in numbers earning bachelor's degrees, by more than 60% in numbers earning master's degrees, and by more than 100% in numbers earning doctoral degrees. Most impressive of all, they increased by more than 550% in numbers earning professional degrees (National Center for Education Statistics, 1980).

Additionally, more women than ever before are earning degrees in male-dominated occupational fields (defined by the National Center for Education Statistics as fields in which men earned more than 80% of all degrees awarded in 1971). By 1979, women accounted for more than 20% of all bachelor's degrees awarded in such traditionally masculine fields as business and management, computer and information sciences, and the physical sciences. They also accounted for nearly 20% of the master's degrees awarded in these fields and more than 10% of the doctoral degrees. These figures represent increases of 100% and more since 1971 in the number of women earning degrees in these male-dominated occupations (National Center for Education Statistics, 1980). Changes in

Peg Downey and Patricia Hyer also contributed to the development of this chapter.

470

the aspirations and achievement of women students in postsecondary education cannot be disputed.

At the same time, as impressive as are the increases in the number of women earning degrees in male-dominated occupational fields, most degrees earned by women continue to be concentrated in the lower-status, lower-salaried occupational areas that women have traditionally dominated. The single most popular degree for women at all levels continues to be education. In 1980, women earned more than 70% of the bachelor's and master's degrees awarded in education and nearly half the doctoral degrees (National Center for Education Statistics, 1980). The fact that women are earning more advanced degrees but that they are earning them for the most part in lower-status, lower-salaried occupational fields may help explain why the gaps between the sexes in income and occupational status have actually been increasing over time rather than decreasing (National Center for Education Statistics, 1981b).

Just as with women students, the status of women faculty members highlights the elusiveness of equity in postsecondary institutions. Although the increased enrollment of women students would imply an increased need for women teachers, mentors, and role models, women continue to experience restricted access to employment and promotion. Furthermore, within all types of institutions the status of women faculty members is similar. Women are concentrated in assistant professorships, lectureships, and instructorships—mostly untenurable and untenured ranks—at the same time that men continue to dominate the professorships and tenure-track positions. Women constitute 19% of the faculties of public and private universities, where they are 45% of the instructors and 43% of the assistant professors but only 17% of the associate professors and 6% of the professors. Women are 27% of the faculties of other 4-year colleges, where they are 54% of the instructors and 36% of the assistant professors but only 21% of the associate professors and 12% of the professors. In 2-year colleges, women are 36% of the faculties—specifically, 50% of the instructors, 40% of the assistant professors, 30% of the associate professors, and 23% of the professors (National Center for Education Statistics, 1982).

In salary as in rank, women faculty members continue to be at a disadvantage in comparison with men. Women professors in public and private universities earn, on the average, $3,000 less than their male colleagues in an academic year; women associate and assistant professors average $1,000 less in yearly earnings. Similar disparities between women and men are apparent in the average salaries of both in other 4-year and 2-year institutions (National Center for Education Statistics, 1981c). Regardless of rank, type of institution, or discipline, women earn less than men.

Women administrators are similarly few in number and concentrated in entry- and middle-level positions. Even when exceptionally successful, they are promoted to such posts as assistants to the president, the chancellor, or the provost. Only rarely do they become president, chancellor, or provost (Sandler, 1979). Additionally, for women administrators, as for women faculty members, the more prestigious the institution the fewer the number of women in senior positions (Moore, 1982).

This chapter examines conditions, policies, and practices that may help explain why sex inequities continue to exist in the education and employment of women in postsecondary institutions and offers some recommendations for specific actions that can be taken to accelerate change toward equity. The analysis is based in part on a comprehensive study of perceptions of sex discrimination conducted in conjunction with the development and dissemination of an *Institutional Self-Study Guide on Sex Equity for Postsecondary Educational Institutions* (Bogart, Flagle, Marvel, & Jung, 1981) with the support of Carnegie Corporation of New York and the Fund for the Improvement of Postsecondary Education. This study involved interviews with more than 200 individuals knowledgeable about the treatment of women in postsecondary institutions, including administrators, faculty members, students, women's advocates, researchers, plaintiffs, and attorneys. Others knowledgeable about postsecondary education were surveyed by mail. Reviews of the literature and of legal precedents were conducted, and complementary efforts taking place elsewhere were identified (Bogart, 1981).

Solutions proposed for addressing perceived inequities are based on recommendations in the self-study guide and numerous other publications and on the exemplary programs and practices of different institutions. The actions that specific institutions are taking to remedy sex inequities are not described. However, *Everywoman's Guide to Colleges and Universities* (Howe, Howard, & Strauss, 1982) evaluates nearly 600 colleges and universities in terms of the programs and environments available to women. Additionally, *Toward Equity: An Action Manual for Women in Academe* (Bogart, 1984), developed with a grant from Carnegie Corporation of New York, describes nearly 150 programs and policies in progress at colleges and universities that promote equity for women in the academic community and are adaptable by other institutions.

The focus in this chapter is on voluntary institutional change. The need for voluntary change has become increasingly important as a result of the February 1984 Supreme Court decision limiting the coverage of Title IX to programs and activities that receive federal financial assistance. Voluntary change has often been impeded, however, by lack of information about the conditions, policies, and practices that perpetuate sex inequities and by lack of information about solutions that can address them. This chapter identifies many of these postsecondary barriers and solutions. A related article by Klein and Bogart (in press) describes some additional sex equity solutions at the elementary and secondary school levels that may be transferable to postsecondary education.

Because the issues involved are complex, only a few are discussed and only a few of many possible solutions are proposed. For further treatment of the issues, other resource materials are referenced throughout the chapter. The discussion is organized around analysis of factors influencing sex equity for students, faculty, administrators, and staff and the social-educational climate within which women and men study and work.

ACHIEVING SEX EQUITY FOR STUDENTS

Admissions. The increased enrollment of women in postsecondary institutions is undoubtedly attributable not only to changes in the aspirations of women but also to changes in admissions policies and practices. In good part thanks to Title IX, few institutions today have quota systems for women and men, although these were common only a decade ago (Astin, 1976; Sandler, 1975). Even without such overt sex discrimination, women may continue to be treated differently, often inadvertently (Sandler, 1979). Some faculty members may make assumptions about appropriate areas of study for men and women that may affect admissions or limit enrollment in nontraditional courses and programs. One student interviewed in conjunction with the development of the *Institutional Self-Study Guide on Sex Equity* related:

> I was told that women are too great a risk to be accepted by this department, despite the admission that my qualifications were equal to or above those of the average candidate. They recommended that I go back to literature where I belong. Namely, where women belong!

Officials may be reluctant to admit many women because they believe women to be less serious or capable than men, particularly at the graduate level. Some institutions adhere to traditional structures, especially regarding class scheduling, residency requirements, and transfer of credit, which may make access difficult for older students, many of whom are women.

There are multiple ways to eliminate sex inequities in admissions. At the undergraduate level, if they are not already doing so, institutions can handle applications for men and women together, so that the best are admitted, instead of the best of each sex (Sandler, 1975). They can periodically review undergraduate admissions practices for possible sex bias, study the admissions and attrition rates of students by sex, age, race, and ethnicity, and take remedial action where necessary.

Because more subjective judgment is involved in graduate admissions, there is greater opportunity for sex discrimination than in undergraduate admissions. It is not uncommon for those responsible for graduate admissions to consider a woman's marital status and whether or not she is "serious" about her career—questions which might not be raised about male applicants.

While subjective judgment cannot be eliminated from the graduate admissions process, institutions can maintain safeguards against the inequitable use of these judgments. They can provide faculty and others who evaluate candidates with guidelines for eliminating sex-related criteria. They can evaluate practices by examining the number of women and men by race, ethnicity, and age who apply to each department and the institution as a whole, and the number who are admitted. They can make a special effort to recruit women in general, and specifically minority women, as both graduate and undergraduate students. (For a discussion of the effects of admissions policies on reentry women students, see chapter 22.)

Financial Aid.   Access to postsecondary education is influenced not only by admissions policies and practices but also by the availability of financial aid. Women students receive fewer dollars than men students do from public sources of financial aid, despite the fact that they have greater financial need (Moran, 1983). Women students are more likely to enroll part-time than men students are because they do not have the financial resources for full-time study, but part-time enrollment disqualifies them from a number of federal aid programs that are limited to full-time students. Women students also continue to report that decisions made by institutions about scholarships, fellowships, and assistantships are influenced by sex-related criteria:

> The same professor who had previously discouraged my entering his department was responsible for the termination of my fellowship after one year, allegedly because I was not "serious." The charge was unjustified from every consideration, and the episode has left me extremely bitter.

> Each year that I was a graduate student, I did not receive a teaching assistantship until the last minute even though my grades were among the highest. I was told that my husband had a job, so I did not need the money. (Bogart, 1981)

Interviews with administrators, faculty, and students (Bogart, 1981) suggest that women students may be denied student loans because of their anticipated lower potential for paying them back; that men are sometimes awarded more prestigious graduate fellowships, while equally qualified or superior women are awarded assistantships; and that the greater financial obligations of older students, who are increasingly women, are not always taken into account in evaluating financial need.

To eliminate sex-related inequities in financial aid programs covered by Title IX under the February 1984 *Grove City College v. Bell* Supreme Court decision, institutions can take a variety of actions. They can make financial aid available to part-time students, many of whom are minorities and women. They can take child and other family costs into account in assessing financial need, both for nonfederal grants and loans and for federal grants and loans where allowed. They can publicize financial aid resources for women. They can conduct reviews to determine the possibility of sex bias in decisions and practices related to financial aid and take remedial action where necessary.

The Curriculum.   Female and male students continue to study a traditional curriculum, which often does not include content on or contributions by women (Howe, 1977, 1980, 1981; Howe & Lauter, 1980; Lauter & Howe, 1978). Students have observed:

Courses taught by women about women are the only place where women are taken seriously either in terms of course content or as participants. Most faculty are not even comfortable with the use of inclusive language with respect to humanity. (Bogart, 1981)

Although male professors give lip service to including "female" development and female authors, they still consider women a "special topic." They treat "it" as they treat other special topics, devoting one lecture either to a guest lecturer who is a woman or to the subject of women. Few female authors are included in the bibliographies. (Bogart, 1981)

Institutions can encourage faculty, particularly in the humanities, social sciences, and biological sciences, to transform traditional courses to include the new scholarship on and by women. Projects at the Wellesley College Center for Research on Women, the University of Arizona, the University of Maine at Orono, Montana State University, Wheaton College, and the University of Colorado, to mention only a few, have also experimented with ways to encourage faculty members to introduce scholarship on and by women into their courses (Bogart, 1984).

Counseling and Guidance. Counseling and guidance may contribute to the problem women often have in achieving support as well as advancement. Some women students are still advised that careers and advanced degrees are not important for women; that women cannot or should not combine careers with marriage and family; or that they should not pursue nontraditional careers.

Personal counseling and guidance services can include peer counseling, which women often find helpful, as well as groups and centers for women with similar needs, such as reentry women or minority women. Career planning services can provide information on occupations traditionally considered "male," as well as workshops to interest women in the professions. Counselors can be encouraged to use a variety of educational materials, many of which have been developed under the sponsorship of the Women's Educational Equity Act Program to meet the needs of different groups of women (for example, Ekstrom, 1981a, 1981b, 1982; Eliason, 1981; Perun, 1982; Project on the Status and Education of Women, 1980; Tittle & Denker, 1980).

Support Services and Facilities. Many colleges and universities are sensitive to the educational and related needs of women and offer a variety of courses and programs for different groups of students, but the opportunities to take advantage of them may be reduced by inadequate support services and facilities. One student reported:

There was space available that could be a day care center that would meet state regulations but there was not enough time to put together a program. By the time female faculty and students had organized to start a day care center, the space had been given to another department. More college support should have been invested in helping to start a day care program so more women could attend college. (Bogart, 1981)

A commission on the status of women can review the status of women on campus. Preventive measures can be taken to increase campus safety, such as nighttime escort service, campus-wide bus service operating during the day and night, adequate lighting throughout the campus, self-defense courses, and information on campus safety and on preventing sexual assault. Health care services can include gynecological care. Institutions can offer child care services, information, and referral. They can allocate space to women and women-related programs, such as a women's center, a center for continuing education, and a center for research on women.

ACHIEVING SEX EQUITY FOR MEMBERS OF THE FACULTY, ADMINISTRATION, AND STAFF

Advertising, Recruitment, and Employment.   Over the last few years, women have increasingly sought employment in higher education as faculty members, researchers, counselors, librarians, deans, vice-presidents, provosts, presidents, and chancellors. Although some have succeeded in obtaining positions at entry or middle management levels, women are still few in number, especially at senior levels of responsibility. In part, this reflects the fact that there are few positions available to men or women at a time when enrollments may be declining and institutional operating costs are increasing. But it may also reflect practices that have a more adverse effect on one sex than on the other (Ekstrom, 1978; National Academy of Sciences, 1979). One faculty member commented:

> A woman professor suggested by memo to the department head that potential job openings be advertised in women's newsletters, such as those of the women's caucuses of professional associations. She listed prices, names, addresses, etc. The response by memo was that women looking for jobs should read the *Chronicle of Higher Education* and the *APA Monitor*. What led up to this incident was that the department chairman had expressed an interest in hiring qualified women candidates "if only we could find them." (Bogart, 1981)

Women are often not part of the informal networks through which many men are identified and recruited for positions. Search committees may not know how to identify women candidates, and ranking procedures may in some instances operate to their disadvantage. For minority women, the barriers imposed by sex are multiplied by barriers having other origins.

Postsecondary institutions can identify, recruit, and hire women as well as men at all levels of responsibility (Bogart, 1981; Gappa, 1977; Gappa & Uehling, 1979; Hays, 1978; Project on the Status and Education of Women, 1978; Touchton & Shavlik, 1978). Positions can be advertised in channels likely to reach prospective women candidates. Positions announcements can invite women, and more specifically minority women, to apply. Senior officials. including trustees, chancellors, presidents, vice-presidents, and deans can regularly search for potential women and minority candidates. Individual women and women's groups can be asked to recommend women for positions. When candidates are interviewed, whether by a committee or an individual, one person may be given the responsibility for seeing that women are included. Efforts can be made to ensure that all candidates are asked the same kinds of questions. A senior administrator can be charged with responsibility for final selection as an alternative to ranking procedures, since such procedures rarely select minorities and women for high-level appointments. Data about the number of position offers, actual hires, and terms and conditions of employment by sex, rank, and race/ethnicity can be collected and evaluated.

Professional Development and Advancement.   For women who are hired, opportunities for professional development and advancement are often few. Women describe few opportunities to receive advice and support from a mentor who is a senior member of the faculty, administration, or staff; few opportunities to establish collegial relationships through research collaboration and other activities; teaching assignments limited to lower division courses; demands placed on them to assume counseling responsibility for a large number of women students due to the few women employed; too many or too few committee assignments; and few opportunities to attend conferences for professional development. In addition, because women's research often focuses on issues of special concern to women, their work is devalued, reducing the chances for promotion.

Professional development, services, and rewards are also limited for women, relative to men, by a variety of factors related to the structure of professional work and the availability of support services. Women, as parents who often have sole or primary responsibility for the care of children, cannot always work without interruption, as can men. Women faculty members, administrators, and staff members share with women students the need for childcare, health, and safety programs.

To improve the status of women members of the faculty, administration, and staff, institutions can collect and evaluate data on teaching and administrative assignments and on opportunities to attend summer institutes, workshops, and conferences for professional development. They can provide release time for unfunded research (Campbell & Brown, 1982). They can determine whether there are explicit written criteria for tenure or promotion. They can encourage members of the faculty, administration, and staff to be familiar with the process by which tenure or promotion is decided. Senior faculty members and administrators can be assigned to help junior staff members prepare for consideration for tenure or promotion. Other mentoring systems can be developed (Rowe, 1981a, 1981b).

Compensation and Fringe Benefits.   The conclusions of numerous studies analyzing salaries of female and male faculty members are consistent: regardless of rank, type of institution, or discipline, women are paid less than men (for example, Trivett, 1978). Although the significantly lower average salaries for women are attributable in part to their concentration in the lower ranks, in 2- and 4-year colleges, and in certain lower-paying disciplines, and to the fact that fewer women than men hold terminal degrees, the differences do not disappear when comparisons are made rank by rank, controlling for type of institution and other personal and institutional factors. These persistent salary discrepancies exist even among new faculty members and constitute an ongoing challenge to salary equity.

Institutions can apply procedures (for example, regression techniques) annually to identify salary inequities and take correction action within a reasonable period of time (Cox & Astin, 1977; Gray & Scott, 1980; Pezullo & Brittingham, 1979; Trivett, 1978). They can provide prorated fringe benefits for part-time and temporary staff members. When such inequities are corrected, adjustments in pensions and other benefits should also be made (Committee W, 1976).

THE SOCIAL-EDUCATIONAL CLIMATE
AND BARRIERS TO SEX EQUITY

Subtle Discrimination. There are a broad range of subtle behaviors and events that perpetuate inequities for women in postsecondary education. These subtle barriers—verbal and nonverbal behaviors that discriminate unintentionally as well as intentionally—are not likely to be formally contested in a court of law. They can be described as "microinequities," or inequities which taken singly seem so insignificant that they may not be identified, much less protested. At the same time, taken together they constitute formidable barriers to equal opportunities for women (Rowe, 1977). They include:

Exclusion: Unintentional and intentional oversights denying women access to events such as departmental functions where information needed for upward mobility may be informally exchanged

Role stereotyping: Expectation of behavior that conforms to sex role stereotypes, such as passivity and deference in demeanor, and traditional course and career choices

The double standard: Differential evaluation of behavior as a function of sex; for example, regarding a man's nonacademic experience as "enriching" and that of a woman as indicating "lack of focus"

Condescension: The apparent refusal to take women seriously as students or colleagues, communicated through posture, gesture, and tone of voice

Sexist comments: Expressions of derogatory beliefs about women, such as the sentiments that women are "inferior," "lacking in originality," "not serious," "not intelligent," and "a distraction"

Hostility: Avoidance, expressions of annoyance, resentment, anger, and jokes and innuendoes at the expense of women

Denial of status and authority: The covert refusal to acknowledge a woman's position or her scope of authority, such as subordinates bypassing a woman staff member to report to her superiors

Invisibility: The failure to recognize the presence or contributions of women; for example, in course content

Tokenism: The discretionary inclusion of one or only a few women; for example, as committee members or speakers

Divide and conquer: The use of tactics that maximize the social distance of women from each other, such as informing a woman that she is superior to other women or to minorities in ability or achievement

Backlash: The rejection of women and men who support efforts to improve the status of women, in such ways as blocking their access to research funds

Women students are subjected to subtle discrimination in the classroom and outside, with the result that they can begin to believe their presence in class is not wanted, their participation in class discussion is not expected, their capacity for intellectual development is limited, and their academic and career goals are not matters for serious attention or concern (Hall, 1982). For example, one student reported:

> Students in one of my classes did a tally and found that male professors called on men more often than on women students. What male students have to say or contribute is viewed as having more importance than what female students have to contribute in class. (Bogart, 1981)

Another student observed:

> In classes, I experienced myself as a person to be taken lightly. In one class, I was never allowed to finish a sentence. There seemed to be a tacit understanding that I never had anything to say. (Bogart, 1981)

For female members of the faculty, administration, and staff, subtle discrimination also represents a major barrier to equitable treatment. A faculty member commented:

> Whenever I am introduced by members of my department, it is "Professor _____, Professor _____, and Mrs. _____," though I have a Ph.D. and am a professor also. (Bogart, 1981)

It is important to educate members of the postsecondary community as to how subtle discrimination expresses itself in both verbal and nonverbal communication (for example, Henley, 1977; Thorne & Henley, 1975) and as to how it may be avoided (for example, International Association of Business Communicators, 1977). Institutions can establish procedures through which students or staff members may express their concerns about subtle discrimination (for example, through administration of surveys or questionnaires inquiring about subtle discrimination or through other informal complaint procedures such as suggestion boxes). An institutional official or office can be delegated responsibility for receiving and responding to expressions of concern regarding subtle discrimination. Institutional officials can also educate and support women in dealing effectively on their own to express their concerns to professors, advisers, or employers.

Multiple Discrimination. For minority women, older women, and disabled women, sex discrimination may be compounded by discrimination on the basis of race, age, or handicap. A minority woman faculty member reported:

> A male student who received a bad grade called me a nigger. This is discrimination, certainly on the basis of race, and possibly of sex. The student most likely would not have made the comment if the institutional climate did not somehow allow this sort of behavior. (Bogart, 1981)

Women subjected to multiple forms of discrimination are least represented as students or staff members and, as members of the postsecondary community, are especially vulnerable to both subtle and overt discrimination. Minority women are often excluded from informal networks, including those of majority women and minority men, and often they cannot locate mentors or role models. Data need to be kept about the status of minority women (that is, data are often collected about the status of women and the status of minorities, but the status of minority women is often obscured). In addition, content on minority women can be included in courses and programs, and members of the faculty, administration, and staff can be sensitized to their needs and interests (Fields, 1981; Project on the Status and Education of Women, 1982b; Scott, cited in *Resources for Change,* 1981). Institutions can also become familiar with programs to identify the needs of and improve the status of minorities, both as students and employees (for example, Chacon, 1982; Scott, cited in *Resources for Change,* 1981) (see also chapter 19).

Data need to be kept about the status of reentry women as students and employees. Content on older women can be included in courses and programs, and training can be provided to members of the faculty, administration, and staff to sensitize them to older women's needs and interests (Astin, 1976; Daniels, 1979; Ekstrom, 1980; Project on the Status and Education of Women, 1980) (see also chapter 22).

Sexual Harassment. There is increasing concern on college and university campuses across the country about the sexual harassment of women students and employees (Crocker, 1982; Diamond, Feller, & Russo, 1981; Franklin, Moglen, & Boring, 1981; Sandler et al., 1981; Till, 1980). This type of harassment ranges from the use of sexual humor and innuendo to physical threats and sexual assaults, including rape. One student reported:

After the quarter was over, he invited me by phone to meet him at a coffee shop, presumably to discuss my paper. Perhaps I was naive, but I was surprised when he did not even bring the paper with him. He proceeded to make various crudely obvious sexual propositions, inviting me to "experiment sexually" with him and to go over that night to his home for dinner . . . trying to put an arm around me, touch, etc.

Another commented:

I was discussing my work in a public setting when a professor cut me off and asked me if I had freckles all over my body. (Bogart, 1981)

Unwanted sexual approaches can produce embarrassment, uneasiness, and fear; feelings of unworthiness; inability to concentrate on studies or work assignments; loss of academic or career counseling opportunities; poor grades and academic failure; and loss of one's job, in the case of employees. Most, if not all, overt sexual harassment can result in legal action against the institution, but the more subtle abuses may not be subject to legal redress.

Institutions can address both overt and subtle sexual harassment through publicized policies and procedures for considering and acting on complaints. They can identify and eliminate sexual harassment by documenting the extent of the problem through surveys, hearings, meetings, or other methods; developing a faculty code of conduct; disseminating written information to students and employees indicating the types of behavior that constitute harassment; imposing sanctions against those who harass students or employees; and developing a procedure to inform new students, faculty members, and employees about their right to be protected against sexual harassment.

Complaint procedures should include both informal and formal grievance channels; be published at least once a year in communication channels likely to reach all members of the campus community; include names or titles of institutional officials who are responsible for responding to reports of harassment; protect the confidentiality of the report; and specify alternative courses of action that may be chosen by a complainant in consultation with institutional officials.

Dissent, Mediation, and Grievance. Although many institutions have grievance procedures, they may not serve as effective channels through which students and staff members can express concerns about conditions, policies, and procedures perceived as contributing to sex discrimination (for example, Abramson, 1975, 1979; DeSole & Hoffman, 1982; Farley, 1981a, 1981b, 1982; McCarthy, 1980; McCarthy & Ladimer, 1981). A faculty member stated:

I have a complaint to make to the department chairman. I cannot confront him directly because that would be tantamount to challenging his authority, yet I have no peers on the staff who will speak for me. My peers are mostly males, and they can see no reason for me to complain, even though I am teaching twice the number of classes for half the pay. (Bogart, 1981)

Channels are needed that maximize the opportunities available to individuals and institutions to resolve concerns peacefully, without escalation into court action. The approaches necessitated by legal procedures are adversarial and do not lend themselves to problem solving. Additionally and unfortunately, litigation rarely produces satisfactory results. Sex discrimination suits against colleges proceed through a series of appeals, often lasting years, consume resources in time and money, and leave both plaintiffs and defendants exhausted and defeated, whatever the outcome of court action.

Institutions can evaluate procedures already in existence for due process and see that they operate in a way that protects all parties from unresponsiveness, delays, complications, failure to protect confidentiality, threats of retaliation, and actual reprisal. Once grievance procedures have been developed that are clear, equitable, and provide adequate due process, administrators should publicize and abide by them.

On some campuses, women faculty members and students have formed their own support groups or networks and have achieved a position within the university system, for example as a review committee for evaluating administrative policies and procedures affecting women. Women need such organizations in order to protect their interests and to learn effective strategies for bringing about change in the practices and policies that disadvantage women. Institutions should recognize this need and support such efforts.

Institutional Leadership. Institutional leadership is the bottom line in efforts to increase sex equity in education and employment. Without support from institutional leaders, the effectiveness of other efforts to improve the status of women will be weakened. To legitimize the concern of others for sex equity, institutional leaders must express their own.

Institutional leaders can identify needs assisted by materials designed for institutional self-study. *The Institutional Self-Study Guide on Sex Equity for Postsecondary Educational Institutions* (Bogart, 1981) is a basic reference for presidents, vice-presidents for academic affairs, deans of students, and other concerned members of the administration, faculty, and staff. Different booklets in easy-to-use checklist format address sex equity for students, faculty members, administrators, and staff members, and the social-educational climate affecting sex equity. Each booklet probes a broad range of practices both subtle and overt, individual and institutional, with and without legal implications, that should be considered when evaluating an institutional response to questions of sex equity. While the self-study guide addresses perceived inequities, regardless of whether or not these are illegal, other self-study materials are intended to facilitate compliance with the law, especially Title IX of the Education Amendments of 1972. These include *Equity Self-Assessment in Postsecondary Education Institutions* (Cloud, 1980); *Mechanisms for the Implementation of Civil Rights Guarantees by Educational Institutions* (Hill & Rettig, 1980); and *Institutional Self-evaluation: The Title IX Requirement* (Taylor & Shavlik, 1975).

Institutions may also seek assistance from a variety of national resources which disseminate information; conduct workshops, minicourses and conferences; provide telephone information and referral; and offer on-site assistance. Among the outstanding programs are the following:

The Project on the Status and Education of Women. The Project on the Status and Education of Women (PSEW), Association of American Colleges, 1818 R Street, NW, Washington, DC 20009, founded in 1971, is the oldest national project concerned with achieving equity for women students, faculty members, and administrators. PSEW monitors litigation and federal legislation and policies affecting women in higher education, develops materials that identify issues and provide numerous recommendations for overcoming barriers to equity for women in higher education, and publishes a quarterly newsletter, *On Campus with Women.* A publications list is available on request.

The Office of Women in Higher Education. The Office of Women in Higher Education, American Council on Education, 1 Dupont Circle, Washington, DC 20036, began their National Identification Program (NIP) in 1977 for the advancement of women in higher education administration. The NIP, a state-based program that is now operational in all 50 states plus Puerto Rico, is a national resource for the identification and promotion of talented women administrators. ACE National Forums, conducted by the NIP, bring together established and emerging education leaders to discuss critical issues related to leadership and management in higher education. The forums are invitational and include women who are ready for college or university presidencies in addition to men and women who already serve as chief executive officers.

The Office of Women also conducts a National Identification Program Focus on Minority Women's Advancement (FMWA). The primary goals of the FMWA are more fully to involve minority women—black, Hispanic, Asian Pacific, and American Indian—in the ongoing National Identification Program and to provide a means for minority women administrators to be identified to one another and to powerful allies who can help them achieve equality of opportunity.

The Higher Education Resource Services. The Higher Education Resource Services (HERS), with branches at the University of Denver, Wellesley College, and the University of Utah, are primarily identified with training in leadership, administrative skills, career-mapping, and networking strategies. Collectively, the HERS programs facilitate the professional development of women in higher education and their advancement into positions of greater authority and responsibility.

Other organizations and publications can also help institutional leaders address needs. The *Handbook for Women Scholars: Strategies for Success* (Spencer, Kehoe, & Speece, 1982) contains chapters by women scholars on strategies to help others, and an assessment of the status of women academic and research professionals and their needs. A resource section provides information on advocacy organizations, women's committees, caucuses of professional organizations, and centers for research on women. *Women in Higher Education: A Contemporary Bibliography* (Moore & Wollitzer, 1979) provides information on research on academic women reported in published and unpublished literature. *Academic Women and Employment Discrimination: A Critical Annotated Bibliography* (Farley, 1982) reviews nearly 200 of the most influential works on employment problems of academic women.

RECOMMENDATIONS

Institutional change to improve the status of women is a slow process. Change often seems to require that an individual or group has studied the problem thoroughly enough to be able to convince institutional leaders of the need for change, that institutional officials are approached with a detailed and reasonable plan of action, and that support be available from a network of concerned women, minorities, and others. The *Institutional Self-Study Guide on Sex Equity* and other materials for self-study; national programs such as the Project on the Status and Education of Women, the Office of Women in Higher Education, and the HERS network; and the solutions that have been introduced elsewhere can help women and minorities work together with institutional officials to achieve equity. The following recommendations are offered to members of the administration, faculty, and staff actually working to achieve change in institutions. They summarize the lessons learned by others in the course of introducing change elsewhere.

1. Women and minorities should work together to achieve common ends. Not only are alliances politically astute, they are more effective. It is easier to engage others by dealing with the issues of race and sex together than by dealing with them one at a time. It is also easier to handle dissension, as well as the perception on the part of women that minorities have made progress but women have not and the corresponding perception on the part of minorities that women have made progress but minorities have not.

2. Change can often be accelerated by bringing a significant outsider onto the campus. The significant outsider, for example, a nationally recognized opinion leader from another campus, can legitimize issues that would otherwise receive little attention from institutional leaders. A corollary to this principle is that it is possible to increase receptivity to change by citing the changes that are taking place elsewhere.

3. Change is influenced by critical factors, including timing, the presence of a critical person who serves as catalyst, and whether or not there is a critical mass of women on campus. Women and minorities can develop the conditions that are needed to facilitate change.

4. In introducing change it is important to be sensitive to the institution's level

of awareness. There are some approaches that are better when awareness is low and others to try when awareness is high and the institution is ready to address more complex problems.

SUMMARY

This chapter has discussed issues and answers with the realization that there are many institutional types and needs and hence many paths to equity. No institution is expected to respond positively to all suggestions, since not all options may be congruent with its mission or viewed as increasing educational quality for that institution or seen as financially feasible. At the same time, it is hoped that postsecondary institutions will define tangible and specific goals for increasing sex equity, establish priorities, and measure progress in addressing equity needs. Additionally, it is hoped that postsecondary institutions will not only improve the status of women and other historically disadvantaged groups, but also serve as models of voluntary social change for other institutions of American society.

REFERENCES

Abramson, J. (1975). *Invisible woman: Discrimination in the academic profession.* San Francisco: Jossey-Bass.
_____. (1979). *Old boys, new women: The politics of sex discrimination.* New York: Praeger.
Astin, H. S. (1976). Continuing education and the development of adult women. *Counseling Psychologist, 6,* 55–60.
Bogart, K. (1981). *Technical manual for the institutional self-study guide on sex equity.* Washington, DC: American Institutes for Research.
Bogart, K. (1984). *Toward equity: An action manual for women in academe.* Washington, DC: Association of American Colleges, Project on the Status and Education of Women.
Bogart, K., Flagle, J., Marvel, M., & Jung, S. J. (1981). *The institutional self-study guide on sex equity for postsecondary educational institutions.* Washington, DC: Association of American Colleges, Project on the Status and Education of Women.
Campbell, P., & Brown, M. (1982). *Survey on the status of educational researchers: A report for the National Institute of Education.* Washington, DC: American Educational Research Association.
Chacon, M. (1982). *Chicanas in postsecondary education.* Stanford, CA: Stanford University, Center for Research on Women.
Cloud, S. (1980). *Equity self-assessment in postsecondary education institutions.* Boulder, CO: National Center for Higher Education Management Systems.
Committee W. (1976). Interim report on equal periodic pension benefits for men and women. *AAUP Bulletin,* 339–342.
Cox, M., & Astin, A. W. (1977). Sex differentials in faculty salaries. *Research in Higher Education, 7,* 289–298.

Crocker, P. L. (1982). *Sexual harassment in higher education: An annotated bibliography*. New York: National Organization for Women, Legal Defense and Education Fund.

Daniels, A. K. (1979). *Welcome and neglect*. Evanston, IL: Northwestern University, Program on Women.

DeSole, G., & Hoffman, L. (Eds.). (1982). *Rocking the boat: Academic women and academic processes*. New York: Modern Language Association.

Diamond, R., Feller, L., & Russo, N. F. (1981). *Sexual harassment action kit*. Washington, DC: Federation of Organizations for Professional Women.

Ekstrom, R. (1978). *Issues in the recruitment, professional development, promotion, and remuneration of women faculty* (Research memorandum). Princeton, NJ: Educational Testing Service.

_____. (1980). Evaluation of women's volunteer and homemaking experiences. *Alternative Higher Education, 4,* 201–211.

_____. (1981a). *Making experience count in sex equity programs*. Princeton, NJ: Educational Testing Service.

_____. (1981b). *Making experience count in vocational education*. Princeton, NJ: Educational Testing Service.

_____. (1982). *Homemaking and volunteer experience skills*. Newton, MA: Education Development Center.

Eliason, N. C. (1981). *Equity counseling for community college women*. Newton, MA: Education Development Center.

Farley, J. (1981a). *Resolving sex discrimination grievances on campuses: Four perspectives*. Ithaca, NY: Cornell University, New York State School of Industrial and Labor Relations, ILR Publications.

_____. (1981b). *Sex discrimination in higher education: Strategies for equality*. Ithaca, NY: Cornell University, New York State School of Industrial and Labor Relations, ILR Publications.

_____. (1982). *Academic women and employment discrimination: A critical annotated bibliography*. Ithaca, NY: Cornell University, New York State School of Industrial and Labor Relations, ILR Publications.

Fields, J. P. (1981). *Factors contributing to nontraditional career choices of Black female college graduates*. Working Paper. Wellesley, MA: Wellesley College, Center for Research on Women.

Franklin, P., Moglen, H., & Boring, P. (1981). *Sexual and gender harassment in the academy: A guide for faculty, students, and administrators*. New York: Modern Language Association.

Gappa, J. M. (1977). *Improving equity in postsecondary education: New directions for leadership*. Washington, DC: U.S. Department of Health, Education, and Welfare.

Gappa, J. M., & Uehling, B. S. (1979). *Women in academe: Steps to greater equality*. Washington, DC: AAHE-ERIC/Higher Education Research Report.

Gray, M. W., & Scott, E. L. (1980). A "statistical" remedy for statistically identified discrimination. *Academe: Bulletin of the AAUP, 66,* 174–181.

Hall, R. (1982). *The classroom climate: A chilly one for women?* Washington, DC: Association of American Colleges, Project on the Status and Education of Women.

Hays, G. (1978). On increasing the number of women in educational administration. *AAHE Bulletin, 31,* 1–3.

Henley, N. M. (1977). *Body politics: Power, sex, and nonverbal communication*. Englewood Cliffs, NJ: Prentice-Hall.

Hill, O. T., & Rettig, R. A. (1980). *Mechanisms for the implementation of civil rights guarantees by educational institutions.* Santa Monica, CA: RAND.

Howe, F. (1977). *Seven years later: Women's studies programs in 1976.* Washington, DC: National Advisory Council on Women's Educational Programs.

———. (1980). Three missions of higher education for women: Vocation, freedom, knowledge. *Liberal Education, 66,* 285–297.

———. (1981). Those we still don't read. *College English, 43,* 12–15.

Howe, F., Howard, S., & Strauss, M. J. (1982). *Everywoman's guide to colleges and universities.* Old Westbury, NY: Feminist Press.

Howe, F., & Lauter, P. (1980). *The impact of women's studies on the campus and the disciplines.* Washington, DC: National Institute of Education.

International Association of Business Communicators. (1977). *Without bias: A guidebook for nondiscriminatory communication.* San Francisco: author.

Klein, S., & Bogart, K. (in press). Achieving sex equity in education: A comparison at the pre- and postsecondary levels. In E. Kahn & I. Robbins (Eds.), Sex equity in academe—A decade of struggle [Special issue]. *Journal of Social Issues.*

Lauter, P., & Howe, F. (1978). The women's movement: Impact on the campus and curriculum. *Current issues in higher education.* Washington, DC: American Association for Higher Education.

McCarthy, J. (Ed.). (1980). *New directions for higher education: Resolving conflict in higher education.* San Francisco: Jossey-Bass.

McCarthy, J., & Ladimer, I. (1981). *Resolving faculty disputes.* New York: American Arbitration Association, Center for Mediation in Higher Education.

Moore, K. (1982). *Leaders in transition:* A national perspective on administrative careers. Paper presented at the annual meeting of the American Association of Higher Education, Washington, DC.

Moore, K., & Wollitzer, P. A. (1979). *Women in higher education: A contemporary bibliography.* Washington, DC: National Association for Women Deans, Administrators, and Counselors.

Moran, M. (1983). *Student financial assistance: Next steps to improving education and economic opportunity for women.* Washington, DC: National Commission on Student Financial Assistance.

National Academy of Sciences. (1979). *Climbing the academic ladder: Doctoral women scientists in academe.* Washington, DC: author.

National Center for Education Statistics. (1980). *Earned degrees conferred, 1979–1980.* Washington, DC: author.

———. (1981a). *Degree awards to women: 1979 update.* Washington, DC: author.

———. (1981b). *Digest of education statistics, 1981.* Washington, DC: author.

———. (1981c). *Faculty salaries, tenure, and benefits, 1980–81.* Washington, DC: author.

———. (1982). *The condition of education: A statistical report.* Washington, DC: author.

Perun, P. S. (Ed.). (1982). *The undergraduate woman: Issues in educational equity.* Lexington, MA: Lexington Books.

Pezzullo, T. R., & Brittingham, B. E. (Eds.). (1979). *Salary equity: Detecting sex bias in salaries among college and university professors.* Lexington, MA: Lexington Books.

Project on the Status and Education of Women. (1978). *Women in higher education administration* (available in packet on Students, Faculty and Administrators [4 papers]). Washington, DC: author.

————. (1980). *Re-entry women* (15 papers). Washington, DC: author.

————. (1982a). *Financial aid: A partial list of resources for women.* Washington, DC: author.

————. (1982b). *Minority women* (5 papers). Washington, DC: author.

Resources for Change, 1981–1982. (1981). Washington, DC: Fund for the Improvement of Postsecondary Education.

Rowe, M. (1977). The Saturn's ring phenomenon: Micro-inequities and unequal opportunity in the American economy. In P. Bourne & V. Parness (Eds.), *Proceedings of the NSF Conference on Women's Leadership and Authority.* Santa Cruz, CA: University of California.

————. (1981a). Building "mentoring" frameworks for women (and men) as part of an effective equal opportunity ecology. In J. Farley, (Ed.), *Sex discrimination in higher education: Strategies for equality.* Ithaca, NY: Cornell University.

————. (1981b). Go find yourself a mentor. In J. Farley, (Ed.), *Sex discrimination in higher education: Strategies for equality.* Ithaca, NY: Cornell University.

Sandler, B. R. (1975). Sex discrimination, admissions in higher education, and the law. *College and University, 50,* 197–212.

Sandler, B. R. (1979). *We've come a long way . . . maybe.* Invited speech, American Educational Research Association, Washington, DC.

Sandler, B. R., et al. (1981). Sexual harassment: A hidden problem. *Educational Record, 62,* 52–57.

Spencer, M. L., Kehoe, M., & Speece, K. (1982). *Handbook for women scholars: Strategies for success.* San Francisco: American Behavioral Research Corporation, Center for Women Scholars.

Taylor, E., & Shavlik, D. (1975). *Institutional self-evaluation: The Title IX requirement.* Washington, DC: American Council on Education.

Thorne, B., & Henley, N. (Eds.). (1975). *She said/He said.* Pittsburgh: KNOW, Inc.

Till, F. J. (1980). *Sexual harassment: A report on the sexual harassment of students.* Washington, DC: National Advisory Council on Women's Educational Programs.

Tittle, C. K.,& Denker, E. R. (1980). *Returning women in higher education: Defining policy issues.* New York: Praeger.

Touchton, J., & Shavlik, D. (1978). Challenging the assumptions of leadership: Women and men of the academy. *New Directions for Higher Education, 6,* 95–106.

Trivett, D. A. (1978). *Compensation in higher education.* Washington, DC: ERIC/Higher Education Research Currents.

25

Summary and Recommendations for the Continued Achievement of Sex Equity in and through Education

Susan S. Klein, Lillian N. Russo,
Carol Kehr Tittle, Patricia A. Schmuck,
Patricia B. Campbell, Peggy J. Blackwell,
Saundra Rice Murray, Carol Anne Dwyer,
Marlaine E. Lockheed, Barb Landers,
and Joy R. Simonson

In this handbook we have brought together a diverse body of knowledge and thought. Educational researchers and practitioners from many fields have reviewed what is known, what still needs to be studied, and the impact on educational equity of current strategies and materials. A reader who began with no information concerning sex equity in education would surely have learned much about the pervasive and persistent nature of sex role stereotyping and subtle sex discrimination in all aspects of our educational system. She or he might well conclude that despite earnest efforts on many fronts, comparatively little progress has been made in the 12 years sex equity in education has existed as a field of inquiry. Clearly there is need for further research, development, evaluation, and improved implementation of what is known.

But fortunately the good news also shines through. Sex equity in education has been recognized as a legitimate goal, and professionals and lay citizens are working toward that goal. We have laws and regulations, research projects and classroom techniques, curricula and instructional materials at every level of education, professional training and revised testing methods, full-time personnel and specialized services, all contributing to increased equity throughout our educational system. The girls and boys, women and men who are students, teachers, administrators, or parents filling many roles in education are benefiting from the equity efforts which lead to wider opportunities and fairer treatment for all.

This chapter describes how sex equity in education has become a new field

The authors acknowledge the assistance of Susan Koen and Marilyn Musumechi.

of inquiry, reviews the importance of achieving sex equity in education, and summarizes strategies used to attain our equity goals. It concludes with recommendations for necessary changes in educational policies, practices, and R&D.

THE EMERGENCE OF SEX EQUITY
IN EDUCATION AS A FIELD OF INQUIRY

This volume provides evidence of the growing maturity of the concerns and achievements of those committed to achieving sex equity in and through education. What was conceived as a collection of the most recent research on sex equity issues and answers has emerged as a viable and vigorous area of study. We have made a start in synthesizing what is known and in identifying what we have yet to learn.

Criteria used to assess the development of a field of disciplined inquiry typically include (1) visible indicators such as university courses, academic degree programs, scholarly documents, textbooks, career specialties, and networks for concerned professionals; (2) shared definitions, theoretical and practical assumptions, goals, and conceptual frameworks; and (3) use of unique and appropriate methods of inquiry (Beauchamp, 1981; Miller, 1980).

Visible Indicators of a Field of Inquiry

At this time, some university courses exist that focus on sex equity in education, along with relevant research studies and books on various topics (such as women and mathematics or sex equity in vocational education). There are also a small number of full-time professional educators who specialize in sex equity in education in research, teaching, or administrative capacities. Educators and social scientists have joined networks of individuals and groups concerned with research and practice on the topic: the nongovernmental participants in this volume, the American Educational Research Association Women's Committee, its Special Interest Group for Research on Women and Education, Women Educators, and the National Coalition for Sex Equity in Education all partially fulfill that function. As these visible indicators of the sex equity field grow, the field will serve as a key resource for the general public and for students, faculty, researchers, and practitioners in education.

Shared Definitions, Assumptions, Goals,
and Conceptual Frameworks

As editors and authors, we have tried to foster the growth of this field of inquiry by conceptualizing the domain of sex equity and systematizing its prescriptive and descriptive perspectives and practices. Our introductory chapter contained a revised version of earlier conceptual frameworks that were used to guide the authors and editors. An analysis of the goals discussed in the chapters shows that the basic sex equity process and outcome goal categories described in chapter 1 were addressed. Almost all chapters focused on process goals such as ensuring equal access to courses and decreasing sex stereotyping of both sexes. In general, these process goals appeared more explicitly and more frequently than the learner outcome goals, such as equalizing females' and males' knowledge of economics or having women and men receive equal satisfaction and rewards from careers in visual arts.

In attending to goals, a small group of authors took a sex-affirmative approach and saw their areas as vehicles for promoting sex equity in society. For example, the authors of the chapter on mathematics, science, and engineering found that it is important and feasible to increase the enrollment of women in math and science courses in order to increase their subsequent participation in careers requiring these skills. Perhaps because there is much less evidence on causal links between attainment of sex equity in many other curricular areas and subsequent outcomes in society, the majority focused more attention on attaining sex equity goals within educational contexts. Thus, it is not surprising that the math/science chapter focused on goals that would result in increasing sex equity in society, while the primary focus of the chapter on physical education and athletics was on attaining fairness within its own domain. It is quite likely that as knowledge of how to achieve sex equity in society accumulates, investigators in domains where inquiry and goals are now primarily focused on fairness in education may acquire increased insights into ways in which educators can promote sex equity in society as well. As sex equity in education continues to emerge as a field of inquiry, the degree of consensus on goals, as well as their specificity and clarity, will increase along with improved knowledge of how to achieve those goals. We predict that much of our future work will focus on clarifying goals related to decreasing sex role stereotyping by paying increased attention to role analyses and related concepts.

Use of Unique and Appropriate Methods of Inquiry

The authors have used three strategies concurrently in examining sex equity. The first strategy involved synthesizing findings from a wide variety of research studies and from evaluations of specific sex equity products and programs. The second involved the collaborative use of peers with relevant expertise as chapter contributors and reviewers. The third strategy was to focus on evidence of effects or causal relationships. Although these strategies are not limited to women or feminists. they are congruent with many feminist views. Indicators of success of the first two strategies are evident in chapter references and the over 200 individuals on the mailing list of participants involved in the development of this book.

The strategy of identifying causal relationships and effects is in an earlier stage of development than the other two modes. This was evident in that virtually all chapter syntheses were quite effective in defining sex equity needs or issues, but they frequently yielded much less guidance on the nature of the causal relationships or the impact of various sex equity policies, practices, products, or programs. In general, although some experiments have been conducted to identify effective strategies, most research in the area has focused on defining problems or issues. As in any emerging area of inquiry, there is a need to become consistent in the definitions and instruments used to measure sex equity. Similarly, there will need to be an increase in studies building on the findings of others using similar designs. Almost all of the evaluation data that exist are from individual, federally funded products and programs. Many of these evaluations were legitimately intended to help guide the development of these sex equity activities; more are needed to determine the degree to which sex equity goals are attained. Thus, many of these evaluations reported that the educators were satisfied with the product, and the next stage will be to show how it changed their lives and their students' lives.

THE IMPORTANCE OF SEX EQUITY IN EDUCATION

Although we have documented some progress over the past decade in attaining equity for females and males in education, consistent, continued instances of sex discrimination and sex stereotyping are found in all areas.

Sex Differences in Outcomes

Inequities in female and male student achievements persist. Most of these disparities are congruent with sex-related stereotypes commonly held by residents of the United States. However, contrary to these stereotypes, sex differences in cognitive test scores and most other ability-related outcomes (excluding differences based on sex differences in body build, such as upper body strength) are very small (about 5%) and never as large as differences in the range of abilities within the same-sex group. These differences between groups of females and males might become even smaller if sex bias were removed from tests that measure the abiliites. Sex differences in some areas of achievement (such as auto repair, mathematics, typing, or childcare) are somewhat larger, because enrollments in many of the courses designed to teach these skills have been unofficially, but predominantly, single-sex. And finally, sex differences in career choices and wages are very large, even where educational attainment and achievement are similar. On the average, females receive 40% less earned income than males.

The pattern is quite clear: there are larger sex differences in outcomes in areas that are most influenced by socialization. The chapter on sex role development described how sex roles and stereotypes have been taught via modeling, reinforcement, and other modes of learning.

Another related pattern is that as sex roles in society become less differentiated and as female and male students receive more similar learning experiences, the sex differences in education-related outcomes decrease. For example, contrary to current stereotypes based on older findings, there is some evidence that female students now do as well as male students on tests of economic knowledge and that male students now score higher on some key measures of verbal ability, including the verbal part of the Scholastic Aptitude Test (SAT). Decreased sex stereotyping in reading and mathematics is associated with increased achievement for boys and girls, respectively.

Authors of several chapters in different parts of this volume have indicated that a major need in their areas is to achieve equity for women employed in education. This was the primary focus in the chapter on school administrators. Although women constitute over 67% of all instructional personnel, with the possible exception of a few female-dominated fields, the higher that education personnel are in rank or salary, the more likely they are to be male. This is a special problem for women in physical education and athletics, many of whom were left with positions subordinate to their male faculty colleagues when female and male physical education and athletic activities were merged. It was a general problem for most other educators, ranging from professors of the social sciences to teacher educators, who found that as they looked up the hierarchy of prestigious jobs they saw many more males than females. Similarly, educators in general are paid less than members of other professions with similar abilities and responsibilities. As these other professions have opened up to women, the quality of educators, particularly women teachers, as measured by tests such as the SAT, has declined (Schlechty & Vance, 1982).

Differences in the Treatment of Female and Male Learners

The most obvious types of sex discrimination in institutional admissions, enrollments, and resource allocations to female and male students have been drastically reduced in response, at least in part, to federal and state laws prohibiting such discrimination. More subtle types of discrimination, however, continue to work against the provision of equal educational opportunities. For example, even in coeducational science, shop, or physical education classes, boys are often expected and taught to do different things than girls. There are many documented sex differences in educational practices which have the effect of favoring males or reinforcing sex role stereotypes that may limit opportunities or benefits for both females and males.

Although there appears to have been some decrease in the amount of sex stereotyping in instruction, many of the chapters document the continued prevalence of stereotyping and the underrepresentation of females in instructional materials (including teacher training materials and student tests) and in interpersonal interaction with learners. There is now extensive evidence showing that sex role stereotyping in instruction negatively affects both female and male students by limiting student motivation to learn in subject areas ranging from reading and mathematics to visual arts or by reinforcing students' learning of sex role stereotypes so that they do not consider nonstereotyped options such as enrolling in advanced science courses or preparing for careers that have been nontraditional for their sex. Sex stereotyping may also cause students to underestimate their abilities in nontraditional areas such as childcare or mechanics, and it presents an inaccurate view of reality, such as the roles women played in our nation's development and the ways that women and men with equal abilities and responsibilities commonly work together, although often without equal pay. Sex role stereotyping of students by teachers via expectations or even biased tests often leads to inaccurate diagnoses of individual student needs and their subsequent inappropriate instruction. Where sex role stereotypes exist, they are also generally exacerbated by similar stereotypes relating to race, socioeconomic class, age, disability, rural or urban status, and so forth. Research on instructional materials has shown that such stereotypes affect students' attitudes and knowledge about sex role behaviors. Nonsexist materials often weaken sex stereotypes, however, even for males who generally stereotype more than females.

Findings of continued subtle sex differences in interpersonal interactions were described in detail in the chapter on classroom organization and climate; however, they are relevant in all the content areas. There appear to be consistent sex differences in how students and teachers interact, with male students generally receiving more attention and criticism. Some of the recent research studies reveal that these differences may be due not as much to teacher discrimination as to the preexisting differences in female and male students' behavior. Male students at all age levels appear to dominate discussions in mixed-sex classes.

Despite some progress in narrowing the gender gap during the past 10 years, there are still sex differences in educational outcomes caused by differences in their educational experiences. The availability of information on specific links between certain types of sex-differentiated treatments and results varies from area to area. In areas with a relatively extensive research base, such as on women and mathematics and career development, specific needs, such as helping girls improve their problem-solving skills, can be identified. Further efforts are needed to identify needs for those working with special populations, such as rural or minority women, because research here has been quite limited and piecemeal. In areas where little is known about equity needs, experts usually respond by addressing priorities identified by the larger community. For example, recently educators of gifted women have put most emphasis on math and science abilities rather than on other aspects of giftedness.

Several equity issues emerged that will warrant future research: (1) How do female or male educators serve as sex role models for their students? (2) What is the role of sexuality in facilitating or constraining cross-sex student-teacher interactions or student-student interactions? (More research on this topic may provide guidance on some causes of sex discrimination.) (3) How can the quality of education be maintained, now that many high-ability women, who formerly would have chosen a career in education, have other attractive, higher-paying options? (4) How do multiple types of discrimination and stereotyping related to gender, race, ethnicity, age, socioeconomic status, handicap, and geographical location function in education? (5) Is there a relationship between the fairly low prestige of education and its stereotype as an occupation for women, and is this compounded in female-dominated areas such as women's studies, early childhood, and art education?

STRATEGIES FOR ACHIEVING SEX EQUITY IN EDUCATION

Many educators and members of the community who care about providing educational equity have used a wide variety of strategies to help equalize educational treatments and outcomes for females and males. This book has provided descriptions of these strategies across many content areas, levels, and domains of education. There is information about the value of many general strategies. One critical strategy is to have and enforce sex equity in education laws or policies. Others include implementing sex-equitable activities as part of existing educational practices, such as sex-fair testing; initiating separate sex-equitable practices such as encouraging girls to enroll in nontraditional vocational courses; and using products or programs specifically designed to help users promote equity for others or attain it for themselves. There is general agreement that equity outcomes are most likely to be achieved by using multiple strategies.

Administrative Strategies for Implementing Sex Equity in Education

Experience indicates that it is important and crucial to have detailed policies and laws such as Title IX regarding sex-fair practices in all organizations related to schools. Mandating equity or creating these policies is, however, crucial but not sufficient. The evidence parallels experience gained from *Brown v. Board of Education,* which indicates that the implementation of the law makes the difference.

After examining the roles of various groups of educational personnel in implementing sex equity policies, it appears beneficial to maintain external assistance organizations such as regional sex equity assistance centers and equity demonstration projects as well as to create more special sex equity jobs and functions within existing educational institutions or agencies. The chief potential implementers of equity, school administrators and teachers, are, however, still striving for sex-equitable treatment for themselves. More needs to be known about the collective roles they play in implementing equity policies to benefit students.

Although there are some commonalities, strategies for implementing sex equity differ when they are intended to change institutions rather than individuals. Commonly used strategies for institutional change have included the development and monitoring of equity policies, technical assistance, and training of key staff. Implementation strategies directed primarily toward individual sex equity personnel, women administrators, and teachers have been dependent upon creating new skills, information, and networks. Future examinations of the role of administrative strategies in implementing sex equity should (1) give more attention to the activities of pressure and community groups such as women's organizations and school boards; (2) place greater emphasis on acquiring stronger and more extensive outcome data; (3) describe how the equity policy mandates link with the administrative implementation strategies; (4) examine the relative advantages of providing specified types of preservice or inservice sex equity training to administrators and teachers (for example, what happens to someone well trained in providing equity when her or his first job is in a school where equity is considered unimportant?); (5) improve our understanding about how to attain greater sex equity within the administrative work force, especially in times of economic retrenchment; and (6) help us learn how women (and men from discriminated-against groups) in educational leadership positions have promoted or may promote equity in the context of their normal administrative, faculty, or R&D management responsibilities.

General Educational Practices for Promoting Sex Equity

Most school instruction in all content areas and at all grade levels is heavily dependent upon the use of general educational procedures such as instructional materials, tests, and classroom dialogue or interaction. All of these practices may be fair or unfair to female and male learners.

Instructional Materials. Substantial evidence has been presented that instructional materials can be a major factor in achieving educational equity (or inequity). Sex-fair materials that represent current reality facilitate sex equity in education, but they are not sufficient to achieve sex equity through education. Thus, sex-affirmative materials that frequently show females and males in nonstereotyped roles can have positive effects, particularly for younger children, and are needed.

A variety of sex-affirmative materials and strategies such as teacher workshops, student hands-on experiences, audiovisual materials suitable for a variety of audiences, and written materials are available from the Women's Educational Equity Act Publishing Center at the Education Development Center in Newton, Massachusetts. Materials and assistance are also available from the regional sex equity assistance centers, special sex equity networks, and organizations or appropriate offices in education agencies at the federal, state, and local levels.

Although more sex-affirmative materials in areas such as mathematics and career and vocational education have been developed and evaluated than in areas such as early childhood education, reading, physical education, visual arts, or for specific populations like Native American or disabled women, the results for all areas were generally positive in progressing toward sex equity goals. Despite the availability of sex-affirmative materials designed to reduce sex discrimination and sex stereotyping in many content areas, most authors reported widespread use of sex-biased materials characterized by underrepresentation or stereotyped representation of females at all ages in the regular curricular materials. Concomitantly, they reported little uniform use of sex-fair or sex-affirmative materials.

The key question is, Since materials can make a difference and guidelines for creating and selecting sex-fair materials are available, why has there been little substantive change in materials? Research needs to be refocused from analysis of materials and their effects to the determination of ways to get better materials used.

   Testing.   Another way to bring about sex fairness in educational practices is to ensure that the criteria and tests selected for judging a learner or an educational employee are free from sex bias. Ways to avoid sex bias in testing range from reviewing for biased content or language to using statistical procedures for measuring bias in test items. As educators routinely check test results for possible sex and race differences, they should also examine the size of any difference. A "known" sex difference that, for example, accounts for less than 1% of the variance should be of little value, either in drawing conclusions or in educational planning. Yet to date, statistically significant differences have been examined more frequently than has the size of the effects. Continued research is also needed in the area of sex differences to determine how much of the difference is real and how much could be due to test factors. Although progress has been made, more work is needed in areas such as developing sex-balanced scales in interest measures, understanding the effects of dual sex norms in vocational tests on career selection, and uncovering possible biases in the use of tests such as the Scholastic Aptitude Test (SAT) and the American College Testing Program (ACT) to predict success in college.

   Interpersonal Interactions, or Classroom Climate.   Although there are some indications that educators and learners themselves have become more sex-equitable in their interpersonal interactions as they become more aware of the need for sex equity, it has been difficult to assess this possible change because the individuals involved are frequently not aware of their inequitable behavior. Strategies used for promoting equity have focused on creating such awareness and then helping those involved learn new equitable behaviors. Additional research is needed to expand our understanding of the role that student-student interaction might play in inequities as well as on any relationship between student-student interaction and variables such as achievement. Since competition appears to be a major component of classroom climate, we need to determine its role in continuing classroom inequity and the possible effects of a cooperative classroom environment on decreasing sex differences in teacher-student and student-student interaction. Additional questions remain about the value of single-sex instructional strategies in hindering or facilitating equitable educational outcomes.

Sex Equity in the Content Areas

   To decrease sex differences in learners' educational opportunities and benefits, educators in the content areas and elsewhere use three basic approaches. First, they try to identify where and how females and males are treated differently and then change whatever is needed so they will treat both sexes the same. This is a frequent response in the area of school practices, career counseling, and visual arts. Second, educators use compensatory strategies to provide the sex that is lower in the desired outcome with extra or different help to surmount its unique barriers. (This is advocated for early education environments and is used in some programs for adult women and to increase the participation of women in mathematics.) Sometimes this extra help is provided in a single-sex, or separate, setting. Third, educators have used other types of strategies, such as creating sex-integrated or coeducational settings in the hope that female and male learners would be treated similarly in the same class. (This is typical in vocational education and physical education.) They may also individualize instruction according to criteria other than sex.

Because the research and evaluation evidence on sex-affirmative strategies in the content areas is not abundant, we need additional work to determine which strategies or practices are most effective. The strategies and materials have showed different effects on sex discrimination or sex stereotyping by age and grade levels. Active, hands-on programs seem to be most successful and most likely to result in cumulative effects. For example, active interventions in math and science led to improvements in female problem-solving skills, more positive female attitudes toward mathematics, and increases in female mathematics enrollments.

Sex Equity Strategies for Specific Populations and Different Educational Levels

With the exception of programs for adult women, very little is known or has been developed to promote sex equity among specific populations of women. However, programs that promote career awareness among general populations of minority women are available, as are programs that improve teacher awareness of the needs of minority women and girls. Strategies targeted at specific ethnic or racial groups are rare. In general, attempts to address unique needs of women from various specific populations are quite piecemeal. For example, although there are some programs for rural women and Asian-American women, there are practically none for girls in these groups. Another basic problem in addressing the unique needs of women from specific populations concerns methods of instructing all students appropriately when many students in a classroom are from diverse groups.

In dealing with the diverse age and educational levels of early childhood environments and postsecondary education, the authors have stressed the importance of making the educational institutions and general school curriculum sex equitable. At the early childhood level, major structural curricular changes are needed to ensure that girls receive the learning experiences they most need but are unlikely to choose voluntarily in unstructured free play time. An entire institutional self-study guide (Bogart, Flagle, Marvel, & Jung, 1981) has been developed to help postsecondary institutions become sex-fair in activities such as admissions, financial aid, and promotion and tenuring of faculty. With the exception of women's studies, postsecondary institutions have taken little initiative in the development or use of sex-affirmative policies, practices, and materials.

In summary, we need to learn if different sex equity activities are more effective when used with females or males, with different populations of women, or at different age levels and what types of policies, practices, products, and programs are most effective in promoting sex equity for whom. We also need to learn how institutional strategies for increasing sex equity can be better articulated with other equity efforts and among educational agencies at different levels of government.

RECOMMENDATIONS AND CONCLUSIONS

Our summary table, "Recommendations for Achieving Sex Equity in and through Education," highlights conclusions from each chapter. Column 1 is designed for readers who want to make educational institutions more sex equitable. Column 2 provides advice to parents and professional educators who are concerned with creating equity for learners. Items in column 3 are directed to educational R&D personnel who would like to use their expertise and resources to further advance disciplined inquiry in the field of sex equity in education.

We urge that members of each of these groups remember that although there is certainly sufficient merit in focusing attention on the achievement of sex equity in educational settings and through this in society, we must point out that work toward this endeavor will result in many other educational improvements as well.

Work toward achieving sex equity improves the general practice of education and is congruent with some of the recent findings about how to create effective, high-quality educational experiences. Additionally, some special services or approaches designed to help women, such as preadmissions counseling for reentry women, have been found to be so valuable that they have been incorporated into many continuing education programs for both men and women. Similarly, strategies designed to help girls see the relevance of mathematics and thus become motivated to enroll in mathematics courses have also been found useful for many males. Educators who have focused on special sex equity needs, such as helping girls with problem solving in mathematics or treating female and male students equally in the classroom, have developed strategies to improve teachers' instructional skills in mathematics and classroom management. Other educators have found that by improving the academic achievement of their female students, the school's total test scores and learning environment have been improved.

Sex equity research improves general educational and social science research. For example, an examination of sex equity problems is helping some researchers recognize the need to integrate the current inconsistent theories of vocational, moral, personality, cognitive, and sex role development into a more integrated theory of human development. Many additional research contributions, such as insights into the teaching profession which do not assume that a male occupational model is an appropriate frame of reference, are illustrated in the chapter on the new scholarship on women.

Work toward developing and implementing policies and activities to institutionalize sex equity in education may be instructive to those trying to understand how to create educational change in less or equally challenging areas. Our work indicates the critical need and value of governmental and institutional policies and programs which specify sex equity goals, criteria, and implementation strategies and which have adequate resources to make these goals reality. Research has shown the value of Title IX and related federally sponsored research, development, and technical assistance in helping eliminate sex discrimination in education. In addition to these federal policies and activities, 30 states have passed some form of sex equity in education law(s), and 42 have established state board policies and/or regulations related to the elimination of sex discrimination and the achievement of educational equity for females and males (Bailey & Smith, 1982). Unfortunately, very few states or localities have comprehensive laws or policies that provide for the infusion of sex equity concepts and processes into the ongoing administrative or R&D functions of their education agencies, and even fewer provide adequate financial incentives or technical assistance to help assure sex equity in the day-to-day operations of schools. Such a comprehensive approach by all levels of government to institutionalize sex equity in education is highly recommended. Similar approaches have been effective in contributing to other types of educational improvements.

In conclusion, our history is one of increasing participation and opportunities for ever-wider groups of the population in both the political and economic spheres. As women—a clear majority in our country—claim, demand, and receive more equitable education, they will achieve an equitable place in society and will contribute more to all of our national efforts. The major movement to achieve sex equity in society through sex equity in education will bring significant gains to American democracy.

Table 17. Recommendations for Achieving Sex Equity in and through Education

	Policy recommendations as they relate to organizational improvement	Educational practice recommendations as they relate to learners	Recommendations for research, development, dissemination, and evaluation
I. ASSUMPTIONS ABOUT THE NATURE AND VALUE OF SEX EQUITY.	I. Articulate and refine process and outcome goals to eliminate sex discrimination and to decrease sex stereotyping. (ch. 1) Use the following types of rationales to justify these goals and subsequent policy: —There is social utility in achieving sex equity in education and in society, and increased emphasis should be given to forming policies which will acknowledge the value (but not total responsibility) of sex equity in attaining desired educational and societal outcomes. The social utility argument may be particularly effective with men who are concerned that women will achieve equity at their expense. (ch. 2)	I. Make conscious efforts to end both overt and subtle sex discrimination and sex stereotyping. (ch. 1) —Make clear to learners the economic needs for sex equity. (ch. 2) —Encourage further philosophical analysis of the ethical issues of sex equity. (ch. 3) —Make use of the above topics as they relate to views of fairness at diverse age levels. (ch. 6) —Mainstream the new scholarship on women in classroom curricula and instructional activities. (chs. 4, 5)	I. Intensify our research on causal relationships to test our assumptions about how to attain sex equity in and through education and to simultaneously refine our sex equity goals. —Place greater focus on answers. In many areas, we have conducted research which describes problems and trends, but we have little research or evaluation of alternative ways to achieve similar sex-equitable goals. Also, examine whether certain activities work better with females or males, members of special populations, or different age and ability levels. —Give increased attention to measuring sex equity processes and outcomes and other indica-

(continued)

501

Table 17. (Continued)

Policy recommendations as they relate to organizational improvement	Educational practice recommendations as they relate to learners	Recommendations for research, development, dissemination, and evaluation
—Based on ethics and justice, women deserve and should demand and claim their human rights and full inclusion in both the public and private spheres. (ch. 3) —The new scholarship on women based on feminism, knowledge gained from women's studies, and sex-equitable, sensitive research methods supports and refines these goals. (ch. 4) —There is no scientific basis for sex discrimination or sex stereotyping based on "natural" or genetic or biochemical sex differences. (ch. 5) —With some exceptions primarily related to physical attributes, sex differences and sex stereotypes are caused by so-		tors of social utility (both short and long term) which may be facilitated by sex-equitable education. (chs. 1, 2) —Work toward greater consensus about operational conceptual frameworks, such as table 1 in ch. 1, and definitions for terms such as "sex-fair" and "sex-affirmative." (ch. 1) —Encourage the growth of all aspects of the new scholarship on women, including feminism, women's studies, and sex-equitable research in all fields; but particularly continue to build the field of inquiry in sex equity in education. (ch. 4) —Continue multidisciplinary and multimethod research on sex equity. Integrate inconsistent theories across disciplines. Meta-

cialization and thus are responsive to instruction. As society changes, sex role stereotypes change. This change is generally slower for men than women, but both need to possess an increasingly wide variety of traits and skills. (ch. 6)

analyses of research studies in some well-researched areas may yield additional insights. (ch. 4)

—Follow the example of work in the areas of sex equity in mathematics where research, development, and evaluation have been closely articulated and have resulted in a fairly rapid understanding of issues and solutions. (ch. 13)

—Increase the opportunities for researchers and practitioners working on sex equity to meet and exchange information and strengthen the relationship between women's studies and education curricula. (ch. 4)

—Increase research on the learning of sex roles at different age levels. Research on genetic or biochemical sex differences does not seem to be very useful to educators. (chs. 5, 6)

(continued)

Table 17. *(Continued)*

Policy recommendations as they relate to organizational improvement	Educational practice recommendations as they relate to learners	Recommendations for research, development, dissemination, and evaluation
II. ADMINISTRATIVE STRATEGIES FOR IMPLEMENTING SEX EQUITY			
II. Develop and implement a comprehensive set of sex equity laws, regulations, and policies which support all our goals at all levels of political and institutional governance.	II. Help educators, community members, and students learn about equity laws and policies and how they can be most effective.	II. Conduct systematic evaluations and research and development of administrative strategies to implement and institutionalize sex equity
—They should be mutually supportive, appropriate to the organization, and effective in accomplishing the sex equity goals. (ch. 7)	—Increase the training of education personnel and parents in sex equity and encourage educators to select equity materials for their students.	—Learn how the institutionalization of sex equity in education is similar to or different from the institutionalization of other educational improvements. Is the role of the community particularly important? (ch. 7)
—Increase, maintain, and strengthen sex equity laws, ranging from the inclusion of women in the federal and state constitutions, to enacting new laws at each level of government, to providing resources and mandates for effective sex equity functions, strategies, delivery mechanisms, and projects.	—Secondary- and postsecondary-level teachers in particular need training in mainstreaming sex equity ideas and practices.	—Provide federal support for the development and operations of sex equity networks and other types of external assistance organizations in a variety of areas to conduct and exchange research and evaluations, provide technical assistance, develop products and practices, and disseminate what is known about sex equity
	—Continue federal and state support for effective efforts to provide technical assistance and information on sex equity to educators and learners.	

504

—Use a comprehensive set of sex equity strategies, ranging from administrator training to site visit monitoring, and use them in a systematic, interactive fashion. Provide increased emphasis on proactive strategies, using knowledge about effective ways to create specific educational improvements and sex equity outcomes.

—Create and support offices and individuals at sufficiently high levels in each bureaucracy with specific responsibility for sex equity functions. If resources are limited, particularly at the learner end of the governmental hierarchy, it would be appropriate to ensure that sex equity functions are at least one key component of a relevant office or educator's responsibility.

—Continue long-term federal, state, and local support for projects that are effective in achieving sex equity in education.

and how to achieve it.

—Develop and disseminate model policies for institutionalizing sex equity in a wide range of governmental operations ranging from teacher evaluation criteria to state policies for sex-affirmative materials. (chs. 7–24)

—Learn more about the roles of female and male educational administrators in promoting sex equity and whether women teachers suffer less tension and burnout with female than with male administrators (ch. 8)

—Conduct additional research on how to surmount internal and external barriers to increasing the number of women in educational administration (ch. 8)

—Study the most effective ways to provide both preservice and inservice teacher training in sex equity. Would these training strategies differ for sex equity in

(continued)

Table 17. (*Continued*)

Policy rcommendations as they relate to organizational improvement	Educational practice recommendations as they relate to learners	Recommendations for research, development, dissemination, and evaluation
Provide positive incentives for institutionalization of these projects or their most effective strategies.		different areas or for teachers with different levels of awareness and commitment to sex equity? (ch. 9)
—Provide increased attention and information about how to achieve sex equity to professional education and community groups, particularly those who are supportive of sex equity. (chs. 7, 9)		—Develop and evaluate incentives to attract and keep highly qualified women in the education professions (chs. 9, 10)
—Relate sex equity policies to other equity policies. (chs. 7, 19–22)		—Learn how administrators and teachers serve as nonsexist sex role models for each other and for their students and about how equity among staff influences student equity. (chs. 9, 10)
—Improve sex equity among educational personnel by drastically increasing the numbers of women with high rank and salary, such as women administrators or full professors; increase the salaries		—Conduct research and develop strategies to help women educators in female-dominated areas equitably survive mergers with male educators in recently integrated areas such as physical and

vocational education (chs. 17, 18)

—Document common patterns of sex-discriminatory treatment of teachers and strategies which may eliminate this discrimination. (chs. 9, 10, 12, 24)

of teachers and the incentives such as part-time employment, which may be particularly effective in retaining, advancing, and obtaining talented women in the education profession. (chs. 8, 24)

—To increase the numbers of women administrators, help them acquire the requisite skills and confidence, but also decrease the structural barriers which have blocked their progress. (ch. 8)

—Use professional accreditation policies and certification requirements to ensure that all curricula for education personnel avoid sex bias and contain adequate training in sex equity and that these personnel are evaluated in part as to how well they helped their organization attain sex equity goals. (ch. 9)

III. GENERAL EDUCATIONAL PRACTICES THAT PROMOTE SEX EQUITY

III. Make sure that institutional, instructional, management, and testing policies and procedures

III. Help educators and students become aware of when they are practicing sex discrimination and

III. Conduct research, development, dissemination, and evaluation (R, D, D, & E) in the area

(continued)

Table 17. (*Continued*)

Policy recommendations as they relate to organizational improvement	Educational practice recommendations as they relate to learners	Recommendations for research, development, dissemination, and evaluation
are clear and congruent with our sex equity goals.	sex stereotyping in testing, school climate and organization, and instructional materials; help them institutionalize sex-equitable practices which at best have positive, and at worst, neutral, effects.	of school practices to promote sex equity.
—Establish policies that prohibit the purchase of sex-biased instructional materials and tests and provide incentives to encourage the purchase of sex-affirmative materials. (chs. 10, 12)	—Review tests for compliance with Title IX, the fair representation of females and males, freedom from sex stereotyping, and sex differences in learner performance. (ch. 10)	—Study the effects of sex-fair interest measurement when it is embedded in well-planned, sex-equitable career counseling programs. (ch. 10)
—Establish specific legislation and policies to encourage equity in school and classroom climate.		—Develop sex-balanced scales in interest measurement and monitor minimum competency, college, professional-level exams, and other tests to ensure their freedom from sex bias. (ch. 10)
—Encourage coeducational or same-sex learning environments as appropriate for meeting sex-fair educational goals. (ch. 11)	—Increase the equity of student and teacher exchanges by making both aware of sex-inequitable patterns and sex segregation. Encourage both students and teachers to interact more equitably, to foster cross-sex cooperation, and to provide leadership oppor-	—Conduct research to determine if and when it is ever effective to have single sex instruction to achieve equitable outcomes. (chs. 11, 13, 14, 17, 20, 22, 24)
		—Study how to increase the use

508

tunities equitably for both sexes. (ch. 11)

—Increase the use of sex-affirmative materials, particularly with younger children. If sex-biased materials must be used, be sure to use them as a lesson against sex stereotyping. (ch. 12)

of sex-fair and sex-equitable tests and instructional materials. (chs. 10, 12)

—Learn how race, ethnic, age, socio-economic and disability group biases are similar to or different from sex biases and develop procedures to eliminate all from tests, instructional materials and classroom interactions. (chs. 10–12)

—Study the role of sexuality in sex discrimination and sex stereotyping at all levels of education, for both students and staff and for interpersonal interactions and instructional materials. (chs. 11, 12)

—Conduct research on how a sex-equitable classroom environment (which provides females with full leadership and participation) affects student outcomes. (chs. 11, 17)

(continued)

Table 17. (Continued)

	Policy recommendations as they relate to organizational improvement	Educational practice recommendations as they relate to learners	Recommendations for research, development, dissemination, and evaluation
IV. SEX EQUITY STRATEGIES IN THE CONTENT AREAS	IV. Eliminate sex discrimination and sex stereotyping in all content areas, whether the areas are currently male-dominated or female-dominated. —For each content area, make a special effort to maintain or develop women's studies curricula and to identify and address the unique needs of female and male students. Simultaneously keep women's studies courses high priority and separate while mainstreaming much relevant information from them in other content courses. Also increase the focus on women's studies in colleges of education and the focus on sex equity in education in women's studies departments. (chs. 4, 9, 15, 16, 24) —Give increased priority to at-	IV. Make both the curriculum content and its implementation sex-equitable. —*General Recommendations:* —Instruction in sex equity and to counter gender stereotyping should be a part of the curriculum in all content areas and in all educational levels. It works! —Learn if female and male learners are treated differently, and then try to treat them the same unless doing otherwise would help them attain more equal learning outcomes. —Use compensatory or special strategies for whichever sex has mastered less of a particular content area to ensure that they obtain a sufficient amount of	IV. Specific R, D, D, and E strategies to increase sex equity in the content areas: —Learn more about how to teach girls to do mathematical problem solving and publicize findings which would generally help all learners in this area. Identify and evaluate strategies that will encourage women to enter and succeed in the "hard" sciences and engineering. (ch. 13) —Learn more about why girls do not score as well as boys on advanced-level verbal tests, and identify and help both sexes speak in the most effective manner, whether or not these patterns have been traditionally sex-linked or not. (ch. 14) —In the social studies, learn

taining sex equity in traditional women's areas such as visual arts and home economics. (chs. 16, 18)

—Use teacher training to dispel myths about sex differences, to help teachers understand how sex stereotypes affect student choices of courses and careers, and to learn how to eliminate sexist attitudes and behaviors in each content area.

—Help the women's art movement increase its impact on elementary and secondary art education. (ch. 16)

—Where there are distinct sex differences such as in physical education and athletics, or in traditions such as in vocational education, make sure that any separate-sex treatments are equal. When the sexes are integrated, do it carefully so that both will receive equal benefits. (Make

instruction to surmount any sex-unique barriers. Occasionally, it may be most efficient to provide this instruction in a single-sex setting; for example, all-male reading classes do not appear to be generally effective, but some all-female math courses appear to have advantages.

—Unless there is a compelling reason to do otherwise, use sex-integrated settings to provide instruction, even in content areas such as physical education or vocational education. As necessary, change the content to increase its appeal to both sexes.

—Teachers often prefer to use sex equity materials which have clear objectives and can be easily used with their other content area lessons. A wide variety of instructional approaches ranging from TV viewing to dramatic role play to lectures have been effective to date, and use of mul-

more about teacher expectations for, and actual student sex differences in, social science knowledge and attitudes, and develop curricula which contain more information on the role of women in government and economics. (ch. 15)

—In visual arts education, what are the advantages of separatist, integrationist, and pluralist approaches to women and art? What are art-related sex differences? Also continue to learn more about the nature of sex bias in art education and develop sex-equitable art education instructional materials and programs. (ch. 16)

—In physical education and athletics, should the curricular content be changed to appeal to both sexes? Is separate but equal treatment possible? (ch. 17)

—Learn more about sex dif-

(continued)

Table 17. (*Continued*)

Policy recommendations as they relate to organizational improvement	Educational practice recommendations as they relate to learners	Recommendations for research, development, dissemination, and evaluation
sure women become head coaches of coed teams or physical education departments and that girls and boys are treated the same way in coed shop classes.)	tiple coordinated strategies is encouraged. —*Chapter-specific Recommendations:* —Improve the achievement of women in math and science by encouraging them to take these courses and by addressing the potential areas of sex differences such as spatial ability, problem solving, and mechanical sophistication. (ch. 13) —Realizing that girls' advantage over boys in verbal tests decreases after puberty, give increased attention to helping girls continue to develop high-level reading and verbal skills. (ch. 14) —For boys, it may be useful to	ferences related to the effectiveness of treatments such as those designed to reduce sex stereotyping of occupations, homemaking, marriage, and parenthood. Also learn more about the generalizability and relationship of findings about beliefs, attitudes, and behaviors in these areas, and develop materials which help students focus on patterns of adult roles rather than on the occupational role in isolation. (ch. 18)

increase the image of reading as an activity appropriate for them. (ch. 14)

—Stop the use of sexist language and jokes in schools. Also help students become aware of sex-linked communication patterns so that they can make a more conscious decision about what patterns to use when. (ch. 14)

—In social studies, practice delivering equity and justice for all learners and make a conscious effort to include more information about women, information about the historical and cultural development of sex stereotypes as well as current status and trends. Also take advantage of women's history celebrations and women's studies courses while mainstreaming all these concerns in all types of social science curricula. Decreased sex stereotyping in students' attitudes also helps increase their self-esteem. (ch. 15)

(continued)

Table 17. (*Continued*)

Policy recommendations as they relate to organizational improvement	Educational practice recommendations as they relate to learners	Recommendations for research, development, dissemination, and evaluation
	—Art educators should teach about women artists and art forms they have dominated and expose female students to male-stereotyped art approaches such as large metal sculpture. (ch. 16)	
	—In physical education and athletics, educators must look carefully at the balance and priority of tradeoffs when they are deciding to provide separate or same-sex or ability groupings. In all cases attention must be given to fairness, avoiding separate but unequal situations and developing each individual's potential. (ch. 17)	
	—Career and vocational education practices should prepare students for the world of tomorrow rather than for past sex stereotyped occupational fields. Career education activities should be se-	

V. SEX EQUITY STRATEGIES FOR SPECIFIC POPULATIONS	lected only if they can demonstrate success in decreasing sex stereotypes of male and female learners and the interrelationships of work and nonwork responsibilities. (ch. 18)		
	V. Make sure that all educational policies are developed and evaluated in terms of their impact on special populations of women.	V. Make sure that sex equity practices are responsive to the needs of diverse groups of learners	V. Conduct R, D, D, and E to achieve sex equity within special populations of women
	—Where possible, have the policies address the unique needs of the special populations of women, while realizing that there are many more unique needs within each group.	—Address the multidimensional equity problems of learners in a sensitive fashion. (chs. 19–22)	—Conduct more research to identify the specific common and unique needs of women members of special populations. Then develop sex equity strategies which are sensitive to the needs of individuals from diverse special populations, simultaneously. (chs. 19–22)
	—The federally supported agricultural extension agent system should play a more active role in helping rural women participate in educational and economic opportunities. (ch. 21)	—Help all students learn about the heritage, contributions, and shared interests of women from various ethnic, geographic, age, socioeconomic and ability backgrounds. (chs. 19–22)	—Programs for special populations of women should combine service to each with research about that population. (chs. 19–22)
	—Institutions should continue their efforts to remove barriers to adult women students by providing, if they do not already do so,	—Make sure that procedures for identifying gifted students are not biased toward males or against females who do not appear to fit traditional sex stereotypes. (ch. 20)	—Conduct research on minority women by minority women. (ch. 19)

(continued)

Table 17. (*Continued*)

Policy recommendations as they relate to organizational improvement	Educational practice recommendations as they relate to learners	Recommendations for research, development, dissemination, and evaluation
courses at convenient times and locations, instructions by modes other than classroom lectures, child care, counseling/information services, and credit for prior experience learning. (ch. 22)	—Practices that have helped women take advantage of formal education opportunities include provision of day care for their family members, women's centers, establishment of supportive networks or chum programs, taking education to the individual rather than the woman to the classroom. (This is particularly important for many rural women.) Among and across the special groups of women, highest priority needs are to learn job-related skills. (chs. 19–22) —Educators should identify demographic and attitudinal changes in the women coming to them and in the women they might serve. They should then modify their programs to meet these changing needs. Current needs include more programs for	—Learn more about the nature and extent of women in gifted student programs and the effects of significant others on female participants in these programs. (ch. 20) —Develop special sex equity programs for rural girls to specifically overcome rural barriers and to exploit rural advantages in favor of equity. (ch. 21) —Develop new methods and materials to assess adult women's prior learning, especially in non-credit courses and in unpaid work, and to relate this learning to formal educational training. (ch. 22)

	employed women, especially programs in cooperation with employers or in the work place; the provision of programs for skill review and renewal, especially in mathematics, prior to admissions testing or enrollment; and programs to help adult women cope with their multiple roles as wives, mothers, workers, and learners and to help women cope with changes such as job loss and retirement. (ch. 22)	VI. Conduct R, D, D, and E to achieve sex equity at different age/educational levels. —Learn more about what different strategies are needed to decrease sex differences and sex stereotyping at different ages and developmental levels. What are the effects of sex equity activities over time, from preschool to continuing education students? —Develop more sex-affirmative instructional materials for use
VI. SEX EQUITY AT DIFFERENT AGE/EDUCATIONAL LEVELS	VI. Make learning environments more responsive to the needs of girls and women at all age levels. —At the early childhood level, provide structure to the free play time to encourage girls to acquire the skills they most need and train teachers to engage in behaviors that will teach students to decrease their stereotyping. (ch. 23) —At the postsecondary level, en-	VI. Since formal educational programs at all age levels were created to meet the educational needs of males, they need to be redesigned to serve women equally well. —At the early childhood level, use teaching strategies to involve children in activities unusual for their sex such as having the teacher remain close to girls when they are engaged in large-muscle activities. Also avoid assigning activities that remedy

(continued)

517

Table 17. (*Continued*)

Policy recommendations as they relate to organizational improvement	Educational practice recommendations as they relate to learners	Recommendations for research, development, dissemination, and evaluation
courage institutions to conduct self-assessments to identify and then eliminate overt and subtle sex discrimination and stereotyping in admissions, financial aid, classroom climate, etc. These institutions should also establish grievance and mediation procedures and criteria and guidelines for students and faculty to use to obtain fair treatment and to avoid sexual harassment and unintentional discrimination. (ch. 24)	problems of boys to all children while allowing activities that remedy problems of girls to be a matter of their own choice. (ch. 23) —At the postsecondary level, encourage the maintenance of women's studies as well as the mainstreaming of sex equity and the new scholarship on women in content, improve sex equity in student-faculty interactions, and provide support services such as nonsexist preadmissions counseling, women's centers, day care facilities, and provisions for student safety. (ch. 24)	with young girls and boys in multiple settings, and develop strategies to mainstream sex equity in secondary schools. (ch. 23) —In postsecondary institutions, routinely collect and report information on the relationships among sex, race, age, handicap, and admissions, graduation, tenure, promotions, etc. Also develop and adopt or adapt effective sex equity practices used by other institutions, such as the *Institutional Self-Study Guide on Sex Equity for Postsecondary Institutions*. Give increased attention to the needs of faculty women. (ch. 24)

REFERENCES

Bailey, S., & Smith, R. (1982). *Policies for the future: State policies, regulations, and resources related to the achievement of educational equity for females and males.* Washington, DC: Council of Chief State School Officers.

Beauchamp, G. A. (1981). *Curriculum theory* (4th ed.). Itaska, IL: Peacock.

Bogart, K., Flagle, J., Marvel, M., & Jung, S. J. (1981). *The institutional self-study guide on sex equity for postsecondary educational institutions.* Washington, DC: Association of American Colleges, Project on the Status and Education of Women.

Miller, T. L. (1980). *Disciplinary and interdisciplinary perspectives in schooling: Implications for program development.* Unpublished doctoral dissertation, Temple University, Philadelphia.

Schlechty, P. C., & Vance, V. S. (1982, February 25–27). *Recruitment, selection and retention: The shape of the teaching force.* Paper presented at the NIE national invitational conference on Research on Teaching: Implications for Practice, Warrenton, VA.

Editors and Major Authors

Institutional affiliations current at the time of publication.

Linda Addison, Consultant, Alexandria, VA

Judith A. Adkison, Division of Public School Administration, North Texas State University, Denton, TX

Susan Bailey, Equity Center, Council of the Chief State School Officers, Washington, DC

Joanne Rossi Becker, Departments of Mathematics and Curriculum and Instruction, Virginia Polytechnic Institute and State University, Blacksburg, VA

Jane Bernard-Powers, School of Education, Stanford University, Stanford, CA

Sari Knopp Biklen, The Education Designs Group, Syracuse, NY

Peggy J. Blackwell, College of Education, University of New Mexico, Albuquerque, NM

Karen Bogart, Consultants for Design and Analysis, Great Falls, VA.

Patricia B. Campbell, Campbell-Kibler Associates, Groton Ridge Heights, Groton, MA

Georgia C. Collins, Art Education, University of Kentucky, Lexington, KY

Esther E. Diamond, Educational and Psychological Consultant, Evanston, IL

Carol Anne Dwyer, Educational Testing Service, Princeton, NJ

Jacquelynne Eccles (Parsons), Department of Psychology, University of Michigan, Ann Arbor, MI

Ruth B. Ekstrom, Division of Education Policy Research and Services, Educational Testing Service, Princeton, NJ

Helen S. Farmer, College of Education, University of Illinois, Champaign, IL

Patricia L. Geadelmann, Office of the Vice-President for Academic Affairs, University of Northern Iowa, Cedar Falls, IA

Georgia S. Glick, Information Mapping, Inc., Waltham, MA

Barbara J. A. Gordon, Office of Program Development and Administration, The American University, Washington, DC

Selma Greenberg, School of Education, Hofstra University, Hempstead, NY

Maxine Greene, Teachers College, Columbia University, New York, NY

Carole L. Hahn, Division of Educational Studies, Emory University, Atlanta, GA

Glen Harvey, The NETWORK Inc., Andover, MA

Susan S. Klein, National Institute of Education, U.S. Department of Education, Washington, D.C.

Nancy Kreinberg, Lawrence Hall of Science, University of California, Berkeley, CA

Barb Landers, California State Department of Education, Sacramento, CA (died Aug. 1984)

Shelby Lewis, Africana Women's Center, Atlanta University, Atlanta, GA

Barbara Lieb-Brilhart, American Society for Medical Technology, Houston, TX

Marcia C. Linn, Lawrence Hall of Science, University of California, Berkeley, CA

Marlaine E. Lockheed, Division of Education Policy Research and Services, Educational Testing Service, Princeton, NJ

Marjory G. Marvel, National Coalition on Older Women's Issues, Washington, DC

Scott McDonald, *Time,* Inc., New York, NY

Saundra Rice Murray, United Planning Organization, Washington, DC

Elizabeth Noble, School of Education, University of Missouri, Kansas City, MO

Anne C. Petersen, College of Human Development, The Pennsylvania State University, College Park, PA

Barbara Peterson, Project Equity, California State University, Fullerton, CA

Stuart A. Rosenfeld, Southern Growth Policies Board, Research Triangle Park, NC

Lillian N. Russo, Consultant, Cherry Hill, NJ

David Sadker, Mid-Atlantic Center for Sex Equity, The American University, Washington, DC

Myra Sadker, School of Education, The American University, Washington, DC

Renee Sandell, Department of Art, George Mason University, Fairfax, VA

Candace Garrett Schau, Department of Educational Foundations, College of Education, University of New Mexico, Albuquerque, NM

Jane Schubert, American Institutes for Research, Palo Alto, CA

Patricia A. Schmuck, College of Education, Lewis and Clark College, Portland, OR

Kathryn P. Scott, College of Education, Florida State University, Tallahassee, FL

Charol Shakeshaft, School of Education, Hofstra University, Hempstead, NY

Ann Sherman, Department of Art Education, University of Kansas, Lawrence, KS

Joan Seliger Sidney, English Department, Eastern Connecticut State University, Willimantic, CT

Joy R. Simonson, Citizens Council on Women's Education, Washington, DC

Elizabeth K. Stage, Lawrence Hall of Science, University of California, Berkeley, CA

Stephen L. Tarason, White Oak Junior High School, Montgomery County Public Schools, Rockville, MD

Carol Kehr Tittle, School of Education, University of North Carolina, Greensboro, NC

Index

AASA. *See* American Association of School Administrators
abortion, 37
academic performance, factors affecting, 69
Academic Women and Employment Discrimination: A Critical Annotated Bibliography, 484
ACCESS, 385–386, 443
achievement tests
  bias against minorities and ethnic groups, 169
  construct validity, 169, 171
  content validity, 169
  face validity, 169
  factors affecting performance, 171–172
  item content, and performance, 170–171
  mathematics, sex differences in, 240
  recommendations
    for research, 173
    for use, 172–173
  representation in, judgments of, 170
  sex differences in, 169–173
  sex equity in, 169–173
  stereotyping in, judgments of, 170
ACT Interest Inventory, 179
activity level, sex differences, 67
administration
  art educators in, 314–315
  barriers to women
    courses and workshops concerned with, 132, 136, 138–139
    external, 130
    illustrative programs for remedying, 135–136
    internal, 130
    legal remedies, 134, 141
    recommendations for remedying, 136–142
    strategies for overcoming, 124–144

courses, for women, 131, 137
creating jobs for women in, 135, 141
hiring policies and practices, people affecting, consciousness raising and assistance for, 134–135, 141
internship, 442
  for women, 133, 139
lack of women in, explanatory models, 129–130
networks, for women, 133–134, 140
political clout of women in, 134, 140
sex equity in, 92–93
strategies for increasing women's access to positions in, 137–141
support systems, for women, 133, 139
women professors of, increasing number of, 131–132, 138
of women's athletic programs, women in, 325
workshops, for women, 131, 137
Administrative Intern, The, 442
administrative strategies, for implementing sex equity, general principles, 91–94
administrators
  female, 471–472
    barriers to, 124–130
    number of, 124–125
  hiring and promoting, sex discrimination in, 129
admissions testing, 175–177
  of adult women, 436
adult basic education, definition, 434
adult education
  definition, 433
  enrollment, 433
adult women
  ambivalence about additional education, 437–438

525

adult women (*continued*)
  counseling, 449
  definition, 432
  diversity, 432
  educational barriers to, 435–438
    institutional, 435–437
    personal, 437–438
    situational, 437
  educational future, 447–448
    research needs, 448
  educational programs for, 431–453
    delivery, 449–450
    flexibility, 450
    recommendations, 448–450
    research recommendations, 450
    types, 433–434
  enrollment, in postsecondary education, 434
  fear of failure, 438
  financial aid for, 436
  importance, as educational group, 434–435
  learners
    characteristics, 432–433
    needs, 433
  life changes, assistance coping with, 449
  self-concept, 438
  stereotypes of, 437
Advanced Placement
  courses, encouraging female participation in,
    401–402
  participation, by sex, 399, 400
advertisements, and sex stereotypes, 54–55
affirmative action, 21, 37, 38
  for women in administration, 134
African-Americans. *See also* blacks
  cultural background, 367
  stereotyping, 375
African-American women
  equity priorities, 379–380
  equity programs, 384–385
aggression
  children's imitation of, 224
  sex differences in, 64, 66–67
agriculture
  doctoral degrees granted to women, 406
  sex segregation in, 425
Alabama, community resource program for rural
    women, 425–426
Alaska
  guidelines for overcoming sex bias, 426
  sex equity legislation and policies, 103
American Association for the Advancement of
    Science, inventory of programs for
    females in science, engineering, and
    math, 247–248
American Association of Colleges, Project on
    the Education and Status of Women, 117
American Association of Colleges for Teacher
    Education, 153

American Association of School Administrators
    (AASA), 132, 136
American College Testing Program (ACT), 175,
    497
American Educational Research Association, 153
American Federation of Teachers, sex equity ac-
    tivities in teacher education, 153
American Institutes for Research, Vocational
    Education Equity Study, 353–354
*Americans in Transition: Life Changes as Rea-
    sons for Adult Learning,* 431
anthropology, doctoral degrees granted to wom-
    en, 406
anxiety. *See also* math anxiety
  and academic performance, 69
  effects on course taking, 245–246
  and learning, 253
  sex differences in, 65
aptitude tests
  assumptions in, 173–174
  recommendations
    for research, 177
    for use, 176–177
  sex differences and sex equity in, 173–177
  uses, 173
  vocational, at secondary level, 174–175
Arendt, Hannah, 29, 41
Armed Services Vocational Aptitude Battery,
    174–175
art. *See also* studio art; women's art movement
  curricular equity for, in public schools, 302–
    303
  in education, status of, 311–312, 314
  feminine identity of, 302–303, 311
  feminist, 305
  interpretation of interest in, 300–301
  performance, sex-related differences in, 300
  role models, 301
  sex stereotyping in, 301–302
  status of women in, 299–300
  traditional values, 301
art criticism, 301–302
Art/Design: Communicating Visually, 310
art education, 511, 514
  classroom practices, 302
  feminist, 306–309
  sex equity efforts, 234–235, 303–311
    art educators in, 312–313
    discipline-specific model, 311–312
    recommendations for, 311–315
  sex equity issues, 298–303
  sex-fair and sex-affirmative content and prac-
    tice, 300–302
  status of women in, 299–300
art educators
  as artists, 314
  as public school teachers, 313–314
  as researchers, 313

sex equity efforts, 312–313
    as supervisors and administrators, 314–315
    as teacher educators, 314
art history, revisionist, courses in, 308
arts and humanities, doctoral degrees granted to
    women, 406
A Sex Equity Handbook for Schools, 212
Asian, Inc., 383
Asian-Americans
    cultural background, 366–367
    distribution, in US, 368–369
    educational attainment, 368, 370
    employment characteristics, 369–371
    income and earnings, 371
    occupations, and educational achievement,
        371
    stereotyping, 375
Asian-American women
    equity priorities, 378
    sex equity programs for, 383–384
Asian Women's Association, 382
Asian Women United, 383
assertiveness, in women, 127
Assisting Women to Advance through Re-
    sources and Encouragement (AWARE),
    132–133, 136, 138, 140
Association for Cross-Cultural Education and
    Social Studies (ACCESS), 385–386
Association for Intercollegiate Athletics for
    Women, 324
Association for Measurement and Evaluation in
    Guidance
    Commission on Sex Bias, 178
athletics, 514. See also physical education
    girls' interest in, 346
    officiating, women in, 326
    sex equity in, 235, 319–337
    sex typing of, 244
athletic scholarships, 324
Atlanta University Center, Transitional Black
    Women's Project, 385
attitudes, definition, 345
AWARE. See Assisting Women to Advance
    through Resources and Encouragement

Bandman, Bertram, 40
Barry, Brian, 38
Becoming, 441
beliefs, definition, 345
Bem Inventory, 81
Better Late Than Never, 436
bias. See also sex bias
    other than sex-related, 165, 218
        experienced by minorities, 376–377
    vs. fairness, 168
biology, doctoral degrees granted to women,
    406
Blackfeet Women's Resource Center, 384

blacks. See also African-Americans
    distribution, in US, 368–369
    educational attainment, by place of residence
        and sex, 423, 425
    employment characteristics, 370
    equity programs for, 384–385
    female, stereotyping, 375
    income and earnings, 371–372
    research on, 361
body language, sex differences in, 273–274
BORN FREE, 352
Bornstein, Rita, "Sexism in American Educa-
    tion," 154
brain organization, sex differences, 58–60
Building Math Confidence in Women, 254
business administration, doctoral degrees
    granted to women, 407
Business Management Training for Rural Wom-
    en, 441

California
    policy on sex-biased instructional materials,
        164
    sex-equity implementation in, 92
    Title IX Assistance Office, Observation/Com-
        mentary/Visitation model, 104–105
California Coalition for Sex Equity in Educa-
    tion, 93, 107–109, 117, 118
    coalition members, 107
    Compliance Measure, 107
    follow-up research, recommendations for,
        121
    high-impact districts, 108
    Institutional Sex Bias test, 107
    long-term effects, 108–109
    purpose, 107
    results, 107–108, 117
California State University, Long Beach, math
    anxiety course, 253
capitalism, 32
CARE. See Curriculum and Research for Equity
career
    achievement, sex differences, 341
    aspirations, sex differences, 341, 343
    choice
        biological, cognitive, and psychosocial fac-
            tors, 68–71
        equity in, social benefits, 53, 71–72
        and gender differences, 55
        mathematics as critical filter in, 234, 239
        sex stereotyping and discrimination in,
            need to reduce, 339–342
    counseling
        changes in, 178
        in postsecondary education, 475
    definition, 338
    development
        for minority women, 378, 381

career (*continued*)
    theory, 339–340, 357
    insignificance of gender in, 71
    scientific, 247
career education, 514
    counseling procedures and practices, 353–354
    curricula, promoting sex equity, 345–354
    educator and community programs and products, 352–354
    elementary school programs and products, 345–347
    employer-based programs, 352
    for gifted girls, 403–408
    high school programs, 349–352
    middle school programs, 347–349
    policy recommendations, 354–357
    sex-equitable, policies aimed at, 344–354
    sex equity in, 235, 338–359
Career Education Act, 233
Career Incentive Education Act, 344
career interest measurement. *See* interest measurement
Career Internship Program, 350
Career-Oriented Modules for Exploring Topics in Science (COMETS), 225
Career Planning for Minority Women, 446
Career Shopper's Guide, The, 441
Careers to Explore, 347
Carnegie Interest Inventory, 177
Catalyst, 440
change
    in institutions, 484, 495
    in society, 431–432
Changing Words in a Changing World, 276
chemistry, doctoral degrees granted to women, 405
childbearing, effects of exercise on, 321, 322
child care, for rural women, 426
children
    differential abilities, experiences, and accomplishments, 459–460
    involvement in activities unusual for their sex, 464
    large muscle development, 462, 464–465
    sex equity programs for, 463–464
    sex-stereotyped behaviors, strategies for reducing, 465–466
    sex-stereotyped knowledge and attitudes, strategies for reducing, 466
Chinese Americans. *See* Asian-Americans
Civil Rights Act (1964)
    funding and support, 100
    local education agency grants, 106
    SDACs, 120
        information dissemination, 116
        research recommendations for, 121

sex equity information and training for teachers, 153
    technical assistance from, 117
    state grants, 105
    Title IV, 96, 97, 98, 119, 344
    Title VII, 24, 99
Civil Service Reform Act (1978), 24
claims, conflicting, 40
classroom
    climate, promoting sex equity in, 497
    environment
        and math anxiety, 253
        race, ethnicity, and perceived ability inequities, 200
    as microcosm of society, 163, 189
    organization and climate
        recommendations for practitioners, 212–213
        research issues, 211–212
        sex-equitable, defining, 189–191
        sex equity in, 189–217
        sex inequities in, 163–165
    peer interaction
        equal status, strategies for promoting, 208–210
        improving, 212–213
        leadership in, 200
        sex inequities in, 199–206
    salience of boys in, 462–463
    sex segregation, 191–196
        classroom discussion of, 207–208
        effect on achievement, 193
        infusion programs, 208
        strategies for reducing, 207–208
        and teacher-directed cross-sex physical adjacencies, 207
        teacher intervention strategy, 212
        and teacher reinforcement of cross-sex play, 207
    teacher intervention strategies, for promoting sex equity, 212–213
    teacher-student interaction. *See* teacher-student interaction
"Classroom Climate: A Chilly One for Women, The," 207
Clement, Catherine, 41–42
coaches, women, 325
coeducation
    inequities in, 189
    vs. single-sex education, 210–211, 248–249
cognition
    sex differences, 59–64, 68
        conclusions about, 63–64
        effects of training and experience, 62–63
    tests, 60-62
cognitive theory, of sex role development, 81, 82–83
college admissions tests, 175–177

College Entrance Examination Board, Advanced Placement tests. *See* Advanced Placement

COMETS. *See* Career-Oriented Modules for Exploring Topics in Science

communication
sex differences in, research, 273–275
sex equity in, 269–279
recommendations for achieving, 277

competitiveness, sex differences, 67

compliance, in sex equity implementation, 116
evaluation for, 116
monitoring, 116

computer sciences, doctoral degrees granted to women, 405

Computers without Fear, 253

confidence, and academic performance, 69

confidence/anxiety, sex differences in, 64–65

conformity
sex differences in, 64, 65
and test performance, 168–169

Congress, funding and support of sex equity, 100

Connections: Women and Work Skills for Good Jobs, 349

Contemporary American Indian Woman: Careers and Contributions, The, 384

continuing education, 434

Continuing Education for Women, 363, 434

Continuing Education for Women: Administrator's Handbook, 440

Control Data Corporation, Small Farm Project, 428

Conway, Jill, 41

Cooperation in Education, 212

Cooperative Extension programs, 427

Cornell University, athletic program, 324

corporate transfers, women's percentage of, 54

Council for the Advancement of Experiential Learning, 443–444

Council of Chief State School Officers Resource Center on Sex Equity, 105

Council on Interracial Books for Children, 310
address, 227, 254

Counseling Adolescents, 404

cross-sex behavior
in classroom, teacher reinforcement of, 207
sex differences in, 191–192, 199–200
in small groups, studies, 201–206
strategies for promoting cooperation in, 208–209

curricular materials. *See also* instructional materials
sexist, and women's career goals, 129
for women in administration, 132–133

curriculum. *See also* instructional materials
approaches to sex equity in, 233

content areas. *See also* specific content area
sex equity in, 233–236, 497–498, 510–515

mathematics and science, to address special needs of women, 254–256

Curriculum and Research for Equity (CARE), 209–210, 213

day care, family, 465

de Beauvoir, Simone, *The Second Sex,* 31

Decisions about Language, 276

Decisions and You, Decisions about Roles, 285

demystification, 15, 42

dependency
sex differences in, 64, 65
and test performance, 168–169

Describimento/Finding Out, 213

Developing Women's Management Programs, 446

developmental theory
adult, 83
of sex role development, 82

Dewey, John, 36–37

DICEL, 132

Differential Aptitude Test (DAT) Battery, 174–175

Directory of Administrators, A, 134

discrimination
multiple, 480
subtle, 478–479

displaced homemakers, 362–363
definition, 432
educational programs for, 440–441
rural, peer counseling, 426–427

Displaced Homemakers: Program Options, 441

Displaced Homemakers Network
address, 440
Program Policy Statement, 440

doctoral degrees, granted to women. *See* specific field; women, degrees earned by

Durkheim, Emile, 50

Earning a Breadwinner's Wage, 444

earth and environmental sciences, doctoral degrees granted to women, 405

Eastern Kentucky University, teacher education module for addressing stereotyping in athletics, 331

economic factors, indicators of equity, 17

economics
doctoral degrees granted to women, 406
gender differences in knowledge and attitudes, 281
sex differences in, 288

education. *See also* adult basic education; adult education; art education; career education; coeducation; continuing education;

education (*continued*)
    single-sex education; vocational education
in art, status of, 311–312, 314
degrees awarded, to women, 471
discrimination in, 39–40
doctoral degrees granted to women, 407
early
    differential impact on boys and girls, 460–463
    educational equity in, 457–469
    —research recommendations, 467–468
    —strategies for creating, 466–468
    myths about sex equity in, 458–463
    sex-equitable environments, strategies for creating, 463–466
    sex equity in, 498–499, 517
effect on wage differential, 24–25
general practices, 163
    sex-equitable, 163
inequity in, 34
multicultural, 150–151
philosophy of, 49
postsecondary
    backlash in, 479
    condescension in, 478
    denial of status and authority to women in, 479
    double standard in, 478
    enrollment of women in, 434
    exclusion from, 478
    grievance procedures, 481–482
    hostility toward women in, 478
    invisibility of women in, 479
    multiple discrimination, 480
    professional development and advancement of women in, 477
    role stereotyping, 478
    sex equity in, 470–488, 498–499, 517–518
    —admissions, 473–474
    —advertising for staff, 476
    —barriers to, 478–480
    —compensation and fringe benefits, 477–478
    —counseling and guidance, 475
    —curriculum, 474–475
    —employment, 476–477
    —financial aid, 474
    —for faculty, administration, and staff, 476–478
    —for students, 473–476
    —institutional leadership toward, 482–483
    —recommendations, 484–485
    —recruitment, 476
    —support services and facilities, 475–476
    sexist comments in, 478
    sexual harassment in, 480–481
    status of women faculty in, 471
    subtle discrimination in, 478
    tokenism in, 479
science and engineering, 26–27
sex-equitable strategies, for sex role learning, 87–88
theoretical work in, 48–50
values, acceptance of, 301
educational administration. *See* administration
educational testing. *See* testing
Education Consolidation and Improvement Act, 344
Education Development Center, address, 227
Education of the Gifted and Talented: Report to the Congress of the United States, 394
educators
    female, numbers of, 125
    inadequate sex equity training, 343
    male, numbers of, 124, 125
Elderhostel, 447
Elementary Curriculum, Women's Studies Program, Berkeley Unified Schools, 284
Embers, 275
empathy, sex differences in, 64, 65–66
employment, of women, in special populations, 363
engineering
    degrees
        male/female ratio, 55, 71, 168, 405
        women earning, 237
    distributions of males and females in, 168
    efforts to increase female participation and achievement in,
        success, 261–262
    females in, 234, 237–268
        intervention programs for increasing, 247–261
        recruitment strategy for, 351
        research on, relationship to research on math, 246–247
        special program for, 251
    spatial ability in, 246
English, doctoral degrees granted to women, 407
environment
    in gender differences, 53–55, 86
    and sex role development, 82
Equal Employment Act (1972), 99
Equality. *See* Project Equality
equal opportunity, 41
Equal Pay Act (1963), 24
Equal Rights Amendments, 8
EQUALS program, 257, 352, 412
Equal Their Chances: Children's Activities for Non-Sexist Learning, 464
equity
    concept of, 17, 18

indicators of, 17
nature of, 25
Equity Demonstration Projects, 93, 101
Equity Institute, Professional Development Project to Encourage the Potential of the Gifted Girl, 392, 410
Equity Self-Assessment in Postsecondary Education Institutions, 482
ERIC System, 116
    teacher education descriptors in, 147
ethics, of sex equity, 30
Everywoman's Guide to Colleges and Universities, 472
Everywoman's Rights, 446
Executive Order 11246, 21
Executive Order 11375, 21
Expanding Your Horizons in Science and Mathematics, conferences, 259–260
Experience-based Career Education, 350

FACET/FACIT, 351
failure, causal attributions about, sex differences in, 65
fairness, 319
fair play, 319
"Fair Play: Developing Self-Concept and Decision-Making Skill," 285
families
    female-headed, 19
        income and earnings, 371–372
    historical context, 32–33
    obstacle to adult women's education, 437
family planning, 19
family protection, 37
family responsibilities, and women's achievement, 127
federal agencies, recommendations for, in integrating sex equity issues into teacher education, 159
Federation of Southern Cooperatives, 425–426
Feinberg, Joel, 40
Female Leaders for Administration and Management in Education (FLAME), 131–141
femininity
    and participation in sports, 321
    vs. masculinity, 80–81
feminism, 30, 31, 45
    definition, 45
    in education, 45
    researchers in, 50
films, effect on behavior, 224
First Mental Measurements Yearbook, 177
FLAME. *See* Female Leaders for Administration and Management in Education
Florida State University, workshops for women on career choices, 132, 136, 138
foreign languages, modern, doctoral degrees granted to women, 407

Freedom for Individual Development
    Counseling and Guidance, 353
    Vocational Education, 353
free play, 461–462
Freestyle, 223, 345–346
From Dreams to Reality, 350
Fund for the Improvement of Postsecondary Education, 100, 445–446
Future Farmers of America, 418

Gall, Joyce and Meredith, "Boys and Girls in School: A Psychological Perspective," 154
GATE, 425
GEM Publications, address, 285
gender consistency, 84
gender constancy, 82, 84
gender differences. *See also* sex differences
    aerobic capacity, 322
    body composition, 322
    causes, heredity and environment in, 53–55
    in cognitive and psychosocial factors, 55
    genetic hypotheses, 53–55
    physical, 322–323
    reported, in mathematics achievement, 54
    research
        bias of researchers, 57
        definition of constructs, 56–57
        magnitude of effects, 55–56
        methodological concerns, 55–57
gender identity, 82, 457
    definition, 79
gender relations, 44–45
gender schema
    cognitive theory, 84
    theory, of sex role development, 82–83
gender stability, 82, 84
genes, and sex differences, 57
genius, studies of, 392–394
gifted, 362, 515
    achievement, sex differences, 408
    career counseling and guidance, 412
    definition, 411
    educational programs for, 398–403
        acceleration, 398–403
        enrichment, 398
        female participation in, 410
        recommendations for, 410–413
        research on, 411–412
    females
        career education and guidance, 403–408
        definitions, 392–396
        in math and science, 401–402
        role models for, 403
    girls
        classroom experience of, 200
        personality traits, 397, 409
    girls and women, in education, 391–415

gifted (*continued*)
  identification, 362, 395–397, 411
    by nomination, 396–397
    by screening, 397
  interaction with teachers, effects of, 408–409
  and interest measurement, 182
  mathematically
    acceleration program for girls, 249–250
    sex differences, 172
    study of, 398–399
  placement, 397
  sex differences in, 234, 240, 271
Gifted and Talented Children's Act (1978), 392, 394–395
Gilligan, Carol, 48, 49, 68
  In a Different Voice, 37–38
Girl Scouts of America, sex equity career education materials, 347, 350
Gollnick, Donna, et al., "Beyond the Dick and Jane Syndrome: Confronting Sex Bias in Instructional Materials," 155
Goucher College, Women's Management Program, 446
Graduate Record Examination, scores, sex differences, 401, 403
Grange, 416, 423
Grove City College v. *Bell*, 94, 97, 474
Growing Up Free: Raising Your Child in the 80's, 464
Growth in Agriculture Through Equality (GATE), 425
Guide for Sex Equity Training, 157
Guidelines for Developing Sex Bias Free Vocational Education Programs in Small Secondary Schools in Alaska, 426
Guide to Social Science Resources in Women's Studies, 49–50

Handbook for Women Scholars: Strategies for Success, 483
handicapped. *See also* women, handicapped
  girls, classroom experience of, 200
HAVE skills, 443
HEAR. *See* Project HEAR
heredity
  and biological sex differences, 60
  in gender differences, 53–55
Higher Education Act (1972), Title IX. *See* Title IX
Higher Education Resource Services (HERS), 483, 484
  The Next Move, 131–132, 139
high school equivalency certificate, 441
Hispanic-Americans
  cultural background, 367
  distribution, in US, 368–369
  educational attainment, 368, 370
    by place of residence and sex, 423, 425

  employment characteristics, 369–371
  income and earnings, 371
  occupations, and educational achievement, 371
  stereotyping, 376
Hispanic-American women
  equity priorities, 378
  equity programs, 385–386
Hobson v. *District of Columbia Public Schools*, 394
Hofstra University
  networking system, for women in administration, 134
  workshops for women, 132, 136, 138
Holland Vocational Preference Inventory, 180
home economics
  courses, 348
    coeducational, 341
    Title IX prohibition of discrimination in, 348
  historical attitudes toward, 416–417
Homemaking and Volunteer Experience Skills, 441
hormones
  developmental changes in, 58
  and sex differences, 57–58
How About a Little Strategy?, 446
Howe, Florence, 46
How to Get College Credit for What You Have Learned as a Homemaker and Volunteer, 443
How to Go to Work When Your Husband Is Against It, Your Children Aren't Old Enough, and There's Nothing You Can Do Anyhow, 440
How Women Find Jobs, 441
Humboldt State University, math course to meet special problems of women, 254

"I Can" competency lists, 443
ICES. *See* Project of Internships, Certification Equity-Leadership, and Support, A
Idaho, Cooperative extension program, women's leadership training, 427
Ideas for Developing and Conducting a Women in Science Career Workshop, 260
independence training, 243
Indians
  American. *See* Native Americans
  Asian. *See* Asian-Americans
industrial arts, courses, 348
  coeducational, 341
  Title IX prohibition of discrimination in, 348
information processing, in sex role development, 82–83
In Her Own Image: Women Working in the Arts, 310
In Search of Our Past, 285

inservice training, in WEEA demonstration projects, 114
Institute for the Study of Anxiety in Learning, 253
Institutional Self-Evaluation: The Title IX Requirement, 483
Institutional Self-Study Guide on Sex Equity for Postsecondary Educational Institutions, 472–473, 483, 484
instructional materials. *See also* curricular materials
   gender-related characteristics, 164–165
   for preservice teachers, promoting sex equity, 154–157
   promoting sex equity in art education, 310–311
   sex-affirmative, 219, 496
   sex bias and sex equity in, 218–232
   sex-biased, 219
      commonly used, 224–225
   sex-biased language in, 219–220
   sex-equitable, 218
      effects on attitudes about sex roles, 220–221
      effects on comprehension, 223–224
      effects on motivation to learn, 222–223
      effects on students' sex-role behaviors, 224
      publication, recommendations for, 226
      recommendations for achieving, 225–228
      research recommendations, 228
      selection, recommendations for, 226–227
      using, 227–228
   sex-fair, 218, 496
   sex role models in, 218
   and sex stereotypes in communication, 275
   strategies for change in, 496–497
   underrepresentation of females in, 493
intellectual action, 41–42
intelligence tests, sex bias in, 393–394
interest measurement
   combined-sex norms, 179–180
   current concerns, 178–182
   dual interest patterns, 181–182
   early history, 177–178
   effects, 181
   and gifted, 182
   and handicapped women, 182
   and minority women, 182
   opposite-sex norms, 179–180
   predictive vs. explorative validity, 180–181
   raw scores vs. normed scores, 180
   recent changes, 178–182
   recommendations
      for research, 183–184
      for use, 183
   and rural women, 182
   same-sex norms, 179–180
   sex-balanced scales, 180
   sex differences and sex equity in, 177–184
interests
   changes in, research recommendations, 356
   definition, 345
International Association for the Evaluation of Educational Achievement (IEA), 171
internships, for adult women, 442
Internships for Women, 441–442
Intersect, 210
Iowa
   sex equity legislation and policies, 104
   teacher accreditation, sex equity criteria, 150
IQ, sex differences, 397
It's Her Future, 353

James, William, 40
Japanese-Americans, educational attainment, 368, 370
Job satisfaction
   related to interest measurement, 180
   and socialization, 181
Johns Hopkins University
   Intellectually Gifted Child Study Group, 404–408
   Study of Mathematically Precocious Youth, 249–250, 398–399, 402–403
Journal of Teacher Education, 153, 160
justice, 35, 37–39, 49
   economic, 40–41
   grounded on mutuality and respect, 41

Kerber, Linda, "The Impact of Women on American Education," 154
Kuder General Interest Survey, 179–181
Kuder Occupational Interest Survey, 178–182
Kuder Preference Record—Vocational, 179

language. *See also* body language
   gender characteristics, effects, 225
   gender-specific, 219
      effects, 220
   gender-unspecified, 219
      effects, 220
   male bias in, 463
   male generic, 219
      effects, 220
   sex-biased, and distortion of pupils' perceptions of reality, 219–220
   sex differences in, 273
   sexist, 513
   sex stereotypes, 274
language arts. *See also* reading; writing
   instruction and learning, sex-equitable, 276
   methods texts, content analysis, 149
   sex differences in, 234
      myths, 269
law, doctoral degrees granted to women, 407
learner characteristics, 3–5

learning
  cooperative, 212
  early childhood, 457
    myths about, 458–463
  experiential
    from prior experience, 441, 443
    programs emphasizing, for women, 441–444
    sponsored, 441–442
    types, 441
  nonformal, acceptance, 433
  observational, 82, 218
Lerner, Gerda, 46
library science, doctoral degrees granted to women, 407
life choices, 339–342
life sciences
  degrees, women earning, 237
  doctoral degrees granted to women, 406
Life Skills for Women in Transition, 441
Lincoln County National Demonstration Project, 208
Los Angeles, school district, sex discrimination suit of women administrators against, 134, 141
Los Angeles County, Infusion Process Model, 106

MacIntyre, Alasdair, 35–36
Making Experience Count in Sex Equity Programs, 443
Making Experience Count in Vocational Education, 443
Management Basics for Minority Women, 446
marriage, values, in career education, 350
Maryland, sex equity activities, 105
masculinity
  and participation in sports, 321
  vs. femininity, 80–81
Massachusetts
  policy on sex-biased instructional materials, 164
  sex equity legislation and policies, 103
math anxiety, 245
  in minorities, 376
Math Anxiety course, 252–253
Mathematical Association of America, Women and Mathematics Program, 258–259
mathematics
  ability, confidence in, 244
  achievement, 512
    affective factors, 245–246
    attitudinal factors, 244–245
    and expectations of parents and teachers, 242–244
    gender differences reported in, 54
    modeling effects, 241–242
    related to spatial skills, 241
    sex differences in, 239, 246
    sex-related differences, 149, 240
    socialization factors, 241–244
  anxiety associated with, 67
  confidence, combined approach to building, 253–254
  as critical filter in career choice, 234, 239
  curriculum, to address special needs of women, 254–256
  degrees, women earning, 237, 405
  efforts to increase female participation and achievement in,
    success, 261–262
  enrollment, 239–240
    programs to increase females' participation, 258
    sex differences in, 246
    after sex equity demonstration project, 115
  females in, 234, 237–268
    intervention programs for increasing, 247–261
    research on, issues identified by, 240–246
  gifted females in, 401–402
  gifted students in, 412
  male superiority in, factors affecting, 165
  methods texts, content analysis, 149
  perceived value of, effects on performance, 245
  problems faced by women, special classes for, 252–254
  quantitative skills, sex differences in, 240
  sex differences in performance, related to coursework, 171–172
  sex typing of, 244–245
  special classes for women, 248–252
  teacher education programs, 256–257
Math for Gifted Girls, 402
Math for Girls, 249
Math/Science Network, 239, 259
Math/Science Resource Center, 260
Math without Fear, 67, 252, 253
maturation, timing, sex differences, 59–60
Maximizing Young Children's Potential, 464
mechanical arts, sex typing of, 244
Mechanisms for the Implementation of Civil Rights Guarantees by Educational Institutions, 482–483
medicine, doctoral degrees granted to women, 406
mentors, for women in administration, 128
Michigan
  CEW program, 434–435
  On-Site Needs Assessment and Long-Range Planning model, 105
Mid-Atlantic Center for Sex Equity, 306
Midwest Center for Race and Sex Desegregation, 306
MINCRIS. See Minnesota Civil Rights Information System

Minnesota
community resource program for rural women, 425
sex equity legislation and policies, 103
teacher accreditation, sex equity criteria, 150
Women in School Administration (WISA), 131 134, 137 141
Minnesota Civil Rights Information System, 103, 116
minorities, 361. *See also* minority women
bias against, 165
career education, 355
classroom environment experienced by, 200
in doctoral fields, 239
educational attainment, 368, 370
employed women from, programs for, 446
employment characteristics, 369–371
geographical distribution, 368–369
income and earnings, 371–372
in programs for the gifted and talented, 410–411
sex equity, unidimensional approach, 376
size of populations, 368–369
stereotyping, 362
types of bias experienced by, 376–377
Minorities and Mathematics Network, 248
minority women, 362. *See also* specific minority
achieving sex equity for, 365–390
multidimensional approach, 386
recommendations, 386–388
communication needs, 381–382
cultural background, 366–368
differential characteristics, 366–373
educational priorities, 366
equity priorities, 377–382
career-related, 378, 381, 388
communication-related, 378, 381–382, 388
contextual, 377–380, 387
need for data base, 377–378, 380–381, 387–388
recommendations for achieving, 387–388
in higher education, 483
and interest measurement, 182
media stereotypes, 381
myth of monolith, 373–374
in postsecondary education, discrimination against, 480
research on, equity priorities in, 380–381
in school administration, 130
sex equity issues, 373–377
stereotyping, reinforced, 374–376
Minority Women in Science Network, 248
Minority Women's Survival Kit, 446
modeling, 218
modern dance, women in, 326–327
mothering, and teaching, 49
Multiplying Options and Subtracting Bias videotapes, 255–256, 258, 262, 352, 412

National Advisory Council on Women's Educational Programs, 97, 98
investigation of educational needs of rural women and girls, 417
National Art Education Association, Women's Caucus, 305–306
National Assessment of Educational Progress, 149, 173, 239, 247, 281
National Association for Girls and Women in Sport, 333
National Association of State Directors of Teacher Education and Certification, sex equity standards, 151 152
National Black Women's Hook-Up, 382
National Coalition for Sex Equity in Education, 118
National Coalition of Women and Girls in Education, 117–118
National Council for Social Studies, 290–292, 293
Special Interest Group for Sex Equity in the Social Studies, 290
National Council for the Social Studies, 153
National Council of Negro Women
Career Exploration Project, 384–385
project to help black women, 446
National Council of Teachers of Mathematics, 153
National Education Association, sex equity activities in teacher education, 153
National Institute of Education, 96, 97, 99
funding and support, 100
Guidelines for the Assessment of Sex Bias and Sex-Fairness in Career Interest Measurement, 178
research program, on women in mathematics, 240
National Science Foundation
Science and Technology Equal Opportunities Act of Fiscal Year 1981, 96, 99
Science Career Workshops, 260
Women in Science Program, 251, 439
National Science Teachers Association, Women Scientists Roster, 259
National Teacher Exam, 150
Native Americans
cultural background, 367–368
distribution, in US, 368–369
educational attainment, 368, 370
employment characteristics, 369–370
income and earnings, 371
stereotyping, 374–375
Native American women
equity priorities, 378–379
sex equity programs, 384
NCAA, 325
Nebraska, sex equity legislation and policies, 103

networking
  cross-ethnic, 382
  in sex equity implementation, 117–118
    recommendations, 120
  for women faculty in postsecondary education, 482
  for women in administration, 133–134, 140
Nevada, cooperative extension program, women's leadership training, 427
New Directions for Rural Women: A Workshop Leader's Manual, 440
New Jersey, policy on sex-biased instructional materials, 164
New Mexico Commission on the Status of Women, Mature Women/Diverse Cultures Employment Awareness/Urban/Rural Project, 385
New Pioneers: A Program to Expand Sex-Role Expectation in Elementary and Secondary Education, 353
New Voices in Counseling the Gifted, 408
New York
  Job Network Information Service, 104
  sex equity legislation and policies, 104
Next Move, The, 131–132, 139
Non-Sexist Teacher Education Project (NSTEP), 154–157
  sex equity materials, 154–155
Northwestern University, Women's Career Program, 445
Nozick, Robert, 35–36
nurturance, 66
Nuts and Bolts of NTO: A Handbook of Recruitment, Training, Support Services, and Placement of Women in Nontraditional Occupations, The, 444

Occupational Choice: Creating Awareness of Alternatives for Asian-American Women and Girls, 383–384
occupations
  of minorities, and educational achievement, 370–371
  nontraditional, programs encouraging women to enter, 444
  sex stereotyping, 178, 343
    development of, 340
Office for Civil Rights, 344
  regional offices, 98, 101
Office of Women in Higher Education, 483, 484
  National Identification Program, 483
    Focus on Minority Women's Advancement, 483
Ohoyo, 382
On Campus with Women, 483
Opening the Doors. *See* Project Opening the Doors
Options: A Curriculum Development Program for Rural High School Students, 350

Oregon
  cooperative extension program, women's leadership training, 427
  sex equity legislation and policies, 104
  teacher education competencies, antidiscrimination knowledge required for, 134, 141
Oregon Women in Educational Administration, 134, 140
Organization of Chinese-American Women, Job Advancement Workshops, 383

parenthood, values, in career education, 350
parents
  expectations, and math involvement, 242
  strategies for creating equity in early education, 466–467
People and Places, U.S.A., 347
Personal Attributes Questionnaire, 81
Persons Involved in Vocational Orientation and Training (PIVOT), 426–427
Peters, R. S., 39
Ph.D., granted to women. *See* specific field; women, degrees earned by
Phi Delta Kappan, 153
Philadelphia, School District Affirmative Action and Equal Educational Opportunity Plan, 106
philosophy, 29
physical education, 514
  coeducational
    effect of teacher attitudes, 327–329
    equity in, 326–330
    girls' self-confidence in, 329, 334
    grouping patterns, 327–328, 332
    social effects, 329
    teacher-student interactions, 329
  curricula, 326–327
  equitable programs and policies, 323–324
  historical philosophical differences, 320–322
  leadership and governance, women in, 324–325, 329–330
  leadership opportunities, establishing guarantees for equality in, 332
  nontraditional settings, support for, 332
  role models
    and performance, 329
    provision of, 331–332
  sex equity, enforcement of laws promoting, 330
  sex equity efforts in, 235
  sex equity in, 319–337
    issues, 320–330
    recommendations for, 333–335
  sex inequities in, 319–320
  stereotyping, teacher education modules for addressing, 331
  student attitudes, 328
  students' attitudes, confrontation of stereotyping in, 330

technical assistance, 332–333
Physical Educators for Educational Equity, 331
physical sciences
  degrees, women earning, 237, 405
  gifted females in, 401–402
  sex typing in, 247
  spatial ability in, 246
physics and astronomy, doctoral degrees granted
    to women, 405
PIVOT, 426–427
*Placing Rural Minority Women in Training Sit-
    uations for Nontraditional Jobs, 441*
political science and public administration, doc-
    toral degrees granted to women, 406
practical arts, 348
Practical Arts Program, 349
professions, doctoral degrees granted to women,
    407
professors, women, 471
Project ACCESS, 443
Project Choice, 392, 408
Project Equality, 345, 346, 347, 466
Project HEAR, 345, 346, 347, 348
Project MOVE, 353, 354
Project on Equal Educational Rights, 105
Project on the Status and Education of Women,
    483–484
  address, 440
Project Opening the Doors, 345, 346, 347
Project of Internships, Certification Equity-
    Leadership, and Support (ICES), 131–
    133, 136–141
Project Re-Entry, 442
Project SPRINT, 333
Project Talent, 247, 394
Project T.R.E.E., 464
psychoanalytic theory, of sex role development,
    81–82
psychology, doctoral degrees granted to women,
    406
puberty, 58–59
public realm
  problematic of, 34–36, 37
  traditional definition, 34
Purdue University
  program for women in engineering, 251
  program for women scientists, 250–251

Queens College, TEAM program, 256

Racism and Sexism Resource Center for Edu-
    cators, 310
RAW, 428
Rawls, John, 35–36, 38
reading, 513
  achievement, and measurement instruments,
    271
  failure, diagnosis, sex differences in, 270,
    271

instruction and learning, sex-equitable, 275
  methods texts, content analysis, 149
  pupil preferences in, 222
  sex differences in, 234
    conclusions, 272–273
    explanations, 272
    myths, 269
    research on, 269–273
    stereotyping, in teacher education texts,
      149
  sex equity in, 269–279
    recommendations for achieving, 277
Reagan Administration, funding and support of
    sex equity, 100
reentry programs, 362–363
  for women in science, 251–252
Re-Entry Women, 440
reentry women, 362–363
  definition, 432
  educational programs for, 438–440
  in postsecondary education, discrimination
    against, 480
Reentry Women Scientists, 439
"Repainting the Sexist Picture: Stereotyping in
    the Fine Arts," 310
*Resource Guide for Vocational Educators and
    Planners: Helping Displaced Home-
    makers Move From Housework to Paid
    Work through Vocational Training, 441*
*Right from the Start: A Guide to Non-Sexist
    Child Rearing, 464*
right(s), claiming, 40
Right-to-Read program, 95
role models
  administrative, 128
  in art, 301
  in classroom learning, 190
  effects, on gifted girls, 403
  in physical education, and performance, 329
role-reversed, definition, 79
Rukeyser, Muriel, 29
Rural American Women (RAW), 428
rural areas
  advantages, 422–423
  conservatism, 417, 419, 428
  isolation, 421–422, 427–428
  labor markets, women in, 420–421
  values, 418–420
rural women and girls, 362, 416–430, 516
  economic opportunities, 420
  economic status, 423–425
  educational attainment, 423–425
  equity issues, research on, 428
  individual, delivery of programs to, 424
  and interest measurement, 182
  isolation, 421–422, 427–428
  peer counseling, 426–427
  in politics, 423

rural women and girls (*continued*)
  rural conditions and, 418–423
  in rural labor markets, 420–421
  self-employment, 420
Rutgers University, science career workshop, 260–261

Sadker, Myra and David, "Between Teacher and Student: Overcoming Bias in the Classroom," 154–155
same-sex, definition, 79
San Francisco State, Center for Mathematics Literacy, 253
Sarah Lawrence College, Summer Institute in Women's History, 292
Schmuck, Patricia and Richard, "Promoting Sex Equity in School Organizations," 155
Scholastic Aptitude Test (SAT), 175–176, 497
  scores, sex differences in, 171, 399–401, 402
  verbal sections, sex differences on, 270–271
school activities
  biological, cognitive, and psychosocial factors, 68–71
  insignificance of gender in, 71
school administration. *See* administration
school administrators. *See* administrators
school boards
  hiring procedures, affecting, 134–135
  rural, 417
school change, methods for, 91
school districts, programs to increase female's participation in mathematics, 258
school performance, research, labeling of constructs, 56
schools, rural, 417
science
  achievement, 246, 512
    related to coursework, 171–172
    sex-related differences, 149, 239
  courses, enrollment, after sex equity demonstration project, 115
  curriculum, to address special needs of women, 254–256
  degrees
    sex ratios, 168
    women earning, 237
  efforts to increase female participation and achievement in,
    success, 261–262
  females' abilities in, 54
  females in, 234, 237–268
    intervention programs for increasing, 247–261
    research on, relationship to research on math, 246–247
  methods texts, content analysis, 149
  problems faced by women, special classes for, 252–254

reentry programs for women, 251–252, 439
retention of women in, 250–251
sex-typing in, 247
socialization effects in, 246
Second Wind: A Program for Returning Women Students, 440
SEEL. *See* Sex Equity in Education Leadership
self-concept
  of adult women, 438
  inequalities in, 339
  and life choices, 342
  positive, development of, 236
  sex differences in, 64, 67, 235
Self-Directed Search, 179–181
self-esteem. *See* self-concept
self-image. *See* self-concept
Sells, Lucy, 239
seniority rule, 20-21
sex, defined, 57
sex-affirmative, definition, 79
"Sex and Gender in the Social Sciences: Reassessing the Introductory Course," 290
sex bias, in career guidance, 178
sex-biased, definition, 79
Sex Desegregation Assistance Centers, 98, 101
sex differences, 14. *See also* gender differences
  in aggression, 64, 66–67
  biological, 57–60
    causal inferences, 60
    and life experiences, 86
    related to career choice, 68–71
    related to school activities, 68–71
    significance, 71
  in career choices, 492
  causal relationships, methodological issues, 68–69
  cognitive, 60–64, 68
    conclusions about, 63–64
    effects of training and experience, 62–63, 70
    methodological issues, 60–61
    related to career choice, 68–71
    related to school activities, 68–71
    significance, 71
  confidence/anxiety, 64–65
  in conformity or dependency, 64, 65
  in educational outcomes, 494
  in empathy, 64, 65–66
  and environment, 86
  facts and assumptions about, 53–77
  genetic factors, 57
  hormonal, 57–58
  implications, 70–71
  in life experiences, 86
  organization of brain, 58–60
  in outcomes, 492–493
  psychological, 239

psychosocial, 64–68. *See also* specific difference
  effects of training, 70
  related to career choice, 68–71
  related to school activities, 68–71
  significance, 71
  summary, 67–68
  training studies of, 67
research on, 165, 235–236
in self-esteem, 64, 67
somatic, 58
in student achievement, 492
in testing. *See* specific test type; testing
in timing of maturation, 59–60
in treatment of learners, 493–494
in wages, 492
sex discrimination
  in education, measuring, 3–6
  in hiring and promoting, in administration, 129
sex-equitable, definition, 79
sex-equitable material, exposure of children to, 87
sex equity
  achievement of, examining, 1–11
  activities, research recommendations, 121
  assumptions about, 13–15, 501–503
  coalitions
    formation, 117–118
    recommendations, 120
  compliance, research recommendations, 121
  development, 117
  economic factors, 18–25
  in education
    administrative strategies, 495–496, 504–507
    compliance, 116
    federal funding for, 100
    as field of enquiry, 490–492
    general practices for promoting, 496–497, 507–509
    goal of, 45, 490–491
    implications of sex role development, 87–88
    importance, 492–495
    and in society, 1–2, 491
    measuring, 3–5
    methods of enquiry, 491–492
    multidimensional approach, 365–366
    progress, 489
    recommendations, 499–518
    related benefits, 499
    and role of government, 95–123
    and sex role development, 78–90
    strategies for achieving, 495–499
  educational research on, 44
  ethical argument for, 13–14
general educational practices for promoting, 163–165
goals, 1, 7, 501
  prescriptive aspects, 7–9
historical context, 30–33
implementing
  administrative strategies for, general principles, 91–94
  and changes in individual behavior, 93–94
  and changes in social system, 92–93
  effect on students, 115
  involvement of professional educators and community, 114–115
  research and evaluation, 118
  technical assistance, 116–117
  working through leaders, 117
information, dissemination, 116
institutionalizing, in education
  administrative strategies, 95–123
  federal policies and activities, 96–100
  federal-regional relationship in, 101–102
  hastening, 118–121
  interrelationships among implementors, improving, 120
  local activities or policies, 98–99
  local school districts in, 106
  regional or multistate activities, 98–99
  relationship among federal, regional, state, and local governments in, 100–101
  research recommendations, 120–121
  state activities and policies, 98–99, 102–106
  strategies linking policy and implementation, 116–118
  studies, findings of, 106–115
interventions, and long-term change, 94
justifications, 36–42
mandates, 91. *See also* specific mandate
networking, 117–118
philosophical argument for, 25
philosophical problem of, 29–43
policies
  evaluation, recommendations, 119
  recommendations, 118–119
programs
  bias in, 377
  replication, 117
research, 47, 499–500
  conceptual framework, 44
research considerations, 9
social utility, 25–27, 501
specialists, working with, 120
for specific populations, 361–364. *See also* specific population
support, recommendations, 119
training, 117
treatment in teacher education, 145–161

Sex Equity Handbook for Schools, 157
Sex Equity in Education, 133
Sex Equity in Education Leadership (SEEL), 131–134, 136–141
sex-equity resources, classroom use, WEEA demonstration project findings on, 113–114
sex-fair, definition, 79
sex-fair reality, portraying, for students, 88
sexism, 47, 298
  in education, 146, 148
sex-linked traits, 57
sex-role reversed, definition, 79
sex roles
  analyses
    role ambiguity, 15
    role proliferation, 15
    role strain, 15
  attitudes, 85–86
    definition, 78–79
    strategies for changing, in children, 87
  attributes, 79
  behavior, 86
    and content of instructional materials, 224
  characteristics, cognitive, 84–85
  conflicts, of adult women, 438
  definition, 78
  development, 218, 457–458
    age patterns, 83–86
    cognitive theories, 81, 82–83
    definition, 78
    gender schema theory, 82–83
    life-span approach, 83
    positive and negative features, 88
    psychoanalytic theory, 81–82
    and sex equity in education, 78–90
    social learning theory, 81, 82
    theories, 81–83
  inventories, 81
  knowledge, 85
    definition, 78
  learning, social learning theory, 84
  norms, 78
  perceived, and athletic performance, 329
  polarized, 83
  prescriptions, 79
  self-concepts, definition, 79
  standards, 78
  stereotypes, 14–15, 69, 70, 72, 79–81, 352
    in athletics, 331
    changing, 81
    children's awareness of, 192–193
    cross-cultural commonality, 80
    and culture, 79–80
    definition, 78, 79
    development of, 340
    discussing, with children, 87
    feminine, 79–80

  masculine, 80
    in physical education, and attitudes of educators, 327–328
    reducing, 356
    —in classes, 351
    and women's achievements in administration, 127
  student's attitudes about, effect of instructional materials, 220–221
  transcendence, 83
  undifferentiated, 83
sex stereotyping, 3. *See also* sex roles, stereotypes
  and advertisements, 54–55
  in children's toys and books, 63
  in education, measuring, 5–6
  in instruction, 493–494
  media reinforcement of, 54–55
  research on, 165
sex-typed, definition, 79
sex typing
  age patterns, 85
  in education, 86
  and processing of sex-related information, 84
sexual harassment, 480–481
Sherman, Nancy, 38
single-sex education, vs. coeducation, 210–211
Smith-Hughes Act, 416
sociability, sex differences, 66
social contract, 36
Social Education, 153
socialization, 70, 72
  effect on mathematics achievement, 241–244
  effect on outcomes, 492
  effects in science, 246
  and job satisfaction, 181
  political, gender differences in, 281, 288
  sex differences, 86
  and test performance, 169
  and women's achievements in administration, 127
social learning theory, of sex role development, 81, 82, 84
social literacy training, 138
social sciences, degrees, women earning, 237, 406
social studies
  gender differences in knowledge and attitudes, 281
  hidden curriculum, 282–283
  methods texts, content analysis, 149
  sex equity curriculum projects, 283–288
  sex equity in, 280–297
    recommendations for achieving, 293–295
    research, 280–281
  sex equity strategies, 513
  sex inequities in, 234
  teacher education, 288–293

textbooks
  inadequacies, 280–281
  —developing curricula to compensate for, 283–288
  recommendations for improving, 293
Social Studies Clearinghouse, 116
social work, doctoral degrees granted to women, 407
society
  as association of persons, 35
  educational system as mirror of, 365
  inequity in, 365–366
  pluralistic view, and sex equity, 53, 71–72
  women in, student knowledge of and attitudes toward, 282
sociology, doctoral degrees granted to women, 406
Solving Problems of Access to Careers in Engineering and Science (SPACES), 254–255
Sources of Strength: Women and Culture, 286
SPACES. See Solving Problems of Access to Careers in Engineering and Science
spatial ability, 59
  and academic performance, 69
  aspects, 61–62
  and education, 246
  relation to mathematics achievement, 241
  sex differences, 61–62, 63, 240–241
  and differential experiences, 243
  tests, 60
spatial memory, sex differences, 61–62
sponsors, for women in administration, 128
Stanford University
  preservice teacher education, in social studies, 289
  Secondary Teacher Education Program, analysis of sex bias in materials, 290–291
  Summer Institute in Women's History, 292
state agencies
  internal activities initiated by, 105–106
  policies for providing assistance to local education agencies, 104–105
  recommendations for, in integrating sex equity issues into teacher education, 159
  relationships with federal and local agencies, 100–102
  research recommendations for, 121
  role in implementing sex equity, 98–99, 102–106
state sex equity legislation and policies, 102–104
state vocational education sex equity coordinators, 98, 105, 118, 344, 352–353
  effectiveness, 111, 112
  individual orientation, 111–112
  research recommendations, 121
  role, recommendations, 119

role assignment, clarity and specificity in laws, 109–111
Statistics without Fear, 253
Stimpson, C., 50
Strong-Campbell Interest Inventory, 178–182, 408
Strong Vocational Interest Blank, revision, for women, 181
studio art, women's studies courses, 306–308
success, causal attributions about, sex differences in, 65
Szewiola and Jones v. Los Angeles United School District, 141

TABS: Aids for Ending Sexism in School, address, 227
teacher accreditation, integrating sex equity issues into, 158–159
teacher certification, sex equity policies, 150
teacher education
  federal resources for sex equity information and training, 152–153
  instructional materials for sex equity, 154–157
  integrating sex equity issues in, 93
  modules, for addressing stereotyping in athletics, 331
  postsecondary, integrating sex equity issues into, 157–158
  professional education association resources for sex equity information and training, 153–154
  programs, addressing issues in mathematics, 256–257
  for programs for gifted students, 408–410
  resistance to sex equity issues, 146
  sexism in
    legal remedies, 150–152
    policy statements, 150–152
  in social studies, 288–293
    inservice, 291–293
    preservice, 289–291
  staffing patterns, 146–147
  state sex equity policies in, 104
  students, attitudes toward sex equity in education, 155–156
  texts
    content analysis, 147–149
    integrating sex equity issues into, recommendations
    —for publishers, 159–160
    treatment of sex equity in, 145–161
    recommendations, 157–160
  women's issues courses, 146
Teacher Education and Mathematics (TEAM), 256
teachers
  ability to visualize mathematics, improving, 256–257

teachers (*continued*)
  attitudes, effect on physical education, 327–329
  awareness of sex equity issues in early education, 463–464
  elimination of sex bias in art education, 313
  equity for, 493
  expectations, and math involvement, 242–244
  female, 34
    career aspirations, 126
    numbers of, 125
    recruitment, 38
  in gifted education, 412–413
  involvement, in sex equity implementation, 114–115
  male, career aspirations, 126
  nomination of gifted students, 396–397
  in rural areas, 419
  same-sex, as role models, 403
  strategies for creating equity in early education, 466–467
  struggle for equality, 34
  use of sex-equitable instructional materials, 227–228
teacher-student interaction
  equitable, strategies for promoting, 210
  with gifted, 409
  improving, 212
  and mathematics achievement, 242–243
  in physical education, 329
  sex differences in, 462–463, 494
  sex inequities in, 193–199
team sports, females in, 326–327
Technical Education Research Centers, 444
television, effect on behavior, 224
Terman, Lewis, 392–394
  Genetic Studies of Genius, 393–394
testing. *See also* achievement tests; admissions testing; aptitude tests; interest measurement
  fairness, definition, 168
  gender differences seen in, analysis, 167–168
  in screening gifted students, 397
  sex bias in, 167, 411
    defining, 168–169
    sources, 168–169
  sex equity in, 167–188
  sex inequities in, 163–165
  sex stereotypes in, 411
  strategies for achieving sex equity in, 497
  unfairness, definition, 168
tests, of developed abilities. *See* aptitude tests
Time for a Change! A Woman's Guide to Non-traditional Occupations, 444
Title IX, 8–9, 21, 94, 95, 96, 97, 98, 118, 119, 148, 150, 164, 167, 175, 233, 342–343, 344, 391, 472, 500
  in athletics, 323–324, 326, 327, 329
    enforcement, 330
  compliance, 105–106
    discovered in California Coalition for Sex Equity project, 107–108
    evaluation, 116
    research recommendations, 121
  coordinators, 98, 105, 117, 118
    administrators, 111, 112
    advocates, 111–112
    apologists, 111, 112
    compared to state sex equity coordinators, 92
    effectiveness, 93, 110, 112–113
    individual orientation, 111–112
    research recommendations, 121
    role assignment, clarity and specificity in laws, 109–111
    roles, recommendations, 119
    and sex equity coordinators, comparison, 109–113
    time spent on Title IX, 110–111
  enforcement, 98, 101
Tobias, Sheila, 252–253
Toward Equity: An Action Manual for Women in Academe, 472
toys, benefits from, sex differences in, 243, 459
Trabahamos: A Bilingual/Multicultural Career Awareness and Language Enrichment Program, 347
Transitional Black Women's Project, 385
Trident Technical College, programs to reduce sex stereotyping, 351

UCEA. *See* University Council of Educational Administration
University Council of Educational Administration (UCEA), 133–134, 139–141
University of Dayton, reentry program for women in science, 251–252
University of Kansas, COMETS project, 255
University of Massachusetts, Project TEAM, 331
University of Minnesota, adult women students, 436
University of Missouri-Kansas City, special classes for women, 250
University of Washington, teacher education program in mathematics, 256–257
Upper Midwest Women's History Center for Teachers, 292
Upper Midwest Women's History Center for Teachers: Elementary Curriculum, 284
U.S. Commission on Civil Rights, 96, 97–100
Utah State University, teacher education program in social studies, 290

verbal abilities, 241. *See also* communication; reading; writing

and academic performance, 69
sex differences in, 59, 61, 234, 269–270
age patterns, 271
myths, 269
tests, 60
Vermont
adult basic education, delivery to individuals, 424
cooperative extension program, use for women's education, 427
Visiting Women Scientists Program, 258–259
visual arts education. *See* art education
Vocational Counseling for Displaced Homemakers: A Manual, 441
vocational education, 514. *See also* career education
areas, 338
curricula, promoting sex equity, 345–354
enrollment, after sex equity demonstration project, 115
experiential learning in, 443
nontraditional, 343
policy recommendations, 354–357
sex discrimination and sex segregation, 342–343
sex-equitable, policies aimed at, 344–354
sex equity in, 235, 338–359
sex stereotyping in, reducing, 422
vs. career education, 338
Vocational Education Act (1963), 119, 233, 344
1976 Amendments, 21, 96–98, 391, 422
provision for coordinator position, 109
sex equity provisions, 9
revision, recommendations for, 354
sex equity aspects, funding and support, 100
Vocational Interest Inventory, 180
voice, pitch, and social attributions, 58
votech centers, women's programs in, 426
Vo-Tech Workshop Guide, 441

wages, female-male differentials, 22–24
Washington
cooperative extension program, women's leadership training, 427
sex equity legislation and policies, 103
Wellesley College, preservice teacher education, in social studies, 289–290
Wesleyan University, Math Anxiety Clinic, 252–253
What to Do with the Rest of Your Life, 440
Wheaton College, preservice teacher education, in social studies, 289
Wherever You Learned It, 443
Who Should test, 115
Wider Opportunities for Women, 440
WIFE, 428
WILL. *See* Women in Leadership Training
WINC. *See* Women in Nontraditional Careers
Wingspread Conference, 290

Winning Justice for All, 284
WISA. *See* Women in School Administration
Wisconsin
teacher accreditation, sex equity criteria, 150
women's programs in votech centers, 426
Wolff, Robert Paul, 35
women. *See also* administrators; adult women; displaced homemakers; minority women; reentry women; rural women and girls
administrators, employment barriers, 92–93
in art and art education, 299–300
artists, 314
degrees earned by, 470–471
by field and decade, 405–407
in doctoral fields, 239
economic status, 13
educators, numbers of, 125
employed, 362
educational programs for, 444–445
employed in education, equity for, 493
enrolled in college, 434
family and home responsibilities, as barrier in educational administration, 127
handicapped, and interest measurement, 182
labor force participation, 18–20, 25
lack of aspiration, as barrier in educational administration, 126
lack of confidence, as barrier in educational administration, 125 126
lack of encouragement, support, and counseling, as barrier in educational administration, 126–127
lack of finances for continuing training, as barrier in educational administration, 128
lack of motivation, as barrier in educational administration, 126
lack of network, as barrier in educational administration, 129
lack of preparation or experience, as barrier in educational administration, 127–128
lack of role models, as barrier in educational administration, 128
lack of sponsorship or mentors, as barrier in educational administration, 128
legal status, 13
level of educational attainment, 18–19, 20–22, 25
new scholarship on, 2, 7, 14, 44–52, 293–294
conceptual framework, 48
evolutionary perspective, 44
goals, 47
methods of inquiry, 50–51
phenomenology, 51
stages, 47–48
vs. old scholarship, 47
within educational thought, 48–50

women (*continued*)
  in nontraditional occupations, programs encouraging, 444
  occupational choice, 21–22
  occupational sex segregation, 13, 20, 21, 22, 86, 341
  older, educational programs for, 446–447
  older/retired, 362
  performance, in military, 331–332, 334
  poor self-image, as barrier in educational administration, 125–126
  in postsecondary education, 470
  pursuing administrative positions, financial assistance for, 131, 137
  recruitment, into administrative preparation programs, 130–131, 137
  relegation to private life, 31–32, 37
  socialization, as barrier in educational administration, 127
  in society, student knowledge of and attitudes toward, 282
  special populations, 361–364. *See also* specific population
    sex equity strategies for, 498–499, 515–517
  unemployment, 20–21
  wages, 22–25
    discrimination in, 24
  without high school diploma, programs for, 441
Women and Mathematics: Balancing the Education, 240
Women Artists, 310
Women in Higher Education: A Contemporary Bibliography, 484
Women in Leadership Training (WILL), 132–133, 139, 140
Women in Nontraditional Careers (WINC), 349, 352
Women in Non-Traditional Jobs, 442
Women in School Administration (WISA), 131–134, 137–141
Women in Science Program, 260
Women Involved in Farm Economics (WIFE), 428
Women in World Area Studies, 285
"Women Make Art: An Androgynous Point of View," 310
Women Moving Up, conferences, 261
Women Moving Up Directory, 261
Women's Action Alliance, address, 227
women's art groups, 303
women's art movement, 511
  as educational force, 303–311

formal education
  at elementary and secondary levels, 309–310
  at higher education level, 306–309
  informal education in, 304–306
  self-education in, 303–304
Women's Caucus for Art, 305
women's colleges, 248–249
Women's Educational Equity Act (1974, 1978), 96, 97, 98, 105, 119, 152, 344, 391–392
  curricular materials developed with funding from, 347, 349, 350, 353
  demonstration projects, 98, 101–102, 106, 117
  follow-up research, recommendations for, 121
  preliminary findings, 113–115
  development sponsored by, 117
  Education Development Center, address, 227
  funding and support, 100
  materials for preservice teacher, 152–153
  support of coalitions and networking, 117
Women's Educational Equity Act Program. *See also* Sex Equity in Education Leadership (SEEL)
  materials for reentry women, 440, 441
  projects addressing early childhood, 463, 464
  for promoting sex equity in classroom, 208
Women's Educational Equity Act Publishing Center, 116
Women's Educational Equity Communications Network, 116
Women's Enterprises of Boston, 444
Women's History Week, 96, 98, 100, 105, 287
Women's Lives/Women's Work, 287
Women's Roots, 286
women's studies, 45–47
  characteristics, 46
  courses, 146
    on issues in art, 306–308
    on women and art education, 309
  goals, 46
  vs. women's movement, 47
Women's Studies Abstracts, 50
Women's Studies Service Learning Handbook: From the Classroom to the Community, 442
Woolf, Virginia, on men's sense of superiority, 34–35
work/study programs, 442
wrestling, females in, 326–327
writing
  children's, sex differences in, 274
  sex equity in, recommendations for achieving, 277

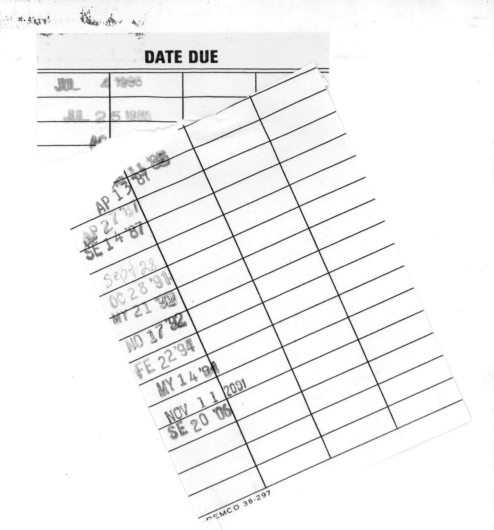